D1705738

# Control of Human Behavior, Mental Processes, and Consciousness

*Essays in Honor of the 60th Birthday of August Flammer*

# Control of Human Behavior, Mental Processes, and Consciousness

## Essays in Honor of the 60th Birthday of August Flammer

Edited by

**Walter J. Perrig**
*University of Bern, Switzerland*

**Alexander Grob**
*University of Basel, Switzerland*

LAWRENCE ERLBAUM ASSOCIATES, PUBLISHERS
2000    Mahwah, New Jersey                    London

The final camera copy for this work was prepared by the editors.

Lawrence Erlbaum Associates, Inc., Publishers
10 Industrial Avenue
Mahwah, NJ 07430

Cover design by Kathryn Houghtaling Lacey

**Library of Congress Cataloging-in-Publication Data**

Control of Human Behavior, Mental Processes, and Consiousness : essays in honor of the 60th birthday of August Flammer / edited by Walter J. Perrig and Alexander Grob.
    p.  cm.
Includes bibliographical references and index.
ISBN 0-8058-2915-6 (hardcover : alk. paper)
1. Control (Psychology) 2. Self-control. 3. Perceptual control theory. 4. Human information processing. I. Flammer, August. II. Perrig, Walter J. III. Grob, Alexander, 1958– .
    BF611.C67    1998
    153—dc21                                    98-32192
                                                    CIP

Books published by Lawrence Erlbaum Associates are printed on acid-free paper, and their bindings are chosen for strength and durability.

Printed in the United States of America
10  9  8  7  6  5  4  3  2  1

# Contents

# VI SOCIALIZATION, SYSTEMS, AND CULTURE

# Preface

"I am not such a productive scientist, that I would deserve such an honor." This sentence paraphrases August Flammer's reaction when he learned about this volume and the authors, friends, colleagues and scientists from around the world who contributed to it in honor of his 60th birthday. We know there are many criteria that may make someone outstanding enough to deserve such an honor. However, there was never a doubt as to whether to proceed with this project. In many respects, Flammer scored highly throughout his career. But it is his productivity in different domains of psychology that makes him outstanding.

Born in 1938, Flammer began his professional career as a teacher at different levels of elementary and high school. He then studied psychology at the University of Fribourg, Switzerland, and in 1970, earned his doctorate in experimental psychology, statistics, and philosophy. His postdoctorate years (1972–1974) brought him first to the Institute for Mathematical Studies in the Social Sciences at Stanford University. There, he worked as a research fellow with a fellowship from the Swiss National Science Foundation. Afterwards, he stayed on as an honorary fellow at the Wisconsin Research and Development Center for Cognitive Learning at the University of Wisconsin, Madison. In 1975, in Switzerland, he was elected professor for experimental and educational psychology at the University of Fribourg. Since 1983, he has been full professor of developmental psychology at the University of Bern (Switzerland). In both Universities he was a dean. Flammer was a visiting professor at the Universities of Melbourne (Australia), Basel (Switzerland), Zurich (Switzerland), Bergen (Norway), and at the Max-Planck Institute for Human Development in Berlin (Germany). He is a member of various scientific organizations and committees and associate editor of several national and international journals. He served several times in the role of organizer for scientific conventions, among them the world congress of ISSBD, 1998, in Bern.

Flammer is—and always was—a busy promoter of scientific psychology. As a 12-year member of the Research Council of the Swiss National Science Foundation, he was responsible for the evaluation of hundreds of grant proposals in the social science and humanities section. At this same institution, his concern for the junior research generation was apparent in his awarding of fellowships to promising candidates. Furthermore, approximately 30 students earned their doctorate degrees under his strict, yet supportive, supervision.

Flammer's bibliography contains more than 200 scientific contributions. The topics reflect chronologically his professional path, which is astonishing in its extraordinary breadth. It begins with educational psychology, individual differences in learning, aptitude-treatment-interaction, test validation, and learning assessment; it also includes experimental work in cognitive psychology, text and discourse processing, and memory; and finally, developmental psychology and developmental tasks and control beliefs across childhood and adolescence. Flammer became an internationally respected scientist publishing laboratory experimental work and broad integrative work. He is a successful representative of the European tradition of a broad education.

Based on Flammer's extraordinary background, we felt proud to edit a volume in honor of his achievements. As his former students, we represent different generations that shared Flammer's earlier interest in experimental cognitive psychology, or his later research in developmental psychology. The publishing of *Control of Human Behavior, Mental Processes, and Consciousness* is justified by Flammer's work and competence. The volume shares Flammer's spirit of keeping broad related topics in mind, and in being precise in both rationale and method. The topic of control is taken from Flammer's main research interests of the 1990s.

We think the topic of control is central to the field of cognitive psychology, and is important enough to be evaluated and elaborated on from many different perspectives. This volume intends to cross the borders of narrow disciplines, and gives the reader a chance to reflect on the concept of control from a variety of perspectives. We embrace the contributions of friends and colleagues of August Flammer, who work in research areas that are close to Flammer's, as well as contributions of leading scientists who are influential in the area of control. There is no doubt that the ideas and elaborations presented here are important and attractive from a theoretical and a practical perspective. Further evaluations and judgments are left to the reader. For us, what remains is the pleasant task of thanking all the authors who shared our commitment to a volume that would not only please the honored, but also be of broad interest to the entire scientific community.

—*Walter Perrig*
—*Alexander Grob*

## ACKNOWLEDGMENTS

The editors thank the Johann Jacobs Foundation and the Swiss Academy of Humanities and Social Sciences for financial support of this project.

# Contributors

| | |
|---|---|
| *Françoise D. Alsaker* | University of Bern, Switzerland |
| *Paul B. Baltes* | Max Planck Institute for Human Development, Berlin, Germany |
| *Albert Bandura* | Stanford University |
| *Nicola Baumann* | University of Osnabrück, Germany |
| *Catherine E. Barton* | Boston College, Chestnut Hill |
| *Thomas R. Bidell* | University of Colorado, Denver |
| *Jochen Brandtstädter* | University of Trier, Germany |
| *Fredi P. Büchel* | University of Geneva, Switzerland |
| *Fabrizio Butera* | University Pierre Mendès, Grenoble, France |
| *Mario von Cranach* | University of Bern, Switzerland |
| *Wolfgang Edelstein* | Max Planck Institute for Human Development, Berlin, Germany |
| *Juan M. Falomir* | University of Geneva, Switzerland |
| *Helmut Fend* | University of Zürich, Switzerland |
| *Frank Fischer* | University of Munich, Germany |
| *Kurt W. Fischer* | Harvard School of Education, Cambridge, MA |
| *Alexandra M. Freund* | Max Planck Institute for Human Development, Berlin, Germany |
| *Volker Gadenne* | Johannes–Kepler–University, Linz, Austria |
| *Cornelia Gräsel* | University of Munich, Germany |
| *Klaus Grawe* | University of Bern, Switzerland |
| *Alexander Grob* | University of Basel, Switzerland |
| *Marina T. Groner* | University of Bern, Switzerland |
| *Rudolf Groner* | University of Bern, Switzerland |
| *Matthias Grundmann* | Max Planck Institute for Human Development, Berlin, Germany |
| *Peter M. Hart* | University of Melbourne, Victoria, Australia |
| *Claude A. Kaiser* | University of Geneva, Switzerland |
| *Franz Kaufmann* | University of Bern, Switzerland |
| *Ruth Kaufmann–Hayoz* | University of Bern, Switzerland |
| *Walter Kintsch* | University of Colorado, Boulder |
| *Julius Kuhl* | University of Osnabrück, Germany |
| *Lieselotte van Leeuwen* | University of Bern, Switzerland |
| *Richard M. Lerner* | Tufts University |
| *Heinz Mandl* | University of Munich, Germany |
| *Alexandra Mies* | Max Planck Institute for Human Development, Berlin, Germany |
| *Gabriel Mugny* | University of Geneva, Switzerland |
| *Philipp Notter* | University of Zürich, Switzerland |
| *Fritz Oser* | University of Fribourg, Switzerland |
| *Margit Oswald* | University of Bern, Switzerland |

*Anne–Nelly*
  *Perret–Clermont*      University of Neuchâtel, Switzerland
*Jean–François Perret*   University of Fribourg, Switzerland
*Meinrad Perrez*         University of Fribourg, Switzerland
*Pasqualina Perrig–Chiello*  University of Bern, Switzerland
*Walter J. Perrig*       University of Bern, Switzerland
*Ursula Peter*           University of Bern, Switzerland
*Alain Quiamzade*        University of Geneva, Switzerland
*Anik de Ribaupierre*    University of Geneva, Switzerland
*Klaus R. Scherer*       University of Geneva, Switzerland
*Norbert K. Semmer*      University of Bern, Switzerland
*Rainer K. Silbereisen*  Friedrich–Schiller–University, Jena, Germany
*François Stoll*         University of Zürich, Switzerland
*Daniel Walther*         University of Bern, Switzerland
*Alexander J. Wearing*   University of Melbourne, Victoria, Australia
*Werner Wicki*           University of Bern, Switzerland
*Margit Wiesner*         Friedrich–Schiller–University, Jena, Germany
*Peter Wilhelm*          University of Fribourg, Switzerland
*Werner Wippich*         University of Trier, Germany
*Hansjörg Znoj*          University of Bern, Switzerland

# I

# Basic Aspects and
# Varieties of Control

# 1

# Emotion, Cognition, and Control: Limits of Intentionality

*Jochen Brandtstädter*

## INTRODUCTION

Psychology has noted for long that the self plays a double role in contexts of control and self-regulation; it is at once the origin as well as the target of self-regulative activity (Bandura, 1989; Flammer, 1990). Skills of self-regulation and self-control are basic requirements of social coexistence; they form the cornerstone of processes of intentional self-development through which we embody conceptions of an "ought" self and of a desirable form of life into our conduct (Brandtstädter, 1998). Many social problems and discontents seem to revolve around difficulties to control one's emotions, thoughts, or behavior:

> Self-regulation failure is the major social pathology of the present time. . . .
> People are miserable because they cannot control their money, their weight,
> their emotions, their drinking, their hostility, their craving for drugs, their
> spending, their own behavior vis-à-vis their family members, their sexual im-
> pulses, and more. (Baumeister, Heatherton, & Tice, 1994, p. 3)

The moral standards that are transmitted through socialization and are installed in particular compartments of the self-system—in the "superego," "ought" self, or wherever—require us to take a reflective and critical stance toward ourselves. Cultured individuals not only have volitions, cognitions, or emotions; they also have meta-volitions, meta-cognitions, and meta-emotions. Once we are capable of evaluating ourselves (or our selves) from a moral or rational point of view, we can form a wish to have, or to not have, particular wishes, beliefs, or intentions, and we may have particular emotional attitudes (such as guilt, shame, or pride) toward our own emotions or affective states. Notions of moral competence and personal freedom presume the potential to form such "second order volitions" (Frankfurt, 1971). Self-discipline is the ability or the skill of translating second order volitions into action; accordingly, "weakness of will" (akrasia) manifests itself not only in the inability to execute one's intentions, but in particular in the failure to regulate one's intentional impulses and behavior according to higher level intentions (cf. Brandtstädter & Greve, in press; Roberts, 1984). "It is good, and also a duty, for us to better ourselves," wrote Kant, who added, however: ". . . but it is foolish to want to improve on what is already beyond our power." (Kant, 1798/1974, p. 104)

Thus, we are held responsible not only for our actions, but to some extent also for our thoughts and feelings. Extending notions of intentionality and control to these latter domains, however, raises certain difficulties which I will discuss in the following. To preview, I will argue that the mental states or processes to which we refer in intentional action explanations cannot be explained throughout within the same intentionalist scheme. Applying theories of personal control to the domain of mental processes thus carries the danger of overstretching concepts and may lead to misorientations in contexts of psychological intervention. In order to prevent misunderstanding, I begin with a few conceptual considerations.

## ACTION, CONTROL, AND INTENTIONALITY

The concepts of action, control, and intentionality are interdependent and to some extent interdefined. We denote as "action" a particular class of behaviors that lend themselves to explanations that refer to the actor's mental states; actions are explained or made understandable by showing how they are intentionally linked to an actor's wishes and beliefs. This basic explanatory scheme also recurs in psychological theories of action (e.g., Feather, 1982); it covers any activity that is goal-oriented, has been selected by the actor from different behavioral options, and is under personal control. The aspect of personal control separates actions from behavioral or physiological events that occur without the actor's intentional involvement, such as blushing, sweating, stumbling, fainting, or awakening from sleep—perhaps even laughing and crying. If we can control such processes, it is in a mediated or technical sense only, that is, by the purposeful arrangement of particular stimulus conditions. For example, one can expose oneself to higher temperatures in order to sweat, or one can set the alarm to wake up at a particular time. This, of course, does not turn sweating, awakening, etc. into a personally controlled action; one may be held responsible for visiting the sauna, but not for perspiring under such conditions.

In psychological theories, control is often defined in terms of the subject's ability to alter the probability of a particular outcome by performing (or not performing) a particular behavior. This definition is unsatisfactory because it confounds the aspect of personal control with that of technical or mediated control. As we have seen, technical control does not imply personal control; if we can affect certain behavioral processes through an intentional arrangement of stimuli, this does not qualify them as intentional, personally controlled activities.

On the other hand, when a given course of action is described as being intentional or under one's personal control, this description will generally not apply to all aspects or elements of the process. Personally controlled actions may have, of course, nonintended or even counterintentional effects: By moving my hand, I inadvertantly frighten away a fly; by eating these delicious mushrooms, I poison myself. Intended action outcomes, too, may entail components which, in and of themselves, were not intended but which are tolerated for the sake of other, positive effects ("periintentional" effects; see Brandtstädter & Greve, in press). Or, consider the following simple case. One rings the doorbell; once the button has been pressed, the bell sounds; thereafter, perhaps someone opens the door. Although one's intentions may pertain to the entire chain of events, the events that are contingent on the initial or basic act of pressing the button of the doorbell are not under one's control in a stricter, personal sense—even if they clearly depend on whether or not the relevant basic act has been performed.

Accordingly, one should distinguish between personally controlled actions and the contextually mediated effects of personally controlled actions (see also Flammer, 1995). Similar reasoning lies behind the differentiation between "competence" and "contingency" (Weisz, 1983), between "action-effect" and "effect–outcome" expectancies (Heckhausen, 1980), between "efficacy expectation" and "response-outcome expectancy" (Bandura, 1977), or between "agency beliefs" and "means–end beliefs" (Skinner, Chapman, & Baltes, 1988). It should be noted, however, that distinctions of this kind cannot be made on an a priori basis for any given activity; they crucially depend on how a given course of action is described and conceptually segmented. For example, one may describe the sequence of "pressing the button" and "producing a tone" as a molar act of "ringing the bell;" at this level of description, the bell's ringing would be a constituent or conceptually implied result of the given act, not a contingent effect. With respect to the more molecular act of pressing the button, however, the produced sound would be a contingent effect. Depending on which elements of the sequence are mentally represented and covered by the actor's intentions, different levels of action identification (Vallacher & Wegner, 1987) may be appropriate. The principle of referential opacity (Quine, 1960) applies to intentions in the same way as it does to other mental states: If an actor intends (believes, wishes) A, and A implies B (by virtue of causal laws, conventions, or conceptual rules), it does not follow that the actor also intends (believes, wishes) B. Whether or not the actor's intending A also covers what is causally or semantically implied by A will of course crucially depend on whether the implications of A are represented in the actor's knowledge base.

It should also be noted at this juncture that actions may dissociate themselves from their original goals and beliefs, even if these continue to provide the rational basis why the actions are performed. This is particularly true for habitualized action patterns. When one routinely stops in front of a red light, one does so intentionally and for good reason. However, if one had to mentally actualize these reasons each time, one would presumably have difficulties to react promptly to the signal. Habitualized behavior obviously can be triggered automatically and without mediating reflection by contextual stimuli that are contingently associated with the behavior (Bargh, 1996); in such cases, intentions may function as mental sets that "allow" a particular class of stimuli to set off a particular behavioral sequence.

## INTENTIONAL CONTROL OF MENTAL STATES

As the given examples illustrate, even intentional, personally controlled action is penetrated throughout with nonintentional and uncontrolled processes. This would also apply to the cognitions and intentions that guide a particular action, if we could consider them as intentional activities, or as the results of such activities. But can mental states or processes be construed this way at all?

The previous differentiation between technical and personal control helps to avoid misunderstanding. Obviously, one can purposefully expose oneself to conditions which foster or prevent the incidence of certain mental states. One can, for example, distract oneself from unwanted thoughts, induce or neutralize emotional states through memorizing particular events or imagining particular scenarios, and more; theories of self-management offer various techniques in that respect (e.g., Karoly, 1993). Thus, there is no doubt that we have, or can acquire, some degree of technical control over our mental states, although we often find ourselves faltering in this kind of self-control. The point at issue rather is whether and to what extent the mental states or processes to which we refer in the explanation of actions can themselves be explained according to the scheme of intentional action.

According to a well-known philosophical argument, a given activity is a personally controlled action if the subject could have done otherwise (e.g., Chisholm, 1971). There are different readings of this criterion. In a first, weaker sense, this would be understood as *one would have done otherwise if one had chosen*. In a more rigorous version, the criterion requires that the subject *could have made a different choice under the very same conditions*. These two variants are similar to the Humean distinction between freedom of action (the freedom to act in accordance with one's wishes and desires) and freedom of the will (i.e., freedom of our volitions from any determination). When intentions, volitions, or beliefs are considered as intentional in origin, freedom of the will and freedom of action apparently become indistinguishable.

Can mental activities, then, be equated with actions over which we have personal control in a strong, nontechnical sense? As indicated above, one can take a critical stance toward one's own beliefs, volitions, or emotions, and one can even attempt to modify them. The idea that we can originate our beliefs, volitions, or emotions in the same intentional way as we can originate our actions, however, apparently has dubious consequences. For one, the forming of intentions would involve an infinite regress: If every intention would require a meta-intention, one would never come to act. The incoherence of this conception becomes even more obvious when one attempts to treat the practical reasoning leading to an action in turn as resulting from an act of practical reflection. One does not reflect to use a mean M in order to achieve a goal G because it seems useful to have this practical thought; due to the "transparency" of the mental, such second-order reflection would already involve the practical thought that it should yield as a conclusion: "You cannot reflect that it would be useful to reflect that p, without reflecting that p, any more than you can remember that you want to remember X, without remembering X." (Müller, 1992, p. 166)[1]

Aside from these more formal reservations, some types of mental states or processes seem inherently intransigent to intentional control. Consider the domain of emotions. It is of course true that emotional reactions crucially depend on the individual's current wishes and beliefs, and it is likewise true that secondary reflections concerning, e.g., the "justifiability" of a current emotional reaction can increase or dampen its intensity. This, however, does not warrant the argument that emotions are, or can be made, a matter of choice. Feelings such as envy, jealousy, wrath, guilt, or pride are not, and cannot be, intentionally actuated, although they clearly induce particular intentional sets (cf. Brandtstädter, 1985; Elster, 1989; Rorty, 1982). This does not render the educational ideals of "cultivating" emotions senseless. As mentioned earlier, we can control our emotions in a technical sense by purposefully creating or avoiding conditions that may intensify or dampen them. Similarly, we may feel an urge or obligation to critically examine the perceptions or beliefs that gave rise to a particular affective state. The motive to do so often arises together with a particular emotional state (the need to carefully examine the facts may be more pronounced in response to aversive emotions than in response to positive ones). In sum: Emotions are not intentionally generated, but "it is not a consequence of the passivity of emotions that they are states with respect to which we are passive." (Gordon, 1987, p. 110)

Emotions are open to some extent to reflection and rational argument because they are inherently related to particular types of cognitions. Generally, emotions vanish together with the cognitions that back them, although it may take some time for the cognitive system to assimilate disconfirming feedback and to override a tendency to negotiate evidence in ways that are consistent with the particular emotion. Though there is consensus that emotions are linked to cognitions and vice versa, it is less clear which kind of relation is involved here. Quite apart from quarrels about whether or not cognitions causally precede emotions (e.g., Lazarus, 1984; Zajonc, 1984), there is the more fundamental question of whether the relation between cognitions and emotions can be conceived at all in causal terms. A short digression may serve to clarify this point.

The concepts that we use to describe or explain human actions and mental states are interrelated; these relationships can be understood as a system of semantic rules that allow or preclude certain combinations of predicates (cf. Keil, 1979). By ascribing a specific emotion, one also ascribes a certain type of cogni-

---

[1]One should be aware of the limitations of this argument. We can certainly form an intention, e.g., to visualize the cathedral of Chartres, without at the same moment having that particular mental image (after all, why should one decide to imagine something that one already is imagining?).

tion; for example, envy implies specific social comparisons, guilt implies the belief of having violated some standard of conduct, anxiety or fear implies the expectation of an aversive event conjoined with doubt of one's chances of preventing its occurence. A particular event can certainly give rise to, and in that sense cause, an emotional state or a change in emotional states; for example, some physical symptom may induce one's fear of having contracted a serious illness, and this fear may vanish after a thorough medical examination. However, a given event or piece of evidence can induce a particular emotion only to the extent that it instantiates the particular type of cognition that is constitutive to that type of emotion, and that latter relation appears to be one of conceptual entailment rather than of causality. Could envy occur without some kind of social comparison? The reason why we deny this possibility is not because it would falsify some assumed causal regularity, but because it seems conceptually incoherent and, in that sense, can be excluded a priori. If, for a given proposition, the falsifying event can be excluded for logical or conceptual reasons, then this proposition becomes a tautology and no longer qualifies as a causal or empirical hypothesis (see Brandtstädter, 1993).

Beyond implying particular types of cognitions, emotions often also involve particular actional tendencies or intentional sets. For example, guilt seems associated with a tendency toward atonement and a readiness to accept some penalty; fear is related to a tendency to eliminate dangerous circumstances or to seek shelter (some kinds of emotion, such as awe, do not seem to carry clear behavioral implications). Again, it is doubtful whether we are dealing here with a causal relationship; for conceptual reasons already, it seems doubtful that a feeling which does not involve a tendency toward atonement could rightly be identified as guilt.

Returning to issues of control and intentionality, two things should be noted. On the one hand, emotions are involved in the generation of action tendencies or intentional sets (cf. Reisenzein, 1996), but on the other hand, neither the emotional reactions, nor the action tendencies that emerge together with an emotion, are intentionally actuated. Whether the induced action tendency is carried out, or how it is carried out, may of course involve reflections and intentional decisions.

In sum, it appears that the format of intentional action explanation is not applicable to the emergence of emotional states, or to the cognitive, motivational, or intentional sets that correspond to particular emotions. Within limits that shall be considered in the following, the same holds for other types of mental states to which we refer in action explanations. Again, there is no doubt that we can to some degree intentionally monitor and modify our mental states; for example, we can decide to activate certain mental contents, we can form an intention to visualize a particular scene, and we may more or less successfully try to suppress disturbing thoughts, though especially such latter attempts may backfire and yield counterintentional results (as Wegner, 1994, has argued, the intention to suppress some thought may activate a mental monitoring mechanism that searches for that very thought, so that the only way to drive away an item from consciousness may be to focus attention on some distractor). Beliefs or preferences, however, are apparently more difficult to control (see also Gilbert, 1993). Though we may attempt to discredit a belief, e.g., by a selective rehearsal of disconfirming evidence, we cannot freely choose to commit ourselves to, or to disengage from, particular beliefs or preferences. We cannot voluntarily adopt certain wishes or opinions or generate certain insights; we may only, with greater or lesser success, try to come to have them. No proof would convince us and no argument could persuade us if we were free to reject or accept it at will. Likewise, one cannot adopt a belief because it seems useful to do so. In particular, we do not decide on the availability of particular thoughts or mental contents in particular situations or emotional states. One can explain to a depressive person, for example, that his or her self-doubts are unfounded, but the problem is that such arguments would not convince the depressive person even if he or she wanted to believe them. Apparently, mechanisms are involved here which are not under intentional control, but rather reflect basic features of the evolved cognitive architecture.

## SELF-DECEPTION, WISHFUL THINKING, AND "SECONDARY CONTROL"

The considerations above might help to clarify problems and paradoxes that are connected to phenomena commonly denoted as self-deception, wishful thinking, and the like (cf. Greve, 1996; Lockard & Paulhus, 1988; Mele, 1987). As the terms are commonly used, wishful thinking occurs when a person, without due deliberation of relevant evidence, believes proposition $X$ primarily for the reason that he or she thinks it would be pleasant or advantageous if $X$ were true. Wishful thinking turns into self-deception when the person accepts or maintains belief $X$ in spite of having evidence that $X$ is not the case. If one individual deceives another, one might say that the deceiver knew better, but how can one bring oneself to believe something that contradicts one's own beliefs?

The phenomena of self-deception and wishful thought seem paradoxical as long as they are seen as personally controlled, intentional acts. If one could acquire a belief at will, it would barely be possible to consider it as something purporting to reflect reality (Williams, 1973). Knowing that one has adopted a belief just for the purpose of calming one's fears would obviously undermine the efficiency of that illusory maneuver. Of course one can decide, for example, to take steps to eliminate residual doubts regarding the truth of an opinion one would like to adopt. Likewise, the probability that an event will occur may be increased under some circumstances by believing that it will occur. This is particularly true in situations in which mental attitudes have some real effect on the relevant processes. For example, an average soccer team can win the tournament because the members of the team were confident of their victory and played with the necessary self-assurance. Similar mechanisms seem involved in self-management strategies such as autosuggestion and "positive thinking" (Johnston, 1995). Proxies such as mental simulation, autosuggestion, use of psychotropic substances, and the like can be strategically employed in order to alter one's proneness to believe or desire something that one otherwise would not be able to wish or believe. Such cases, however, cannot truly be described as instances of wishful thought or self-deception; they illustrate, on the contrary, that the mere intention to have some belief or desire is not sufficient to bring about the intended mental state.

A well-known strategy to resolve the paradox of self-deception (p simultaneously believes a and not-a) is to divide the self into two homuncular sub-selves: into a deceived subsystem or Self 1 which is sufficiently naive and gullible, and a deceiving subsystem or Self 2 which is better informed and carries out the deception. This creates new puzzles, however. How can Self 2 have privileged access to the truth? How can it manipulate the beliefs of Self 1, without the latter noticing, or somehow playing along? Why should Self 2 be interested in deceiving Self 1, and at the same time let it speak or act for the whole person? "Does it like lying for its own sake? Or does it suppose that it knows what is best for the deceived system to believe?" (Johnston, 1995, p. 434). Obviously, this approach leads to bizarre consequences, at least insofar as the involved homuncular subselves are again understood to be intentional agents.

Similar reservations apply to psychological theories of coping and control which often treat phenomena of motivated reasoning as if they were deliberately chosen "strategies" or modes of personal control. The model of "primary" and "secondary" control advanced by Rothbaum, Weisz, and Snyder (1982), for example, posits that in situations involving a loss or restriction of (primary) control, a sense of control can be maintained by specific "secondary" maneuvers such as identifying with powerful others, downgrading expectations, deriving meaning from aversive events, or engaging in fantasies or illusions of control (cf. also Flammer, 1990; Flammer, Züblin, & Grob, 1988; Heckhausen & Schulz, 1995). The different focus of primary and secondary modes of control is epitomized in the distinction of "changing the world" vs. "changing the self" (Rothbaum, Weisz, & Snyder, 1982, p. 103). This conceptualization does not differentiate systematically between intentional and unintentional or subpersonal processes; extending the notion of control to secondary cognitive processes of the mentioned type tends to conflate these processes with purposefully chosen strategies of coping. This leads to the paradoxical implications mentioned above. It also blurs the important difference between intentional actions that aim at changing "the world" (or even "the self") and nonintentional processes through which the goals, beliefs, or self-definitions which feed into intentional action, are changed.

It should be noted at this juncture that the human cognitive system was not designed by evolution to produce illusionary maneuvers, but rather to construe models of reality that are sufficiently veridical to guide efficient behavior. Likewise, the primary function of negative affects or mood states is certainly not to produce wishful thinking, but rather to activate instrumental behavior that—in the phylogenetic course or in the individual's ontogeny—has proven effective in eliminating aversive conditions. As long as the individual is capable to acitvely eliminate a problem, it would be dysfunctional to deny it, or to engage in positive illusions. As far as cognitive biases occur during problem-focused action, they will tend to be consistent with, rather than undermine, the intention to act: There is experimental evidence, for example, that problems become even more aversive (or goals more attractive) when effective goal pursuit is hampered or becomes more difficult (Wortman & Brehm, 1975), and that individuals tend to overestimate their control potentials when they are in an "implemental mind set" (Gollwitzer, 1990; Gollwitzer & Kinney, 1989). Although such mind sets emerge together with the intention to act, they are not intentionally implemented, but automatically induced.

Mental processes that erode the attractiveness of intended goal states or enhance a positive reinterpretation of initially aversive situations should become activated, however, when the goal is definitely blocked. Again, such "accommodative" processes (Brandtstädter & Renner, 1990) are not intentionally induced. Even in cases where the disengagement from a goal or the dissolution of a commitment manifests itself as an intentional decision, the shifts in values or meanings that rationalize such a decision must obviously occur before the decision is formed: "It is doubtful that people can deliberately revise their commitments merely because it seems advantageous to do so" (Lazarus & DeLongis, 1983, p. 251; see also Lazarus, 1985).

Thus, the deeper analysis of accommodative processes through which barren goals and ambitions are relinquished must take into account subintentional mechanisms. For example, when a goal is perceived as uncontrollable, attention tends to shift away from the goal, and auxiliary mechanisms are activated that remove it from working memory (Brandtstädter & Renner, 1990; Carver & Scheier, 1990). Obviously, it would be dysfunctional if unattainable goals continued to draw attention and were shielded against distractive stimuli or competing action tendencies. In cases where the blocked goal is of high personal importance and not easily substituted by other goals, the accommodative process may be impeded such that the attachment to the goal persists and thoughts circle about the blocked goal in a ruminative fashion (cf. Kuhl, 1985; Martin & Tesser, 1989). Accommodation of goals and preferences is further supported by the increased accessibility of cognitive contents that reduce the attractiveness of the blocked goal states or the aversive valence of the actual situation; the tendency to generate such palliative cognitions may be enhanced precisely by their potential to provide comfort and relief (cf. Wentura, 1995). In addition, the search for relevant information may be positively biased in that it is discontinued as soon as the information recovered fits a preferred conclusion; this tendency may be particularly strong when the conclusion in question is attractive enough to compromise a desire of being objectively correct (cf. Bohner, Moskowitz, & Chaiken, 1995; Kunda, 1990).

In summary, a coherent account of "wishful thinking," "self-deception," and related phenomena seems impossible unless one drops the assumption that these phenomena have an intentional character. Mechanisms of the type considered above are not strategically chosen, but rather reflect inherent "tropisms" (Johnston, 1995) of the cognitive system.

## CONCLUSION

The considerations presented above have pointed to limitations of the paradigm of intentional action and personal control. More specifically, it appears that this paradigm is of limited explanatory scope. As purposeful actors, we can certainly reflect upon, and try to influence, our beliefs, wishes, and intentions; we may also develop meta-volitions that neutralize or modify primary intentions and actional tendencies. Ultimately, however, the genesis of mental events that feed into intentional decision and action cannot itself be explained in intentional terms. The formation and change of mental states not only depends on the individual's embedding in social and cultural "action spaces" over which he or she has only limited control (Brandtstädter, 1997), but in particular on mental processes that cannot be considered as intentional. In a certain sense one could perhaps argue that nothing can be more intentional than our intentions as such. However, if we use the term "intentional" to denote behavioral or mental phenomena that are voluntarily originated and result from effective choices of the actor, it appears that large parts of our mental life cannot be described that way.

To what extent do these insights bear on the picture that we construe of ourselves and our world? It may seem that existential and moral attitudes which presume strong notions of freedom and responsibility are rendered questionable by a concept of action that includes subintentional mechanisms. To claim that our beliefs and intentions would not be "ours" unless we had them originated at will, however, would appear equally questionable; in fact, the opposite assertion could be defended (cf. Dennett, 1984). Notions of freedom and responsibility seem to hinge more crucially on the extent to which one can identify with one's desires and actional tendencies (cf. the concept of "embraced desires," Frankfurt, 1971). Furthermore, one might doubt whether the hypothetical freedom to originate particular wants, beliefs, or desires, at will, would still be compatible with notions of personality and moral responsibility (cf. Honderich, 1988).

Another open question is whether and how intentional (personal), and subintentional (subpersonal) perspectives could be theoretically integrated, without confounding categorically different levels of discourse. This question is of course far too complex to be settled in short compass. A helpful notion, however, is that there are different explanatory "stances" from which we can analyze human behavior (Dennett, 1987; see also Bieri, 1987). Within an intentional stance, we explain an activity by relating it, by means of a rational calculus, to particular mental states of the actor. The explanatory concepts of this stance—expectancies, beliefs, desires, goals, and the like—cannot be identified with particular physical states, but rather are ascriptive predicates that can be connected within a rational calculus; within the intentional stance, we ascribe those mental states to an actor which would yield the most consistent rational account of his or her behavior in the given situation. Behavioral processes may also be analyzed from subpersonal (physical, physiological, biological) perspectives, and we may have to adopt this latter stance in cases where the intentional perspective does not provide any consistent account for a given behavior or becomes unproductive and circular. These various explanatory stances are neither exchangeable nor can they be reduced to each other; each level provides a specific conceptual frame that generates its specific questions and answers. Shifts between these explanatory perspectives, however, remain possible and may even be of heuristic value. Similar explanatory shifts are common in everyday practice. For example, to operate a computer or to replace some deficient component, it usually suffices to know the basic functional design; to understand, however, why particular components do, or do not, function as they should, one must have some deeper knowledge of the basic physical processes involved. Such alternations between explanatory levels do not involve a theoretical reduction but rather afford complementary and mutually enriching analytic viewpoints. Accordingly, psychology, and research on action and control in particular, may be well advised to allow for a plurality of explanatory perspectives rather than to continue to pit traditional dichotomies (reasons vs. causes, freedom vs. determinism, explanation vs. understanding) against each other in the search for the one single, appropriate paradigm.

## REFERENCES

Bandura, A. (1977). Self-efficacy: Toward a unifying theory of behavioral change. *Psychological Review, 84,* 191–215.

Bandura, A. (1989). Self-regulation of motivation and action through internal standards and goal systems. In L.A. Pervin (Ed.), *Goal concepts in personality and social psychology* (pp. 19–85). Hillsdale, NJ: Lawrence Erlbaum Associates.

Bargh, J. A. (1996). Automaticity in social psychology. In E.T. Higgins & A.W. Kruglanski (Eds.), *Social psychology: Handbook of basic principles* (pp. 169–183). New York: Guilford.

Baumeister, R. F., Heatherton, T.F., & Tice, D.M. (1994). *Losing control: How and why people fail at self-regulation.* San Diego, CA: Academic Press.

Bieri, P. (1987). Intentionale Systeme: Überlegungen zu Daniel Dennetts Theorie des Geistes. In J. Brandtstädter (Ed.), *Struktur und Erfahrung in der psychologischen Forschung* (pp. 208–252). Berlin: de Gruyter.

Bohner, G., Moskowitz, G. B., & Chaiken, S. (1995). The interplay of heuristic and systematic processing of social information. In W. Stroebe & M. Hewstone (Eds.), *European Review of Social Psychology* (vol. 6, pp. 33–68). Chichester: Wiley.

Brandtstädter, J. (1985). Emotion, Kognition, Handlung: Konzeptuelle Beziehungen. In L. H. Eckensberger & E.-D. Lanter-mann (Eds.), *Emotion und Reflexivität* (pp. 252–261). München: Urban & Schwarzenberg.

Brandtstädter, J. (1993). Struktur und Erfahrung in der psycho-logischen Forschung: Handlungs- und entwicklungstheoretische Aspekte. In U. Gähde & L. Eckensberger (Eds.), *Ethik und Empirie. Zum Zusammenspiel von begrifflicher Analyse und er-*

*fahrungswissenschaftlicher Forschung in der Ethik (pp. 244–267)*. Frankfurt a. M.: Suhrkamp.

Brandtstädter, J. (1997). Action, culture, and development: Points of convergence. *Culture and Psychology, 3*, 335–352.

Brandtstädter, J. (1998). Action perspectives on human development. In R. M. Lerner (Ed.), *Theoretical models of human development* (Handbook of child psychology, Vol. 1, 5th ed., pp. 807–863). New York: Wiley.

Brandtstädter, J. & Greve, W. (in press). Intentionale und nicht-intentionale Aspekte des Handelns. In J. Straub & H. Werbik (Eds.), *Handlungsbegriff und Handlungserklärung: Interdisziplinäre Perspektiven*. Frankfurt/M.: Suhrkamp.

Brandtstädter, J. & Renner, G. (1990). Tenacious goal pursuit and flexible goal adjustment: Explication and age-related analysis of assimilative and accommodative strategies of coping. *Psychology and Aging, 5*, 58–67.

Carver, C. S. & Scheier, M. F. (1990). Origins and foundations of positive and negative affect: A control-process view. *Psychological Review, 97*, 19–25.

Chisholm, R. M. (1971). "Er hätte etwas anderes tun können." *Conceptus, 5*, 13–19.

Dennett, D. C. (1984). *Elbow room. The varieties of free will worth wanting*. Oxford: Clarendon.

Dennett, D. C. (1987). *The intentional stance*. Cambridge, MA: MIT Press.

Elster, J. (1989). *Nuts and bolts for the social sciences*. New York: Cambridge University Press.

Feather, N. T. (Ed.). (1982). *Expectations and actions. Expectancy-value models in psychology*. Hillsdale, NJ: Lawrence Erlbaum Associates.

Flammer, A. (1990). *Erfahrung der eigenen Wirksamkeit. Einführung in die Psychologie der Kontrollmeinung*. Bern: Huber.

Flammer, A. (1995). Developmental analysis of control beliefs. In A. Bandura (Ed.), *Self-efficacy in changing societies* (pp. 69–113). New York: Cambridge University Press.

Flammer, A., Züblin, C., & Grob, A. (1988). Sekundäre Kontrolle bei Jugendlichen. *Zeitschrift für Entwicklungspsychologie und Pädagogische Psychologie, 20*, 239–262.

Frankfurt, H. G. (1971). Freedom of the will and the concept of a person. *Journal of Philosophy, 68*, 5–20.

Gilbert, D. T. (1993). The assent of man: Mental representation and the control of belief. In D.M. Wegner & J. W. Pennebaker (Eds.), *Handbook of mental control* (pp. 57–87). Englewood Cliffs, NJ: Prentice-Hall.

Gollwitzer, P. M. (1990). Action phases and mind-sets. In E. T. Higgins & R. M. Sorrentino (Eds.), *Handbook of motivation and cognition: Foundations of social behavior* (Vol. 2, pp. 53–92). New York: Guilford Press.

Gollwitzer, P. M. & Kinney, R. F. (1989). Effects of deliberative and implemental mind-sets on illusion of control. *Journal of Personality and Social Psychology, 56*, 531–542.

Gordon, R. M. (1987). *The structure of emotions. Investigations in cognitive philosophy*. New York: Cambridge University Press.

Greve, W. (1996). Erkenne dich selbst? Argumente zur Bedeutung der "Perspektive der ersten Person". *Sprache & Kognition, 15*, 104–119.

Heckhausen, H. (1980). *Motivation und Handeln*. Heidelberg: Springer.

Heckhausen, J. & Schulz, R. (1995). A life-span theory of control. *Psychological Review*, *102*, 284–304.

Honderich, T. (1988). *A theory of determinism. The mind, neuroscience, and life-hopes*. Oxford: Clarendon.

Johnston, M. (1995). Self-deception and the nature of mind. In C. Macdonald & G. Macdonald (Eds.), *Philosophy of psychology. Debates on psychological explanation* (Vol.1, pp. 433–460). Oxford: Blackwell.

Kant, I. (1974). *Anthropology from a pragmatic point of view* (Transl. M. J. Gregor). The Hague: Nijhoff (original work published in German, 1798).

Karoly, P. (1993). Mechanisms of self-regulation: A systems view. *Annual Review of Psychology*, *44*, 23–52.

Keil, F. C. (1979). *Semantic and conceptual development: An ontological perspective*. Cambridge, MA: Harvard University Press.

Kuhl, J. (1985). Volitional mediators of cognition-behavior consistency: Self-regulatory processes and action vs. state orientation. In J. Kuhl & J. Beckmann (Eds.), *Action control. From cognition to behavior* (pp. 101–128). Berlin: Springer.

Kunda, Z. (1990). The case for motivated reasoning. *Psychological Bulletin*, *108*, 480–498.

Lazarus, R. S. (1984). On the primacy of cognition. *American Psychologist*, *39*, 124–129.

Lazarus, R. S. (1985). Toward an understanding of efficiency and inefficiency in human affairs: Discussion of Schönpflug's theory. In M. Frese & J. Sabini (Eds.), *Goal directed behavior: The concept of action in psychology* (pp. 189–198). Hillsdale, NJ: Lawrence Erlbaum Associates.

Lazarus, R. S. & DeLongis, A. (1983). Psychological stress and coping in aging. *American Psychologist*, *38*, 245–254.

Lockard, J. S. & Paulhus, D. L. (Eds.). (1988). *Self-deception: An adaptive mechanism?* Englewood Cliffs, NJ: Prentice-Hall.

Martin, L. L. & Tesser, A. (1989). Toward a motivational and structural theory of ruminative thought. In J.S. Uleman & J.A. Bargh (Eds.), *Unintended thought* (pp. 306–326). New York: Guilford Press.

Mele, A. (1987). Recent work on self-deception. *American Philosophical Quarterly*, *24*, 1–17.

Müller, A. (1992). Mental teleology. *Proceedings of the Aristotelian Society*, *92 (Part 1)*, 161–183.

Quine, W. V. O. (1960). *Word and object*. Cambridge, MA: MIT Press.

Reisenzein, R. (1996). Emotional action generation. In W. Battmann & S. Dutke (Eds.), *Processes of the molar regulation of behavior* (pp. 151–165). Lengerich: Pabst Science Publishers.

Roberts, R. C. (1984). Will power and the virtues. *Philosophical Review*, *93*, 227–247.

Rorty, R. (1982). Contemporary philosophy of mind. *Synthese*, *53*, 323–348.

Rothbaum, F., Weisz, J. R., & Snyder, S. S. (1982). Changing the world and changing the self. A two-process model of perceived control. *Journal of Personality and Social Psychology*, *42*, 5–37.

Skinner, E. A., Chapman, M., & Baltes, P. B. (1988). Control, mean-ends, and agency beliefs: A new conceptualization and its measurement during childhood. *Journal of Personality and Social Psychology, 54*, 117–133.

Vallacher, R. R. & Wegner, D. M. (1987). What do people think they're doing? Action identification and human behavior. *Psychological Review, 94*, 3–15.

Wegner, D.M. (1994). Ironic processes of mental control. *Psychological Review, 101*, 34–52.

Weisz, J. R. (1983). Can I control it? The pursuit of veridical answers across the life span. In P. B. Baltes & O. G. Brim, Jr. (Eds.), *Life-span development and behavior* (pp. 233–300). New York: Academic Press.

Wentura, D. (1995). *Verfügbarkeit entlastender Kognitionen. Zur Verarbeitung negativer Lebenssituationen.* Weinheim: Psychologie Verlags Union.

Williams, B. (1973). Deciding to believe. In Williams, B. (Ed.) *Problems of the self* (pp. 136–151). Cambridge: Cambridge University Press.

Wortman, C. B. & Brehm, J. W. (1975). Responses to uncontrollable outcomes: An integration of reactance theory and the learned helplessness model. In L. Berkowitz (Ed.), *Advances in experimental social psychology* (Vol. 8, pp. 278–336). New York: Academic Press.

Zajonc, R. B. (1984). On the primacy of affect. *American Psychologist, 39*, 117–123.

# 2

# Self-Efficacy: The Foundation of Agency[1]

## *Albert Bandura*

## INTRODUCTION

People have always striven to exercise control over events that affect their lives. They seek control because it provides them with countless personal and social benefits. Uncertainty in things that have significant personal consequences is highly unsettling. To the extent that people are able to influence their outcomes, they are better able to predict them. Predictability fosters foresightful and adaptive preparedness. By influencing events over which they command some control, people can better realize desired futures and forestall undesired ones. Inability to exert influence over things that adversely affect one's life breeds apprehension, dysfunction, apathy and despair.

The accelerated pace of informational, social and technological evolution has placed a premium on people's capabilities to exert a strong hand in their own development and functioning throughout the life course. Consider a few examples. With the rapidly-growing information systems, students now have well-organized instruction and the best libraries, laboratories, museums, and other sources of knowledge at their fingertips, regardless of time and place. This enables them to educate themselves on whatever interests them. The recent years have witnessed a major change in the conception of health from a disease model to a health model. By exercising control over health habits people live longer, healthier, and slow the process of aging. In the modern workplace, knowledge and technical skills are quickly outmoded unless they are updated. Employees have to take charge of their self-development over the full course of their worklife. Efficacious innovativeness and adaptability has become a premium at the organizational level as well. These new realities place increasing demands on individual and collective efficacy to shape personal destinies and the national life of societies.

Because of the centrality of control in people's lives, many theories about it have been proposed over the years. Much of this research is tied to general measures of perceived control and search for their correlates. In social cognitive theory,

[1]Preparation of this article was supported by grants from the Grant Foundation and the Spencer Foundation. Portions of this chapter contain revised and expanded material from the book, Self-Efficacy: The Exercise of Control, 1997. New York: Freeman.

perceived self-efficacy is embedded in a theory of human agency (Bandura, 1986; 1997).

People make causal contribution to their lives through mechanisms of personal agency. Among the mechanisms of agency, none is more central or pervasive than people's judgments of their efficacy. Perceived self-efficacy refers to beliefs in one's capabilities to organize and execute the courses of action required to produce given levels of attainments. Unless people believe they can produce desired effects by their actions, they have little incentive to act. Efficacy belief is, therefore, the foundation of agency. The events over which self-influence is exercised vary widely. It may entail regulating of one's own motivation, thought processes, affective states and actions, or changing environmental conditions, depending on what one seeks to manage (Bandura, 1995, 1997; Maddux, 1995; Schwarzer, 1992).

## STRUCTURE AND FUNCTION OF EFFICACY BELIEFS

Human competencies are developed and manifested in many different forms. These diverse areas of functioning demand different knowledge and skills. One cannot be all things; hence, people differ in their sense of efficacy across different activity domains. Social cognitive theory treats the efficacy belief system not as an omnibus trait, but as a differentiated set of self-beliefs linked to distinct realms of functioning. Comparative studies show that domain-linked measures of perceived efficacy are good predictors of motivation and action (Bandura, 1997). Omnibus global measures have little explanatory and predictive value.

A central question in any theory of cognitive regulation of motivation, affect and action concerns the issue of causality. Do efficacy beliefs operate as causal factors in human functioning? This issue has been examined by a variety of experimental strategies. In each approach, perceived efficacy is systematically varied to differential levels by nonperformance means and the effects of instated efficacy beliefs on performance are measured. Causal contribution has also been tested using prospective multivariate designs with structural modeling verifying the independent and mediated impact of perceived self-efficacy on performance.

These diverse causal tests have been conducted with different modes of efficacy induction, diverse populations, using both interindividual and intraindividual verification, in all sorts of domains of functioning, and with microlevel and macrolevel relations (Bandura, 1997). The evidence is consistent in showing that perceived self-efficacy contributes significantly to level of motivation and performance accomplishments.

## EFFICACY-ACTIVATED PROCESSES

Efficacy beliefs regulate human functioning through four major processes. They include cognitive, motivational, emotional, and selection processes. These are reviewed briefly in the sections that follow.

*Cognitive Processes.* Efficacy beliefs affect thought patterns that can enhance or undermine performance. These cognitive effects take various forms. Much human behavior is regulated by forethought in the form of cognized goals. The stronger the perceived efficacy, the higher the challenges people set for themselves and the firmer their commitment to meeting them. Challenging goals raise motivation and performance attainments (Bandura, 1991; Locke & Latham, 1990).

People's beliefs in their efficacy also influence the anticipatory scenarios and visualized futures they construct and use to guide their actions. Those of high efficacy visualize success scenarios that provide positive guides for performance, whereas those who doubt their efficacy visualize failure scenarios that undermine performance by dwelling on how things might go wrong. Moreover, in appraising situations, people who are assured in their efficacy focus on the opportunities worth pursuing rather than dwell on risks (Krueger & Dickson, 1993; 1994). They take a future time perspective in structuring their lives (Eppel, Bandura, & Zimbardo, in press).

A major function of thought is to enable people to predict events and to exercise control over those that are important to them. People of high efficacy show greater cognitive resourcefulness and strategic flexibility. Discernment of predictive rules governing events and good operative rules for changing them enables people to manage their environment more effectively and productively (Wood & Bandura, 1989).

*Motivational Processes.* Efficacy beliefs play a central role in the self-regulation of motivation. Most human motivation is cognitively generated. There are three forms of cognitive motivators, around which different theories have been built. These include *causal attributions, outcome expectancies*, and *cognized goals*. The corresponding theories are attribution theory, expectancy-value theory, and goal theory. Efficacy beliefs play a key role in each of these motivational systems.

Much human motivation and behavior is regulated anticipatorily by the outcomes expected for given actions (Feather, 1982). Courses of action likely to produce positive outcomes tend to be adopted and used, whereas those that bring unrewarding or punishing outcomes are usually discarded. However, there are many activities which, if done well, produce valued outcomes, but they are not pursued by people who doubt they can do what it takes to succeed. Such exclusions of large classes of options are made rapidly on efficacy grounds, with little thought of costs and benefits. Rational models of decision making that exclude efficacy judgment sacrifice explanatory and predictive power (Bandura, 1997). Moreover, making decisions in no way ensures that the needed courses of action will be executed successfully, especially in the face of difficulties. A psychology of decision making requires a psychology of action grounded in enabling and sustaining efficacy beliefs (Harré, 1983).

The capacity to exercise self-influence by personal challenge through goal setting and evaluative reaction to one's own performances provides another major cognitive mechanism of motivation and self-directedness. Once people commit themselves to valued goals, they seek self-satisfaction from fulfilling them and intensify their efforts by discontent with substandard performances. It is partly on the basis of efficacy beliefs that people choose which goal challenges to undertake, how much effort to invest and how long to persevere in the face of difficulties (Bandura, 1991; Locke & Latham, 1990). When faced with obstacles, setbacks and failures those who doubt their abilities slacken their efforts, give up, or settle for mediocre solutions. Those who have strong belief in their capabilities redouble their effort and figure out better ways to master the challenges.

The causal attributions people make for their performances also affect their motivation (Weiner, 1986). Efficacy beliefs influence causal attributions, regardless of whether the activities involve cognitive attainments, interpersonal transactions, physical performances, or management of health habits. People who regard themselves as highly efficacious ascribe their failures to insufficient efforts, inadequate strategies or unfavorable circumstances (Alden, 1986; Courneya & McAuley, 1993; Grove, 1993; Matsui, Konishi, Onglatco, Matsude, & Ohnishi, 1988; McAuley, Duncan, & McElroy, 1989; Silver, Mitchell, & Gist, 1995). Those of low efficacy attribute their failures to low ability. The effects of causal attributions on achievement strivings are mediated almost entirely through efficacy beliefs (Relich, Debus, & Walker, 1986; Schunk & Gunn, 1986; Schunk & Rice, 1986).

*Affective Processes.* People's beliefs in their coping capabilities also affect how much stress and depression they experience in threatening or taxing situations. There are four major ways in which efficacy beliefs regulate emotional states (Bandura, 1997). They do so by influencing how threats are cognitive processed, supporting coping actions that alter the threats, exercising control over perturbing thought patterns and by alleviating aversive affective states.

Efficacy beliefs influence how threats and taxing demands are perceived and cognitively processed. People who believe they can manage threats are not distressed by them. Those who believe they cannot control them experience high anxiety, dwell on their coping deficiencies, view many aspects of their environment as fraught with danger, magnify possible risks and worry about perils that rarely happen. By such thinking they distress themselves and impair their functioning (Bandura, 1997; Sanderson, Rapee, & Barlow, 1989).

People who have a high sense of coping efficacy lower their stress and anxiety by acting in ways that transform threatening environments into benign ones. The stronger the sense of efficacy the bolder people are in tackling the problems that breed stress and anxiety, the greater is their success in shaping the environment to their liking (Bandura, 1997; Williams, 1992).

People have to live with a psychic environment that is largely of their own making. Many human distresses result from failures to control disturbing, ruminative thoughts. Control of one's thought processes is, therefore, a key factor in self-regulation of emotional states. The process of efficacious thought control is summed up well in the proverb: *"You cannot prevent the birds of worry and care from flying over your head. But you can stop them from building a nest in your hair."* What causes distress is not the sheer frequency of disturbing thoughts, but the perceived helplessness to turn them off (Kent, 1987; Kent & Gibbons, 1987). Hence, the frequency of aversive cognitions is unrelated to anxiety level when the influence of perceived thought control efficacy is removed, whereas perceived thought control efficacy is strongly related to anxiety level when frequency of aversive cognitions is removed.

In addition, people can exercise control over their affective states in palliative ways without altering the causes of their emotional arousal. They do things that bring relief from unpleasant emotional states when they arise. People who believe they can relax, get engrossed in activities, calm themselves by reassuring thought, and seek support from friends, family, and others, find unpleasant emotional states less aversive then those who feel helpless to relieve their emotional distress (Arch, 1992, a, b).

Perceived inefficacy to control things one values also produces depression. As in the case of anxiety arousal, perceived inefficacy contributes to depression in varied ways. One route is through unfulfilled aspirations. People who impose on themselves standards of self-worth they judge they cannot attain drive themselves to depression. Depression, in turn, weakens people's beliefs in their efficacy creating a downward cycle (Kavanagh & Bower, 1985).

A second route to depression, is through a low sense of social efficacy to develop social relationships that bring satisfaction to one's life and make chronic stressors easier to manage and to bear. A low sense of social efficacy contributes to depression both directly and by curtailing development of social support. Perceived efficacy and social support operate bidirectionally in human adaptation and change. Social support is not a self-forming entity waiting around to buffer harried people against stressors. Rather, people have to go out and find or create supportive relationships for themselves. Individuals of high perceived social efficacy create more supportive environments for themselves than those who distrust their social capabilities (Holahan & Holahan, 1987a, b). Supportive relationships, in turn, can enhance personal efficacy. Enabling supporters raise efficacy in others in several ways. They can model effective coping attitudes and strategies for managing problem situations, demonstrate the value of perseverance, and provide positive incentives and resources for efficacious coping. Mediational analyses reveal that social support has beneficial effects only to the extent that it raises perceived coping efficacy (Cutrona & Troutman, 1986; Major, Mueller, & Hildebrandt, 1985).

The third route to depression is through thought control efficacy. Much human depression is cognitively generated by dejecting, ruminative thought (Nolen-Hoeksema, 1991). A low sense of efficacy to control ruminative thought contributes to the occurrence, duration, and recurrence of depressive episodes (Kavanagh & Wilson, 1989).

*Selection Processes.* The preceding discussion documents how efficacy beliefs enable people to create beneficial environments, modify them and control them. People are partly the product of their environment. By choosing their environments, they can have a hand in what they become. Efficacy beliefs can, therefore, play a key role in shaping the courses lives take by influencing the types of activities and environments people choose to get into. In self-development through choice processes, personal destinies are shaped by selection of environments known to cultivate valued potentialities and lifestyles.

The power of efficacy beliefs to affect life paths through selection processes is most clearly revealed in studies of career choice and development (Lent, Brown, & Hackett. 1994). Occupational choices are of considerable import because they structure a major part of people's everyday reality, provide them with a source of personal identity and determine whether their worklife is repetitively boring, burdensome and distressing, or lastingly challenging and fulfilling. People who have a strong sense of personal efficacy consider a wide range of career options, show greater the interest in them, prepare themselves better for different careers and have greater staying power in their chosen pursuits. Even as early as junior high school, children's beliefs in their occupational efficacy, which are rooted in their patterns of perceived efficacy, have begun to crystallize and steer their occupational considerations in directions congruent with their efficacy beliefs (Bandura, Barbaranelli, Caprara, & Pastorelli, 1997).

In sum, people who have a low sense of efficacy in a given domain of life shy away from difficult tasks, which they perceive as personal threats. They have low aspirations and weak commitment to the goals they choose. They turn inward on their self-doubts instead of thinking about how to perform successfully. When faced with difficult tasks they dwell on obstacles, the negative consequences of failure and their personal deficiencies. Failure makes them lose faith in their capabilities because they attribute it to personal inadequacies. They slacken their efforts or give up quickly in the face of difficulties. They are slow to recover their sense of efficacy after failures or setbacks and easily fall victim to stress and depression.

People who have a strong sense of efficacy, by contrast, approach difficult tasks as challenges to be mastered rather than threats to be avoided. They set challenging goals and sustain strong commitments to them. They concentrate on how to perform successfully not on themselves and disruptive personal concerns when they encounter problems. They attribute their failures to lack of knowledge or skill, faulty strategies or insufficient effort, all of which are remediable. They redouble their efforts in the face of difficulties, display low vulnerability to stress and depression and quickly recover their sense of efficacy after failures or setbacks. Success usually comes through renewed effort after failed attempts. It is resiliency of personal efficacy that counts. This type of affirmative outlook sustains motivation, promotes accomplishments and lowers vulnerability to stress and depression.

## VERIDICALITY OF SELF-APPRAISAL: SELF-AIDING OR SELF-LIMITING?

There has been some dispute about whether people are bettered served by veridical or optimistic self-belief (Colvin & Block, 1994; Taylor & Brown, 1988; 1994). These debates fail to make important distinctions that specify when optimistic judgment of capabilities is beneficial and when veridical judgment is self-limiting. Tenacious strivers should be differentiated from wishful dreamers. Wistful optimists lack the efficacy strength to put up with the uncertainties, disappointments and drudgery that are required for high accomplishments. Tenacious strivers believe so strongly in themselves, that they are willing to exert extraordinary effort and suffer countless hardships and disappointments in pursuit of their vision. They abide by objective realism about the normative reality, but subjective optimism about their chances of success. That is, they do not delude themselves about the tough odds of high attainments, but they believe they have what it takes to beat those odds.

The functional value of veridical self-appraisal also depends on the nature of the pursuits. In activities where the margins of error are narrow and missteps can produce costly or injurious consequences, people had better be accurate in judging their efficacy. It is a different matter where difficult accomplishments can produce substantial personal or social benefits and the personal costs involve time, effort, and resources. Individuals have to decide for themselves which abilities to cultivate, whether to invest their resources and efforts in ventures that are difficult to fulfill, and how much hardship they are willing to endure in pursuits strewn with obstacles and uncertainties.

The realities of everyday life are strewn with difficulties. In a world full of disappointments, impediments, adversities, failures, setbacks, frustrations, and inequities, optimistic self-efficacy is an adaptive judgmental bias not a cognitive failing to be eliminated. Evidence shows that human accomplishments and positive well-being require an optimistic sense of personal efficacy to override the numerous impediments to success. Indeed, the striking characteristic of people who have achieved success in their fields is an inextinguishable sense of efficacy and a firm belief in the worth of what they are doing (Shepherd, 1995; White, 1982). So-called realists forsake difficult pursuits or become cynical about the prospects of change.

Early rejection is the rule, rather than the exception, in virtually all innovative and creative endeavors. A resilient self-belief enables people to override repeated early rejections of their work. People who are successful, innovative, sociable, nonanxious, nondepressed, and effective social reformers take an optimistic view of their efficacy to influence events that affect their lives (Bandura,

1997). If not exaggerated, such self-beliefs raise aspirations, and enhance and sustain the level of motivation needed for personal, and social, accomplishments.

Societies enjoy the considerable benefits of the accomplishments in the arts, sciences and technologies of its efficacious persisters and risk takers. To paraphrase the astute observation of George Bernard Shaw, since reasonable people adapt to the world and unreasonable ones try to alter it, human progress depends on the unreasonable ones. It is not all that difficult to produce veridical self-appraisal in which people's beliefs in their efficacy match their current performances but they do not strive for something higher. Simply punish optimism (Oettingen, 1995). We study extensively the costs of mistaken actions that are taken. But we ignore the costs of promising actions not taken because of under-confidence. Yet, people have greater regrets about the career opportunities not pursued, personal relationships not cultivated, and risks not taken, than regrets about the actions they have taken (Hattrangadi, Medvec, & Gilovich, 1995). The heavy preoccupation with the risks of optimistic self-beliefs reflects a pervasive conservative bias in psychology.

## FORMS OF AGENCY

The exercise of human agency can take different forms. It includes production of effects through *direct personal agency*; through *proxy agency* relying on the controlling actions of intermediaries; and by *collective agency*, operating through shared beliefs of efficacy, pooled understandings, group aspirations, and collective action. Each of these expressions of agency is rooted in belief in the power to make things happen. The preceding analyses of the origins, operative processes, and diverse effects of efficacy beliefs address the direct expression of personal agency. The vast literature and wide-ranging applications of self-efficacy theory to diverse spheres of life are reviewed in considerable detail in *Self-Efficacy: The Exercise of Control* (Bandura, 1997). The sections that follow examine the role of proxy efficacy and the growing importance of collective efficacy in people's lives.

*Proxy Agency.* In many spheres of life, people do not have direct control over social conditions and institutional practices that affect their lives. Under these circumstances, they seek their well-being and security through proxy agency by getting those who wield influence and power to act on their behalf to get what they want (Bandura, 1997). Moreover, people often turn to proxy control in areas in which they can exert direct influence because they have not developed the means to do so, they believe others can do it better, or they do not want to saddle themselves with the burdens that direct control imposes. Effective proxy control requires a high sense of personal efficacy to influence intermediaries who, in turn, operate as the agents of desired outcomes.

Many theorists regard the striving for control as an expression of an inborn drive (Adler, 1956; Deci & Ryan, 1985; Skinner, 1995; White, 1959). In fact, personal control is neither universally desired nor universally exercised. There is an onerous side to direct personal control that can dull the appetite for it. The exercise of control requires mastery of knowledge and skills attainable only through long hours of arduous work. Maintaining control also requires continued investment of time, effort and resources in self-renewal to fit the changing times. A noted composer put it succinctly when he said, *"The toughest thing about success, is that you've got to keep on being a success."* In addition to the hard work of continual self-development, in many situations the exercise of personal control carries heavy responsibilities, stressors, and risks. For these many reasons, people often opt for proxy control rather than exercise direct control. But part of the price of proxy agency is a vulnerable security that rests on the competence, power, and favors of others.

*Collective Agency.* Conceptions of human agency have been essentially confined to individual agency. However, people do not live their lives as isolates. They work together to produce the results they desire but cannot accomplish on their own. Social cognitive theory extends the analysis of mechanisms of human agency to collective agency. People's shared beliefs in their collective power to produce desired outcomes is a crucial ingredient of collective agency. Group performance is the product of interactive and coordinative dynamics of its members. Therefore, perceived collective efficacy is not simply the sum of the efficacy beliefs of individual members. It is an emergent, group-level attribute. A group, of course, operates through the behavior of its members. It is people acting collectively on a shared belief not a disembodied group mind that is doing the cognizing, aspiring, motivating and acting.

Personal and collective efficacy differ in the unit of agency but, in both forms, efficacy beliefs serve similar functions and operate through similar processes. People's shared beliefs in their collective efficacy influence the type of futures they seek to achieve; how well they use their resources; how much effort they put into their group endeavor; their staying power when collective efforts fail to produce quick results or meet forcible opposition; and their vulnerability to discouragement.

Some people live their lives in individualistically-oriented social systems. Others do so in collectivistically-oriented ones (Triandis, 1995). Some writers inappropriately equate self-efficacy with individualism and pit it against collectivism. In fact, a high sense of personal efficacy contributes just as importantly to group-directedness as to self-directedness. To work together successfully, members have to perform their roles with a high sense of efficacy. Chronic self-doubters are not easily formed into a collective efficacious force. Personal efficacy is valued, not because of reverence for individualism, but because a strong sense of efficacy is vital for successful functioning regardless of whether it is achieved individually or by group members working together.

Group achievements and social change are rooted in self-efficacy. Cross-cultural research confirms the universal functional value of efficacy beliefs (Earley, 1993; 1994). In these studies, efficacy beliefs contribute to productivity by members of collectivist cultures just as they do by those raised in individualistic cultures. But cultural values shape how efficacy beliefs are developed, the purposes to which they are put, and the social arrangements through which they are best expressed. Members of individualistic cultures feel most efficacious and perform best under an individually-oriented system. Those from collectivistic cultures judge themselves most efficacious and work most productively under a group-oriented system. But the critical factor is not collectivism per se. When collectivists of different ethnicity have to work together they distrust their collective efficacy and perform poorly.

Cultures are not as homogeneous as the stereotypic portrayals would lead one to believe. Collectivistic systems, such as those founded on Confucianism, Buddhism or Marxism favor a communal ethic, but they differ from each other in the values, meanings and customs they promote (Kim, Triandis, Kâgitçibasi, Choi, & Yoon, 1994). Nor are so-called individualistic cultures a uniform lot. Americans, Italians, Germans and the British differ in their particular brands of individualism. Even within an individualistically-oriented culture, such as the United States, the New England brand of individualism is quite different from the Californian version or that of the Southern region of the nation.

There are collectivists in individualistic cultures, and individualists in collectivistic cultures. Regardless of cultural background, people achieve the greatest personal efficacy and productivity when their personal orientation is congruent with the social system. For example, U. S. collectivists do better under a group-oriented system, Chinese individualists do better under an individually-oriented system.

The personal orientation rather than the cultural orientation is a major carrier of the effects. Both at the societal and individual level of analysis, a strong sense of efficacy fosters high group effort and performance.

Neither individualistic nor collectivistic cultures are static, uniform entities. People express their cultural orientation conditionally rather than invariantly. The members of different cultures vary in how collectivistic or individualistic they are across generations, across different facets of life, interpersonal relationships, social contexts, socioeducational levels and over time (Matsumoto, Kudoh, & Takeuchi, 1996). For example, those in collectivistically-oriented societies are highly communal with ingroup members but not so with outgroup members. But in the presence of negative sanctions against free riders they become as communal with outsiders as do people in individualistic cultures (Yamagishi, 1988). Both intracultural and conditional variation in styles of behavior underscore the need to specify mechanisms through which cultural influences exert their effects. Cultural orientations must be treated as multifaceted dynamic influences rather than as categorical entities. Research based on global classifications that gloss over intracultural variation may do more to perpetuate cultural stereotypes than to clarify the role of sociocultural influences in human adaptation and change.

## UNDERMINERS OF COLLECTIVE EFFICACY
## IN CHANGING SOCIETIES

Life in the societies of today is increasingly shaped by transnational interdependencies (Keohane & Nye, 1977; Keohane, 1993). Because of the interconnectedness, what happens economically and politically in one part of the world can affect the welfare of vast populations elsewhere. The transnational forces, which are hard to disentangle let alone control, challenge the efficacy of governmental systems to exert a determining influence on their own economic and national life. The growing interdependence of social and economic life requires effective collective action at local, national and transnational levels. As the need for efficacious collective effort grows so does the sense of collective powerlessness. Many of the contemporary conditions of life undermine the development of collective efficacy.

Global market forces are restructuring national economies and shaping the social life of societies. Some of the transnational market forces may erode or undermine valued aspects of life. There are no handy social mechanisms or global agencies through which people can shape and regulate transnational practices that affect their lives. As nations wrestle with the loss of control, the public expresses disillusionment and cynicism over whether their leaders and institutions can work for them to improve their lives. The crisis of leadership and governmental efficacy affects most nations nowadays. People strive to regain some control over their lives by seeking to shape their local circumstances, over which they have some influence. The retreat to localism, fueled by public disillusionment with its national systems, ironically comes at a time calling for strong national leadership to manage powerful influences from abroad to shape their nation's own destiny.

Under the new realities of growing transnational control, nation states increase their controlling leverage by merging into larger regional units such as the European Union. Other regional nation states will be forced to merge into larger blocks, otherwise they will have little bargaining power in transnational relations. These regional marriages do not come without a price. Paradoxically, to gain international control nations have to negotiate reciprocal pacts that require some loss of national autonomy and changes in traditional ways of life (Keohane, 1993). Some members of the society gain from the agreements, others lose. This creates disputes within nations between the winners and losers. The major challenge to leadership is to build a national sense of efficacy to take advantage of the opportunities of globalization, while minimizing the price that the changes extract from local cultures.

Modern life is increasingly regulated by complex technologies that most people neither understand, nor believe they can do much to influence. The very technologies that people create to control their life environment, can become a constraining force that, in turn, controls how they think and behave. As an example of such paradoxical consequences, the citizens of nations that are heavily dependent on deteriorating atomic plants for for their energy feel powerless to remove this catastrophic hazard from their lives, even though they acknowledge the grave danger. The devastating consequences of mishaps do not respect national borders.

The social machinery of society is no less challenging. Bureaucracies thwart effective social action. Many of the bureaucratic practices are designed more to benefit the people who run the social systems than to serve the public. Those who exercise authority and control wield their power to maintain their advantage. Long delays between action and noticeable results discourage efforts at change. Most people relinquish control in the face of institutional and bureaucratic obstacles.

Social efforts to change lives for the better require merging diverse self-interests in support of common core values and goals. Disagreements among different constituencies create additional obstacles to successful collective action. The recent years have witnessed growing social fragmentation into separate interest groups, each exercising its own power. Pluralism is taking the form of antagonistic factionalism. In the more extreme forms of social fragmentation, countries are being dismantled with a vengeance along racial, religious, and ethnic lines. In addition, mass migration of people fleeing tyranny or seeking a better life is changing cultural landscapes. As migration changes the ethnic composition of populations, societies are becoming more diverse and harder to unite around a national vision and purpose.

The magnitude of human problems also undermines perceived efficacy to find effective solutions for them. Profound global changes, arising from burgeoning populations, deforestation, desertification of croplands, ozone depletion, and rapid extinction of species by razing their habitats are destroying the intertwined ecosystems that sustain life. These changes are creating new realities requiring a high level of collective efficacy to devise and implement transnational remedies. Worldwide problems of growing magnitude instill a sense of paralysis, that there is little people can do to reduce such problems. Global effects are the products of local actions. The strategy of "Think globally, act locally" is an effort to restore in people a sense of efficacy, that they can make a difference.

Macrosocial applications of modeling principles via the electronic media illustrate how a small collective effort can have a huge impact on global problems. The soaring population growth and the environmental devastation it produces is the most urgent global problem. The world population is doubling at an accelerating rate. Radio and television dramatic serials founded on social cognitive principles are raising people's efficacy to exercise control over their family lives, enhancing the status of women and lowering the rates of childbearing internationally (Singhal & Rogers, 1989; Vaughn, Rogers, & Swalehe, 1995; Westoff & Rodriguez, 1995).

## INTERDEPENDENCE OF PERSONAL AGENCY AND SOCIAL STRUCTURE

Human agency operates within a causal structure involving triadic reciprocal causation (Bandura, 1986). In this transactional view of self and society, personal factors in the form of cognitive, emotional and biological events; behavior patterns; and environmental events all operate as determinants that influence each other bidirectionally. Human adaptation and change are rooted in social systems. Therefore, personal agency operates within a broad network of social structural influences. For the most part, social structures represent authorized social practices carried out by human beings occupying designated roles (Giddens, 1984). Within the societal rule structures there is a lot of personal variation in their interpretation, adoption, enforcement, circumvention or active opposition (Burns & Dietz, in press). This interactive relationship is not a static dualism between a disembodied social structure and personal agency, but a dynamic interplay between individuals and those who preside over the institutionalized operations of social systems.

Sociostructural theories and psychological theories are often regarded as rival conceptions of human behavior, or as representing different levels of causation. Human behavior cannot be fully understood solely in terms of sociostructural factors or psychological factors. A full understanding requires an integrated perspective in which social influences operate through psychological mechanisms to produce behavioral effects. When analyzed within a unified causal structure, sociostructural influences produce behavioral effects largely through efficacy self processes rather than directly (Baldwin, Baldwin, Sameroff, & Seifer, 1989; Bandura, Barbaranelli, Pastorelli, & Caprara, 1996, 1997; Elder, & Ardelt, 1992). The effects of sociostructural influences on the functioning of social systems are also in large part mediated through the perceived collective efficacy of the operators of the systems (Bandura, 1997).

The self system is not merely a conduit for external influences, however. People are producers as well as products of social systems. By exercising self-influence, human agency operates generatively and proactively rather than just reactively. Social structures are created by efficacious human activity. The structural practices, in turn, impose constraints and provide resources and opportunity structures for personal development and functioning. Given this bidirectionality of influence, social cognitive theory rejects a dualism between social structure and personal agency.

## CONCLUSION

Diverse lines of research verify that beliefs of personal efficacy play an influential role both in mediating the impact of environmental conditions on behavior and in the production of environmental conditions. Belief in the power to make things happen operates through direct personal agency, proxy agency, and collective agency. The value of a psychological theory is judged not only by its explanatory and predictive power, but also by its operative power to bring about psychosocial changes. Social cognitive theory provides prescriptive knowledge on how to alter beliefs of personal and collective efficacy that enable people to change their lives for the better.

## REFERENCES

Adler, A. (1956). In H. C. Ansbacher & R. R. Ansbacher (Eds.), *The individual psychology of Alfred Adler*. New York: Harper & Row.
Alden, L. (1986). Self-efficacy and causal attributions for social feedback. *Journal of Research in Personality, 20*, 460–473.
Arch, E. C. (1992a). Affective control efficacy as a factor in willingness to participate in a public performance situation. *Psychological Reports, 71*, 1247–1250.
Arch, E. C. (1992b). Sex differences in the effect of self-efficacy on willingness to participate in a performance situation. *Psychological Reports, 70*, 3–9.
Bandura, A. (1986). *Social foundations of thought and action: A social cognitive theory*. Englewood Cliffs, NJ: Prentice-Hall.
Bandura, A. (1991). Self-regulation of motivation through anticipatory and self-regulatory mechanisms. In R. A. Dienstbier (Ed.), *Perspectives on motivation: Nebraska symposium on motivation* (Vol. 38, pp. 69–164). Lincoln: University of Nebraska Press.
Bandura, A. (1995). *Self-efficacy in changing societies*. New York: Cambridge University Press.
Bandura, A. (1997). *Self-efficacy: The exercise of control*. New York: W. H. Freeman.
Bandura, A., Barbaranelli, C., Caprara, G. V., & Pastorelli, C. (1996). Multifaceted Impact of self-efficacy beliefs on academic functioning. *Child Development, 67*, 1206–1222.
Bandura, A., Barbaranelli, C., Caprara, C. V., & Pastorelli, C. (1997). *Efficacy beliefs as shapers of aspirations and career trajectories*. Stanford University.
Burns, T. R., & Deitz, T. (in press). Human agency and evolutionary processes: Institutional dynamics and social revolution. In B. Wittrock (Ed.), *Agency in social theory*. Thousand Oaks, CA: Sage.
Colvin, C. R., & Block, J. (1994). Do positive illusions foster mental health? An examination of the Taylor and Brown formulation. *Psychological Bulletin, 116*, 3–20.
Courneya, K. S., & McAuley, E. (1993). Efficacy, attributional, affective responses of older adults following an acute bout of exercise. *Journal of Social Behavior and Personality, 8*, 729–742.
Cutrona, C. E., & Troutman, B. R. (1986). Social support, infant temperament, and parenting self-efficacy: A mediational model of postpartum depression. *Child Development, 57*, 1507–1518.
Deci, E. L., & Ryan, R. M. (1985). *Intrinsic motivation and self-determination in human behavior*. New York: Plenum.
Earley, P. C. (1993). East meets West meets Mideast: Further explorations of collectivistic and individualistic work groups. *Academy of Management Journal, 36*, 319–348.
Earley, P. C. (1994). Self or group? Cultural effects of training on self-efficacy and performance. *Administrative Science Quarterly, 39*, 89–117.

Elder, G. H., Jr., & Ardelt, M. (March 18–20, 1992). *Families adapting to economic pressure: Some consequences for parents and adolescents.* Paper presented at the Society for Research on Adolescence, Washington, D.C.

Eppel, E. S., Bandura, A., & Zimbardo, P. G. (in press). Escaping homelessness: Influence of self-efficacy and time perspective on coping with homelessness. *Journal of Applied Social Psychology.*

Feather, N. T. (Ed.) (1982). *Expectations and actions: Expectancy-value models in psychology.* Hillsdale, NJ: Lawrence Erlbaum Associates.

Giddens, A. (1984). *The constitution of society: Outline of the theory of structuration.* Cambridge, MA: Polity Press; Berkeley, CA: University of California Press.

Grove, J. R. (1993). Attributional correlates of cessation self-efficacy among smokers. *Addictive Behaviors, 18,* 311–320.

Harré, R. (1983). *Personal being: A theory for individual psychology.* Oxford: Blackwell.

Hattiangadi, N., Medvec, V. H., & Gilovich, T. (1995). Failing to act: Regrets of Terman's geniuses. *International Journal of Aging and Human Development, 40,* 175–185.

Holahan, C. K., & Holahan, C. J. (1987a). Self-efficacy, social support, and depression in aging: A longitudinal analysis. *Journal of Gerontology, 42,* 65–68.

Holahan, C. K., & Holahan, C. J. (1987b). Life stress, hassles, and self-efficacy in aging: A replication and extension. *Journal of Applied Social Psychology, 17,* 574–592.

Kavanagh, D. J., & Bower, G. H. (1985). Mood and self- efficacy: Impact of joy and sadness on perceived capabilities. *Cognitive Therapy and Research, 9,* 507–525.

Kavanagh, D. J., & Wilson, P. H. (1989). Prediction of outcome with a group version of cognitive therapy for depression. *Behaviour Research and Therapy, 27,* 333–347.

Kent, G. (1987). Self-efficacious control over reported physiological, cognitive and behavioural symptoms of dental anxiety. *Behaviour Research and Therapy, 25,* 341–347.

Kent, G., & Gibbons, R. (1987). Self-efficacy and the control of anxious cognitions. *Journal of Behavior Therapy & Experimental Psychiatry, 18,* 33–40.

Keohane, R. O. (1993). Sovereignty, interdependence and international institutions. In L. Miller & M. Smith (Eds.), *Ideas and ideals: Essays on politics in honor of Stanley Hoffman* (91–107). Boulder, CO: Westview Press.

Keohane, R. O., & Nye, J. S. (1977). *Power and interdependence: World politics in transition.* Boston: Little, Brown.

Kim, U., Triandis, H. D., Kâgitçibasi, C., Choi, S., & Yoon, G. (1994). *Individualism and collectivism: Theory, method, and applications.* Thousand Oaks, CA: Sage.

Krueger, N. F., Jr., & Dickson, P. R. (1993). Self-efficacy and perceptions of opportunities and threats. *Psychological Reports, 72,* 1235–1240.

Krueger, N., Jr., & Dickson, P. R. (1994). How believing in ourselves increases risk taking: Perceived self-efficacy and opportunity recognition. *Decision Sciences, 25,* 385–400.

Lent, R. W., Brown, S. D., & Hackett, G. (1994). Toward a unifying social cognitive theory of career and academic interest, choice, and performance. *Journal of Vocational Behavior, 45,* 79–122.

Locke, E. A., & Latham, G. P. (1990). *A theory of goal setting and task performance.* Englewood Cliffs, NJ: Prentice-Hall.

Maddux, J. E. (Ed.) (1995). *Self-efficacy, adaptation, and adjustment: Theory, research and application.* New York: Plenum.

Major, B., Mueller, P., & Hildebrandt, K. (1985). Attributions, expectations, and coping with abortion. *Journal of Personality and Social Psychology, 48*, 585–599.

Matsui, T., Konishi, H., Onglatco, M. L. U., Matsuda, Y., & Ohnishi, R. (1988). Self-efficacy and perceived exerted effort as potential cues for success-failure attributions. *Surugadai University Studies, 1*, 89–98.

Matsumoto, D., Kudoh, T., & Takeuchi, S. (1996). Changing patterns of individualism and collectivism in the United States and Japan. *Culture & Psychology, 2*, 77–107.

McAuley, E., Duncan, T. E., & McElroy, M. (1989). Self-efficacy cognitions and causal attributions for children's motor performance: An exploratory investigation. *The Journal of Genetic Psychology, 150*, 65–73.

Nolen-Hoeksema, S. (1991). Responses to depression and their effects on the duration of depressive episodes. *Journal of Abnormal Psychology, 100*, 569–582.

Relich, J. D., Debus, R. L., & Walker, R. (1986). The mediating role of attribution and self-efficacy variables for treatment effects on achievement outcomes. *Contemporary Educational Psychology, 11*, 195–216.

Sanderson, W. C., Rapee, R. M., & Barlow, D. H. (1989). The influence of an illusion of control on panic attacks induced via inhalation of 5.5% carbon dioxide-enriched air. *Archives of General Psychiatry, 46*, 157–162.

Schunk, D. H., & Rice, J. M. (1986). Extended attributional feedback: Sequence effects during remedial reading instruction. *Journal of Early Adolescence, 6*, 55–66.

Schwarzer, R. (Eds.); (1992). *Self-efficacy: Thought control of action.* Washington, D.C.: Hemisphere.

Shepherd, G. (Ed.); (1995). *Rejected: Leading economists ponder the publication process.* Sun Lakes, AZ: Thomas Horton.

Silver, W. S., Mitchell, T. R., & Gist, M. E. (1995). Responses to successful and unsuccessful performance: The moderating effect of self-efficacy on the relationship between performance and attributions. *Organizational Behavior and Human Decision Processes, 62*, 286–299.

Singhal, A., & Rogers, E. M. (1989). Pro-social television for development in India. In R. E. Rice & C. K. Atkin (Eds.), *Public communication campaigns* (2nd ed., pp. 331–350). Newbury Park, CA: Sage.

Skinner, E. A. (1995). *Perceived control, motivation, & coping.* Thousand Oaks, CA: Sage.

Taylor, S. E., & Brown, J. D. (1988). Illusion and well-being: A social psychological perspective on mental health. *Psychological Bulletin, 103*, 193–210.

Taylor, S. E. & Brown, J. D. (1994). Positive illusions and well-being revisited: Separating fact from fiction. *Psychological Bulletin, 116*, 21–27.

Triandis, H. C. (1995). *Individualism and collectivism.* Boulder, CO: Westview Press.

Vaughan, P. W., Rogers, E. M., & Swalehe, R. M. A. (1995). *The effects of "Twende Na Wakati," an entertainment-education radio soap opera for family planning and HIV/AIDS prevention in Tanzania.* Unpublished manuscript, University of New Mexico, Albuquerque.

Weiner, B. (1986). *An attributional theory of motivation and emotion.* New York: Springer-Verlag.

Westoff, C. F., & Rodriguez, G. (1995). The mass media and family planning in Kenya. *International Family Planning Perspectives, 21*, 26–31,36.

White, R. W. (1959). Motivation reconsidered: The concept of competence. *Psychological Review, 66*, 297–333.

White, J. (1982). *Rejection.* Reading, MA: Addison-Wesley.

Williams, S. L. (1992). Perceived self-efficacy and phobic disability. In R. Schwarzer (Ed.), *Self-efficacy: Thought control of action* (pp. 149–176). Washington, D.C.: Hemisphere.

Wood, R. E., & Bandura, A. (1989). Impact of conceptions of ability on self-regulatory mechanisms and complex decision making. *Journal of Personality and Social Psychology, 56*, 407–415.

Yamagishi, (1988). The provision of a sanctioning system in the United States and Japan. *Social Psychology Quarterly, 51*, 265–271.

# 3

# The Orchestration of Selection, Optimization, and Compensation: An Action–Theoretical Conceptualization of a Theory of Developmental Regulation

*Alexandra M. Freund*

*Paul B. Baltes*

## INTRODUCTION

Throughout the life span, people react to and proactively create opportunity structures that foster and constrain their development. We posit that whether the dynamic interaction of opportunity structures and resources results in a positive ratio of gains (positive outcomes) to losses (negative outcomes) depends on the orchestration of three component processes of developmental regulation: selection, optimization, and compensation. The meta-theory of selective optimization with compensation (SOC-theory, P. B. Baltes, 1997; P. B. Baltes & Baltes, 1990; M. M. Baltes & Carstensen, 1996; Freund & Baltes, 1997; Marsiske, Lang, Baltes, & Baltes, 1995) provides a general framework for the understanding of developmental continuity and change across different periods of the life span, different levels of analysis, and across different domains of functioning. In this vein, we argue that the explication of selection, optimization, and compensation carries the potential of evolving into a general theory of development.

In this chapter, we take an action–theoretical perspective conceptualizing selection, optimization, and compensation as strategies of individual life-management. Before doing so, we will first address three basic assumptions of lifespan developmental psychology underlying the SOC-theory, namely the limitation of resources such as time and energy across the entire life span, multidirectionality and multifunctionality of development, and development as a dynamic interaction of person and environment. We will then provide a definition of selection, optimization, and compensation as general-purpose mechanisms of successful development.

Finally, as we embed these processes into an action-theoretical framework, the topic of a psychology of control (Flammer, 1990) comes to the fore. In our SOC approach, processes of goal-setting and goal pursuit are central. The same is true for the psychology of control where the entire process of action planning, action regulation, and action outcome are seen as an integrated ensemble (e.g., Bandura, 1996a; Flammer, 1990; Rotter, 1966; Skinner, Chapman, & Baltes, 1988). In a similar vein, in the present chapter we take an approach of action control conceptualizing the entire action process as the orchestration of the three processes of selection, optimization, and compensation. Thus, as outlook, we will briefly address the interplay of selection, optimization, and compensation.

## Basic Assumptions Underlying The Model of Selection, Optimization, and Compensation

Before defining the three component processes of developmental regulation selection, optimization, and compensation, we want to briefly address three basic assumptions about human development underlying the SOC-theory (for a more detailed discussion of see P. B. Baltes, 1997; P. B. Baltes, Lindenberger, & Staudinger, 1997): (a) resources for behavioral and developmental engagement are constrained and limited across the lifespan. (b) development is multidirectional and multifunctional in trajectories of adaptive fitness (i.e., multifunctionality: changes in adaptive fitness include growth and decline; multifunctionality: outcomes are associated with a multitude of consequences). (c) development is a dynamic process of both reacting to and proactively shaping one's environment as well as one's internal mental representations.

(a) An individual's internal and external resources are constrained and limited at every point of his or her lifespan. We define resources as factors that help persons to interact with their environments. Such resources include biological-genetic characteristics (e.g., general activity level), psychological characteristics (e.g., self-efficacy), and social-cultural characteristics (e.g., education system). A first set of constraints and limitations derives from the unique potentials of the genome (e.g., human senses evince specific sensitivities). A second set of constraints and limitations is associated with change over the lifespan (P. B. Baltes, 1997; Lerner, 1991). For instance, although some, if not all, of these resources are constrained and limited across the entire lifespan after biological maturation, the level of limitation increases with age.

(b) Lifespan psychology holds that development is best described as multidirectional, that is, as comprising growth and decline, gains and losses (P. B. Baltes, 1997; P. B. Baltes et al., 1997; Brandtstädter & Wentura, 1995; Lavouvie-Vief, 1981). In addition, developmental outcomes are conceptualized as having multiple consequences (multifunctionality). Another perspective consistent with the multidirectional and multifunctional argument is to view lifespan change as involving continuous change in adaptive fitness and associated trade-offs (Brandtstädter, 1984; Magnusson, 1996; Flammer, 1996). Although this gain-loss dynamic is less obvious in child development, where the focus is on growth (i.e., acquiring new skills), even children are subject to developmental losses (e.g., approximately after the age of 12, children are unable to learn a new language with the competence of a native speaker, Levelt, 1989). The *ratio* of gains to losses, however, becomes less positive with age. This is at least partly due to the fact that, although resources promoting growth are limited throughout the entire lifespan, this limitation increases with age (P. B. Baltes, 1997; J. Heckhausen, Dixon, & Baltes, 1989). This lifespan script suggest that with age, individuals need to invest more and more of their time and resources into maintenance and resilience of functioning rather than into processes of increased adaptive fitness or growth (P. B. Baltes, 1997; Staudinger, Marsiske, & Baltes, 1995).

(c) A third basic assumption of the SOC-theory that has almost gained the status of being trivial is that people do not only react to environmental demands to achieve a good person-environment fit but also shape their internal and external environment actively and proactively, placing themselves into an existing environment or creating opportunity structures that fit best their needs (e.g., Lawton, 1989; Labouvie-Vief, 1981; Lerner, 1991). These two aspects of development are not unique to the SOC-theory (cf., Brandtstädter, 1997; Carstensen, 1993; J. Heckhausen & Schulz, 1995; Rothbaum, Weisz, & Snyder, 1982). As discussed next, the assumption of personal development as an ongoing person-environment transaction with internal and external loci of change is necessary for conceptualizing developmental regulation in terms of selecting developmental pathways, optimizing one's level of functioning in selected domains, and compensating for loss or decline.

## Selection, Optimization, and Compensation as General-Purpose Processes

The main purpose of the SOC-theory is to conceptualize lifespan processes of adaptive development (M. M. Baltes & Carstensen, 1996; P. B. Baltes, 1997; P. B. Baltes & Baltes, 1990; Freund & Baltes, 1997; Marsiske et al., 1995). The SOC-theory provides a general framework for the understanding of developmental change across *different stages of life*. Each stage of life or point in the life course evinces both continuity and change due to the special constellations of age-graded, history-graded, or nonnormative developmental tasks. The SOC-theory is intended to permit developmental-adaptive conceptualization across *different levels of analysis* ranging from the molar level (e. g., societal) to the microgenetic level (e. g., differentiation of cells). Finally, the SOC-theory also applies to *various domains of functioning* (e.g., cognition, motivation, self and personality). In this chapter, we will apply the general-purpose processes selection, optimization, and compensation to the domain of personal goals.

Let us first briefly define these developmental processes on a general level. The SOC-theory posits that selection, optimization, and compensation form fundamental processes underlying successful development, where successful development is defined as the simultaneous minimization of losses and maximization of gains (M. M. Baltes & Carstensen, 1996; Brandtstädter & Wentura, 1995).

Regarding *selection*: The constraints and limitation of resources such as brain potentialities, time, and energy innate to human existence necessitates selection throughout the lifespan. On the most general level, selection refers to narrowing the range of alternative ecologies, domains of functioning, or goals from the pool of available options. Without selection there would be no direction in development and energy would be diffused in many areas instead of directed and focused on certain domains. Thus, selection is a necessary precondition for achieving higher levels of functioning (P. B. Baltes & Baltes, 1990; Carstensen, Hanson, & Freund, 1995; Marsiske et al., 1995). The second component process, *optimization*, refers to applying means aimed at achieving optimal functioning or desired outcomes. Optimization involves the acquisition and coordination of means (resources) required for goal-attainment. The aspect of decline and management of loss is addressed by the process of *compensation*. To maintain a given level of functioning under conditions of loss or decline in goal–relevant means threatening one's level of functioning, compensatory processes need to take place. In the prototypical case, compensation involves substitution of means (this is often feasible because of equifinality in development) or use of external aids such as hearing aids (see also Dixon & Bäckman, 1995).

These definitions might easily be misunderstood as implying that selection, optimization, and compensation are conceptualized as active, intentional, and conscious processes. This is, however, not the case. Selection, optimization, and compensation can vary along the dimensions active – passive, internal – external, and conscious – non-conscious.

So far, we have defined selection, optimization, and compensation as universal processes of developmental regulation that vary phenotypically depending on socio-historical and cultural context, domain of functioning, as well as on characteristics of the system or unit of interest (e.g., person, group, society). The "meta-theory" of SOC (P. B. Baltes & Baltes, 1990) needs to be embedded in a specific theoretical framework for applying it to particular developmental phenomena. In the following section, we will embed the SOC-theory in an action-theoretical framework (Boesch, 1976, 1991; Brandtstädter, 1997; Eckensberger, 1997; Flammer, 1990; Gollwitzer & Bargh, 1996) that we believe to be most useful when interested in the domain of personal goals. As mentioned above, the active and conscious selection, pursuit, and maintenance of goals is the primary focus of this chapter.

## AN ACTION THEORETICAL VIEW ON DEVELOPMENTAL REGULATION: SELECTION, OPTIMIZATION, AND COMPENSATION AS STRATEGIES OF SELF-MANAGEMENT

How do people successfully manage to attain some of their goals and, furthermore, how do people maintain a high level of functioning when faced with loss and decline? In an action–theoretical approach, selecting, pursuing and maintaining personally relevant goals is an integral aspect of successful development.

Goals, that are "desired states that people seek to obtain, maintain, or avoid" (Emmons, 1996, p. 314), can be viewed as an important source of motivation that guide behavior and action (Bandura, 1996a), as giving direction to development. Note that we conceptualize successful development not as a static outcome (goal achievement) but instead as an ongoing process of attaining a positive balance of gains and losses in one's interaction with the environment and one's construction of self representations (see also M. M. Baltes & Carstensen, 1996). What constitutes a gain and what constitutes a loss, however, cannot be objectively defined. Ultimately, the definition of gains and losses depends not only on individual values and preferences but also on historical, societal, religious, and economic parameters. Taking the individual person as the unit of analysis is but one of the possible ways to conceptualize development. We view this as the starting point from which one might proceed to more complex levels of analyses of development (e.g., on the level of dyads, groups, societies, etc.).

Taking an action–theoretical approach to development, our focus is on *personal goals*; both *goal-setting* (elective selection)—that is, developing and choosing goals—and *goal-striving*—that is, investing means for pursuing these goals, and improving one's level of performance in selected domains (optimization), as well as employing means for maintaining one's performance when faced with loss or decline in goal-relevant means (compensation). Decline or loss, however, can be of a nature that it leads to a skill–demand mismatch that is so great that compensatory efforts become a fruitless investment of one's resources (an aspect of compensation often neglected but highlighted by Bäckman and Dixon, 1992). Under such conditions, a more adaptive response than continued compensatory striving is the selection of another goal (loss-based selection). In the following sections, we will address each of the processes of developmental regulation as applied to the domain of personal goals in more detail.

## SELECTION

Selection denotes the processes involved in developing, choosing and committing oneself to goals. Goals both guide behavior and give direction and meaning to people's lives (Klinger, 1977). To fulfill these functions, however, the mere presence of goals is probably not sufficient. They have to be organized into a *hierarchy of coherent goals*. Such a hierarchy comprises different levels of goal-representation, ranging from subordinate (low level, proximal) goals specifying action plans to superordinate (high level, distal) goals providing a purpose or implication of goal-related actions (Boesch, 1991; Carver & Scheier, 1995; Emmons, 1996; H. Heckhausen, 1991). Sheldon and Kasser (1994) showed that two types of coherence of goals are related to indicators of subjective well-being. Vertical coherence refers to the degree to which proximal or subordinate goals serve also more distal or superordinate goals. Horizontal coherence, on the other hand, refers to the degree to which attainment of a goal also contributes to attainment of goals at the same level. Based on the findings reported by Sheldon and Kasser (1994), we expect both aspects of coherence, that is, vertical and horizontal, to enhance the likelihood of optimization efforts to be successful.

Which is the best *level of goal-representation* for successful goal pursuit? Are people who represent and identify their goals primarily on a superordinate level more likely to develop successfully because they strive for meaning rather than for little, everyday accomplishments? There is no clear answer to the question of which level of representation of goal is most adaptable for its successful pursuit. Locke and colleagues (Locke, Shaw, Saari & Latham, 1981) contend that specific goals lead to higher goal performance. They propose four positive effects of having specific (subordinate) goals: (a) directing attention, (b) mobilizing effort, (c) increasing persistence, and (d) helping in strategy development. Pursuing primarily specific (subordinate) goals, however, might also have also costs. Little (1989) described the dynamics between identifying one's goals primarily on a higher ("magnificent obsessions") versus a lower ("trivial pursuits") level of abstraction as a trade-off between manageable and meaningful goals. According to Vallacher and Wegner (1985), goals will always be identified on the highest possible level (i.e., the level that provides direction and meaning). Only when action plans fail or a goal is blocked, will the next lower level in the goal-hierarchy be identified in order to be able to find the best way to solve the problem.

The value of high level goals is illustrated in the concept of possible selves. Possible selves are defined as "personalized representations of one's self in the future" (Cross & Markus, 1991, p. 230) and are proposed to function as links between cognition and motivation in that they represent enduring self-relevant goals to achieve or to avoid certain states or possibilities of oneself. Possible selves can thus be conceptualized as a person's frame for change over time (Markus & Nurius, 1986; Cross & Markus, 1991; Ryff, 1991). As possible selves represent self-relevant superordinate goals they might motivate proactive adaptive behavior to predicted changes in the environment (e.g., retirement) and oneself (e.g., decline in health with increasing age). Possible selves can hence serve as guides for selection processes "in deciding which domains and activities to pursue and which ones to abandon" (M. M. Baltes & Carstensen, 1991, p. 257).

Possible selves, however, are too abstract to be easily translated into actions, or to use the terms by Carver and Scheier (1995), they do not provide "do goals" (cf. B. R. Little, 1989). Therefore, Bandura (1996b) argues that a simultaneous representation on higher and lower levels in the goal-hierarchy might be most adaptive:

> In the pursuit of goals requiring hard work, success is best achieved by combining a long-range vision with proximal subgoals that get one there. Distal goals alone are too far removed in time to exert much control over current behavior. (p. 22)

The possible counterproductive effects of distal goals when occurring in form of positive fantasies were highlighted by Oettingen (1996). Oettingen demonstrated in a series of studies that positive, distal goals (fantasies) undermine optimization efforts unless they are confronted with the (negatively) discrepant reality.

Level of goal-representation also plays an important role in determining success or failure in goal pursuit because goals provide standards against which persons evaluate their performance (Carver & Scheier, 1995). The more abstract a goal (i.e., high level of goal representation), the more outcomes are consistent with it. This might lead to a higher likelihood of satisfaction with one's own performance because there are more possible outcomes qualifying as goal achievement. Consistent with this argument, Klein, Whitener, and Ilgen (1990) found that goal-specificity (here defined as the range of performance levels) was related to higher level of performance on a simple computer task when goal difficulty was held constant. Interestingly, with increasing task difficulty, participants in their study showed a tendency to define their goals less specifically (i.e., to allow for a broader range of acceptable outcomes). Participants might have tried to enhance their chances for goal achievement by broadening the range of acceptable values defining success. High achievement on a simple computer task, however, is still a specific, lower level goal when compared to such an abstract, higher level goal as being a good person.

The central issue seems one of consistency between levels of goal articulation. As abstract goals do not specify clear criteria for success, it is more difficult to determine when one has reached the goal, and hence one might never get the satisfaction of actually having achieved one's goal. Thereby pursuing superordinate goals might undermine one's optimization efforts in the long run because of lacking reinforcement for goal achievement. In this sense, more specific, low-level goals are likely to be positively related to optimization efforts. High level goals or possible selves, however, are important to provide directionality to development. Thus, in the long run it seems most effective to articulate a goal system with convergent linkages across levels of analysis and generality. A lifespan developmental approach would suggest further that such convergence needs to consider temporal linkages as well, such as that earlier goal attainments need to involve means that are also useful at later stages (cf., positive developmental transfer).

Another important distinction regarding the representation of goals is their framing as *approach or avoidance* goals (Emmons, 1996; H. Heckhausen, 1991; Hobfoll, 1989; Klinger, 1977). Although logically, the framing of a goal as an approach or avoidance goal is symmetrical ("I do want to become a competent person" vs. "I do not want to become an incompetent person"), psychologically they are not. Approach goals direct attention to a possible positive state. Becoming or attaining something desired, such as achievement of an approach goal should therefore lead to positive affect. Avoidance goals, on the other hand, focus one's attention on avoiding negative states. Although achievement of avoidance goals might lead to the absence of negative affect, it is unlikely to contribute to positive affect. Approach goals might be more attractive, thereby mobilizing efforts of goal pursuit and persistence, because they promise positive reinforcement whereas the best outcome of avoidance goals is the absence of a negative event.

An interesting developmental dynamic is whether optimization of gains is considered as more important than avoidance of loss. On the one hand, Emmons (1996) reports several studies consistently showing that persons holding primarily avoidance goals show lower subjective well-being (lower positive mood, less life satisfaction, more anxiety; physical symptomatology) compared to persons with primarily approach goals. In a recent study, Elliot and Sheldon (1997) found that avoidance motivation in the achievement domain is negatively related to goal-relevant outcomes as well as general well-being. Moreover, Elliot, Sheldon, and Church (1997) demonstrated in a longitudinal study that persons with low perceptions of their life skills were also more likely to form avoidance goals. A higher proportion of avoidance goals, in turn, were associated with a decrease of subjective well-being. Similarly, Coats, Janoff-Bulman, and Alpert (1996) found negative correlations between number of avoidance goals, optimism, and self-esteem, and a positive correlation between number of avoidance goals and depression. Approach goals were negatively related to depression, but—contrary to hypotheses—not associated with optimism or self-esteem.

On the other hand, especially with aging and a changing lifespan script from growth to maintenance and management of loss, the significance of avoidance of loss may increase in importance. More research is needed to investigate the effects on motivation dependent on the framing of goals: Is it most motivating to have a goal framed simultaneously as both approach and avoidance goal? Does the framing of goals have different effects depending on the level of representation?

Taking a lifespan developmental perspective, we believe that the overall dynamic between approach and avoidance goals might change with age. However, at the same time we suggest that approach goals might contribute more to successful development than avoidance by providing a clearer direction and also a sense of meaning and accomplishment when achieving them. Yet, given the increase of losses and the decrease of gains over the lifespan as reflected in subjective developmental expectations (J. Heckhausen et al., 1989), goals might gradually shift from being predominantly approach goals in earlier phases of the lifespan ("I want to become a lawyer") to either maintenance goals ("I want to stay healthy") or avoidance goals in later life ("I do not want to become dependent"); (cf., Staudinger et al., 1995). Evidence for such a shift in framing of goals was empirically supported in a study by J. Heckhausen (reported in Heckhausen, 1998) who found that younger adults reported more goals that reflected a striving for gains and less goals of avoiding losses than middle-aged and old adults. This shift in the framing of goals might partly account for the finding of a decrease in positive emotions in old age, while there are no age-related differences regarding negative emotions (Smith, Fleeson, Geiselmann, Settersten, & Kunzmann, 1996).

So far, we have focused on qualitative characteristics of the goal system, such as its congruence, the level of representation, and the framing of goals as approach or avoidance goals. An important quantitative aspect is the degree of *commitment* to a goal. In a diary study, Emmons (1986) found that goal commitment was positively related to life satisfaction. Beyond direct effects, the degree of goal commitment likely moderates the functions of the characteristics of goals discussed above. For instance, in a longitudinal study Brunstein (1993) found goal commitment to moderate the relationship between perceived goal attainability and changes in well-being. If participants (in this study, students) judged goal attainment favorably they reported particular high well-being when they were highly committed to these goals. High commitment had a negative effect on well-being, however, when the likelihood of goal attainment was perceived as low.

Thus, it is important to commit oneself to goals that one also perceives as likely to be achieved (cf. H. Heckhausen, 1991). In order to be able to evaluate the likelihood of achieving a goal, it is important to take both personal characteristics (e.g., skills) as well as opportunity structures and constraints (e.g., educational system) into account (Cantor, 1994). Thus, to avoid the negative effects of premature goal commitment, that is, committing to a goal without having tested possibly better fitting alternatives, a phase of careful evaluation of possible goal-paths is important (this refers to the aspect of "developing goals" in Table 3.1).

Turning to another quantitative aspect, the *number of goals* to which a person feels committed, we find more questions than answers. For example, is there an optimal number of goals to promote development? Does the optimal number of goals vary across individuals and/or change with age? Is there an optimal ratio of superordinate to subordinate goals best for guiding behavior and providing direction to development? Again, does the optimal ratio change with age? Some answers to these questions are provided by Staudinger's work (Staudinger & Freund, 1997) on personal life–investment: Personal life-investment, defined as the amount of self-reported investment (thought and action) across a number of goal–domains, decreases in old age. Moreover, being more selective (i.e., investing in fewer domains) is related to subjective indicators of well-being in old age. This finding is consistent with one of the central hypotheses of the SOC-theory, namely that it is adaptive to narrow the pool of alternatives (domains of functioning, goals) on which to focus one's optimization efforts when resources become increasingly limited, as is the case in old age.

In this section, we conceptualized selection in an action–theoretical framework as setting personal goals. Based on research on personal goals, we highlighted the importance of the following aspects of selection for successful goal pursuit: (a) Goals need to be integrated into a hierarchy of coherent goals; (b) Goals need to be represented both on a superordinate and a subordinate level in order to provide meaning and guide behavior; (c) The hierarchy and coherence of goals needs to consider temporal developmental contexts; (d) Framing goals as approach goals might be more adaptive than framing them as avoidance goals, although this conclusion may be less true for old age where avoidance of loss looms in comparison; (e) Successful goal pursuit is more likely when committing oneself to goals that are one perceives as having a high probability of being achieved; and (f) When resources become increasingly limited, it is important to narrow the number of goals one wants to pursue.

TABLE 3.1
*Selection, Optimization, and Compensation Embedded in an
Action–Theoretical Framework
(after P. Baltes, M. Baltes, Freund, & Lang, 1995; Freund & Baltes, 1997)*

| Selection (goals/preferences) | Optimization (goal–relevant means) | Compensation (means/resources for counteracting loss/ decline in goal–relevant means) |
|---|---|---|
| *elective selection* | – attentional focus | – substitution of means |
| – specification of goals | – seizing the right moment | – use of external aids/help of others |
| – goal system (hierarchy) | – persistence | – use of therapeutic intervention |
| – contextualisation of goals | – acquiring new skills/resources | – acquiring new skills/resources |
| – goal-commitment | – practice of skills | – activation of unused skills/resources |
| | – effort/energy | |
| *loss-based selection* | – time allocation | – increased effort/ energy |
| – focusing on most important goal(s) | – modelling successful others | – increased time allocation |
| – reconstruction of goal hierarchy | | – modelling successful others who compensate |
| – adaptation of standards | | – neglect of optimizing other means |
| – search for new goals | | |

## OPTIMIZATION

Selecting and committing oneself to certain goals is an important step in the action- process. Goal-setting, however, is only the first step in the process of eventually achieving the desired outcome (P. B. Baltes & Baltes, 1990; Boesch, 1976, 1991; Oettingen, 1996). The very engagement in goal pursuit has positive impact on affect, particularly when the goals are personally important (Fleeson & Cantor, 1995). In this section, we will describe in more detail what processes are involved in goal pursuit. To do so, we again chose an action-theoretical framework. Within this framework, the model of action-phases (Boesch, 1976, 1991; H. Heckhausen, 1991) appears particularly fruitful for examining the "ingredients" of optimization (see Table 3.1 for a summary of typical instances of optimization).

According to the model of action-phases, the "preactional" phase (after having selected a goal and before actually engaging in goal-relevant actions) consists primarily of *planning the implementation* of intentions as to how, when, and where to start goal-relevant actions and means. In a number of studies, Gollwitzer and his colleagues (for an overview see Gollwitzer, 1996) demonstrated that implementation intentions contribute to goal achievement. Implementation intentions specify goal-related *means* and actions, *situations* in which to apply those means, and also the right *timing* of acting on a given goal. Moreover, implementation intentions have important cognitive effects ("implemental mindset"): They focus attention on goal-relevant information and ward off distractions (including questioning the value of the selected goal), they heighten the accessibility of situational cues allowing goal-related actions (thereby enhancing the likelihood of seizing the right moment and opportunity), and lead to being particularly optimistic about achieving the goal. All of these characteristics of planning enhance the likelihood of initiating and completing intended goal-related actions or applying goal-related means (Gollwitzer & Brandtstädter, 1997).

What kinds goal-related means do we subsume under the notion of optimization? Initially, there are two general issues to consider. First, there is rarely a fixed set of means that are necessary conditions for goal attainment. Rather, goals can be reached through multiple and often substitutable pathways. Equifinality (Kruglanski, 1996) is the rule rather than the exception. Second, which means are most appropriate for enhancing the likelihood of achieving a given goal, depends on the content (domain) of the goal, a person's developmental status, and characteristics of the socio-cultural context (Cantor, 1994). For instance, the particular means that help a child to learn to read in a culture that provides elementary school education are different from the means that help a grandfather to establish a good relationship to his granddaughter in a patriarchal society.

On a more abstract level, however, we have identified a number of means likely to contribute to successful goal attainment across a large variety of domains (see Table 1). Such relatively global instances of optimization are the investment of time and energy, acquiring new skills or resources, the practice of skills, modeling successful others, and high self-efficacy beliefs. In addition, the pursuit of long-term goals usually requires persistence in one's efforts to achieve the goal. Persistence, in turn, requires self-regulation skills such as the abilities to delay gratification (Mischel, 1996) and to engage in extended forms of deliberate practice (Ericsson, 1996). Let us briefly explain why we believe the optimization means listed above to be essential for most forms of successful goal pursuit.

*Investment of time and energy* is necessary to both acquire and practice skills. The literature on expertise shows that level of performance is directly related to the amount of time spent on deliberate practice (Ericsson, 1996). Practice leads to the refinement of skill components, to their smooth orchestration or integration, and to their automatization. Automatization of skills enhances overall performance because tasks become less resource-demanding and thus free resources such as attention that can be devoted to other goal-related means (cf., Bargh & Gollwitzer, 1994). As automatic process are not operating under conscious control, however, it is difficult to alter them even if they lead to suboptimal performance. Thus, when acquiring a new skill it is important to monitor the practice of its components closely (either by self-monitoring or by a supervisor) to ensure that they are learned properly before becoming automatic.

*External supervision and learning to monitor oneself* are part of most "institutionalized" programs of skill acquisition (e.g., school, sports training, musical education). This is less the case, however, for skills that are usually not explicitly taught, such as social competence or coping strategies. It might happen much more frequently in these latter domains - in which goals also tend to be less explicit and more vague, and performance-criteria are less clear - that suboptimal means are practiced (though probably rarely deliberately) and automatized.

Optimization in such domains as social relations (for a discussion of optimization in this domain see Marsiske et al., 1995, p. 58/59), might thus be more difficult than optimization in achievement related domains. For instance, the best means for attaining a trusting, satisfying, intimate long-term relationship are neither as well understood nor taught as calculus is, even though the latter is probably a much less important goal for most people. An important way of optimizing one's level of functioning in domains lacking explicit training, is *modeling successful others*. Since the early work by Bandura (1969, 1996a), watching others perform has been shown to be a powerful tool for learning and acquisition of skills as well as for the activation of unused skills. Watching a model not only provides information about how a certain skill or behavior is to be performed, it also provides the observer with information about contextual contingencies as well as its social and/or instrumental consequences. Thereby, observers acquire means-ends beliefs without having to try out all possible—including the many unsuccessful—means for achieving a goal themselves.

The role of control beliefs for planning and performing goal-related actions has been particularly stressed by Flammer (1990). High beliefs in one's ability to control oneself and one's environment appear to have positive effects on subjective well-being in and on themselves (e.g., Grob, 1991). More important in the current context, control-beliefs also have positive effects on engaging in the specific actions required for goal-attainment (Bandura, 1996a; Flammer, 1990; Flammer, Kaiser, Lüthi & Grob, 1990). The impact of control beliefs on goal attainment was for instance demonstrated in several studies and across sociocultural contexts for children's academic achievements (for overviews see T. D. Little, 1998; Oettingen, 1995).

Beliefs regarding which means lead to which outcomes (i.e., means-ends beliefs, Skinner et al., 1988) are important for forming intentions and for planning.

However, it is not only important to know *what* to do, but also *when* and in *what situation*. While observing a model, for instance, might help to learn how to link certain situational cues to specific behaviors that serve one's goals (i.e., for forming means-ends beliefs), one also needs to attend to those situational cues for initiating the goal-related actions. As long-term goals cannot be pursued in one given moment but require persistent action over time, the critical issue is to not let opportunities for goal pursuit pass by. Planning to act on the goal when the specified situational cues are present, helps to keep them cognitively accessible which in turn is reflected in perceptual readiness to detect a good opportunity when it presents itself (see Gollwitzer, 1996). In addition, reminding oneself of the goal and one's intention to apply certain means in specified situations, helps to keep one's attention focused on the goal. Moreover, by consciously and repeatedly activating a goal in a certain situation, the association of situational cues and a given goal becomes automatic (Bargh & Gollwitzer, 1994). Thus, a goal can be automatically triggered by situational features without consuming attentional resources that can therefore be devoted to engaging in goal-related actions.

Once goal-related actions are initiated, how is the *process of goal pursuit maintained, changed, or stopped*? In early work on this topic, Boesch (1976, 1991) elaborated on the notion of a monitoring comparison between cognitively represented "action models" (Handlungsmodelle) and realized action toward the goal. In fact, Boesch identified a discrepancy between imagined and realized action phases as the essential reason for a regulatory effort. In this vein, in most if not all cases, successful goal pursuit entails a number of actions that need to be tuned to the nature and amount of the discrepancy between the actual and the desired state. One way to conceptualize the process of *monitoring progress* (or the lack thereof) towards a goal is a feedback-loop model (Miller, Galanter, & Pribram, 1960). According to a feedback-loop model monitoring is an ongoing comparison of the actual and the desired state resulting in feedback about the discrepancy. This feedback can be used to maintain or change one's goal-related means accordingly (Carver & Scheier, 1995). Although comparing the actual with the desired state might at times be a conscious form of balancing, it more often occurs outside of awareness (Wegner, 1992) leading to adjustments in goal-related behavior that may also not be conscious. For example, the child grasping for a cup adjusts the movement of her arm, hand and fingers to the exact location of the cup relative to her own position without consciously controlling the sequence of this movement and the fine-tuning of the muscles involved.

As ontogenetic development is extended to include lifespan dimensions (time and space), the pursuit of long-term goals requires *persistence* in goal-related actions. It is not likely that such longterm trajectories occur automatically, because the goal-related actions themselves are effortful to maintain or because other attractive goals might occur that compete for the resources invested in goal-related means. Unsurprisingly, therefore, lifespan investments require organized efforts at reflexivity, planning, and management (Smith, 1996). Numerous factors contribute to persistence of goal pursuit in the face of attractive alternatives. Which of two competing goals will be pursued depends on a number of factors, such as the value (importance) of each of the two opposing goals (Lewin, 1935), the temporal distance to achieving either of the goals (here the ability to delay gratification is very important, Mischel, 1996), the perceived likelihood of the realization of each of the goals (H. Heckhausen, 1991), the strength of control beliefs related to the two goals, such as control expectancies, means-ends beliefs, and personal agency beliefs (e.g., Skinner et al., 1988), and self-efficacy beliefs (Bandura, 1996a). Although each of these factors have been investigated separately in numerous studies in a variety of domains and with varying age-groups, it is as yet unknown how these factors interact with each other in the case of a goal-conflict, and how their interaction might develop over the lifespan. Being a necessary condition for achieving long-term goals (Ericsson, 1996; Mischel, 1996), persistence is probably one of the most important aspects of optimization contributing to successful development.

Recently, attempts have been made to include in the consideration of relevant factors the role of social contexts and interactive minds (P. B. Baltes & Staudinger, 1996). As people develop, they are part of a collection of cohorts and subgroups which share in the estimation and attainment of goals. This notion of social ensembling is at the center of the concept of collective SOC (M. M. Baltes & Carstensen, in press) as well as that of collective efficacy (Bandura, 1996a). A lifespan perspective highlights the role of socially organized, joint action as coliving persons such as couples and friendship networks attempt to maximize gains and minimize losses. Persistence in this case is also socially constituted. Note in this context that such collective conditions can also spell failure rather than success (Staudinger, 1996).

In this section, we elaborated the process of optimization within an action-theoretical framework as the employment of means aimed at goal achievement. We identified the following aspects as particularly important for successful goal pursuit: (a) Forming intentions and planning where, when and what goal-related means should be applied in order to achieve one's goal; (b) The investment of time and energy appear to be building blocks for achieving high levels of performance; (c) External supervision and learning to monitor oneself ensure the necessary adjustments of goal-related actions during the process of goal pursuit; (d) Modeling successful others contributes to forming means-ends beliefs as well as to the acquisition of goal-relevant skills; (e) Pursuit of long-term goals requires persistence and high self-regulatory skills; (f) Success in pursuit of longterm goals is facilitated by social context and the conjoint or collective action of social ensembles or networks.

## COMPENSATION

From a lifespan developmental point of view, conceptualizing developmental regulation is incomplete if not both aspects of development are addressed, gains (growth) *and* losses (decline). Whereas optimization is motivated by consideration of processes related to growth, compensation addresses the aspect of losses and decline. This does not mean, however, that the consequences of compensation are a loss in functioning. On the contrary, compensation denotes the application of means in the interest of *maintaining* a given level of functioning when confronted with a loss in goal-relevant means (P. B. Baltes & Baltes, 1990; Carstensen et al., 1995).

Our definition of compensation as a response to loss or decline is narrower than the one proposed by Bäckman and Dixon (1992) who define compensation on a very general level as the attempt to overcome a mismatch between skill and demand. If we were to accept their definition, it would be even more difficult to distinguish between optimization and compensation. We want to confine compensation to those instances of mismatch that are due to loss or decline in previously available goal-relevant means. In our view, this qualification is important because different motivational and cognitive processes are involved in trying to achieve a new goal versus trying to regain or maintain a previous level of functioning the face of loss or decline in goal-related means.

Framing the identical outcome as loss or gain has been shown to be most influential on people's willingness to take risks (Tversky & Kahneman, 1981; see also Hobfoll's [1989] conservation of resources model). In order to prevent a loss, people are more willing to take risks than in order to achieve a gain. According to prospect theory, people's response to losses are more extreme than their response to gains because they attach a greater value to loss (Tversky & Kahneman, 1981). Thus, even though the means employed in optimization and compensation can be the same, counteracting losses appears to be a motivationally and functionally distinct process from optimization (cf. the above distinction of approach and avoidance goals and their assumed differential affective consequences). Similar arguments for the uniqueness of compensation can be made for cases where compensation involves new means (such as a hearing aid) where there are no substitutive means available that stem from internal resources.

Losses in goal-relevant means can be due to the (increased) limitation in resources that are needed for the maintenance of the level of functioning in a certain domain or that affect the execution of the respective goal-related behavior. For example, cognitive plasticity—a resource for learning new cognitive skills and improving performance on cognitive tasks—decreases beginning in adulthood (Kliegl, Smith, & Baltes, 1989; Lindenberger & Baltes, 1997). Taken together, the likelihood of loss and decline increase with age, enhancing the need for compensation for maintaining levels of functioning (cf., Staudinger et al., 1995). Similarly, in the area of personal care and maintenance of autonomy, older adults may opt for the compensatory use of social and technical support in order to free up resources for goals involving optimization (M. M. Baltes, 1996). Another source of loss can be negative transfer (within or between domains of functioning). For instance, having to drive one's car on the left side of the street might be negatively affected when having learned to drive one's car on the right side of the street all one's life. Negative transfer might also increase with age (cf., Kliegl & Lindenberger, 1993), possibly because of a higher degree of automatization of overlearned skills with increasing age. Finally, people can directly lose the relevant means for goal attainment (such as when a car accident results in paraplegia). As morbidity increases and sensory functioning decreases in old age (e.g., Marsiske, Klumb, & Baltes, 1997), such direct losses of goal-relevant means might be more prominent in old than in younger age-groups.

Many means that were discussed in relation to optimization, can also function as compensatory means when they are aimed at counteracting an actual or anticipated loss in goal-relevant means (see table 3.1). This is so because of equifinality and multiple pathways to goal attainment (Kruglanski, 1996). Many means have substitutive power. On the surface, then, and taking a functional perspective, the very same means can either constitute optimization or compensation, depending on the context. For a final evaluation of whether a given behavior is optimization or compensation, therefore, it is important to understand the action context in which the behavior is displayed.

To give another example: Practicing phonetic articulation might be an optimization strategy for language acquisition in children but a compensatory strategy for an adult with damage to the speech production areas of the brain. And moreover, having practiced phonetic articulation in a compensatory setting does not exclude that the skills acquired at a later point may be used for purposes of optimization of another and quite distinct action goal. Only if the means are applied *in order to counteract loss* in goal-relevant means to maintain functioning in the same (goal-)domain, do we define them as compensatory. If these two criteria (response to loss, serving the same goal) are not rigorously applied to the definition of compensation, the concept loses its usefulness as every goal-related behavior could ultimately be defined as compensatory (Carstensen & Freund, 1994; Uttal & Perlmutter, 1989).

Compensation for the loss in goal-relevant means can be achieved also by increasing the time, effort, and energy when engaging in goal-relevant means. For instance, spending more time practicing piano in a more concentrated way can help to maintain a very high level of functioning even when faced with the loss of flexibility, speed and strength of one's fingers (see the "Rubinstein"-example in P. B. Baltes & Baltes, 1990). Thus, the replacement of means does not have to encompass the acquisition of new means (e.g., skills) but can also be accomplished by activating previously acquired but unused means. When facing loss in goal-relevant means, drawing on a set of already existing functionally equivalent means, is probably the easier (i.e., less effortful and time-consuming) form of compensation (Freund, 1995).

There are two broad classes of external forms of compensation, that is, of employing means that do not lie inside the person: (a) the use of technical aids, and (b) assistance from other people. A good example for the first class is the use of a hearing aid that can compensate, at least partly, for loss in hearing (Tesch-Römer, 1997). A major component of external compensatory efforts is social. For instance, there is strong evidence in the literature on social support that the informal or formal help of other people can be regarded as a powerful means for compensating for loss or decline in goal-relevant means (cf., Schwarzer & Leppin, 1992). As Lang (e.g., Lang & Baltes, 1997) showed, not only the availability of social resources but also their effective management can provide an important source for compensation in old and very old age.

As does optimization, compensation itself draws on resources (e.g., time, energy, social network) that are limited (cf. Hobfoll, 1989). Hence, one way to compensate is to focus one's efforts on the most promising means to achieve the level of performance threatened by loss or decline instead of investing time and energy in various possible means. To concentrate one's remaining resources on the refinement and improvement of those means that are best suited to one's abilities and the maintenance of a given level of performance, instead of spending one's resources on pursuing various compensatory means, seems a more parsimonious compensatory strategy. In lifespan theory, finding the most effective composition of compensatory means to maintain adequate function is paramount.

As we discussed ways and means of optimization and compensation, we have perhaps neglected the fact that both, of course, can evince negative consequences; true to the gain-loss dynamic of lifespan theory and multifunctionality. Let us hasten to add, therefore, that, although the maintenance of one's level of functioning is generally viewed as a positive form of adaptation to a threat caused by loss or decline in goal-related means, there also exists the possibility of maladaptive compensatory efforts (e.g., Bäckman & Dixon, 1992; Carstensen et al., 1995). Three forms of mis-compensation can be distinguished: (a) under-compensation, that is, not investing enough means in order to counteract the effect of loss or decline in goal-related means, (b) criterion-inadequate compensation, that is, investing in means that do not lead to the desired effect, and (c) over-compensation (i.e., "overdoing it"; for instance, a gymnast who tries to compensate for age-related loss in flexibility by doubling hours of training, which eventually leads to irreversible damage of the joints). As is true for optimization, monitoring the effectiveness of employed compensatory means is essential for successful compensation.

## LOSS-BASED SELECTION

If the costs of compensatory efforts permanently outweigh the benefits, the most adaptive response to loss is disengaging from the respective goal and instead engaging in loss-based selection. Loss-based selection occurs in response to decline or loss of previously available means or resources and encompasses such processes as the reconstructing the goal-hierarchy, focusing on the most important goals, adapting standards, and searching for new goals (see table 3.1).

Quitting fruitless compensatory efforts is particularly difficult when a person is highly committed to the respective goal or when the social context is organized to reinforce that goal. Moreover, the more resources a person has already invested in compensatory efforts, the harder it becomes to think of the invested resources as sunk costs that should be cut. Instead they continue trying to repair their losses and invest even more resources (e.g., Whyte, 1993). In such a case, it is more adaptive to disengage from the goal and select a goal that is more likely to be achieved.

In this vein, Brandtstädter and his colleagues have pointed out, that flexible goal-adjustment or accommodative coping styles are more adaptive for successful development when goals are blocked (e.g., Brandtstädter & Wentura, 1995). According to Brandtstädter, people will first try to invest in instrumental, goal-relevant means in order to attain their goals when they are blocked (i.e., compensatory efforts). Only when these assimilative efforts fail (i.e., goals remain blocked), accommodative processes such as disengagement from goals or adjustment of standards are invoked. Disengaging from permanently blocked goals and engagement in new, alternative goals are also central to the concept of compensatory secondary control as proposed by J. Heckhausen (1998). According to their model of primary and secondary control, these secondary control strategies contribute to adaptiveness in that they buffer the negative emotional and motivational effects of failure or loss.

There is also some empirical evidence that is consistent with the proposed adaptiveness of loss-based selection given the failure of compensatory striving. For instance, Brandtstädter and Renner (1990) provide cross-sectional evidence for an age-related increase in flexible goal-adjustment, supposedly because losses in goal-related means increase with age. In addition, in a recent study, Wrosch and Heckhausen (in press) demonstrated that people downgrade goals when they encounter opportunity structures that are detrimental for goal attainment. To our knowledge, however, there exists no *direct* empirical evidence speaking to our hypothesis that loss-based selection may be more adaptive than continued investment in compensatory efforts in cases when goals are permanently blocked. Empirical studies need to address whether some goals might be subjectively so central for a person's sense of leading a meaningful life that giving them up would lead to even stronger feelings of loss than continuing to engage in (fruitless) compensatory efforts.

## CONCLUSION

*Outlook: The Orchestration of Selection, Optimization, and Compensation.* In this chapter, we have discussed the processes of selection, optimization, and compensation as separate processes contributing to successful development. As pointed out by Flammer (1996), however, a full understanding of development requires the coordinated integration of the three developmental processes. In agreement with Flammer's view, we contend that a conceptualization of developmental regulation also requires the investigation of the interplay of selection, optimization, and compensation (P. B. Baltes & Baltes, 1990; Marsiske et al., 1995). To reflect an action-theoretical perspective we use the metaphor of orchestration. In the remainder of this chapter, we want to briefly address the question of the orchestration of selection, optimization, and compensation within an action-theoretical framework.

As was already pointed out above, goal-setting (selection) is a necessary but not a sufficient condition for goal-striving (optimization and compensation). The investment of one's resources, however, is more likely to lead to optimal levels of functioning when it is goal-directed. Thus, again based on one of the fundamental assumptions underlying the SOC-theory, namely, the limitation of resources throughout the lifespan, the concentration of means in a select number of domains of functioning should enhance the likelihood of achieving or maintaining a high level of functioning. In other words, the more goals a person pursues at the same time, the less resources can be invested in each of them, thereby decreasing the likelihood of achieving an optimal level of functioning in the various domains. Similarly, when facing loss or decline in goal-relevant means, a person is more likely to successfully use compensatory strategies if the resources of time and energy do not have to be distributed among a large number of domains of functioning. Thus, selection is important not only in choosing initial goals but in making the best of limited resources for optimizing gain and if necessary, compensating for loss.

Optimization and compensation are likely to be positively related to each other. As the difference between optimization and compensation does not lie in the means but in the conditions under which they are employed, we expect that a person who frequently and consistently engages in optimizing strategies to be likely to use similar means when confronted with loss or decline in goal-relevant means. To achieve an overall positive balance, then, wise investment in both, optimization and compensation, seems necessary.

Finally, we argue, of course, that the simultaneous and lifelong coordination of all processes is the peak of adaptive fitness across the lifespan. In this spirit, we propose that selection, optimization, and compensation can also be conceptualized as three facets of one combined and orchestrated process, namely, the process of 'selective optimization with compensation'. Marsiske et al. (1995) have argued that selective optimization with compensation always "operate dynamically as a unit or as a package." (p. 44). Because it takes the directionality of development (selection) as well as the fact that all development is associated with gains (optimization) *and* losses (compensation) into account, a conceptualization of SOC as one dynamic and orchestrated process of developmental regulation consisting of three distinct yet interrelated facets, appears theoretically most promising. This theoretical perspective, however, is but an opening. Its elaboration will require much further work, theoretical and empirical.

## REFERENCES

Bäckman, L., & Dixon, R. A. (1992). Psychological compensation: A theoretical framework. *Psychological Bulletin, 112*, 1–25.

Baltes, M. M. (1996). *The many faces of dependency in old age.* New York: Cambridge University Press.

Baltes, M. M. & Carstensen, L. L. (1991). Possible selves across the life span: Commentary. *Human Development, 34*, 256–260.

Baltes, M. M., & Carstensen, L. L. (1996). The process of successful aging. *Aging and Society, 16*, 397–422.

Baltes, M. M., & Carstensen, L. L. (in press). Social psychological theories and their application to aging: From individual to collective social psychology. In V. L. Bengtson & K. W. Schaie (Eds.), *Handbook of theories of aging.* New York: Springer.

Baltes, P. B. (1997). On the incomplete architecture of human ontogeny. Selection, optimzation, and compensation as foundation of developmental theory. *American Psychologist, 52*, 366–380.

Baltes, P. B., & Baltes, M. M. (1990). Psychological perspectives on successful aging: The model of selective optimization with compensation. In P. B. Baltes & M. M. Baltes (Eds.), *Successful aging. Perspectives from the behavioral sciences.* (pp. 1–34). New York: Cambridge University Press.

Baltes, P. B., Lindenberger, U., & Staudinger, U. M. (1997). Life-span theory in developmental psychology. In R. M. Lerner (Ed.), *Handbook of child psychology: Vol. 1. Theoretical models of human development* (pp. 1029–1143). New York: Wiley.

Baltes, P. B. & Staudinger, U. M. (1996). Interactive minds in a life-span perspective: Prologue. In P. B. Baltes & U. M. Staudinger (Eds.), *Interactive minds: Life-span perspectives on the social foundation of cognition.* (pp. 1–32). New York: Cambridge University Press.

Bandura, A. (1969). *Principles of behavior modification.* New York: Holt, Rinehart, & Winston.

Bandura, A. (1996a). *Self-efficacy: The exercise of control.* New York: Freeman.

Bandura, A. (1996b). Failures in self-regulation: Energy depletion of selective disengagement? *Psychological Inquiry, 7*, 20–25.

Bargh, J. A., & Gollwitzer, P. M. (1994). Environmental control of goal-directed action: Automatic and strategic contingencies between situations and behavior. In W. D. Spaulding (Ed.), *Nebraska Symposium on Motivation: Vol. 41. Integrative views of motivation, cognition, and emotion.* (pp. 71–124). Lincoln, NE: University of Nebraska Press.

Boesch, E. E. (1976). *Psychopathologie des Alltags.* Bern: Huber.

Boesch, E. E. (1991). *Symbolic action theory and cultural psychology.* Heidelberg: Springer.

Brandtstädter, J. (1994). Personal and social control over development: Some implications of an action perspective in life-span developmental psychology. In P. B. Baltes & O. G. Brim, Jr. (Eds.), *Life-span development and behavior,* (Vol. 6, pp. 1–32). New York: Academic Press.

Brandtstädter, J. (1997). Action theory in developmental psychology. In R. M. Lerner (Ed.), *Handbook of child psychology: Vol. 1. Theoretical models of human development* (pp. 807–866). New York: Wiley.

Brandtstädter, J., & Renner, G. (1990). Tenacious goal pursuit and flexible goal adjust-ment: Explication and age-related analysis of assimilative and accommodative strate-gies of coping. *Psychology and Aging, 5,* 58-67.
Brandtstädter, J., & Wentura, D. (1995). Adjustment to shifting possibility frontiers in later life: Compensatory adaptive modes. In R. A. Dixon & L. Bäckman (Eds.), *Psy-chological compensation: Managing losses and promoting gains* (pp. 83–106). Hillsdale, NJ: Lawrence Erlbaum Associates.
Brunstein, J. C. (1993). Personal goals and subjective well-being: A longitudinal study. *Journal of Personality and Social Psychology, 65,* 1061-1070.
Cantor, N. (1994). Life task problem solving: Situational affordances and personal needs. *Personality and Social Psychology Bulletin, 20,* 235-243.
Carstensen, L. L. (1993). Motivation for social contact across the life span: A theory of socioemotional selectivity. In J. Jacobs (Ed.), *Nebraska Symposium on Motivation: Vol. 40. Developmental perspectives on motivation* (pp. 209–254). Lincoln, NE: Uni-versity of Nebraska Press.
Carstensen, L. L. & Freund, A. M. (1994). The resilience of the aging self. *Developmental Review, 14,* 81-92.
Carstensen, L. L., Hanson, K. A., & Freund, A. M. (1995). Selection and compensation in adulthood. In R. A. Dixon & L. Bäckman (Eds.), *Compensating for psychological deficits and declines: Managing losses and promoting gains* (pp. 107-126). Hillsdale, NJ: Lawrence Erlbaum Associates.
Carver, C. S., & Scheier, M. F. (1995). *On the self-regulation of behavior.* Cambridge, England: Cambridge University Press.
Coats, E. J., Janoff-Bulman, R., & Alpert, N. (1996). Approach versus avoidance goals: Differences in self-evaluation and well-being. *Personality and Social Psychology Bul-letin, 22,* 1057–1067.
Cross, S., & Markus, H. (1991). Possible selves across the life span. Human Develop-ment, 34, 230–255.
Dixon. R. A. , & Bäckman, L. (Eds.), *Psychological compensation: Managing losses and promoting gains.* Hillsdale, NJ: Lawrence Erlbaum Associates.
Eckensberger, L. H. (1997). The legacy of Boesch's intellectual oeuvre. *Culture and Psychology, 3,* 277–298.
Elliot, A. J. & Sheldon, K. M. (1997), Avoidance achievement motivation: A personal goals analysis. *Journal of Personality and Social Psychology, 73,* 171–185.
Elliot, A. J., Sheldon, K. M., & Church, M. A. (1997). Avoidance personal goals and subjective well-being. *Personality and Social Psychological Bulletin, 23,* 915–927.
Emmons, R. A. (1986). Personal strivings: An approach to personality and subjective well-being. *Journal of Personality and Social Psychology, 51,* 1058–1068.
Emmons, R. A. (1996). Striving and feeling. Personal goals and subjective well-being. In P. M. Gollwitzer & J. A. Bargh (Eds.), *The psychology of action: Linking cognition and motivation to behavior* (pp. 313–337). New York: Guilford Press.
Ericsson, K. A. (1996). *The road to excellence: The acquisition of expert performance in the arts and sciences, sports, and games.* Mahwah, NJ: Lawrence Erlbaum Associ-ates.
Flammer, A. (1990). *Erfahrung der eigenen Wirksamkeit.* Bern: Huber.
Flammer, A. (1996). *Entwicklungstheorien: Psychologische Theorien der menschlichen Entwicklung.* Bern: Huber.
Flammer, A., Kaiser, F. G., Lüthi, R., & Grob, A. (1990). Kontrollmeinungen und Selbstwissen. *Schweizerische Zeitschrift für Psychologie, 49,* 159-172.
Fleeson, W. W., & Cantor, N. (1995). Goal relevance and the affective experience of daily life: Ruling out situational explanations. *Motivation and Emotion, 19,* 25–57.
Freund, A. M. (1995). *Die Selbstdefinition alter Menschen. Inhalt, Struktur und Funktion.* Berlin: Edition Sigma.

Freund, A. M., & Baltes, P. B. (1997). *Selection, optimization, and compensation as strategies of life-management: Correlations with subjective indicators of successful aging.* Manuscript submitted for publication.

Gollwitzer, P. M. (1996). The volitional benefits of planning. In P. M. Gollwitzer & J. A. Bargh (Eds.), *The psychology of action* (pp. 287–312). New York: Guilford Press.

Gollwitzer, P. M., & Bargh, J. A. (Eds.), *The psychology of action.* New York: Guilford Press.

Gollwitzer, P. M., & Brandstätter, V. (1997). Implementation intentions and effective goal pursuit. *Journal of Personality and Social Psychology, 73,* 186–199.

Grob, A. (1991). Der Einfluß bedeutsamer Lebensereignisse auf das Wohlbefinden und auf bereichsspezifische Kontrollmeinungen von Jugendlichen. *Schweizerische Zeitschrift für Psychologie, 50,* 48–63.

Heckhausen, H. (1991). *Motivation and action.* New York: Springer.

Heckhausen, J. (1998). *Developmental regulation in adulthood: Age-normative and sociostructural constraints as adaptive challenges.* New York: Cambridge University Press.

Heckhausen, J., Dixon, R. A., & Baltes, P. B. (1989). Gains and losses in development throughout adulthood as perceived by different adult age groups. *Developmental Psychology, 25,* 109–121.

Heckhausen, J., & Schulz, R. (1995). A life-span theory of control. *Psychological Review, 102,* 284–304.

Hobfoll, S. E. (1989). Conservation of resources. A new attempt at conceptualizing stress. *American Psychologist, 44,* 513–524.

Klein, H. J., Whitener, E. M., & Ilgen, D. R. (1990). The role of goal-specificity in the goal-setting process. *Motivation and Emotion, 14,* 179–193.

Kliegl, R., & Lindenberger, U. (1993). Modeling intrusions and correct recall in episodic memory: Adult age differences in encoding of list context. *Journal of Experimental Psychology: Learning, Memory, and Cognition, 19,* 617–637.

Kliegl, R., Smith, J., & Baltes, P. B. (1989). Testing-the-limits and the study of age differences in cognitive plasticity of a mnemonic skill. *Developmental Psychology, 26,* 894–904.

Klinger, E. (1977). *Meaning and void. Inner experience and the incentives in people's lives.* Minneapolis: University of Minnesota Press.

Kruglanski, A. W. (1996). Goals as knowledge structures. In P. M. Gollwitzer & J. A. Bargh (Eds.), *The Psychology of action: Linking cognition and motivation to behavior* (pp. 599–618). New York: Guilford Press.

Labouvie-Vief, G. (1981). Proactive and reactive aspects of constuctivism: Growth and aging in life-span perspective. In R. M. Lerner & N. A. Busch-Rossnagel (Eds.), *Individuals as producers of their development.* (pp. 197–230). New York: Academic Press.

Lang, F. R., & Baltes, M. M. (1997). Being with people and being alone in late life: Costs and benefits for everyday functioning. *International Journal of Behavioral Development., 21,* 729–746.

Lawton, M. P. (1989). Behavior-relevant ecological factors. In K. W. Schaie & C. Schooler (Eds.), *Social structure and aging: Psychological processes.* (pp. 57–78). Hillsdale, NJ: Lawrence Erlbaum Associates.

Lerner, R. M. (1991). Changing organism-context relations as the basic process of development: A developmental contextual perspective. *Developmental Psychology, 27,* 27–32.

Levelt, W. J. M. (1989). *Speaking: From intention to articulation.* Cambridge, MA: MIT Press.

Lewin, K. (1935). *A dynamic theory of personality.* New York: McGraw-Hill.

Lindenberger, U., & Baltes, P. B. (1997). Intellectual functioning in old and very old age: Cross-sectional results from the Berlin Aging Study. *Psychology and Aging, 12,* 410–432.

Little, B. R. (1989). Personal projects analysis: Trivial pursuits, magnificent obsessions, and the search for coherence. In D. M Buss & N. Cantor (Eds.), *Personality psychology: Recent trends and emerging directions* (pp. 15–31). New York: Springer.

Little, T. D. (1998). Sociocultural influences on the development of children's action-control beliefs. In J. Heckhausen & C. S. Dweck (Eds.), *Motivation and self-regulation across the life span.* New York: Cambridge University Press.

Locke, E. A., Shaw, K. N. , Saari, L. M., & Latham, G. P. (1981). Goal setting and task performance: 1969–1980. *Psychological Bulletin, 90,* 125–152.

Magnusson, D. (Ed.). (1996). *The life-span development of individuals: Behavioural, neurobiological, and psychosocial perspectives.* Cambridge, England: Cambridge University Press.

Markus, H., & Nurius, P. (1986). Possible Selves. *American Psychologist, 41,* 954–969.

Marsiske, M., Klumb, P., & Baltes, M. M. (1997). Everyday activity patterns and sensory functioning in old age. *Psychology and Aging, 12,* 444–457.

Marsiske, M., Lang, F. R., Baltes, M. M., & Baltes, P. B. (1995). Selective optimization with compensation: Life-span perspectives on successful human development. In R. A. Dixon & L. Bäckman (Eds.), *Compensation for psychological defects and declines: Managing losses and promoting gains* (pp. 35–79). Hillsdale, NJ: Lawrence Erlbaum Associates.

Miller, G. A., Galanter, E., & Pribram, K.-H. (1960). *Plans of structure of behavior.* New York: Holt, Rinehart, & Winston.

Mischel, W. (1996). From good intentions to willpower. In P. M. Gollwitzer & J. A. Bargh (Eds.), *The psychology of action* (pp. 197–218). New York: Guilford Press.

Oettingen, G. (1995). Cross-cultural perspectives on self-efficacy. In A. Bandura (Ed.), *Self-efficacy in changing societies* (pp. 149–176). New York: Cambridge University Press.

Oettingen, G. (1996). *Psychologie des Zukunftsdenkens. Erwartungen und Phantasien.* Göttingen: Hogrefe.

Rothbaum, F., Weisz, J. R., & Snyder, S. S. (1982). Changing the world and changing the self: A two-process model of perceived control. *Journal of Personality and Social Psychology, 42,* 5–37.

Rotter, J. B. (1966). Generalized expectancies for internal versus external control of reinforcement. In G. A. Kimble (Ed.), *Psychological Monographs: General and applied* (Vol. 80, pp. 1–28). Washington, DC: American Psychological Association.

Ryff, C. D. (1991). Possible selves in adulthood and old age: A tale of shifting horizons. *Psychology and Aging, 6,* 286–295.

Sheldon, K. M., & Kasser, T. (1994). Coherence and congruence: Two aspects of personality integration. *Journal of Personality and Social Psychology, 68,* 531–543

Skinner, E. A., Chapman, M., & Baltes, P. B. (1988). Children's beliefs about control, means-ends, and agency: Developmental differences during middle childhood. *International Journal of Behavioral Development, 11,* 369–388.

Smith, J. (1996). Planning about life: Toward a social-interactive perspective. In P. B. Baltes & U. M. Staudinger (Eds.), *Interactive minds: Life-span perspectives on the social foundation of cognition.* (pp. 241–275). New York: Cambridge University Press.

Smith, J., Fleeson, W., Geiselmann, B., Settersten, R., Kunzmann, U. (1996). Wohlbefinden im hohen Alter: Vorhersagen aufgrund objektiver Lebensbedingungen und subjektiver Bewertung. In K. U. Mayer & P. B. Baltes (Eds.), *Die Berliner Altersstudie* (pp. 497–523). Berlin: Akademie Verlag.

Schwarzer, R., & Leppin, A. (1992). Social support and mental health: A conceptual and empirical overview. In L. Montada, S.-H. Filipp, & M. J. Lerner (Eds.), *Life crises and experiences of loss in adulthood* (pp. 435-458). Hillsdale, NJ: Lawrence Erlbaum Associates.

Staudinger, U. M. (1996). Wisdom and the social-interactive foundation of the mind. In P. B. Baltes & U. M. Staudinger (Eds.), *Interactive minds: Life-span perspectives on the social foundation of cognition* (pp. 276–318). New York: Cambridge University Press.

Staudinger, U. M., & Freund, A. M. (1997). *Krank und "arm" im hohen Alter und trotzdem guten Mutes? Untersuchungen im Rahmen eines Modells psychologischer Widerstandsfähigkeit.* Manuscript submitted for publication.

Staudinger, U. M., Marsiske, M., & Baltes, P. B. (1995). Resilience and reserve capacity in later adulthood: Potentials and limits of development across the life-span. In D. Cicchetti & D. Cohen (Eds.), *Developmental psychopathology: Vol. 2. Risk, disorder, and adaptation* (pp. 801–847). New York: Wiley.

Tesch-Römer, C. (1997). Psychological effects of hearing aid use in older adults. *Journal of Gerontology: Psychological Sciences, 52B*, 127–138.

Tversky, A., & Kahneman, D. (1981). The framing of decisions and the psychology of choice. *Science, 211*, 453–458.

Uttal, D. H., & Perlmutter, M. (1989). Toward a broader conceptualization of development: The role of gains and losses across the life span. *Developmental Review, 9*, 101-132.

Vallacher, R. R., & Wegner, D. M. (1985). *A theory of action identification.* Hillsdale, NJ: Erlbaum.

Wegner, D. M. (1992). You can't always think what you want: Problems in the suppression of unwanted thoughts. In M. Zanna (Ed.), *Advances in experimental social psychology* (Vol 25, pp. 193–225). San Diego, CA: Academic Press.

Whyte, G. (1993). Escalating commitment in individual and group decision making: A prospect theory approach. *Organizational Behavior and Human Decision Processes, 54*, 430–455.

Wrosch, C., & Heckhausen, J. (in press). Being on-time or off-time: Developmental deadlines for regulating one's own development. In A. N. Perret-Clermont, J. M. Barrelet, A. Flammer, D. Miéville, J. F. Perret, & W. Perrig (Eds.), *Mind and time.* Göttingen: Hogrefe & Huber.

# 4

# Freedom of the Will—the Basis of Control[1]

## *Mario von Cranach*

> *"Whoever has control could exercise it if he or she would be willing to do so." (Flammer, 1990, p. 78)*[2]

## INTRODUCTION

In his comprehensive textbook on the control belief ("Erfahrung der eigenen Wirksamkeit"), Flammer (1990, p. 78) defines control on the basis of action psychology. "Whenever a behavior is executed as consciously planned, we speak of *action*. Actions are a partial set of behavior, and only this partial set is of interest in the following." He defines the elements of control as:

- knowing a certain goal
- accepting it as a goal for oneself
- knowing a way by which the goal can be reached
- the ability to go this way (and to know about it)
- to really go this way.

*Having control* consists of the first, third and fourth elements above; exercising control consists of all of these elements. Understanding the exercise of control as an action implies responsibility:

> If exercising control is understood as an action the goal of which is known and the execution of which is decided upon, responsibility can be ascribed to the controlling person; according to the principle of causation, he or she can be obliged to bear the consequences of the action. (Flammer, 1990, p. 80)

---

[1]I am grateful to Adrian Bangerter for critical comments and revisions of my English formulations.

[2]All quotations from Flammer (1990), Rochat & Modigliani (1996), Dörner (1996), v. Cranach (1996), and Kuhl (1996) are my translations; the emphases in the quotations are taken from the original text.

And responsibility is based on the assumption of action freedom: "If actions are executed consciously and because of their goals, this includes that the person would have, in any case, also the possibility not to execute this action" (p. 77). Our concept of control also implies *freedom of action.* Action, control and responsibility imply, so I see it, a minimum of freedom of action" (Flammer, 1990, p. 81).

Freedom of action can be based on two preconditions, *external circumstances* (which allow the agent to follow his or her intentions) and the *internal freedom of choice,* namely freedom of volition (Steinvorth, 1987; v. Cranach, 1996a). Therefore the assumption of freedom of volition is the basis of the concept of controlling as well as of the control belief; I find the same idea in Flammer's statement which I have used as an introducing quotation. Similar assumptions apply to related concepts, like that of degrees of freedom (Hacker, 1986) or autonomy (Hackman & Oldham, 1974); in work psychology, reactance (Brehm & Brehm, 1981), self-regulation (Kanfer, 1987), or learned helplessness (Seligman, 1975).

What are however the consequences of the assumption of freedom of volition for psychology? Are we obliged to take it into account as a *psychological concept,* should we refine it, build models of it, investigate it empirically? Flammer does not go so far to draw this consequence:

Strictly speaking, action freedom is a postulate of a corresponding image of man and cannot be empirically proved or demonstrated in its existence. Also, introspection is not conclusive here. Since I want however assume that people can basically or at least occasionally take responsibility or partial responsibility, and that in principle they are entitled to the merits of good deeds as well as guilt, the principal possibility of action freedom is indispensable.

This is where I take a different standpoint. I think that, since action and volition have become theoretical and empirical topics of psychology again, and since freedom of action and volition form the implicit basis of so many important theoretical notions, including control, we should also explore them as *psychological topics.* Here, we should proceed as we do with other important sociopsychological matters: taking individual experiences into account without taking them for granted, but as possible parts of the ongoing processes; being aware that they may sometimes and partly be, but not always and totally, illusions. We should look at naive theories and social knowledge as possible sources; we should think about functions and build models of possible processes, and think of ways to obtain empirical evidence. We should be aware of philosophical considerations, but also of the fact that philosophers cannot resolve our problems for us (even if they can answer their own questions). In the following pages, I shall report about some psychological concepts of freedom of action and volition which have been recently developed.

## PSYCHOLOGICAL MODELS OF FREEDOM OF VOLITION

In 1993, Klaus Foppa and myself organized a conference on the topic. About 20 well-known German-speaking psychologists participated. During two and a half days, they were involved in lively and partly heated discussions. The proceedings of the conference became a book (v. Cranach & Foppa, 1996). As to be expected, there was a wide variation in the use and understanding of terms like freedom of action and volition, determination and indetermination, causality and of the body-mind problem; I shall not go into this debate here. It is perhaps not very surprising that all authors of the books' fifteen chapters consider the experience of freedom of volition as an important topic for scientific psychology. As to the question whether there is a real basis for this experience, whether there exist in fact psychological processes which produce something like free choices and decisions, two positions can be distinguished.

Some colleagues do not consider freedom of volition a possible problem for scientific psychology. Two main lines of argument are used to support this point of view:

1. that the assumption is deleterious to science, since it mixes *two different language games* or "jargons," namely the scientific jargon serving the explanation of the world through laws of general validity and the "freedom of volition-jargon" of everyday life which serves the establishment of social responsibility.
2. that there are *logical difficulties* leading to the assumption that actions and thus also freedom of volition can not be objects of empirical investigations: to do so would be a categorical mistake. This assumption is mainly based on arguments which have been developed in philosophy of mind.

There is however a strong faction which thinks that freedom of volition results from the complicated systemic order of human action, motivation, emotion and information processing. These authors reject the classical view of causality which is contained in the first argument as all too narrow, emphasize that the human mind is also part of nature, stress the importance of intentional terms as scientific terms, reject the "self-stultification" which would result from a gap between man as the researching scientist and his "image of man." They also deny, for various reasons, the appropriateness of a purely logical analysis. Thus they conclude that freedom of volition should be an indispensable object of psychological research. There are, however, also generally accepted precautions, namely that conscious experience of ongoing psychological processes, although a valuable source of information, should be considered as cautiously as the results of perception in general; and that the naive realism of everyday language should not be introduced into the scientific treatment of the phenomenon.

As a conceptual basis for the investigation of the psychological processes underlying what we call freedom of the will in everyday life, four different models

(Rochat & Modigliani, Dörner, v. Cranach and Kuhl, all 1996) have been proposed. I shall now present the essence of these models, finally compare and discuss them.

## Free Decisions May Occur in Sequences of Small Steps

Rochat & Modigliani (1996) performed a series of reanalyses of the well-known Milgram– experiments on obedience to authority (Milgram, 1974). To remind the reader, in these studies the subject is put into the role of a "teacher" and induced by the experimenter to administer a long series of electroshocks of increasing strength to an invisible "learner." A lot of attention was elicited by the repeated finding that many subjects finally administered obviously painful and dangerous shocks to their innocent and helpless victim; others resisted the instructions of the experimenter. In general, no personality differences between obedient and resistant subjects were found.

Rochat & Modigliani where interested in the question of why certain subjects *did not conform* to the experimenters' instructions. Using sequential content analysis of the videotaped interactions between experimenter and "teacher", they reconstructed the typical pathways that lead to obedience or resistance. It turns out that typical phases—a cooperative phase, a tension phase, a divergence phase and finally a conformance/confrontation phase (participants either submit to or refuse the experimenters demands) could be distinguished.

In order for the situation to constitute one of free decisions, conditions would have to be fulfilled which the authors call *capability, awareness, and the absence of coercion.* The authors conclude that these conditions were fulfilled for most of the obedient and all of the defiant participants; so the experiments are relevant for the problem of freedom of volition. Now, what are the characteristics of the observed decision processes? Rochat & Modigliani observe a typical *inertia effect:* once a person has made a choice to resist or to remain obedient, subjects tend to maintain their stance.

This is related to an additional finding:

> Free will and behavioral inertia are connected. It appears that participants may well "discover" their free will through acting it out behaviorally. In the very process of acting resistant, they demonstrate to themselves that they are deeply opposed to the experimenter's demands. . . . In the very process of acting in compliance with the experimenters demands, acquiescent participants demonstrate to themselves that, on balance, they want to continue. . . (p. 295)

So the subjects learn about their possibilities, but also about their own motivation. This has the effect that they tend to remain in their track: "*The longer one stays in the road of obedience, the more likely on is to stay on that road.. . .* Conversely, once participants begin questioning and objecting to the experimental procedure, they usually continue to resist . . ." (p. 296)

So we can formulate as a general result from these studies, that free decisions may occur in sequences of small steps, and that there is an impact of "behavioral inertia." In mastering this pathway, the agent may undergo and experience perceptual and motivational changes which make him another person. Or, as I formulated it some years ago:

> The experience of action freedom reinforces itself. Part of this circular process is the motivation for control; which is also an essential precondition of the state and process of action freedom. While learning to experience ourselves as acting free, we also learn to act more free. (v. Cranach, 1991, p. 22)

## Freedom of Decision as the Result of an Internal Dialogue

Dörner's (1996) model is based on the presumptions that (a) *thinking is an internal dialogue* which occurs in memory; that (b) *consciousness is self-reflexivity*, constant monitoring and elaborating of the own cognitive activity; and that (c) the results of self-reflexive processes are stored in a *protocol memory*. His aim is to show that the processes of freedom of volition are fully determined, but that the details of this determination are not given in advance, but that they unfold during the process and are unpredictable (crypto-determinism). These processes start from an equilibrium of competing motives which, to the frustration of the would-be agent, impedes action.

These motives are conceived according to the well-known value-expectancy model. In order to overcome the impediment, the subject enters into an *antagonistic dialogue*, during which various arguments, which speak in favor or against the competing motives, are debated; any argument can either increase or decrease the value or the probability of one of the competing motives. The dialogue can also be raised to meta- or meta-meta-levels, like for example considering strategies of how the conflict could be resolved. In the language of cognitive psychology, the arguments can be considered as operators in the algorithm of the antagonistic dialogue. The whole process takes place merely in the cognitive system, no other personality system has to be postulated; it is self-reflective, and its aim and end is *redetermination* in respect of the original motive conflict.

Where is freedom of volition now, and what does it mean? Here we must take a closer look at the nature of redetermination:

> To experience consciously to be free in one's decisions is nothing but the knowledge that such processes of redetermination are possible and occur in dependence from the given motivational situation. . . . Redetermination means that the decision does not just depend on certain given determinants. . . . but that the determinants change during the process. The landscape of determinants constantly changes, and this process can lead to the effect that finally quite different dimensions determine the decision than those visible in the beginning. . . . The process of redetermination itself is fully determined; there is however a difference between this form of determination and "ordinary" deter-

mination. Here there is not only one decision and its determinants, but the determinants are themselves determined." (Dörner, 1996, p. 143)

So the results of this analysis are, that "the free will is not indeterminate, but can be conceived as being fully determined. . . However, when the process begins, nobody, even not the agent, can see how the whole procedure will end. . . the outcome of the process is not predictable." (Dörner, 1996, p. 147)

**Freedom of Volition as Personal Self-Organization Involving Social Knowledge**

Cranach (1991, 1992, 1996) has developed a model of "action decision freedom;" the name indicates that it is mainly focused on action situations. The model resembles that of Dörner (1996) in many respects. The individual process also departs from motivational conflict, runs off in recursive loops and is conceived as consciously monitored. On the other hand, there are considerable differences: v. Cranach's model is much more comprehensive (and therefore more complicated), since it takes the social embeddedness of the individual into account, involves not only cognition but several personal subsystems, considers the conscious representation of alternatives and their voluntary reinforcement as determinants of the final decision and sees the agent as capable of learning to handle situations of "underdetermination."

Figure 4.1 depicts the basic features of the model. Here are more details: From his social supersystem, the person has acquired knowledge, values and convictions, including what Flammer (1990) calls "control belief" about the possibilities and the value of decision freedom, which are integrated into his personality. This knowledge also refers to conditions of the environment and the situation which are appropriate for free decisions. If, in such a situation, the agent simultaneously experiences two or more equally strong conflicting action tendencies, he will find himself in a state of *underdetermination*. (Underdetermination can be *partial*, so that a part of the alternative to be chosen is clear, another part unclear: P is determined to marry, but has difficulties to chose between Anne or Mary; or he does not know whether to marry, but if so only Anne comes into consideration. And underdetermination is normally *local*, which means that only specific pieces of decision-related information are in contradiction: P may doubt whether he makes enough money to have a family, or whether he can be faithful to one woman, or whether he is at all the person to be married and so on). If he also stays under a *pressure to act*, underdetermination will be consciously experienced as a *disagreeable state of conflict and disability*. In this case he will start a *search for information which could resolve the conflict*, either in the environment or in his own stock of knowledge. If he finds such information, he is again determined and able to act; if not, especially if he finds again incommensurable information, he will again be in a state of underdetermination. The search will proceed in *recurrent loops*, which will eventually include the value system and the self-concept. During this search, an increasing *pressure for a solution*, namely decision, resolve, and action, will be experienced.

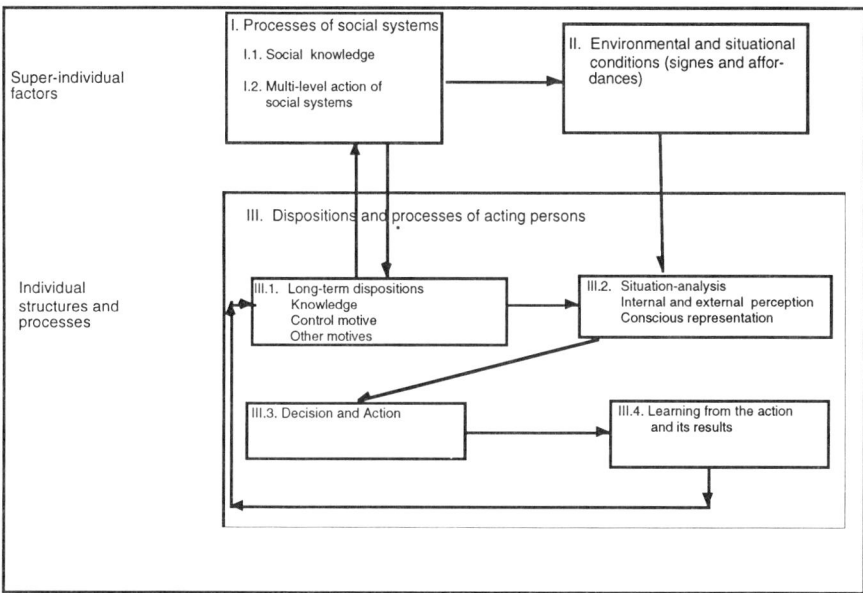

Legend: The knowledge and processes of social systems and their results (I) influence as well the environmental and situational conditions of the action-decision-situation (II) as also the long-term dispositions of the decider (III.1.). On this basis, the person perceives and analyses the situation (III.2.), decides and acts (III.3.). From the process of decision and action and its results, the person learns (III.4.) and changes his or her own dispositional basis (III.1.) and under appropriate conditions also the knowledge of the social systems (I.1.). Adapted from v. Cranach (1996).

*FIG. 4.1. A schema of the process of action decisions.*

How can the person finally find criteria? He may either make a voluntary choice according to the principles of the volition processes (e.g. Kuhl 1996; paragraph 3.4.). Or his attention will be involuntarily caught by a relevant cognitive element which is in this moment consciously experienced. (Here, v. Cranach refers to the *emergency function* of consciousness (v. Cranach & Ochsenbein, 1985; Ochsenbein, 1989) which allows to predict that cognitive elements which are needed in an action situation are likely to be consciously represented). Thus the first relevant criterion which becomes consciously represented is likely to become decisive. But in order to operate efficiently, this choice is likely to become reinforced by *voluntary strategies* like situation control, stimulus control, emotion control and so on (Kuhl, 1983).

Finally the model assumes that the results of the whole process are consumed and evaluated like many actions. The resulting experiences are used in future decision situations: the control motive is reinforced, knowledge about one's own decision processes is gained, well-tried perceptual schemata, concepts (for example parts of the self-concept) and strategies become more salient. "In the final result, personality differences are developed: persons which fear decisions and see themselves at the mercy of their environment, and others which calmly expect (or even search for) decisions, and for which their own decision freedom is self-evident and important" (v. Cranach, 1996).

Where is the "freedom" in this model? Obviously, the essentials of Dörner's argumentation can be applied here. All the details of the ongoing processes seem determined, but the results gradually develop and cannot be predicted. The person experiences freedom because he or she cannot foresee his or her own cognitive and emotional processes and its outcome, classifies it as free and values it highly according to his acquired social knowledge. And these tendencies will be reinforced or inhibited in the processes of personal self-organization which ensue.

## Processes of Volition and the Experience of Freedom

Kuhl (1996) discusses the problems of objective and subjective freedom of volition and of determination on the basis of the comprehensive theoretical and empirical studies of the topic of volition, which he and his group have performed during more than a decade. He emphasizes the differences between a phenomenological perspective of freedom of volition and a functionalistic view based on experimental studies: the further can be explained on the basis of the latter. Consequently Kuhl criticizes philosophical and psychological standpoints which concentrate on experiences of freedom of volition.

To understand the problem we must take into account that volition is the joint function of a multitude of subsystems which are related to the execution of intentions:

> In a preliminary way, we can describe *volition* as a system of processes, which can be decomposed, and which, in addition to their specific functional particularities, have in common that they are directed towards the maintenance and realization of an actual action intention.

As examples of such subsystems, he names volitional functions as intention memory, attention control, impulse control, emotional, motivational, and temperamental control, and planning. Their cooperation demands for a leading and coordinating central instance:

> We have identified the *I* or *self* with a knowledge basis which is specialized on a distinct kind of knowledge, namely highly inferent knowledge about the states of various partial systems or functions (e.g. memory, attention, emotion, motivation, temperament), on the meaning of these (at any given time) registered system configurations to reach the best realization of the intention

and of the possibilities to influence the partial systems. . . The I can be connected to the function of a volitional leading center. (Kuhl, 1996, p. 199)

In addition, the *I* can also function as a "self-reflexive, linguistically encoded knowledge basis which preferably orients itself also according to social norms and previous decisions and, so to speak, generates the commission of coordination for the real system of volition" (pp. 199–200). Different persons identify in different situations different system configurations with the *I*. The partial systems are involved in an activity, the more an action is experienced as really willed. Empirical research has identified a number of criteria which seem to be active if a person experiences volition. However, there are also indications that the activation alone is not sufficient for the experience of subjective freedom: the personality characteristics of *action orientation* and *state orientation* operate as mediating factors (pp. 204–205).

Kuhl finally comes to this theoretical generalization:

> *Concept of freedom:* If the system expects to be able to control . . . the *I* will call itself *free* to succeed with any chosen action. This *explicit* experience of freedom is completed by an *implicit* experience of freedom which is as stronger as more subsystems participate at the coordination order generated by the *I*: After defeating strong aversions one may *consciously* experience oneself as free, although one *feels* unfree insofar as one is aware that many Aspects of the Self have not sustained the own behavior.
> *Constraint (feeling unfree):* If the behavior is determined by forces which are known to be uncontrollable, the system designates itself as *unfree*... (Kuhl, 1996, p. 209)

Here, the relation of experienced freedom to the control belief is made explicit.

Kuhl (1996) also argues that a classical *indeterminism*, leaving however room for a "systemic determinism", seems the appropriate stance for psychology: linear causality, sufficient conditions, predictability, repeatability of constellations of conditions are not fulfilled. However the principal causation by a complex pattern of conditions can be accepted and proved in the model, although it cannot be proved in any single case.

It seems that Kuhl's considerations relating to the problem of determination can be reconciled with those of Dörner. In contrast to v. Cranach, Kuhl remains on the individual level, but he also introduces personal subsystems. His model is more strongly sustained than those of Dörner and v. Cranach, since it is based on a rich basis of theoretical and empirical research.

## CONCLUSION

In this paper, I have first argued that control presupposes freedom of action and the will. This led us to the question of how these grand themes of philosophy and of everyday parlance and experience could be conceived in scientific psychology. In order to answer this question, we have outlined four psychological models of freedom of decisions and volition. These models do not exclude each other, although some of them partially overlap.

The models are at last partially aiming to different cases. In an analysis of the philosophical discussion of the will, Arendt (1977), and Erpenbeck (1993) have distinguished between three conceptions of volition:

(a) volition as a *strong form of motive or drive*, which is used to execute an action against internal or external resistance. This is the underlying concept of Kuhl's model.

(b) volition as a *constitutive moment in the decision between alternatives*. This is the main theme of Rochat, Dörner and v. Cranach.

(c) volition as a *principle of creative self-realization*, the faculty to begin something new. This is a consequence of v. Cranach's model.

Rochat & Modigliani's research demonstrates that what looks and is experienced as a single important decision may in fact be a result of many small steps, although the pathway may contain decisive phases. The details of psychological functioning within these small steps may partially be explained by the other models. The concept of behavioral inertia is however missing in the other models. Dörner's and v. Cranach's models show how we can conceive of decisions as lawful processes which are determined in detail but unpredictable in outcome, and related to the persons experienced freedom of decision. v. Cranach and Rochat & Modigliani point to the aspect of personality development through the exercise of decisions which are experienced as free. v. Cranach's model includes some of the volition processes outlined by Kuhl. Dörner; v. Cranach and Kuhl see the function of these processes likewise in redetermination or, in Kuhl's terms, reestablishment of the ability to act. In Kuhl's and v. Cranach's models, the control motive and control belief play an explicit role. All of these models work with constructs which are more or less generally known and used in psychology.

Finally, it seems noteworthy that in all of these models, the processes which underlay the experience of freedom differ from the naive, but also from the philosophical concept of freedom of action, decision, and volition: Freedom is no longer identified with indetermination. It is seen as resulting from determined processes, but also as principally unpredictable. It has gained a specific meaning which makes sense in the context of scientific psychology. Thus, also the concept of control is provided with a stronger basis.

## REFERENCES

Arendt, H. (1977). *The life of the mind. Vol. 2: Willing*. New York: Harcourt Brace.

Brehm, S. S. & Brehm, J. W. (1981). *Psychological reactance. A theory of freedom and control*. New York: Academic Press.

Cranach, M. v. (1991). Handlungsfreiheit und Determination als Prozess und Erlebnis. *Zeitschrift für Sozialpsychologie, 22*, 3–24.

Cranach, M. v. (1992). Handlungs-Entscheidungsfreiheit als psychologischer Prozess. *Zeitschrift für Sozialpsychologie, 23*, 287–294.

Cranach, M. v. (1996). Handlungs-Entscheidungsfreiheit: ein sozialpsychologisches Modell. In M v. Cranach & K. Foppa (Eds.), *Freiheit des Entscheidens und Handelns* (253–283). Heidelberg: Asanger.

Cranach, M. v. & Ochsenbein G. (1985). "Selbstüberwachungssysteme" und ihre Funktion in der menschlichen Informationsverarbeitung. *Schweiz. Zeitschrift für Psychologie, 44,* 221–235.

Cranach, M. v. & Foppa K. (Eds.), (1996). *Freiheit des Entscheidens und Handelns.* Heidelberg: Asanger.

Dörner, D. (1996). *Der freie Wille und die Selbstreflexion.* In M. v. Cranach & K. Foppa (Hrsg.), *Freiheit des Entscheidens und Handelns* (125-150). Heidelberg: Asanger.

Erpenbeck, J. (1993). *Wollen und Werden.* Konstanz: Universitätsverlag Konstanz.

Flammer, A. (1990). *Erfahrung der eigenen Wirksamkeit. Einführung in die Psychologie der Kontrollmeinung.* Bern: Huber.

Hacker, W. (1986). *Arbeitspsychologie.* Berlin, VEB Deutscher Verlag der Wissenschaften.

Hackman, J.R. & Oldham, G.R. (1974). The job diagnosis survey: An instrument for the diagnosis of jobs and the evaluation of job redesign projects *Technical report, 4,* Yale University.

Kanfer, F. (1987). Selbstregulation und Verhalten. In H. Heckhausen, P. M. Gollwitzer & F. Weinert (Hrsg), *Jenseits des Rubikon. Der Wille in den Humanwissenschaften* (286–299). Berlin, Heidelberg: Springer.

Kuhl, J. (1996). Wille, Freiheit, Verantwortung: Alte Antinomien aus experimentalpsychologi-scher Sicht. In M. v. Cranach & K. Foppa (Hrsg.), *Freiheit des Entscheidens und Handelns* (186–218). Heidelberg: Asanger.

Milgram, S. (1974). *Obedience to authority: An experimental view.* New York: Harper.

Rochat, F. & Modigliani, A. (1996). Obedience to authority and free will. In M. v. Cranach & K. Foppa (Hrsg.), *Freiheit des Entscheidens und Handelns* (284–301). Heidelberg: Asanger.

Seligman, M. E. P. (1975). *Helplessness: On depression, development and death.* San Francisco: Freeman.

Steinvorth, U. (1987). *Freiheitstheorien in der Philosophie der Neuzeit.* Darmstadt: Wissenschaftliche Buchgesellschaft.

# II

# Conscious, Automatic, and Controlled Processes

# 5

# Automatic and Controlled Uses of Memory in Social Judgements

*Werner Wippich*

## INTRODUCTION

The notion of control or of control processes has a long standing tradition in human memory research. For example, once upon a time memory was thought to consist of at least two stores, namely, a short-term store and a long-term store (Atkinson & Shiffrin, 1968). The transfer of information from the short-term store to the long-term store was seen to be at least partly under the control of the subject. For example, rehearsal has been interpreted as a control process by which information residing in the short-term store may be copied into the long-term store. For sure, this view has proven to be too simple, and the control process of rehearsal was found to differ according to the goals subjects may pursue (Craik & Watkins, 1973). Similarly, memory research has favored the idea that subjects may control which information they are willing to forget at the time of encoding. Research on the phenomenon of intentional or directed forgetting has revealed that forgetting can be affected by voluntary mechanisms that may be utilized by the person with varying effectiveness (Epstein, 1972). On the other hand, the levels of processing approach has shown that later demonstrations of memory do not require an intention to learn or to store information at the time of encoding (Craik & Lockhart, 1972). Even more importantly, some information seems to be stored automatically at the time of encoding. By the standard definition, automaticity provides a basis for rapid responding, does not require attentional capacity, and does not require intent (e.g., Hasher & Zacks, 1979; Posner & Snyder, 1975).

   In recent years, the concept of a short-term store was found to be too simple and has been replaced by the notion of a working memory system (Baddeley, 1986). Within this research domain, we may mention a further notion of the concept of control that is interpreted to be operating either intentionally or automatically, too (Holley & McEvoy, 1996). For example, one model of cognition proposes that, together with goals, inhibitory mechanisms control some aspects of the contents of consciousness and of action. They determine which activated representations gain entrance into working memory, they suppress those representations in working memory that are no longer relevant, and they help to prevent prepotent or recently rejected candidates for responses from gaining control over thought and action before weaker alternative candidates can be considered (Hasher & Zacks, 1988; Zacks & Hasher, 1994). When inhibitory control is inefficient, a broader range of information will enter working memory, information that is no longer relevant will continue to remain active, and the frequency of inappropriate overt responses and of momentarily irrelevant or marginally relevant thoughts will increase. Recent work strongly suggests that inhibitory control may be less efficient for depressed and stressed young adults relative to age–mate controls (Linville, 1996), as it may be for younger children relative to older children (Dempster, 1992), for people with schizophrenia (Frith, 1979), and for patients with frontal lobe damage (Shimamura, 1995). Inhibitory control is also considerably less efficient for older adults than for younger adults (Dempster, 1992). For example, older adults are likely to form multiple inferences in situations in which younger adults do not (Hamm & Hasher, 1992). Furthermore, older adults, relative to younger adults, are less able to abandon no-longer-relevant thoughts and action plans from working memory (Zacks & Hasher, 1994).

Traditionally, the notion of control or of inhibitory control as well as assumptions about automaticity have been applied to the encoding stage of information processing and to the processing of incoming information. In this article, however, we are interested in research suggesting that the *retrieval* of previously studied information may be based on controlled uses of memory as well as on automatic or unconscious uses of memory. The distinction between intentional and incidental retrieval of information from memory has proven to be a very important one. First, we will introduce this distinction by discussing some research that has been devoted to so-called implicit or indirect memory tests as opposed to traditional explicit or direct memory tests. Some interpretations of implicit memory tests have equated performance on these tests with an automatic, unconscious, or incidental retrieval orientation whereas performance on explicit tests has been attributed to a controlled, conscious, or intentional retrieval orientation. Recently, however, it has become clear that subjects in an implicit test condition may, for whatever reason, invoke recollective or controlled strategies to solve the problems they are given. This contamination of implicit tests by the intentional or controlled use of memory has been the primary concern of researchers, but in our opinion the converse problem—incidental or automatic retrieval affecting performance on explicit tests—is at least as likely (indeed, we believe more likely under most circumstances, see Wippich, 1992). Therefore, we will describe next a procedure that is aimed at separating controlled uses of memory from automatic uses as they operate within a single task. This approach, the so-called process dissociation procedure (Jacoby, 1991), may be seen as a refinement of implicit memory research. Finally, we will report the results of some experiments that have used this procedure in an attempt to separate consciously controlled and automatic retrieval processes in social judgments. In concluding, we will evaluate some shortcomings of this approach. In our opinion, however, the distinction between automatic and controlled uses of memory promises to remain an important topic not only for memory research.

## IMPLICIT VERSUS EXPLICIT MEMORY TESTS

In many ways the primary paradigm for studying implicit memory is quite similar to the customary way of studying explicit memory in laboratory experiments. In both cases, subjects are exposed to material (usually a list of discrete words or pictures) in a first phase. In a later test phase, subjects in an explicit memory task are asked to recall words or pictures or to recognize them amongst plausible lures; in either case, they are asked to consciously retrieve the prior experiences. Thus, the consequences of previously experienced events are expressed as conscious recollections. In an implicit memory task, subjects are not directed to intentionally recollect the items presented earlier; rather, they are given some ostensibly unrelated task, such as identifying fragmented forms of the pictures or words or identifying them from brief displays. The finding is that subjects can name the fragmented forms of the stimuli better if they have recently studied them than if not. This facilitation is termed priming. Thus, memory is expressed as a change in performance that does not entail explicit retrieval of the learning episode.

The original reason that cognitive psychologists became excited about the study of priming on implicit memory tests was the observation that performance on these tests seems resistant to the dramatic forgetting sometimes seen on explicit tests. Densely amnesic patients, who perform very poorly on standard recall or recognition tests, were found to show normal patterns of priming on implicit memory tests (Parkin, 1987; Shimamura, 1986). This pattern of performance has led to the conclusion that implicit tests assess different processes, information, or systems than explicit tests. This conclusion is bolstered by other reports in which researchers have shown intact priming in groups of subjects or under experimental conditions in which conscious recollection is impaired.

For example, although subjects under the influence of alcohol have been found to perform poorly on explicit tests of retention, they show levels of priming equivalent to those of sober subjects on implicit tests (Hashtroudi, Parker, DeLisi, Wyatt, & Mutter, 1984). Similarly, both the aged (Light & Singh, 1987) and children (Greenbaum & Graf, 1989; Wippich, Mecklenbräuker, & Brausch, 1989) show this same pattern of impaired explicit but relatively intact implicit test performance. Subjects exposed to information when under anesthesia have also shown priming on implicit memory tests when they have shown absolutely no ability to recall or to recognize the material (Jelicic, Bonke, Wolters, & Phaf, 1992). For these reasons, at least certain implicit memory tests seem to reveal a form of retention that is quite different from that measured on explicit memory tests such as recall or recognition.

In normal human subjects, the majority of studies have focused on demonstrating differences between the two types of test. Furthermore, most theoretical accounts of the relations between implicit and explicit tests have been formulated primarily to explain the differences between the two types of test (see Richardson-Klavehn & Bjork, 1988, and Roediger & McDermott, 1993, for reviews). For example, most of the early research on implicit memory has demonstrated that priming is uninfluenced by various encoding (e.g., levels of processing) and retrieval manipulations that affect explicit memory performance (Jacoby & Dallas, 1981). Furthermore, implicit memory effects can be surprisingly long-lasting (Mitchell & Brown, 1988), and the two types of memory performance can be statistically independent of one another (Eich, 1984).

In a general sense, priming on implicit memory tests indicates an ubiquitous effect of specific past experiences. These experiences bias the current perception or comprehension of repeated or similar events, and they make current processing of those events more efficient, rapid, or fluent. According to Jacoby and his co-workers (e.g., Jacoby, Lindsay, & Toth, 1992), the fluent processing of repeated information is attributed to a source, thereby giving rise to a particular subjective experience. Errors in this attribution process can result in a variety of memory-based illusions. For example, when previously heard and new sentences must be judged against a white noise background of varying loudness, then the background noise appears less loud when the sentences are old (and, presumably, are processed more fluently) than when they are new (Jacoby, Allan, Collins, & Larwill, 1988). A host of other experiments demonstrated such memory-based illusions. For instance, effects of prior experiences can also be misattributed to an object being more aesthetically pleasing (Kunst-Wilson & Zajonc, 1980), a statement being true (Begg, Anas, & Farinacci, 1992), an answer being correct (Kelley & Lindsay, 1993), or a problem being easy (Jacoby & Kelley, 1987). Each of these phenomena shows that influences of the past can affect the subjective experience of the present. Another interesting memory-based illusion has been explored for the first time by Neely and Payne (1983) who reported that subjects were more likely to judge both a nonfamous and a famous name as being famous if the name had been encountered recently.

A reliably higher rate of false alarms (i.e., erroneous fame judgments) for previously studied nonfamous than for new nonfamous names defines this so-called *false fame effect*. The false fame effect has been investigated systematically by Jacoby and his associates (Dywan & Jacoby, 1990; Jacoby, Kelley, Brown, & Jasechko, 1989; Jennings & Jacoby, 1993). Jacoby suggested that the earlier reading of a nonfamous name increases how familiar it appears, presumably because prior reading influences the ease of processing during the judgment task that can be considered as an implicit test of memory. The more familiar a name appears, the higher is the probability that it is later mistaken for a famous name. This influence of familiarity may reflect an unconscious or automatic influence of memory because conscious recollection of its prior presentation should allow one to attribute the familiarity correctly and thus avoid the judgment bias.

The findings of many dissociations between performance on explicit and implicit memory tests in studies of patients with neurological deficits as well as of normal subjects and the findings of memory-based illusions in judgment tasks (such as the false fame effect) have led to a resurgence of interest in conscious (or controlled) and unconscious (or automatic) processes in retrieval. Typically, unconscious processes or automatic uses of memory have been equated with performance on implicit tests or judgment tasks, and conscious processes or controlled uses of memory with performance on explicit tests. However, this form of definition is problematic, because conscious processes may contaminate performance on implicit tests (Reingold & Merikle, 1990) and, less obviously, unconscious processes might contaminate performance on explicit tests (Jacoby, Toth, & Yonelinas, 1993). Rather than equating processes with tasks, as is usually done by the explicit versus implicit test distinction, one strategy has been to gain estimates of the contributions of each type of process to performance on a single task. Next, we will briefly introduce a so-called process dissociation procedure that is aimed at separating controlled uses of memory from automatic uses (Jacoby, 1991).

## THE PROCESS DISSOCIATION PROCEDURE

The main difficulty in separating intentional or controlled retrieval processes from incidental or automatic processes is that both are expected to facilitate performance in the standard tests. That is, if subjects are given an (incidental) word stem completion test after studying a list of words, they could show facilitation in completing the word stems with a word from the list either from *priming* (incidental retrieval), *conscious recollection* (intentional retrieval), or some combination of the two. The process dissociation procedure developed by Jacoby (1991) accomplishes a separation of these processes by comparing two test conditions in which instructions to subjects differ.

We will introduce the procedure within the context of a false fame experiment. After studying a list of nonfamous names, subjects may be given a fame judgment task. Subjects have to judge old as well as new nonfamous names. Under *exclusion* test conditions the experimenter correctly informs the subjects that all of the names they had read in the study list were nonfamous. Therefore, if they recognize a name from the study list during the fame judgments, they can be sure that the name is nonfamous and exclude it from the set of names called famous. The automatic influence of memory such as an increased familiarity of old nonfamous names could thus be opposed by conscious recollection of the fact that the name had appeared on the study list. Given that automatic and controlled uses of memory make independent contributions to fame judgments, the probability of calling an old, nonfamous name famous on an exclusion test may be given as $Exc = A (1 - C)$, where A stands for automatic and C stands for controlled influences of memory. Unless controlled uses of memory are fully eliminated, the exclusion test scores would underestimate the effects of automatic influences of memory, however. In order to estimate separately the contributions of controlled and of automatic uses of memory, Jacoby (1991) therefore suggested to compare the exclusion test performance to judgments in an *inclusion* test in which both controlled and automatic uses of memory operate "in concert." For example, subjects in the fame judgment task can be misinformed that all names from the study list are famous names. Therefore, it can be expected that an old name is called famous if it is recollected by a controlled use of memory or if, in the absence of recollection, the name appears familiar (i.e., an automatic influence of memory). Thus, the probability of calling an old nonfamous name famous on an inclusion test can be given as Inc = C + A (1 − C). Under certain assumptions it follows from this reasoning that it should be possible to estimate the probability of calling a name famous on the basis of a controlled use of memory by simply subtracting the probability of calling a name famous in the exclusion test from the probability of calling a name famous in the inclusion test. Finally, given an estimate for the probability of a controlled use of memory, the probability of an automatic influence of memory may also be estimated (see Jacoby, 1991).

Jennings and Jacoby (1993) used the process dissociation procedure to examine the effects of aging on automatic and controlled uses of memory in a fame judgment task. A group of elderly adults was compared with a group of younger adults in either a full-attention or in a divided-attention condition. Both age and divided attention had detrimental effects on controlled uses of memory but left the automatic component largely unaffected. This seems to be strong evidence in favor of the assumptions that automatic or unconscious uses of memory are spared by aging and are important in order to invoke the false fame effect. Very similar results have been reported by Squire and McKee (1993) for amnesic patients who were also shown to have great problems in recognizing previously presented names. Next, we will describe some research from our laboratory which used the names of nonfamous or famous people as stimuli for intentional or incidental retrieval. More importantly, some of these experiments explored the process dissociation procedure in order to gain further evidence on automatic and controlled uses of memory in various social judgment tasks.

## AUTOMATIC AND CONTROLLED USES OF MEMORY: EXPERIMENTS ON THE INTENTIONAL, OR INCIDENTAL RETRIEVAL OF NAMES

Proper names have a frustrating propensity to be forgotten. A considerable amount of laboratory and naturalistic data has demonstrated this vulnerability of proper names to memory errors both in learning new names and in retrieving familiar names. Moreover, retrieval of familiar proper names is especially impaired in old age and in some cases of aphasia (see Cohen & Burke, 1993). The vulnerability of names to memory errors in intentional retrieval attempts, as well as the negative social evaluations of such errors (in general, it is socially not acceptable if one cannot name a known person or an acquaintance), make this kind of information interesting for memory as well as for social cognition research. Moreover, it may be speculated that automatic uses of memory are an essential component in the retrieval of names. Because intentional retrieval of names seems to be difficult and error-prone, there is room for automatic and unconscious influences of name information. And because names can designate social categories (such as the gender of a person), they may be seen as interesting stimuli in research of stereotyping or of other social phenomena.

Proper names are more difficult to learn than other biographical information about a person who is encountered for the first time (Cohen & Faulkner, 1986). Although proper names are, on average, lower in frequency of occurrence in language than other classes of words, this does not seem to be the source of the learning deficit. Using name–occupation homophones such as *Baker – baker*, McWeeny, Young, Hay, and Ellis (1987) tested recall of names and occupations paired with pictures of unfamiliar men. Recall of occupations was superior to recall of names, even though the same words were used in each category across subjects. Cohen (1990) has argued that the relative meaninglessness of proper names compared to other words is a source of vulnerability in memory because names such as Baker cannot be encoded in such a rich semantic network as words like baker. That is, many more semantic propositions about the *occupation* baker than the *name* Baker are available.

In a first study, we wanted to demonstrate a learning deficit for names in an incidental learning situation and with an explicit test of memory. Because all of the previous studies have used paired-associate paradigms (with faces as stimuli), we used a recognition paradigm in order to find out if the learning of names per se is hampered (i.e., a form of response learning). Using name-occupation homophones such as *Baker – baker*, 30 critical items (such as *Baker – baker*) were presented to the subjects either embedded in the context of other occupations or in the context of other typical surnames. Without any learning instructions, subjects had to rate each item for its familiarity. In the following recognition test, the 30 critical items were presented together with 30 lures. First of all, the same items were judged to be more familiar when presented in the context of other occupations (60% of the items judged to be familiar) than in the context of other surnames (48% familiar). Thus, and in agreement with Cohen (1990), proper names seem to be less meaningful to subjects compared to other words. Consequently, recognition testing revealed a significant advantage for occupations (a hit rate of 90%), compared to names (a hit rate of 71%). Most interestingly, recognition of occupations was superior to recognition of names for those items judged to be less familiar to the subjects. Thus, we have found empirical support for the thesis that even response learning of names *as names* is suboptimal, and that the relative meaninglessness of names is a source of vulnerability in memory.

In a second study, we wanted to confirm the false fame effect for German subjects. Given that names are difficult to learn (as noted here), the chances to find such a bias in a social judgment task were judged to be good. In the study phase, we presented 32 names of famous persons (e.g., Kurt Waldheim) and 32 names of nonfamous persons (e.g., Hugo Lauscher). Some subjects were asked to read the names whereas others were asked to make fame judgments in the study phase. Twenty-four hours later, the old names were mixed with new famous and nonfamous names. First, all of the subjects were required to make fame judgments. Next, a test of recognition was performed with the same names. The results demonstrated a clear and significant false fame effect. Old nonfamous names were judged to be famous more frequently than new nonfamous names (18% vs. 14%, respectively). A similar effect was found for famous names (79% of the old and 74% of the new names were judged to be famous). The orienting task in the study phase (reading the names vs. judging the fame) did not influence these results. Thus, this bias seems to be a robust phenomenon and can be observed even under elaborate encoding conditions (i.e., fame judgments in the study phase). On the other hand, recognition was found to be superior following the elaborate study condition compared to the simple reading of the names. Finally, and more importantly, a signal detection analysis revealed that prior presentation did not affect the discrimination between famous and nonfamous names, but rather the criterion subjects used for judging a name famous. Thus, the bias was manifested in the use of a lower criterion for responding famous to old relative to new names.

The latter result seems to be important because Banaji and Greenwald (1995) have shown that the false fame phenomenon is potentially useful for diagnosing implicit (and in their view, unconscious) stereotypes. In four experiments, they observed a false fame effect with male or female subjects. Most importantly, the increase in fame for old names was significantly larger for male than for female names. A signal detection analysis demonstrated that this gender bias was manifested in the use of a lower criterion for responding "famous" to old male relative to female names. According to the authors, there is an implicit association of the concept of fame with the male gender. Thus, the increased familiarity of old names may be more readily attributed to fame in the case of male than of female names. The application of a lower criterion to old male relative to female names may be an expression of this (implicit) association.

In a third study, we used the process dissociation procedure in order to investigate the presumed unconscious basis of this gender bias more directly. In the study phase, male as well as female subjects judged the familiarity of nonfamous male and female names. Twenty-four hours later, the subjects performed a fame judgment task with old and new nonfamous names, and with new famous names. In an exclusion test, subjects were informed correctly that old names were indeed nonfamous. In an inclusion test, however, old names were declared to belong to famous persons (for more details, see Buchner & Wippich, 1996). As described earlier, the process dissociation procedure renders it possible to estimate automatic (or unconscious) and controlled (or conscious) uses of memory. A general analysis of both estimates did not reveal any gender bias. However, a reanalysis of the data as a function of the sex-role orientation of the subjects (Bem, 1974) did reveal important differences between the groups.

Subjects with a stereotypically male-oriented belief system did show an unconscious gender bias with significantly higher estimates for male than for female names for an automatic use of memory. Subjects with a stereotypically female-oriented belief system did not show the gender bias. If one assumes that in stereotypically male-oriented belief systems male gender and the concept of fame are more strongly associated than in stereotypically female-oriented belief systems, this result seems to be plausible. Most importantly, the gender bias was found for the automatic and not for the controlled use of memory. Thus, we have detected an unconscious bias that may be based on implicit stereotypes (see Greenwald & Banaji, 1995).

There may be, however, another reason for the nonconscious gender bias detected in fame judgment tasks. The world of names was traditionally male-dominated (for example, women adopted the name of their husbands after the marriage). Therefore, subjects may have a general (and possibly unconscious) bias to attribute the familiarity of a name to a male source. In investigating this hypothesis, in a fourth study the process dissociation procedure was employed again. In the study phase, subjects judged the surnames of nonfamous people according to how melodious the names sounded. In the test phase, they were required to identify either male or female persons under either inclusion test or exclusion test instructions. For example, some of the surnames from the study phase were repeated in the test phases. Subjects who were to detect male persons were informed that repeated names would belong to male persons *(inclusion test)* or would belong to female persons *(exclusion test)*. Estimates of a controlled use of memory were low (with a mean of 0.30), and did not reveal any differences among the experimental conditions. Estimates of an unconscious or automatic influence of memory, however, revealed a significant gender bias for both male and female subjects. In identifying male persons, the automatic influence of memory (0.50) was significantly stronger than in identifying female persons (0.32). Thus, the increased familiarity of repeated surnames was attributed more readily to the male than to the female domain, possibly because there is better match or stronger feeling of belongingness between the evoked familiarity and the predominating notion of "maleness" of names.

A similar bias has been detected by Wippich (1994) in a fifth study where subjects were required either to search for people originating from the Eastern parts of Germany, or search for people originating from the Western parts of Germany. Again, the process dissociation procedure was used and the subjects were to search under either inclusion or exclusion test instructions. For subjects from the Western part of the country, the results revealed a strong and automatic bias favoring the detection of Western people (0.61) compared to Eastern people (0.39). A similar bias was not found for the controlled use of memory (0.49 and 0.46, respectively; see Wippich, 1994). Thus, feelings of familiarity, such as that produced by prior exposure to a name, are attributed by an unconscious, or automatic use of memory to a greater extent to those categories of judgment that seem to be more familiar to the subjects (e.g., to Western rather than to Eastern people for subjects from the Western part of the country).

## CONCLUSION

We have shown that the intentional retrieval of names is error-prone and suboptimal (study 1). Therefore, and because names refer to social categories, they can be recommended as interesting stimuli for social judgment tasks. Study 2 replicated the false fame effect with names and revealed that this bias is due to the use of a lower criterion for responding "famous" to old, relative to new names. More importantly, study 3 demonstrated a gender bias in fame judgments that was based on an unconscious and automatic use of memory. In our view, the results of these two studies are compatible. A criterion shift in terms of signal detection analysis (study 2) may result from an unconsious or automatic use of memory (study 3). A similar view has been proposed by Erdelyi (1985). The gender bias in fame judgments may be partly due to the fact that people share an unconscious bias to attribute names to male rather than female persons (study 4). Finally, we have shown that an unconscious bias can be detected in other social judgment tasks, namely, the categorization of people as belonging to Western or Eastern parts of Germany (study 5).

There are, of course, a number of reasons as to why one could be interested in whether the false fame phenomenon, the gender bias in fame judgments, or other biases are based primarily on controlled or automatic and unconscious uses of memory. For example, if the assumption is correct that most stereotypes bias judgments in an unconscious mode of processing, then the negative effects of stereotyping should be counteracted by means that differ from those one would use if the biases were conscious. Given that at least some biases are not under the control of persons (see Devine, 1989, for a further example), but result from an automatic use of memory, it does not seem to be useful to overcome effects of stereotyping by means of strategies that invoke a controlled or conscious use of memory. Over the last several decades, concerns about the prevalence of social discrimination in employment or education have led to the proposal and implementation of antidiscrimination strategies that fall into three categories (Greenwald & Banaji, 1995).

*Consciousness raising* encourages the social person to have heightened awareness of potential biasing cues. According to our results, such a strategy that is based on controlled uses of memory is deemed to be inefficient in most cases. *Blinding* denies the social person access to potentially biasing information. In our view, effective blinding is often not achievable in practice. Furthermore, we have found an unconscious bias in judgments even under conditions where the biasing information (i.e., male or female first names) was not provided (see study 4). The third strategy, *affirmative action*, has a deliberate compensatory component: An attribute that is known to be responsible for adverse discriminations is treated instead as if it were a positive qualification. This strategy appears to qualify as a fool-proof method of avoiding negative discrimination. But negative side-effects of this strategy are unavoidable, too.

Do our results warrant a discussion about the implementation of antidiscrimination strategies? Most of the presented research has used the process dissociation procedure and is thus based on a certain measurement model and on a specific interpretation of this model. Recently, Buchner, Erdfelder, and Vaterrodt-Plünnecke (1995), took a multinomial modeling approach in order to estimate the parameters representing an automatic and a controlled use of memory. Furthermore, these authors developed an extended model differing from Jacoby's (1991) original suggestion in that it includes guessing parameters. Buchner et al. have shown that their model results in parameter estimates that are less contaminated by biases resulting from guessing than the parameters of Jacoby's original model. Even more importantly, we have shown (see Buchner & Wippich, 1996) that seemingly automatic or unconscious influences of memory in social judgments (such as the gender bias in fame judgments) are due to the guessing parameters, according to the extended model of the process dissociation procedure. In our view, this is not consequential for a general interpretation of the results. Guessing can, and was, seen as based on a primarily automatic or unconscious use of memory. Thus, it may not have important practical consequences whether the biases observed are attributed to the automatic or to the guessing component of the measurement model. On the other hand, this ambiguity and certain other conceptual as well as practical problems of the procedure (see e.g., Buchner, 1997; Graf & Komatsu, 1994; Richardson-Klavehn, Gardiner, & Java, 1995), indicate that we have reason to be cautious in applying the procedure and in interpreting its results.

In sum, we are convinced that it is useful to distinguish between an automatic and a controlled use of memory. In our view, the evidence in favor of this distinction is overwhelming. We are less convinced, however, whether it is justified to equate an automatic use of memory with an unconscious and unintentional state of the subject, or to equate a controlled use of memory with a conscious and intentional state of the subject (as it is done by Jacoby). Nevertheless, it seems to be evident that memory is used automatically very often, and that an automatic use of memory can have important consequences that cannot be controlled by the social person.

## REFERENCES

Atkinson, R. C., & Shiffrin, R. M. (1968). Human memory: A proposed system and its control processes. In K. W. Spence & J. T. Spence (eds.), *The psychology of learning and motivation, Vol. 2*, 89-195. New York: Academic Press.

Baddeley, A. (1986). *Working memory*. New York: Oxford University Press.

Banaji, M. R., & Greenwald, A. G. (1995). Implicit gender stereotyping in judgments of fame. *Journal of Personality and Social Psychology, 61*, 181–198.

Begg, I. M., Anas, A., & Farinacci, S. (1992). Dissociation of processes in belief: Source recollection, statement familiarity, and the illusion of truth. *Journal of Experimental Psychology: General, 121,* 446–458.

Bem, S. L. (1974). The measurement of psychological androgyny. *Journal of Consulting and Clinical Psychology, 42,* 155–162.

Buchner, A. (1997). Consciousness, intention, and the process dissociation procedure. *Sprache & Kognition, 16,* 176–182.

Buchner, A., Erdfelder, E., & Vaterrodt-Plünnecke, B. (1995). Toward unbiased measurement of conscious and unconscious memory processes within the process dissociation framework. *Journal of Experimental Psychology: General, 124,* 137–160.

Buchner, A., & Wippich, W. (1996). Unconscious gender bias in fame judgments? *Consciousness and Cognition, 5,* 197–220.

Cohen, G. (1990). Why is it difficult to put names to faces? *British Journal of Psychology, 81,* 287–297.

Cohen, G., & Burke, D. M. (1993). Memory for proper names: A review. *Memory, 1,* 249–263.

Cohen, G., & Faulkner, D. (1986). Memory for proper names: Age differences in retrieval. *British Journal of Psychology, 4,* 187–197.

Craik, F. I. M., & Lockhart, R. S. (1972). Levels of processing: A framework for memory research. *Journal of Verbal Learning and Verbal Behavior, 11,* 671–684.

Craik, F. I. M., & Watkins, M. J. (1973). The role of rehearsal in short-term memory. *Journal of Verbal Learning and Verbal Behavior, 12,* 599–607.

Dempster, F. N. (1992). The rise and fall of the inhibitory mechanisms: Toward a unified theory of cognitive development and aging. *Developmental Review, 12,* 45–75.

Devine, P. G. (1989). Stereotypes and prejudice: Their automatic and controlled components. *Journal of Personality and Social Psychology, 56,* 5–18.

Dywan, J., & Jacoby, L. L. (1990). Effects of aging on source monitoring: Differences in susceptibility to false fame. *Psychology and Aging, 5,* 379–387.

Eich, E. (1984). Memory for unattended events: Remembering with and without awareness. *Memory & Cognition, 12,* 105–111.

Epstein, W. (1972). Mechanism of directed forgetting. In G. Bower (ed.), *The psychology of learning and motivation, Vol 6.* New York: Academic Press.

Erdelyi, M. H. (1985). *Psychoanalysis: Freud's cognitive psychology.* New York: Freeman.

Frith, C. D. (1979). Consciousness, information processing, and schizophrenia. *British Journal of Psychology, 134,* 225–235.

Graf, P., & Komatsu, S. (1994). Process dissociation procedure: Handle with caution! *European Journal of Cognitive Psychology, 6,* 113–129.

Greenbaum, J. L., & Graf, P. (1989). Preschool period development of implicit and explicit remembering. *Bulletin of the Psychonomic Society, 27,* 417–420.

Greenwald, A. G., & Banaji, M. R. (1995). Implicit social cognition: Attitudes, self-esteem, and stereotypes. *Psychological Review, 102,* 4–27.

Hamm, V. P., & Hasher, L. (1992). Age and the availability of inferences. *Psychology and Aging, 7,* 56–64.

Hasher, L., & Zacks, R. T. (1979). Automatic and effortful processes in memory. *Journal of Experimental Psychology: General, 108,* 356–388.

Hasher, L., & Zacks, R. T. (1988). Working memory, comprehension, and aging: A review and a new view. In G. H. Bower (ed.), *The psychology of learning and motivation, Vol. 22,* 193–225. San Diego: Academic Press.

Hashtroudi, S., Parker, E. S., DeLisi, L. E., Wyatt, R. J., & Mutter, S. A. (1984). Intact retention in acute alcohol amnesia. *Journal of Experimental Psychology: Learning, Memory, and Cognition, 10,* 156–163.

Holley, P. E., & McEvoy, C. L. (1996). Aging and inhibition of unconsciously processed information: No apparent deficit. *Applied Cognitive Psychology, 10,* 241–256.

Jacoby, L. L. (1991). A process dissociation framework: Separating automatic from intentional uses of memory. *Journal of Memory and Language, 30,* 513–541.

Jacoby, L. L., Allan, L. G., Collins, J. C., & Larwill, L. K. (1988). Memory influences subjective experience: Noise judgments. *Journal of Experimental Psychology: Learning, Memory, and Cognition, 14,* 240–247.

Jacoby, L. L., & Dallas, M. (1981). On the relationship between autobiographical memory and perceptual learning. *Journal of Experimental Psychology: General, 110,* 306–340.

Jacoby, L. L., & Kelley, C. M. (1987). Unconscious influences of memory for a prior event. *Personality and Social Psychology Bulletin, 13,* 314–336.

Jacoby, L. L., Kelley, C. M., Brown, J., & Jasechko, J. (1989). Becoming famous overnight: Limits on the ability to avoid unconscious influences of the past. *Journal of Personality and Social Psychology, 56,* 326–338.

Jacoby, L. L., Lindsay, D. S., & Toth, J. P. (1992). Unconscious influences revealed. *American Psychologist, 47,* 802–809.

Jacoby, L. L., Toth, J. P., & Yonelinas, A. P. (1993). Separating conscious and unconscious influences of memory: Measuring recollection. *Journal of Experimental Psychology: General, 122,* 139–154.

Jelicic, M., Bonke, B., Wolters, G., & Phaf, R. H. (1992). Implicit memory for words presented during anesthesia. *European Journal of Cognitive Psychology, 4,* 71–80.

Jennings, J. M., & Jacoby, L. L. (1993). Automatic versus intentional uses of memory: Aging, attention, and control. *Psychology and Aging, 8,* 283–293.

Kelley, C. M., & Lindsay, D. S. (1993). Remembering mistaken for knowing; Ease of retrieval as a basis for confidence in answers to general knowledge questions. *Journal of Memory and Language, 32,* 1–24.

Kunst-Wilson, W. R., & Zajonc, R. B. (1980). Affective discrimination of stimuli that cannot be recognized. *Science, 207,* 557–558.

Light, L. L., & Singh, A. (1987). Implicit and explicit memory in young and older adults. *Journal of Experimental Psychology: Learning, Memory, and Cognition, 13,* 531–541.

Linville, P. W. (1996). Attention inhibition: Does it underlie ruminative thought? In R. S. Wyer (ed.), *Advances in social cognition: Ruminative thoughts, Vol. 9,* 121–133. Mahwah, NJ: Lawrence Erlbaum Associates.

McWeeny, K. H., Young, A. W., Hay, D. C., & Ellis, A. W. (1987). Putting names to faces. *British Journal of Psychology, 78,* 143–149.

Mitchell, D. B., & Brown, A. S. (1988). Persistent repetition priming in picture naming and its dissociation from recognition memory. *Journal of Experimental Psychology: Learning, Memory, and Cognition, 14,* 213–222.

Neely, J. H., & Payne, D. G. (1983). A direct comparison of recognition failure rates for recallable names in episodic and semantic memory tests. *Memory & Cognition, 11,* 161–171.

Parkin, A. J (1987). *Memory and amnesia.* Oxford: Blackwell.

Posner, M. I., & Snyder, C. R. R. (1975). Attention and cognitive control. In R. L. Solso (ed.), *Information processing in cognition: The Loyola Symposium* (pp. 55–85). Hillsdale, NJ: Lawrence Erlbaum Associates.

Reingold, E. M., & Merikle, P. M. (1990). On the inter-relatedness of theory and measurement in the study of unconscious processes. *Mind and Language, 5,* 9–28.

Richardson-Klavehn, A., & Bjork, R. A. (1988). Measures of memory. *Annual Review of Psychology, 39,* 475–543.

Richardson-Klavehn, A., Gardiner, J. M., & Java, R. I. (1995). Memory: Task dissociations, process dissociations, and dissociations of consciousness. In G. Underwood (ed.), *Implicit cognition* (pp. 85–158). Oxford: Oxford University Press.

Roediger, H. L., & McDermott, K. B. (1993). Implicit memory in normal human subjects. In H. Spinnler & F. Boller (eds.), *Handbook of neuropsychology, Vol. 8,* 63–131. Amsterdam: Elsevier.

Shimamura, A. P. (1986). Priming effects in amnesia: Evidence for a dissociable memory function. *Quarterly Journal of Experimental Psychology, 38A,* 619–644.

Shimamura, A. P. (1995). Memory and frontal lobe function. In M. S. Gazzaniga (ed.), *The cognitive neurosciences* (pp. 803–813). Cambridge, MA: MIT Press.

Squire, L. R., & McKee, R. D. (1993). Declarative and nondeclarative memory in opposition: When prior events influence amnesic patients more than normal subjects. *Memory & Cognition, 21,* 424–430.

Wippich, W. (1992). Implicit and explicit memory without awareness. *Psychological Research, 54,* 212–224.

Wippich, W. (1994). Unbewußte Effekte und Voreingenommenheiten bei Urteilen zu Personen-namen. *Zeitschrift für experimentelle und angewandte Psychologie, 41,* 154–172.

Wippich, W., Mecklenbräuker, S., & Brausch, A. (1989). Implizites und explizites Gedächtnis bei Kindern: Bleiben bei indirekten Behaltensprüfungen Altersunterschiede aus? *Zeitschrift für Entwicklungspsychologie und Pädagogische Psychologie, 21,* 294–306.

Zacks, R. T., & Hasher, L. (1994). Directed ignoring: Inhibitory regulation of working memory. In D. Dagenbach & T. H. Carr (eds.), *Inhibitory processes in attention, memory, and language* (pp. 241–264). San Diego: Academic Press.

# 6

# Are Controlled Processes Conscious?

*Margit E. Oswald*
*Volker Gadenne*

## INTRODUCTION

In cognitive psychology, it has become common to equate controlled with conscious processes, and to oppose them to automatic processes (cf. Wegner & Bargh, 1997; Reingold & Goshen-Gottstein, 1996). This is, at the same time, a widely accepted view of the role of consciousness in cognitive processes: Cognitive processes are controlled processes, and consciousness functions as supervision and control. Controlled and automatic processes, respectively, are defined by a number of characteristics of information processing: The former tend to be more slow, unspecific, errorprone, flexible, sequential and limited in capacity whereas the latter are comparably fast, domain specific, reliable, rigid, parallel, and without any limit of capacity (as compared to controlled processes). Typical examples of controlled processes are attentive problem solving and careful decision making. Typical automatic processes are the detection of features in character recognition, and the control of overlearned motor activities.

Controlled, or conscious, processes are often attributed the functions of selection and control in case of conflict (Shallice, 1972); e.g., sensory processes offer a rich choice of information which may be interpreted in many different ways. A choice has to be made between different interpretations. And, in motor activity, the function of selection and control serves the purpose of avoiding the simultaneous activity of processors which would inhibit each other, or, in case of conflict, would give an impact which helps a certain direction of activity to succeed.

The differentiation between controlled and automatic processes may be tied to arguments from the theory of evolution: Rigid programs of behavior control are effective, although fitted only for very specific situations and requirements. In the environment of any organism, there may occur problems for the solution of which its repertoire of rigid programs does not suffice. And, if it comes to structural changes in the environment, this repertoire may fail completely. Thus, a new kind of information processing has proven useful in the evolution of organisms which is less specific but highly flexible. Consciousness is the highest developed version of these flexible processes. It works slowly, and more error-prone than the automatic programs, but it is applicable to any problem.

Although this assumption has been widely accepted, it is theoretically not well elaborated and contains several problems. In our view, it is, actually, *not* the result of careful analyses, but reflects a certain intuition of lay psychology which is a solid part of the image of man in our culture: Consciousness is the central agent of mental processing. Even if it has no access to all mental processes, it still controls and supervises these processes.

In the following, we will address those problems which are associated with the assumption that controlled processes may be equated with conscious processes. The first problem does not challenge this assumption so far but presupposes that it can be shown how states of information processing are related to states of consciousness. However, the second problem makes clear that the assumption discussed cannot be maintained as it is: Conscious processes are not to be equated with controlled ones. A more differentiated conception has to be developed. Above all, it is important to distinguish between cognitive contents and procedures, and, furthermore, between different levels of representation.

## CONSCIOUSNESS, COGNITION, AND LANGUAGE GAMES

The first one of the two problems concerns the entanglement of different language games. The concept of "consciousness" roots in a language game about persons, their states of consciousness, and their actions. A person may perceive something, desire something, intend something. And he or she may be conscious of several things, may have conscious perceptions, imaginations, desires, etc. On the other hand, we have the language of information processing about systems and subsystems, information stores, processors, operators and programs. Problems arise if we mix concepts from these two languages (without prior clarification), and if we say, e.g., that an information processing system may possess consciousness, or may be conscious of an issue. The following quotation demonstrates that even leading authors in cognitive psychology commit such "errors in category." Bobrow & Norman (1975, p. 147) present an information processing system implying a hierarchical structure of processors, and they describe the organization of this system as follows:

> We believe that all these considerations together require that the system be guided from the top by a single central mechanism, one with awareness of its own processes and of the information sent to it by lower order schemata. We believe this central conscious mechanism controls the process that schedules resources, initiates actions by making decisions among the alternatives presented to it, and selects which conceptualizations to pursue and which to reject. . . . We believe this

central evaluating mechanism is probably serial, probably slow, and probably re-
source-limited.

With respect to such statements, there pertains a strange situation in current
psychology: Everybody knows that such statements of this kind are problematic
(cf. Herrmann, 1982), and yet they exist in abundance in the professional literature. Sometimes it is possible to avoid the difficulty by showing that the respective statement has been meant only metaphorical, and how it may be made more
to the point. For example, one does not have to say that a scheme of the visual
systems "sees something" but one may choose the wording that it is activated by
certain feature detectors, and that further schemes are activated this way, etc. But
there is a topic where this procedure is not possible, i.e., if we are concerned with
consciousness itself. There we find statements which relate consciousness to
concepts from cognitive psychology, like working memory, focal attention, controlled processes, or just to the central processor or the executive. And, in most
contributions of this kind, the problem is not even explained, and so much less
searched, for a solution.

What is the problem? The central processor does not possess any consciousness, no consciousness of anything, and neither is it a "conscious mechanism." If
such statements are supposed to serve any purpose at all in the context of psychological theory, they have to be translated into completely different statements.
It is the problem of cognitive psychology, as far as it talks about consciousness,
that it does not promote this translation in any way, and that it does not deal with
the individual questions which have to be answered before such a translation
becomes feasible.

## CONSCIOUSNESS AND COGNITION: CLARIFYING THE ISSUE

In another publication, we have discussed in detail how cognitive theory can be
related to the description of consciousness (Gadenne & Oswald, 1991, chap. 7;
Gadenne, 1996, pp. 85f.). To summarize the result of this study: First, we have to
elaborate whether cognitive psychology intends to give a new definition of "consciousness" without any reference to the phenomenological aspect, as it has been
done e.g., with the concepts "controlled processing" and "automatic processing"
in term of sequential vs. parallel processing, etc. We could define conscious
processes as mental processes characterized by the following attributes: relatively slow, unspecific, errorprone, flexible, sequential, and limited in capacity.
Thus, the concept of consciousness would be redefined, and applicable to information processing systems in general. Former meanings of "conscious" had to be
avoided carefully in cognitive psychology. Is this intended?

For two reasons, this can be denied: First, it can be clearly seen that theorists of cognitive psychology, when talking about consciousness, refer to something which is well known by experience. Therefore, they frequently talk about phenomenological aspects in connection with consciousness. Shiffrin and Schneider (1977, p. 157), e.g., supposed: "The phenomenological feeling of consciousness may lie in a subset of short–term store (STS), particularly in the subset that is attended to and given controlled processing." The concept of consciousness is intended to refer to phenomenal events, to events of subjective experience. Hypotheses of this kind would not make sense if the problem at stake was a problem of definition. In addition, a new concept of "conscious" would be completely redundant if it could be defined by means of concepts of information processing. Anything that could be expressed by it could as well be expressed by means of concepts already in use, e.g., as "controlled processing." It would contribute nothing to the explanatory power of cognitive theories. And thus, it could only produce embarrassment such that it would be advisable to avoid it.

The question of how cognition and consciousness are related presupposes several levels of description. Most generally, the same subject, or the same series of events may be described from different points of view, e.g., from the perspective of neural science, of cognitive psychology, and of subjective experience. And it is possible to look for relations between these levels, e.g., between certain activities of information processing and certain conscious events. This holds, in particular, when we realize that it is the same brain that does the information processing, and also produces consciousness. We suppose that certain brain activities represent a certain kind of information processing while the respective person experiences conscious acts and states. In that case, certain conditions in the brain, certain steps of information processing, and certain states of consciousness are lawfully connected and take place in parallel. Figure 6.1 demonstrates this relation.

| Conscious events | | | $C_1$ | | $C_2$ | | $C_3$ |
|---|---|---|---|---|---|---|---|
| | | | $\mid$ | | $\mid$ | | $\mid$ |
| Events of information processing | $I_1$ | $I_2$ | $I_3$ | $I_4$ | $I_5$ | $I_6$ | $I_7$ |
| | $\mid$ | $\mid$ | $\mid$ | $\mid$ | $\mid$ | $\mid$ | $\mid$ |
| Brain events | $B_1$ | $B_2$ | $B_3$ | $B_4$ | $B_5$ | $B_6$ | $B_7$ |

FIG. 6.1. Relations between consciousness, information processing, and brain events.

Let $I_1$ through $I_7$ be a sequence of states, represented in the language of information processing. We assume that $B_1$ through $B_7$ are the states of the brain that enact $I_1$ through $I_7$. In accordance with the assumption that not all mental events are conscious, we here assume that not every state I corresponds to a state of consciousness C.

Neuropsychology asks for the relations between levels B and I, and partly also for those between B and C. Cognitive psychology may as well ask for relations between I and C. With this approach, the aforementioned problem does not occur. There are no concepts from one level applied in the other. For example, it is not proposed that person p creates a new knot in his or her semantic network, nor that the central processor possesses consciousness of its activities. An admissible statement may be of the format: Person p is in the conscious state C if (or if and only if) the information processing system is in state I. Both parts of this statement are understandable at their respective levels: They express states, and then it is said that one state occurs if (or if and only if) the other one obtains.

Here we don't have to presuppose an answer to the body–mind problem. If there is a parallelism or lawful relation between B and C, i.e., if certain types of B events and C events always occur simultaneously, it is not the task of psychology to decide whether this relation is based on an identity between mind and brain. If C events are identical with certain B events, there would be actually only one real level (which would be brain processes for the identity theorist of today), and the two other levels would be only different approaches to this reality. However, a parallelism would also be compatible with the view that there is no identity, and that the property "conscious" is not reducible to B events although it may only occur in connection with them (cf. Gadenne & Oswald, 1991, chap. 4). During the last three decades, there has been a development away from reductive physicalism, but, at the same time, one tries not to fall back to substance dualism. An approach to the relations between the three levels which is favored by ourselves is the following: The brain processes, i.e. level B, are real. These may as well be described in the language of information processing. We may develop theories in the language of information processing even if we do not know very much about level B, assuming that it is the brain processes that enact the I processes in man. The C level is real as well, however, not as a mental substance but as mental properties. "Conscious" is an emergent property of mental events. Events with this property occur simultaneously with certain highly complex brain processes. Based on this approach, we have to assume that there are also relations between levels I and C.

The mind–body problem cannot be decided empirically. For the psychology of consciousness, another question is in focus: What do these I events have in common which are related to C events, as opposed to those I events for which there are no corresponding C events? Are there certain features at the level of information processing which always obtain if simultaneously consciousness occurs? Are these I events which are associated with conscious processes maybe characterized as sequential and slow processes with small capacity? This is not an empirical study of the usual kind, but neither a purely theoretical analysis, for we have to respect the facts of subjective experience: What exists in human consciousness, and what are its features? Is there a structural similarity of consciousness to controlled processes rather than to automatic processes?

## STATES OF CONSCIOUSNESS AND THEIR FEATURES

"Conscious" is a property of certain (but not of all) mental events. A mental event is conscious if it is experienced, i.e., if one has the impression of immediately "feeling" that this mental event takes place just now with its characteristic features. In the current philosophy of psychology which is intensively concerned with the topic of consciousness, the experienced qualities of mental events are called "qualia." What may be conscious in this sense? Examples include sensations, perceptions, images, and emotions. Furthermore, according to common belief, thinking is conscious. Concentrated thinking is even considered paradigmatic for consciousness.

The consciousness of a person at a given interval in time is the totality of his or her mental events during that time interval. *Consciousness is neither an instance nor a container.* The favorite way of saying something be "in consciousness," may be translated by saying that the respective mental event possesses the property of being conscious.

Consciousness is not the same as attention. More precisely, not only those contents may become conscious which are in the focus of attention. James already pointed out that each state of consciousness possesses a center and a periphery. Certain contents are more central, others more peripheral; sometimes there is a continuous transition from the center to the outermost rims of experiencing. James talked about the "fringe" of consciousness (James, 1890, pp. 258f). A person regards, for example, a vase, and the largest part of attention rests on it, the background is formed by a table and a wall. At the fringe of attention he or she notices, for a tiny moment, a fly, and the faint frou-frou of paper. The latter events, too, are conscious ones since one experiences such subtle perceptions.

Now, do conscious events, understood this way, have the properties of controlled processes, in contrast to the properties of automatic processes?

## CONSCIOUSNESS IN CONTROLLED AND AUTOMATIC PROCESSING

First, we study the case of controlled processing, with the example of careful concentrated thinking as it is applied to problem solving, and frequently also with the formation of judgment. Assume the subject of thinking would be a detective case to be solved. The detective in charge of the case thinks sequentially of several potential offenders and tests whether there may be a connection between them and the victim. He or she gets the idea that a suspect (S) might have had a motive, and he tests whether S might have had the possibility of committing the crime. After some reasoning he finds out that S, to do so, would have to cover, within five minutes, a distance for which even a fast runner would need thirty minutes. S now drops out as a potential culprit.

Such a reasoning process demonstrates certain aspects which may be found in all cases of problem solving, as in trying to prove a theorem in algebra: You focus on a mathematical equation, think which algebraic operations might be appropriate for the proof, perform the operations, reason what to do with the result, etc. This is a *sequential* process which proceeds *relatively slowly* as compared to automatic processes which we will consider later. The procedures of information processing, like the heuristic principles of thinking, or rules of reasoning, are rarely tied to specific fields of application, but rather are applicable to very different problems (cf. Nisbett, 1993). Furthermore, controlled activities require a high degree of attention, and the *capacity of attention* is limited. The process is relatively flexible, i.e., the thinking person may try several ways of solution, discard strategies of a solution previously selected, or modify it. And, unfortunately, we are more errorprone in doing so than we wish.

Could we say that such a controlled process takes place completely consciously? Without any doubt, certain states in this process are very clear states of consciousness, and accompanied by high attention, e.g., when the detective suddenly thinks "S has the motive of jealousy," or "S drops out as the offender". But is really *everything* conscious in a thinking process? It could be, e.g., that the detective thought of S as a probable offender, in the first place, because person S, with his or her characteristics, "seemed to fit well" the offence. Maybe the detective's thinking was guided, in this phase, by the *representative heuristic* which produces the perception of a causal relation between events or objects just because of existing similarities (cf. Oswald, 1986). And the conclusion at the end of the thinking process according to which S drops out is the modus tollens: If A, then B; now B does not obtain, thus neither does A. (There are theories according to which persons are not capable of formal principles of reasoning; but according to these theories, the thinking of persons is guided by other procedures, like heuristics or cognitive schemes, cf. Gadenne, 1993, and the following elaboration holds for these as well.) We will call those procedures or heuristics which control the run of a sequential cognitive process during a certain time interval the "active procedures." The respective active procedures, in our example the representative heuristic and the modus tollens, are *part of the controlled process.* And the active procedure is never content of consciousness. This can be seen just from the fact that most persons, in general, do not know which cognitive procedures they are applying in detail. But even the few ones who ever think about heuristics and logical conclusions are not conscious of the current active procedures. We *may* as well think about rules of reasoning or about heuristics, and make these contents of consciousness. But even if this happens, the thinking is guided, at this moment, by procedures which are not at the same time contents of consciousness (although they may correspond to those one is just concerned with). It follows that there is necessarily something about a controlled process which is not conscious: the active procedure.

This argument is based on the distinction between *contents* and *procedures.* The theory of controlled and automatic processes assumes a cognitive system for which this distinction is necessary. This distinction does not apply only when dealing with a system that does not contain any data store but only interconnected processors. *Contents* (or data) refers to all information that is at least temporarily represented in a memory store. A *procedure* is a description of the way a processor works. It has to be emphasized that the currently active procedure belongs to the process. A cognitive process is not just defined by means of a sequence of cognitive contents; rather, the same sequence might be part of a different process, just dependent on which procedure it is based on. The same pieces of information or contents of thinking may be part of an inductive or deductive reasoning, of an unbiased perception, of a confirmation strategy with respect to a certain hypothesis, etc.

Now, let us take a look at automatic processes: First, consider a case where a gradual transition from controlled to automatic processing takes place. Such processes of learning may be described in terms of *declarative* and *procedural* knowledge. Declarative knowledge corresponds to what we have just termed cognitively represented contents. Such knowledge is accessible to consciousness. It may become the contents of working memory. The corresponding pieces of information stored in long term memory are activated, and, in general, it is roughly possible to verbalize this knowledge. Opposed to this is a kind of knowledge which shows up in the behavior of a person but which cannot be presented in the form of propositions or images. Persons manage numerous complex procedures of action without being able to name and reproduce the partial action and their consecution when asked for it. The production of language is an impressive example. Persons are able to produce grammatically (approximately) correct sentences but are not conscious of any rule of grammar, neither can they name such rules. As well, you do not have to enroll in a class on logic and learn rules of logic by heart to be able to argue logically. The base of such activities is *procedural knowledge*. It is not accessible to consciousness, it is not knowledge about anything (cf. Oswald & Gadenne, 1984). And people find it, mostly, very difficult to describe their procedural knowledge in language. It is dealt with mechanisms of processing which take place during an automatic cognitive or motor process.

In the acquisition of procedural knowledge we may roughly distinguish three phases (cf. Anderson, 1983). During the *cognitive* phase, *declarative* knowledge is acquired, and the learning person tries to store this knowledge in memory. Let us consider the process of learning how to drive a car without an automatic transmission. The student has acquired declarative knowledge and tries to re-member: Push down the clutch, start the engine, get into first gear, release the clutch softly, and push down the accelerator easily. In this phase, the action re-quires much conscious attention corresponding to the declarative knowledge acquired. To a high degree, the control of behavior takes place by means of con-trolled processes. In the second, *associative* phase, procedural knowledge devel-ops by means of exercise. The student does not have to focus attention to each detail any more, some are already automatic. The motor or cognitive activities become more fluent. They can be executed at higher speed. The precision in-creases, errors diminish. Since the procedural control mechanisms are not yet completely stored and not always reliably available, the student uses frequently declarative knowledge, as a support, and to bridge possible hazards in the auto-matic process.

During the third, *autonomous* phase, the respective activity is controlled by *automatic* processes. The starting of the car happens fluently and fast, and the driver can devote his or her attention more than before to the traffic. As time passes by, also the processing of information from the traffic becomes more and more automatic, and the driver is increasingly occupied by things which just happen to pass through his or her head. Conscious attention only gives the im-petus of the whole sequence of actions, and everything else runs automatically.

It is similar with all motor activities which are practiced. In the beginning, a piano player has difficulties to position the fingers on the right keys, and he or she has to devote conscious attention to the successive scores and finger move-ments. With much practice, the player is finally able to master a difficult run where the movements of the fingers succeed so fast that it would not be possible to control them individually consciously. The control of the movement of one finger does not interfere with the processing capacity for the control of the others as soon as the state of an automatic process is reached. Controlled processes take place even in experienced persons but they occur at a higher level of the organi-zation of action, they consist of higher order components.

The three phases are not sharply separated from each other but pass fluently to each other. In general, we can say that in passing the phases the learned activ-ity becomes increasingly more effective, and is enacted with less expenditure and strain. *As far as consciousness is concerned, we find that it shifts during the run through the phases.* At the beginning, the consciousness is occupied by various details. At the end, the conscious states are more located in a higher level of the organization of action. There is more capacity of attention available for sudden occurring events which cannot be coped with by automatic procedures.

Now, the crucial question is: In an activity like car driving, when the third phase has been reached, are the individual driving movements all unconscious? And is it the case that the driver stops at a red traffic light without consciously perceiving the red? Does he or she react to most of the visual information concerning the traffic without having to notice the respective conditions consciously? Every skilled driver who studies this problem given his or her own routine will find the following: It is indeed true that one does not pay much attention to particular driving movements, and processes information from traffic lights and other vehicles without having it in the focus of attention. But it would be mistaken to equate this to the fact that they are not conscious at all. The driving movements continuously lead to short kinesthetic perceptions, and also the visual and auditive perception from the traffic are accompanied by short transitory conscious experiences.

Maybe part of this information input takes really place without consciousness, but another part is accompanied by conscious experiences. Above, we pointed at the difference between focal and peripheral consciousness. There are mental events which are experienced for fractions of a second but which are not paid attention, and which can be remembered only if one is asked for them immediately afterward.

Now, we consider an activity which is characteristic for experiments in cognitive psychology, and, for that purpose, we choose a well known and influential experimental paradigm. Neisser (1964) has shown that *parallel processes* take place during pattern recognition. Subjects are visually presented a set of 200 characters (50 rows of 4 characters each). (cf. fig. 6.2).

EHYP

SWIQ

UFJC

WBYH

OGKX

etc.

*FIG. 6.2. Stimulus material for subjects; explanation in the text.*

The task was to scan this picture from top to bottom as fast as possible, and to search for the letter K, and push a button on finding it. The letter K, the target, was in a different position in each trial. The measurement of reaction time showed that subjects scanned, on the average, ten rows per second, i.e., 40 characters per second. When the task was modified such that a K or a Z had to be found, the search time did not increase which indicates that the processes work in parallel.

In this case, we are concerned with very fast automatic processes. According to the theory which we discuss they should be unconscious. More precisely, there should be a conscious decision to start the task and to search for K, and also at the moment when the K is found there should be conscious perception. But everything in between should run unconscious. The reader is challenged to try the experiment. You do not have to measure reaction times since they are not relevant for the question we are dealing with. Is everything that happens in between completely unconscious? Indeed, we have no consciousness of the individual comparison processes which take place, according to the theory, at a tearing pace. That is, one does not have the experience of making a conscious decision at each single letter: Is it a K, yes or no? Is it a Z, yes or no? If not, then search on. However, it is not true that everything in this process be unconscious. As a searching subject, one may find for oneself that one passes through the rows at a high speed, and that one sees at least a certain set of characters for a cursory moment. One has the experience to see, at a time, several letters simultaneously, not as single characters but as parts of a larger Gestalt. These cursory perceptions are different from the longer sustained state of consciousness which finally occurs when the search process ends: "Here is the K." But they are still visual experiences. It cannot be proven that the subject has seen all letters consciously; but what should be emphasized here is that it is not very plausible that the entire search process should be completely unconscious.

Next, we are going one step further into automatic processing. To recognize characters, in visual perception features are processed which are more elementary than characters. An "A", e.g., consists of three elementary features: Two slanted lines (Λ) and a crossbar (-), which are interconnected according to a certain rule. To recognize an A, the cognitive system needs *detectors* for such elementary features. The detector for the letter A reacts after an appropriate combination of elementary feature detectors has reacted. This theory of pattern recognition is supported by experimental findings according to which person, after a short presentation, particularly frequently mixes up letters which are subvisibly different. Moreover, this theory is in agreement with knowledge about the physiological processes in vision (cf. Lindsay & Norman, 1977).

A corresponding theory exists for *auditory* perception. Spoken words consist of *phonemes*. Like visual patterns, also phonemes are distinguished by means of certain features which are related to how the phonemes are produced. Among these features are consonance, voicedness, and point of articulation. Experimental studies have shown that these features serve the identification of phonemes (Miller & Nicely, 1955).

It is clear that we are concerned with *non-conscious* processes both in the visual and in the auditive detection of elementary features where highly specialized detectors are at work which operate very fast. In contrast to the automatic processes presented before, it is here rather unambiguous that no aspect of the process corresponds to a conscious experience. The analysis of features does not occur in experience, it is not only sometimes or frequently unconscious but happens completely beyond the processing of information which is accompanied by conscious states. To put it metaphorically: If it really happens as the theory of pattern recognition pretends, then this is an event to which consciousness simply has no access.

It is time to present an intermediate balance: It is not completely correct to equate controlled processes with conscious ones since controlled processes do contain a component which is not conscious: the process controlling procedure. Besides that it is not correct that automatic processes run all the way unconscious. There are automatic processes for which this holds. But there are other ones in which individual events of the process are conscious even if they are not given a high degree of attention.

## CONCLUSION

It should have become clear by now what the main problem is with the theory which pretends that conscious processes in human information processing are those with properties of controlled processes, and non-conscious ones those with properties of automatic processes. This theory lacks the distinction between contents and procedures. Talking only about controlled (or automatic) processes, events, or corresponding processing does not clarify whether it is concerned with contents, procedures, or both. Therefore, statements which produce a connection to consciousness become false, or at least so imprecise that they lead to serious misunderstandings.

Let us state, in the first place, how consciousness is related to contents and procedures. We may express this relation about this way: In a cognitive process, the active procedure is never conscious. Miller (1962, p.56) worded this insight (following Lashley, 1956) by means of the thesis that it is "the result of thinking, not the process of thinking that appears spontaneously in consciousness." However, more unambiguous is it to say that the active procedure that controls the process does not occur in consciousness. For, also the contents represented belong to the process as a whole. And, of course, not only the final result of the thinking process is conscious but also many intermediate steps (which is compatible with that there might exist non-conscious intermediate steps).

If we want to distinguish the levels of description introduced above precisely, we would have to say: *To the active procedures at the level of information processing, there is no correlate at the level of conscious experiences.* This holds for procedures in controlled processes as well as for those in automatic ones. At this point the distinction controlled versus automatic is irrelevant for the question of consciousness.

Now, are contents always conscious? Or are the contents of controlled processes conscious but not those of automatic ones? Here, too, the situation is more complicated than assumed in the simple initial theory. Even the assumption that the contents of controlled processes are always conscious has been questioned. Also the cognitively represented abstract concepts and propositions belong to these contents. For many centuries, philosophers and psychologists doubted whether abstract concepts and propositions are conscious. Is it possible, e.g., to think of the concept of dog without using the sound image "dog" and without producing a visual imagination? Psychologists from the Würzburg School held the position that they had proven the existence of unimagined states of consciousness in their experiments. Do concepts and propositions belong to these unimagined contents which are easily overlooked as contents of consciousness? Or are thoughts actually only conscious because their imaginable carriers are conscious, i.e., auditive and visual "images"? We have dealt with this question in another publication (cf. Gadenne & Oswald, 1991), and leave this question open. It may be stated here that at any rate numerous contents of cognitive processes are conscious. And the propositions are at least indirectly represented in consciousness, namely as far as the language representations connected to them are conscious as "inner speech".

Are all contents of automatic processes unconscious? At this point, it is important to distinguish several levels of representation. In the field of vision, e.g., features like corners and edges belong to the outermost peripheral level, together with their respective feature detectors. In the auditive field, we find at the peripheral level the aforementioned features of phonemes. What happens in the peripheral field of perception, and also of motor control, is neither conscious nor accessible to consciousness. There, information processing is accomplished by means of highly specialized parallel processors. Thus, it is correct that everything in these automatic processes runs unconscious.

But there are further levels of representation where also automatic processing takes place which are but accompanied by experiences of a certain kind. This has been explained above by means of the example of car driving. There are numerous cognitive and motor activities which become automatic after some practice, and then require very little attention. In contrast to the processes at the outermost peripheral level, the run of such processes does not take place without any experience. On the contrary, at least parts of the process are related to conscious events. Also, it is possible to follow an automatic process of this kind consciously (which proves sometimes disturbing) which is not possible with the outermost peripheral processes. Consciousness is not the same as high attention and concentration, rather, there are also the aforementioned cursory experiences, and we find them where automatic processes run, acquired by practice, which are (partly) correlated with cursory sensory impressions.

At the beginning of this analysis we mentioned that the conception that consciousness has control over mental events corresponds to a widely accepted image of man. Do the results cause us to consider consciousness as peripheral? And what is the function of consciousness if it is not identical to controlled processes?

The goal of this article was to demonstrate that the widespread theory that conscious events could be equated to controlled processes as opposed to automatic processes is not correct in its simplicity. More detailed analyses are necessary to determine exactly which states and processes at the level of information processing are related to consciousness. From this does not follow that consciousness does not have relation at all to controlled processes. *There are relatively more conscious states in that part of information processing which deals more with slow, sequential processes and which are accompanied by high attention.* And they are not at all found in most specialized processes for which there are possible innate procedures.

*If the run of conscious events is not controlled by conscious procedures, it does not follow that mental representations which correspond to conscious contents do not have any influence of their own.* A conscious mental representation may be, e.g., the result of a reasoning process, and it may depend on it whether the respective person performs action A or B. Or it may be a goal representation which influences his or her actions for a longer time decisively.

As to the question of what is the function of consciousness, it may be deluding to start exactly from one function, and then search for it in working memory, attention, or, as discussed here, in controlled processes. Consciousness has more to do with controlled processes than with automatic ones, but, at the time being, there is no cognitive theory which might correlate all mental events with the quality of experience (qualia) exactly and convincingly to certain kinds of information processing.

## REFERENCES

Anderson, J. R. (1983). *The architecture of cognition.* Cambridge, MA: Harvard University Press.

Bobrow, D. G., & Norman, D. A. (1975). Some principles of memory schemata. In D. G. Bobrow und A. Collins (Hrsg.), *Representation and understanding.* New York: Academic Press.

Gadenne, V. (1993). Deduktives Denken und Rationalität. In Hell, W., K. Fiedler und G. Gigerenzer (Hrsg.), *Kognitive Täuschungen* (S. 161–188). Heidelberg: Spektrum.

Gadenne, V. (1996). *Bewusstsein, Kognition und Gehirn: Einführung in die Psychologie des Bewusstseins*. Bern: Huber.

Gadenne, V., & Oswald, M. (1991). *Kognition und Bewusstsein*. Berlin: Springer.

Herrmann, Th. (1982). Über begriffliche Schwächen kognitivistischer Kognitionstheorien: Begriffsinflation und Akteur-System-Kontamination. *Sprache und Kognition, 1*, 3–14.

James, W. (1890). *The principles of psychology*, Vol. I. New York: Holt.

Lashley, K. (1956). Cerebral organization and behavior. In H. Solomon, S. Cobb und W. Penfield (Hrsg.), *The brain and human behavior*. Baltimore: Williams und Wilkins.

Lindsay, P. H. & Norman, D. A. (1977). *Human information processing: An introduction to psychology*. New York: Academic Press.

Miller, G. A. (1962). *Psychology: The study of mental life*. New York: Harper and Row.

Miller, & Nicely, (1955).

Neisser, U. (1964). Visual search. *Scientific American, 210*, 94–102.

Nisbett, R.E. (1993). *Rules for reasoning*. Hillsdale, N.J.: Lawrence Erlbaum Associates.

Oswald, M. (1986). Urteile über den Repräsentationsheurismus. *Archiv für Psychologie, 138 (2)*, 113–125.

Oswald, M., & Gadenne, V. (1984). Wissen, Können und künstliche Intelligenz. Eine Analyse der Konzeption des deklarativen und prozeduralen Wissens. *Sprache und Kognition, 3*, 173–184.

Reingold, E. M. & Goshen-Gottstein, Y. (1996). Separating consciously controlled and automatic influences in memory for new associations. *Journal of Experimental Psychology, Learning, Memory, and Cognition, 22 (2)*, 397–406.

Shallice, T. (1972). Dual functions of consciousness. *Psychological Review, 79*, 383–393.

Shiffrin, R. M., & Schneider, W. (1977). Controlled and automatic human information processing: II. Perceptual learning, automatic attending, and a general theory. *Psychological Review, 84*, 127–190.

Wegner, D. M., & Bargh, J. A. (1997). Control and automaticity in social life. In D. T. Gilbert, S. T. Fiske, & G. Lindzey (Eds.), *Handbook of social psychology* (4/e). Boston: McGraw-Hill.

# 7

# Intuition and Levels of Control: The Non-Rational Way of Reacting, Adapting, and Creating[1]

*Walter J. Perrig*

## INTRODUCTION

A living organism survives because of, and sometimes despite, its environmental conditions. These conditions embrace everything that is perceived as physically or psychologically distinct from the person and the self.

If this environment supplies the necessary alimentary resources, the individual organism can use them in a quite passive and established way, without effort. If this environment does not fulfill its basic needs the organism either has to change itself, adapt, or actively do something to have better conditions. It is assumed that human beings not only adapt or react to present situation demands by reflexive responses, but that they use to a rather large degree their stored experiences from the past to deal either with actual conditions or with anticipated conditions of the future.

This is what psychology is all about. As a philosophical or as an empirical science, psychology investigates human nature to obtain functional descriptions and explanations of the determinants or the logic of observable behavior and mental processes. There are many notions like perception, learning, memory, emotion, motivation, thinking, and intelligence that have received the status of scientific terminology to explain human states or actions. By the dominance of the behaviorist tradition in the first part of this century the focus was mainly on the action part, on performance. Cognitive psychology changed this focus and psychological studies started to contain lengthy elaborations on mental architecture and processes.

The concept of control is a prominent example of this change of the scientific focus in psychology. August Flammer who is honored by this book dedicated large parts of his scientific endeavors to the concept of control beliefs and their impact on motivation, performance and social interactions of humans (Flammer,

[1]The preparation of this article was supported by grant 1114–050947.97 of the Swiss National Science Foundation.

1995; Flammer, 1990; Flammer, Grob & Lüthi, 1989). In one of his major publications (Flammer, 1990) he relates the concept of control belief to other concepts like causality, attribution or helplessness for instance. But of course control belief is also related to what the belief is about. This embraces all mental and real actions that make a person believe he or she has an influence on himself or herself, on others, or in general on problems to solve, or goals to reach.

In this contribution I refer to the processes where control beliefs might come from. In this perspective we have to investigate control itself. In this sense any human phenomenological experience and any behavior is controlled by some precedences or ongoing processes. Although it is in many respects important to think about the causes, consequences and the nature of the processes that are intrinsically related to control beliefs, I concentrate in this chapter on a form of processes that are under poor subjective control, but nevertheless control human behavior and experience to very substantial degrees.

I will refer to these processes with the term *intuition*. First a terminological discussion, and then the rationale for using this notion as a scientific term will be given. Later, a few examples for intuitive behavior will be presented. In the final discussion, I question whether these processes that seem very poorly related to subjective rationality could nevertheless constitute important elements in subjective control beliefs.

## INTUITION AS A TYPE OF CONTROL OF HUMAN BEHAVIOR

Intuition obviously serves an important communicative function in our natural language. The word is important enough to have dictionary entries. In science we have a broad literature in philosophy, some in the psychoanalytical tradition, but little in experimental psychology. From what is presented below, I will conclude that the phenomenon of intuition represents an identifiable form of control of human behavior that has its own characteristics. Among human forms of behavioral control we have simple automatic reflexes, but also complex reasoning that precedes decisions and actions. The basic difference between these two forms of behavioral control is the degree to which the individual behaves consciously and intentionally. This variability brings in the concepts of *consciousness, rationality*, or—what is more convenient in psychology—*attention* and *effort*. It is the state of the art in psychology that in human information processing automatic, implicit, non-analytic, or perceptual forms are distinguished from effortful, explicit, analytic, rational, or conceptual types (Posner & Snyder 1975; Hasher & Zacks, 1979; Schneider & Shiffrin, 1977; for overviews see: Kihlstrom, 1987; Perrig, Wippich & Perrig-Chiello, 1993). The terms referring to these differences in characteristics vary, but as descriptive terms, they do not imply more detailed explanational differences, and the common idea behind them seems valuable enough to be transferred to practical applications (Epstein, 1994; Grawe, 1998).

In some theoretical approaches, controlled or effortful behavior is opposed to automatic processing (Posner & Snyder, 1975; Hasher & Zacks, 1979; Schneider & Shiffrin, 1977). The relevant dimension for this distinction is related to phenomenology, to intention, attention, consciousness, or effort of the subject. If we take these experiential dimensions seriously, we can reserve control as a general term, and specify different types of control in terms of this other dimension, representing subjective experience. Under this assumption and with respect to available research domains and data, it is reasonable to distinguish different types of processes that control human behavior:

*Innate automatic processes* occur without intention, and are never objects of consciousness in terms of knowledge or content. They constitute the fundamental transformations from external physical energy to organismic responses. These processes do not benefit from practice and show limited developmental trends. Reflexes, spreading activations in associative nets, habituation, conditioning and priming might be phenomena that are based on this kind of processes.

*Learned automatic processes* are overlearned behavioral patterns, that have become automatic after long practice. Performances and actions can be the result of this kind of complex skills that do not require attention or mental capacity.

*Reasoning,* in contrast, implies conscious decision, effort, will and intention. While automatic processes do not put a strain on attention and effort, reasoning processes constitute our conscious contents and are heavily restricted in capacity.

*Intuitive processes* are considered as a combination of automatic processes and reasoning processes. They come into play when goal-oriented actions, decisions, or interpretations have to be realized under conditions of uncertainty or lack of knowledge. It will argue below, that intuition is a function of consciousness, or a form of reasoning, that determines or guides behavior on the basis of processes or structures that themselves are not yet, or will never be, the content or objects of consciousness. One might argue that all our reasoning and thinking is the product of structures and processes that are outside of our phenomenal awareness or inspection. The most important assumption here is that intuition is the ability to become aware of automatic or unconscious processes or automatic sensorial activity, the results of which will never be the categories of knowledge or insight.

Most realistically, it can be assumed that in naturalistic settings most performances are the result of a combination of all of these forms of control, and we are not aware of what kind of processes lead to what kind of effects. A more analytical consideration, which I will present below, leads to the conclusion that a hierarchical order relates the different types of control, by which human beings react to physical stimulation, adapt to environmental requirements or create new ways of thinking and behaving. We can speak of levels of control. Each level of the three distinquished forms of control: automatization, intuition, and reasoning can serve in the function of reaction, adaptation or creation. In the following I will concentrate on intuitive processes. First, I will concentrate on definitional and theoretical problems. Second, I will deal with the possibility of the experimental investigation of intuitive behavior, and third, an effort will be made to integrate experimental findings into a coherent theoretical framework.

## The Phenomenon and the Definition of Intuition

Writing about intuition or intuitive behavior poses first the problem of terminology and conceptual distinction between what is meant by "intuition" and other forms of behavioral control as distinguished above. While the distinction between automatic and controlled processes has become state of the art in psychology, it does not capture what is meant by intuition. For defining intuition, we have to elaborate on the central dimensions that are used—sometimes more implicitly than explicitly—for distinguishing between automatic and controlled processes. These dimensions are attention, effort, and insight. Thus, the most distinctive feature between automatic and controlled processes is related to the amount of phenomenological experience or consciousness.

Of course, there is still the question of whether there is a phenomenon like intuition at all to be explained. The fact is that we have this word in natural language, and it serves a valuable communicative function. Empiricism of everyday observations must have constructed a common basis of understanding each other when speaking about intuition. This could be reason enough to study the phenomenon of this understanding scientifically. More than this justification I believe that intuition is a special form of human information processing and behavior, and that understanding intuitive behavior will add substantially to our knowledge about human nature.

According to the Oxford English Dictionary, intuition is "The immediate apprehension of an object by the mind without the intervention of any reasoning process." More generally it is sometimes defined as "Direct or immediate insight." These definitions have their roots in philosophical thinking. They clearly imply that intuition is a means of detecting, understanding or discovering basic truths without any conscious rationality of the mind. This meaning with its positive connotation mirrors closely what is communicated in natural language. If we speak of intuition in everyday context, we refer to a special kind of phenomenological experience that we have sometimes when we are confronted with some task. We report about lack of knowledge or insight that prevents understanding and about feelings or impressions that help us to do the right things. Without having clearer insight into the nature of these processes, it is rather believed than known that in certain cases of decision making or problem solving, behavior seems related more to emotion, or "the heart," than the rationality of the brain. I am focusing rather on this aspect of intuitive feeling than on having sudden insights.

But what is the exact nature of this phenomenon? Is it the additional influence of automatic or emotional processes that support decision making or reasoning? Whatever the answer to this question will be in detail, it seems obvious that intuitive behavior can not be substituted neither by the category of automatic processes, where consciousness is not a constituent, nor by reasoning in terms of rational inferencing or decision making. A theory about intuition has to take into account that subjects are confronted with a problem or some task demand, for the solution of which they do not have the necessary explicit knowledge available. On the other hand they are not simply using information that is processed on an automatic or unconscious basis. Rather at some point people become aware that they are using such information that has been made available by automatic or unconscious processes, in the form of vague impressions or feelings.

Given this analysis I define intuition in a first attempt as a function of consciousness, or a form of reasoning, that determines or guides behavior on the basis of processes or structures that themselves are not yet, or do not become at all, the content or objects of consciousness. One might argue that all our reasoning and thinking is the product of structures and processes that are outside of our phenomenal awareness or inspection. The most important assumption here is that intuition is the ability to become aware of automatic or unconscious processes either before cognizing, recognition or insight is possible, or—and what I believe is more important—to be aware of automatic sensorial activity, the results of which will never be the categories of knowledge or insight. If this rationale is correct, intuition is a combination of automatic control and conscious control of behavior in the sense that high-level cognition like thinking and deciding picks up or monitors automatic low-level cognition by discriminative impressions or feelings and not by insight. If it comes to insight or discovery, intuition as defined here can belong to the antecedents, but this is not necessarily the case. The process of something coming to mind, or of knowledge becoming conscious, or simply knowledge activation, is not intuition. *Heurekas* in discovery might partly be the result of intuition. Here we reserve the term intuition to faint feelings and behavior that are adaptive or correct in absence of a rational justification by the subject. Before I elaborate further on this idea, I want to concentrate first on available theoretical and empirical approaches of studying behavior that has been called intuitive.

**Theoretical Approaches to the Study of Intuition**

I do not claim to be complete in reviewing work that has been done or could be relevant to the concept of intuition as I tried to define it above. I will give a rather rough estimate on the question whether and from what direction we have contributions from the past, and on the actual research. While there is little literature in psychology related to the topic of intuition, there is a long philosophical tradition about intuition. I am unable to do justice to all the relevant insight that might come from philosophy.

Nevertheless, I will mention just a few meanings of the term that have been given important roles in philosophical discussions. Rorty (1967) distinguishes four principal meanings of intuition: (a) Intuition as unjustified true belief not preceded by inference; (b) intuition as immediate knowledge of the truth of a proposition, where *immediate* means not preceded by inference; (c) intuition as immediate knowledge of a concept that does not entail the ability to define the concept; and (d) intuition as nonpropositional knowledge of an entity. This can be sense perception, considered as a product of a cognitive faculty distinct from the faculty of forming judgments concerning the entity sensed. This meaning also embraces intuitions of universals or insensible particulars as time and space and mystical or inexpressible intuitions that do not make possible knowledge of the truth of propositions about the entities intuited.

From this classification it is difficult to infer what could be constituent parts of my rationale concerning intuitive behavior developed above. Also, it would not be easy to take this taxonomy as a basis for empirical psychological investigation. Nevertheless the broadest definition of intuition given in philosophy delivers a basis for scientific discourse and analysis. In the general range of uses, intuition is considered *immediate apprehension*. Apprehension covers states as disparate as sensation, knowledge, or mystical rapport. Immediate may signify the absence of inference, the absence of causes, the absence of the ability to define a term, the absence of justification, the absence of symbols, or the absence of thought. In this most general meaning, intuition is the true belief not preceded by inference. In a most common sense intuition means a *hunch*. What is most astonishing from the psychological point of view is the fact that for philosophy the existence of hunches is uncontroversial and therefore, as mentioned by Rorty (1967), not of philosophical interest. In contrast, it would be a most valuable contribution to psychology to explain what the exact basis of these hunches are, and what their functional value is.

In psychology pioneering investigations by the Gestalt psychologists using the concept of insight looked promising for studying productive, creative, or intuitive thinking. However, the paradigm of behaviorism could not deal in a really forthcoming way with the too heavy, mental load of this concept. Consciousness as well as intuition became highly emotive words in psychology and had been all but excluded from serious study. An esoteric and mystique connotation of these concepts seemed to prevent an empirical investigation. Also in cognitive psychology the preference for the "harder" behavioral data dominated the "softer" reports about awareness, states, or contents of consciousness. Experimentation and assumptions on cognition, thinking, imaging, problem-solving or remembering predominantly focused on product-oriented verbal or nonverbal output-behavior, and parallel verbal reports, e.g., in problem-solving, were immediately questioned in their validity (Nisbett & Wilson, 1977). Considering these facts, it is no wonder that there are no elaborated concepts on consciousness or intuition to agree on. When making intuition the object of scientific analysis, one should describe a unique set of its attributes.

Bastick (1982) has undertaken one of the rare attempts to find a set of properties satisfying a consensus meaning of intuition and from which an operational definition and theory may be developed. His analysis results in attributes that contrast intuition with abstract reasoning, logic, or analytic thought. Attributes like *sudden appearance, preconscious processing*, or *understanding by feeling* refer to phenomenological discriminations. We can easily follow this undertaking, but what would be needed is the unfolding of the underlying mechanisms of these phenomenological discriminations.

The current scientific development in the research of cognition could strengthen this perspective. There is a fast-growing literature, revealing the impact of consciousness on the individual's experience, thought and action (Kihlstrom, 1987; Perrig, Wippich & Perrig, 1993). In memory research for instance, the most prominent distinction is made between conscious memory for facts and events and various forms of nonconscious memory, including skill and habit learning, and simple, classical conditioning and priming (Squire, Knowlton & Musen, 1993). These indirect demonstrations of memory, usually referred to by the term *implicit memory*, are all instances where memory is expressed through performance rather than by recollection (Graf & Masson, 1993). Subliminal perception (Marcel, 1983), automatization (Schneider & Shiffrin, 1977; Hasher & Zacks, 1979), grammar learning (Reber, 1989; Servan-Schreiber & Anderson, 1990), and social cognition (Lewicki, 1986) are other domains where human performances are conceptualized in direct relation to the degree of the subjects' ability to verbalize awareness or conscious interpretations. And there is cumulating evidence for predictable systematization in the control of behavior outside of consciousness. On this broad empirical basis it seems imperative to explicitly conceptualize consciousness within the framework of human cognition. Approaches toward this goal (Tulving, 1985; Tulving & Schacter, 1990; Schacter, 1990) seem to be good ways to ask better questions and to proceed to a more adequate understanding of human cognition. Formal accounts of cognitive processes, information flow, and representation do not only have to explain reasoning or rational decision-making, but also have to explain the processes underlying emotion and unconscious mental processes that operate on knowledge structures and on representation structures  that do not bear the characteristic of knowledge but are—as I believe—related to intuitive behavior. A most significant approach for the rationale presented here is the distinction between accessible content and accessibility experience. In this context Schwarz (in press) elaborates on the interplay of declarative and experiential information and different strategies in judgment (systematic processing vs. heuristic processing). Although the phenomena discussed by Schwarz are not related to the concepts of control and intuition I consider them as being directly relevant for the theoretical proposal outlined here.

## EXPERIMENTAL APPROACHES TO
## THE STUDY OF INTUITION

In experimental psychology we do not have an established theoretical framework that guides empirical investigations of intuition. Nevertheless we have experimental approaches that tackle the notion of intuition. These available studies should help us to proceed to a clearer understanding of intuition. In this section I therefore describe a selection of studies that disclose central characteristics of intuitive behavior.

## Intuition in the Context of Discovery and Justification

In contrast to assumptions about the positive effects of intuition, some studies concerned with intuition have emphasized the errors of intuitive judgment in the context of justification (Kahneman, Slovic & Tversky, 1982; Ross, 1977). But there are also experimental demonstrations of higher-than-chance correctness in responses, where the subjects do not have an adequate rational explanation or decision criteria for their performance. Bowers, Regehr, Balthazard & Parker (1990) is a good example of a demonstration of this kind of intuitive judgment behavior. In a Gestalt-closure task subjects were shown slides of paired drawings. One of the drawings represented a fragmented picture of a familiar object, whereas the other was constructed by rotation of these elements, destroying the coherent Gestalt fragments. The subjects' task was to identify the more coherent drawing. The data showed that the subjects' selection of the coherent structure was well above chance, although they were not able to identify the pictured objects. Subjects rather frequently report some form of intuitive reliance on some kind of familiarity impressions.

How can we deal with the inconsistency that in one type of investigation, intuition is considered to be irrationality serving as the source for errors in judgment, while in another series of studies, intuition guides people to correct responses or to detect coherence they could not identify? What then is the value or the validity of intuition? The answer to this question by Bowers et al. (1990) is convincing. These authors assume that intuition is better suited in a context of discovery than in a context of justification. This is certainly the case as long as the judgments to be made can and should be based on normative considerations, rational inference, and knowledge. In contrast, if judgments or justifications are made when there is a lack of applicable knowledge or normative considerations, intuition may take over as the process of generating hunches or hypotheses that will require further testing before they are accepted as valid. Bowers et al. (1990) assume that in a *guiding* phase the network of memory and experience is aroused unconsciously by spreading activations until in the *integrative* phase sufficient activation has accumulated to cross a threshold of awareness. This can be experienced as Gestalt-like perception, hunches or insight that has to be validated further. Investigating intuition requires the creation of circumstances that permit reasonably clear access to these preanalytic phases of information processing.

I believe that we can tap this intuitive stage of information processing in several domains of implicit memory research. In indirect or implicit memory tests, we can find above-chance correctness or improvement in responses or performances because of an intuitive awareness of experience or perception that does not reach the level of insight in terms of knowledge. We also have captured this distinction in theoretical two-stage models of recognition, where performance can be the result of memory recognition, or the feeling of familiarity (Mandler, 1980; Jacoby & Dallas, 1981).

## Intuition in Recognition

Recognizing episodes or stimuli is usually considered to indicate that knowledge has been reactivated. Recognition is used systematically as a direct test of memory to measure the amount of conscious recollective experience. But Kunst-Wilson & Zajonc (1980), for instance, used recognition to show that their subjects could not discriminate on a recollective basis stimuli that had been presented before for milliseconds from new stimuli, but that their subjects selected (above the level of chance) more old items on an emotional basis, when they were instructed to pick the one from two items (one old, one new) that they liked better. Other studies show that recognition decisions rely on different sources. Gardiner & Java (1990) not only asked for the recognition response, but also investigated further the recollective experience of the subjects. They demonstrated that "remember"-responses depend on qualitatively different memory processes than "know"-responses. The remember responses share the features of explicit episodic memory while the know responses seem to obey the laws of implicit or semantic memory.

Direct evidence that subjects also use phenomenological impressions in absence of any remembering to make their recognition decision had been presented by Johnston, Dark & Jacoby (1985). New words that had to be identified as quickly as possible were more often judged as old when they were identified quickly than when they were identified more slowly. In this case, no memory trace or any trace of previous experience had been used to make the judgment. Obviously the impression of fluency in identification was the reason for misjudging an item as old. We can suppose that this feeling of fluency is related to the impression of familiarity in the sense of: "If it is so easy, it could have been presented just before." It is important to note the difference of the source of information for the *old* response to old items, in contrast to the *old* response to new items. In the case of an *old* judgment with an old item in absence of remembering, we nevertheless do attribute the feeling of familiarity to some kind of implicit traces of memory or experience. This is not the case with the old responses to new items.

To further investigate the effects of this different response basis, I conducted a recognition experiment (see Perrig & Wippich, 1990) with difficult–to–remember, non-semantic material (pictures of snow crystals). Together with the old/new response, we collected a justification by the subjects for their old/new decisions. In an incidental and an intentional learning condition (that produced no difference in recognition performance) digitized black and white photographs of snow crystals were presented to subjects on a computer screen. In the recognition test, old and new pictures of crystals were presented, and the subjects had to decide whether they had seen the snow crystal in question before or not. After giving a yes or no response, subjects had to select one of the following three categories as a justification for their choice:

(1) Remember–response ("I remembered a feature of a seen item" after a yes-response, or "I detected a feature not seen before" after a no-response),

(2) Know–response ("I know somehow it was there or it was not there without remembering or detecting any feature"), and finally,

(3) Guessing ("I just guessed").

Thus, beside the categories *remember* and *know* (Gardiner & Java, 1990) the subjects had the possibility to say that they had guessed. It follows from our rationale that the response distribution and the sensitivity of discrimination are influenced by different principles, dependent on whether an old item or a new item has to be judged. The identification of an old item (and thus the difference between the number of hits and misses) should be especially good in the remember category, and less accurate or absent in the categories of know and guess. Because in the new items no episodic memory information is available, a correct rejection must be based on a different source of information, e.g. of the phenomenological impression of not remembering. This should produce more correct rejections than false alarms in all three categories of justification.

The results show exactly this pattern. The responses were rather equally distributed over the three categories of justification, with 31%, 31% and 38%; and 30%, 32% and 38% for *remember, know*, and *guess* for the old and the new items, respectively. The subjects gave correct or false responses dependent on their awareness of remembering and the type of items. Within the old items, subjects had significantly more hits than misses only in the case where they signalled recollective experience and said that they remembered some features of the snow crystals. Within the new items, on the other hand, in all three categories of explanation we have significantly more (and above chance level) correct rejections than false alarms. Thus, even in the situations where the subjects stated that they had guessed, they clearly show discriminative behavior. With this non-meaningful material of pictures of snow crystals which are non-recallable units, and difficult to remember, the power for discrimination clearly seems to come from the ability to reject new information. Overall, the hit-rate is 54% (within the chance level) while the correct rejection average is above chance level (63%). It seems that in situations where little knowledge can be reactivated perceptual information can be used to reject new information.

Above we reserved the term intuition to faint feelings and behavior that are adaptive or correct in absence of a rational justification of the subject. Consequently we assume that people are able to "feel" a more fluent processing of old information that is used to discriminate old from new information. But why does familiarity not lead to a higher hit rate compared to the miss responses in the categories of knowing and guessing? The reason for this could lie in the phenomenological impression of not remembering that we suppose to be responsible for the high correct-rejection rate. The feeling of not remembering can also be the cause for increased miss rates in the know and the guess categories. From this reasoning it follows that not only the false alarm rate, but under the condition of not remembering, also the hit rate is dependent on the ability to correctly reject new information. The result of this analysis has several consequences on the application of the signal detection theory to recognition data. In the traditional analysis of recognition data the signal detection model allows to distinguish discrimination sensitivity from response bias. The calculation of the discrimination index combines hit and false alarm rates without making any assumptions on differential processing of old and new items. However, from the data presented here we conclude that beside remembering the ability to identify new information is a separate and powerful function that has to be considered when we calculate discrimination scores. I do not want to elaborate this point in this contribution. Rather I will resume this chapter with a speculation on the question why the ability to correctly identify new information is basic from an evolutionary point of view. From an evolutionary perspective our finding might tap a harm-preventing function. For the goal of surviving, new situations are more dangerous than old ones, because the old situation has already been survived at least once. And in absence of any knowledge and remembering this kind of discrimination between old and new is a powerful adaptive mechanism.

**Intuition in Perception**

In a perceptual experience episodic information can be extracted as conceptual meaning that represents the subjective phenomenal identification or recognition of objects or events. Our findings on the recognition of snow crystals do suggest that perceptual traces that do not constitute meaningful features can be used to discriminate old from new objects for which memory representations that go beyond the previous episode of stimulus presentation do not exist. In this case decision making represents the feature of intuition, because it is based either on perceptual representations that directly mirror the physical characteristics of the input stimuli, or on phenomenological qualities of the process of perception itself.

So far we had demonstrations of intuitive behavior that used traces of previous experience. In this section we demonstrate how humans are able to structure and to organize their physical environment purely on a perceptual basis.

*Method.* The experimental paradigm that is presented here has been developed by a collaborator in his master thesis (Fumasoli, 1992). He demonstrated that his subjects could classify non-meaningful line drawings on a basis of similarity judgments without being able to justify their performance with identifiable features. The author argued that the impression of similarity was based solely on perceptual regularity that was produced by mathematical functions which were used to distort original figures in the coordinate net. Because there is no psychological theory at hand that could explain this effect, and because only one experiment had been presented, I did a series of replications which will be presented here.

*Material.* The material was taken from Fumasoli (1992) and consisted of 30 geometric-like and meaningless line drawings. These figures were distorted by five different mathematical functions. Out of this material, 20 complex pictures were constructed, each containing six drawings. Five of them were distorted by the same, one by another function.

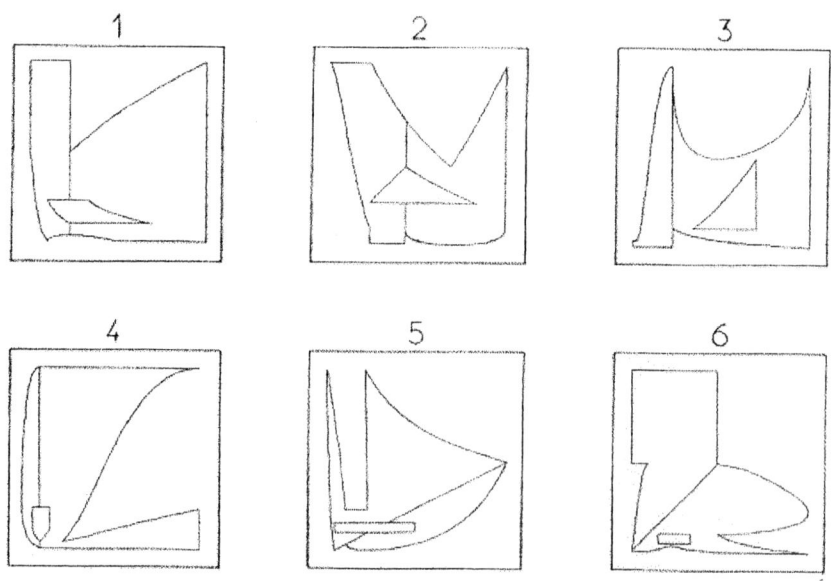

*FIG. 7.1. Example task with rule-based geometrical distortions (same function: No. 1, 3, 4, 5, and 6; different function: No. 2).*

*Procedure.* The subjects were presented the complex pictures, one after another, for 10 seconds each. They were instructed that the drawings would represent artistic products. From the six figures they should select the one figure that fits the least with the others. In doing so they were advised not to concentrate on formal aspects, but rather that they should decide from a stylistic and holistic point of view. An example of such a stimuli is presented in figure 7.1.

*Subjects and Test Conditions.* Four experiments were conducted in different settings of classes, with different subjects and different numbers of tasks.

*Results.* The data show that subjects are able to select the one drawing that is constructed by a different rule compared to the five other figures, without reference to meaningful discriminative features. The observed hit rates are well above chance level in all four experiments as is shown in table 7.1. This performance is astonishing because from the visual appearance of the figures, subjects do not identify obvious features that distinguish one figure from another.

*TABLE 7.1*
*Hit rates in target selection of rule-deviant figures*
*(one out of six) in experiments 1 to 4*

| Experiment | Hits Expected (Rate) | Hits Observed (Rate) | Binomial Test |
|---|---|---|---|
| Experiment 1: 49 subjects; 20 tasks | 49 x 20 x 1/6 = 163 (16.66%) | 259 (26%) | z = 8.2, p < 0.001 |
| Experiment 2: 21 subjects; 5 tasks | 21 x 5 x 1/6 = 17 (16.66%) | 40 (38%) | z = 5.92, p < 0.001 |
| Experiment 3: 38 subjects; 5 tasks | 38 x 5 x 1/6 = 32 (16.66%) | 72 (38%) | z = 7.85, p < 0.001 |
| Experiment 4: 61 subjects; 20 tasks | 61 x 20 x 1/6 = 203 (16.66%) | 365 (30%) | z = 12.42, p < 0.001 |

Nevertheless, some kind of phenomenological perceptual correspondence must have guided the selection process. As long as we do not have a deeper understanding about the physiological or psychological process that mirrors the invariance of the line construction produced by the mathematical formula, it is difficult to say what exactly enables this selective behavior. In this situation we have to be especially cautious to establish the reliability of the phenomenon, which we are actually trying to do by continuing to work with this paradigm.

From the experience we have collected so far, we are inclined to believe that we have succeeded in producing physical invariance that is extracted by the visual system to the level of phenomenological discriminations. This invariance is outside of categorical or semantic domains. But nevertheless if we are forced to select one part of a picture on the basis of perceptual correspondence we are able to do so above chance level. According to our rationale this is done by intuition, which uses phenomenological impressions that reflect automatic organizing or discriminative processes in perception.

## THE ARCHITECTURE OF LEVELS OF CONTROL

I have presented experimental investigations of intuitive judgments in the domains of justification, discovery, recognition and perception. The question remains how we can explain this intuitive behavior that we consider as a characteristic and unique form of behavioral control, which we distinguished from automatic processes and reasoning. The basic assumption given in the introduction of this article considers intuitive control of behavior as a combination of automatic processes and reasoning processes. This form of control comes into play when goal-oriented actions, decisions, or interpretations have to be realized under conditions of uncertainty or lack of knowledge. This behavior is related to phenomenological qualities like hunches or feelings, rather than insights, identification, or recollection.

Related to the dimension of time in which information is processed and meaning and knowledge is activated one can assume that intuitive control can be restricted to a short and critical period, while in other situations the information in the environment is so restricted that intuitive behavior is the final level that can be reached.

This assumption implyes a hierarchical order, or levels of control. Each level of automatization, intuition and reasoning can serve in the function of reaction, adaptation or creation. In experimental investigations of sequences of human behavior we can identify human reactions to stimuli or stimulations as automatic, intuitive, or logically inferred. Whether such reactions will be adaptive or creative will be judged later in a historical view by the criteria of novelty and/or success. Learning can be considered as adaptive behavior that is responsive in a reactive or anticipative way. And again this learning can be (a) automatic (perceptual and/or semantic priming), (b) intuitive by the use of phenomenological information, or (c) rational in the sense of consciously controlled behavior. The hierarchy of these levels of control range from automatic processes over intuition to rational control progresses, and from low-level to high-level cognition. The most important criteria for the distinction of these levels is the concept of consciousness. Here we might identify the weakest point of this rationale because psychology indeed does not have an elaborated concept of consciousness to agree on. This fact however does not prevent the need for introducing consciousness as a core faculty of human beings into an architecture of cognition that does explain primitive automatic responsive as well as complicated logical inference activities. Levels of control thus vary basically on the amount of experienced control.

At this point we have to characterize a framework of cognition, including the concept of consciousness, that allows to integrate or to explain observable human behavior, thinking, or feeling. For this reason I want to elaborate further on a conceptualization that was presented earlier in Perrig, Wippich and Perrig-Chiello (1993). That framework relates behavior to consciousness, and memory. Within memory a perceptual and a conceptual memory are distinguished. *Perceptual memory* represents experience that connects properties of stimuli with involuntary, automatic responses based on genetic programs of biological functioning. This automatic *associative reaction function* leaves traces and thus changes continuously the representational status of this stimulus-response experience. The concept of *consciousness* embraces all phenomenological experiences, from states of awareness over feelings, to reasoning and thinking. *Conceptual memory* is constituted of and is uniquely the result of these conscious interpretations. Consciousness is considered as the *constructive interpretation function* in humans. Consciousness has access to transformed forms of reality in the process of perceiving. Cognizing, recognizing and remembering are the results of conceptual memory retrieval in form of knowledge, meaningful experience or memories of the past. Perceptual memory can only be accessed indirectly by consciousness through the phenomenological correlates of experience in use, that is when perceptual memory or experience is activated and used by data-driven, automatic processes.

By means of this processing the organism does not only rely on an automatic adaptive response behavior, that e.g. is manifested in perceptual and/or semantic priming, but it can use phenomenological information that is not knowledge yet to initiate behavior, besides behavior that results from knowledge-based reasoning. In the intuitive mode of control phenomenological categories are discriminative in the form of being aware or in the form of feeling. Intuition in this view is based on preconscious discrimination processes. The phenomenological discriminations, feelings, or emotions are a mediating form of information about the environment that is not yet knowledge. Intuition in this sense can be  considered as instinctive or based on incomplete knowledge, or as understanding through feeling. It is assumed that in this type of behavioral control human beings use hunches, vague hypotheses or phenomenological experiences like e.g. feelings of familiarity, easiness, reduced uncertainty, or impressions of clarity, contrast, or consistency that accompany either the process of automatic information processing or correlate with the products of it. This view can be related to older feed-back theories of emotion and to the concepts of *fluency of processing* and *familiarity* proposed by Jacoby and collaborators (Jacoby & Dallas, 1981; Jacoby & Whitehouse, 1989; Whittlesea, Jacoby & Girard, 1990) to dissociate automatic from controlled processes. The experimental demonstrations of those authors show that previous experience can influence perceptual fluency leading to savings or priming that are automatic and unconscious effects, bare of any recollective experience. Moreover, their data demonstrates that in forced choice decisions subjects rely on feelings of familiarity for their responses, which can influence the hit-rate of the recognition data or to erroneous attributions, like in the "false fame" effect, where subjects judge names as famous more frequently only because they had been presented 24 hours earlier, which subjects had forgotten (Jacoby, Kelley, Brown & Jasechko, 1989).

In terms of our framework of level of control and the hypothesized architecture of cognition that distinguishes perceptual memory, conceptual memory and consciousness, I come to the following interpretation of perceptual fluency and familiarity effects: Perceptual fluency is a reduction in processing load by means of automatic processing in perceptual or conceptual memory, that results in priming or saving in behavioral measures. This variability in fluency of processing is experienced by consciousness which enables the switch from automatic control to the level of intuitive control. This intuitive control can—dependent on the task, and the context information available—lead to more correct responses like in recognition or to misattributions like in the false fame example. Fluency of processing can be manipulated by previous experience, but also by stimulus characteristics such as clarity and contrast. It was convincingly demonstrated that these characteristics influence preference judgments by the means of enhanced perceptual fluency rather than by the stimulus characteristics per se (Reber, Winkielman, & Schwarz, 1998).

In terms of learning, perceptual memory saves sensorial experience, representing reality directly and automatically according to the neurophysiological principle of each biological sensory system. Receptive activity, considered as the package of stimulus and automatic responses, inevitably changes the representational basis of perceptual memory, and thus constitutes the basic requisites of learning. On this basis the organism is able to distinguish between old and new without knowledge or semantic categories. But this low-level cognition already is of great adaptive power enabling automatic forms of learning including skill and habit learning, simple classical conditioning and priming.

This conceptualization of human information processing leads to critical questions. From the epistemological perspective we need to know how high-level cognition, knowledge and meaningful categorization develop and how they are related to the mechanisms of low-level learning. From the developmental perspective we have to ask the same question, namely how the newborn, with its innate reflexive responses, proceeds to the abstract knowledge structures of the adult. A hypothetical answer can be inferred from our theoretical framework. I assume that the very same processes that enable intuitive control mediate between low-level and high-level cognition. Intuition is considered as a mechanism that connects automatic perceptual stimulus-response associations with consciousness.

Changes in physiological states can vary with phenomenological discriminations in consciousness. The conscious interpretation function must consist of a highly sensitive system that mirrors difference, contrast, and change in subjective phenomenological experience which copies a multitude of physiological processes from the physical world. In relation to learning this proposed covariation of awareness, constituting conscious interpretations, and feelings on one hand, with innate biological stimulus-response activities on the other hand, must be considered as the basic function of recoding or duplicating discriminative information from lower to higher levels of cognition. It is a fundamental principle of learning that explains how epistemological development proceeds from sensorial body responses to modality-independent thinking.

Another question tackles the relation between intuition and emotion. In our theory intuitive control is the result of phenomenologically being aware of discriminative physiological states or processing. Of course, this has to do with feelings, but we are not equating intuition with emotion. Intuitive behavior is the result of subtle conscious interpretations. The input for such interpretations can come either from emotional processing or from cognitive computations. Both emotion and rational thinking, have to be integrated into our general concept of cognition. In this view the proprioceptive sensation of biological stimulus-response activities can become the subject of meaningful interpretations as well as activated knowledge or emotional reactions.

## CONCLUSION

Any activity of a human organism is under some kind of control. The concept of levels of control presented in this contribution distinguishes between an automatic, an intuitive and a rational control of human behavior. The relevant criteria for this distinction are related to phenomenological experience, insight, intention, attention, and effort of the subject. This fact led to the introduction of the concept of consciousness into a broad architecture of cognition. Consciousness in this framework is given the core function in explaining human behavior. The terminology of the proposed levels of control should enable the description of simple automatic and unconscious reactions, as well as explaining complicated logical inference activities. A hierarchy is proposed that leads from automatic processes over intuition to rational control, in a way a taxonomy of behavior is described that characterizes low-level and high-level cognition, and its interaction.

While the contrast of automatic and controlled processes has received a lot of attention in psychology I concentrate here on intuition, which so far has received little thought in experimental psychology. Focusing on the phenomenon that is called *intuition* asks for an integrated view of low-level and high-level cognition. It is assumed that in this type of behavioral control human beings use hunches, vague hypotheses, or phenomenological experiences like feelings of familiarity, easiness, reduced uncertainty, or impressions of clarity, contrast, or consistency that accompany either the process of automatic information processing or correlate with the products of it. The proposed covariation of conscious experience with physiological stimulus-response activities is considered not only as the mechanism explaining intuition but also as the basic function that recodes or duplicates discriminative information processing from lower levels to higher levels of learning. Of course, we have to assume that in the process of knowledge retrieval or problem-solving automatic processes are always at the basis. In this activation of knowledge or previously learned solutions we have to assume that all conditions for intuitive behavior would be fulfilled only for a short, critical period of time. If we tap this short time frame by adequate experimental procedures like in close-to-threshold presentations in the paradigm of subliminal perception, we can study the characteristic of intuitive control. But in successful activation of knowledge lies insight, clarity, and certainty which have different consequences on behavior than intuition. I believe that in all everyday and professional performances intuitive control is not less frequent than automatic control and rational control.

The research paradigms, the empirical results, and the framework of levels of control presented here focus on unconscious and intuitive information processing in describing its relationship to automatic processing and reasoning. There is not yet a study that simulates the whole intuitive process. At the current state of research different approaches and studies demonstrate pieces of the characteristic attributed to intuitive thought and behavior. The psychological processes that enable intuitive control are considered at the same time to constitute a fundamental principle of learning that explains how epistemological development proceeds from sensorial body responses to modality-independent thinking. The framework of levels of control also gives a functional description for the distinction of a conceptual memory that can be retrieved and remembered and a perceptual memory that is automatically used in form of unconscious experience. This framework also explains data that is collected in the research domain of implicit memory and subliminal perception, and it also explains the concepts of perceptual fluency and familiarity of the process-dissociation paradigm, and effects that contrast procedural experience and declarative knowledge.

After this elaboration on the more objective forms of control of human behavior, thought, and consciousness I only can try to speculate on how these different types of control might influence subjective control beliefs. The belief of having a high level of control—self control, or control over the environment—can be the result of a person's experience or attribution that he or she himself/ herself was responsible for doing something efficiently he/she intended to do. From such an assumption we could conclude that in terms of the levels of control distinguished in the framework presented here, especially the rational level of control would be important and influential, because there are all dimensions of reasoning, interpretation, and self-reflection available. I do hesitate to adopt this conclusion too quickly. We rather have to consider that virtually all complex performance is the result of combinations of these different levels of control. Even the results of unconscious and automatic processes can become the subject of reasoning and attribution. On the level of intuitive control, we already have large amounts of phenomenological experience available that can be used for the development of control beliefs. It is also plausible to distinguish different types of control beliefs that relate to the levels of control distinguished here. We also have to assume that there are substantial individual differences in the self-perception of personality or cognitive style. The distinction between an intuitive-experiential and an analytical-rational style of thinking might be a promising dimension to measure individual differences in self report, and to study its relation to control beliefs. The consideration of more objective task performances and its theoretical implications could help to validate such a research approach.

## REFERENCES

Bastick, T. (1982). *Intuition. How we think and act.* New York: Wiley.
Bowers, K. S., Regehr, G., Balthazard, C. & Parker, K. (1990). Intuition in the context of discovery. *Cognitive Psychology, 22,* 72–110.
Epstein, S. (1994). Integration of the cognitive and the psychodynamic unconsciousness. *American Psychologist, 49,* 709–724.
Flammer, A. (1990). *Erfahrung der eigenen Wirksamkeit.* Bern: Huber.
Flammer, A. (1995). Developmental analysis of control beliefs. In A. Bandura (Ed.), *Self-efficacy in Changing Societies* (pp. 69–113). Cambridge, MA: Cambridge University Press.
Flammer, A., Grob, A. & Lüthi, R. (1989). Swiss adolescents' attribution of control. In J.P. Forgas & J.M. Innes (Eds.), *Recent advances in social psychology.: An international perspective.* North Holland: Elsevier Science Publishers.
Fumasoli, C. (1992). *Implizites Wissen oder das unbewusste Erfassen von Invarianz in komplexen Stimuluskonfigurationen.* Lizentiatsarbeit. Institut für Psychologie, Universität Basel.
Gardiner, J. M. & Java, R. I. (1990). Recollective experience in word and nonword recognition. *Memory & Cognition, 18,* 23–30.
Graf, P. & Masson, M. E. J. (1993). *Implicit memory: New directions in cognition, development, and neuropsychology.* Hillsdale, N.J.: Lawrence Erlbaum Associates.
Grawe, K. (1998). *Psychologische Therapie.* Göttingen: Hogrefe.
Hasher, L. & Zacks, R. T. (1979). Automatic and effortful processes in memory. *Journal of Experimental Psychology: General, 108,* 3, 356-388.
Jacoby, L.L. & Dallas, M. (1981). On the relationship between autobiographical memory and perceptual learning. *Journal of Experimental Psychology: General, 110,* 306–340.
Jacoby, L. L. & Whitehouse, K. (1989). An illusion of memory: False recognition influenced by unconscious perception. *Journal of Experimental Psychology: General, 118,* 126–135.
Jacoby, L. L., Kelley, C. M., Brown, J. & Jasechko, J. (1989). Becoming famous overnight: Limits on the ability to avoid unconscious influences of the past. *Journal of Personality and Social Psychology, 56,* 326–338.
Johnston, W. A., Dark, V. J. & Jacoby, L. L. (1985). Perceptual fluency and recognition judgments. *Learning, Memory and Cognition. 11,* 3–11.
Kahneman, D. S., Slovic, P. & Tversky, A. (Eds.) (1982). *Judgment under uncertainty: Heuristics and biases.* Cambridge, MA: Cambridge University Press.
Kihlstrom, J.F. (1987). The cognitive unconscious. *Science, 237,* 1445–1452.
Kunst-Wilson, W. R. & Zajonc, R. B. (1980). Affective discrimination of stimuli that are not recognized. *Science, 207,* 557–558.
Lewicki, P. (1986). *Nonconscious social information processing.* New York: Academic Press.
Mandler, G. (1980). Recognizing: The judgment of previous occurence. *Psychological Review, 87,* 252–271.
Marcel, A. (1983). Conscious and unconscious perception: Experiments on visual masking and word recognition. *Cognitive Psychology, 15,* 197–237.
Nisbett, R. E. & Wilson, T. D. (1977). Telling more than we can know: Verbal reports on mental processes. *Psychological Review, 84,* 231–259.
Perrig, W. J. & Wippich, W. (1990). Intuition in the context of perception, memory and judgment. In B. Boothe, R. Hirsig, A. Helminger, B. Meier & R. Volkart

(Eds.). *Swiss Monographs in Psychology* (Volume 3: pp. 21-31). Bern: Hans Huber.

Perrig, W., Wippich, W. & Perrig-Chiello, P. (1993). *Unbewusste Informationsverarbeitung*. Bern: Hans Huber.

Posner, M. J. & Snyder, R. R. (1975). Attention and cognitive control. In R. L. Solso (Ed.), *Information processing and cognition*. Hillsdale, NJ: Lawrence Erlbaum Associates.

Reber, A. S. (1989). Implicit learning and tacit knowledge. *Journal of Exprimental Psychology: General, 118*, 219–235.

Reber, R., Winkielman, P. & Schwarz, N. (1998). Effects of perceptual fluency on affective judgments. *Psychological Science, 9*, 45–48.

Rorty, R. (1967). Intutition. In P. Edwards (Ed.), *The Encyclopedia of Philosophy*, (vol. 4, 204–212). New York: McMillan.

Ross, L. (1977). The intuitive psychologist and his shortcomings: Distortions in the attribution process. In L. Berkowitz (Ed.), *Advances in experimental social psychology, 10* (pp. 173–220). New York: Academic Press.

Schacter, D. L. (1990). Toward a cognitive neuropsychology of awareness: Implicit knowledge and agnosia. *Journal of Clinical and Experimental Neuropsychology, 12*, 155–178.

Schneider, W. & Shiffrin, R. M. (1977). Controlled and automatic human information processing: I. Detection, search, and attention. *Psychological Review, 84*, 1–66.

Schwarz, N. (in press). Accessible content and accessibility experiences: The interplay of declarative and experiential information in judgment. In J. Metcalfe & F. Strack (Eds.), Metacognition. Special issue of *Personality and Social Psychology Review*.

Servan-Schreiber, E. & Anderson, J. R. (1990). Learning artificial grammars with competitive chunking. *Journal of Experimental Psychology: Learning, Memory and Cognition. 16*: 592–608.

Squire, L. B., Knowlton, B. & Musen, G. (1993). The structure and organization of memory. *Annual Review of Psychology, 44*, 453–495.

Tulving, E. (1985). Memory and consciousness. *Canadian Journal of Psychology, 26*, 1–12.

Tulving, E. & Schacter, D. L. (1990). Priming and human memory systems. *Science, 247*, 301–306.

Whittlesea, B. W. A., Jacoby, L. L. & Girard, K. (1990). Illusions of immediate memory: Evidence of an attributional basis for feelings of familiarity and perceptual quality. *Journal of Memory and Language, 29*, 716–732.

# III

# Perception, Knowledge, Memory, and Learning

# 8

# The Issue of Control in Sensory and Perceptual Processes: Attention Selects and Modulates the Visual Input

*Rudolf Groner*
*Marina T. Groner*

## INTRODUCTION

Sometimes it has been assumed that sensory and perceptual processes are automatic in the sense that, once established, they invariably proceed always in the same manner and cannot be modified in the course of the ongoing process. The intention of this paper is to show that such a view is basically wrong. Specifically, the claim is that already at relatively early levels of visual information processing, the organism is capable of actively controlling and, consequently, also structuring its input. The main function of this mechanism, called "attention," is to reduce the flood of incoming information, for the purpose of adapting the organism optimally to a highly complex environment.

There are various ways of achieving such a goal, each associated with a particular way of tuning the visual system to some aspects of the optical input. However, one must in mind that some of these attentional tuning mechanisms are not specific to the visual system but are linked to more general aspects of human information processing. In the following, we give first an overview of the different kinds of attentional processes, and subsequently concentrate on the special case of visual information processing.

## "ATTENTION" IN DIFFERENT LOCI OF HUMAN INFORMATION PROCESSING

Figure 8.1, modified after Groner, 1989, presents some elements of a taxonomy of the concept of attention. To avoid complexities unnecessary in the current context, we only consider those main categories where successive branching leads to relevant dimensions with respect to the topic of this chapter: Attentional processes restricted to the visual modality.

A.   Concepts of Attention

        A.1. *General*                  A.2. *Specific*

        A.2.1. Ressources Allocation     A.2.2. Orientation

B.   Properties

| | | |
|---|---|---|
| B.1.1. overt | - | B.1.2. covert |
| B.2.1. conscious | - | B.2.2. unconscious |
| B.3.1. voluntary | - | B.3.2. reflexive |
| B.4.1. controlled | - | B.4.2. automatic |
| B.5.1. endogenous | - | B.5.2. exogenous |
| B.6.1. top down | - | B.6.2. bottom up |

*FIG. 8.1. Taxonomy of attentional processes. The upper part presents a hierarchic classification of current research topics (omitting further distinctions in those branches not relevant for this chapter, e.g., divided attention). The lower part indicates essential properties which are stated as dichotomies, although they apply in a varying degree to all attentional processes.*

On the most general level we can distinguish between *specific forms of attention* as opposed to attention conceived as *a general state of the activity level* of the organism. Under the heading "activation" (Duffy, 1962), "arousal" (Magoun, 1963; Pribram & McGuiness, 1975; Thayer, 1989), "vigilance" (e.g., Mackie, 1977), or "sustained attention" (Warm, 1984) a lot of relevant research has been done in this area, often providing links to various neurobiological correlates, e.g., the reticular formation and the limbic system (Routtenberg, 1968).

    Among the specific forms of attention, an important group centers around the metaphor of allocating processing resources for a demanding task (e.g., Schneider & Shiffrin, 1977; Navon & Gopher, 1979; Wickens, 1984). It is assumed that, out of a hypothetical pool of processing resources, controlled processing selects a larger amount and more specific attentional resources than automatic processing.

    Another group of approaches conceives attention as some activity of *orienting* in the sense of an alignment of the sensory input (Posner, 1978). If this orientation can be observed externally, e.g., as an orienting response (Sokolov, 1975; Pribram & McGuiness, 1992) or as eye movements (Groner & Groner, 1989), it is described as *overt orienting*, as opposed to *covert orienting* where no behavioral correlate can be observed, but rather a metaphorical inference is drawn comparing attention to "the mind's eye movements" (Jonides, 1980).

    The next three polarities: *conscious* versus *unconscious*, *voluntary* versus *involuntary*, and *controlled* versus *automatic*, are assumed by most theorists (Kahneman, 1973; Posner & Snyder, 1975; Shiffrin & Schneider, 1977; LaBerge, 1981; Marcel, 1983) to be closely related aspects of two common processes, although despite of the properties they share, there is certainly a difference in function and diversity among them (Allport, 1988; Allport, 1993; Neumann, 1996).

A further distinction can be drawn between the two potential sources eliciting an attentional process: It might be initiated by an *endogenous* source within the information processing system, e.g., expectation or intention; or—on the other hand—it might be initiated by an *exogenous* source, e.g., the onset of a stimulus or a salient stimulus property. Endogenous has been related to *voluntary*, and exogenous to *reflexive* by several authors (James, 1890; Sereno, 1992; and Kingstone & Klein, 1993). Ultimately, these terms can also be related to the particular mode of information processing (Groner & Groner, 1989): endogenous is identical with the so-called *top-down* mode of information processing, whereas exogenous equals the *bottom-up* approach (Norman, 1968).

One main aspect of specific attentional processes is their selective role in an early stage of visual information processing. Based on neurobiological evidence (Trevarthen, 1968; Held, Ingle, Schneider & Trevarthen, 1968; Breitmeyer & Ganz, 1976; Ungerleider & Mishkin, 1982), two different subsystems have been proposed for stimulus selection based on an early pre-processing over a wide range of the optic input (the "ambient", "locating", "transient" or "where" system), followed on a second stage by a system performing a qualitatively different analysis (the "focal", "identifying", "sustained", or "what" system). This distinction was followed up by other authors on the basis of psychophysical evidence,Treisman & Gelade (1980) distinguishing between feature extraction and object identification; and Julesz (1984) calling it "preattentive" and "attentive" visual processes. It is evident that, as a consequence of the qualitatively different nature of the processing on the first and second stage, attention introduces a *modulating* effect on visual information processing, whereas the *selective* effect is given by the result of the first process (i.e., the locating process results in a spatial location within the stimulus array where a target object is selected for the subsequent process of identification).

In the following, we will focus on the paradigm of overt visual attention, assessed by eye movement recording.

## ATTENTION AND SACCADIC EYE MOVEMENTS

The experimental situation of instructing a subject to pay attention to a defined stimulus, and recording saccadic eye movements during this activity, is the classical paradigm of *voluntary eye movements*. However, already Wundt (1903) and Helmholtz (1909) made the claim that it is possible to dissociate the locus of attention from the actual point of eye fixation, a phenomenon which has extensively used by modern experimentalists like Posner (e.g. Posner & Snyder, 1975; Posner, 1980), and Fischer (1986; Fischer & Breitmeyer, 1987) for investigating the relation between attentional and oculomotor processes. Furthermore, neuro-physiological evidence (Goldberg & Wurtz, 1972; Wurtz & Mohler, 1976) suggests that specific, but different, areas in the colliculus superior account for spatial attention and saccadic eye movements. Burkhart Fischer's theory of attentional engagement and disengagement (Fischer, 1986; Breitmeyer & Braun, 1990) claims that attentional processes control the execution of saccadic eye movements in the sense that attentional engagement must precede a saccade, and blocks the execution of a consecutive execution of a saccade for a short period of time, which must be followed by an attentional disengagement in order to permit the execution of a next saccade. However, his theory has been challenged by other authors (e.g., Findlay, 1992; Kingstone & Klein, 1993a, 1993b), mainly by criticizing his crucial assumption about the existence of a special class of very fast saccades, so called "express saccades" which are assumed to be executed by the saccadic system in a state of attentional disengagement. Although the majority of experiments by several authors tend to support the notion of express saccades (see Biscaldi, Weber, Fischer & Stuhr, 1995) still more experimental and theoretical work has to be done for settling the issue, or at least for silencing the critics.

All research reported above has been done under conditions of extremely restricted stimulation, i.e. the onset of a very simple stimulus (a dot, cross, or square, etc, in front of a homogeneous background). Although this issue is hardly ever discussed, the implicit assumption is that the stimulus elicits exogeneously an oculomotor response that is assumed to be driven by a bottom-up information processing model. With respect to the category *voluntary vs. reflexive*, the situation is not completely clear . Since, as outlined above, observers can be instructed to suppress voluntarily a saccade towards the stimulus or even perform a saccade into the opposite direction *(antisaccade)*, one is inclined to subsume the behavior investigated in these experiments under the heading *voluntary*. On the other hand, since most of the models are based on human and animal experiments, and taking into account their very simple nature as well as the usual procedure of collecting the data over hundreds of trials in a highly automatized setting, the characterization of "voluntary" becomes questionable. Similar arguments can be made with respect to *conscious vs. unconscious*. Obviously, more conceptual analysis and directed experimental work has to be done to shed light on this issue.

## Bottom-Up Processing and Overt Visual Attention

In this section we will summarize some of the experimental work that deals with stimuli of more complexity than, e.g., dots against a homogeneous background, where at least some selection within the optic input is involved, but the task of the observer is simple enough to allow for bottom-up processing.

In a series of experiments, Menz & Groner (1987) used patches of random dots with varying dot densities which were arranged in equal excentricity from the initial fixation point. If two targets are displayed simultaneously in a distance of 2 degrees of visual angle, the distribution of the landing points of the elicited saccades has its peak value in the median range in between the two patches. If the separation of the patches becomes larger, the distribution of landing positions becomes bimodal, concentrating on either patch. However, the temporal latency of the onset of the saccade is not affected, independently, whether there are one or two targets, and whether they are close to each other or further apart. This result has been interpreted by the authors, in agreement with other findings, as evidence for an automatic bottom-up process elicited by the stimulus within a critical area, analogous to receptive fields in single-cell recordings.

With more complex stimuli, it can be expected that some salient perceptual features serve as target for saccadic responses. There are only very few results available from research about the attentional salience of different perceptual features with respect to exogenous attentional reactions, assessed by saccadic responses. The main reasons for the lack of systematic research in this area are probably the methodological difficulties of a direct procedure, to name just a few: (a) it is only possible to assess a measure of *relative* salience of some feature in competition with others on the same stimulus display, (b) the excentricity relative to the point of fixation plays a crucial role, and the excentricity of every position on the display changes as a result of each saccade, (c) as a consequence of the second point, the only suitable method is to start from an empty display with a fixation point, instructing the subject to fixate it, and then replacing it by the stimulus display and to record only the first saccade. This procedure is time consuming and somehow artefactual, as compared to free looking behavior, but the only direct access to the question about the relative saliency of different perceptual dimensions. In this way the effect of contrast, brightness, and spatial frequency content was investigated by Groner, von Mühlenen & Groner (1997). A series of natural images were either high-pass filtered, thus containing only the high spatial frequency components, or low-pass filtered, containing only low spatial frequencies. In a full 2 x 2 x 2 factorial design, all eight combinations of spatial frequency content, contrast (high versus low), and brightness (bright versus dark) were created for each image and arranged in equal excentricity around the point of initial fixation. The analysis of the landing position of the first saccade demonstrated significant main effects of contrast and spatial frequency, but not of brightness which only showed an interaction with spatial frequency. With respect to the question of saliency it was concluded that high spatial frequencies are more salient than low spatial frequencies, and high contrast is more salient than low contrast. Brightness per se has no effect, it enhances saliency only in combination with high spatial frequency components.

As outlined above, the disadvantage of the direct assessment procedure is its restriction to a highly artefactual display and to the use of initial fixations only.

For an alternative to the direct assessment procedure, one might investigate the salience of perceptual features indirectly by displaying successively images of different perceptual qualities, recording eye movements for each of them, and comparing the statistics of oculomotor parameters. In this way Groner, von Mühlenen, & Groner (1995) investigated the effect of spatial frequency filtering on saccadic amplitude and fixation duration. Spatial frequency had a significant effect on the size of saccades, in the sense that oberservers showed longer saccades when looking at low-pass filtered images as compared to unfiltered and high-pass filtered images. With respect to fixation duration, there was an increase under the condition of high-pass filtering especially for those pictures which already had a greater extent of high spatial frequencies before filtering. However, it should be noted that it is debatable whther the results of this experiment should be sub-sumed under the heading "bottom-up" processing, when there was 10 seconds' processing time allowed per picture, and the instruction given to the observers was to find a name for the picture as a whole. It might be argued that such a task leads, perhaps after a few initial fixations, very soon to some kind of internal representation of the stimulus at an early stage, and therefore in need of further corroboration. In consequence, such a view leads to the concept of hypothesis testing implemented in a top-down information processing mode.

## Top-Down Processing: Attention as Hypothesis Testing

In the current context it is interesting to note that, some time before the concept of endogeneous attention was re-examined in psychology after the cognitive revo-lution, the "New Look" was proposed by Bruner and Postman (1948; Postman & Bruner, 1948), conceiving perception as hypothesis testing. Another research impulse, theoretical as well as experimental, came later from the combination of cognitive with eye movement research (Groner, 1975; 1978) where it was de-monstrated that it is possible, based on formal models, to derive detailed empiri-cal predictions from basic assumptions about hypothesis testing strategies, thus linking perceptual to cognitive and (oculo-) motor processes. In this context, eye movements serve as empirical indicators of the sensory input controlled by the subject. It is obvious that such an approach implies top-down modeling. One and the same cognitive model, which minimized memory load on the cost of repeated visual scanning, was quite sucessful in predicting frequency distributions of sac-cadic path length and solution latencies, as well as error probabilities (for a re-view, see Groner & Groner, 1982; 1987).

Another influential top-down model for visual information storage and re-trieval was introduced by Lawrence Stark and his group (Noton and Stark 1971a, 1971b, 1971c; Stark & Ellis, 1981; Ellis & Smith, 1985). The core concept of the model is the *scan-path* as a regular sequence of eye fixations which, once de-veloped during the encoding of a stimulus, will be stored as a feature ring (i.e., a sequence of foveal images plus the motor codes of the saccades linking them), and reproduced for the purpose of recognizing that stimulus on latter occasions.

However, an exclusive top-down approach bears the danger to emphasize too much top-down processing on the cost of neglecting the monitoring unexpected aspects of the environment by bottom-up processes. In our own research, after realizing this shortcoming, we attempted to reformulate scan-path theory in order to entail both bottom-up and top-down processing.

## Combining Bottom-Up with Top-Down Processes: The Interaction of Local and Global Scan-Paths

In an experiment on the perception and recognition of human faces (Groner, Walder & Groner, 1984) we found empirical evidence for two different kinds of statistical regularities in the time course of eye fixations. There were regular patterns of *consecutive* fixations (e.g., fixating first the left eye, then the right eye, then the nose, etc.) which were analyzed by counting the sequences of three consecutive fixations *(triplets)* and, when their frequency was beyond random expectation, were called *local* scan-paths. These local scan-paths are identical to the scan-paths of Noton & Stark (1971a, b, c); in disagreement with these authors, however, Groner et al. (1984) argued that they are caused by exogenous factors in the stimulus, and therefore should be modelled by bottom-up processes. For the implementation of top-down processes, Groner et al. (1984) suggested what they called *global scan-paths*, i.e. characteristic distributions of fixations on a larger time scale.

Global scan-paths can be assessed by dividing the whole inspection period into parts of equal length, and comparing the respective frequency distributions of fixations which were centered on different parts of the image. In the experiments of Groner et al. (1984) the observers, when inspecting a human face for 10 seconds, fixated on the left eye more frequently in the first third of the inspection time as compared to the remainder of time. The authors also noted that different observers showed quite idiosyncratic local and global scanpaths which were consistent within the same subject, but varied considerably over different subjects.

These findings were replicated in a study (Groner & Menz, 1985) using a complete factorial design with the factors: (a) stimulus variation, (b) task requirements, and (c) individual diffferences between observers. In agreement with the hypothesis of top-down control of global scanpaths, it was shown that the nature of the task (free inspection vs. searching for a small target vs. concept identification), had a significant influence on global scanpaths. As already in the previous study, a strong moderating effect of individual differences on local and global scanpaths was found, which makes this experimental paradigm almost intractable for general psychology (in the sense of proposing information processing strategies which are equally valid for *all* individuals), but a rich potential source for differential psychology or cognitive style research.

## CONCLUSION

In this chapter we demonstrated that the attentional system serves as some kind of intelligent interface between individual and environment, regulating the sensory input in accordance with the dynamic external world and the internal representations within the organism. We focussed on processes of overt visual attention, assessed by eye movement recording, where there is the unique possibility of an empirical access to the postulated processes by time-related measures of saccades and fixations. Since the control processes have to converge at one moment of time into one single input unit (= saccade plus fixation), the situation becomes an interesting example of simultaneous control processes. In our modelling we investigated the dynamics of these simultaneous bottom-up and top-down control processes by means of local and global scan-paths, and found, in addition, a strong moderating effect of individual differences on attentional processes.

Our current research hast two main directions: (a) Developing an experimental paradigm which allows for more direct experimental control of the exogenous and endogenous aspect, and (b) implementation of these aspects into very explicit bottom-up and top-down processes within computational models of visual information processing.

## REFERENCES

Allport, D. A. (1988). What concept of consciousness? In A. J. Marcel & E. Bisiach (Eds.) *Consciousness in contemporary science*, 159–182. Oxford: Clarendon Press.

Allport, D. A. (1993). Attention and control: Have we been asking the wrong questions? In D. E. Meyer & S. Kornblum (Eds.), *Attention and Performance, 14* , 183-218. Cambridge, MA: MIT Press.

Biscaldi, M., Weber, H., Fischer, B., & Stuhr, V. (1995). Mechanisms for fixation in man: Evidence from saccadic reaction time. In J.M. Findlay (Ed.) *Eye movement research*. Amsterdam: Elsevier-North Holland.

Breitmeyer, B., & Braun, D. (1990). Effects of fixations and attention on saccadic reaction time. In R. Groner, G. d'Ydewalle & R. Parham (Eds.) *From eye to mind: Information acquisition in perception, search, and reading*. Amsterdam: Elsevier-North Holland.

Breitmeyer, B. G., & Ganz, L. (1976). Implications of sustained and transient channels for theories of visual pattern masking, saccadic suppression and information processing. *Psychological Review, 83*, 1–36.

Bruner, J., & Postman, L. (1948). An approach to social perception. In W. Dennis (Ed.) *Current trends in social psychology*. Pittsburgh: University of Pittsborgh Press.

Duffy, E. (1962). *Activation and behavior*. New York: Wiley.

Ellis, S. R., & Smith, J. D. (1985). Patterns of statistical dependencies in visual scanning. In R. Groner, G.W. McConkie & Ch. Menz (eds.) *Eye movements and human information processing*. Amsterdam: Elsevier-North Holland.

Findlay, J. M. (1992). Programming of stimulus-elicited saccadic eye movements. In K. Rayner (Ed.) *Eye movement and visual cognition*. New York: Springer.

Fischer, B. (1986). The role af attention in the preparation of visually guided eye movements in monkey and man. *Psychological Research, 48*, 251–257.

Fischer, B., & Breitmeyer, B. (1987). Mechanisms of visual attention revealed by saccadic eye movements. *Neuropsychologia, 25*, 73–83.

Goldberg, M. F., & Wurtz, R. (1972). Activity of superior colliculus in behaving monkey: Effects of attention in neuronal responses. *Journal of Neurophysiology, 35*, 560–574.

Groner, M., von Mühlenen, A., Groner, R. (1995). Do spatial-frequency channels control eye movement? *Perception, 24*, Suppl. 71.

Groner, R. (1975). Verallgemeinerte Hypothesenmodelle für Ordnungsaufgaben und Konzepter-werb. In W. H. Tack (Hrsg.) *Bericht über den 29. Kongress der Deutschen Gesellschaft für Psychologie in Salzburg 1974, 1*, 341–346. Göttingen: Hogrefe.

Groner, R. (1978). *Hypothesen im Denkprozess. Grundlagen einer verallgemeinerten Theorie auf der Basis elementarer Informationsverarbeitung*. Bern, Stuttgart & Wien: Huber.

Groner, R. & Groner M. T. (1982). Towards a hypothetico-deductive theory of cognitive activity. In R. Groner & P. Fraisse (Eds.) *Cognition and eye movements*. Amsterdam: Elsevier-North Holland.

Groner, R. & Groner M. T. (1987). Hypothesis theory—a review. In E. van der Meer & J. Hoffmann (Eds.) *Knowledge aided information processing in human beings*. Amsterdam: Elsevier-North Holland.

Groner, R. & Groner M. T. (1989). Attention and eye movement control: an overview.*European Archives of Psychiatry and Neurological Sciences, 239*, 9–16.

Groner, R., von Mühlenen, A., & Groner, M. (1995). Top-down versus bottom-up processing of saccades in texture perception. *Perception, 26*, Suppl. 93.

Groner, R., & Menz, C. (1985). The effects of stimulus characteristics, task requirements and individual differences on scanning patterns. In R. Groner, G. W. McConkie & C. Menz (Eds.) *Eye movements and human information processing*. Amsterdam: Elsevier-North Holland.

Groner, R., Walder, F., & Groner, M. (1984). Looking at faces: Local and global aspects of scanpaths. In A. G. Gale & F. Johnson (Eds.) *Theoretical and applied aspects of eye movement research*. Amsterdam: Elsevier-North Holland.

Held, R., Ingle, D., Schneider, G. E., & Trevarten, C. B. (1967). Locating and identifying: two modes of visual information processing. *Psychologische Forschung, 31*, 44–62; 299–348.

Julesz, B. (1984). Toward an "axiomatic" theory of preattentive vision. In G. M. Edelman, W. E. Gall, & W. M. Cowan (Eds.), *Dynamic aspects of neocortical function*. New York: Wiley.

Helmholtz, H. von (1909) *Handbuch der physiologischen Optik*, 3. Auflage. Hamburg: Voss.

James, W. (1890). *The principles of psychology*. New York : Holt.

Jonides, J. (1980). Towards a model of the mind's eye movements. *Canadian Journal of Psychology, 34,* 103–112.

Kingstone, A., & Klein, R. M. (1993a). What are human express saccades? *Perception & Psychophysics, 40,* 431–273.

Kingstone, A., & Klein, R.M. (1993b). Visual offsets facilitate saccadic latency: Does predisengagement of visuospatial attention mediate this gap effect? *Journal of Experimental Psychology: Human Perception and Performance, 19,* 1251–1265.

Kahneman, D. (1973). *Attention and effort.* Englewood Cliffs, NJ: Prentice Hall.

LaBerge, D. (1981). Automatic information processing: A review. In J. Long & A. Baddeley (Eds), *Attention and Performance, 9,* 173-186. Hillsdale, NJ: Lawrence Erlbaum Associates.

Mackie, R. (1977). *Vigilance: Theory, operational performance, and physiological correlates.* New York: Plenum.

Magoun, H. W. (1963). *The waking brain.* Springfield: Thomas.

Marcel, A. J. (1983). Conscious and unconscious perception: An approach to the relations between phenomenal experience and perceptual processes. *Cognitive Psychology,15,* 238–302.

Menz, C., & Groner, R. (1987). Saccadic programming with multiple targets under different task conditions. In I. J. K. O'Regan & A. Lévy-Schoen (Eds.) *Eye movements: From physiology to cognition.* Amsterdam: Elsevier-North Holland.

Navon, D., & Gopher, D. (1979). On the economy of the human processing system. *Psychological Review, 86,* 214–255.

Neumann, O. (1996). Theorien der Aufmerksamkeit. In O. Neumann & A. F. Sanders (Hrsg.) *Aufmerksamkeit. Enzyklopädie der Psychologie C-II- 2,* 559–644. Göttingen : Hogrefe.

Norman, D.A. (1968) Towards a theory of memory and attention. *Psychological Review, 75,* 522–536.

Noton, D., & Stark, L. (1971a). Eye movements and visual perception. *Scientific American, 224,* 34–43.

Noton, D., & Stark, L. (1971b). Scanpaths in eye movements during pattern perception. *Science, 171,* 308–311.

Noton, D., & Stark, L. (1971c). Scanpaths in saccadic eye movements while viewing and recognizing patterns. *Vision Reasearch, 11,* 929–942.

Posner, M. I. (1978). *Chronometric explorations of mind.* Hillsdale, NJ : Lawrence Erlbaum Associates.

Posner, M. I. (1980). Orienting of attention. *Quarterly Journal of Experimental Psychology, 32,* 3–26.

Posner, M. I., & Snyder, C. R. R. (1975). Attention and cognitive control. In R. Solso (Ed.), *Information processing and cognition*: The Loyola symposium. Potomac: Lawrence Erlbaum Associates.

Postman, L., & Bruner, J. (1948). Perception under stress. *Psychological Review, 55,* 314–323.

Pribram, K. H., & McGuinness, D. (1975). Arousal, activation, and effort in the control of attention. *Psychological Review, 82,* 116–149.

Routtenberg, A. (1968). The two-arousal hypothesis: Reticular formation and limbic system. *Psychological Review, 75,* 51–80.

Sereno, A. B. (1992). Programming saccades: The role of attention. In K. Rayner (Ed.), *Eye movement and visual cognition,* 89–107. New York: Springer.

Sokolov, E. N. (1975). The neuronal mechanism of the orienting reflex. In E.N. Sokolov & O.S. Vinogradova (Eds.), *Neuronal mechanisms of the orienting reflex,* 217–238. New York: Wiley.

Stark, L., & Ellis, S. R. (1981). Scanpaths revisited: Cognitive models direct active looking. In D. F. Fisher, R. A. Monty & J. W. Senders (Eds.) *Eye movements: Cognition and visual perception.* Hillsdale, NJ: Lawrence Erlbaum Associates.

Treisman, A., & Gelade, G. (1980). A feature-integration theory of attention. *Cognitive Psychology, 12,* 97–136.

Trevarthen, C. B. (1968). Two mechanisms of vision in primates. *Psychologische Forschung, 31,* 299–337.

Ungerleider, L. G., & Mishkin, M. (1982). Two cortical visual systems. In D. J. Ingle, M. A. Goodale, & R. J. W. Mansfield (Eds.), *Two cortical visual systems.* Cambridge, MA: MIT Press.

Warm, J. S. (1984). *Sustained attention in human performance.* Chichester: Wiley.

Wickens, C. D. (1984). Processing ressources in attention. In R. Parasuraman & R. Davis (Eds.), *Varieties of attention,* 63–102. New York: Academic Press.

Wundt, W. (1903). *Grundzüge der physiologischen Psychologie, Band III.* 3. Auflage. Leipzig: Engelmann.

Wurtz, R., & Mohler, C. W. (1976). Organisation of monkey superior colliculus: Enhanced visual response of superficial layer cells. *Journal of Neurophysiology, 39,* 745–765.

Schneider, W., & Shiffrin, R. M. (1977). Controlled and automatic human information processing: I. Detection, search, and attention. *Psychological Review, 84,* 1–66.

Thayer, R. E. (1989). *The biopsychology of mood and arousal.* Oxford: Oxford University Press.

# 9

# The Control of Knowledge Activation
# in Discourse Comprehension

*Walter Kintsch*

Knowledge activation in discourse comprehension is uncannily accurate. As long as we stay on a familiar topic, the appropriate background knowledge that we need to interpret what we hear or read comes to us readily and without apparent effort. Even more amazing is what does not come to us: In each situation, there are numerous associated bits of information that are useless in this particular context and that could distract us—but somehow we manage not to think of these, we manage not to be swamped by this flood of intruding irrelevancies.

How does the mind achieve this miraculous adaptability? The classic answer is that control structures called schemata manage the information flow in comprehension, making sure that only contextually relevant knowledge and experiences are activated and filtering out whatever is not needed and not wanted. However, some researchers, including myself (e.g., Kintsch, 1988; 1998), have argued against this view, which is too inflexible to either account for human knowledge use or to provide a workable computational framework. An alternative possibility is to view knowledge activation as a two-stage process: a bottom-up construction process under local control that promiscuously generates a network of contextually relevant as well as irrelevant information, and an integration process that turns this network into a coherent mental representation, ridding it of the irrelevancies and contradictions that were originally included. This is achieved via a spreading activation, or constraint satisfaction process: Those pieces of knowledge that fit in with the text and each other are retained, while the others become deactivated. Hence the name construction-integration model.

The construction processes involved in knowledge activation are of two types: Automatic associative knowledge activation via retrieval structures, and controlled search processes that may be strategic, effortful, and resource demanding. Normal comprehension is characterized by automatic knowledge activation. When this process misfunctions, problem solving activity takes over, which may be quite extensive and demanding and may take an unpredictable variety of forms. I shall focus here on automatic knowledge activation.

Knowledge activation means that some item of information (the *cue*) in the comprehender's focus of attention (alias short-term memory or consciousness) retrieves (makes available in short-term working memory) an item of knowledge or personal experience from long-term memory. How this can happen automatically is explained by the theory of long-term working memory (Ericsson & Kintsch, 1995; Kintsch, 1998). If there exists a stable link in long-term memory between a cue and an item in long-term memory (a retrieval structure) this item is quickly and effortlessly accessible—it is part of what we have called long-term working memory. Hence, the capacity of working memory is greatly expanded: it consists not only of the strictly capacity limited short-term working memory, but also of the potentially much larger long-term working memory accessible via retrieval structures from cues held in short-term working memory. This expansion is conditional, however, on the existence of appropriate retrieval structures—memory structures that have to be acquired over long periods of time, with significant amounts of practice. Such structures are available only in domains where we are experts. For example, chess masters have developed retrieval structures for encoding chess games, scientists or medical doctors have retrieval structures that allow them to rapidly and reliably access their knowledge and experience in their domains of expertise. And we all have developed retrieval structures in the domain where we all are expert: everyday language use. These retrieval structures mediate knowledge activation in comprehension.

The first retrieval structure that was studied scientifically and in detail was one developed by a memory artist for the purpose of memorizing random strings of digits (Chase & Ericsson, 1981). Further examples of retrieval structures from a variety of domains are discussed in Ericsson and Kintsch (1995). The retrieval structures that permit automatic knowledge activation in everyday discourse comprehension are the very structures that the comprehender generates in comprehension, for the mental representation of a text that is the result of the comprehension process at the same time also functions as a retrieval structure. Thus, memory for text is incidental: the very act of comprehension ensures that we can remember what we have comprehended. Comprehension is structure–building, and the comprehension structure and the memory structure are one and the same.

Human knowledge can be conceptualized as a high-dimensional semantic space. Comprehending a text implies building a mental representation of this text that is embedded in this semantic space. The semantic space, then, functions as the retrieval structure that permits automatic access to relevant information: items of knowledge and experience close to the text structure in the semantic space are readily accessible, while more distant items require potentially resource demanding and time consuming search processes. How we can approximate this semantic space via Latent Semantic Analysis (LSA), is described below.

## KNOWLEDGE STRUCTURE AND THE LSA SPACE

Human knowledge is the result of our interaction with the world. The nature of that interaction is constrained by the nature of the human body and human mind. Human knowledge contains information at different levels of representation, starting with the level of action and sensory experience which we share with some animals, to linguistically coded information and the abstract-symbolical level which are distinctly human. Language has come to be a dominant factor in the way human knowledge is encoded and structured. It is certainly not the case that all human knowledge is linguistic, but much of what we know is indeed represented linguistically, either because the original information was in linguistic form or because we have recoded linguistically a type of experience that was non-linguistic to begin with: an action, sensation, emotion, or abstraction. Thus, while human knowledge may take on many forms, linguistic representations play a particularly important role. While I can do no more here than briefly summarize these claims about the nature of knowledge representations, the arguments and the literature for and against this view have been discussed in some detail in Kintsch (1998).

How can such a knowledge based system be modeled? Since it is too large and too opaque for hand coding, the only way would be to design an algorithm that acquires knowledge through experience in the way humans do. However, because computers are, by nature, very different from humans, they cannot interact with the world and learn from it in the way humans do. I see no solution to this dilemma.

There is a solution, however, to a more limited problem. Suppose we model not all of human knowledge, but only its linguistically encoded component, or more precisely, only that part of human knowledge that is reflected in written language. While this is undoubtedly a nontrivial restriction, the portion of human knowledge that is representable by the written word is a large one. It does not comprise all knowledge, and the written representation may sometimes introduce distortions—but if we could successfully model this section of human knowledge, this would be a major advance. LSA permits us to do so.

LSA is a fully-automatic computer method for the construction of a knowledge representation in the form of a high-dimensional semantic space based on the analysis of a large corpus of written text. The computer reads a large amount of text—several millions of word tokens—consisting of many thousands of documents and many thousands of word types. From this input it constructs a huge word-by-document matrix, the entries of which are the frequencies with which each word type appeared in each document. Thus, word co-occurrences are the input to LSA. This input is processed and transformed in two ways: first, through the mathematical technique of singular value decomposition, and then through dimension reduction. Singular value decomposition is a technique which allows one to express any matrix as the product of three matrices, one of those being the singular values matrix. If one multiplies the three matrices together, one simply gets back the original one. But we do not want the original matrix of word co-occurrences, because that matrix contains too much information. The fact that an author used this particular word in this particular place is not important; rather, we want to know what kinds of words could be used in that place. In other words, we want to represent the basic meaning relationships, not particular word choices. LSA achieves that through dimension reduction: It throws away

most of the information it has computed and retains only the information associated with the approximately 400 largest singular values of the matrix. Thus, it
keeps the essence of the semantic relationships in the texts it has read, but dis-
cards the incidental and irrelevant detail.

The rationale for this analysis and its details are described elsewhere (Deerwester, Dumais, Furnas, Landauer, & Harshman, 1990; Landauer & Dumais,
1997; Landauer, Foltz, & Laham, in press). Here, I give only a simple example
to indicate the flavor of this method. For instance, in a large corpus of texts, the
singular and plural forms of a noun are not very highly correlated: in general,
when we talk about a particular *mountain* we do not also talk about *mountains* in
the same context, and vice versa. Thus, the correlation between *mountain* and
*mountains* is probably low in the texts that LSA reads, perhaps around r = .1 or
.2; after dimension reduction, however, this correlation is much higher (r = .84 in
this case): LSA has inferred that *mountain* and *mountains* are closely related
semantically (though are by no means identical).

Although LSA starts with word co-occurrences (much like a child listening to
an adult's speech), it infers from these a space that reflects the meaning relationships among words and sentences, no longer their co-occurrences. The result of
dimension reduction is an abstract knowledge space representing the structure of
the information underlying the texts it had read.

Having constructed a high-dimensional semantic space of typically 300-400
dimensions in this way, we can express words, sentences, and whole texts as
vectors in that space, with all the advantages this mathematical representation
affords. That is, we can readily compute the semantic relatedness of vectors in
terms of the cosine (a measure that can be interpreted much like the familiar
correlation coefficient), and we can find out what other vectors are located in the
semantic neighborhood we are interested in. For instance, around *mountain* we
find *peaks, rugged, ridges,* and *climber,* whereas around *mountains* we find
*peaks, rugged, plateaus,* and *foothills.* This is the kind of information we need to
model knowledge activation in comprehension.

## KNOWLEDGE ACTIVATION AS SAMPLING
## FROM A SEMANTIC NEIGHBORHOOD

According to the construction–integration model of text comprehension (Kintsch,
1988; 1998) knowledge activation is a bottom-up, associative process, followed
by contextual integration. LSA permits us to model the bottom-up associative
component of this two-stage process objectively and in detail. We assume that
the LSA space is the retrieval structure within which automatic knowledge activation in comprehension takes place. (Controlled knowledge activation will not
be considered here.)

Specifically, each word in a text will activate associated knowledge by random sampling from its semantic neighborhood. Sampling probabilities are proportional to the cosine between the source vector and the target vectors.[1]

Propositions, in addition to words, also activate knowledge from their semantic neighborhood, in the same way as words do. For LSA, propositions are disambiguated and appropriately parsed word groups. Examples will be described later in the chapter.

Macro-units of a text can also be represented as vectors in the LSA space. Indeed, once a text has been parsed into its constituent words and propositions, the vector representing the text as a whole is simply the centroid of the constituent vectors. Thus, the macrostructure of the text is given for free as soon as the text's microstructure has been computed (assuming that the appropriate macro-units are clearly signaled in the text). Hence macro-units can also participate in the knowledge activation process, exactly as words and propositions do. Indeed, items activated from the neighborhood of macro-units will usually turn out to be particularly important for the final interpretation of the text (the situation model that is constructed from the text), because they will tend to be widely interconnected. In contrast, locally activated knowledge items may become deactivated in the integration process if they are not linked to other items in the text.

How much knowledge elaboration does occur in comprehension? Technically speaking, how many items are sampled from the semantic neighborhood of each text unit? These are not questions that can be answered in general. Reader activity will depend on many factors. In the extreme case of no elaboration, the resulting mental representation of the text will be a pure textbase; if a substantial amount of knowledge elaboration occurs, the mental representation is called a *situation model*, in the terminology of Kintsch (1998).

Once a textbase has been constructed and knowledge has been activated in the manner described above, a constraint-satisfaction or integration process takes over according to the construction-integration model. Integration ensures that only related items play a role in the final knowledge representation, and that all the irrelevant and contradictory information that necessarily has been included in the bottom-up construction process is rejected.

There are two kinds of links in the network that has been constructed at this point: text links and knowledge links. Text links result from linguistic information in the text. For example, propositions that share a common argument (word concept) are related, or propositions that are explicitly linked by a sentence connective. In addition, there are the semantic links between texts units, between text units and retrieved knowledge units, and among the retrieved knowledge units

---

[1]In order to focus the sampling process on the most related items one might consider making sampling probabilities proportional to the square, or even the cube, of the cosine. Thus, distantly related items could be neglected in modeling the retrieval process.

themselves. Text links must be weighted more heavily than semantic links in modeling the integration phase so as not to distort the meaning of the text.

## SOME ILLUSTRATIVE EXAMPLES

To illustrate the control of knowledge activation according to the CI model, consider a simple sentence like

*The band played a waltz.*

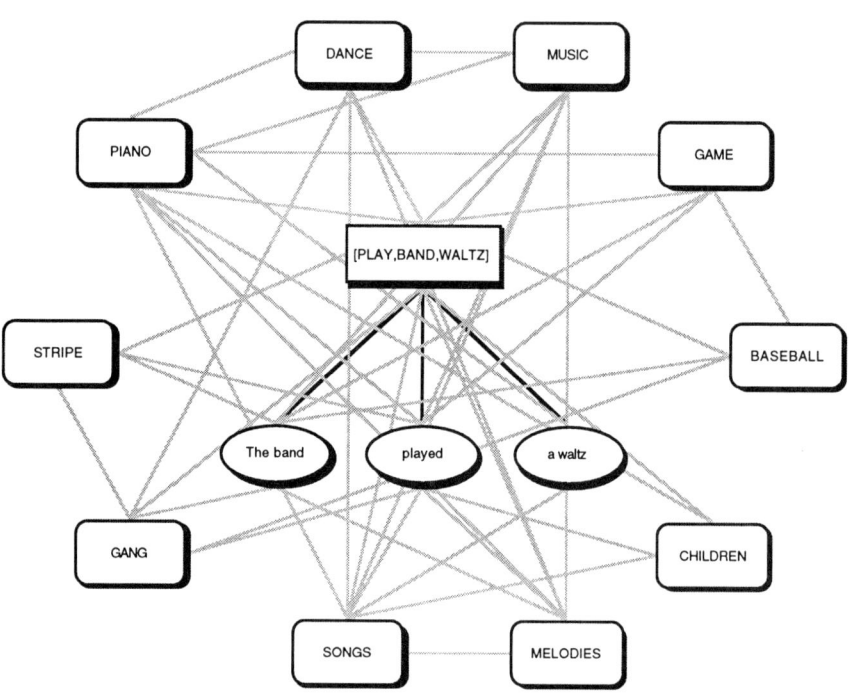

*FIG. 9.1. Knowledge activation for the sentence The band played a waltz. Words are enclosed by ovals, the underlying proposition by a rectangle, and the concepts retrieved from long-term memory by rounded rectangles. Only links above a certain strength are shown.*

According to the CI model, we first construct a network representing the sentence itself as well as the items of knowledge that were retrieved from long-term memory by the text elements. Figure 9.1 shows the three word groups that make up the sentence as well as the corresponding proposition. I have also indicated knowledge activation in figure 9.1: three close neighbors for each of the four original sentence constituents were selected (with some overlap, so that the total number of items is less than 12) and connected to their sources and each other with links whose strengths were set equal to the cosines of the corresponding vector pairs in the LSA space. The links between the three content words and the proposition node, on the other hand, were assigned a strength value of 1 to make sure that they will dominate the resulting network. Note that the network thus constructed contains relevant (e.g., *dance*) as well as irrelevant (e.g. *game*) nodes. After integration, however, the irrelevant nodes are deactived (their activation values are low), while the relevant knowledge items as well as the original sentence constituents remain strongly activated, as seen in figure 9.2. A network with strength values as in figure 9.2 would be the situation model the CI model has formed, given that the LSA space functions as the retrieval structure and given that the particular knowledge items were sampled as in figure 9.1. We can express this situation model as a vector in the LSA space, too: The vector representation of the sentence is the centroid of all the component vectors, weighted by the activation values shown in figure 9.2.

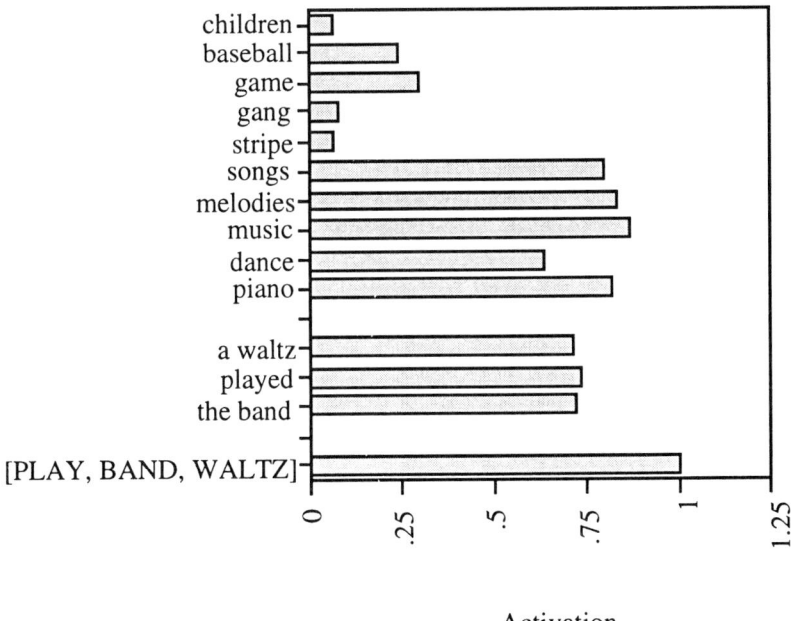

Activation

FIG. 9.2. Final activation values for the nodes in figure 9.1.

Now consider the two-sentence mini-text:

*The band played a waltz. Mary loved to dance.*

There are no direct links between these two sentences, but the sentences are nevertheless indirectly coherent (Kintsch, 1998). LSA lets us assign a non-arbitrary value to the coherence link between these two sentences, the cosine between their corresponding vectors, which turns out to be .45 in this case. No inference is required to connect these sentences: the very fact that they both are situated in the same semantic space provides a link of a certain strength between them.

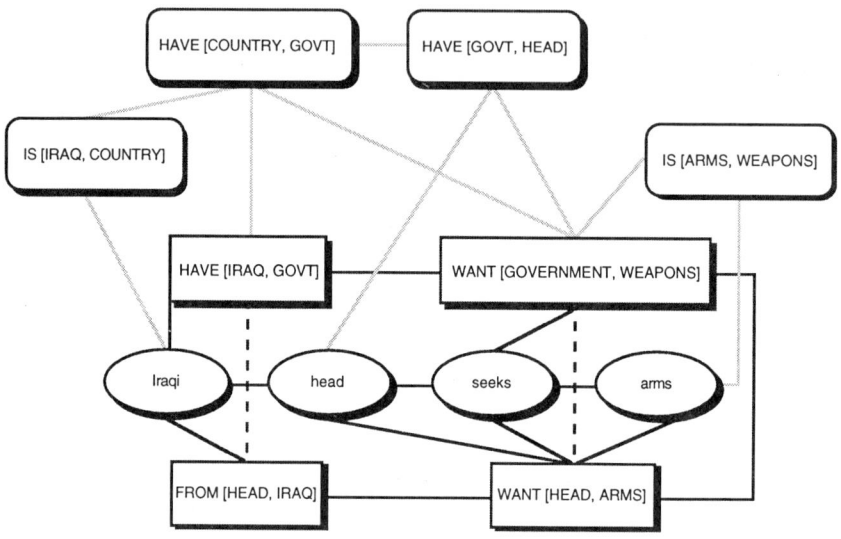

FIG. 9.3. The sentence "Iraqi head seeks arms" with two opposing propositional interpretations and bridging inferences. Words are enclosed by ovals, the propositions by rectangles, and inferred propositions by rounded rectangles.

A slightly more complex case, the often-cited newspaper headline *Iraqi head seeks arms* is shown in figure 9.3. There are two propositional interpretations[2] of this sentence: *A head from Iraq seeks arms*, which does not make any sense, and *The government of Iraq wants weapons*, which is the intended meaning. The two propositional interpretations interfere with each other (the broken lines indicate a link strength of -1). If the network consisting only of the sentence and the two antagonistic propositions is integrated, neither interpretation wins out. Further-more, the process of associative knowledge elaboration, in this case, fails to

---

[2]In figure 9.1 the proposition was not really needed—the sentence itself would have served just as well. In general, propositions are needed to clarify the psychologically most relevant meaning relations in complex or ambiguous sentences, neglecting, however, some semantic and syntactic detail.

disambiguate this sentence. If we add, as in figure 9.1, three associates from the neighborhood of each node (not shown in figure 9.3), the integration process is not helped. What is needed in this case is a more directed inference process: Not only the propositions shown in rectangular boxes must be constructed as part of the original parsing process, but also the intermediate propositions shown in the rounded-off rectangles that provide the missing links between the words and the eventual propositions (*Iraq is a country; countries have governments; governments have heads*, etc.). If these inferences are included in the network, the network settles on the intended interpretation: the *want-government-weapons* proposition receives a final activation value of .89, the *have-Iraq-government* proposition ends up with .66, and both unintended propositions receive an activation value of zero.

## CONCLUSION

The two examples discussed here illustrate both how the control of knowledge activation can be modeled with LSA providing the knowledge representation and the CI model the comprehension process. In the first example the LSA-CI model provided a good account of the process of knowledge activation. However, as the second example shows, this is not always sufficient: Sometimes the process of bottom-up associative knowledge elaboration must be supplemented by more a goal-directed inference process to generate a coherent representation of a text. LSA is a model of knowledge representation and it must be combined with theories that specify the precise processes that operate on this representation. The CI model—specified in detail in Kintsch (1998)—is one such process theory, but to completely model human thinking and language understanding, more than that will be required—for instance, an explicit account of how sentences are parsed in the first place, as well as the analytic, goal–directed problem solving that is involved in the formation of inferences in text comprehension.

In spite of these reservations and limitations, it is worth pointing out that the CI model and LSA together provide a serious and testable account of many of the phenomena of knowledge activation, and the control of knowledge activation, in human understanding.

## REFERENCES

Chase, W. G., & Ericsson, K. A. (1981). Skilled memory. In J. R. Anderson (Eds.), *Cognitive skills and their acquisition.* Hillsdale, NJ: Lawrence Erlbaum Associates.

Deerwester, S., Dumais, S. T., Furnas, G. W., Landauer, T. K., & Harshman, R. (1990). Indexing by Latent Semantic Analysis. *Journal of the American Society for Information Science, 41*, 391–407.

Ericsson, K. A., & Kintsch, W. (1995). Long-term working memory. *Psychological Review, 102*, 211–245.

Kintsch, W. (1988). The use of knowledge in discourse processing: A construction-integration model. *Psychological Review, 95*, 163–182.

Kintsch, W. (1998). *Comprehension: A paradigm for cognition.* New York: Cambridge University Press.

Landauer, T. K., & Dumais, S. T. (1997). A solution to Plato's problem: The Latent Semantic Analysis theory of acquisition, induction and representation of knowledge. *Psychological Review, 104*, 211–240.

Landauer, T. K., Foltz, P., & Laham, D. (in press). An introduction to Latent Semantic Analysis. *Discourse Processes.*

# 10

# Working Memory and Attentional Control[1]

*Anik de Ribaupierre*

## INTRODUCTION

The first question that can be asked is "Why address the concept of working memory in a book whose general topic is that of control?" As will be apparent throughout this book, the concept of control can be used very differently. One of these uses, in cognitive psychology, consists in speaking of "controlled processes." It would lead us too far to discuss in detail the concept of controlled processes in this chapter, all the more as a whole section of this book is devoted to this issue; it suffices to say that they have often been considered to be synonymous with conscious, or attentional, or effortful processes, while being opposed to automatic processes.[2] The common characteristic of all these quasi-synonyms is that they involve limited resources. This is also the main defining property of working memory (WM). Indeed, although WM is defined differently in different models, there is a general consensus that it is a system with very limited resources, for temporarily maintaining and processing information for use in other cognitive tasks. Thus, the essential characteristic of WM is not so much its memory (or storage) component, but the fact that it consists in temporarily

[1]This paper is in part based on research made possible by a grant from the Fonds National Suisse de la Recherche Scientifique (grant no 14-040465.94). I would like to thank Laurence Poget, as well as our two editors, Alexander Grob and Walter Perrig, for their useful comments.

[2]Automatic processes are considered to be fast processes, operating in parallel, requiring no attentional capacity, and placed under the control of stimuli rather than intention. This definition is often post hoc and circular (see Jacoby, Ste-Marie, & Toth, 1993). Indeed, as soon as results tend to attest to serial processing, or to age effects (e.g., Hasher & Zacks, 1979), it will be concluded that controlled processes are also at work. Jacoby has suggested a procedure, the process dissociation procedure, to overcome this circularity effect, by considering that all tasks require automatic and controlled processes, albeit in a different weight, rather than assigning processes to tasks in a one-to-one correspondence. Therefore, he suggests that the best possible way to disentangle them is to devise tasks where they work in concert, and tasks in which they work in opposition.

holding information on line, while being severely limited; much work has been devoted to examining the limits of these resources (working memory capacity), particularly among developmentalists.

Although research on WM finds its origins in memory approaches, and more particularly short-term memory, at least as concerns adult cognitive psychology, it can now be considered to lie at the confluent of different streams of research, as indicated by the title of this chapter: memory research, research on attention, and research on controlled vs. automatic processes. Moreover, as will be developed below, WM is also of interest for the study of executive functions, another somewhat fuzzy, but rapidly extending, concept.

A perhaps more direct indication that WM is closely linked to controlled processes and to the field of attention in general, is the suggestion made by Baddeley (1986) that the Central Executive (i.e., one subcomponent of his model of WM) acts as an "attentional controller". Moreover, Baddeley (1993) has considered the possibility to relabel Working Memory as Working Attention. Similarly, developmentalists, in particular neopiagetians, have used almost indifferently the concept of working memory or that of attentional capacity. Generally speaking, the idea that attentional resources are limited, and that this limitation can be assessed with some measure of memory span is not new and dates back at least to the end of the 19th century.

This chapter will be devoted to reviewing a few models of WM, which all consider that WM is an attentional system. After a brief definition, four different models of WM will be considered, each of which is anchored in a different research tradition[3] while nevertheless emphasizing the relation of WM with attention and controlled processes: (a) Baddeley's model of WM, grounded in adult, experimental psychology; here, the emphasis will be on the Central Executive subcomponent, (b) Engle's work on WM as an activation/inhibition resource hypothesis that finds its origin in an individual differences approach, (c) Pascual-Leone's developmental model of mental attention, and (d) neuropsychological models of executive functions such as Robert and Pennington's. Although these models may first appear to be very different from one another, whether from a methodological or from a theoretical point of view, it will be argued, in the conclusion, that they present a large degree of theoretical overlap. It is only fitting, in a book dedicated to August Flammer, that such a broad perspective be adopted. Indeed, during his fruitful career, August has worked in a number of

---

[3]The classification used here is somewhat arbitrary, because the frontiers between the different approaches are not all that clear. For instance, the experimental model of WM has, in good part, been based on neuropsychological findings; likewise, Engle's approach, classified as individual differences, could just as well be characterized as an experimental approach. Moreover, developmental approaches, in particular aging ones, will also be mentioned in the other sections.

areas, and has attempted to coordinate experimental psychology with differential and developmental psychology.

## CONSENSUAL DEFINITION OF WORKING MEMORY

As mentioned above, WM is defined as a system, or a set of processes, that serve to process and maintain temporary information for use in other cognitive tasks. There are clearly two different perspectives, those that consider that WM is a memory "system" in the sense of constituting a distinct structural component, and those that suggest that WM only consists in a temporarily activated subset of long-term memory. Baddeley's model can be classified in the first group. Likewise, Schacter and Tulving (1994) propose that WM, or primary memory, is one of five different memory systems. In contrast, other authors (e.g., Cowan, 1988; Ericsson & Kintsch, 1995) suggest that WM designates only either an activated subset of long-term memory, or a set of processes at work in WM tasks. For instance, Moscovitch (1994) proposes that WM would be more appropriately labeled as "working with memory." Pascual-Leone's model, which will be discussed here, also belongs to this latter perspective. Still other authors, such as Daneman and Carpenter (1980), have not discussed whether WM constitute a separate system, and are satisfied with an operational definition of WM as a combination of processing and storage.

Richardson (1996) has recently summarized different approaches by a number of theoretical statements, some of which are certainly still open to controversy. Nevertheless this sets the stage for a presentation of different WM models. The propositions are the following:

1.  Working memory is a *complex system*[4] responsible for the storage and processing of information;
2.  WM is structurally and functionally distinct from the different forms of permanent and long-term memory. As already mentioned, this point is probably the most controversial. A statement according to which the processes at work in WM tasks are not the same as those underlying long-term memory would probably be more appropriate.
3.  The contents of WM consist in a set of representations that are currently being activated by interpretive processes in long-term memory.
4.  *The capacity of WM is constrained* by limitations in the amount of activation that can be distributed and by limited attentional resources available to activate and maintain task-relevant information, while inhibiting task-irrelevant information. Obviously, there is here a distinction (also apparent in Engle's work, see below) between an automatic and an attentional type of activation.

---

[4]The emphasis is mine.

5. The core of the system is a *central processor*, involved in a wide variety of executive functions.
6. Some of the storage functions of the Central Executive (CE) can be discharged to auxiliary subsystems.
7. WM is fundamental in understanding intellectual performance; in laboratory tasks as well as in everyday situations.

## BADDELEY'S MODEL OF THE CENTRAL EXECUTIVE

Baddeley and Hitch (1974) suggested a tripartite model, consisting of two subsidiary and slave systems (the phonological loop and the visuo-spatial sketchpad, responsible for the holding and manipulation of verbal and visuo-spatial information, respectively), and of a coordinating component, the CE. In 1986, Baddeley, drawing after Norman and Shallice's model of attentional control, suggested that the CE functions as an attentional controller.

Baddeley (1993) makes it clear that attention, in this context, means *integration of information and control of action*, in contrast with *perceptual selection*, which is the focus of study in many models of attention. Although the distinction is not always very easy to draw, clearly the CE is concerned with the former type of control. Likewise, Shallice & Burgess (1993) distinguish attentional control of cognitive processes from attentional control of perceptual processes. According to Norman and Shallice (1980; quoted in Baddeley, 1986; Shallice, 1982), control of cognitive processes or of ongoing action can be further decomposed in two hierarchized mechanisms. The *Contention Scheduling* mechanism involves selection among well–learned competing schemas. The *Supervisory Attentional System* (SAS), serves to cope with novelty, and modulates the action of contention scheduling by additional activation and/or inhibition of certain schemas. This supervisory system is considered necessary in five types of situations, which can be identified by different types of tasks: planning or decision-making, correction of errors, novelty, technical difficulty (or dangerous situations), and overcoming of a strong habitual response.

For a number of years, the CE remained a sort of global entity, or even a "black box." Most empirical studies within Baddeley's model concentrated on demonstrating the functioning of the phonological loop, or the independence of the two slave systems. The CE was invoked when the two slave systems were not sufficient to account for the data, in particular when performances in dual tasks showed larger impairment than that predicted on the basis of either slave system alone.

This was particularly true of performances in visuo-spatial tasks, leading a number of researchers to suggest that the visuo-spatial sketchpad is less independent from the CE than the phonological loop (e.g., Logie & Marchetti, 1991; Morris, 1987; Quinn, 1991). However, Baddeley (1993, 1996) suggested recently that the CE should be further fractionated into a number of component functions:

1. The capacity to coordinate performance on separate tasks, capacity which seems to be particularly impaired in Alzheimer's patients (Baddeley et al., 1991; Baddeley & DellaSala, 1996);
2. The capacity to switch retrieval plans or strategies. The example most often offered by Baddeley is that of the random generation task, in which subjects have to generate rapidly a random sequence of letters or numbers. This task has often been used as a concurrent, secondary task, to examine its effect on a verbal task, a visuo-spatial task, or a complex cognitive task. A task such as the Wisconsin Card Sorting Task, almost routinely used in neuropsychological studies, could probably be placed in the same category;
3. The capacity to attend to a stimulus and inhibit the interfering aspect of others; in this case, Baddeley refers to tasks in which subjects have to process visually presented stimuli while ignoring other stimuli presented concurrently.[5]
4. The capacity to activate and retrieve information from long-term memory. This last function was considered by Baddeley to correspond to the accounts offered by Hasher et al. (Hasher, Stoltzfus, Zacks, & Rypma, 1991; Hasher & Zacks, 1988), or by Engle (1996), in terms of selective attention.

This classification was described by Baddeley as four approaches toward a fractionation of the CE; they tend nevertheless to be interpreted as four functions, resulting in a certain confusion between tasks and processes. I would like to argue that they can best be summarized by saying that they essentially call for three types of processes: *Activation* (general definition of working memory, and functions 1 and 2 above), *inhibition* (functions 3 and 4), and executive processes such as planning or coordinating (functions 1 and 2), in the sense of Pascual-Leone's executive schemes (Pascual-Leone, Goodman, Ammon, & Subelman, 1978; see below), or Sternberg's metacomponents (Sternberg, 1983). I would further suggest that these three sets of processes are at work in all the complex WM tasks, although their relative weight might vary. Such a definition brings the CE component very close to the North American tradition of WM research, as well as to neuropsychological studies of executive functions.

---

[5]It should be noted that this type of task is very close to the tasks used in studies of attention considered by Baddeley (1993, see above) as dealing with the control of perceptual processes, showing that the line between these two types of attention is rather difficult to draw.

## INDIVIDUAL DIFFERENCES IN WM AND ATTENTIONAL RESOURCES: THE EXAMPLE OF ENGLE'S STUDIES

Most of the North American research on WM in adults has been concerned with individual differences in the capacity of WM and their predictive power with respect to other cognitive tasks, following initial work by Daneman and Carpenter (1980).[6] It has indeed been shown that WM capacity is associated with performance in a wide variety of cognitive tasks, such as reading and listening comprehension, vocabulary, or complex learning, in young adults as well as in children or in older adults. Also, most North American researchers have, implicitly or explicitly, acknowledged that their conception of WM is equivalent to Baddeley's idea of a central executive. Among them, Engle and his colleagues have made a number of proposals, the most recent of which are perhaps of greatest interest for the present chapter. They first proposed a *General Capacity Theory*, according to which the relationships between WM capacity and higher level cognitive tasks are mediated by a general mechanism of *activation* (Cantor & Engle, 1993; Conway & Engle, 1996; Engle, Cantor, & Carullo, 1992). WM is defined as a subset of long-term memory, and the contents of WM consist of either temporary or permanent memory units that are active above some threshold. Because individuals differ as to the amount of activation available to their systems, individual differences are accounted for in terms of the number of memory units that are activated. In this theory, activation was considered to spread quickly, almost automatically, and without conscious or controlled attention.

This theoretical proposal was backed up by a number of empirical studies, attesting not only to the generality of WM by means of between-task relationships (Engle et al., 1992), but also showing that activation seemed indeed to spread more quickly in high-span subjects, that is, in subjects with higher WM capacity. For instance, low-span subjects presented a larger fan effect; this result was interpreted as showing that they had less activation available to spread among the different items.

In a Sternberg-type task of speeded recognition, the slope relating set size with recognition time was steeper in low-span subjects, pointing again to a smaller amount of activation available. Likewise, verbal fluency, considered to reflect semantic activation, was lower in low-span subjects.

However, in the same set of studies, Engle et al. also suggested that high- and low-span subjects differ less in the amount of automatic activation than in terms of controlled attention. Using modifications of the tasks just mentioned, they showed that high-span subjects were superior to low-span subjects essen-

---

[6]It is interesting to point out that the Reading Span task proposed by Daneman and Carpenter (1980) and considered as one of the first valid measures of the capacity of WM, was partly modeled after Case's Counting Span task (e.g., Case, Kurland, & Goldberg, 1982). This points to a greater similarity of the different approaches than is usually thought.

tially when some type of inhibition was called for. For instance, Conway and Engle (1994) observed that the difference in slope initially observed, in a speeded recognition task, between high- and low-span subjects, disappeared when each of the stimulus was used only once across the task. Repeating the same stimuli (e.g., digits), in different associations may indeed create interference effects, since some associations are irrelevant in a given trial and have to be suppressed. As an example, presenting a set of digits such as 924 and asking whether the digit 7 belongs to the set proved to be a more difficult task if the digit 7 was associated with 2 and/or 4 (e.g., 724) in a preceding trial than if any of the digits was presented only once; in the former case, the association which was formed between the digits 7, 4, and 2 has to be inhibited. Overlap in set membership had an effect on the low-span subjects only, who were considerably slowed when a same stimulus belonged to different sets; this result points to a more controlled processing in the high-span subjects, who appear to be better able to resist to irrelevant associations. In the same vein, using a verbal fluency task in a dual condition (combining retrieval of animal names with responding to digits, or with a preload condition) had an effect on high-span subjects only (Engle, 1996), as if these subjects process the task in a more controlled, attentional way. The interpretation goes as follows: If they are free to assign their attentional resources to processing the primary task (verbal fluency in this case), high-span subjects reach high performances; when their attentional resources have to be divided, as in the dual task, their performances in the primary task decline. In contrast, because they process the primary task in a less controlled way, low-span subjects are not as sensitive to a situation calling for division of attention.

These different studies, as well as others (e.g., Engle, 1996; Engle, Conway, Tuholski, & Shisler, 1995) led Engle to replace the General Capacity Theory by an *Inhibition-Resource Hypothesis*, according to which high- and low-span subjects differ in terms of controlled or central-executive processes. High-span subjects are considered to engage in a more controlled processing than low-span subjects in a number of tasks, resulting in higher performances. It is not clear, at this point, whether Engle suggests that high-span subjects have more attentional resources available, or whether they merely choose to engage in more deliberate strategies. Also it should be remarked that the performances of the high-span subjects remained superior, even in the non interfering tasks; this shows probably that a hypothesis in terms of individual differences in amount of activation should not be totally dismissed. In any case, these studies clearly demonstrate a strong link between attentional processes and working memory. Engle's proposal that individual differences would be most clearly revealed in tasks involving some level of interference is also congruent with proposals made by developmentalists or by cognitive aging researchers, that inhibitory processes play an important part in cognitive changes with age (e.g., Bjorklund & Harnishfeger, 1990; Harnishfeger & Bjorklund, 1994; Hasher et al., 1991), whether in general cognition or in WM.

## PASCUAL-LEONE'S MODEL OF MENTAL ATTENTION

Pascual-Leone's model of mental attention was developed in the context of the Piagetian theory, to account for cognitive development, and initiated the so-called *neopiagetian perspective* (e.g., Case, 1992).

Although distinct from one another, the different neopiagetian approaches share nevertheless common postulates (e.g., Case, 1995; de Ribaupierre, 1997), in particular with respect to attentional capacity: Limits in attentional capacity or in WM[7] impose severe constraints on cognitive performances and are of a general nature, in the sense of operating across a broad range of situations. These limits increase with age, due both to maturational and to experiential factors. In turn, this increase can be considered to be a causal factor of cognitive development. The limits in attentional capacity define general stages; the concept of stage corresponds here not so much to the type and form of behavior observed within a given age range, but rather to the complexity of the maximal performances which can be achieved. Indeed, all neopiagetians, although perhaps not to the same extent, stress the importance of individual and situational variability, the upper limit of which is set by the limits in WM. Most models have focused on WM capacity and its assessment in order to study its predictive power with respect to cognitive development. Pascual-Leone's model is certainly, among the neopiagetian models, the one that addressed in most details the functional characteristics of WM, in addition to its capacity. Given the breadth and the complexity of the model, it will only be very cursorily summarized, with a focus on the definition of mental attention that it offers.

Pascual-Leone's model is multidimensional (i.e., suggests that there are a number of independent, underlying mechanisms that function as activators, or possibly deactivators, of schemes) and offers a dynamic view of processing (e.g., Pascual-Leone, 1970, 1983, 1990; Pascual-Leone & Ijaz, 1989). Three nested levels of activation are described. Firstly, when an input arrives, a number of schemes (defined as information-carrying functional units or structures) are activated in the repertoire, via their own propensity to be activated and via affective operators; this is referred to as the general field of activation, denoted H\*. Second, a subset of more highly activated schemes is created, by means of relevant executive schemes and of a number of silent mechanisms, whose role is to activate (deactivate) schemes. This subset is sometimes labeled WM by Pascual-Leone (e.g., Pascual-Leone & Baillargeon, 1994; Pascual-Leone & Ijaz, 1989); thus, in this model, WM merely reflects a subset of the subject's repertoire of schemes which is highly activated by a number of factors. Third, and depending whether

---

[7]Different, albeit very similar concepts have been used by neopiagetian researchers, such as working memory, attentional capacity (Chapman, 1987), M- space or M-power (Pascual-Leone, 1987), Short-Term Storage Space (STSS) (Case, 1985), processing space or resources (Halford, 1993). They all point to the fact that processing resources are very limited, and increase with age.

the situation is misleading,[8] some activated schemes must be actively inhibited, while others require supplementary activation. This last subset defines the *field of Mental Attention*. Mental attention, in this model, is not unitary but consists of three mechanisms:

1. the *M operator* that serves to boost task-relevant schemes which are not directly activated by the display or by other mechanisms. M-capacity, or *M-power*, is a limited resource that increases, up until adolescence, in a stage-wise manner;
2. an inhibition mechanism, the *I-operator*, which is responsible for actively inhibiting or interrupting less relevant or irrelevant schemes. This operator is considered to be important in the management of attention, ensuring that schemes activated by M become dominant and determine performance;
3. executive schemes, recently labeled the *E-operator*, which consists of a set of plans of actions and regulatory controls directing the mental process.

A fourth operator, the *F operator*, is considered to be important for the selection of action in attentional processing. Its function is to produce as performance a single integrated whole, by activating the set of schemes that is both minimally complex and maximally adaptive.

Most empirical studies conducted within Pascual-Leone's model have been developmental in nature, addressing the increase of the M operator with age as well as the predictivity of *M*-capacity measures with respect to performances in complex cognitive tasks. As concerns the relationship between WM and attentional control, which is the topic of this chapter, Pascual-Leone's model makes a number of important and interesting suggestions. First, neither WM nor mental attention are unitary constructs, but correspond to the combined activation of several processes. Second, WM should not simply be equated with mental attention (defined in a strict sense, as controlled attention), but includes it as a subset. This is why we have suggested elsewhere (de Ribaupierre & Bailleux, 1994) that WM in Pascual-Leone's model corresponds to Baddeley's three subsystems of WM, while the field of mental attention seems to correspond to the Central Executive. Third, precise developmental predictions have been made with respect to the increase of the field of mental attention with age. Finally, this model also makes it possible to combine a developmental with a differential perspective.

---

[8]Misleading situations are those in which different silent operators activate incompatible sets of schemes, one of which is often more highly activated while leading to an incorrect solution. A good example is the piagetian tasks of conservation, in which a perceptual dimension (such as length in the task of conservation of substance, in which a ball of plasticine has been transformed into a sausage) is highly activated and competes with a correct response based on invariance. In contrast, in facilitating situations, different sets of schemes are activated which all concur to a correct solution.

From a developmental perspective, a number of operators, such as $M$ and $I$, are hypothesized to grow in an endogenous manner with age; the $E$-operator and the whole repertoire of schemes also grow with age, both quantitatively and qualitatively (that is, they become more complex), but under the influence of experiential factors, as well as in interaction with the endogenous increase of $M$. From a differential perspective, the relative weight of some operators, in particular the $F$- and $C$-operators, varies across individuals (e.g., Pascual-Leone, 1989; de Ribaupierre, 1989).

## WORKING MEMORY AND EXECUTIVE FUNCTIONS

The study of executive functions finds its origins in neuropsychology to account for the impaired behavior presented by frontal patients, so much so that the term executive functions (or tasks) is often used interchangeably with that of *frontal* or *prefrontal functions* (or tasks). Although there is no clear theoretical definition of what executive functions exactly entail, there is a general consensus that (a) they consist of a (possibly consciously) controlled behavior, (b) they enable a person to engage in independent, purposive self-serving behavior (Lezak, 1995), (c) they are particularly drawn on in novel tasks, and (d) they are subserved by prefrontal functions, although they can also call upon different regions of the brain. There is no space in the present chapter to develop this large and somewhat fuzzy domain of study (e.g., Eslinger, 1996). It suffices to mention that different components have been defined, such as volition, planning, purposive action, and effective performance (Lezak, 1995), or such as planning, execution, self-regulation, maintenance, spatiotemporal segmentation, and sustained mental productivity (Daigneault, Braun, & Whitaker, 1992; Rabbitt, 1997).

The theoretical overlap of executive functions with attention is thus considerable (e.g., Morris, 1996), all the more as there has been recently an increasing interest for the study of executive functions in non–patient populations on the part of experimentalists or developmentalists. Moreover, and of interest to this chapter, recent models have also linked executive functions with WM. This is of course the case of Baddeley's model as was discussed here.[9] This is also the case of recent theories and computational models that attempt to provide a more unified account of frontal or prefrontal functioning (Cohen & Servan-Schreiber, 1992; Fuster, 1997).

These models suggest that, in addition to serving a coordinative function, prefrontal processes consist of the ability to maintain and manipulate short-term information needed for generating upcoming action (working memory) and the ability to inhibit inappropriate action (Roberts & Pennington, 1996). According

---

[9]Baddeley (e.g., 1986, 1996) has guarded against the danger of identifying the central executive with the frontal functions, and suggested to replace the structural, neuroanatomical concept of a frontal syndrome, with the functional concept of a dysexecutive syndrome.

to Pennington et al. (Pennington, Bennetto, McAleer, & Roberts, 1996), WM is critical for understanding what various executive tasks have in common, as well as for understanding the functions of the prefrontal cortex. They propose thus an interactive framework for understanding executive functions, which is very close to Pascual-Leone's perspective: The selection of a relevant action results from a dynamic interaction among a person's WM resources (WM being defined in terms of capacity, maintenance over time, and moment-to-moment activation), a task's WM demand, and the strength of prepotent, misleading action, or response alternatives, i.e., inhibition. Their proposal remains still essentially theoretical, and has not yet received empirical support. Nevertheless, there have been some studies showing that increasing the WM demand of a task decreases inhibition while augmenting the probability of committing incorrect prepotent responses. Roberts and Pennington quote studies by Diamond (e.g., Diamond, 1988) for instance, in which an increase in delay in a WM task (i.e., an increase in the requirement for maintaining information over time) results in an increase in errors. Likewise, Roberts, Hager, & Heron (1994) showed that increasing the WM demand by combining a concurrent task with a primary anti-saccade task results in more errors. In the same vein, although in the context of experimental psychology rather than neuropsychology, Engle (1996; Engle et al., 1995) has shown that a negative priming effect (tapping the efficiency of inhibitory processes) is diminished, and even disappears, when a WM task is introduced.

The interest of a model such as Roberts and Pennington's is two-fold. On the one hand, and from a theoretical perspective, they postulate a very small set of core processes at work in executive tasks, which may nevertheless account for a wide variety of normal and disorganized behaviors. On the other hand, their model makes it possible to directly address some of the measurement problems, in particular the problem of discriminant validity, encountered by most of the executive function tasks (e.g., Lehto, 1996; Pennington et al., 1996; Rabbitt, 1997).

## CONCLUSION

The objective of this chapter was to briefly present four models of working memory (WM) developed within different research perspectives—cognitive experimental, individual differences, developmental, and neuropsychological. Given the breadth of each domain, this overview could only be very cursory, by singling out models within a large range of different propositions. At first glance, it may also appear as a mere juxtaposition of widely divergent models developed within historically separate research traditions. My claim is that the models reviewed here are much closer than is usually considered, even though their divergence remains real on a number of issues. The first part of this conclusion will therefore consist in outlining their similarities. The necessity to maintain or not a distinction between WM, attentional or controlled processes, and executive functions will then be discussed.

A first, and perhaps superficial reason to consider that these models make similar propositions is the existence of cross-references among them, particularly between Baddeley's and the neuropsychological approaches, or between Baddeley's and Engle's work. Moreover, some references to Pascual-Leone's developmental model begin to appear in the cognitive, experimental perspective (e.g., Richardson, 1996).

Second, as has hopefully been demonstrated above, all four models postulate a close relationship between the three constructs of working memory, attention, and executive functions. In Baddeley's model of WM, the CE subcomponent is considered to be an attentional controller; an impairment of this subsystem may lead to a so-called *dysexecutive syndrome*. The focus of Engle's work is placed on individual differences in the capacity of WM; recent work has shown that these differences may be due to individual differences in the amount of attentional re-sources. Although not explicitly focusing on executive functions, Engle makes it clear that his conception of WM is closer to the CE subcomponent than to either of the other two subcomponents in Baddeley's model. In Pascual-Leone's devel-opmental model, the focus is on the increase with age of the field of mental attention, defined as a subset of WM, itself defined as a set of schemes currently activated by a number of operators. Within the field of mental attention, execu-tive schemes play an important role, in determining which schemes receive addi-tional activation by the $M$ and $I$ operators. Neuropsychological approaches or recent modelizations that center on executive or so-called prefrontal functions not only consider that such functions are attentional in nature, but also assign an important role to WM.

Third, and beyond what may still appear as a rather superficial resemblance in terminology, these different models suggest similar underlying processes or mechanisms. This is perhaps clearest as concerns the perspectives adopted by Engle, Pascual-Leone, and Roberts and Pennington, or by recent computational modeling of the frontal functions such as Cohen and Servan-Schreiber's.

Baddeley remains more elusive as to which mechanisms underlie the four ap-proaches or functions recently used to fractionate the CE. In all of these models, two mechanisms seem essential for the correct functioning of an attentional system, namely activation and inhibition. Engle suggested initially that individ-ual differences in WM are due to the amount of available activation; more re-cently, he stressed the importance of inhibitory processes. In Pascual-Leone's model, the role of the $M$ operator is to enhance the activation of a number of schemes, while the $I$_operator serves to actively decrease or interrupt the activa-tion of irrelevant, highly activated schemes. Roberts and Pennington suggest that executive tasks call for both on-line holding of information, which amounts to saying that this information must be continuously activated, and for inhibition of prepotent actions.

A proposal according to which activation and inhibition are both necessary components of an attentional system is in line with other cognitive approaches which do not specifically address the issue of WM; Bjork (1989), for instance, considers that inhibitory processes are just as important as excitatory ones in information processing. This proposal also makes it possible to overcome the controversy that has emerged in developmental psychology between authors who claim that cognitive development (cognitive aging) consists in an increase (decrease) in WM capacity construed as the possibility to maintain and process a certain amount of information, on the one hand, and authors who assign most of the developmental changes to an increase in the efficiency of inhibition, on the other hand. It leaves open, however, a number of unresolved issues, that will require close scrutiny in the years to come, some of which also bear practical implications in terms of assessment (both developmental and neuropsychological) or/and measurement. To mention just a few, it should be stressed that the two mechanisms of activation and inhibition remain too general and need to be operationalized. For instance, I suggested elsewhere (de Ribaupierre, 1996) that the construct of activation could be indirectly measured by using processing speed tasks; it is indeed very difficult to measure the number of items activated. It is also important to assess whether these mechanisms are general or universal in nature, in the sense of operating across a broad range of situations, or whether they are situation specific. Although a number of developmental researchers speak of changes in inhibition with age, there is presently very little empirical support for the generality of this mechanism. On the contrary, results of studies in which several inhibition tasks were used conjointly point to only very weak between-task correlations, if any; this is also the case in an ongoing research project in our laboratory, in which we used four inhibition/interference tasks. This lack of correlations stands in strong contrast with the results obtained with processing speed tasks, particularly in the field of cognitive aging (e.g., Salthouse, 1996); it could be due to poor measurement properties of the tasks used, but it could also point to a certain specificity of inhibitory processes.

Another, theoretically important question that should be raised is whether working memory, controlled processing, and executive functions (EF) should still be distinguished. As concerns the latter distinction, between controlled and EF processing, Rabbitt (1997) makes the case that the stringent criteria proposed by Schneider and Shiffrin to define controlled vs. automatic processing (e.g., sensitivity to information load, amount of practice, generalization versus task specificity, etc.) seem to have been forgotten. As a result, controlled processing is more and more frequently equated with EF processing, and automatic with non–EF processing. This is not to say that the distinction between EF and non–EF processing is easier to establish; the same circularity problem may well apply (see footnote 1), all the more so as the construct of EF processing is based on types of tasks rather than on the analysis of underlying processes. Moreover, because the only remaining criterion seems to be that of novelty versus extended practice, Rabbitt suggests that these two types of processing ( i.e., executive or controlled on the one hand, and non executive or automatic processing, on the other hand) would best be defined as two hypothetical endpoints on a continuum running from novelty to extended practice, rather than as qualitatively different.

There is certainly also a large overlap between WM and executive functions (EF), also exemplified by the fact that most authors who have recently addressed the topic of EF seem to consider that WM is systematically involved (e.g., Phillips, 1997). I would like to suggest that it may be worthwhile to retain a distinction, but that it should be made in terms of tasks rather than in terms of underlying processes; continuing to speak of WM and EF as if they were structurally distinct systems is bound to maintain or even to increase the present confusion. In line with a number of models, it seems indeed more appropriate to consider that WM refers to a set of temporarily and highly activated items of information (whether individual items, pointers to chunks of information and/or between-item connections) rather than to a structural entity; the generality of WM, as attested by a number of correlational studies, would be due to limits in the size of this activated set, that is, to the quantity of information that can be integrated, rather than to the actual processes at work. Likewise, there is no evidence for a single, structural, system responsible for executive processing; even apparently well-defined functions such as planning or coordinating do not seem to generalize across tasks. Moreover, it has recently been suggested that, after all, executive processing is not that different from the concept of fluid intelligence (e.g., Rabbitt, 1997). No one would defend the idea that fluid intelligence corresponds to a neuropsychologically distinct and unitary structural entity.

A distinction in terms of tasks may be useful, however, because both types of tasks probably pursue slightly different objectives. Although they are both likely to rely on similar mechanisms such as activation or inhibition, to call for controlled processing and even to be both subserved by the frontal lobe, they may differ by the relative weight of the processes at work. WM tasks are those tasks in which subjects have to *temporarily* hold in mind (i.e., activate) relevant information, while suppressing, when necessary, irrelevant information; information is deemed relevant because it will have to be retrieved at a later time (as in a short-term memory task) or because it will be necessary in concurrent, or subsequent cognitive, processing. The main objective of WM tasks is to assess the amount of attentional resources available to the subject. Such tasks do not call for very elaborated executive schemes, nor for a very extensive knowledge base; on the contrary, they are usually rather simple, which makes it possible to control for a number of individual differences.

Congruent with the literature, and particularly with Pascual-Leone's and Engle's recommendations, the best WM tasks to measure attentional limits are probably short-term memory tasks involving simple and novel information (so that no chunks can be made) or/and tasks in which some amount of inhibition is required like in a dual task paradigm or in a task calling for both processing and storage; such procedures should indeed ensure that the material to be retained is attentionally processed. EF tasks—referring to tasks such as the Wisconsin Sorting Card Test, or tasks of verbal fluency or, more generally, planning tasks which are typically identified with executive functions (e.g., Shallice & Burgess, 1993)—probably call for the same attentional resources as WM tasks, namely activation of the relevant information (e.g., the current sorting criterion in the WCST, or the category name and exemplars already retrieved in a verbal fluency task), and inhibition of irrelevant information (preceding sorting criteria, or other categories); however, in such tasks, the prepotency of irrelevant information may be stronger than in WM tasks, calling for still more efficient inhibitory processes and greater flexibility. They require additional processing as well, such as planning or temporal ordering. As a result, EF tasks are usually more complex than WM tasks; they may also be closer to everyday tasks and may call for a more extensive knowledge base. As recently pointed out by a number of authors, EF tasks raise, however, a number of methodological and theoretical difficulties, not the least being lack of reliability and of validity; careful task analyses, in terms of underlying cognitive processes, should help in clarifying this issue.

## REFERENCES

Baddeley, A. (1986). *Working memory*. Oxford: Oxford University Press.

Baddeley, A. (1996). Exploring the central executive. *The Quarterly Journal of Experimental Psychology, 49A*, 5–28.

Baddeley, A. D. (1993). Working memory or working attention? In A. D. Baddeley & L. Weiskrantz (Eds.), *Attention, selection, awareness, and control. A tribute to Donald Broadbent*. (pp. 152–170). Oxford: Clarendon Press.

Baddeley, A. D., Bressi, S., Della Sala, S., Logie, R. H., & Spinnler, H. (1991). The decline of working memory in Alzheimer's disease. *Brain, 114*, 2521–2542.

Baddeley, A., & DellaSala, S. (1996). Working memory and executive control. *Philosophical Transactions of the Royal Society of London Series B-Biological Sciences, 351*(1346), 1397–1403.

Baddeley, A., & Hitch, G. J. (1974). Working memory. In G. Bower (Ed.), *Recent advances in learning and motivation, Vol. 8*. (pp. 47–70). New York: Academic Press.

Bjork, R.A. (1989). Retrieval inhibition as an adaptative mechanism in human memory. In H.L. Roediger & F.I.M. Craik (Eds). *Varieties of memory and consciousness*. (pp. 309–330). Hillsdale, NJ: Lawrence Erlbaum Associates.

Bjorklund, D. F., & Harnishfeger, K. K. (1990). The resources construct in cognitive development: diverse sources of evidence and a theory of inefficient inhibition. *Developmental Review, 10*, 48–71.

Cantor, J., & Engle, R. W. (1993). Working memory capacity as long-term memory activation: an individual-differences approach. *Journal of Experimental Psychology: Learning, Memory, and Cognition, 19*, 1101–1114.

Case, R. (1985). *Intellectual development. Birth to adulthood*. New York: Academic Press.

Case, R. (1992). Neo-piagetian theories of intellectual development. In H. Beilin & P. B. Pufall (Eds.), *Piaget's theory: prospects and possibilities*. (pp. 61–104). Hillsdale, NJ: Lawrence Erlbaum Associates.

Case, R. (1995). Capacity-based explanations of working memory growth: A brief history and reevaluation. In F. E. Weinert & W. Schneider (Eds.), *Memory Performance and Competencies —Issues in Growth and Development*. (pp. 23–44). Hillsdale, NJ: Lawrence Erlbaum Associates.

Case, R., Kurland, D. M., & Goldberg, J. (1982). Operational efficiency and the growth of short-term memory span. *Journal of Experimental Child Psychology, 33*, 386–404.

Chapman, M. (1987). Piaget, attentional capacity and the functional implications of formal structures. In H. W. Reese (Ed.), *Advances in child development and behavior, Vol. 20.* (pp. 289–334). Orlando,FL: Academic Press.

Cohen, J. D., & Servan-Schreiber, D. (1992). Context, cortex, and dopamine: A connectionist approach to behavior and biology in schizophrenia. *Psychological Review, 99,* 45–77.

Conway, A. R., & Engle, R. W. (1994). Working memory and retrieval: a resource-dependent inhibition model. *Journal of Experimental Psychology, General, 123,* 354–373.

Conway, A. R. A., & Engle, R. W. (1996). Individual differences in working memory capacity: More evidence for a general capacity theory. *Memory, 4(6),* 577–590.

Cowan, N. (1988). Evolving conceptions of memory storage, selective attention, and their mutual constraints within the human information-processing system. *Psychological Bulletin, 104,* 163–191.

Daigneault, S., Braun, C. M. J., & Whitaker, H. A. (1992). An empirical test of two opposing theoretical models of prefrontal function. *Brain and Cognition, 19,* 48–71.

Daneman, M., & Carpenter, P. A. (1980). Individual differences in working memory and reading. *Journal of Verbal Learning and Verbal Behavior, 19,* 450–466.

Diamond, A. (1988). Differences between adult and infant cognition: Is the crucial variable presence or absence of language? In L. Weiskrantz (Ed.), *Thought without language.* (pp. 337–370). Oxford, MA: Clarendon Press.

Engle, R. W. (1996). Working memory and retrieval: An inhibition-resource approach. In J. T. E. Richardson, R. W. Engle, L. Hasher, R. H. Logie, E. R. Stoltzfus, & R. T. Zacks (Eds.), *Working memory and human cognition.* (pp. 89–119). New York: Oxford University Press.

Engle, R. W., Cantor, J., & Carullo, J. J. (1992). Individual differences in working memory and comprehension: a test of four hypotheses. *Journal of Experimental Psychology: Learning, Memory, and Cognition, 18,* 972–992.

Engle, R. W., Conway, A. R. A., Tuholski, S. W., & Shisler, R. J. (1995). A Resource Account of Inhibition. *Psychological Science, 6(2),* 122–125.

Ericsson, K. A., & Kintsch, W. (1995). Long-term working memory. *Psychological Review, 102(2),* 211–245.

Eslinger, P. J. (1996). Conceptualizing, describing, and measuring components of executive function: A summary. In G. R. Lyon & N. A. Krasnegor (Eds.), *Attention, memory, and executive function.* (pp. 367–395). Baltimore: Paul H. Brookes.

Fuster, J. M. (1997). *The prefrontal cortex: Anatomy, physiology, and neuropsychology of the frontal lobe (3rd ed.).* Philadelphia: Lippincott-Raven.

Halford, G. S. (1993). *Children's understanding: The development of mental models.* Hillsdale, NJ: Lawrence Erlbaum Associates.

Harnishfeger, K. K., & Bjorklund, D. F. (1994). A developmental perspective on individual differences in inhibition. *Learning and Individual Differences, 6(3),* 331–355.

Hasher, L., Stoltzfus, E. R., Zacks, R. T., & Rypma, B. (1991). Age and inhibition. *Journal of Experimental Psychology: Learning, Memory, and Cognition, 17,* 163–169.

Hasher, L., & Zacks, R. T. (1979). Automatic and effortful processes in memory. *Journal of Experimental Psychology: General, 108,* 356–388.

Hasher, L., & Zacks, R. T. (1988). Working memory, comprehension, and aging: A review and a new view. In G. H. Bower (Ed.), *The psychology of learning and motivation.* (pp. 193–225). San Diego: Academic Press.

Jacoby, L. L., Ste-Marie, D., & Toth, J. P. (1993). Redefining automaticity: Unconscious influences, awareness, and control. In A. D. Baddeley & L. Weiskrantz (Eds.). *Attention: Selection, awareness, and control. A tribute to Donald Broadbent.* (pp. 261–282). Oxford: Oxford University Press.

Lehto, J. (1996). Are executive function tests dependent on working memory capacity? *The Quarterly Journal of Experimental Psychology, 49A(1),* 29–50.

Lezak, M. D. (1995). *Neuropsychological assessment (3rd ed.).* New York: Oxford University Press.

Logie, R. H., & Marchetti, C. (1991). Visuo-spatial working memory: Visual, spatial or central executive? In R. H. Logie & M. Denis (Eds.), *Mental images in human cognition.* (pp. 105–115). Amsterdam: North Holland.

Morris, N. (1987). Exploring the visuo-spatial scratch pad. *The Quarterly Journal of Experimental Psychology, 39A,* 409–430.

Morris, R. D. (1996). Relationships and distinctions among the concepts of attention, memory, and executive function: A developmental perspective. In G. R. Lyon & N. A. Krasnegor (Eds.), *Attention, memory, and executive function.* (pp. 11–16). Baltimore: Paul H. Brookes.

Moscovitch, M. (1994). Memory and working with memory: Evaluation of a component process model and comparisons with other models. In D. L. Schacter & E. Tulving (Eds.), *Memory systems 1994.* (pp. 269–310). Cambridge, MA: The MIT Press.

Pascual-Leone, J. (1970). A mathematical model for the transition rule in Piaget's developmental stages. *Acta Psychologica, 32,* 301–345.

Pascual-Leone, J. (1983). Growing into human maturity: Toward a metasubjective theory of adulthood stages. In P. B. Baltes & O. G. Brim (Eds.), *Life-span development and behavior.* (pp. 117–156). New York: Academic Press.

Pascual-Leone, J. (1987). Organismic processes for neo-Piagetian theories: A dialectical causal account of cognitive development. *International Journal of Psychology, 22,* 531–570.

Pascual-Leone, J. (1989). An organismic process model of Witkin's field-dependence-independence. In T. Globerson & T. Zelniker (Eds.), *Cognitive style and cognitive development.* (pp. 36–70). Norwood, NJ: Ablex.

Pascual-Leone, J. (1990). Reflections on life-span intelligence, consciousness and ego development. In C. N. Alexander, E. J. Langer, & R. M. Oetzel (Eds.), *Higher stages of development: Adult growth beyond formal operations.* (pp. 258–285). New York: Oxford University Press.

Pascual-Leone, J., & Baillargeon, R. (1994). Developmental measurement of mental attention. *International Journal of Behavioral Development, 17(1),* 161–200.

Pascual-Leone, J., Goodman, D. R., Ammon, P., & Subelman, I. (1978). Piagetian theory and neo-Piagetian analysis as psychological guides in education. In J. McCarthy Gallagher & J. A. Easley (Eds.), *Knowledge and development.* (pp. 243–289). New York: Plenum.

Pascual-Leone, J., & Ijaz, I. (1989). Mental capacity testing as a form of intellectual-developmental assessment. In R. J. Samuda, S. L. Kong, J. Cummins, J. Pascual-Leone, & J. Lewis (Eds.), *Assessment and placement of minority students.* (pp. 143–171). Toronto: C.J. Hogrefe.

Pennington, B. F., Bennetto, L., McAleer, O., & Roberts, L. J. (1996). Executive functions and working memory: Theoretical and measurement issues. In G. R. Lyon & N. A. Krasnegor (Eds.), *Attention, memory, and executive function.* (pp. 327–348). Baltimore: Paul H. Brookes.

Phillips, L.H. (1997). Do "frontal tests" measure executive function? Issues of assessment and evidence from fluency tests. In P. Rabbitt (Ed). *Methodology of frontal and executive function* (pp. 191–213). Hove: Psychology Press.

Quinn, G. (1991). Encoding and maintenance of information in visual working memory. In R. H. Logie & M. Denis (Eds.), *Mental Images in human cognition.* (pp. 95–104). Amsterdam: North Holland.

Rabbitt, P. (1997). Introduction: Methodologies and models in the study of executive function. In P. Rabbitt (Ed). *Methodology of frontal and executive function* (pp. 1–38). Hove: Psychology Press.

de Ribaupierre, A. (1989). Operational development and cognitive style: A review of french literature and a neo-Piagetian reinterpretation. In T. Globerson & T. Zelniker (Eds.), *Cognitive style and cognitive development.* (pp. 86–115). Norwood, NJ: Ablex.

de Ribaupierre, A. (1996). *From child development to life-span development.* Paper presented at the XIVth ISSBD Meetings, Quebec City, August 12-16.

de Ribaupierre, A. (1997). Les modèles néo-piagétiens: Quoi de nouveau? *Psychologie Française, 42(1),* 9–21.

de Ribaupierre, A., & Bailleux, C. (1994). Developmental change in a spatial task of attentional capacity: An essay toward an integration of two working memory models. *International Journal of Behavioral Development, 17,* 5–35.

Richardson, J. T. E. (1996). Evolving issues in working memory. In J. T. E. Richardson, R. W. Engle, L. Hasher, R. H. Logie, E. R. Stoltzfus, & R. T. Zacks (Eds.), *Working memory and human cognition.* (pp. 120–147). New York: Oxford University Press.

Roberts, R. J., Hager, L. D., & Heron, C. (1994). Prefrontal cognitive processes: Working memory and inhibition in the antisaccade task. *Journal of Experimental Psychology, General, 123,* 374–393.

Roberts, R. J., & Pennington, B. F. (1996). An interactive framework for examining prefrontal cognitive processes. *Developmental Neuropsychology, 12(1),* 105–126.

Salthouse, T. (1996). The processing-speed theory of adult age differences in cognition. *Psychological Review, 103,* 403–428.

Schacter, D. L., & Tulving, E. (1994). What are the memory systems of 1994? In D. L. Schacter & E. Tulving (Eds.), *Memory systems 1994.* (pp. 1-38). Cambridge, MA: MIT Press.

Shallice, T. (1982). Specific impairments of planning. *Philosophical Transactions of the Royal Society, 298,* 199–209.

Shallice, T., & Burgess, P. (1993). Supervisory control of action and thought selection. In A. D. Baddeley & L. Weiskrantz (Eds.), *Attention: Selection, awareness, and control.* (pp. 171–187). Oxford, MA: Oxford University Press.

Sternberg, R. J. (1983). Components of human intelligence. *Cognition, 15,* 1–48.

# 11

# Problem-Oriented Learning: Facilitating the Use of Domain-Specific and Control Strategies Through Modeling by an Expert

*Heinz Mandl*

*Cornelia Gräsel*

*Frank Fischer*

### INTRODUCTION

A main question in instructional psychology has been how to overcome the problem of 'inert knowledge.' With the constructivist turn in instructional psychology and the view of learning as an active, constructive and highly situated process, problem-oriented learning has recently had a kind of renaissance (Bransford, Sherwood, Hasselbring, Kinzer, & Williams, 1990; Cognition and Technology Group at Vanderbilt, 1991, 1992, 1993; Collins, Brown, & Newman, 1989; Gerstenmaier & Mandl, 1995; Resnick, 1987). The main idea of problem-oriented learning is that knowledge acquired in the context of meaningful and authentic problems can be more easily transferred to real life situations than knowledge acquired in an abstract and systematic way. Of course, the idea of teaching applicable knowledge through problem-oriented learning has a long tradition: For example, at the end of the 19th and at the beginning of the 20th century, the Reformpädagogik (reform pedagogy) implemented instructional models which resemble the constructivist view of learning and teaching (e.g., Gaudig, 1922; Kerschensteiner, 1912; see Mandl, Gruber, & Renkl, 1996). The concepts of *discovery learning* (Bruner, 1961) and *case-based learning* (see Williams, 1992) also share basic ideas of problem-oriented learning.

All these approaches share the assumption that authentic and complex tasks should lead students to engage themselves in constructive and mindful learning activities. In the more recent constructivist approaches the term strategies is referred to for learning activities (e.g., Collins et al., 1989). First, the importance of domain-specific learning and problem-solving strategies to effective problem-oriented learning is emphasized; furthermore the importance of metacognitive control strategies is stressed, particularly the detection of comprehension failures and mistakes during the learning process. Unfortunately, research results show that the assumption that learners successfully employ appropriate strategies seems to be too optimistic and cannot be supported by findings in this straightforward sense. Findings from our previous studies in the field of medical education indicated that students were overwhelmed by the complexity of problems and had difficulties with constructive and mindful learning (Gräsel & Mandl, 1993). Students especially used ineffective domain-specific strategies when dealing with complex medical problems. Studies in other domains, e.g., in the domain of business management showed similar results (Renkl, Gruber, Mandl, & Hinkofer, 1994; Stark, Graf, Renkl, Gruber, & Mandl, 1995). There has been as of yet little reasearch on which, if any, difficulties arise in the use of control strategies in problem-oriented learning. However, research on text comprehension has shown that even experienced learners have difficulties with metacognitive control, particularly the detection and correction of comprehension failures (Schneider & Pressley, 1989).

Thus, we concluded that students should be given instructional support in order to foster their use of adequate domain-specific and control strategies in problem-oriented learning environments. Since our work is concerned with problem-oriented learning in medicine, we specifically asked how the strategy use of medical students in problem-oriented learning environments can be supported.

## DOMAIN-SPECIFIC AND CONTROL
## STRATEGIES IN PROBLEM-ORIENTED LEARING
## IN THE DOMAIN OF MEDICINE

Problem-oriented learning in medicine means that students deal with medical cases presented on paper, video, or computer. How medical education can be improved by the extension of problem-oriented learning currently is a question of interest in Germany (Bundesministerium für Gesundheit, 1993) as well as in other countries (ACME-TRI Report, 1993; Albanese & Mitchell, 1993). In order to determine adequate strategies for learning with medical cases, we orientated ourselves towards the research on problem-based learning in the domain of medicine (e.g., Elstein, Shulman, & Sprafka, 1978; Patel, Groen, & Norman, 1993):

*Domain-Specific Strategies.* Domain-specific strategies comprise the strategies for learning through problem-solving as well as the "tricks of the trade" for a specific domain. Theoretical and empirical works show that students' success in learning with medical cases is associated with the use of strategies subsumed under the concept of hypothetico-deductive proceeding (Hmelo, Gotterer & Bransford, 1994; Patel et al., 1993). Hypothetico-deductive proceeding consists of the following strategies: *(A) Construction of initial hypotheses.* The first impression of the patient and some first information should lead to the construction of early hypotheses. *(B) Goal-directed selection of information.* Further information about the patient should be collected in a goal-directed manner, meaning that the learner should have a reason for each question he/she asks and for each physical examination he/she performs. *(C) Formulation of competing hypotheses.* Medical students should think of more than one possible hypothesis. They should avoid pinning themselves down to one—possibly wrong—diagnosis. *(D) Establishing coherence.* An important strategy is to construct a coherent representation of the case. Establishing coherence means connecting information about the patient and drawing conclusions from findings which support certain hypotheses on the basis of pathophysiological knowledge.

*Control Strategies.* One main idea of problem-oriented learning is the exploration of the learning environment with a minimum of external control. Learners therefore have to observe their own learning process and correct themselves when necessary. Thus, the application of adequate metacognitive control strategies in such an environment is very important. Based on the research on metacognition, Collins et al. (1989) distinguish three kinds of control strategies for problem-oriented learning: *(A) Monitoring*, meaning the observation and evaluation of one's own learning process. As long as no difficulties arise (positive monitoring, see Chi, Bassok, Lewis, Reimann, & Glaser, 1989), the application of further control strategies is not necessary. But when obstacles, contradictions or comprehension failures are noticed by the learner (negative monitoring), the application of further control strategies is important. *(B) Self-diagnosis* is necessary in order to find the cause of an obstacle or a comprehension failure. If the learner sees the cause in a lack of his own knowledge, the next step is the regulation of his own learning process. *(C) Self-regulation* comprises the use of additional information (for example glossary texts) as well as the mindful activation of prior knowledge.

Since learners in problem-oriented learning environments experience very little external control, it is important that they regulate comprehension failures if the cause is seen in a deficiency of knowledge. This use of control strategies can be called the *use of error-regulating control strategies.* By comparison, if negative monitoring ends in neither self-diagnosis nor self-regulation, this use of *error-ignoring control strategies* is problematic, because the opportunity to rethink and expand one's own proceeding or knowledge is not taken.

Prawat (1993) bemoans the fact that instructional designers assume implicitly that learners become aware of their comprehension failures and correct themselves optimally. In fact, it cannot be taken for granted that learners use adequate control strategies in problem-oriented learning environments: Findings in the research of metacognition show that adequate monitoring and regulation is often difficult for learners (Schneider & Pressley, 1989). Thus, problem-oriented learning environments should be designed in a way that fosters the use of domain-specific and control strategies.

## FOSTERING THE USE OF STRATEGIES IN PROBLEM-ORIENTED LEARNING WITH STRATEGY MODELING BY AN EXPERT

An important instructional method for fostering the use of strategies in problem-oriented learning environments is strategy modeling: An experienced practitioner shows how to proceed adequately when learning with complex and authentic problems. Above all, the Cognitive Apprenticeship approach (Collins et al., 1989) uses strategy modeling as instructional support. Furthermore, other instructional models based on constructivism use expert models in the design of problem-oriented learning environments (Cognition and Technology Group at Vanderbilt, 1992; Honebein, Duffy & Fishman, 1993; Jones, Knuth, & Duffy, 1993). Two forms of strategy modeling can be distinguished:

*Strategy Modeling by Articulations of an Expert.* Central to strategy modeling in Cognitive Apprenticeship is that learners get insight into the expert's proceeding while he/she is dealing with authentic problems. The reason for this is that these processes so far remain inaccessible to learners in many instructional settings. In medical education, for example, learners rarely have the opportunity to see the way physicians came up with their diagnoses, the hypotheses they discarded or the errors they made and recognized—in short: The use of strategies in the process of diagnosing. Therefore, the core of modeling in the sense of Cognitive Apprenticeship is that an *expert articulates his or her thoughts* when dealing with complex and authentic problems. These articulations should comprise the use of domain-specific strategies as well as the use of control strategies. Thus, learners have insight not only to adequate strategies, but also to the conditions of their adequate use. Considering findings of strategy training—especially of training of metacognitive strategies—it is to question, whether a simultaneous articulation of domain-specific *and* control strategies is effective. It is well known that especially the change of metacognitive strategies is dependent on prerequisites of learners and often needs intensive training (Friedrich & Mandl, 1992).

*Strategy Modeling with Expert Maps.* Another approach to strategy modeling involves learning with expert maps. While working on a specific problem, an expert structures its content by means of graphic tools. In this process, maps evolve through different stages, which can be used as modeling components in learning environments. Comparing the results of one's own learning process with expert results or expert solutions is assumed to be an important element in apprenticeship learning (Brown, Collins, & Duguid, 1989; Collins & Brown, 1988). Maps and other kinds of graphical representations may be regarded as important learning results in cognitive domains (e.g. Greeno & Goldman, 1997; Pea, 1994).

Moreover, expert maps have been successfully employed in *fostering conceptual understanding* in empirical studies (e.g. Jüngst, 1995; see Jonassen, Beissner, & Yacci, 1993). *Facilitating the use of strategies by modeling with expert
maps* has been distinctly less systematically investigated thus far. It seems very
promising to model strategy use in problem-oriented learning with a series of
expert maps for different stages in problem management, since this kind of support allows a visual demonstration of how the expert sequentially structures
complex problem information and how he or she relates this information to their
prior knowledge.

## RESEARCH QUESTIONS

We conducted two studies concerned with the following questions: To what extent does strategy modeling by an expert effect the use of domain-specific and
control strategies ? And are there correlations between strategy use in problem-
oriented learning environments and diagnostic competence? Study 1 is concerned
with strategy modeling by articulations of an expert, Study 2 with modeling with
expert maps.

## STUDIES

### Learning Environment

In both studies the multimedia learning system 'PlanAlyzer' (Lyon et al., 1990)
was used as the central component of the problem-oriented learning environment.
The cases presented in the program deal with anemia (the lack of hemoglobin).
The learner has the possibility of obtaining information about the patient's
symptoms, medical history and the results of a physical examination and can
request additional information about related concepts from a glossary.

### Study 1: Strategy Modeling by
### Articulations of an Expert

The main question of Study 1 is, to what extent modeling by articulations of an
expert has an effect on the learners' use of strategies. Two different forms of
strategy modeling were compared: *(a) Modeling of domain-specific strategies.* A
physician *articulated domain-specific strategies* while working on a case. She
explained why and how to construct initial hypotheses based on initial complaints and the first impression of the patient. The selection of further data was
goal-directed and well-grounded. Working with the case, she formulated competing hypotheses and gave reasons for them. Findings were clustered on the basis
of pathophysiological knowledge; all findings were associated to hypotheses.
*(b) Combined modeling of domain-specific and control strategies.* In the second
treatment, the physician *demonstrated the domain-specific strategies and, in addi-*

*tion, she showed how to use control strategies adequately.* She especially attached importance to the regulation of comprehension failures. Whenever she noticed contradictions or obstacles or became aware of errors, she regulated her own proceeding: She tried to rethink the problem, activated prior knowledge, or used the glossary to get additional information. This kind of simultaneous demonstration of strategy use is suggested by Cognitive Apprenticeship. The question was, which kind of modeling would be more effective in fostering the learners' strategy use.

*Design.* Thirty-six fourth-year medical students participated in the study. Only students who had completed all courses concerning the content of anemia were asked to participate. After a pretest (factual knowledge of anemia and solutions of short paper-and-pencil cases), learners were introduced to the PlanAlyzer program. Then all participants had to solve a *baseline case* without instructional support. Afterwards the whole group was divided into three experimental groups who worked with the treatment case under the following conditions: Modeling of domain-specific strategies (n = 12), combined modeling of domain-specific and control strategies (n = 12) and control group (n = 12). In the two treatment groups the articulations of an expert were presented to the learners; additionally her actions on the computer program were shown to them on the screen. Subjects in the control group worked on the same case without any additional help; time on task was equal in the three groups (60 minutes). Finally, learners had to work with a *transfer case* by themselves. The baseline and the treatment case were very similar (anemia due to iron deficiency), the transfer case differed concerning the findings, the hypotheses and the underlying concepts (anemia due to leukemia). Thus, it could be insured that learners with the expert models had no advantage of non-strategy-related concepts which the models might have had explained.

*Measurement of Strategy Use.* In many studies, strategies are assessed by questionnaires after learning. Yet, this kind of reflecting self-evaluation has some methodological problems (e.g. biases in self-assessment). Therefore, we decided to measure strategy use during the learning process in both studies. Learners were asked to think aloud while working on the cases. Think-aloud protocols were analyzed with regard to the *domain-specific strategies*: The construction of initial hypotheses was indicated by the number of hypotheses mentioned after the first impression of the patient. Goal-directed selection was indicated by the amount of considered relevant findings, and the formulation of competing hypotheses by the number of different diagnoses learners took into account. In order to measure the strategy of establishing coherence, the expressed relations within findings and between findings and diagnoses were counted.

Think-aloud protocols were also analyzed with regard to control strategies. Sequences in the protocols, where comprehension failures were verbalized and regulated, were coded as *error-regulating control strategies*; sequences, where comprehension failures were verbalized but not regulated, were coded as *error-ignoring control strategies*.

*Assessment of Diagnostic Competence.* With the correctness of possible hypotheses at the end of the transfer case we assessed the diagnostic competence. At the end of the program, learners had to weight a given list of diagnoses with respect to the probability of the diagnosis. The weightings of the students were compared with the rating of an expert and received a grade with respect to corresponding weightings.

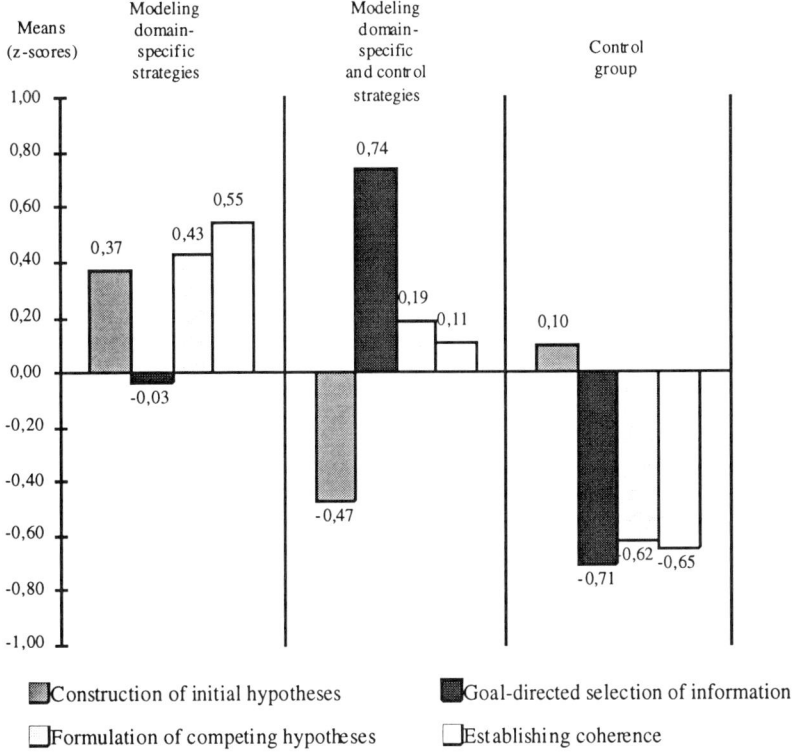

FIG. 11.1. *Effects of strategy modeling by articulations of an expert on the use of domain-specific strategies.*

*Results.* The first research question was, whether the strategy modeling had an effect on the use of strategies. To compare the three treatment groups, we calculated adjusted means of the strategy use: The means of the strategy use in the transfer case were adjusted by the strategy use in the baseline-case. The modeling of domain-specific strategies had a positive effect on the use of two domain-specific strategies. Analyses of variance show that the group with this treatment differed from the control group in the formulation of competing hypotheses and the strategy of establishing coherence (see figure 11.1). In contrast, the combined modeling of domain-specific and control strategies had a positive effect only on the strategy of goal-directed selection. Learners in this group used the strategy of goal-directed selection significantly more often than learners in the control group.

Figure 11.2 shows the results for the use of *control strategies*. As expected, the combined modeling of domain-specific and control strategies had an effect on the use of control strategies: Group comparisons show that learners in this treatment group corrected their comprehension failures more often using prior knowledge or additional information from the computer program. Moreover, they were less likely to ignore errors than learners in the other groups. Additional analyses showed that there was no treatment effect on the frequency of positive monitoring (e.g., "oh, that works without any problem").

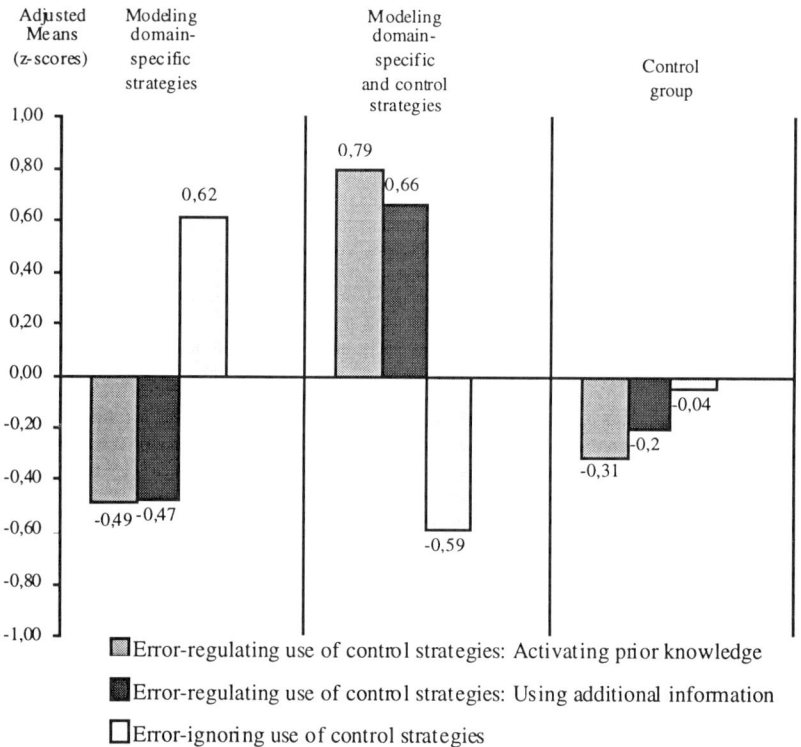

□ Error-regulating use of control strategies: Activating prior knowledge

■ Error-regulating use of control strategies: Using additional information

□ Error-ignoring use of control strategies

*FIG. 11.2. Effects of strategy modeling by articulations of an expert on the use of control strategies.*

The second question of the study was, whether there are significant correlations between the use of strategies and diagnostic competence. It was assumed that both, the use of domain-specific and the use of error-regulating control strategies, are positively correlated, and the use of error-ignoring control strategies is negatively correlated with diagnostic competence. However, findings only partly supported this assumption. With respect to the domain-specific strategies, the formulation of competing hypotheses ($r = .59$) and the strategy of establishing coherence ($r = .54$) was significantly correlated with diagnostic competence. No substantial correlation could be found for the strategies of construction of initial hypotheses ($r = .09$) and goal-directed selection ($r = .21$). Furthermore, neither the use of error-regulating control strategies nor the use of error-ignoring control strategies is significantly correlated with diagnostic competence (see Gräsel, 1997).

*Discussion.* The two kinds of modeling by articulations of an expert had different effects on the strategy use of the learners: The domain-specific modeling influenced the use of those domain-specific strategies which were associated with diagnostic competence: The formulation of competing hypotheses and the strategy of establishing coherence. In contrast, the modeling involving domain-specific and metacognitive strategies fostered goal-directed selection compared to the control group, but not the other domain-specific strategies. Therefore, learners in this group selected more information about the patient than learners in the other groups—but they did not differ in organizing symptoms into meaningful clusters or drawing conclusions with respect to hypotheses. One can conclude that, compared to the domain-specific modeling, the combined modeling of domain-specific and control strategies, adversely influenced the use of domain-specific strategies. But as predicted, the additional modeling of control strategies had an effect on the use of control strategies by learners: After they saw how the physician dealt with her comprehension failures, they showed more use of error-regulating and less use of error-ignoring control strategies.

However, the expected correlations between the use of control strategies and diagnostic competence could not be found. It can be assumed that the *quantity* of control strategy use was enhanced, but not the *quality*. Detailed case studies supported this supposition (Gräsel, 1997): The critical point for learning is to become aware of important comprehension failures—for example to recognize misconceptions—and to regulate these comprehension failures in a *truly adequate manner*. Whereas metacognitive modeling had an effect on the quantity of control strategie, it can be argued that the quality was not affected.

Two conclusions can be drawn from the study: (a) Modeling by articulations of an expert can facilitate the use of domain-specific strategies in problem-oriented learning environments. However, showing learners the use of domain-specific and control strategies simultaneously seems to pose a problem. Thus, the use of adequate control strategies has to be trained or supported more intensively. (b) In order to analyze the relevance of control strategies it is important to grasp qualitative aspects of comprehension failures and their regulation.

## Study 2: Strategy Modeling with Expert Maps

In the second study we explore the effects of modeling with expert maps on strategy use in problem-oriented learning. The expert maps were developed as following: While working on a PlanAlyzer case, a medical teaching expert demonstrated how to apply domain-specific strategies by visualizing important findings and relevant working diagnoses at different stages using *InStructure-Tool*, a computer-based concept-mapping tool (F. Fischer, Gräsel, Kittel, & Mandl, 1996). Basically, the procedure of learning with expert maps involves two main steps: After each stage in the PlanAlyzer case, the learner first develops his/her own map using InStructure-Tool. The learner is then asked to compare his or her map with that of the expert. In our study we compared two forms of modeling with expert maps: Maps *without* explicitly explaining the strategies, which were applied by the expert, and maps *with additional strategy instructions*, which named and explained the domain-specific strategies employed by the expert.

The strategies to be fostered in this study were already described in Study 1 (construction of initial hypotheses, goal-directed selection, formulation of competing hypotheses and establishing coherence). The main research question of Study 2 was: How can strategy use be facilitated by *modeling with expert maps*? Like in Study 1 we also asked whether there are substantial correlations between strategy use and diagnostic competence.

*Design.* Twenty-four advanced (fourth-year) medical students worked individually on a series of 4 case problems of the case-based multimedia system *PlanAlyzer Anemia:* A baseline case to measure the initial strategy use; two treatment cases, and one transfer case. In baseline and transfer, all participants worked under the same conditions. As an additional component, the InStructure-Tool was integrated into the learning environment. Using this tool, domain-specific strategies were modeled as follows: The expert integrated a number of relevant working diagnoses using "hypothesis cards" at the beginning of the case (construction of initial hypotheses). On "finding cards" he integrated findings into the map, which could be seen as evidence for or against already existing working diagnoses (goal-directed selection). Throughout the whole process, the expert worked with a number of hypotheses, the actual relevance of which was visualized by the size of the hypothesis card (formulation of competing hypotheses). He graphically related all important findings to one or more hypotheses, which may explain them; moreover, he demonstrated the grouping of findings into symptom complexes by clustering the finding cards into meaningful groups (establishing coherence).

During treatment cases four instructional conditions were implemented: *1. Expert maps*. The learners' task in this treatment condition was first, to represent his/her own view graphically. Second, the learner was asked to compare his/her own solution with that of the expert. The domain-specific strategies used by the expert were not explicitly named or explained. *2. Expert maps and additional strategy-instruction texts*. Learners in this group were also asked to visualize relevant findings and working diagnoses after each stage of the case. In addition to the expert maps they were provided with instructional texts which named and explained the domain-specific strategies which should be used in working with the learning cases. *3. Strategy-instruction texts only*. Learners in this group were only provided with strategy-instruction texts to control for the effects of this kind of additional support. *4. Control group*. Learners in the control group were asked to visualize relevant findings and working diagnoses with the InStructure-Tool after each stage of the case, but were not provided with any kind of additional instructional support.

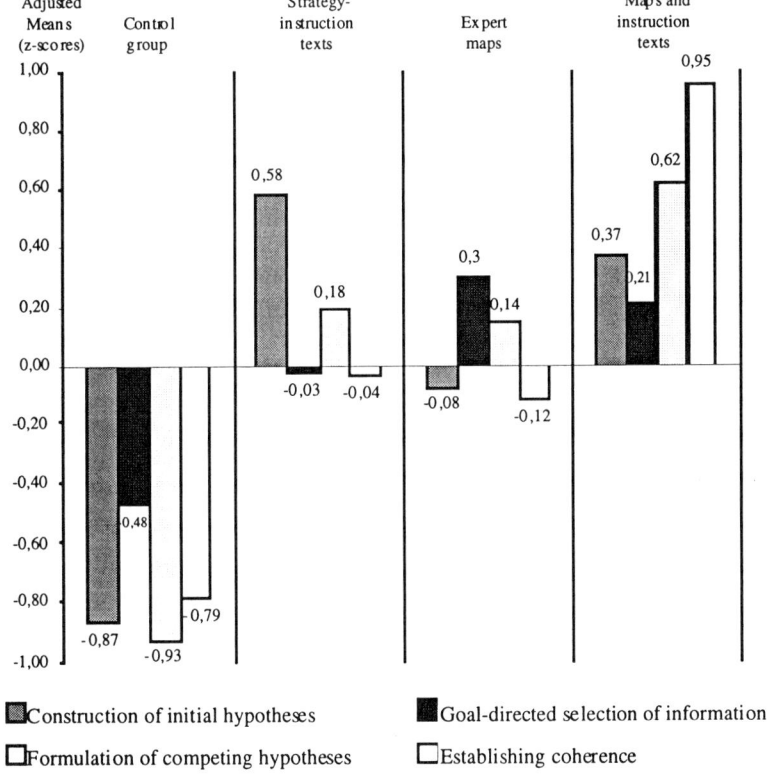

FIG. 11.3. *Effects of strategy modeling with expert maps on the use of domain-specific strategies.*

In all treatment groups learners had the possibility to make changes in their own map before proceeding to the next step in the PlanAlyzer case.

*Measurement of Strategy Use and Diagnostic Competence.* *Domain-specific strategies* were measured with the classification system used in Study 1, except for the strategy of constructing initial hypotheses: In Study 2 we used the number of hypotheses generated in first impression *and* patient interview as an indicator for the use of this strategy. *Control strategies* were only measured for the two groups in which the learners compared their own graphical interpretation with those of the expert during treatment cases. For the assessment of control strategies the same measures as in Study 1 were used. The correctness of the final diagnoses in the transfer case was, as in Study 1, chosen as an indicator for *diagnostic competence*.

*Results.* Modeling with expert maps had substantial effects on the use of domain-specific strategies in a transfer case. More specifically, the strategies of *establishing coherence* and of *formulating competing hypotheses* could be facilitated in both groups which were provided with the expert maps. There were no treatment effects on the strategy of *goal-directed selection.* For the strategy of *construction of initial hypotheses*, only the instruction texts showed a significant effect (see figure 11.3).

It is of interest that there were no substantial differences in strategy use between the group with strategy-instruction texts and the group with expert maps, whereas both groups differed substantially from the control group concerning the strategies of establishing coherence and of formulating competing hypotheses. There were no interaction effects between the two forms of instructional support. Thus, in the group with expert maps and strategy-instruction texts both kinds of instructional support contributed additionally to the total treatment effect. Learners in this group showed substantially more strategy use than the learners in the other groups.

The *use of control strategies* was assessed during treatment cases for those two groups in which the learners were provided with the expert maps. The two groups differed substantially in the application of control strategies: In the group with expert mapping the detection of a comprehension failure (negative monitoring) was followed by error-regulating control strategies in one third of the cases. In the group with additional strategy instruction texts containing only domain-specific strategies, negative monitoring resulted in error-regulation in approximately two thirds of the cases.

*Diagnostic Competence.* There were significant effects from both kinds of treatments on diagnostic competence. Again, like with the variables of domain-specific strategies, the group with both kinds of instructional support outperformed the other groups, and the modeling group with expert maps but without additional strategy-instruction texts differed only slightly from the group which was only provided with the strategy-instruction texts.

*Correlation Between Strategy Use and Diagnostic Competence.* There is significant correlation for three of the four strategy variables: Establishing coherence and the construction of initial hypotheses showed the strongest correlation with the variable of diagnostic competence ($r = .50$ and $r = .48$). The formulation of competing hypotheses was less strongly—but nevertheless substantially related with the criterion ($r = .36$). Only the strategy of goal-directed selection was not significantly correlated with diagnostic competence ($r = .19$). Additionally, it could be shown that strategy use may be considered as a mediator between treatment and diagnostic competence (see F. Fischer, 1997; F. Fischer, Kittel, Gräsel, & Mandl, 1997). In the two groups control strategies were assessed; there was neither the expected positive correlation with error-regulating nor the expected negative correlation with error-ignoring control strategies. However, as in Study 1, there were indications that the successful learners tended to recognize and correct their *fundamental* mistakes more thoroughly.

*Discussion.* The results of Study 2 showed that strategy modeling with expert maps facilitated strategy use. The condition with expert maps and additional strategy-instruction texts was shown to be the most effective. Strategy-instruction texts contributed cumulatively to the effects of modeling with expert maps regarding central domain-specific strategies. In the case of diagnostic competence a positive effect of modeling with expert maps could be shown. In addition, a positive correlation between domain-specific strategies and diagnostic competence was found. Learners in the group with modeling by expert maps *and* strategy-instruction texts used error-regulating strategies most frequently and corrected the more important errors in their diagnostic process.

The results for the two different forms of modeling with expert maps implemented in Study 2 indicate, that just demonstrating may not be enough, at least for some learners. Concerning the facilitation of strategy use, modeling with expert maps is no more effective than the isolated strategy-instruction texts. As the studies of Rogoff (1990) showed, it is not simply the demonstration of how to handle a problem, but the additional explication of how and why to apply a given strategy in handling a problem which is connected with individual transfer in cognitive domains. The instructional texts for the domain-specific strategies seemed to be adequate additional explications in that sense.

The modeling procedure with strategy explanations used in this study can be regarded as a theory-based way of fostering the learners' mindful engagement by facilitating important externalization processes with the visualization task, and by eliciting reflection processes in the task of comparing the self-constructed maps with those of an expert (Collins, 1991; Collins & Brown, 1988).

Moreover, the procedure of modeling with expert maps employed in Study 2 can be considered an economic and practical way of instructional support in multimedia learning environments. Initial implementations of this kind of support in multimedia learning environments in medicine has already been realized (M. Fischer et al., 1996).

## CONCLUSION

*Strategy Use can be Facilitated with Modeling.* The results of our studies show that it is possible to support learners when they are dealing with authentic and complex problems. Especially the use of domain-specific strategies can be facilitated by instructional support. For our domain—learning with medical cases—strategy modeling seems to be a promising way of promoting the use of adequate domain-specific strategies. Especially the important strategies of establishing coherence and formulating competing hypotheses were effected. In contrast, the facilitation of metacognitive control strategies seems to be more difficult. Results of both studies indicate that the quantity of metacognitive control strategies was effected by modeling, but not the quality.

*The Use of Domain-Specific Strategies is Associated with the Correctness of Diagnoses.* In both studies, evidence could be found that the use of domain-specific strategies is correlated with diagnostic competence in problem-oriented learning of advanced medical students. At first glance, this seems to contradict the findings in medical expertise research (e.g. Patel & Groen, 1990). These findings emphasize the relative importance of domain knowledge as compared to strategies for the criterion 'diagnostic competence.' It has been argued that strategies could not replace lacking knowledge. In our studies, advanced medical students are employed as subjects who are supposed to already have the relevant prior knowledge. This supposition was confirmed by prior knowledge test results in both of our studies, which indicate that students have already acquired large quantities of concepts relevant in the area of anemia and related diseases. More importantly, most of the students participating in our studies had the relevant concepts for the solution of the diagnostic problems posed in the experiment. In the baseline case, however, only few learners were able to construct a coherent interpretation and accurate diagnoses. Researchers in the field of medical expertise have often used simplified text cases, in which the learner gets all the case information at once without having to ask the patient for additional information or to request relevant laboratory tests. In these cases, the application of prior knowledge may be much easier and the use of domain-specific strategies is less relevant than in the authentic cases used in our studies. Considering this difference, the use of the domain-specific strategies may be seen as facilitating the application of domain knowledge on complex and authentic medical problems.

Concerning the relation of strategy use and diagnostic competence, the results of Study 1 could be replicated in Study 2 in three out of four domain-specific strategies (goal-directed selection, formulating competing hypotheses, and establishing coherence). The studies differed in the results concerning the strategy of constructing initial hypotheses. Whereas the finding of a substantial correlation in the second study is in accordance with findings from medical education as well as from medical expertise research on the important role of early hypotheses, the lack of this correlation in Study 1 may be due to operationalization: The first stage in PlanAlyzer cases (first impression) may contain too little information to induce the formulation of the correct diagnoses in advanced medical students. As shown in Study 2, by considering a longer interval for the strategy of constructing initial hypotheses, a substantial correlation between this variable and the diagnostic competence variable could be found.

Concerning *control strategies*, the two studies revealed consistent findings: The simple amount of error-regulating control strategies does not seem to be a crucial factor in problem-oriented learning. We assume that subjects frequently used monitoring strategies correcting *minor* mistakes in the diagnostic process. More detailed analyses showed that the more critical point for learning is to notice *important* comprehension failures. It may have been disadvantageous to model the use of control strategies for one case and to ask the learner to apply these strategies for another case. This procedure did not provide learners with the possibility to compare their own use of control strategies with that of the expert *in relation to a specific content*. Concerning control strategies, our results confirm training studies in the field of metacognition which indicate that fostering metacognitive control, needs intensive instructional suuport, for example coaching by an experienced person.

***Conclusions for Educational Practice.*** Previous work with problem-oriented learning environments has shown that learners are often overwhelmed by this complex form of learning—especially when they are not used to it. To avoid these difficulties it is not necessary to reduce authenticity or complexity of the problems, or to wholly discard the problem-oriented learning approach. With adequate instructional support, problem-oriented learning seems to be a promising approach to closing the gap between knowledge and action. Domain-specific strategies are useful for learning with authentic and complex cases in medicine. Our findings support the claim made by some researchers of in the field of problem-based learning, that the application of these strategies in medical education should be taught. Modeling with expert articulation and with expert maps has shown to be an adequate instructional support in facilitating strategy use. Moreover, strategy modeling by experts is an economical and practicable way of realizing effective instructional support in *problem-oriented multimedia learning environments*.

## REFERENCES

ACME-TRI Report (1993). Educating medical students. Assessing change in medical education—the road to implementation. *Academic Medicine, 68* (6, Supplement), 1–48.

Albanese, M. A. & Mitchell, S. (1993). Problem-based learning: A review of literature on its outcomes and implementation issues. *Academic Medicine, 68,* 52–81.

Bransford, J. D., Sherwood, R. D., Hasselbring, T. S., Kinzer, C. K., & Williams, S. M. (1990). Anchored instruction: Why we need it and how technology can help. In D. Nix & R. J. Spiro (Eds.), *Cognition, education, and multimedia: Exploring ideas in high technology* (pp. 163–205). Hillsdale: Lawrence Erlbaum Associates.

Brown, J. S., Collins, A., & Duguid, P. (1989). Situated Cognition and the culture of learning. *Educational Researcher, 18,* 32–42.

Bruner, J. S. (1961). The act of discovery. *Harvard Educational Review, 61,* 21–32.

Bundesministerium für Gesundheit (1993). *Bericht der Sachverständigengruppe zu Fragen der Neuordnung des Medizinstudiums* [Report of the expert group for questions of restructuring medical education]. Bonn: Bundesministerium für Gesundheit.

Chi, M. T. H., Bassok, M., Lewis, M. W., Reimann, P., & Glaser, R. (1989). Self-explanations: How students study and use examples in learning to solve problems. *Cognitive Science, 13,* 145–182.

Cognition and Technology Group at Vanderbilt (1991). Technology and the design of generative learning environments. *Educational Technology, 31* (5), 34–40.

Cognition and Technology Group at Vanderbilt (1992). The Jasper series as an example of anchored instruction: Theory, program, description, and assessment data. *Educational Psychologist, 27,* 291–315.

Cognition and Technology Group at Vanderbilt (1993). Designing learning environments that support thinking: The Jasper series as a case study. In T. M. Duffy, J. Lowyck, D. H. Jonassen, & T. M. Welsh (Eds.), *Designing environments for constructive learning* (pp. 9–36). Berlin: Springer.

Collins, A. (1991). Cognitive apprenticeship and instructional technology. In L. Idol & B. F. Jones (Eds.), *Educational values and cognitive instruction: Implications for reform* (pp. 121–138). Hillsdale, NJ: Lawrence Erlbaum Associates.

Collins, A. & Brown, J. S. (1988). The computer as a tool for learning through reflection. In H. Mandl & A. Lesgold (Eds.), *Learning issues for intelligent tutoring systems* (pp. 1–18). New York: Springer.

Collins, A., Brown, J. S., & Newman, S. E. (1989). Cognitive apprenticeship: Teaching the crafts of reading, writing, and mathematics. In L. B. Resnick (Ed.), *Knowing, learning, and instruction. Essays in the honour of Robert Glaser* (pp. 453–494). Hillsdale, NJ: Lawrence Erlbaum Associates.

Elstein, A. S., Shulman, L. S., & Sprafka, S. A. (1978). *Medical problem solving: An analysis of clinical reasoning.* Cambridge, MA: Harvard University Press.

Fischer, F. (1997). *Mappingverfahren als Werkzeug für das problemorientierte Lernen. Entwicklung und empirische Untersuchung eines computerbasierten Mappingverfahrens in der Domäne Medizin* [Concept mapping as a tool for problem-oriented learning. Development and evaluation of a computer-based mapping technique]. Unveröff. Diss., Ludwig-Maximilians-Universität, München.

Fischer, F., Gräsel, C., Kittel, A., & Mandl, H. (1996). Entwicklung und Unter-suchung eines computerbasierten Mappingverfahrens zur Strukturierung kom-plexer Information [A computer-based mapping technique for structuring complex information: Development and some preliminary data]. *Psychologie in Erziehung und Unterricht, 43,* 266–280.

Fischer, F., Gräsel, C., Kittel, A., & Mandl, H. (1997). Strategien zur Bearbeitung von Diagnoseproblemen in komplexen Lernumgebungen [Strategies for working with diagnostic problems in complex learning environments]. *Zeitschrift für Entwicklungspsychologie und Pädagogische Psychologie, 29,* 62–82.

Fischer, M., Schauer, S., Gräsel, C., Baehring, T. Mandl, H. Gärtner, R., Scherbaum, W., & Scriba, P. C. (1996). Modellversuch CASUS. Ein computergestütztes Autorensystem für die problemorientierte Lehre in der Medizin [CASUS. A com-puter-based authoring system for problem-oriented medical education]. *Zeitschrift für ärztliche Fortbildung, 90,* 385–389.

Friedrich, H. F. & Mandl, H. (1992). Lern- und Denkstrategien—ein Problemaufriß [Learning and thinking strategies—a critical overview]. In H. Mandl & H. F. Frie-drich (Hrsg.), *Lern- und Denkstrategien. Analyse und Intervention* (S. 3–54). Göt-tingen: Hogrefe.

Gaudig, H. (1922). *Die Schule im Dienste der werdenden Persönlichkeit* [Schools for the development of personality]. Leipzig: Teubner.

Gerstenmaier, J. & Mandl, H. (1995). Wissenserwerb unter konstruktivistischer Per-spektive [Knowledge acquisition from a constructivist perspective]. *Zeitschrift für Pädagogik, 41,* 867–888.

Gräsel, C. (1997). *Problemorientiertes Lernen. Strategieanwendung und Gestaltungsmöglichkeiten* [Problem-oriented learning. Strategy use and possi-bilities for design]. Göttingen: Hogrefe.

Gräsel, C. & Mandl, H. (1993). Förderung des Erwerbs diagnostischer Strategien in fallbasierten Lernumgebungen [Fostering the acquisition of diagnostic strategies in case-based learning environments]. *Unterrichtswissenschaft, 21,* 355–370.

Greeno, J. G. & Goldman, S. (Eds.). (1997). *Thinking practices: Math and science learning.* Mahwah, NJ: Lawrence Erlbaum Associates.

Hmelo, C. E., Gotterer, G. S., & Bransford, J. D. (1994, April). *The cognitive effects of problem-based learning: A preliminary study.* Paper presented at the Annual Meeting of the American Educational Research Association, New Orleans.

Honebein, P. C., Duffy, T. M., & Fischman, B. J. (1993). Constructivism and the design of learning environment: Context and authentic activities for learning. In T. M. Duffy, J. Lowyck, D. H. Jonassen, & T. M. Welsh (Eds.), *Designing envi-ronments for constructive learning* (pp. 87-108). Berlin: Springer.

Jonassen, D. H., Beissner, K., & Yacci, M. (1993). *Structural knowledge. Techniques for representing, conveying and acquiring structural knowledge.* Hillsdale, NJ: Lawrence Erlbaum Associates.

Jones, B. F., Knuth, R. A., & Duffy, T. M. (1993). Components of constructivist learning environments for professional development. In T. M. Duffy, J. Lowyck, D. H. Jonassen, & T. M. Welsh (Eds.), *Designing environments for constructive learning* (pp. 125–137). Berlin: Springer.

Jüngst, K. L. (1995). Studien zur didaktischen Nutzung von Concept Maps [Studies on the didactical use of concept maps]. *Unterrichtswissenschaft, 3,* 229–250.

Kerschensteiner, G. (1912). *Begriff der Arbeitsschule* [The concept of the working school]. Leipzig: Teubner.

Lyon, H. D., Healy, J. C., Bell, J. R., O'Donnell, J. F., Shulth, E. K., Wigton, R. S., Hirai, F., & Beck, J. R. (1990). *PlanAlyzer. Cases on hematology.* Hanover: Dartmouth Medical School.

Mandl, H., Gruber, H., & Renkl, A. (1996). Learning to apply: From "school garden instruction" to technology-based learning environments. In S. Vosniadou, E. de Corte, R. Glaser, & H. Mandl (Eds.), *International perspectives on the design of technology-supported learning environments* (pp. 307-321). Hillsdale, NJ: Lawrence Erlbaum Associates.

Patel, V. L., Groen, G. J., & Norman, G. R. (1993). Reasoning and instruction in medical curricula. *Cognition and Instruction, 10,* 335–378.

Pea, R. D. (1994). Seeing what we build together: Distributed multimedia learning environments for transformative communications. *Journal of the Learning Sciences* (Special Issue: Computer support for collaborative learning), *3,* 285–299.

Prawat, R. S. (1993). The value of ideas: Problems versus possibilities in learning. *Educational Researcher, 22* (11), 5–16.

Renkl, A., Gruber, H., Mandl, H., & Hinkofer, L. (1994). Hilft Wissen bei der Identifikation und Kontrolle eines komplexen ökonomischen Systems? [Does knowledge support the identification and control of a complex economical system?] *Unterrichtswissenschaft, 22,* 195–202.

Resnick, L. B. (1987). Learning in school and out. *Educational Researcher, 16* (9), 13–20.

Rogoff, B. (1990). *Apprenticeship in thinking: Cognitive development in social context.* Oxford, MA: Oxford University Press.

Schneider, W. & Pressley, M. (1989). *Memory development between 2 and 20.* New York: Springer.

Stark, R., Graf, M., Renkl, A., Gruber, H., & Mandl, H. (1995). Förderung von Handlungskompetenz durch geleitetes Problemlösen und multiple Lernkontexte [Fostering action competence by guided problem solving and multiple learning contexts]. *Zeitschrift für Entwicklungspsychologie und Pädagogische Psychologie, 27,* 289–312.

Williams, S. M. (1992). Putting case-based instruction into context: Examples from legal and medical education. *The Journal of the Learning Sciences, 2,* 367–427.

# 12

# The Role of Cognitive Structure in the Development of Behavioral Control: A Dynamic Skills Approach

*Thomas R. Bidell*
*Kurt W. Fischer*

## INTRODUCTION

Imagine trying to control an automobile without the structure of a steering wheel, steering column, or mechanical linkage to the front wheels. Or, imagine trying to ride a horse without reins or a bit with which to communicate your intentions and guide its movements. Such mundane examples point up the inseparable relation between structure and control in everyday life. Given this obvious relationship, it is surprising to find that theories of cognitive development have typically provided very little explanation of how the development of cognitive structure is related to the development of behavioral control. Instead, structural theories of cognitive development have tended to project formal and universalist concepts of cognitive structure like Piagetian stages or Chomskian competencies. Such concepts are so static and abstract that they offer little insight as to how cognitive structure might function in the control of actual behavior which is always dynamic and concrete. As a consequence, there has been little basis for relating cognitive structural development with processes of behavioral control.

In this chapter we present a brief critique of static concepts of cognitive structure showing why such concepts limit our understanding of the relations between structure and control in behavioral development. We then draw on a dynamic systems approach coupled with neo-Piagetian principles of cognitive structural development, to present an alternative concept of cognitive structure associated with dynamic skills theory (Fischer, 1980; Fisher & Bidell, 1997). Finally, we show how the concept of dynamic skills can provide a theoretical and empirical basis for understanding the links between structure and control in behavioral development.

## LIMITATIONS OF THE STRUCTURE-AS-FORM PARADIGM

Cognitive structure is the organizational aspect of human behavior. Behavior, defined as goal-oriented activity, necessarily involves an organizational or structural dimension. If it were not structured, behavior would degenerate into random acts, incapable of reaching goals or communicating meaning. In principle, this unity of structure and control in behavior has been understood by cognitive scientists at least since Lashley's (Jeffress, 1951; Gardner, 1985) critique of associative chain models. Lashley showed that complex behaviors such as speech, involving sequences of actions cannot simply be bound together by individual links between the parts. Instead, the individual actions *must* be governed by some kind of structure of the whole that can ensure each action is performed in its proper sequential relation with all the others. In a sentence such as "Please pass the salt" some means must be in place to assure that "Please" comes before "pass," that "salt" comes at the end, and so on. Such a structure must be simultaneous in nature since the set of sequential relations must be anticipated as a whole at the same time that each of the individual actions (words uttered) is executed in its turn.

This principle applies not just to language but to all forms of human behavior. Consider, for example, executing a routine set of errands after work: picking up your children at daycare, picking up the laundry, getting groceries for dinner, filling the car with gas. To be successful, these errands must be planned using a cognitive structure that holds them in a simultaneous set of temporal, spatial, and categorical relations (Bidell & Fischer, 1994). The daycare closes at 6:00 p.m., but the cleaner is closer so you need to stop there first, and it is easier to grocery shop before picking up the children, so you go there next knowing it is past the cleaner, but you can get gas with the children staying in the car so this can be done last, after stopping at the daycare. Any failure to hold these items and their multiple interrelations in a simultaneous mental organization will result in a failure to control the behavioral sequence of actions that must be performed.

In examples such as this, it is easy to see that cognitive structure must be *dynamic* since it is the organizational aspect of living systems of activity (including thinking activity). Planning processes like the one above require the ability to flexibly reorganize one's conception of the relations among actions in the face of new contingencies like the early closure of the clothes cleaner, or a traffic blockage that demands a re-ordering of the sequence in which one's actions must be executed. In such events, rigidly determined rules or scripts would be worse than useless. To rigidly repeat a sequence of events simply because it is the way one has always done it is a dysfunctional approach to life. A hallmark of human intelligence is that we can flexibly adapt to changing situations by quickly restructuring our understanding to guide us in novel behavioral approaches to the world.

However, traditional theories of cognitive development have failed to capture the dynamism of cognitive structure. Instead, cognitive theories have typically fallen into a conceptual error in which dynamic structure is reductionistically separated from real living activity and treated as a static, predetermined form. Such reification of structure as form extends back at least to the Platonic belief in universal forms of ideas said to pre-exist and determine the specific concepts developing in a individual. Although Plato's description of the general form of key thought patterns in Western culture achieved a powerful abstraction from the dynamics of everyday living, Plato made the mistake of giving his abstractions an independent life of their own. He projected his abstraction of forms of thought as separately existing universal entities endowed with the power to create the very patterns of thinking activity from which he had abstracted them in the first place!

The philosopher of science Pepper (1942) identified form as one of the primary metaphors or "world hypotheses" through which Western culture has interpreted mind. Although Pepper's metaphors of mechanism, organicism, and historicism have been more commonly applied to metatheory in psychology, we believe that the tendency to view dynamic structure through the lens of static form is so pervasive in Western thought that it merits designation as the *structure-as-form* paradigm. In the section below, we outline ways in which the structure-as-form paradigm has influenced three common models of cognitive structure, Piagetian stages, Chomskian competences, and competence–performance models, and show how the confounding of form with structure in these models has limited our understanding of the relation between cognitive structure and behavioral control.

First, it is essential to distinguish between the use of the concept "form" as a metaphor for dynamic structure and the use of formal abstraction as a tool in scientific analysis. It is only the former that we are criticizing here. Obviously, the abstracting of formal descriptions from a complexly structured dynamic system is an invaluable tool for scientific inquiry, allowing us to take "snapshots" of key moments or general patterns in system dynamics. Indeed, a key tool in our own and other's work on dynamic systems in cognitive development is the use of formal mathematical equations to model change in such systems. What we object to is not use of formal abstraction at the methodological level, but the confounding of static formal abstractions with the real dynamic structure of cognitive systems at the theoretical and metatheoretical level. To held maintain this important distinction, the term "formal" is used in the following discussion to refer to specific descriptive tools such formal mathematical models, formal logics, or formal rule systems derived from the empirical study of cognitive systems. The term "formalist" is used in a way similar to the term "universalist" to characterize broad theoretical models of cognitive structure which we believe conform to the structure-as-form paradigm.

## Piagetian Stage Theory

Classical Piagetian stage theory provides a clear illustration of why formalist models of cognitive structure obscure real relations between cognitive structure and behavioral control.

In Piagetian stage theory, cognitive structures are characterized in terms of universal *logical forms* emerging in a developmental sequence. At each stage, children's behavior is more or less predetermined by the logical structure existing at that time: a pre-operational child will act illogically and a concrete operational child will act logically (in concrete situations). The conception of the relations between cognitive structure and behavioral control is one-directional and rigid. The form of the logic determines the type of behavior. There is little in this model of structure to support an understanding of how cognitive structure helps guide everyday activities such as planning, how cognitive structures may change and adapt to changing circumstances, or how such functional involvement might contribute to the development of new kinds of cognitive structure.

In this regard it is important to make a distinction between two contradictory aspects of Piaget's theory: his *constructivist epistemology* and his *formalist stage model*. Piaget's constructivist epistemology is a very dynamic approach to knowledge which includes a dynamic conception of structure as a "system of relations" (Piaget, 1970a). Piaget made a strong distinction between dynamic structure and static form, and laid the epistemological foundations for understanding cognitive structure as the product of self organization (Piaget, 1977). However, in moving from Piaget's epistemological position to the stage model of cognitive structure that he developed, one finds that dynamic definition of structure does not carry over. In his the stage model, Piaget (1970b) represented cognitive structures in terms of universal formal logics. Toward the end of his career Piaget tried to rectify this problem, seeking more dynamic conceptions of cognitive structure derived from the *logic of meaning* and other contemporary work. However, Piaget never succeeded in providing a workable dynamic model of cognitive structure at the psychological (as opposed epistemological) level. Consequently, formalist stage structures became the default assumption in most of the of cognitive developmental work inspired by Piaget's theory. This concept of logical stages has remained quite platonic: emerging universal forms of logic that pre-determine the type of behavior an individual will exhibit across various tasks and contexts.

## Chomskian Competence Theory

Although frequently contrasted with Piaget's stage theory, Chomsky's theory of innate universal competencies simply represents another version of the structure-as-form paradigm.

Instead of an emerging sequence of formal logics, an emerging set of genetically coded formal rules (or scripts or principals) determines the organization of linguistic behavior across situational or cultural contexts. Indeed, formal logics and formal rule systems have in common that they abstract the *form* of some dynamic living activity like reasoning or communicating, and project it as a static entity isolated from the real activity and context from which it was abstracted. Piagetian theory abstracts a formal description of a logical stage, like pre-operations, from the dynamic and highly variable reasoning activity of myriad young children across a vast array of tasks and contexts. Similarly, Chomskian theory abstracts formal grammatical rules from myriad instances of actual speech. In reality, each individual instance of reasoning or speech differs from all others in its organization, goal, and outcome. Of course, each instance of actual reasoning or communication *is* organized. But the organization of real behavior is dynamic and thus inevitably varies from formalist descriptions which, by their nature, are static abstractions.

It is for this reason that the biggest shortcoming of both Piagetian and Chomskian theories has been their inability to account for variability in the data of cognitive development. Although both theories have been good at predicting *general* trends in behavior and development, they have been notoriously bad at predicting or accounting for variations in linguistic or cognitive behavior across differing individuals and across situational and cultural contexts. It is now well established that individuals who measure at one cognitive level on a given task, such as number conservation, can display an entirely different cognitive level on other tasks such as spatial conservation; or, their cognitive level may even change on the same task if the materials or procedures have changed or if the individuals own emotional, nutritional, or attentional processes have changed. Similarly, the ages at which children acquire new cognitive abilities can vary greatly depending on task materials, external support conditions, or cultural context. None of these widely documented types of variation is either predicted or explained by the theory that cognitive structure in individuals consists in formal logical stages.

**Competence-Performance  Theory**

The recognition that formal logics and rule systems cannot account for the variability inherent in real contextualized activity led some theorists (Chomsky, 1968; Flavell & Wohlwill, 1969) to introduce a third approach to cognitive structure: the competence-performance distinction. On this view, each person possesses certain "underlying" abilities or competences which take the form of pre-existing rule-systems or logics. Although these covert competences remain essentially constant, they somehow give rise to overt performance which varies with specific circumstances. Superficially this distinction appears reasonable: One may have an ability and not exercise it. Yet, on closer examination, the competence-performance distinction adds nothing of explanatory value to the formalist theories it seeks to amend. It simply makes explicit, the implicit schism between structure and behavior found in all formalist models of cogntive structure.

Moreover, by raising the dualistic divsion between cognitive structure and behavior to the level of a theoretical premise, competence-performance models create the need to explicate implicit deterministic mechanisms in an attempt to explain how these underlying structures relate to behavioral outcomes. This puts researchers in the absurd position of attempting to show how real behaviors can be derived from formal abstractions which were drawn from the real behavior patterns to begin with. An example of this approach comes from Greeno, Riley, and Gelman (1984) who attempted to explain children's mathematical performance by formally deriving behavioral sequences from competence structures.

We use Chomsky's (e.g. 1965) method of analyzing competence with formal derivations that connect postulated competence with properties of performance. Our analysis differs from Chomsky's and other linguistic analyses in the objects that are derived. In linguistic analyses, the derived objects are sentences, corresponding to sequences of behavior. We derive cognitive procedures, which are capable of producing sequences of behavior. . . In our analysis, the relation between competence and performance structures has the form of derivations in which performance structures are consequences of competence structures, derived by a planning system (p. 104).

An unfortunate consequence of this approach is that it effectively depicts behaviors as the product of a one-way deterministic chain of events with formal competence at the determining end of the chain, and individual's behavior mechanically "derived" from these. From a scientific perspective, such models fail to provide testable explanations of variability in behavior since, for every newly observed variation in performance, a new "derivative" mechanism can simply be added to the model (Chandler, 1991; Tang & Ginsberg, 1997). Consequently competence-performance models, like their predesessors, leave us with the same unanswered questions about why children's cognitive performance varies across contexts, and how children's own goal-oriented adaptive activity in everyday situations might contribute to the development of cognitive structure in the first place.

In summary, formalist models of cognitive structure have failed to explain how cognitive organization is tied to the control of real contextualized behavior. At best, stage and competence models are one directional, dictating what behavior should be based on formal logics or rules. As such, there is no room for the give and take between structural organization and the highly dynamic adaptive activity of human cognitive systems. What is needed is a model of cognitive structure that helps to explain variability in everyday behavior and helps to illuminate the role played by cognitive structure in the control of behavior.

## THE DYNAMIC STRUCTURE OF COGNITIVE SKILLS

An important alternative source of concepts about cognitive structure is dynamic systems theory. Scientists studying dynamic systems in a range of disciplines have recognized that the apparent randomness or "chaos" observed in phenomena such as weather, coastal erosion, and cardiac pathology, are in fact the result of complexly organized dynamic systems. By building models of the complex dynamics inherent in such systems, scientists have made new advances in understanding the organization of seemingly chaotic phenomena. As researchers in developmental psychology have increasingly recognized the inadequacy of formalist models in accounting for evidence of variability in cognitive development, there has been a growing interest in dynamic systems models of cognitive development (Fischer & Bidell, 1997; Lewis, 1994; Thelen & Smith, 1994; van Geert, 1994).

Because dynamic systems theory assumes that systems are both complexly organized and dynamic (Thelen & Smith, 1994), there is no need posit abstract formal entities, existing separately from the dynamic organization of the system itself. This means that the troublesome distinctions between formal logics or competencies and behavioral control can be dropped. Instead of dichotomizing formal competence and real performance, the structure that controls behavior can be seen as simply the dynamic organization inherent in cognitive activities themselves. Instead of accounting for variablity in performance as an aberration from some underlying "true" competence, variability is seen as a natural outcome of a complexly organized dynamic system. The theoretical task then becomes to explain observed variability as a consequence of the structural dynamics of the cognitive system, instead of devising rationales to explain away empirical departures from a formalist model.

### Dynamic Skills Theory

Dynamic skills theory (Fischer, 1980; Fischer & Bidell, 1997) provides a useful framework by which to apply dynamic systems principles to the explanation of variability in cognitive functioning and development. The term *skill* denotes and connotes many characteristics of the dynamic organization of human activities. A skill is the ability to act in an organized way in a specific context. Skills are always concrete and contextualized: a skill for playing tennis, playing chess, telling stories, or communicating with others. Although some skills, like isolation-of-variables reasoning, may be adaptable to a broad range of contexts, there are no universal, context-free skills.

The notion of skill is useful for conceptualizing the dynamic organization of human activities because real concrete skills necessarily integrate many levels of systems. A skilled story teller in a given cultural setting must integrate and unite systems of emotion, memory, planning, speech, and gesture, as well as sociocultural systems involving cultural norms for story pattern and audience participation. Because it entails such interrelations among systems, the concept of skill helps cut through artificial dichotomies between cognitive structure and behavioral control. And for the same reason, the skill concept facilitates the study of dynamic relations among multiple interrelating systems and the patterns of variation in behavior which they produce.

## How Dynamic Skills Explain Variability

Let us consider several characteristics of cognitive skills that help explain variablity in human activities.

*Integration.* Skills are integrated living systems, not atomistically composed heaps of behaviors (Bidell & Fischer, 1997). Sub-systems participate in each other and in the skill as a whole. Therefore, changes in one subsystem often result in changes in other subsystems. An individual's tennis-playing skill will vary considerably with the player's emotional condition, nutritional status, cognitive readiness, and physical conditioning. Because all these systems are integrated in the skill of playing tennis, changes in any of these interrelated systems can result in variation in any of the other systems and in level of performance on a given day.

*Context Specificity.* Human activity systems are organized to function in specific settings. The particular constellation of integrated sub-systems that functions well in one setting does not automatically function as well in another: good baseball players do not make good basketball players without extensive training and reintegration of skills for eye-hand coordination, physical conditioning, and conceptualization of the game. An individual with high level discourse skills in one language and culture will fumble awkwardly in an unknown cultural context. Indeed the sociocultural support system in which cognitive skills function may be seen as one of the integrated component systems of that skill. Therefore, from a dynamic skills perspective, it follows that cognitive performance should vary greatly across situational and cultural contexts (Fischer, Bullock, Rothenberg, & Raya, 1993). Yet, formalist stage and competence theories have been at a loss to explain such variation.

*Self-Regulation.* An important source of the dynamics of cognitive systems is that, as living systems, they are self-regulating and self-organizing. From the perspective of self-regulation, cognitive systems are adaptive and must actively adjust their functioning to changes in the contexts in which they participate. For example, a child who is skilled at working puzzles but is working collaboratively with an adult who selects pieces for her, may only need to organize her cognitive activity minimally—just enough to find the matching contours. But if the adult leaves, the child must suddenly adapt by organizing a more complex set of cognitive activities that include those the adult had been performing. This adaptive response involves a variation in the whole activity system including both the behavior and its cognitive organization. Thus, in the dynamic skills approach, variation in performance is natural consequence of the dynamics functioning of cognitive skills, not a conundrum to be resolved by dichotomizing structure and performance.

*Self-Organization.*    An extension of the self-regulatory aspect of cognitive skills is self-organization. Since skills are dynamic living systems, new kinds of skill organization arise not from the unfolding of predetermined forms, but from a self-actualizing process in which existing skills are integrated or *coordinated* to construct new skills with new dynamic structures (Bidell & Fischer, 1997). For example, around three to four years of age children typically have constructed two separate interpersonal skills, one for controlling "nice" behavior (as evidenced by doll play) and one for controlling "mean" behavior. Typically these skills function independently, with children being unable to control both nice and mean behavior in a single situation. Gradually, however, children show evidence of coordinating these two skills into a single skill. Initially, when presented with dolls acting both nice and mean, children shift back and forth from controlling one behavior to controlling the other. Eventually, they succeed in fully integrating the component skills and can make a doll act both nice and mean in the same situation.

Like self-regulation, the process of self-organizing leads naturally to variablity in skill development. For one thing, self-organization, as a real constructive activity, does not simply uncover pre-formed ideas, but involves a *microdevelopmental* (microgenetic) process of integration taking place over time and often showing leaps or regressions (Bidell & Fischer, 1994; Granott, 1993). Thus a child who has recently succeeded in constructing a skill for simultaneous control and of nice and mean behaviors in a familiar setting, may not be able to hold together the component skills when faced with an unfamiliar environment. Or, a child who has gradually worked at integrating nice and mean concepts without success, may suddenly succeed, shifting to a new level of cognitive skill all at once. Again, such sudden changes in skill level are easily understood as a natural part of the constructive process, but are difficult to explain at all on the basis of formal competencies which predicts that individuals should possess only one underlying level of ability in a given domain until the next level is somehow revealed.

*Multilineality.*    Finally, it follows from the context-specific and self-organizing nature of cognitive skills that they need not conform to a single developmental pathway. Formalist models of cognitive structure imply a unilinear developmental pathway since development is conceptualized as an unfolding or uncovering of a necessary sequence of formal logics or competencies. The core metaphor for change in such models is the developmental *ladder* in which each new competence represents another step up toward a predetermined outcome. Even where "domain-specificity" is recognized, formalist models characterize

developmental progress as a linear climb up the developmental ladder for each
domain.

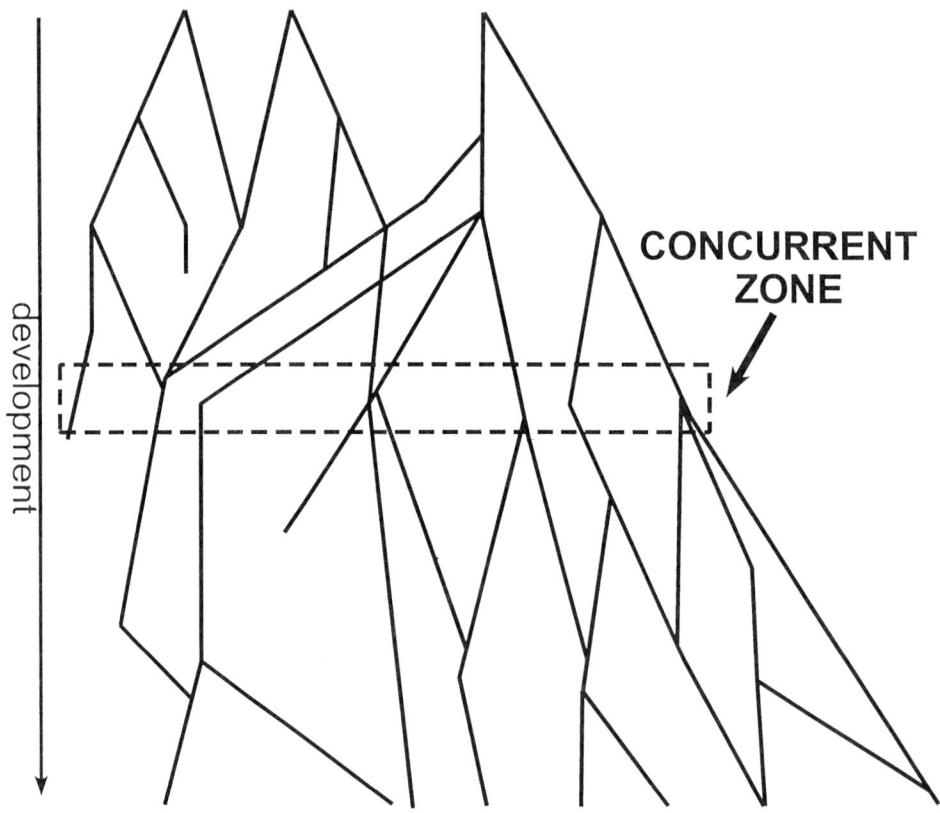

*FIG. 12.1. A developmental web showing concurrent discontinuities across
strands. The metaphor of a web represents development as a constructive, self-
organizing, multilineal process. Each strand represents a domain of developing
activity. Concurrent construction of similar skills along different strands can
create a stage-like effect. Adapted from Fischer & Kennedy (1997).*

In contrast, skill development is better characterized with the metaphor of a
developmental *web* (Bidell & Fischer, 1992) shown in figure 12.1. The web

metaphor is meant to show how the development of cognitive skills can take a branching, multilineal set of directions as skills constructed in one context are reconstructed to create new skills for new situations and contexts.

As an example, consider a child who has constructed two separate sensori-motor skills: grasping objects, and waving an arm back and forth. Both these skills were constructed in the context of lying in its cradle. Now, the infant finds itself in a new context: a parent regularly holds the infant and offers it toys such as rattles. In order to participate in this new context by taking the offered rattle and shaking it, as modeled by the parent, the infant must coordinate the component grasping and waving skills to create the more inclusive skill of shaking the rattle by grasping it and waving its arm at the same time.

Thus, the active integration of component skills extends the child's cognitive repertoire in two directions: the hierarchical inclusion of component skills under a common control structure (represented by the vertical dimension of the web), and the ability to participate in a new environmental context (represented by the horizontal dimension of the web). This "strand" can then become the basis for further branching in the web. For instance, the child may construct a primitive pencil-use skill by applying the gaping-waving skill to a pencil, and coordinating this skill with the skill of pressing the pencil downward against a sheet of paper. Or the skill may branch in another direction as the infant constructs a skill for grasping the string of a pull-toy and pulling it in, extending his or her participation to another context of activity.

The web metaphor also supports thinking about stablity in development without reducing it rigid consistency as do formalist models. Thus, in dynamic skills theory an individuals cognitive level of skill for a given tasks is described in terms of a *developmental range* of skill levels, the upper limit of which is determined by the highest level of complexity yet constructed for that task and the lower limit by the degree of external support and internal systemic resources available at a given moment.

Moreover, this range itself varies in its upper limit across tasks, contexts, and content areas. Thus, instead of fixed levels of competence that cut across tasks and contexts, children's dynamic skills develop across concurrent zones (represented by the box cutting across strands in figure 12.1) in which the similarity in upper limit of skills is due to relative similarities in the constructive process, but in which skill levels can nevertheless vary greatly.

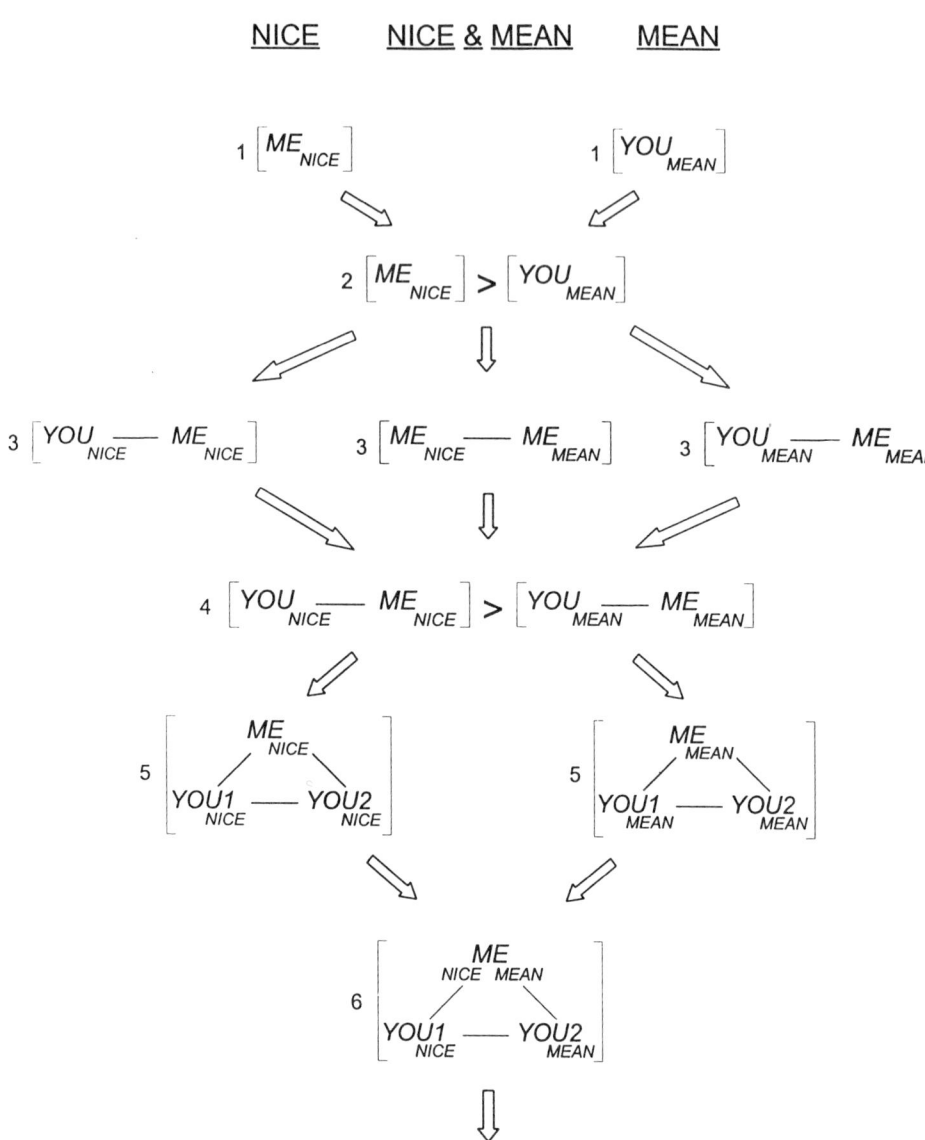

FIG. 12.2a. *Developmental web for understanding nice and mean interactions in nonmaltreated children.*

Although examples such as these represent the construction of a within-individual web of cognitive skills, the metaphor of the constructive web can also be used to analyze multilineality in developmental pathways across individuals. One example comes from research on the development of concepts of nice and mean from childhood through adulthood (Fisher & Ayoub, 1994). Figure 12.2a. presents a developmental web tracing the pathways by which normal children typically construct skills for controlling stories about nice and mean acts by themselves and others. As figure 12.2a. suggests, children first construct simple skills for controlling stories about a nice act by me, a nice act by you, a mean act by me, etc. These simple cognitive skills then serve as components in the construction of more complex skills for controlling multiple components in a single story, such as a nice act by you, complemented by a nice act by me; or an act that is both nice and mean at the same time. Note that in this web concepts of equal complexity are controlled at about the same time (as represented by parallel position in the vertical dimension of the web) whether they represent nice or mean acts.

Figure 12.2b., however, shows a distinctly different developmental web. This web traces the construction of nice and mean concepts in a group of children who have suffered from abuse and neglect. Note that conceptual development is strongly biased toward mean concepts. Although these children start with the same components and eventually construct the same concepts, they come to understand stories involving meanness much sooner. Thus, an analysis of the relative differences in constructive pathways across two groups of children reveals ways in which the dynamic construction of skills in differing contexts leads to variability across persons in the rate of development of cognitive structures.

In summary, the high degree of variablity inherent in the constructive process of cognitive skill development contrasts directly with the assumptions of formalist models of cognitive structure. Formalist models assume a fixed structure and therefore a fixed level of competence. At any given point in development, an individual is thought to have achieved a specific, invariant, level of ability which, by implication, should support behavioral performance of specific levels of complexity. From this point of view, variability in actual performance is problematic and is typically treated as a nuisance: annoying data complicating an otherwise elegant theory. Thus Piaget argued that gaps in performance levels were due to differential types of environmental "resistance," but was never able to offer a theory descriptive of specific types of resistance or predictive of how such resistance would systematically affect behavior. Similarly, Chomsky (1968) introduced the distinction between underlying competence and actual performance in an attempt to explain away variability in performance, and was never able to offer an specific theory to show why specific variations in performance occur at a given time an place.

NICE              NICE & MEAN              MEAN

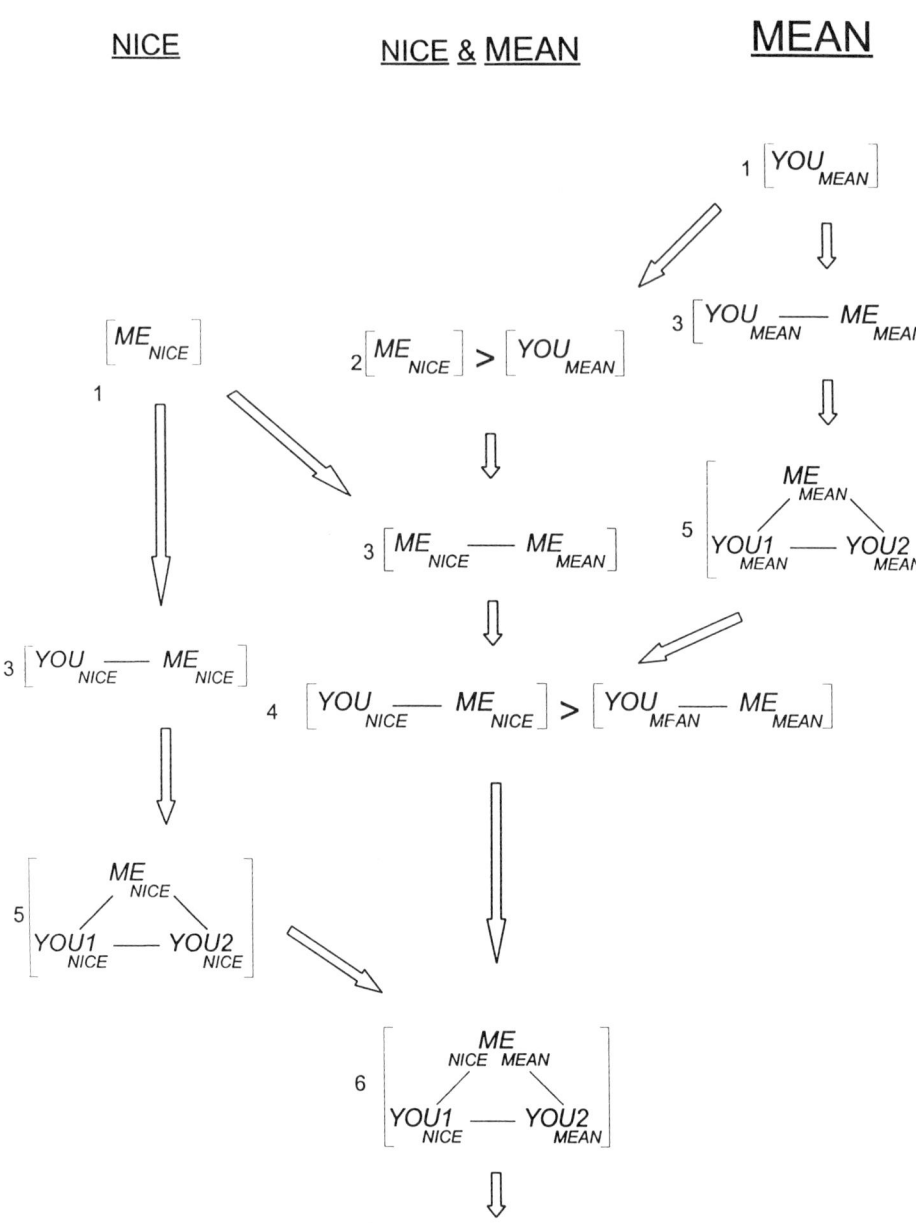

FIG. 12.2b. *Developmental web biased toward mean interactions in abused children.*

The assumptions of dynamic skill theory are just the opposite. Since structure is defined not as a fixed competence, but as the organizational aspect of real dynamic systems of activity, structure and performance are no longer portrayed as separate but as unified dimensions of behavioral systems. Cognitive structure simply is the way activity, including thinking activity, is dynamically organized. As with other types of dynamic systems models, the goal in dynamic skills theory is not to explain why behavior varies from the predictions of a formalist model, but to describe the actual dynamic organization of complex systems. Of course, all systems must possess stability and relative consistency if they are to maintain themselves as systems. As noted earlier, this is the fundamental role of structure in cognitive organization. However, formalist models of structure, by rafting structure, obscure its dynamic nature and mislead researchers into false dichotomies like the competence-performance distinction.

## RETHINKING RELATIONS BETWEEN COGNITIVE STRUCTURE AND BEHAVIORAL CONTROL

Having outlined the differences between static, formalist models of cognitive structure and the dynamic systems models exemplified by skill theory, it should now be apparent why formalist models have been of little help in understanding the relations between cognitive structure and behavioral control. When cognitive structure is conceived of as abstract, formal, unchanging, and separated from actual performance, as in the competence–performance distinction, then the only relation to performance possible is deterministic. This leads to a marionette model in which cognitive structure is viewed as determining the outcome of behavior from afar. Moreover, since the strings operate in only one direction, the marionette model cannot offer useful accounts of the cognitive structure arising out of behavioral activity—only behavior being determined by underlying structure (Greeno et. al. (1984), competence–performance model of children's counting, cited earlier).

Dynamic skills theory offers an alternative approach to the relation between cognitive structure and behavioral control which avoids the misleading assumptions and rigid determinism of formalist models. Since, in skill theory, cognitive structure is not separated from concrete performance but resides in the concrete activity itself (as the organizational aspect of that activity) there is no need to posit marionette strings of determination bridging the gap from reified structure to behavior. On the contrary, since skills are self-organizing systems of activity, cognitive structures are self-determined by the constructive efforts of the person. Therefore, in the dynamic skills approach, the relation between cognitive structure and behavioral control is not determination but enablement. Since action must be organized to achieve goal directed behavior, structure is an inherent part of the dynamic behavioral control system itself. The origin of new cognitive structure is a natural outcome of the functioning of the cognitive behavioral system as it reorganizes to meet new challenges. Individuals do not construct cognitive structures and then translate them into behavioral actions, but instead, construct webs of cognitive–behavioral skills which are structured and restructured to enable action in specific environments.

The shift from determinism to self-determination in our understanding of relations between cognitive structure and behavioral control hold important implication s for research on this topic. Since formalist models mistakenly portray behavior as determined by separately existing formal structures, research efforts tend to get sidetracked into attempts to verify the formal model by explaining away the high degree of variability found in real contextualized behaviors. This has led to endless futile debates about what is the "real" age of acquisition for a given cognitive skill, or which task "truly" evaluates such a skill. In this debate, variability and change—which should be the focus of scientific research—have been treated as a nuisance in the quest to validate static formalist models of cognitive structure.

By contrast, the general research goal in the dynamic skills approach is to understand how the actual dynamic cognitive-behavioral systems are in fact organized, and how this organization changes, by describing the range and patterns of variability and change in real activity. From this perspective, variability in performance is anything but a nuisance. On the contrary, variability provides a valuable set of clues for researchers in their attempts to describe the full range of complexity and dynamics in developing cognitive–behavioral systems.

An example comes from work on computer modeling of the dynamics of developing systems. Figure 12.3. shows a family of growth curves produced by a structural equation constructed to model developmental change in self-in-relation concepts and performance among Korean adolescents (Fischer & Kennedy, 1997). Structural equation modeling of this type allows researchers to represent the outcomes of multiple interconnections of a complex web-like system to be represented as families of growth curves (Fischer & Bidell, 1997; van Geert, 1994). Figure 12.3. shows a range of growth patterns, all produced by the same structural model, representing different developmental pathways adolescents may follow under differing conditions or domains.

Development is measured on a 12-step skill theory scale in which each step represents a new structural level in the ability to conceptualize one's relations with others (Fischer, Kenny, & Pipp, 1990; Kennedy, 1994). The five *domains* represent different self-in-relation conditions including relations with mother, father, best friend, romantic friend, and teacher. The *optimal* and *functional* sets of curves model high and low support conditions respectively (high support conditions are those most conducive to good performance on a given task, such as encouragement or modeling; low support is independent performance). Only two typical domains are shown in the functional condition to improve readability of the graph.

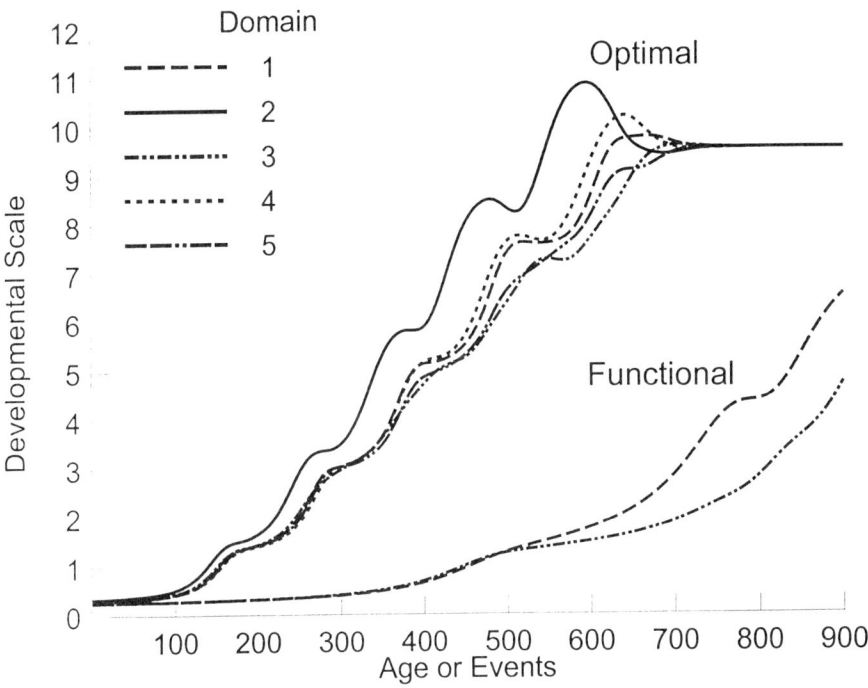

*FIG. 12.3. Optimal and functional levels in a dynamic model of development of self-in-relationships among Korean adolescents. The model illustrates how patterns of variability in the development of a concept depend on both domain (who the individual relates to) and support conditions (optimal versus functional). In five different domains (relationships), optimal levels show a sequence of regulated stage-like discontinuities, but functional levels (illustrated for only two domains to keep the graph clear) show neither systematic discontinuities nor clear regulation. Adapted from Fischer & Kennedy (1997).*

The family of curves in figure 12.3. represent the wide range of variability possible in the development of a cognitive-behavioral system. This variability within a family of curves reflects findings of the study with Korean as well studies with American adolescents. Under optimal conditions development shows steep growth marked by stage-like discontinuities. Under functional conditions, growth is more gradual and monotonic. Moreover, within either of these conditions, there is variability in growth curves depending on the type of relationship (domain) involved. Since each of the curves in this family is systematically related to others by specific developmental relations predicted by the theoretical model, the family as a whole represents variability in development produced by the web-like interconnections in the developing cognitive-behavioral system under study. Such models provide tools for researchers to step out of the limiting assumptions of formalist models, which predict linear, ladder-like progression for the development of a given concept, and begin to describe the web-like complexity and dynamics of real developmental systems.

Models of this kind also have important practical consequences for understanding the developmental of behavioral control. Under the linear assumptions of formalist models, it is easy to assume that Korean adolescents lag American adolescents in the development of the ability to talk about themselves. However, the present example indicates that the situation is much more complex. Korean adolescents are capable of a range of developmental patterns. Under conditions of high support, their skills in this important area of behavioral control show developmental patterns quite comparable to those of American adolescents—contrary to a widely held cultural stereotype.

## CONCLUSION

The study of behavioral control and the study of cognitive structural development are two very closely related scientific disciplines that have been artificially made to seem distant by the misleading assumptions of formalist models of cognitive structure. When cognitive structure is viewed as dynamic and constructive instead of formal and static, then the relation ship between cognitive structure and behavioral control becomes interactive and enabling instead of one-directional and deterministic. Research tools aimed at the description of variability in cognitive development can then be applied to the problem of describing the ways in which behavioral control systems, or cognitive skills, are constructively adapted and reorganized during their development.

## REFERENCES

Bidell, T. R. & Fischer, K. W. (1992). Beyond the stage debate: Action, structure, and variability in Piagetian theory and research. In R. J. Sternberg & C. A Berg (Eds.), *Intellectual Development*. NY: Cambridge Press University.

Bidell, T. R. & Fischer, K. W. (1994). Developmental transitions in children's early on-line planning. In M. M. Haith, J. B. Benson, R. J. Roberts Jr., & B. F. Pennington (Eds.), *The development of future oriented processes*. Chicago: University of Chicago Press.

Bidell, T. R., & Fischer, K. W. (1997). Between nature & nurture: The role of human agency in the epigenesis of intelligence. In Sternberg, R. J., & Grigorenko, E. (Eds.), *Intelligence, Heredity, & Environment*. Cambridge, MA: Cambridge University Press.

Chandler, M. (1991). Alternative readings of the competence-performance relation. In M. Chandler & M. Chapman (Eds.), *Criteria for competence: Controversies in the conceptualization and assessment of children's abilities*. Hillsdale, NJ: Lawrence Erlbaum Associates.

Chomsky, N. (1968). *Language and mind*. New York: Harcourt Brace.

Jeffress, L. A. (1951). *Cerebral mechanisms in behavior: The Hixon Symposium*. New York: Wiley.

Fischer, K.W. (1980). A theory of cognitive development: The control and construction of hierarchies of skills. *Psychological Review, 87,* 477–531.

Fischer, K. W., & Ayoub, C. (1994). Affective splitting and dissociation in normal and maltreated children: Developmental pathways for self in relationships. In Cicchetti & S. L. Toth (Eds.), *Disorders and dysfunctions of the self* (Vol. 5, pp. 149–222). Rochester, NY: University of Rochester Press.

Fischer, K. W., & Bidell, T. R. (1997). Dynamic development of psychological structures in action and thought. In W. Damon (Ed.) *Handbook of child psychology. Vol 1.*

Fischer, K. W., Bullock, D., Rotenberg, E. J., & Raya, P. (1993). The dynamics of competence: How context contributes directly to skill. In R. Wozniak & K. Fischer (Ed.), *Development in context: Acting and thinking in specific environments* (pp. 93–117). Hillsdale, NJ: Lawrence Erlbaum Associates.

Flavell, J. H., & Wohlwill, J. F. (1969). Formal and functional aspects of cognitive development. In D. Elkind & J. H. Flavell (Eds.), *Studies in cognitive development: Essays in honor of Jean Piaget* (pp. 67–120). New York: Oxford University Press.

Gardner, H. (1985). *The mind's new science: A history of the cognitive revolution.* New York: Basic Books.

Granott, N. (1993). *Microdevelopment of co-construction of knowledge during problem-solving: Puzzled minds, weird creatures, and wuggles.* Unpublished doctoral dissertation, MIT, Cambridge, MA.

Knight, C. C., & Fischer, K. W. (1992). Learning to read words: individual difference-sin developmental sequences. *Journal of Applied Developmental Psychology, 13,* 377–404.

Lewis, M. D. (1994). Reconciling stage and specificity in neo-Piagetian theory: Self-organizing conceptual structures. *Human Development, 37,* 143–169.

Pepper, S. C. (1942). *World hypotheses: A study in evidence.* Berkeley: University of California Press.

Piaget, J. (1970). *Structuralism.* New York: Harper & Row.

Piaget, J. (1977). *The development of thought: Equilibration of cognitive structures* (A. Rosin, trans.). New York: Viking. (Originally published in 1975).

Piaget, J. (1970). Piaget's theory. In P. H. Mussen (Ed.), *Carmichael's manual of child psychology* (Vol. 1). New York: Wiley.

Siegler, R. S., & Crowley, K. (1991). The microgenetic method: A direct means for studying cognitive development. *American Psychologist, 46,* 606–620.

Tang, E., & Ginsberg, H. P. (1997). *Reconceptualizing the competence-performance distinction: Mathematical thinking in preschoolers.* Paper presented at the biennial conference of the Society for Research in Child Development, April 5th, Washington, DC.

Thelen, E. & Smith, L. B. (1994). *A dynamic systems approach to the development of cognition and action.* Cambridge, MA: MIT Press.

van Geert, P. (1994). *Dynamic systems of development: Change between complexity and chaos.* London: Harvester Wheatsheaf.

# 13

# Metacognitive Control in Analogical Reasoning[1]

## Fredi P. Büchel

## INTRODUCTION

The main purpose of this chapter is to demonstrate the importance of metacognitive control in analogical reasoning. In the first part, I present a review of metacognitive theory with a special emphasis on verbal methods for assessment and training of metacognition. In the second part, analogical reasoning is introduced as a paradigm for transfer of learning. In the last part, I attempt to link the two research domains, metacognition and analogical reasoning, by describing some examples that show how metacognition supports analogical reasoning.

## METACOGNITION

The concept of metacognition refers to two different things: Metacognitive knowledge on the one hand and executive functions on the other. Flavell & Wellman (1977) defined metacognitive knowledge as the knowledge learners have about themselves, about task characteristics, and about strategies. According to Brown, Bransford, Ferrara & Campione (1983, 106–107) this special knowledge is stable, statable ("one can reflect on the cognitive processes involved and discuss them with others"), often fallible (a person "can perfectly well know certain facts about cognition that are not true"), and late-developing. Executive functions include planning, monitoring, and checking. These activities are task and situation dependent but "not necessarily statable, somewhat unstable, and relatively age independent" (Brown et al., 1983, 106–107).

### Metacognitive Knowledge

The concept of metacognition was introduced by Flavell to explain memory development. "What, then, is memory development the development of? It seems in large part to be the development of intelligent structuring and storage of input, of intelligent search and retrieval operations, and of intelligent monitoring and

---

[1]The author acknowledges valuable editorial support by Ursula Scharnhorst, University of Geneva, Patrick Büchel and Laura Loder, University of Fribourg, and Jean Dumas, Purdue University.

knowledge of these storage and retrieval operations—a kind of "metamemory", perhaps. Such is the nature of memory development" (Flavell, 1971, 277). It is interesting to note that in this very first formulation of metacognitive theory, Flavell focused more on the procedural than on the declarative aspect of metacognitive control whereas in later publications he emphasized declarative aspects and neglected procedural ones. Flavell never really proposed a fully elaborated model of metacognition as was done later, e.g. by Kluwe (1980) or Cavanaugh & Perlmutter (1982). These authors postulated that metaknowledge represents the knowledge base of procedural functions which, in turn, control what Flavell (1971) called "intelligent search and retrieval operations."

In their "Interview Study of Children's Knowledge about Memory," the first and most quoted study about metaknowledge, Kreutzer, Leonard, and Flavell (1975) proposed a definition that reduces metamemory to its declarative aspect. According to these authors, metamemory can be "broadly defined as the individual's potentially verbalizable knowledge and awareness concerning any aspect of information storage and retrieval". In this study we also find a first version of Flavell's ideas about metacognitive variables, which were later elaborated by Flavell & Wellman (1977) and provided an important and widely accepted model.

Kreutzer et al. (1975) started with the question of "what variables interact in what ways to affect the quality of a person's performance on a retrieval problem," and postulated "at least three broad and overlapping categories of such variables. One has to do with the person himself. A second category has to do with the data and task demands . . . third, the child has the possibility of acquiring an almost limitless repertoire of deliberate and conscious memory strategies . . . finally, these variables always interact with one another . . ." (p.1–2). With respect to task demands, Brown (1975) emphasized that "there exists a hierarchy of tasks varying in the degree to which strategic intervention can be fruitfully applied." The different variables can be summarized in table 13.1.

In his description of metacognitive variables, Flavell distinguished different levels of consciousness. He used the word "repertoire" to refer to strategies, which are seen as tools that can be deliberately chosen by the learner. Flavell further attributed knowledge to the learner that accounts for general psychological features and task-specific characteristics. Various cognitive states of knowledge (e.g., the recency of some knowledge) to which the learner "may become increasingly sensitive" are recognized and differentiated by so-called "mnemonic sensations " (Kreutzer et al., 1975, 2).

TABLE 13.1
*Important variables of metaknowledge (according to Kreutzer et al., 1975;*
*Flavell & Wellman, 1977)*

| |
|---|
| *1. Person variables* |
|     1.1. General awareness of one's own cognitive activity. |
|     1.2. Knowledge about intra- and interindividual differences. |
|     1.3. General knowledge about human memory. |
|     1.4. Sensations about mnemonic states of knowledge. |
| *2. Task variables* |
|     2.1. Knowledge about retrieval effects of data properties. |
|     2.2. Knowledge about retrieval effects of task demands. |
| *3. Memory strategies* |
|     3.1. Repertoire of storage strategies. |
|     3.2. Repertoire of retrieval strategies. |
| *4. Interactions* |

## Executive Control

Flavell's work focused on metacognitive knowledge or metaknowledge (in his first publications, he used the word "metamemory"), but did not develop the concept of executive functions. Executive functions were proposed in early theories of human information processing. In their well-known model of human memory, Atkinson & Shiffrin (1968) introduced several control processes which "are not permanent features of memory, but are instead transient phenomena under the control of the subject" (p. 168). According to Shiffrin (1975) these control processes are *selective mechanisms* responding to the limited capacity of the short term store. He distinguishes *cognitive processing*, which is under the subject's control, from *systemic processing* referring "to those stages of processing which occur automatically, with or without the subject's attempted control" (p. 170). Cognitive processing includes "control processes like scanning, rehearsal, coding, and decisions carried out on the information in short term store" (p. 171). Some form of executive control of cognitive processes was postulated in most of the early information processing models, but the concept was never elaborated fully. For example, in her "information-processing model of short-term memory", J. S. Reitman (1970) introduced an "executive routine" which is "the longest in running, and the most important," but nevertheless "the shortest in length" although "it is this executive routine that makes the whole thing go" (p. 147).

The idea of a central executive control was later taken up in the training paradigm of developmental psychology by Butterfield and his colleagues (e.g. Butterfield, Wambold, & Belmont, 1973; Belmont, Butterfield, & Ferretti, 1980) and
by A. L. Brown (1974, 1975). With regard to strategy training in persons with
mental retardation, Brown (1974, 102) stated, after an extended review of the
strategy training literature, that "the next step would be to devise techniques to
train children with retardation to monitor their own strategy production and to
evaluate realistically the interaction between the task demands and their own
capacity and repertoire of specific skills." Brown (1975) mentioned the "intention
to be strategic" or, the fact that subjects have a "plan to form a plan." Persons
have some knowledge about the usefulness of a strategic approach in different
tasks ranging from very simple tasks that require the use of very few strategies to
"tasks which require complex strategic intervention involving the flexible application, *monitoring, and control* of a variety of complex cognitive operations" (p.
134, italics added). It seems that for A. L. Brown, the strategic intention and the
monitoring of cognitive processes were the main aspects of executive functioning. Brown & Barcley (1976, 71) stated that "on a more general level, both the
overall intention to be strategic and the efficient monitoring of memorial processes appear to be required in any intelligent attempt to remember."

On a more process oriented level, Butterfield et al. (1973) had observed, in a
series of cumulative rehearsal studies, that "retarded subjects did not lack the
memory processes for accurate performance . . .," but "spontaneous access to the
processes and coordination among them." These authors were convinced that in
persons with mental retardation "this failure of executive control is transsitua-
tional," and they suggested that future research should focus on "the level of
selecting, sequencing, and coordinating processes" and therefore "train executive
functions instead of the particular skills . . ." (p. 668).

Butterfield & Belmont (1977, p. 314) defined executive functions as follows:
"Executive function is exhibited when the subject changes a control process or
sequence of control processes as a reasonable response to an objective change in
an information-processing task." In a famous paper, Belmont et al. (1982) then
extended their propositions to instruct *self-management skills* and they postulated
three "general skills such as goal-setting, strategy planning, and self-
monitoring." Most other authors replaced goal-setting by the concept of anticipation. According to Brown & DeLoache (1978, p. 14), for example, "the basic
skills of metacognition include predicting the consequences of an action or event,
. . ."

In a more cognitive-behavioral tradition, executive functions were subsumed
under the concept of self-regulation. According to Whitman (1990, p. 349) "the
self-regulatory system consists of self-monitoring, self-evaluation, and self-
reinforcement responses. Self-regulation is different from automatic processing in
that it requires focused attention and continuous decision-making." Similar
propositions had been made by Meichenbaum and collaborators (e.g. Meichenbaum & Asarnow, 1979). It seems that the activation of metaknowledge is trig-

gered in some way by verbal mediation. Even in the Kreutzer et al. (1975) defini-tion, metamemory was described as a "potentially verbalizable knowledge and awareness of . . ." It is therefore not surprising that cognitive researchers also used self-verbalization to instruct metacognitive control. For example, Bork-owski & Kendall–Varnhagen (1984) compared a self-instructional with a tradi-tional direct instruction format for teaching anticipation and paraphrase strategies to children with mental retardation. While in immediate learning and maintenance no differences were found, the self-instructional format facilitated strategy trans-fer.

In summary, metaknowledge is supposed to be the knowledge base of execu-tive functions (metacognitive level) which, in turn, control cognitive processes (cognitive level). These functional relations are represented in table 13.2.

*TABLE 13.2*
*Functional relations between metacognitive and cognitive processes*

| |
|---|
| *Metacognitive level*<br>METAKNOWLEGE:<br>Knowledge about one's own cognitive functioning<br>Knowledge about task specificities<br>Knowledge about strategies<br><br>*is the basis of:*<br><br>EXECUTIVE FUNCTIONS:<br>Anticipation<br>Planning<br>Control<br><br>*coordinate and control:*<br><br>*Cognitive level*<br>COGNITIVE PROCESSES:<br>Coding – Rehearsal<br>Comparison and classification<br>Induction – deduction<br>Memorization – recall |

## CONTROL, CONTROL-BELIEFS AND METACOGNITIVE CONTROL

It would be interesting to compare the concept of executive control with the more general concept of control as proposed by Flammer (1990). It is somewhat sur-prising that the concepts of metacognition and metacognitive control do not appear in this book about control and control-beliefs. Control, according to Flammer (1990, pp. 19–22), is an action. It consists of a series of procedures that one can apply in order to change one state into another. Control is goal-oriented and more or less conscious.

Because consciousness is an important element of control, the concept can be applied to human beings only. To describe a similar activity in animals, Flammer proposes the concept of regulation. Another important aspect of control is its specificity. On one hand, all of us apply a lot of control in some domains but less or none at all in others. On the other hand, control is not only domain-specific, it varies as well with respect to its objectivity. Flammer distinguishes between objective control and subjectively perceived control (control-beliefs) which is more important to a human's well being. "Control-beliefs are defined as subjective representations about one's own ability to influence things around and with oneself" (Flammer & Scheuber-Sahli, 1995, p. 50), or "as belief in having one's own control of situations" (Flammer et al., 1996, p. 277).

In opposition to Flammer's action-oriented control-beliefs, the concept of executive control, as introduced in information processing and metacognitive theories, is not oriented towards actions but towards cognitive processes, as illustrated in table 13.2. According to Atkinson & Shiffrin (1968) we have to distinguish conscious cognitive control from automatic systemic control. A similar distinction has been proposed by Flammer: conscious control in human beings and unconscious regulation in animals. Control-beliefs, according to Flammer, are "subjective representations about one's own ability to influence things." Control-beliefs thus resemble what is called in the metacognitive framework, metaknowledge, or "knowledge about one's own cognitive functioning." There exists, nevertheless, a difference between these two concepts: While control-beliefs are intrinsically oriented towards concrete execution of control, metaknowledge is in some way more static. Metaknowledge consists of the general representation about knowledge acquisition, elaboration and storage, and of more idiosyncratic representations about one's own functioning (academic self-concept). Incomplete general knowledge or a negative academic self-concept may decrease the conscious part of executive control (cognitive processing) but not necessarily the automatic part (systemic processing). That is exactly what has been found in students with mental retardation. For example, with respect to the cumulative rehearsal paradigm, Butterfield et al. (1973) presented students with and without mental retardation with several lists of letters and measured the amount of cumulative rehearsal. Learning without rehearsal was called *passive learning*, and learning with rehearsal was called *active learning*. They found that "all people, regardless of age and IQ, use their passive systems about equally well." But while most of the students without mental retardation used a combination of the passive and the active system, students with mental retardation used the active system only after extended and explicit instructions. In later studies, Butterfield and his colleagues interpreted this observation as a consequence of a lack of metacognition.

Before finishing this short comparison of Flammer's control concept with the metacognitive one, it may be interesting to pose the epistemological question of how the introduction of these two concepts is justified. Why, in a more general framework of psychological theory, is the concept of control useful? According to Flammer, control is a basic need of all human beings, and experience of one's own control is some kind of natural and basic life experience[2]. In metacognitive theory, the control concept is justified in a more restricted but also more technical way. In information processing models (e.g. Lindsay & Norman, 1977) executive control has to be postulated because short term memory capacity is limited. Only very little information can therefore be processed simultaneously. However, sensory systems are continuously attacked by millions of bits of information. In order to prevent a system overload, some instance has to transform the information flow into manageable units and put them into a sequence. This is a matter of executive control. It seems evident that the system needs some knowledge about different ways of putting information into units treatable by the system (strategy variables according to Flavell), and it needs some knowledge and awareness of its own functioning and the system limits (person variables, according to Flavell) as well. If the information theory had postulated intelligence models without any processing limitations, there would be no need of metacognitive control. But such kinds of models would have some problems explaining and predicting human cognition.

## VERBAL METHODS FOR ASSESSING AND TRAINING OF METACOGNITION

The methodological question of how to assess metacognitions has a significant impact on the theoretical questions of the emergence of metacognition and the causal relations between metacognitive and cognitive processes. At what age does metacognitive awareness develop? Is executive control necessarily and exclusively a conscious process, or can we observe signs of executive control before the emergence of metacognitive awareness? What kind of verbal statements or what kind of directly or indirectly observable data can be interpreted as metacognitive? What kind of instruction can be called metacognitive? Kreutzer et al. (1975) showed that some metacognitive knowledge can be expected from Kindergarten children, but that this knowledge was not very stable and reliable. And we do not know if the data of this study really reflect the children's actual state of knowledge and not only their limited ability to verbalize their knowledge. Brown et al. (1983) pointed to the fact that the reliability and validity of developmental data (mostly verbal data obtained through questionnaires or interviews) are rarely discussed. Most likely, questionnaires and interview protocols cannot furnish objective data, but these methods can be interesting for training purposes. On the

---

[2]"Kontrollerfahrung ist eine Lebensgrunderfahrung; und alle Menschen streben natürlicherweise nach einem Kontrollanteil." (Flammer, 1990, p.7)

other hand, thinking aloud data can be fairly objective and their quality depends on the quality of the given instruction and on the subjects' age (Büchel, 1983[3]; Ericsson & Simon, 1979a) and cognitive level (Büchel, 1990[4]; Scharnhorst & Büchel, 1990).

Most research on metacognitive knowledge is based on assessment methods like interviews, questionnaires, thinking aloud protocols or spontaneous private speech. Further, executive control is often inferred from task analysis or overt behavior, such as, eye movements.

Reliability and validity of retrospective verbal data were analyzed by Ericsson & Simon (1978) from a human information processing perspective, and by Huber & Mandl (1982) from the point of view of action theory. Starting from the Nisbett & Wilson (1977) hypothesis that human beings are not capable of objective introspection, Huber & Mandl (1982) developed a two-dimensional taxonomy of verbal data that allows an estimation of the importance and direction of possible biases. Regarding the timing of data collection, they distinguish preactional, periactional and postactional access. Periactional verbalizations are generally said to be closest to the actions they control. According to Ericsson & Simon (1978), postactional verbalizations are highly influenced by long term memory (LTM) contents.

Subjects tend to create some coherence between their values (LTM contents) and the justification of their actions. Preactional verbalizations are close to planning behavior, and there is no guarantee that actions are completely controlled by previous plans. Huber & Mandl (1982) conclude that all verbal data tend to be confounded with processes of interpretation and justification. The second dimension of their taxonomy concerns the level of structuring of the data collecting method (high level–low level).

There is a general agreement in the literature that highly structured methods tend to induce the expected answers more than less structured methods. As a third dimension, not included in their taxonomy, Huber & Mandl discuss the level of specificity of the questions (interview) or instructions (thinking aloud method). As a source of lack of validity, Brown et al. (1983) note that most questions about metacognition are stated in very general terms, and we therefore cannot be sure that subjects interpret them in the same way as the experimenter.

In an earlier study, I have argued that thinking aloud protocols are probably the most reliable source of verbal data because "thinking-aloud-statements pass only through short-term memory, but not through long-term memory, and would therefore be free of systematic adaptations, as attributed to long-term memory" (Büchel, 1988, p. 133). In the literature, thinking aloud data are often quoted and criticized without any attention to the theoretical basis of this data collection

---

[3]The reported research was supported by the Swiss National Science Foundation (Grant  4.323.0.79.10).

[4]The reported research was supported by the Swiss National Science Foundation (Grant  1.981–0.84).

method. Based on human information processing models and, in particular, on the work of Ericsson & Simon (1978; 1979a; 1979b), I proposed (Büchel, 1983, pp. 114–138) a model of the thinking aloud method in which thinking aloud statements are synonymous with overt rehearsal in short-term memory (STM). According to the model, thinking aloud statements (a) are necessarily STM contents, (b) do not consume very much attention, and (c) are not conscious and planned. If conscious and planful construction of a verbal statement can be inferred from its syntax, then the statement should be excluded from the protocol analysis because it no longer conforms to the above definition of thinking aloud.

It seems that this kind of data corresponds to what Belmont & Butterfield (1977, p. 447) called "direct measurement." After a critical synthesis of instructional studies in developmental psychology, these authors postulated that researchers should observe "as directly as possible how a person is thinking while performing a criterion task." But, as Huber & Mandl (1982, p. 18) stated, even thinking aloud data has to be interpreted with caution. Ericsson & Simon (1979a) mentioned three critical arguments:

1. The effect-of-verbalization argument: The nature of cognitive processes changes if simultaneous verbalization is elicited. This may be true if the subjects' instruction does not prevent short-term memory overload, and if other statements than overt rehearsal are interpreted as thinking aloud instances.

2. The incompleteness argument, for which Huber (1982) mentions four possible reasons: 2.1. Some perceptual processes are highly automatic. The results of such processes may be transferred into LTM without going through STM. 2.2. Cognitive overload of STM may result in a lack of verbalization. 2.3. If the given information is non-verbal, translation into a verbal code may be too difficult. 2.4. Subjects may believe that some information is not interesting. According to the proposed thinking-aloud model (Büchel, 1983), argument 2.1. has to be accepted. The lack of thinking aloud statements about some process does not allow the conclusion that it did not occur. Argument 2.2. and 2.3. are often relevant in research with persons with mental retardation. The level of task difficulty is difficult to estimate, and therefore STM overload cannot always be avoided. Some persons with mental retardation have important difficulties in verbalization. That's the reason why the thinking aloud method is often very disappointing with this population. Argument 2.4. can be prevented by an adequate thinking aloud instruction.

3. The irrelevance argument states that thinking aloud statements are activities running parallel to the thinking processes, and that they have only the status of epiphenomena. Different methods (e.g., Belmont & Butterfield, 1977) demonstrated that rehearsal processes always accompany thinking processes. Even if the hypothesis of a simple parallelism cannot be ex-

cluded, the postulate of a functional relation between thinking and rehearsal seems rather coherent with cognitive theories.

However, it has also been demonstrated that thinking aloud instructions slow
down the execution of simultaneous thinking processes (Ericsson & Simon,
1979a; Kluwe & Reimann, 1983; Reimann & Kluwe, 1983). Further, positive
effects of verbalization instructions on problem solving performance have been
reported (e.g., Merz, 1969; Franzen & Merz, 1976). According to Dörner (1981)
verbalization has a stabilizing effect on thinking processes.

In order to identify metacognitive elements in analogical reasoning protocols,
the following verbal methods are of special interest:

- Preactional data collection: high to low structured interviews, spontaneous
  private speech.
- Periactional data collection: thinking aloud protocols, clinical interview
  questions (as used by the Piagetian school) immediately following actions, spontaneous private speech.
- Postactional data collection: interviews, confrontation with protocols (e.g.
  video), spontaneous private speech.

Verbal methods have also been suggested for intervention purposes. Certain
verbalizations seem to activate metacognitive processes and therefore have some
control effects on analogical thinking. This is especially true for self-
verbalizations in a self-regulatory context. "Self-regulation was suggested to
basically be a linguistically guided process" (Whitman, 1990, p. 347). The following methods are the most promising with respect to training effects:

- Preactional verbalizations: highly structured interview questions may induce the required behavior. Preactional verbalizations triggered by interview questions can be used by the child for goal setting and other planning activities.
- Periactional verbalizations: thinking aloud instruction may reduce impulsivity because they generally slow down the thinking processes. The importance of cognitive tempo for metacognitive control has been emphasized by several authors. For example, Borkowski, Peck, Reid, & Kurtz
  (1983, p. 459) found "a relationship between cognitive tempo and the
  ability to use strategies in new contexts." Clinical interview questions
  about relations should increase metacognitive awareness and therefore have
  a stabilizing effect on the understanding of these relations.
- Postactional verbalizations: Confrontation with protocols (e.g. video)
  should increase metacognitive awareness and checking activities.

## ANALOGICAL REASONING

Although analogical reasoning is a topic approached from different perspectives in different disciplines (e.g. philosophy, experimental psychology, artificial intelligence, education) it is possible to identify some key components of a general definition of analogy. According to Vosniadou & Ortony (1989, p. 6) "there is a general agreement that analogical reasoning involves the transfer of relational information from a domain that already exists in memory (usually referred to as the *source* or *base* domain) to the domain to be explained (referred to as the *target* domain)." Solving an analogical problem requires that one finds some similarity between source and target domain. Comparing two situations or problems and detecting some similarity between the two is a very basic cognitive activity in intelligent behavior. "The ability to perceive similarities and analogies is one of the most fundamental aspects of human cognition" (Vosniadou & Ortony, 1989, p. 1). Similarly, Holyoak (1984) states that "analogical thinking is a pervasive component of human intelligence and manifests itself in many forms throughout most of the lifespan." Expectations regarding the first manifestations of analogical thinking had to be corrected and extended to include early childhood. According to Chen, Sanchez, & Campbell (1997, p. 790) "Analogical problem solving may be one of the major accomplishments during the 1st year of life." It is therefore not surprising that analogical problems were included in intelligence tests from the very beginning of the intelligence testing tradition (e.g., Burt, 1911; Thurstone, 1938). "Analogical reasoning performance represents a prototypical measure of Spearman's g" (Pellegrino & Goldman, 1983, p. 143). Spearman (1923) found three main processes included in analogical reasoning, i.e., apprehension, education of relation, and education of correlates. In more recent writings, these three processes are called encoding, detection of similarities between components of the source domain, and mapping of the detected relations to the target domain. The study of analogical reasoning is not only justified by the extended use of analogies in intelligence tests. "Analogical reasoning is an important vehicle of human thought and merits investigation in its own right" (Mulholland, Pellegrino, & Glaser (1980, p. 252).

With respect to a formal definition, Pellegrino (1985, p. 198) quotes Aristotle who defined analogy as "an equality of proportions (involving) at least four terms . . . when the second is related to the first as the fourth is to the third." Generally, analogies are composed of four terms, two in the first part (source domain) and two in the second (target domain). They are represented in a linear format as A:B::C:D or in a corresponding matrix format.

Some authors distinguish analogy from matrix tasks (Pellegrino & Glaser, 1980; Klauer, 1989). Vosniadou & Ortony (1989, p. 7) distinguish analogies *between-domain* (metaphorical analogies) from analogies *within-domain* (literal analogies). In the first type of analogy, "items are drawn from conceptually different or remote domains," whereas in the second "items are drawn from the same domain, or at least from conceptually very close domains."

Regarding the basic processes of analogical reasoning, most authors follow the componential theory proposed by Sternberg (1977). He distinguishes six sequentially ordered processes:

1. Attribute discovery or encoding.
2. Inference (establish a relationship between A and B).
3. Mapping (correspondence between A and C, i.e. establish a relationship between A and C).
4. Application (of the analogical rule to D).
5. Justification.
6. Execution (an overt response).

## Analogical Reasoning, Intelligence, Learning, Transfer, and Metacognition

There is increasing evidence that the concepts of analogical reasoning, general intelligence, learning capacity, transfer, and metacognition are closely connected one with another. According to Belmont, Butterfield, & Ferretti, (1982) we have to "instruct self-management skills" if we want to "secure transfer of training". These authors postulate a functional relationship between transfer and executive functions. A significant correlation between metamemory and generalization was found by Kendall, Borkowski, & Cavanaugh (1980).

On the other hand, Butterfield & Ferretti (1986, pp.195–196) explain interindividual differences in IQ with differences in short term memory, knowledge base, strategies, metaknowledge, and executive control. The last three of these factors are metacognitive variables. They therefore postulate strong correlations between metacognition and intelligence.

The relation between transfer, general intelligence and learning capacity has been studied by different authors. Campione, Brown and their collaborators furnished some empirical evidence for "intelligence related differences in learning and transfer propensity" (Campione, Brown, Ferrara, Jones, & Steinberg, 1985, p. 298). In a first study, they presented three types of analogical matrices to groups of MA-matched students with retardation (IQ, WISC = 72; CA = 14.5) and without retardation (IQ, Peabody = 118; CA = 9.1) and taught three task specific rules to solve these problems. No significant group-differences were found in the learning and training phase when the tasks were presented in a block-ordered format (task type 1 to 3). However, in the maintenance and transfer tests, tasks were presented in random order. In this condition, children without retardation performed significantly better than children with retardation; they needed less help and made fewer errors. These results indicate that a clear relationship exists between intelligence, maintenance and transfer. On the other hand, no learning differences were found in this study. The authors explain the successful learning of the students with mental retardation by the fact that the tasks were presented in a blocked format: The same rule could be applied for all tasks of a block. This format facilitates learning-to-learn effects. But in other studies (e.g., Campione, Brown, Ferrara, & Bryant, 1984, for children without retardation; Büchel, Schlatter, & Scharnhorst, 1997,[5] for students with mental retardation), intelligence-related differences were found even in the learning phase.

Gholson, Morgan, Dattel, & Pierce (1990, 269) do not only see a relationship of similarity but even of identity between transfer and analogical reasoning. They define analogical reasoning as "the transfer of existing knowledge to new but closely related problems and situations." And according to Holyoak (1984, p. 201) "the function of analogy is to allow transfer of knowledge from a known situation to a novel one, even if the two situations are superficially dissimilar. Such transfer is central to learning and reasoning."

In the next section, the main focus will be on the relation between metacognition and analogical reasoning.

## THE IMPORTANCE OF METACOGNITION IN ANALOGICAL REASONING

A special problem in analogical theories is the explanation of the process of mapping. In Piagetian theory, it is the question of second-degree (Inhelder & Piaget, 1958) operations or higher order relations (Piaget, Montangero, & Billeter, 1977). After having decoded the two terms (A, B) of the first part of the analogy, and inferred the A-B relation, how does a person retrieve an analog in from memory? For the case of within-domain analogies, the concept of surface similarity or "a mere appearance match" (Gentner, 1983, p. 161) was suggested. Sternberg & Gardner (1979, 5) also think that "analogical reasoning may be considered a kind of similarity judgment between concepts." If the detection of surface similarity can be viewed as a more or less automatic process, things become more difficult if we consider the mapping process in the case of between-domain analogies. In this case, consciously controlled analysis seems to be required. According to Vosniadou & Ortony (1989, p. 8) "plans and goals may play an important role in access." If this is true, metacognition would be an important component of the mapping process in analogies in which "the source domain is remote from the target domain" (p. 8).

Metacognitive control has not received much attention and discussion in the analogical literature. It is mainly discussed with respect to developmental and training effects. Brown (1989, pp. 404–405) explains the fact that "older children assigned to unassisted conditions transfer more readily than younger ones" by assuming differences in knowledge, in basic mental capacities, and in learning strategies. "Once one has ruled out knowledge and capacity, one is left with learning strategies and metaconceptual competence; and perhaps it is advances in these general factors that underlie the improvements we see". Gholson et al. (1990, p.

[5]The reported research was supported by the Swiss National Science Foundation (Grant No. 11–25463.88).

303) refer to "meta-conceptual competence" as proposed by Borkowski & Kurtz (1984) to explain where strategies of analogical thinking originate. "These kinds of metaconceptual competencies, of course, involve exactly the kinds of activities we have identified as reflecting the use of specific strategies."

In training studies, one important question is whether different kind of induced verbalizations increase analogical reasoning performance. Generally, a positive effect has been found, but it is not always clear if the nature of this effect can be interpreted as metacognitive. For example, Welsh (1987, 52) conducted a verbal labeling training with 5th- and 6th grade-students and found "that the verbal labeling procedures have a positive influence on figural matrix problem solving," but she also observed that impulsive children profited less than reflective children, and she explained this with "a deficit in the metacognitive skills of impulsive children" (p. 54). "Metacognitive awareness of *strategy* and *task* variables may contribute to one's appreciation of the intent of an imposed instructional set and to one's translation of this appreciation into effective cognitive activity" (pp. 54–55). In a series of studies, Carlson and Wiedl (e.g., 1978; 1980) demonstrated that feedback and self-verbalization can significantly increase performance in the CPM (Raven, 1965) in learning disabled and children without handicap.

The verbalization effect can be explained by metacognitive theory. Guided discovery, verbalization and self-reflection, as well as verbal self-instruction (VSI; Meichenbaum & Goodman, 1971) are the three training methods recommended by Klauer (1993) for the application of his inductive reasoning training. Masendorf & Klauer (1987) used the VSI method to train learning disabled students (CA 10;3–13;9) that involved series completion and analogy tasks. Masendorf & Maihack (1986) used VSI for an inductive training of students with language disorders. In both studies, VSI proved to be a very effective training method.

In an earlier study of metacognitive regulation in problem solving, we presented (Büchel & Scharnhorst, 1989; Scharnhorst & Büchel, 1990) students with mental retardation some tasks in which geometrical figures had to be identified in clouds of dots ("organization of dots;" Rey & Dupond, 1953; Feuerstein, Rand, Hoffman, & Miller, 1980). A special video system allowed us to record the visual focus with respect to significant task elements. We also collected thinking aloud and clinical interview data, and analyzed typical errors in the solutions provided by the subjects. This combination of several methods allowed us to construct a two-dimensional taxonomy of "problem solving components for organization-of-dots tasks." Regarding the direction of control, top-down components were distinguished from bottom-up components. With respect to the object of control, we distinguished components for exploration, elaboration, planning, checking, execution, and social interaction.

Metacognitive knowledge is mainly contained in the top-down planning components, while executive functions are mainly found in the bottom-up checking components. Most of these components can also be expected in analogical reasoning protocols, and the following provisional indicators of metacognitive control in analogical reasoning can therefore be suggested:

Planning indicators
*Metaknowledge (all top-down)*
- knowledge of task characteristics
- knowledge of personal processing capabilities
- knowledge of strategy effectiveness

*Executive control (all top-down)*
- Selection of a starting point for problem solution
- Justification of the starting point
- Change of solution strategy

Checking indicators
*Executive control*
- verbalizing imaginary solutions (top-down)
- expressing doubt (top-down)
- comparison with a model (bottom-up)

## AN EXAMPLE OF A DYNAMIC ASSESSMENT PROCEDURE SUPPORTING ANALOGICAL REASONING WITH METACOGNITIVE HINTS

Following the main topic of this chapter, the demonstration of the importance of metacognitive control in the assessment and training of analogical reasoning, I present some examples of verbal interactions from the ARLT[6] manual in order to analyze them with respect to their metacognitive nature.

The ARLT has been developed to assess learning capacity in analogical reasoning of persons with moderate mental retardation[7] (Schlatter, Büchel, & Thomas, 1997;[8] Schlatter, Scharnhorst, & Büchel, 1997). It is a dynamic assessment

---

[6]This research is supported by the Swiss National Science Foundation (Grant 11–45541.95). The authors acknowledge the valuable collaboration of all members of the reasearch team, which includes Nadja Scerri, Didier Strasser, and Laurence Thomas (research assistants), Aline Comoli, Joëlle Cosman, Manuela Ghilardi, David Imboden, Lara Magrini, Diana Steenbergen, and Valérie Suter (student collaborators).

[7]During the period when August Flammer wrote his book *Individuelle Differenzen im Lernen*, I was an assistant in special education at the same university institute, and Flammer attempted without success to convince me to study the dynamic assessment literature. Many years later, reading his book again, I finally understood that, engaged in mental reatardation research, I had to do some dynamic assessment. It seems that important things are not always obvious at first.

[8]In the introduction to *Individuelle Unterschiede im Lernen* (Flammer, 1975), a

instrument in which the student's responses are supported and optimized by means of a standardized social interaction. The procedure includes five different phases: (a) Training of comparisons (A:B), (b) training of simplified analogies (A:B::A':B'), (c) learning (A:B::C:D), (d) maintenance, and (e) near and far transfer.

The following statements are examples of how the experimenter tries to optimize student performance in analogical reasoning by fostering metacognitive awareness:

*Training of comparison:* "That's very good." "You did understand very well." Positive feedback of this kind does not serve the function of simple reinforcement as it is commonly recommended in the cognitive–behavioral tradition, but it is an indirect invitation to self-checking that is a metacognitive function. Possible variations of such feedback are "That's almost correct," and "That's not the right answer, let's try once again."

"Do you know what you will have to put here?" This question invites the student to anticipate the process of inference and to select some criterion for the A-B-relation (starting point for problem solving).

*Simplified analogies:* "You see, big becomes small (A-B); if we make the same transformation here (A'-B'), . . ." The opening phrase "You see" and respective pointing invites the student to compare A'-B' with A-B (the model). According to our model (table 13.3) this is a bottom-up process controlled by metacognitive knowledge (of task characteristics).

"Now, it's getting a little bit more difficult." This announcement should activate some metaknowledge of task characteristics and prepare the student to select an appropriate strategy.

"That's correct. You understand this problem very well." This comment is meant to activate knowledge of personal processing capabilities; the student's approach is confirmed, and he or she is encouraged to engage in executive control.

"In order to find the correct answer, you have to look what changes happen from the left side to the right side, . . ." The student is invited to develop a com-

---

book that influenced my own thinking in many ways, Flammer deplored the fact that experimental and differential psychology resisted to enrich one another, and proposed a model of interdependences between general, clinical, and differential psychology. His proposition has been repeated since by several researchers in the field of clincal-differential psychology (e.g. Guthke, 1990; Sternberg, 1977).

When I began to study inductive reasoning, I made a similar experience: I was surprised to see that two domains of psychological theory, inductive reasoning and metacognition, were treated in a completely independent way one from another, although relations from different point of views are obvious. The writing of this chapter proved to me that it is not easy to conceptualize and demonstrate these relations, and I understand in some way the authors who published in both domains, but never attempted to put the two domains together.

parative strategy to detect possible attributes that may lead him or her to infer the relevant A-B relation.

*Learning phase:* "You have seen that the big apple becomes small (A:B). Now, let's do the same thing here (C:D)." The student's attention is focused on the A-B-relation. He or she is invited to use A-B as a model for making a similarity judgment concerning C:D.

These few examples should demonstrate the presence of metacognitive elements in standardized instructions of a dynamic assessment instrument. They confirm that the most important help in such a problem solving situation consists in the activation of the student's metacognitive knowledge and in the invitation to engage in executive control.

## CONCLUSION

In a number of studies, Klauer (e.g., 1989; 1996) attempted to show that inductive training increases specific inductive processes, and that the observed transfer effects that results from training cannot be explained by more general components of thinking, e.g., metacognition or motivation. However, the relation between inductive thinking and metacognition can also be discussed from another, more positive point of view, as we tried to do it in this chapter. Metacognition can be seen as a kind of general guideline for inductive thinking. In order to study the special case of analogical reasoning, a distinction between several processing phases in which different processes (or components) are dominant has been suggested (e.g., Sternberg, 1977). The present review of the literature reveals that mapping is the most difficult process to explain as it raises several important research questions: What kind of sub-processes are involved in mapping? Why is mapping so difficult for some persons, particularly persons with lower IQ? What kind of training elements facilitate mapping in different populations? It seems that the importance of metacognitive processes that support and enable the mapping process has been underestimated. An explicit exploration of one's own knowledge regarding the A:B-term is a prerequisite for good mapping. The same is true for the planning and checking of the correspondence of the A-C and B-D relations as well as for the anticipation of incorrect answers that violate the analogical proportion. With the help of some ARLT-examples we attempted to show how we think analogical reasoning can be supported by forms of social interaction that incorporate elements of metacognitive theory.

## REFERENCES

Atkinson, R. C. & Shiffrin, R.M. (1968). Human memory: A proposed system and its control processes. In K. W. Spence & J. T. Spence (Eds.). *The Psychology of Learning and Motivation* (pp. 89–195). New York: Academic Press.

Belmont, J. M., & Butterfield, E. C. (1977). The instructional approach to developmental cognitive research. In R. V. Kail & J. W. Hagen (Eds.), *Perspectives on the development of memory and cognition* (pp. 437–481). Hillsdale, NJ: Lawrence Erlbaum Associates.

Belmont, J. M., Butterfield, E. C., & Ferretti, R. P. (1982). To secure transfer of training, instruct self–management skills. In D. K. Detterman & R. J. Sternberg (Eds.), *How and how much can intelligence be increased?* Norwood, NJ: Ablex.

Borkowski, J. G. & Kendall Varnhagen, C. (1984). Transfer of learning strategies: Contrast of self–instructional and traditional training formats with EMR children. *American Journal of Mental Deficiency, 4,* 369–379.

Borkowski, J. G. & Kurtz, B. E. (1987) Metacognition and executive control. In: J.G. Borkowski & J. Day (Eds.) *Cognition in special children* (pp. 123–152). Norwood, NJ: Ablex.

Borkowski, J. G. & Peck, V. A., Reid, M. K. & Kurtz, B. E. (1983). Impulsivity and strategy transfer: Metamemory as mediator. *Child Development, 54,* 459–473.

Brown, A. L. (1974). The role of strategic behavior in retarded memory. In N. R. Ellis (Ed.), *International review of research in mental retardation.* (Vol. 7, pp. 55–111). New York: Academic Press.

Brown, A. L. (1975). The development of memory: Knowing, knowing about knowing, and knowing how to know. In H. W. Reese (Ed.), *Advances in child development and behavior.* (Vol. 10, pp. 103–151). New York: Academic Press.

Brown, A. L. (1989). Analogical learning and transfer: What develops? In S. Vosniadou & A. Ortony (Eds.). *Similarity and analogical reasoning* (pp. 369-412). Cambridge, MA: Cambridge University Press.

Brown, A. L. & Barclay, C. R. (1976). The Effects of Training Specific Mnemonics on the Metamnemonic Efficiency of Retarded Children. *Child Development, 47,* 71–80.

Brown, A. L., Bransford, J. D., Ferrara, R. A., & Campione, J. C. (1983). Learning, remembering, and understanding. In J. F. Flavell & E. M. Markman (Eds.), Carmichael's manual of child psychology (Vol. 3, pp. 515–529). New York: Wiley.

Brown, A. L. & DeLoach, J. S. (1978). Skills, Plans, and Self-Regulation. In R. S. Siegler (Ed.). *Children's Thinking. What Develops?* (pp. 3–35). Hillsdale, NJ: Lawrence Erlbaum Associates.

Büchel, F. P. (1983). *Lernstrategien bei Jugendlichen und Erwachsenen in der beruflichen Ausbildung.* Unveröffentlichte Habilitationsschrift. Phil.–hist. Fakultät der Univ. Basel.

Büchel, F. P. (1988). Training of memory strategies with adolescents and adults in vocational schools. In F. W. Weinert, & M. Perlmutter (Eds.), *Memory development: Universal changes and individual differences* (pp. 131–144). Hillsdale, NJ: Lawrence Erlbaum Associates.

Büchel, F. P. (1990). Analyse des processus d'apprentissage médiatisés auprès d'enfants présentant des difficultés d'apprentissage. *Revue de Psychologie Appliquée, 40, 4,* 407–424.

Büchel, F. P. & Scharnhorst, U. (1989). Metacognitive regulation in problem solving with mentally retarded: The development of a descriptive system. *Archives de Psychologie, 57,* 323–336.

Büchel, F. P., Schlatter, C., & Scharnhorst, U. (1997). Training and assessment of analogical reasoning in students with severe learning difficulties. *Educational and Child Psychology, 14 (4),* 83–94.

Burt, C. (1911). Experimental tests on higher mental processes and their relation to general intelligence. *Journal of Experimental Pedagogy, 1,* 93–112.

Butterfield, E. C. & Belmont, J. M. (1977). Assessing and improving the executive cognitive functions of mentally retarded people. In I. Bialer & M. Sternlicht

(Eds.), *The psychology of mental retardation: Issues and approaches* (pp. 277–318). New York: Psychological Dimensions Inc.

Butterfield, E. C. & Ferretti, R. P. (1987). Toward a Theoretical Integration of Cognitive Hypotheses about Intellectual Differences among Children. In J. G. Borkowski & J. D. Day (Eds.). *Cognition in Special Children: Comparative Approaches to Retardation, Learning Disabilities, and Giftedness* (pp. 195–233). Norwood, NJ: Ablex.

Butterfield, E. C., Wambold, C., & Belmont, J. M. (1973). On the Theory and Practice of Improving Short-Term Memory. *American Journal of Mental Deficiency, 77, 5,* 654–669.

Campione, J. C., Brown, A. L., Ferrara, R. A., & Bryant, N.R. (1984). The zone of proximal development: Implications for individual differences and learning. In B. Rogoff & J. Wertsch (Eds.), *Children's learning in the zone of proximal development* (pp. 77–91). San Francisco: Jossey–Bass.

Campione, J. C., Brown, A. L., Ferrara, R. A., Jones, R. S. & Steinberg, E. (1985). Breakdowns in flexible use of information: Intelligence–related differences in transfer following equivalent learning performance. *Intelligence, 9,* 297–315.

Carlson, J. S. & Wiedl, K. H. (1978). Use of Testing-the-Limits Procedures in the Assessment of Intellectual Capabilities in children with Learning Difficulties. *American Journal of Mental Deficiencies, 6,* 559–564.

Carlson, J. S. & Wiedl, K. H. (1980). Applications of a dynamic testing approach in intelligence assessment: empirical results and theoretical formulations. *Zeitschrift für differentielle und diagnostische Psychologie, 1 (4),* 303-318.

Cavanaugh, J. C. & Perlmutter, M. (1982). Metamemory: A critical examination. *Child Development, 53,* 11–28.

Chen, Z., Sanchez, R. P., & Campbell, T. (1997). From Beyond to Within Their Grasp: The Rudiments of Analogical Problem Solving in 10- and 13-Month-Olds. *Developmental Psychology, 33 (5),* 790–801.

Dörner, D. (1981). Sprache und Denken. *Nova acta Leopoldina, 245,* 627–635.

Ericsson, K. A. & Simon, H. A. (1978). *Retrospective verbal reports as data.* CIP Working Paper 388. Carnegie Mellon University.

Ericsson, K. A. & Simon, H. A. (1979a). *Thinking–aloud protocols as data.* CIP Working Paper 397. Carnegie Mellon University.

Ericsson, K. A. & Simon, H. A. (1979b). *Sources of evidence on cognition: An historical overview.* CIP Working Paper 406. Carnegie Mellon University.

Ferrara, R. A., Brown, A. L. & Campione, J. C. (1986). Children's learning and transfer of inductive reasoning rules: A study of proximal development. *Child development, 57,* 1087–1099.

Feuerstein, R., Rand, Y., Hoffman, M. B., & Miller, R, (1980). *Instrumental Enrichment. An intervention program for cognitive modifiability.* Baltimore: University Park Press.

Flammer, A. (1975). *Individuelle Unterschiede im Lernen.* Weinheim: Beltz.

Flammer, A. (1990). *Erfahrung der eigenen Wirksamkeit.* Bern: Huber.

Flammer, A., Ito, T., Lüthi, R., Plaschy, N., Reber, R., Zurbriggen, L., & Sugimine, H. (1996). Coping with control-failure in Japanese and Swiss adolescents. *Swiss Journal of Psychology, 54 (4),* 277-288.

Flammer, A., & Scheuber-Sahli, E. (1995). Selective recall as intervention to modify control-beliefs in an academic achievement setting. *Swiss Journal of Psychology, 54 (1),* 50–56.

Flavell, J. H. (1971). First discussant's comments: What is memory development the development of? *Human Development, 14,* 272–278.

Flavell, J.H. & Wellman, H. M. (1977). Metamemory. In R. V. Kail & J. W. Hagen (Eds.), *Perspectives on the Development of memory and cognition* (pp. 3–33). Hillsdale, NJ.: Lawrence Erlbaum Associates.

Franzen, U. & Merz, F. (1976). Der Einfluss des Verbalisierens auf die Leistung bei Intelligenzprüfungen: Neue Untersuchungen. *Zeitschrift für Entwicklungspsychologie und Pädagogische Psychologie, 8,* 117–139.

Gentner, D. (1983). Structure-Mapping: A Theoretical Framework for Analogy. *Cognitive Science, 7,* 155–170.

Gholson, B., Morgan, D., Dattel, A. R., & Pierce, K. A. (1990). The Development of Analogical Problem Solving: Strategic Processes in Schema Acquisition and Transfer. In D.F. Bjorklund (Ed.). *Children's Strategies* (pp. 269–308). Hillsdale, N.J.: Erlbaum.

Guthke, J. (1990). Les tests d'apprentissage comme alternative ou complément aux tests d'intelligenc: un bilan de leur évolution. In F. Büchel & J.-L. Paour (Eds.). Assessments of Learning and Development Potential: Theory and Practices. Special issue of *European Journal of Psychology of Education, V,2,* 117–133.

Holyoak, K. J. (1984). Analogical Thinking and Human Intelligence. In R. J. Sternberg (Ed.). *Advances in the Psychology of Human Intelligence* (pp. 199–230). Hillsdale, NJ: Erlbaum.

Huber, O. (1982). *Entscheiden als Problemlösen.* Bern: Huber.

Huber, G. L. & Mandl, H. (1982). Verbalisierungsmethoden zur Erfassung von Kognitionen im Handlungszusammenhang. In G. L. Huber & H. Mandl (Eds.). *Verbale Daten* (pp. 11–42) Weinheim: Beltz.

Inhelder, B. & Piaget, J. (1958). *The growth of logical thinking from childhood to adolescence.* New York: Basic Books.

Kendall, C. R., Borkowski, J. G., & Cavanaugh, J. C. (1980). Maintenance and generalization of an interrogative strategy by EMR children. *Intelligence, 4,* 255–270.

Klauer, K. J. (1989). *Denktraining für Kinder, I. Ein Programm zur intellektuellen Förderung.* Göttingen: Hogrefe.

Klauer, K. J. (1993). *Denktraining für Jugendliche. Ein Programm zur intellektuellen Förderung.* Göttingen: Hogrefe.

Klauer, K. J. (1996). Denktraining oder Lesetraining? Über die Auswirkungen eines Trainings zum induktiven Denken sowie eines Lesetrainings auf Leseverständnis und induktives Denken. *Zeitschrift für Entwicklungspsychologie und Pädagogische Psychologie, XXVIII, 1,* 67–89.

Kluwe, R. H. (1980). *Metakognition: Komponenten einer Theorie zur Kontrolle und Steuerung eigenen Denkens.* Unveröffentlichte Habilitationsschrift. Universität München.

Kluwe, R. & Reimann, H. (1983). *Problemlösen bei vernetzten, komplexen Problemen: Effekte des Verbalisierens auf die Problemlöseleistung.* Unveröffentlichter Bericht aus dem FB Pädagogik, Abt. Psychologie. Hochschule der Bundeswehr Hamburg.

Kreutzer, M. A., Leonard, C. Sr., & Flavell, J. H. (1975). An interview study of children's knowledge about memory. *Monographs of the society for research in child development.* Serial No. 159, Vol. 40, 1.

Lindsay, P. H. & Norman, D. A. (1977). *Human Information Processing.* New York: Academic Press.

Masendorf, F. & Klauer, K. J. (1987). Intelligenztraining bei lernbehinderten Sonderschülern. *Psychologie in Erziehung und Unterricht. 34,* 14–19.

Masendorf, F. & Maihack, V. (1986) Intelligenztraining bei Behinderten. *Rehabilitation, 25,* 116–122.

Meichenbaum, D., & Asarnow, J. (1979). Cognitive-behavioral modification and metacognitive development: Implications for the classroom. In P. Kendall & S. Hollon (Eds.). *Cognitive-behavioral interventions: Theory, research and practice.* New York: Academic Press.

Meichenbaum, D. & Goodman, J. (1971). Training impulsive children to talk to themselves: A means of developing self–control. *Journal of Abnormal Psychology, 77,* 115–126.

Merz, F. (1969). Der Einfluss des Verbalisierens auf die Leistung bei Intelligenztestaufgaben. *Zeitschrift für experimentelle und angewandte Psychologie, 16,* 114–137.

Mulholland, T. M.; Pellegrino, J. W., & Glaser, R. (1980). Components of Geometric Analogy Solution. *Cognitive Psychology. 12,* 252–284.

Nisbett, R. E. & Wilson, T. C. (1977). Telling more than we can know: Verbal reports on mental processes. *Psychological Review, 84,* 231–259.

Pellegrino, J. H. (1985). Inductive reasoning ability. In R. J. Sternberg (Ed.), *Human abilities. An information–processing approach* (pp. 195–225). New York: Freeman.

Pellegrino, J. W. & Glaser, R. (1980) Components of Inductive Reasoning. In: R.E. Snow, P.–A. Federico & W.E. Montague (Eds.) *Aptitude, Learning, and Instruction* (pp. 177–217). Hillsdale, NJ: Lawrence Erlbaum Associates.

Pelegrino, J. W. & Goldman, S. R. (1983). Developmental and Individual Differences in Verbal and Spatial Reasoning. In R. F. Dillou, & R. R. Schmeck (Eds.). *Individual Differences in Cognition* (Vol. 1, pp. 137–180). New York: Academic Press.

Piaget, J., Montangero, J., & Billeter, J. (1977). Les correlats. L'abstraction réfléchissante. Paris. PUF.

Reimann, H. & Kluwe, R. (1983). *Effekte des Verbalisierens auf die Problemlöseleistung beim Umgang mit komplexen Systemen.* Unveröffentlicher Bericht aus dem FB Pädagogik, Abt. Psychologie. Hochschule der Bundeswehr Hamburg.

Reitman, J. S. (1970). Computer Simulation of an Information-Processing Model of Short-Term Memory. In D. A. Norman (Ed.). *Models of Human Memory* (pp. 117-148). New York: Academic Press.

Rey, A. & Dupond, J. B. (1953). Organisation des groupes des points en figures géométriques simples. *Monograhpies de Psychologie Appliquée.* Neuchâtel: Delachaux et Niéstlé.

Scharnhorst, U., & Büchel, F. P. (1990). Cognitive and Metacognitive Components of Learning: Search for the Locus of Retarded Performance. In. F. P. Büchel & J.-L. Paour (Eds.), Assessments of Learning and Development Potential: Theory and Practices. Numéro spécial du *Journal Européen de Psychologie de l'Education, Vol. 5, 2,* 207–230.

Schlatter, C. & Büchel, F. P. (in press). Dynamic Assessment of Analogical Reasoning in Adolescents with Moderate Mental Retardation. *Journal of Cognitive Education* (submitted).

Schlatter, C., Büchel, F. P., & Thomas, L. (1997). Test d'apprentissage de la pensée analogique pour adolescents handicapés mentaux modérés. *Revue francophone de la déficience intellectuelle, 8 (1),* 37–54.

Schlatter, C., Scharnhorst, U., & Büchel, F. P. (1997). *Dynamic Assessment and Training of Analogical Reasoning in Students with Moderate Mental Retardation: A Stepping or a Stumbling Stone to Higher Cognitive Functioning?* Paper presented at the 7th Conference for Research on Learning and Instruction (EARLY), Athens, Greece.

Shiffrin, R. M. (1975). The Locus and Role of Attention in Memory Systems. In P. M. Rabbitt, & S. Dornic (Eds.). *Attention and Performance* (Vol. 5, pp. 168–193). New York: .Academic Press.

Sternberg, R. J. (1977) *Intelligence, information processing, and analogical reasoning: The componential analysis of human abilities.* Hillsdale, NJ: Lawrence Erlbaum Associates.

Sternberg. R. J. & Gardner, M. K. (1979). *Units in Inductive Reasoning.* Technical Report, No. 18. Yale University, Department of Psychology, New Haven, CT.

Spearman, C. (1923). *The nature of intelligence and the principles of cognition.* London: Macmillan.

Sternberg, R. J. & Gardner, M. K. (1979). *Units in Inductive Reasoning.* Technical Report No. 18. Department of Psychology, Yale University, New Haven, CT.

Thurstone, L. L. (1938). *Primary mental abilities.* Chicago: University of Chicago Press.

Vosniadou, S. & Ortony, A. (1989). Similarity and analogical reasoning: a synthesis. In S. Vosniadou & A. Ortony (Eds.). *Similarity and analogical reasoning* (pp. 1-17). Cambridge, MA: Cambridge University Press.

Welsh, M. (1987). Verbal Mediation Underlying Inductive Reasoning: Cognitive Tempo Differences. *Cognitive Development, 2,* 37-57.

Whitman, T. L. (1990). Self-Regulation and Mental Retardation. *American Journal of Mental Retardation, 94 (4),* 347-362.

# IV

# Emotion, Motivation, and Action

# 14

# Emotional Expression: A Royal Road for the Study of Behavior Control[1]

*Klaus R. Scherer*

> "...*Laughter is involuntary for the same reason that other emotional displays are involuntary. ...The brain broadcasts an honest, unfakable, expensive advertisement of a mental state by transferring control from the computational systems underlying voluntary action to the low level drivers of the body's physical plant.*"
>
> *Steven Pinker in* How the Mind Works

## INTRODUCTION

This quote was published as a vignette in a recent issue of Science (24 October, 1997; Vol. 278, p. 595) nicely demonstrating the appeal of emotional expression, and in particular laughing and crying, as intriguing demonstrations of involuntary behavior control. In fact, emotional expression raises some fascinating issues with respect not only to the underlying "low level drivers" of our behavior, but also with respect to the elaborate regulation or control mechanisms which are used to bring the involuntary motor commands emanating from the emotion system in line with cultural norms and expectations or strategic considerations. Unfortunately, the role of emotion in behavior control and regulation has not been a favorite theme of emotion theorists or researchers. The elicitation of emotion specific expressive behavior has been largely taken for granted, ascribing it to neural circuits or neural motor programs (Ekman, 1992b; Panksepp, 1982, 1989; Tomkins, 1962, 1963, 1984). Similarly, the regulation of emotion-

[1]The author gratefully acknowledges the contributions of Grazia Ceschi and Marcel Zentner to this chapter.

ally expressive behavior, once triggered, has been dealt with rather summarily by postulating cultural display rules (Wundt, 1905, p. 85; Ekman, 1972). It has been only recently that strong interest in emotion regulation has appeared, particularly from a developmental point of view (Eisenberg, & Fabes, 1992; Malatesta-Magai, 1991). In this chapter, I examine some of the issues that future theorizing and research in this area will need to take into consideration. In order to ground this discussion, I briefly describe the emotion model which I have proposed and which will serve as a basis to examine the issues linked to control and regulation of emotional expression.

## A COMPONENT PROCESS MODEL OF EMOTION

Adopting a line of functional reasoning, and stressing phylogenetic continuity, I see emotion as having superseded rigid reflex and/or innate releasing mechanisms. This evolutionary development has created a highly flexible, adaptational mechanism which decouples stimulus and response, providing latency time to choose an optimal behavioral response, while at the same time preparing the organism for action. More specifically, I have proposed a *component process model* of emotion (Scherer, 1981, 1984a,b, 1986). This model proceeds from the assumption that emotion needs to be conceptualized as a *process of adaptation* consisting of patterns of state changes in five major functional subsystems of an organism. These subsystems correspond to the functions and components of emotion as postulated by most emotion theorists. The evaluation function is served by an *information processing subsystem* with the system states characterized by perception, memory, prediction, or evaluation of situations, relationships, facts, events, or actions. Internal regulation is the task of the *support subsystem*, which controls neuroendocrine, somatic, and autonomic states. The *executive subsystem* is responsible for planning, decision making, and the preparation of action, as well as arbitrating between conflicting motives or plans. The *action subsystem* regulates neuromuscular states and processes and is thus responsible for motor expression and overt behavior. A *monitoring subsystem*, finally, is conceptualized as a control system determining the deployment of attention and reflecting the current states of all other subsystems. At least in humans, some elements of these representations constitute awareness or consciousness; in the case of emotion—subjective feeling states.

Put briefly, the component process model defines emotion as a sequence of interrelated and synchronized changes in the states of the functional subsystems described above in response to the evaluation of an external or internal event as highly significant to the organism (see Scherer, 1984b, 1993a). How does this model explain the elicitation and differentiation of emotion?

Following the pioneering work of Arnold (1960) and Lazarus (1968), many emotion theorists have, more or less explicitly, assumed that differentiated emotional experiences result from the outcome of an organism's appraisal or evaluation of a stimulus or event in terms of its significance for survival and well being. This tradition of thought about emotion–antecedent evaluation is currently referred to as *appraisal theories*, including theorists such as Ellsworth, Frijda, Lazarus, Roseman, Scherer, and Smith, who arrived, largely independently, at converging models of emotion (see Scherer, in press). In an attempt to analyze the criteria used in this emotion-antecedent evaluation and to underline its nature as a recursive process, I have suggested a *sequence theory of emotional differentiation* as part of the component process model (Scherer, 1981, 1984a,b, 1987) which postulates that each organism's information processing subsystem continuously scans external and internal stimulus input and performs a series of *stimulus evaluation checks* (SECs). The theory specifies the following five SECs, which are expected to always occur in the same sequential order:

*Novelty Check*
Determines whether there is an abrupt change in the pattern of external or internal stimulation, particularly whether a novel event occurred or is to be expected.
*Intrinsic Pleasantness Check*
Determines whether a stimulus event is pleasant, inducing approach tendencies, or unpleasant, inducing avoidance tendencies based on innate feature detectors or learned associations.
*Goal/need Significance Check*
Determines whether a stimulus event is relevant to important goals or needs of the organism *(relevance subcheck)*, whether the outcome is consistent with or discrepant from the state expected for this point in the goal/plan sequence *(expectation subcheck)*, whether it is conducive or obstructive to reaching the respective goals or satisfying the relevant needs *(conduciveness subcheck)*, and whether there is an urgent need to respond to the event *(urgency subcheck)*.
*Coping Potential Check*
Determines the causation of a stimulus event *(causation subcheck)* and the coping potential available to the organism, particularly the degree of control over the event or its consequences *(control subcheck)*, the relative power of the organism to change or avoid the outcome through fight or flight *(power subcheck)*, and the potential for adjustment to the final outcome via internal restructuring *(adjustment subcheck)*.
*Norm/Self Compatibility Check*
Determines whether the event, particularly an action, conforms to social norms, cultural conventions, or expectations of significant others *(external standards subcheck)*, and whether it is consistent with internalized norms or standards as part of the self concept or ideal self *(internal standards subcheck)*.

A specific emotional state is the end result of the respective outcomes of these checks; for example, fear may result from evaluating an event as novel, unpleasant, hindering goal achievement, and requiring flight to cope with. If the outcome of the coping potential check indicates, that one's power is sufficient to fight an obstacle, on the other hand, the reaction to the very same event might be

anger. A more detailed description of the sequence theory of emotional differentiation and the different SECs can be found elsewhere (Scherer, 1984a,b, 1986,
1987, 1988, 1993b).

If it is justified to assume that the outcomes of the major evaluation checks
determine the structure of human experience, it seems plausible, and from an
adaptive phylogenetically oriented point of view indeed necessary, to assume that
these outcomes also determine the pattern of change in the physiological and the
motivational systems. I have developed a *componential patterning theory*, as part
of the component process model, in which I have proposed, partly based on the
literature and partly on speculation about functionality, detailed predictions concerning the response patterning to be expected in the autonomic and somatic
systems and in the bodily, facial, and vocal modalities.

The theory assumes that the outcome of each evaluation check elicits a specific functional response pattern in both the support and action subsystems. Of
course, since the evaluation sequence is processed very rapidly, it is often not
possible to observe such specific changes in isolation since they are overlayed by
the effects of the subsequent checks. The total response patterning at a particular
point in time, then, is the *net result* of the effects of the outcomes of preceding
SECs in the information processing subsystem (a "value-added" notion) and of
the total effect of the changes in other subsystems (which also affect response
patterning). A detailed example of this theoretical approach, resulting in concrete
predictions, has been elaborated for the vocal expression of emotion (Scherer,
1986). Recent empirical work has confirmed many of these theoretical predictions
(Banse & Scherer, 1996). Similar approaches for facial expression and physiological response patterning, as based on Scherer (1984a,b, 1987, 1992), are currently being pursued in our laboratory (van Reekum, Johnstone, & Scherer,
1997; Wehrle, Kaiser, Schmid, & Scherer, submitted).

How does this model relate to other emotion theories focussing on the response subsystems? Arousal theories have focussed almost exclusively on gross
activation. In the component patterning theory this is seen in a more differentiated manner—the closest to the classical arousal notion is probably the assumption in the model that major ergotropic or trophotropic shifts (Gellhorn, 1963,
1967; Hess, 1954) are generated by the results of the goal/plan conduciveness
check, related to the degree of activity or effort needed to reach a goal. The present
theory differs from discrete emotion theories (Ekman, 1984, 1992a; Izard, 1971,
1990, 1993; Tomkins, 1962, 1963) in that it does not endorse the notion of hard-
wired integrated response mechanisms for a few discrete emotions that are triggered as a whole, yielding a completely organized response pattern (requiring the
notion of mixing or blending of such patterns in order to explain complex states
that do not conform to one of the basic emotions). Yet, I do not claim that the
discrete patterns that these theories highlight do not exist at all. I think that they,
and the basic emotion labels that refer to them, are phylogenetically old patterns
of prototypical outcome configurations of evaluation sequences that occur very
frequently in the life of organisms (such as encountering pleasant events, frustra-

tions, loss, etc.). For this reason, I suggested to denote these overarching emotion families as *modal* emotions (Scherer, 1987, 1994). While I would also conceive of parts of these prototypical patterns to be hard-wired I would be hesitant to assume that the whole pattern is.

In summary, the component patterning model predicts that efferent motor commands are triggered by the respective patterns of appraisal, based on phylogenetically evolved, adaptive mechanisms. While this conceptualization goes further than most other emotion theories in trying to explain the mechanism and allow concrete predictions of expressive behavior patterns as a result of antecedent appraisal, it clearly does not do justice to the complex reality of control and regulation of emotional behavior. Some of the complicating factors will now be addressed.

## DETERMINANTS OF EMOTIONAL EXPRESSION

To begin, the simple version of a component patterning model assumes that emotionally expressive behaviors are always spontaneous, triggered automatically by the appraisal of the situation and the adaptive mechanisms that are brought into play by the outcomes of the evaluation. This is obviously not true of all observed emotional expressions. These can be produced voluntarily or intentionally (although apparently not very easily, see Galati, Scherer, and Ricci-Bitti, 1997) in the service of a variety of strategic goals in social interactions. One could argue that such voluntary or intentional expressions need not be dealt with by an emotion theory trying to explain the control of emotional expression and behavior in the case of *non-intentional, spontaneous* emotion arousal. In this sense, voluntary production of emotional expression would be comparable to any other kind of voluntary action, and thus a class in itself. Unfortunately, reality is likely to be more complicated than that. Contrary to the customary treatment of emotion as a state, in reality emotion is a process with constantly varying inputs and reactions. Once the emotion process has started, the resulting patterning becomes itself subject to appraisal (see also Frijda, 1993) and thus subject to different kinds of regulation. Furthermore, emotion, while originally elicited in a spontaneous fashion, may, in the ongoing process of emoting, become of strategic importance in interaction. Aristotle was the first to insist on one having to be able to express anger at he right time, in the right intensity and towards the right person in order not to be seen as a social fool (Aristotle, 1941). Thus, once the emotion process is ongoing, one might expect various mixtures of spontaneous (automatic) and voluntary (intentional) affect expression, depending on the nature of the situation, the strategic goals of the actor, and his or her cognitive and social development. In consequence, one of the major issues to be dealt with in the study of behavior control under emotion is the relative mix of spontaneous vs. voluntary aspects of behavior control.

Even assuming that the ongoing process and the behavior patterns triggered by appraisal results is mostly spontaneous, it is unlikely that the resulting pattern of responses is completely determined by what Scherer, Helfrich, & Scherer (1980) have called *push* factors, i.e., the "pushing out" of motor patterns from the inside, based entirely on phylogenetically evolved adaptive neuro-motor reactions. It is highly likely that *pull* factors, determined by cultural norms, expectations, or context factors, also play a role (see Kappas, Hess, & Scherer, 1991; Scherer, 1985, 1988; Scherer, & Kappas, 1988). Pull effects are not limited to controlling expressive reactions that have been triggered in order to correspond to some kind of cultural display rule. For example, Leyhausen (1967) has convincingly shown that the patterns of expressive signals are not only determined by the underlying motivational state of animals but also by the expectations of receivers in a communication system. Thus, one can demonstrate a very close phylogenetic link between ex̲pression and im̲pression. The details of the effects of such push or pull factors on emotional expression are largely unexplored. They are likely to be very important, however, since emotional expression is, in fact, an important signaling system, subject to the constraints of any such communication system (see Hauser, 1996).

Another issue likely to be of great importance is the onset of *regulation or control* of triggered expressive behavior. This is different from the two issues discussed above, in that the focus here is entirely on eliminating or changing a particular expressive pattern once triggered. This is not necessarily voluntary, it can also occur in an automatic or spontaneous fashion. Nor is it necessarily determined by pull effects, as in the case of polite smiles serving as masking stimuli. Rather, regulation may work in the sense of mimicking other push effects. Thus, this dimension extends between the extremes of *raw* expressions on the one hand, unhampered by regulation efforts, and *regulated* expressions that are consistently monitored and changed from what the raw expression would be. It is important to insist that this does not have to be either voluntary or conscious—regulation can work in a very automatic fashion.

The *consciousness or awareness* dimension crosscuts the dimensions described above. Regulation efforts do not necessarily have to be conscious and even voluntary productions might occur in a less than completely conscious fashion. While there may be a tendency for voluntary production, regulation, and pull effects on the one hand to be more conscious than spontaneous production, push effect action, and raw expression on the other hand, degree of consciousness or awareness would seem to be an independent dimension worthy of study in its own right. Table 14.1 summarizes these dimensions underlying the production of the expressive behavior which all require independent conceptualization and operationalization in empirical research.

*TABLE 14.1*
*Dimensions underlying the production of expressive behavior*

| Production dimension | Description |
| --- | --- |
| Spontaneous vs. voluntary production | To what extent is the expression initiated by concrete goal states |
| Push effects vs. pull effects | To what extent is the expressive pattern determined by physiological effects or by socially shared models |
| Raw vs. regulated unfolding | To what extent does the expression follow the initial impulse vs. being controlled and regulated |
| Conscious vs. unconscious processes | To what extent is the person aware of the push effects or message intention and/or potential regulation efforts |

## NEUROMOTOR CONTROL OF EMOTIONAL EXPRESSION

Remarkable progress has been made in understanding the hierarchical structure of behavior control for relatively simple motor actions (see Gallistel, 1980, Kelso, 1995). So far, nothing approaching the sophistication of the respective models or the research associated with them has been developed in the area of motor expression of emotion (see Jürgens, 1979; Ploog, 1988; Rinn, 1984, 1991). This is probably partly the case because of the predominantly spontaneous nature of emotional expression. However, efforts in this direction will need to be undertaken if we are to progress in our understanding of behavior and motor control in emotional expression. This is all the more so since one might well imagine that the different control dimensions as reviewed above will affect different stages of the efferent outflow from central command structures to the musculature. One will need to think of hierarchical models allowing impact on the control sequence from different determinants at different points. Although this is not my area and I have not yet done the necessary groundwork with respect to the existing literature, in figure 14.1, I venture to present a very preliminary and highly speculative outline of what such a model might need to address. I hasten to add that what is displayed in figure 14.1 does not claim to be a model of the process. It obviously does neither include the different levels of processing nor the recursive effects. Rather, it is to provide a simple illustration of some of the determinants likely to be operative. The basic assumption is that either automatic, adaptive mechanisms controlled directly by appraisal results, or voluntary expression intentions, will produce patterned motor commands at the highest level. As the command is being encoded in an integrated pattern of movement there is likely to be a complex mixture of push and pull effects of a largely unconscious nature.

Muscle innervation is then produced by neuro-physiological mechanisms, which are again outside of awareness. Once the nature of the motor output is fed back to the central control mechanism through proprioceptive feedback, awareness of the efferent pattern may set in and regulation mechanisms are likely to be applied. Obviously, this type of model will need to be greatly elaborated and brought in line with ongoing discoveries in the motor control literature.

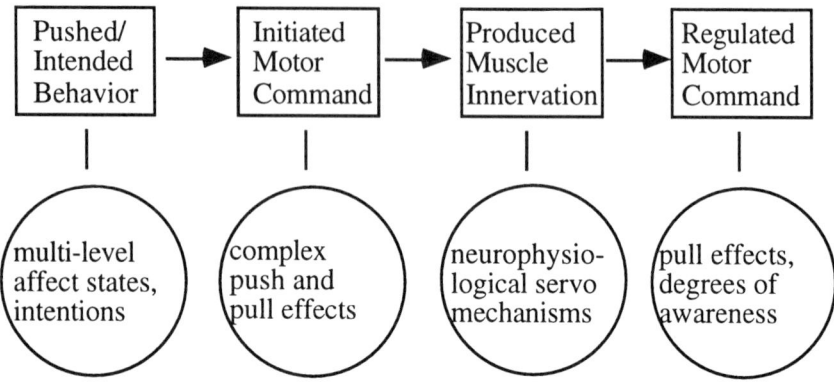

FIG. 14.1. Outline of a working model for the multi-level sequential organization of expressive behavior.

It is well known that volitional motor behavior in general is controlled by cortical regions (supplementary motor cortex and cingulate gyrus) since lesions in this area will abolish voluntary movement whereas electrical stimulation can produce coordinated movement (Halgren, & Malinkovic, 1995). This is equally true for expressive behavior. Rinn (1991) illustrates on the basis of neurological disorders that volitional or "instrumental" facial behavior is controlled by the pyramidal system through the cortical motor control areas. Spontaneous, reactive facial expressions on the other hand are controlled through subcortical regions, via the extrapyramidal system. There is massive evidence for spontaneous emotional expressions in man and animals being controlled by the limbic system (Jürgens, 1979; Rinn, 1984, 1991; Robinson, 1976). However, as shown above, it is unlikely that the regulation of the expressive motor behavior will be entirely volitional (in a cold, instrumental sense) or entirely spontaneous (as automatic "fixed-action patterns"). It has been pointed out that in many cases of volitional behavior there is a "coupling" to the limbic system (Hutton, 1972) providing affective coloring (see Scherer, & Wallbott, 1990). Similarly, one can think of the cortical motor control areas being "coupled" to motor efference produced by the limbic system in the case of emotional regulation, such as the suppression or modification of a "pushed-out" expression. Other kinds of coupling can be observed in the integration of cortical, volitional and subcortical, emotional control in activities such as speech. For example, Rinn (1991) points out that speakers are generally unaware of their abrupt eyebrow movements that "punctuate" speech (Ekman, 1979) and have difficulty reproducing them voluntarily in the same manner. Thus, in most cases of expressive behavior we can expect a very intricate intermingling of cortical and subcortical determinants subserved by a very complex recursive regulation mechanism.

Given the complexity of the recursive, hierarchical control structure outlined above, empirical research in this area is unlikely to be a trivial affair. In fact, the very complexity of the issues has probably been responsible for researchers being reticent to invest themselves in this area. However, it will be necessary to start empirical research on these questions in order to advance our theoretical understanding of the issues involved. This will have to be done in a piecemeal fashion trying to assemble the pieces of an immensely complex puzzle. In what follows, I shall describe some recent studies conducted in our laboratory which attack, in a very modest way, some of the topics mentioned above.

## ILLUSTRATIVE EMPIRICAL RESEARCH
## FROM OUR LABORATORY

One of the important tasks in this line of research will be to try to disentangle the relative importance of push versus pull effects on emotional expression. Since most, but not all, push effects are likely to be psycho-biologically determined, rather than the result of socialization or strategic planning, a developmental approach to the issue seems promising. In other words, the ontogenetic study of the expression of emotion in different modalities should allow us to determine which aspects of expression are determined by psycho-biologically determined push factors before one would expect cultural norms or strategic concerns to regulate the observable expression (Izard, Fantauzzo, Castle, Haynes, et al., 1995). However, only very rudimentary and primitive push effects can be studied in this manner since with the maturation of cognitive functioning, leading to more complex appraisal and thus more elaborated push effects, the child will also acquire knowledge and competencies with respect to pull-effect governed regulation strategies.

### Development Of Emotional Expression In Infants

In a series of experiments (conducted in collaboration with Pierre Mounoud and Daniel Stern), we attempted to determine to what extent we could experimentally demonstrate the effect of manipulated emotional states on facial and vocal expression as well as gaze behavior. Contrary to the assumption that emotional expression would be present from birth (as postulated by discrete emotion theorists, e.g. Izard, 1971, 1990) it was assumed (in line with an appraisal theoretical approach to the explanation of emotion elicitation and differentiation, see Scherer,

1984b; Scherer & Zentner, submitted) that the nature of the emotional reaction to particular experimental manipulations would depend on the type of evaluation an infant would be able to perform at a certain age, given its state of ontogenetic maturity.

We studied infants of 5–, 7–, 9–, 11–, and 14–months old in a cross sectional design. The experimental manipulations were violations of expectancy of different kinds. In one paradigm the infant was encouraged to pick up objects from a table in front of it. While the objects remained stationary in the control condition, in the violation condition the experimenter moved the object surreptitiously by operating a lever underneath the table. In another manipulation, the infant is presented with a little figure that moves back and forth through a tunnel (in the control condition).

In the violation condition, one type of figure will go into the tunnel and another type of figure will come out. Our particular interest in the present context concerns the third manipulation where we used computer filtering of the voice of the experimenter while talking to the infant. This violates the expectancy of stability of the visual and vocal aspects of the other person. In addition, the effect of the filtering is a rather unpleasant sounding, raspy voice. Thus, using the stimulus evaluation checks described above, one could hypothesize that the evaluation of the infant should be one of novelty (since such a discrepancy between vocal and visual cues is unlikely to have been observed before), and of intrinsic unpleasantness (given the nature of the filtering of the voice). In addition one could expect an evaluation of goal hindrance with respect to possible effects of the voice change on the interaction between infant and experimenter. As mentioned above, one of the issues in this study was to check to what extent these evaluations can be produced by the infant given the degree of cognitive maturation. For example, it would seem that in order to be able to evaluate the significance of a discrepancy between the visual and vocal aspects of another person, stable person schemata would need to have been established.

The component patterning theory, as described above, theoretically postulates the expected facial and vocal expressions for each of the results for the checks described above. The detailed observation of the infant's facial and vocal reactions to the experimental manipulations were therefore seen as privileged means of access to or inference of the underlying evaluative process. Furthermore, this type of approach should allow us to evaluate whether, at least at this rudimentary level, the expected push effects, uninfluenced by cultural or strategic pull effects, can be demonstrated empirically.

The experimental sessions with 58 infants studied in this research were videotaped in their entirety and analyzed by trained coders. We used the Baby-FACS (Oster, & Rosenstein, 1989), the infant version of the Facial Affect Scoring System developed by Ekman and Friesen (1978), to code the observable facial expressions. In addition, we developed a code to measure the infant's gaze toward the object that occupied the center of attention, toward the experimenter, or toward other point in the room. The vocalizations of the infants were to be analyzed by digital analysis of the voice (Scherer, 1989). However, it was quickly obvious that many of the infants did not vocalize at all or only very rarely, which lead us to drop the vocal modality in the analyses.

The data for the gaze results are relatively straightforward to interpret. With increasing age the infant seems to be able to recognize that the cause for the unexpected change in the auditory impression of the voice must be sought in the experimenter, leading to a redirection of the gaze toward the experimenter. The data for the facial action units are less easy to interpret. While there is a definite effect of age, and while some of the theoretically postulated action units are observed, the total number of coded expressions is relatively low and does not allow to systematically evaluate the theoretical predictions (see Scherer Mounoud, Stern, Kappas, et al., 1994).

This finding was all the more surprising since viewing of the videotapes strongly supports the impression that the infants did, in fact, react to the experimental manipulation. Intensive inspection of the pertinent portions of the tapes showed that the scarcity of facial expressions was due to an abundance of *freezing* responses in the infants. As is well documented in the literature on both animals and young infants and children, freezing is a typical response to both novel information, requiring *focussed attention* on a stimulus, or threat, producing anxiety, in situations where flight is not the privileged option (Archer, 1976; Fraiberg, 1982; Miller & Blaich, 1988; Takahashi, Turner, & Kalin, 1991). In order to examine the possibility that many of the infants in our study had reacted with freezing rather than a discrete facial expression, we had a group of 15 judges observe the tapes and press a button whenever a freezing period, as operationalized by a list of criteria given to the judges, was observed. Using an empirically derived agreement criterion, we then determined the amount of perceived freezing for each infant. The pattern of results shows a very clear quadratic age effect (the amount of freezing decreasing from 7 to 9 months, then increasing again toward 11–, 12– and 14–months), indicating that the push effects on this type of behavior seem to be determined, at least in part, by the respective stage of cognitive maturation of the infant.

How can this pattern of results be explained? One might assume that freezing diminishes from 7– to 9–months since the 9–month old infants have a larger number of schemata that could accommodate sudden changes and discrepancies. The renewed increase in freezing toward ages 11 and 14 could be explained by the increasing sophistication of the schemata and growth in working memory for the older infants, allowing them to recognize that a specific schema is being violated (for further details, see Scherer, Zentner, Scherer, Mounoud et al., 1997).

With respect to the issue of push factors mentioned above, these findings seem to indicate that one of the push factors involved seems to be the need for attention to significant stimuli leading to both freezing of the behavior of the organism, to allow focusing of attention, and redirection of gaze, to obtain information on potential causes.

Clearly, these data are preliminary and will need to be replicated and extended to allow us to make more educated guesses about the nature of pure push effects in early infancy. However, they demonstrate a potential avenue for addressing some of the issues involved.

## The Regulation Of Laughter In Children

A doctoral thesis by Grazia Ceschi recently completed in our laboratory, addresses the issue of pull effects in interaction with powerful push effects. Ceschi studied 7– and 10–year–old school children whom she showed a live clown performance in individual sessions. All children were told to watch the clown's performance, which would probably make them laugh a lot. Half of the children of both ages, the experimental group, were told in addition *not to show* their laughter. In other words, the children in this dissimulation group were expected to control the spontaneously induced laughter in a systematic fashion. Again, a developmental approach is used to try to understand the operation of control strategies motivated by pull effects. While research in the traditional "theory of mind" approach (Harris, 1989) has demonstrated that children as young as 4 years old have a clear understanding of the difference between felt and expressed emotions either with respect to their meta-theory of emotions attributed to fictive character in a story or to their own emotional expressions (for example not to show disappointment when being given an unwanted present by a favorite aunt). There is also evidence that the knowledge about the strategies to be used develops after 5 to 6 years of age, and increases in complexity between 7 and 10 years.

While Ceschi was able to replicate earlier results in this literature concerning the developmental progression of *knowledge* about emotion regulation (i.e. her 7–year–old children were less sophisticated than the 10 year old ones, particularly with respect to the use of mental strategies) there were no differences with respect to the actual ability to control their laughter in response to the clown's antics. This suggests that, for functional purposes, the pull effects linked to expression control in a voluntary fashion are well established by 7 years even though these children have imperfect knowledge, from a cognitive perspective, what exactly they are doing when they are trying to control. This could be taken as an example of automatically occurring, non-conscious regulation determined by pull factors.

With respect to an understanding of the nature of expression regulation, it is of interest to study the motor behaviors that were used by the children in both age groups to control their laughter. Ceschi had videorecorded the facial expressions of her children and had coders trained in Ekman and Friesen's FACS system as described above. The results show that it is particularly the muscles in the lower area of the face, particularly *m. orbicularis oris* that seem to have been involved in the regulation attempts. The type of muscular action most frequently used can be described as *lip press*. Ceschi's detailed analysis of the muscular movements involved in voluntary control behavior are of great significance in an attempt to understand some of the details in the hierarchical control structure as sketched out in figure 14.1. One might postulate on the basis of these results that the voluntary innervation of control movements might actually consist of a systematic innervation of the muscles producing results *opposite* from those that have produced the spontaneous expression. If this were the case, the systematic study of *voluntary* control could be informative with respect to the study of *spontaneous* expression patterns as produced by push effects (which are normally extremely difficult to investigate).

## Voluntary Facial Expression
## Of Emotion In The Blind

I will conclude the sampling of studies from our laboratory that are pertinent to this issue by briefly describing a study on the voluntary facial expression in sighted and blind subjects which was conducted in collaboration with Dario Galati and Pio Ricci-Bitti (Galati, Scherer, & Ricci-Bitti, 1997). Galati had asked groups of naive sighted and congenitally blind subjects to produce typical facial expressions of emotion in response to a number of scenarios, which had been chosen to be equally evocative for both sighted and blind people. The expressions produced by the subjects were photographed with a high-speed camera. Judges were used to isolate the most representative still photograph for the expressive sequence. These photos were then coded by trained FACS coders to obtain an indication of the facial action units that had been produced by the subjects. In addition, judges were asked to rate or recognize the emotions expressed or portrayed by the sighted and blind subjects. As one might expect on the basis of literature that seems to suggest that the neuro-muscular capacities of blind subjects might be impaired (Rinn, 1991), making it more difficult for them to spontaneously produce facial expressions, the recognition rate for expression of the blind was below that of the sighted subjects.

However, a detailed analysis of the facial action units actually produced by the two groups of posers, failed to reveal any major significant difference. The differences that were found were mostly due to the use of tic-like facial movements, such as closing the eyelids or rolling the eyes that are often produced by blind persons. It is likely that these movements have confused the judges, accounting for the lower recognition rate.

The results of this experiment indicate that the voluntary control of expression is independent of visual-motor feedback or of the knowledge concerning the external appearance of the desired expressive patterns. At the same time, the results show that the performance of both the sighted and the blind group was rather poor with respect to the production of highly differentiated and prototypical expression patterns (as postulated, for example, by Ekman and Friesen, 1978). Since this was one of the very first studies to systematically study the ability of non-trained persons to produce prototypical facial expressions, these results raise the important issue of the nature of the schemata and the command structures that are used by persons asked to voluntarily portray a particular facial expression. It would seem that research of this type might yield interesting data for researchers interested in voluntary and spontaneous motor control of the facial expression of emotion.

## CONCLUSION

Theory and research on the expression of emotion has been responsible for insti-gating the renaissance of emotion research in general following a long period of neglect during the heydays of behaviorism and cognitivism (Ekman, Sorensen, & Friesen, 1969; Izard, 1971, 1977; Tomkins, 1962, 1963, 1984). This is not surprising since expression is in many ways central to the component process that constitutes emotional episodes. Expressive behavior is situated between the functional changes produced in the individual organism for the purpose of adapta-tional behavior and the signaling of the emotional state to the social environ-ment. Furthermore, most expressive behavior shows at least some degree of discrete patterning allowing to differentiate and define qualitatively and quantitati-vely different emotional states. Emotional expression is concurrent to other pro-cesses in emotional episodes and can thus serve, due to its observability, as an index to other, less accessible aspects or components of the emotion process (see Scherer, 1992, 1993a). Finally, the mounting evidence for the existence of some kind of proprioceptive feedback from expression to the subjective feeling compo-nent, although probably of limited range and power (Buck, 1980; Cappella, 1993; Laird, & Bresler, 1992; Tourangeau & Ellsworth, 1993), suggest that expression plays a central role in the organization of emotional responding.

Given the importance of expression for the general study of emotion, it is reasonable to assume that the study of emotional expression can also turn out to be a royal road to increasing our understanding of some of the thornier issues in psychological research such as neuromotor control of behavior and the role of consciousness, awareness, and intention. In this chapter, I provide some prelimi-nary pointers for possible directions of future theorizing and research. Clearly, in order to make inroads into this complex area, expression research will have to move from the almost exclusive reliance on perception or decoding studies to carefully planned, experimentally oriented, encoding or production studies. Given the complexity and the multiple interactions of the factors or determinants in-volved on several levels of behavioral control, this will be a formidable task. In consequence, it might be advisable to adopt a developmental research strategy as advocated above, beginning with simpler control systems in infants and young children before moving up to the extraordinary complexity of adult behavior regulation. However, such a developmental strategy will only bear fruit if the current lack of communication between researchers working on infants, children, adolescents, and adults of various ages, respectively, can be remedied. Typically, researchers congregate according to the age of the groups studied. In order to use fruitfully the developmental approach as a research strategy, new forms of collaboration need to be forged. The study of the behavioral regulation of emotional expression across the life span would be a promising beginning.

## REFERENCES

Aristotle. (1941). Ethica Nicomachea. In R. McKeon (Ed.), *The basic works of Aristotle* . New York: Random House.

Archer, J. (1976). Aggression and fear in vertebrates. In P. P. G. Bateson, & P. H. Klopfer (Eds.), *Perspectives in ethology.* Vol. 2 (pp. 231–298). New York and London: Plenum.

Arnold, M. B. (1960). *Emotion and personality. (Vol.1). Psychological aspects.* New York: Columbia University Press.

Banse, R. & Scherer, K. R. (1996). Acoustic profiles in vocal emotion expression. *Journal of Personality and Social Psychology,* 70(3), 614–636.

Buck, R. (1980). Nonverbal behavior and the theory of emotion: The facial feedback hypothesis. *Journal of Personality and Social Psychology, 38*(5), 811–824.

Cappella, J. N. (1993). The facial feedback hypothesis in human interaction: Review and speculation. Special Issue: Emotional communication, culture, and power. *Journal of Language and Social Psychology, 12*(1–2), 13–29.

Ceschi, G. (1997). *Le contrôle du rire: Entre savoir et savoir faire.* (The control of laughter: Between knowing and knowing to do). Ph.D. Thesis, University of Geneva, Geneva, Switzerland.

Eisenberg, N., & Fabes, R. A. (1992). Emotion, regulation, and the development of social competence. In S. C. Margaret (Ed.), *Emotion and social behavior. Review of personality and social psychology, Vol. 14* (pp. 119–150). Newbury Park, CA: Sage.

Ekman, P. (1972). Universals and cultural differences in facial expression of emotion. In J. R. Cole (Eds.), *Nebraska Symposium on Motivation* (pp. 207–283). Lincoln: University of Nebraska Press.

Ekman, P. (1979). About brows: Emotional and conversational signals. In M. v. Cranach, K. Foppa, W. Lepenies, & D. Ploog (Eds.), *Human ethology* (pp. 169–202). Cambridge, MA: Cambridge University Press.

Ekman, P. (1984). Expression and the nature of emotion. In K. R. Scherer & P. Ekman (Eds.), *Approaches to emotion* (pp. 319-344). Hillsdale, NJ: Lawrence Erlbaum Associates.

Ekman, P. (1992a). An argument for basic emotions. *Cognition and Emotion*, 6(3/4), 169–200.

Ekman, P. (1992b). Facial expressions of emotion: New findings, new questions. *Psychological Science, 3*(1), 34–38.

Ekman, P., & Friesen, W. V. (1978). *The Facial Action Coding System (FACS): A technique for the measurement of facial movement.* Palo Alto, CA: Consulting Psychologists Press.

Ekman, P., Sorenson, E. R., & Friesen, W. V. (1969). Pan-cultural elements in facial displays of emotion. *Science, 164,* 86–88.

Fraiberg, S. (1982). Pathological defenses in infancy. *Psychoanalytic Quarterly, 51*(4), 612–635.

Frijda, N. (1993). The place of appraisal in emotion. *Cognition and Emotion, 7,* 357–387.

Galati, D., Scherer, K. R., & Ricci-Bitti, P. (1997). Voluntary facial expression of emotion: Comparing congenitally blind to normal sighted encoders. *Journal of Personality and Social Psychology, 73,* 1363–1380.

Gallistel, C. R. (1980). *The Organization of Action: A New Synthesis*. Hillsdale, NJ: Lawrence Erlbaum Associates.

Gellhorn, E. (1967). *Principles of autonomic-somatic integration*. Minneapolis: University of Minnesota Press.

Gellhorn, E., & Loofbourrow, G. N. (1963). *Emotions and emotional disorders*. New York: Harper & Row.

Halgren, E., & Marinkovic, K. (1995). Neurophysiological networks integrating human emotions. In M. S. Gazzaniga (Ed.), *The cognitive neurosciences* (pp. 1137–1151). Cambridge, MA: MIT Press.

Harris, P. L. (1989). *Children and emotion : The development of psychological understanding*. Oxford: Basil Blackwell.

Hauser, M. D. (1996). *The evolution of communication*. Cambridge, MA: MIT Press.

Hess, W. R. (1954). *Das Zwischenhirn. Syndrome, Lokalisationen, Funktionen*. [The diencephalon: Syndromes, localizations, functions]. Basel: Schwabe.

Hutton, R. (1972). Neurosciences: Mechanisms of motor control. In R. N. Singer (Ed.), *The psychomotor domain: Movement behavior* (pp. 349–384). Philadelphia: Lea & Ferbiger.

Izard, C. E. (1971). *The face of emotion*. New York: Appleton-Century-Crofts.

Izard, C. E. (1991). *The psychology of emotions*. New York: Plenum.

Izard, C. E. (1993). Four systems for emotion activation: Cognitive and noncognitive processes. *Psychological Review, 100*(1), 68–90.

Izard, C. E., Fantauzzo, C. A., Castle, J. M., Haynes, O. M., & et al. (1995). The ontogeny and significance of infants' facial expressions in the first 9 months of life. *Developmental Psychology, 31*(6), 997–1013.

Jürgens, U. (1979). Vocalization as an emotional indicator: A neuroethological study in the squirrel monkey. *Behaviour, 69*, 88–117.

Kappas, A., Hess, U., & Scherer, K. R. (1991). Voice and emotion. In B. Rimé & R. S. Feldman (Eds.), *Fundamentals of nonverbal behavior* (pp. 200-238). Cambridge and New York: Cambridge University Press.

Kelso, S. J. A. (1995). *Dynamic patterns: The self-organization of brain and behavior*. Cambridge, MA: MIT Press.

Laird, J. D., & Bresler, C. (1992). The process of emotional experience: A self perception theory. In M. S. Clark (Ed.), *Review of personality and social psychology* . Newbury Park, CA: Sage.

Lazarus, R. S. (1968). Emotions and adaptation: Conceptual and empirical relations. In W. J. Arnold (Ed.), *Nebraska Symposium on Motivation* (Vol. 16, pp. 175–270). Lincoln, NE: University of Nebraska Press.

Leyhausen, P. (1967). Biologie von Ausdruck und Eindruck (Teil 1). [Biology of expression and impression—Part 1]. *Psychologische Forschung, 31*, 113–176.

Malatesta-Magai, C. (1991). Development on emotion expression during infancy: General course and patterns of individual difference. In J. Garber & K. A. Dodge (Eds.), *The development of emotion regulation and dysregulation* (pp. 49–68). Cambridge: Cambridge University Press.

Miller, D. B., & Blaich, C. F.(1988). Alarm call responsivity of mallard ducklings: VII. Auditory experience maintains freezing. *Developmental Psychobiology, 21*(6), 523–533.

Oster, H., & Rosenstein, D. (1989). *Baby FACS: Analyzing facial movement in infants* (New York University: Unpublished report).

Panksepp, J. (1982). Toward a general psychobiological theory of emotions. *Behavioral and Brain Sciences, 5*(3), 407–467.

Panksepp, J. (1989). The neurobiology of emotions: Of animal brains and human feelings. In A. Manstead & H. Wagner (Eds.), *Handbook of social psychophysiology. Wiley handbooks of psychophysiology.* (pp. 5–26). Chichester: Wiley.

Pinker, S. (1997). *How the mind works*. New York: Norton.

Ploog, D. (1988). Neurobiology and pathology of subhuman vocal communication and human speech. In D. Todt, P. F. D. Goedeking, & F. Symmes (Eds.), *Primate Vocal Communication* (pp. 195–212). Berlin/Heidelberg: Springer.

Rinn, W. E. (1984). The neuropsychology of facial expression: A review of the neurological and psychological mechanisms for producing facial expressions. *Psychological Bulletin, 95,* 52–77.

Rinn, W. E. (1991). Neuropsychology of facial expression. In R. S. Feldman & B. Rimé (Eds.), *Fundamentals of nonverbal behavior* (pp. 3–30). Cambridge, MA: Cambridge University Press.

Robinson, B. W. (1976). Limbic influences on human speech. *Annals of the New York Academy of Sciences, 280,* 761–776.

Scherer, K. R. (1981). Wider die Vernachlässigung der Emotion in der Psychologie. [Against the neglect of emotion in psychology]. In W. Michaelis (Ed.), *Bericht über den 32. Kongress der Deutschen Gesellschaft für Psychologie in Zürich 1980* (pp. 304–317). Göttingen: Hogrefe.

Scherer, K. R. (1984a). Emotion as a multicomponent process: A model and some cross-cultural data. In P. Shaver (Ed.), *Review of Personality and Social Psychology* (Vol. 5, pp. 37–63). Beverly Hills, CA: Sage.

Scherer, K. R. (1984b). On the nature and function of emotion: A component process approach. In K. R. Scherer & P. Ekman (Eds.), *Approaches to emotion* (pp. 293–318). Hillsdale, NJ: Lawrence Erlbaum Associates.

Scherer, K.R. (1985). Vocal affect signalling: A comparative approach. In J. Rosenblatt, C. Beer, M.-C. Busnel, & P. J. B. Slater (Eds.), *Advances in the study of behavior*, Vol. 15. (pp. 189–244). New York: Academic Press.

Scherer, K. R. (1986). Vocal affect expression: A review and a model for future research. *Psychological Bulletin, 99,* 143–165.

Scherer, K. R. (1987). Toward a dynamic theory of emotion : The component process model of affective states. *Geneva Studies in Emotion and Communication, 1,* 1–98.

Scherer, K. R. (1988). On the symbolic functions of vocal affect expression. *Journal of Language and Social Psychology, 7,* 79–100.

Scherer, K. R. (1989). Vocal correlates of emotion. In A. Manstead & H. Wagner (Eds.), *Handbook of Psychophysiology: Emotion and social behavior* (pp. 165–197). London: Wiley.

Scherer, K. R. (1992). What does facial expression express? In K. Strongman (Ed.), *International Review of Studies on Emotion.* Vol. 2 (pp. 139–165). Chichester: Wiley.

Scherer, K. R. (1993a). Neuroscience projections to current debates in emotion psychology. *Cognition and Emotion, 7,* 1–41.

Scherer, K. R. (1993b). Studying the emotion-antecedent appraisal process: An expert system approach. *Cognition and Emotion, 7*(3/4), 325–355.

Scherer, K. R. (1994). Toward a concept of "modal emotions". In P. Ekman & R. J. Davidson (Eds.), *The nature of emotion: Fundamental questions* (pp. 25–31). New York–Oxford: Oxford University Press.

Scherer, K. R. (in press). Appraisal theories. In T. Dalgleish, & M. Power (Eds.). *Handbook of Cognition and Emotion.* Chichester: Wiley.

Scherer, K. R., & Kappas, A. (1988). Primate vocal expression of affective states. In D. Todt, P. Goedeking, & E. Newman (Eds.), *Primate vocal communication* (pp. 171–194). Heidelberg: Springer.

Scherer, U., Helfrich, H., & Scherer, K. R. (1980). Internal push or external pull? Determinants of paralinguistic behaviour. In H. Giles, P. Robinson, & P. Smith

(Eds.), *Language: Social psychological perspectives* (pp. 279–282). Oxford: Pergamon.

Scherer, K. R., Mounoud, P., Stern, D., Kappas, A., Zinetti, A., & Ceschi, G. (1994, June). *Emotional reactions to experimentally manipulated voice changes: A lab report on a cross sectional study of infants between 5 and 14 months.* Paper presented at the International Conference on Infant Studies, Paris, France.

Scherer, K. R., Zentner, M., Scherer, U., Mounoud, P., & Stern, D. *"Freezing" als emotionale Reaktion bei Kleinkindern: Experimentelle Befunde einer Querschnittuntersuchung* (Growth functions of freezing and of visual fixation for expectancy violations in infancy). Paper presented at the 13. Tagung für Entwicklungspsychologie, Wien, Austria.Tomkins, S. S. (1962). *Affect, imagery, consciousness: Vol. 1. The positive affects.* New York: Springer.

Scherer, K. R., & Wallbott, H. G. (1990). Ausdruck von Emotionen. In K. R. Scherer (Hrsg.). *Enzyklopädie der Psychologie. Band C/IV/3 Psychologie der Emotion.* (pp. 345–422). Göttingen: Hogrefe.

Scherer, K. R., & Zentner, M. (submitted). The development of emotion-antecedent appraisal: Inferring cognitive prerequisites from facial expression, gaze, and freezing. University of Geneva, Switzerland: Manuscript submitted for publication.

Takahashi, L. K., Turner, J. G., Kalin, N. H.(1991). Development of stress-induced responses in preweanling rats. *Developmental Psychobiology, 24*(5), 341–360.

Tomkins, S. S. (1962). *Affect, imagery, consciousness: The positive affects. (Vol. 1).* New York: Springer.

Tomkins, S. S. (1963). *Affect, imagery, consciousness: The negative affects. (Vol. 2).* New York: Springer.

Tomkins, S. S. (1984). Affect theory. In K. R. Scherer & P. Ekman (Eds.), *Approaches to emotion* (pp. 163–196). Hillsdale, NJ: Lawrence Erlbaum Associates.

Tourangeau, R., & Ellsworth, P. C. (1979). The role of facial response in the expression of emotion. *, 37*(9), 1519–1531.

van Reekum, C. M. & Scherer, K. R. (1997). Levels of processing for emotion-antecedent appraisal. In: G. Matthews (Ed.), *Cognitive science perspectives on personality and emotion.* (pp. 259–300). Amsterdam: Elsevier Science.

van Reekum, C., Johnstone, T., & Scherer, K. R. (1997). *Multimodal measurment of emotion induced by the manipulation of appraisals in a computer game.* Presented at the 3rd European Conference of Psychophysiology, Konstanz, Germany.

Wehrle, T., Kaiser, S., Schmidt, S. & Scherer, K. R (submitted). Exploring the relation between emotion and facial expression with synthetic faces.

Wundt, W. (1905). *Grundzüge der physiologischen Psychologie* (5th ed.). [Fundamentals of physiological psychology] Leipzig: Engelmann.

# 15

# Control Psychology Under the Control of Questionnaires? The Search for an Alternative Assessment Procedure[1]

*Meinrad Perrez*

*Peter Wilhelm*

## INTRODUCTION

The concept of control psychology, when it started with the early contributions of J. B. Rotter in the fifties, was strongly related to behavioural theoretical assumptions integrating cognitive constructs such as "expectancies" or "internal versus external locus of control reinforcement." Empirical research on the development of expectancies for internal and external control of reinforcement under natural conditions proved difficult; nevertheless theoretical assumptions dealt with learning of expectations under natural conditions, as did the contribution on social learning theory by Bandura (1973), or Mischel (1973).

The theoretical contributions of Rotter and many others begun later to focus on the concept of *generalized* expectancies and on *individual differences.* All these developments were important and represent a real evolution in psychological theory succinctly described by August Flammer's book "Erfahrung der eigenen Wirksamkeit. Einführung in die Psychologie der Kontrollmeinung" (Flammer, 1990). The rich abundance of control psychology which later followed was for a great part centred around these topics, with exception of the experimental approaches (Averill, 1973; Seligman, 1975).

These latter topics on generalized expectancies, individual differences, and field-specific control beliefs (such as control beliefs concerning health behavior; Lefcourt & Davidson-Katz, 1991) are based on questionnaire data. Questionnaires are an appropriate method for such theoretical questions.

It is interesting to speculate why we know so much about the correlations of generalized control beliefs with other psychological features, and why so little, based on data gathered in concrete daily life situations, about the function of control expectancies as hot cognitions, for behavior regulation in everyday life.

---

[1]We are indebted to Ian Law for his capable programming work and Regula Berger, Monique Horner and Dominik Schoebi for their precious support.

One possible answer is that in psychology, theoretical topics, which can be treated with questionnaires, attract more empirical attention than topics, such as posed by the early Rotter, which are methodologically more complicated to deal with. As so often in research, not only theoretical assumptions stimulate methodological developments, but methods inspire also theoretical ideas and influence the selection of research topics.

The dominance of questionnaires is clearly reflected in the literature. In the PsycLIT search system we found, for example, under Journal Articles (1974–1997), by combining the following keywords "internal-external-locus of control," and "questionnaire or scale or inventory, but not experiment" 2615 indications. For the combination of "internal-external-locus of control" and "experiment or behavioral assessment" PsycLIT offered 371 articles. About 7 times more publications are based on questionnaire data than on experimental or behavioral assessment data.

The same observation can be made for the development of psychological research in the domain of causal attribution. Causal attribution processes were theoretically considered as cognitive processes which take place under specific conditions and which can influence emotions. The majority of the research focused on questionnaire data is dealing with the cognitive self-representation of the subjects' causal attributions. They rely on indicators of how subjects think they would attribute causalities in hypothetical situations or how they remembered that they attributed causalities in experienced situations with other measures, such as measures on motivation. Alternative approaches are developed e.g., by the group of Scherer (1993) for predicting emotions by attributional and appraisal processes.

In the following, we describe briefly the development of a method, which allows another access to control and attribution related psychological phenomena and which allows new theoretical questions which are difficult to test with traditional questionnaires. Typical trait oriented questionnaires for revealing individual differences, e.g. concerning locus of control, query the subjects' generalised cognitive representation of his of her beliefs, behavior, emotional reaction etc. They usually do not record concrete beliefs in concrete situation, concrete behavior in concrete situation or specific emotions in specific situations, and if they do so, they rely heavily on the subjects' memory. They inform on the subjects representation or belief on how they act, behave etc. Cold and not hot cognitions or emotions are at stake.

## DEVELOPMENT OF A COMPUTER-AIDED SELF-MONITORING ASSESSMENT UNDER FIELD CONDITIONS

In order to avoid the impairing effects on validity of usual—and especially of retrospective—self-report data, we need assessment strategies which meet the three following criteria: (A) The procedure should allow assessing positive mood and emotions as well as stressful episodes in daily life and the social and environmental conditions in which these states and events occur. (B) The time lag between the stressful event and its being recorded should be as short as possible, in order to minimise memory distortions. It must be easy to record information when the subjects are still in the state of emotional arousal for storing "hot emotions" and "hot cognitions." (C) The method should assess psychological relevant data, not using a diary free text self description, but structured, according to the theoretical framework.

With this aim we have recently developed a systematic self observation method, based on the use of pocket computers. This approach to psychological data can be seen in the tradition of self recording procedures as developed by the group of Larson and Richards (1994) in the United States or by Brandstätter (1983) in Germany, working with booklets. Pawlik and Buse (1982) or Fahrenberg (1994) are examples of researchers who also worked with pocket computers. The book "Ambulatory Assessment" (Fahrenberg & Myrtek, 1996) gives an overview on the development of these methods in Europe. The assessment procedure, still undergoing refinement, and whose current development we will briefly discuss, is built on the experience of the COMRES (COMputer REcording System), that Perrez and Reicherts (1989, 1992, 1996) developed and evaluated in earlier projects on recording of individual stress experiences and coping with them. The pocket computer is used as an external memory for stress, that is applied directly in stressful, but also in agreeable, situations to record emotions and other information. This allows us to minimise problems of memory and the subjective retrospective distortion. Alongside the computer version, a booklet variant was developed.

## What Is Self-Recorded?

Table 15.1 summarises the different information types and item formats assessed by the family-self-monitoring system (FASEM).

Part of this information is recorded at every observation and part depends on previously stored information. For example, the program only asks questions on adaptive reactions (coping responses) if there is a need for adaptation, depending on the answers to preceding questions about mood and emotions (negative mood or emotions, and challenge). Furthermore, the questions on social coping depend on the involvement of other people in the situation. For situations, requiring adaptation without social involvement, only the individual coping items are presented.

*TABLE 15.1*
*FASEM information types and item formats*

| Information on: | Item Format |
|---|---|
| 1.  Mood | 1 item, 10 degrees |
| 2.  Emotions | 13 items, 3 degrees |
| 3.  Setting and evaluation of the setting | 5 categories<br>2 categories (familiar to strange) |
| 4.  Presence of other persons | 11 categories |
| 5.  Actual activity<br>Valency of activity | 7 categories<br>1 item, 4 degrees |
| 6.  Concerns of mood and emotions (is physical, psychic, social or economic integrity positively or negatively at stake?)<br>Self evaluation<br>If others are involved:<br>Evaluation of others<br>Evaluation of interaction | <br><br><br><br>8 categories<br><br>12 categories<br>2 categories (with/without conflict) |
| 7.  Causal attribution<br>Internal or external attribution<br>Other persons | <br>4 items, 3 degrees<br>12 items, 3 degrees |
| 8.  Control expectation<br>by myself or by other persons | <br>12 items, 3 degrees |
| 9. Coping, if there is need for adaptation<br>Individual coping<br>Social coping | <br>8 items, 3 degrees<br>14 items, 3 degrees |
| 10. Evaluation of the behavior of other persons (if involved) | 12 items, 3 degrees |

## Sampling Method

The system works with a time sampling method supplemented with an event sampling strategy. The events are breakfast, lunch, and dinner, which all subjects have to record. The computer alerts the subject acoustically every two hours to record his current mood and the other information mentioned above. This sampling schedule assures 7 observations per day (3 event- and 4 time-sampling). In this way we have simultaneous self recording of both members of the couple and their teenage children. This group self-monitoring procedure is done over a 7-day period.

## Technical Aspects

The palmtop computer, an HP 200 LX, is about the size and weight of a note pad, 16 x 8.64 x 2.54 cm and 312 grams. Its performance corresponds to that of a desktop computer some 5 years ago. The output device is a monochrome LCD display with a maximum resolution of 600 * 400 points. The input device is a compact, but complete QWERTY keyboard. No mouse or other pointing device is present.

These characteristics make it possible to carry it during everyday activities and allow the immediate entry of information in a structured format. All subjects have been trained in self observation before the observation period.

To minimize the reactivity the questioning should be as brief as possible. For this reason, every reply is immediately recorded and the possibility is not given to correct the data entry. We accept that the user may sometimes make a simple typing mistake. However, our pre-tests showed this to be relatively rare, due to simplicity of the task and the initial user training. It is also impossible that a user misses completely or incorrectly fills in a question, as it sometimes occurs in the booklet version. The computer also allows the questionnaire to be readily personalised for each family, using the individual names of all family members.

For the development of the questionnaire our program separates the questionnaire interpreter from the questionnaire specification. This allows preparation of the questionnaire without any knowledge of computer programming. It also allows easy adaptation to different languages, important in Switzerland, with four official languages. Improvements in display or in user input (for example use of a pointer device if available on later laptops) can also be incorporated without changing the questionnaire specification.

## Methodological Characteristics

Using the data of the pilot study (N = 70) with the booklet version *split-half reliability* measures were calculated.

The 49 sampling points were divided into odd and even (Pawlik & Buse, 1996). For each half either the mean for the interval scaled variables or the percentages scores for categorial variables were calculated for each individual. The values from both halves were correlated with one another and evaluated according to Spearman-Brown. To calculate the mean split half reliability for the items belonging to one question, the coefficient were subjected to a Fisher's-Z-transformation. The mean reliability lies between $r = .63$ (estimation of the "correctness" of the behavior of the interaction partner) and $r = .96$ (presence or absence of other family members). For the mood the split half reliability was $r = .93$, for the emotion items $r = .89$.

The split-half reliability calculated over all items was $r = .90$. This is a meaningful indication of the high reliability of the aggregated values.

The most critical problem of self monitoring as assessment method concerns its possible *reactivity*. It must be clarified whether the question branching leads the subjects, to adapt their protocol behavior to a more comfortable answer modus. Good mood has a shorter answer sequence because the coping questions are not posed.

There is no statistically relevant daily difference to observe over time, in the frequencies of negative, neutral, or positive mood. This indicates that the response style was not influenced over time by the easy option of a shorter questionnaire. For more details see Perrez, Berger and Wilhelm (1998).

With regard to the exactness of the protocol, we can use, as an indicator for the *objectivity*, the inter-subjective agreement, when more than one subjects make at the same observation sampling point, the same statement about objective questions. This is the case, when the person states where they are and who else is present.

For each family member the concordance percentage was calculated with the remaining family members. The means of the concordance percentages for the parents and the adolescents were then calculated separately.

It could be seen that the place, at which the person is found, gives a very high agreement between the family members (parents 96%, adolescents 99%). The agreement with the data about the presence of the other family members is somewhat smaller (parents 87%, adolescents 82%) and much lower when the presence of people who do not belong to the family, are coded (parents 70%, adolescents 65%).

The accurateness of the inter-observer objectivity can be rated as very good, the data about the presence of other people is satisfactory. A more detailed description of these results can be found in Perrez et al. (1998).

Data from 68 subjects of the recent study, who had the computer version, inform on the *accuracy and duration of recording*. The palmtop computer stores automatically the real recording time and the duration of every assessment. This allows strong control on the subject's commitment to their self-observation task. Figure 15.1 shows the distribution of the time lag between the prescribed and the real observation time on the base of the time sampling observation points (four per day; 11:00, 15:00, 17:00, and 21:00 o'clock). About the half of the observations (48%) were executed at the prescribed time (deviation +/- five minutes).

Concerning the *duration* to answer the questions, the mean needed time (average over the intra-individual means) for the short version was 2.96 minutes (SD = 0.95), and for the complete version 5.17 minutes per protocol (SD = 1.98).

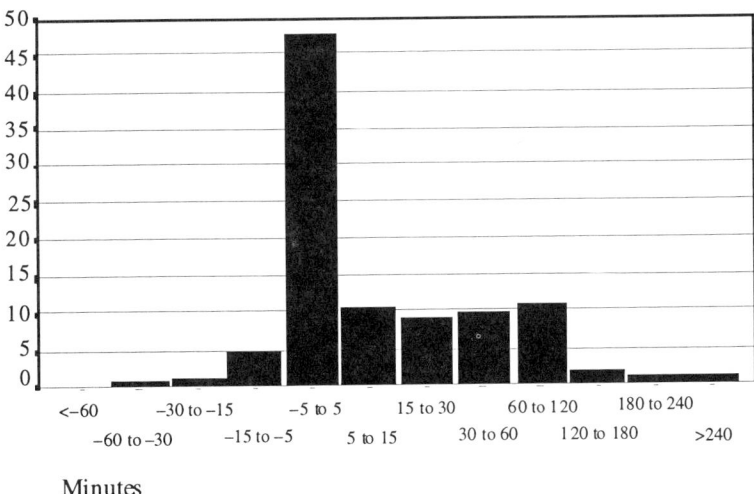

*FIG. 15.1. Difference between prescribed and real observation in minutes (N = 68)*

## SOME FIRST RESULTS ON CONTROL EXPECTANCIES AND CAUSAL ATTRIBUTIONS IN DAILY LIFE OF ADOLESCENTS AND PARENTS

### Family Recruiting

For family selection we applied the following criteria: Each family should consist preferable of both parents and at least one adolescent older than 12 years, living together in the same household. We also took care that the self observation took place during a normal family week, and not during the holidays or while moving.

We found through the German- and French-speaking parent associations of the secondary schools of the canton Fribourg, and the town population control, information freely available to the public, 99 families (355 subjects) in total with adolescents, that fulfil the criteria mentioned and accepted to participate in the study. For the final analysis we could work with 339 subjects from 96 families. Thirty-three German speaking families, 50 French-speaking families, and 13 Italian-speaking families: 96 mothers, 81 fathers, 76 sons, and 86 daughters. The mean age of the parents was 45.2 (*SD* = 4.63), ranging from 32 to 60 years; the mean age of the children was 16.7 (*SD* = 2.14), ranging 13 to 26 years. One part of the subjects worked with the booklets, the other with the palmtop computers (20 families, n = 68).

## Principles Of The Data Analysis

As we asked each of the 339 subjects to give us 49 observations, our row data-matrix consists of 16,611 cases minus a certain level of missing observations, which varied between 3.8% and 7.1% according to the question asked.

For the further analysis, special situations of interest were selected and then the data were aggregated, so that each person was represented once in the new aggregated data matrix. For continuous variables the aggregation function was the mean or the standard deviation, for categorial variables the percentage of occurrence was used. For a discussion of the advantages and drawbacks of aggregated data see Larson & Delespaul (1992).

These aggregated data were then treated as dependent variables in different significance test procedures to examine effects of generation (parents vs. adolescents), of sex and mood state. A detailed description of the data preparation and significance testing is given for each set of hypotheses.

## Control Expectancies In Daily Life Situations

According to different studies and reviews, *gender differences* covering generalized control expectancies are not evident (Krampen, 1991). Nearly all available studies refer to locus of control as a generalized control belief and we could not find any study that assessed control expectancies in daily life situations with a self monitoring method.

In order to explore the question of gender differences covering locus of control and other properties (mono-causal and multi-causal expectancies) the data in field situations were analyzed to help answer these questions. A further question concerns the control expectancies as a function of the development, in particular the comparison of adolescents with adults.

Hypotheses about differences between adults and adolescents:

1. For adolescents, the peer group is more important than the family. Therefore their external control expectancies are more often focused on persons outside the immediate family.

2. The external control expectancies of the parents are more directed to other family members.

*Operationalization and Data Analysis.* When the person's current mood was bad, the question was asked: "who could change the situation in a positive way." If the person answers, that *only* he or she could change the situation, we get an indicator for internal control expectancy. If the person answered that *only* a member of the family or that *only* people outside the nuclear family could change the situation, we get different aspects of external control expectancy. Possible are also mixed control expectancies. This is the case if the person answers at the same time that the situation could be changed by him or herself *and* someone else.

Negative moods were rare events. Only 1,080 situations (6.8%) were reported in which the mood was negative. In 594 (55.0%) events with a negative mood, the person had the expectation that somebody could change the situation. In 409 (37.9%) of the cases, they had no control expectation. 77 answers (7.1%) were missing. The 594 situations with a control expectation were selected, and for each person the percentage of the occurrence of the different types of control expectations were computed. We collected valid data from 218 persons (46 fathers, 61 mothers, 45 sons, 66 daughters) out of 91 families, which were based on different number of situations per person (80 people had one situation, 52 had two, 27 had three and 59 had four or more situations). As the percentage scores did not correspond to the normal distribution, we used the Mann-Witney-U-test to examine the sex differences and the differences between parents and adolescents ( $\alpha$ < .05; one tailed for explicit hypotheses, two tailed for exploratory purposes).

TABLE 15.2
Differences in the relative frequencies (percent per person) of different control expectancies between females and males

| types of control expectancies | females (n = 127) | | males (n = 91) | | M-W-U |
|---|---|---|---|---|---|
| | M | SD | M | SD | p-Value |
| only oneself | 12.9 | 26.3 | 13.1 | 28.4 | .624 |
| only family members | 10.9 | 25.2 | 13.4 | 28.9 | .702 |
| only persons outside the family | 25.3 | 38.2 | 15.6 | 29.4 | .581 |
| self and family members | 20.0 | 31.4 | 19.9 | 32.4 | .967 |
| self and persons outside the family | 18.6 | 31.5 | 25.9 | 38.8 | .278 |

The Mann-Witney-U-test proposes the independence of the sampling units. Because the data stem from family members they are not independent. In general, data from family members are more or less positively correlated with each other. This leads to the consequence that significance tests for independent data tend to be conservative (Rosenthal & Rosnow, 1991). As alternative procedures that treat family members as dependent from each other would also have had disadvantages (e.g. loss of subjects that can not be paired adequately) we took the risk of making too conservative decisions.

*Results.* As Table 15.2 shows there were no sex differences in any of the control expectancies types.

*TABLE 15.3*
*Differences in the relative frequencies (percent per person) of different control
expectancies between parents and adolescents*

| types of control expec-<br>tancies | parents<br>(n = 107) | | adolescents<br>(n = 111) | | M-W-U |
|---|---|---|---|---|---|
| | M | SD | M | SD | p-Value |
| only oneself | 12.6 | 23.8 | 13.4 | 30.1 | .476 |
| only family members (*) | 18.9 | 33.0 | 5.1 | 16.4 | <.001 |
| only persons outside the family (*) | 10.6 | 26.5 | 31.6 | 39.1 | <.001 |
| self and family members | 31.4 | 36.9 | 9.0 | 20.7 | <.001 |
| self and persons outside the family | 15.6 | 29.7 | 27.4 | 38.5 | .017 |

(*) The test for these variables was one-tailed.

We find significant results, as predicted, between the two generations. In the parents' perception, other family members or themselves together with other family members, could most often change the situation. Adolescents on the other hand expect, that someone outside the nuclear family or themselves together with a non-family member have most often control over the situation. Concerning the internal control-expectation there is no difference between generations.

## Causal Attributions In Daily Life Situations

In the following we describe the procedure and the results concerning the analysis of factors influencing causal attributions: mood, sex, and generation. Here again, the distribution of the data restricts the analysis to nonparametric procedures. Therefore we could not test the influence of the factors simultaneously.

*Operationalisation of the Causal Attributions.* The subjects were asked at the beginning of every observation about their current mood state. A later question asked: "Who or what is the cause of your situation?" (see Table 15.1) Similar to the control expectancies classification we get an indicator for internal (i.e., self-) attribution, if the person answers, that *only* he or she is the cause for the situation.

If the person answers that *only* a member of the family or that *only* persons outside the nuclear family could change the situation, we get different aspects of external person directed attribution. Possible is also the attribution on impersonal circumstances, (*only* external circumstances, weather or chance, are chosen). We get a general external attribution, if the person attributes to other persons *or* to non-personal circumstances.

The simultaneous use of different attribution types is also quite common. If the person attributes to him- or herself *and* also to other persons *or* external circumstances, we get an indicator for a kind of interactional attribution type.

*Hypotheses About Attributions Concerning Different Mood States.*

1. Self attributions should be less common concerning negative than concerning positive mood states.

2. External attributions (to external circumstances or to other persons) should be more common concerning negative than concerning positive mood states.

Both reactions are functional to maintain the homeostasis of the self-esteem.

*Data analysis.* To examine the hypothesis about attributions in different mood states, the data were aggregated under the condition that the mood was good and once again under the condition that the mood was bad. The two files were matched so that the data could be treated with repeated measurement procedures. The data matrix contains 267 subjects (57 fathers, 77 mothers, 61 sons and 72 daughters) out of 93 families, which had at least reported one observation in a negative mood state.

Here again the percentage scores were multimodal distributed. We therefore used the Wilcoxon-test to test our hypothesis (alpha < .05, one-tailed). Beside the variables for which we had hypotheses about, we did an exploratory look on some further attribution-types of interest and on sex and generation differences, using the Mann-Witney-U-test again (alpha < .05, two-tailed).

*Results.* As figure 15.2 shows, there are significant mood-dependent differences between the attribution types in the predicted direction. Concerning good mood states, self-caused attributions are twice as common as those concerning bad mood states while external attributions are half as frequent. The most frequent type is the attribution to oneself and to external causes at the same time. Here a mood difference also exists that fits the direction of our expectancies: Concerning good mood this kind of attribution is more frequent.

The exploratory analysis of the subgroups of external attribution reveals an interesting pattern. While there is not a substantial mood difference in attributing to external circumstances or people outside the family, the attribution to family members almost only occurs for bad mood states.

On the left side of the gap the three main types of causal attributions are shown. On the right side three subcategories of exclusively external attributions are shown. Differences were tested with the Wilcoxon-test (one-tailed for only self, and only external attributions, two-tailed for the other variables).

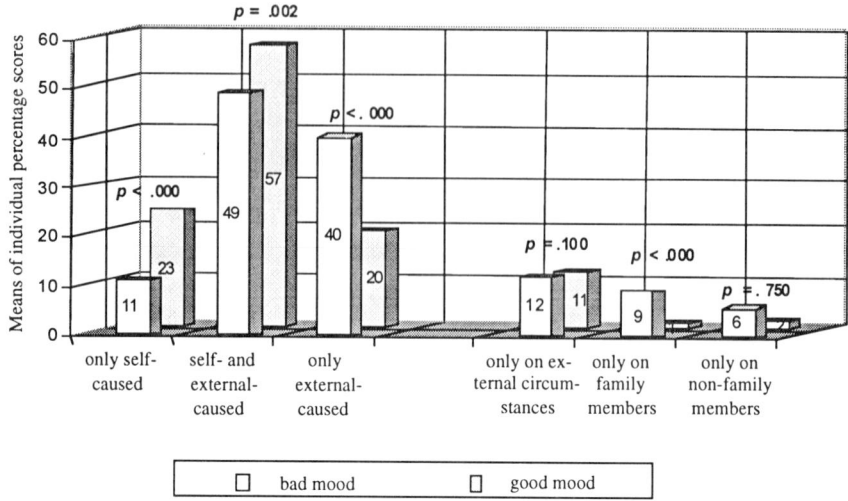

*FIG. 15.2. Mean percentage of attribution types concerning bad mood and good mood states (N = 267).*

The examination of the generation effects reveals that parents attribute the cause of their bad mood more often to external sources and less often to themselves than adolescents do. Parents also attribute more often to other family members, both for bad mood and for good mood. (Table 15.4). For positive mood states adolescents are more likely to attribute these to external circumstances than to parents.

## Hypotheses About The Effects Of Specific Attributions On The Change Of Negative Mood

Because external attributions with respect to negative mood are more likely to maintain the self-esteem, they should be more prone to change the mood in a positive direction than internal attributions.

1. We predict as a short-term-effect that positive mood swing between the previous observation x0 and the following observation x1 will be larger, if the subject reports at observation x0 external attributions, and it will be lower, if it reports an internal attribution.

*Data Analysis.* To test the short-term effect on mood regulation the mood of observation, x0 was subtracted from the mood at observation x1 (under the condition that both observations were made at the same day). First, all situations with a bad mood and only external attributions at observation x0 were selected and than aggregated. Second, all situations with a bad mood and only internal attributions at observation x0 were selected and also aggregated. After matching

the two files together, 32 subjects (7 fathers, 4 mothers, 11 sons, and 10 daughters) out of 27 families were left, who had at least one pure external and one pure
internal attribution concerning a negative mood. As these data were approximately normal distributed, the mood difference could be analyzed with a t-test for
paired samples (one-tailed, alpha < .05).

TABLE 15.4

*Differences between parents (n = 134) and adolescents (n = 133) in the use of
causal attributions concerning bad and concerning good mood states*

| Causal attributions | for bad mood | | | for good mood | | |
|---|---|---|---|---|---|---|
| | parents M | adoles M | M-W-U p-val. | parents M | adoles M | M-W-U p-val. |
| self-caused | 8.7 | 13.0 | .032 | 22.0 | 23.3 | .865 |
| self- and external caused | 45.1 | 53.2 | .140 | 58.8 | 54.7 | .192 |
| only external caused | 46.2 | 33.7 | .023 | 19.2 | 22.0 | .233 |
| only external circumstances | 13.4 | 10.7 | .629 | 10.4 | 13.1 | .025 |
| only family members | 11.7 | 6.7 | .016 | 1.9 | 0.8 | .010 |
| only non family members | 5.5 | 5.9 | .642 | 1.9 | 1.9 | .948 |

We didn't find significant and substantial sex differences in the use of causal
attributions.

***Results.*** The intrapersonal comparison shows - matching our prediction -
that after external attributions the positive mood change is significantly larger
than after internal attributions (internal: $M = 2.6$, $SD = 1.6$; external: $M = 3.3$,
$SD = 1.4$; $p = .020$, one-tailed). One may doubt that this result is due to differences in the mood state at observation x0. We checked that also with a t-test for
paired samples. No mood difference could be found. This result clearly supports
our hypothesis.

## CONCLUSION

We consider, on the basis of the current trial, that this method provides reliable and useful data on self observed cognitive, emotional, and social processes. Nevertheless, different problems are inherent to this approach which limit its methodological power. The main methodical problem, that this method has to take into account, is that of *reactivity*. Just as the data of retrospective are liable to be impaired by memory distortions, here, the important question is how far the observed behavior is changed by the observation method. This reactivity could prevent the collection of reliable and useful data. Stern (1986) could show for the method developed by Pawlik and Buse that the behavior reactivity can be strongly observed, when only a single behavior type is studied in isolation rather than several, and when people find themselves in unfamiliar surroundings rather than when they find themselves in a habitual setting. Our observation setting is above all the familiar surrounding of the family and professional life and several behavioral types are simultaneously observed, and therefore the reactivity should be limited in this method. This interpretation is supported by the data for certain reactivity aspects which we have discussed above. (For a more detailed discussion of the reactivity problem, we refer to Perrez, Horner & Morval, submitted).

A second problem concerns the *limited information on objective properties* of the situations in which subjects are involved while storing their covert and overt behaviour. For some aspects of situations this problem may be less important, e.g., for the setting or for the presence or absence of other people. For the analysis of coping with stressful situations, information on objective properties of stressors would be important. A third problem consists of the question, if the *sample* of stored behavior is *representative* for the person. One week is a long self observation period, but for certain questions it may be too short for assuring representative data of the subjects' experience and behaviour.

We have found that the *acceptance of the method*, using computer aided self recording, to be surprisingly high. After the data collection, all the co-operating subjects fill in, a questionnaire to estimate their experience with the investigation. We pose the question: "What, in your opinion, is the ideal length of the self observation?" Seventy percent answered that one week or more would be the ideal duration. Only a minority of 30% pleads for a shorter observation time. This method of data collection, however, demanded an appropriate coaching of the participating subjects.

We described above some results on control expectancies and causal attributions assessed with FASEM in everyday life. On the basis of the data from self observation of daily life experiences, the results on locus of control expectancies by adolescents confirm, for example, the hypothesis, that peers are expected to be more helpful for aid with personal problems than parents or other family members. This finding is in accordance with results of other studies, for example those, that deal with the decreasing importance of parents as supporting partners in stressful situations. Fend (1990) observed in a longitudinal study of 1,790 adolescents a continuous decrease of the adolescents' preference to address themselves to their parents for personal or social problems over the 12- to 16-year-old period.

Concerning causal attributions, we compared different types with reference to mood states, gender and generation. The self evaluation maintenance may in general favor internal causal attributions for bad mood (Tesser, Pilkington & MacIntosh, 1989). The general tendencies seem to be mediated by social, respectively generation influences.

These examples of results are based on systematic self observation of concrete experiences in daily life. They do not reflect generalized cognitions (such as locus of control tendencies or causal attribution tendencies) and possible connections of such cognitions with other properties of the subjects. They therefore provide a new means of access to properties of the behavioral stream.

With reference to the question posed in the introduction, self-monitoring under natural conditions opens new and complementary theoretical perspectives for the psychology of control and causal attribution. The described assessment procedure can help to answer questions on the specificity of behaviour in every day life, questions on behavior consistency (Pawlik & Buse, 1996), questions on short-term and on mid-term effects on emotional reactions and well being of different types of appraisal processes etc. Furthermore, this assessment procedure allows analyzing dynamic aspects of behavior such as questions on periodicity of mood over time. It permits new possibilities in analysing social interactions, as Larson and Richards (1994) have already demonstrated. It opens new theoretical perspectives for predicting behavior under natural conditions, taking into account proximal variables like hot emotions, hot cognitions, behavioral, and setting variables.

## REFERENCES

Averill, J. (1973). Personal control over aversive stimuli and its relationship to stress. *Psychological Bulletin, 80,* 286–303.

Bandura, A. (1973). *Aggression: A social learning analysis.* Engle-Wood Cliffs, NJ: Prentice Hall.

Brandstätter, H. (1983). Emotional responses to other persons in every day life situations. *Journal of Personality and Social Psychology, 45,* 871–883.

Dalbert, C. (1992). Subjektives Wohlbefinden junger Erwachsener: Theoretische und empirische Analysen der Struktur und Stabilität. *Zeitschrift für Differentielle und Diagnostische Psychologie, 4,* 207–220.

Fahrenberg, J. (1994). Ambulantes Assessment. Computerunterstützte Datenerfassung unter Alltagsbedingungen. *Diagnostica, 40,* 3, 195–216.

Fahrenberg, J. & Myrtek, M. (Eds.). (1996). *Ambulatory assessment. Computer-assisted psychological and psychophysiological methods in monitoring and field studies.* Seattle/Toronto: Hogrefe & Huber.

Fend, H. (1990). *Vom Kind zum Jugendlichen. Bd. 1.* Bern: Huber.

Flammer, A. (1990). *Erfahrung der eigenen Wirksamkeit. Einführung in die Psychologie der Kontrollmeinung.* Bern: Huber.

Krampen, G. (1991). *Fragebogen zu Kompetenz- und Kontrollüberzeugungen (FKK).* Göttingen: Hogrefe.

Larson, R. & Delespaul, P. A. E. G. (1992). Analyzing experience sampling data: A guide book for the perplexed. In M.W. de Vries (Ed.), *The experience of psychopathology: Investigating mental disorders in their natural settings.* Cambridge, MA: Cambridge University Press.

Larson, R. & Richards, M. (1994). *Divergent realities. The emotional lives of mothers, fathers, and adolescents.* New York: Basic Books.

Lefcourt, H. M. & Davidson-Katz, K. (1991). Locus of control and health. In C. R. Snyder & D. R. Forsyth (Eds.), *Handbook of Social and Clinical Psychology* (pp. 246-266). New York: Pergamon.

Mischel, W. (1973). Toward a cognitive social learning reconceptualization of personality. *Psychological Review, 80,* 252–283.

Pawlik, K. & Buse, L. (1982). Rechnergestützte Verhaltensregistrierung: Beschreibung und erste psychometrische Überprüfung einer neuen Erhebungsmethode. *Zeit-schrift für Differentielle und Diagnostische Psychologie, 3,* 101–118.

Pawlik, K. & Buse, L. (1996). Verhaltensbeobachtung im Labor und Feld. In K. Pawlik (Hrsg.), *Grundlagen und Methoden der Differentiellen Psychologie. Enzyklopädie der Psychologie. Bd. C/VIII/1.* Göttingen: Hogrefe

Perrez, M. & Reicherts, M. (1989). Belastungsverarbeitung: Computerunterstützte Selbstbeobachtung im Feld. *Zeitschrift für Differentielle und Diagnostische Psychologie, 10,* 2, 129–139.

Perrez, M. & Reicherts, M. (1992). *Stress, coping, and health: A situational-behavior approach. Theory, methods, applications.* Seattle; Toronto; Bern; Göttingen: Hogrefe & Huber.

Perrez, M. & Reicherts, M. (1996). A computer-assisted self-monitoring procedure for assessing stress-related behavior under real life conditions. In J. Fahrenberg & M. Myrtek (Eds.), *Ambulatory Assessment. Computer-assisted psychological and psychophysiological methods in monitoring and field studies* (pp. 51–71). Seattle; Toronto: Hogrefe & Huber.

Perrez, M., Berger, R. & Wilhelm, P. (1998). Die Erfassung von Belastungserleben und Belastungsverarbeitung in der Familie: Self-Monitoring als neuer Ansatz. *Psychologie in Erziehung und Unterricht, 45,* 19–35.

Perrez, M., Horner, M. & Morval, M. (submitted). Comment mesurer le stress: Une nouvelle approche: l'auto-observation systématique au moyen d'un ordinateur de poche.

Rosenthal, R. & Rosnow, R. L. (1991). *Essentials of behavioral research. Methods and data analysis (2nd ed.).* New York: McGraw-Hill.

Scherer, K. R. (1993). Studying the emotion-antecedent appraisal process: An expert system approach. *Cognition and Emotion, 7,* 325–355.

Seligman, M. E. P. (1975). *Helplessness. On depression, development and death.* San Francisco: Freeman.

Stern, E. (1986). *Reaktivitätseffekt in Untersuchungen zur Selbstprotokollierung des Verhaltens im Feld.* Phil. Diss., Universität Hamburg. Frankfurt: Lang.

Tesser, A., Pilkington, C. J. & McIntosh, W. D. (1989). Self-evaluation maintenance and the mediational role of emotions: The perception of friends and strangers. *Journal of Personality and Social Psychology, 57*, 442–456.

# 16

# The Control of Unwanted States and Psychological Health: Consistency Safeguards

*Hansjörg Znoj*

*Klaus Grawe*

## INTRODUCTION

This contribution is mainly motivated by the question how disruptive life events and their consequences affect peoples' lives and feelings. In the last ten years, the diagnosis of post-traumatic stress disorder has become a main topic among researchers and clinicians. The inclusion of post-traumatic stress disorder in the DSM-III was an important milestone in psychiatric nomenclature. Prior to this, the signs and symptoms of stress response had appeared in descriptions of traumatic neuroses, and combat neuroses. Symptoms of post-traumatic stress disorder include intrusions, avoidance, hypervigilance, and general failure to adapt to changing circumstances. These signs occur not only after unusual events, such as combat experience, hurricanes, and cruel accidents, but also after more common events, such as bereavement. What happens after experiencing a personal loss or an extremely stressful event, is that the old working models of the world no longer apply to the new circumstances. In addition, a person often experiences psychological conflicts involving unresolved issues and contradictory views of themselves and others. Due to such conflicts, feelings of guilt after surviving an accident where a close person died, often lead to complicated and prolonged forms of grief. Blaming others or believing that one`s real self is far discrepant from an ideal self are other possible reactions.

Discords between internal beliefs and external reality make it emotionally difficult to integrate the personal meanings of stressor events and to plan new adaptive behaviors (Horowitz, Bonanno, Holen, 1993; Stroebe & Stroebe, 1993). Alarming emotional pangs (Horowitz, Stinson, & Fridhandler, 1991) may be due to the mismatch between new and enduring prior relationship models of the self and others. People who have many persisting contradictions in their schematic organization of working models and beliefs about the self and others will have more emotional trouble in working through the loss.

Recent epidemiological studies (e.g., Kessler, Sonnega, Bromet, Hughes, & Nelson, 1995) found a relative high lifetime incidence of PTSD after several types of trauma as shown in table 16.1. The lifetime prevalence after Kessler et al., (1995) is higher for women (10.4%) than for men (5.0%); these rates exceed the numbers that were reported in earlier studies and are typical for many surveys (Maercker, 1997). Possible explanations for these findings are better instruments and the higher likelihood to report trauma and trauma related crimes. In Europe the reported rates are usually smaller but this could be due to the relative ignorance among many health providers and the unwillingness to report trauma-related psychological problems (Schnyder, Valach, & Hofer, 1996).

TABLE 16.1
Frequencies of various traumas and onset of PTSD
after a representative American sample. (Kessler et. al., 1995).

| Type | Occurrence of Trauma (%) | Lifetime Incidence after Trauma (%) |
|---|---|---|
| Rape | 5.5 | 55.5 |
| Sexual harassment | 7.5 | 19.3 |
| War | 3.2 | 38.8 |
| Threat with weapons | 12.9 | 17.2 |
| Physical violence | 9.0 | 11.5 |
| Accidents | 19.4 | 7.6 |
| Eye-witness (accidents, violence) | 25.0 | 7.0 |
| Fire, natural disasters | 17.1 | 4.5 |
| Childhood trauma | 4.0 | 35.4 |
| Neclect in childhood | 2.7 | 21.8 |
| Other life threatening situations | 11.9 | 7.4 |
| Other traumas | 2.5 | 23.5 |
| Some trauma | 60 | 14.2 |

In this chapter we will focus on psychological processes that may lead to pathological reactions. We will focus especially on the coping process following disruptive life-events, how the self protects itself against threats of internal regulation. We will suggest that the discrepancy between expected perceptions and experience of loss of expected perceptions can lead to formation of psychological disorder. Consistency safeguards—the postulated control processes—may help to reduce the immediate threat caused by this discrepancy. Theoretically we draw from various sources, from psychodynamic view to information theory, from coping to defense mechanisms. We postulate observable strategies people use to regulate unwanted states and will, finally, present first results with a recently developed self-report measure.

## STRIVING FOR CONSISTENCY AND EMOTIONAL REGULATION

Disorders caused by traumatic stress are the result of a breakdown in the adaptability of the individual. In accordance with Epsteins integrative theory of personality (Epstein, 1991) and with Powers theory of control (1973), we regard the striving for consistency between actual perceptions and expectations as one of the most fundamental principles of the human information processing system. In the face of traumatic events, many people fail to assimilate the actual perceptions to their fundamental beliefs and specific perceptual readiness. The consequence is a persisting inconsistency warning signal, accompanied by strong negative emotions which result in the psychological system being constantly preoccupied with the enduring inconsistency. These continual attempts to assimilate what cannot be assimilated find their expression amongst other things in the intrusions into both waking and sleeping states so typical to the post-traumatic stress disorder. In this specific case, the futile struggle for consistency is an inherent part of the disorder. In our opinion, raised levels of inconsistency in psychological functioning play a less obvious but equally important role in the emergence of other psychological disorders. Psychological disorders in general can be seen as a sign that the quest for consistency was not successful.

When a person fails to bring about perceptions which are consistent with their goals and expectations—we could also use the expression motivational schemas—a state of inconsistency comes into being. We can call this type of inconsistency external inconsistency, as it affects the individual's adaptation to external events.

A common reason for a person's inability to bring about perceptions which are congruent with his or her goals is that, opposing the positive motivational (or intentional) schemas, which are aimed at the satisfaction of the individual's needs, are avoidance schemas, which evolved as means of protecting the individual from violations of his or her basic needs. Situations which are relevant to the satisfaction of a basic need simultaneously activate the intentional schemas developed to satisfy that need and the respective avoidance schemas. The need cannot be satisfied and therefore persists. The continual activation of the intentional schemas however, leads to an equally persistent activation of the avoidance schemas. The result is an enduring conflict-tension due to internal inconsistency. Neither the approach-tendency nor the avoidance-tendency can exert a determining influence on psychological functioning. Therefore, psychological activity adopts a not definitely ordered, fluctuating state at a level of high tension. The cause of this psychological situation lies in a persistingly high inconsistency of psychological functioning. Psychological activity is not determined by definite organizational patterns of motivation.

In this situation, new organizational patterns can emerge and be differentially reinforced by the ensuing reduction of inconsistency-tension. These new organizational patterns are not aimed at the reduction of need-related tension, but at the reduction of inconsistency-related tension. We consider psychological disorders to be such qualitatively new patterns in the organization of psychological functioning, which emerge from a situation of persistently raised inconsistency levels. After its formation due to the reduction of existing inconsistency-tension and differential reinforcement, a psychological disorder can develop its own dynamics and detach itself from the original conditions of its development. The disorder then becomes functionally autonomous and persists even after the inconsistency-tension has been dispersed one way or the other.

According to this view (for a more detailed description, see Grawe, 1998), continually raised levels of inconsistency in psychological functioning pose a serious risk to psychological health. They can become the substrate for psychological disorders.

A psychologically healthy person should therefore be equipped with means to prevent the development of persistently high levels of inconsistency-tension. People have such means at their disposal if they have well-developed intentional schemas to satisfy their basic needs and if the opposing avoidance schemas are relatively weak in comparison. However, inconsistency in psychological functioning due to conflicting motivational constellations cannot be completely avoided. As inconsistency jeopardizes the efficiency of interactions with the environment, it makes sense that, in the course of their development, people acquire consistency-safeguards which secure psychological functioning when it is threatened by a rising level of inconsistency. Such consistency-safeguards include e.g., emotion-oriented coping as according to Lazarus and Folkman (Folkman & Lazarus, 1988), or repression, as understood by Freud. Repression ensures the indviduals capacity for conscious action by protecting consciousness from too high level of inconsistency. The perceptions, cognitions, and emotions which are not admitted to consciousness then influence psychological functioning implicitly. This involves the danger that the processes pertaining to the implicit and the conscious mode of functioning may be inconsistent and that on a long-term basis, the inconsistency in the system is raised even higher. Consistency-safeguards can therefore play a positive or a negative role in psychological functioning, i.e., there are favorable and less favorable mechanisms for securing consistency. Favorable consistency-safeguards lead to a reduction of inconsistency without impairing the need-related interactions of the individual and his or her environment. Unfavorable consistency-safeguards may lead to a short-term reduction of inconsistency (this allows them to emerge), but on a long-term basis, they hinder effective interactions with the environment and in turn contribute to a further increase in the level of inconsistency.

Inconsistency is accompanied by negative emotions. Mechanisms serving to regulate negative emotions can therefore be also regarded as consistency-safeguards. They arent necessarily part of conscious experience and can proceed within the implicit mode of functioning. Their positive function is that they prevent the individual from being hindered by unmanageably high levels of inconsistency. To this end, it is sometimes even necessary that they do not become conscious. In the course of his or her socialization, a person can however also develop unfavorable mechanisms of emotion-regulation of which he or she is not conscious.

A person's emotional regulation can therefore play a positive or a negative role with regard to his or her psychological health. It can have a protective effect by preventing the development of high levels of inconsistency without impairing the capacity for action. It can, however, also contribute to a deterioration of psychological health, respectively become a correlate of psychological ill-health.

It is this functional relevance of emotion-regulation mechanisms for psychological health which is the basis of our scientific interest in these mechanisms. In the following, we will first review the most important previous contributions dealing with the functional relevance of emotional control-mechanisms, or consistency-safeguards, for psychological health. Subsequently, we will report on a possible empirical approach developed in our laboratory.

## COPING AND CONSISTENCY—SOME CONSIDERATIONS

Emotional turbulence may reach such high levels that self protective mechanisms help to forestall incoming information. This is in line with the idea behind the psychoanalytic term *defense mechanisms* (Anna Freud, 1936) and with more recent ideas of coping processes focussing on palliative strategies (Zeidner & Endler, 1996; Parker & Endler, 1996). Such mechanisms—whether we call them defense mechanisms or coping—are part of a general striving for consistency. Psychological theories of balanced structures or motives go back to Lewin's (1935) dynamic theory of personality, Heider's (1946) structuralistic view of personality (see also Allport, 1964), Festinger's (1957) theory of cognitive dissonance, and to approaches trying to graph structural balance (Cartwright & Harary, 1956; Peak, 1958). Recently, Thagard (1989) proposed a neural network approach to simulating explanatory coherence which he sees as a main factor in the justification of action and decision. The common theme of these efforts is the view that human functioning should be balanced between different forces, needs or motives. The more balanced an action or decision is, the more reliable and stable is the output of the system, be the system a person, group, or technical device.

The inhibition of information processing may be a main factor in the development of serious complications and of pathology (Hayes, Wilson, Gifford, Follette, & Strosahl, 1996), therefore the psychological aspects of processing information or inhibiting the "normal" way of information processing, are of high clinical relevance, not only for post-traumatic stress disorders, but for all disorders involving the development of inner conflicts. Here, we propose that coherence, a state of minimal conflict, is necessary for psychological health

(Antonovsky, 1990; Moos & Schaefer, 1986). Antonovsky (1990) sees three main components of coherence: A sense of *comprehensibility*, a sense of *manageability*, and a sense of *meaningfulness*. A good sense of coherence, a feeling that life in general follows certain rules, is manageable and meaningful, can be seen partly as the result of personality (Antonovsky, 1993) but also as the effect of good coping strategies for dealing with stressful events. A prerequisite for comprehensibility are consistent experiences, whereas to develop a sense of manageability, strains need to be well-distributed and one needs the possibility of taking part in socially well-recognized decisions. An upbringing which includes both challenges and protection seems to be a necessity in this concept of coherence. Because of the high negative correlations usually reported for coherence and psychological symptoms, it is, however, possible that a good sense of coherence is just the opposite of feeling emotionally distressed (Antonovsky, 1993).

Emotional alarm reactions caused by conflicts must be reduced in order to integrate information which in turn leads to adaptation to new circumstances and to enhanced coherence. Assuming that there is a limited capacity for processing novel and stressful events, codings of discrepant information remain in the active memory (Horowitz, 1986), and information processing is not completed. This leads to experiences of intrusion, e.g., nightmares, or unwanted graphical memories. To avoid entry in such states of mind, controls are activated to modify the cognitive processes (Horowitz, 1991). Following Horowitz (1986), the path from active memory storage to representation and processing can be inhibited, which reduces anxiety. Reduced anxiety reduces the motivation for controls and the tendency of active memory toward representation reasserts itself, leading to a typical cycle between states of avoidance and states of hyperarousal often found in people suffering from reactions of trauma. The progressive modifications of the meaning of recently aquired information, and the progessive modification of preexisting models are ways to enhance coherence that can be both adaptive and maladaptive (for a discussion of adaptive vs. maladaptive see Zeidner & Saklovske, 1996). In making this distinction, we hope to avoid some of the confusion that has plagued earlier scales of emotion focused coping (Stanton, Danoff-Burg, Cameron, & Ellis, 1994).

The distinction of adaptive and maladaptive ways for controlling unwanted psychological states was based on theory and clinical experience. Studies by Pennebaker and others (e.g., Pennebaker, 1993, Pennebaker, Kiecolt-Glaser, & Glaser, 1988) show some evidence that verbal expresion of distressing content may indeed enhance psychological functioning and physical health. Adaptive items of content of thought included speaking in depth about emotionally important topics; expressing strong feelings clearly; bringing up stressful topics when talking to a close friend. Maladaptive strategies can provide a short term emotion stifling effect at the expense of long term dysfunction. Examples for maladaptive strategies on the content level are: Putting distressing facts out of attention; making use of distractions to avoid painful memories, making jokes about topics that are hard to handle with, or overreacting emotionally.

In the following, we will explain how emotional regulation is related to information inhibition and distortion in order to protect the individual from overwhelming states.

## SCHEMAS, OR WHAT HAPPENS WHEN INFORMATION DOES NOT MEET ONE'S EXPECTATIONS

Many of our ideas on emotional regulation are based on the constructivist school of cognitive psychology. We use the term constructivist in the broadest sense here, meaning the way by which people generally construct a mental reality which may not, and usually does not correspond exactly with reality. One of the earliest and most influential contributions in this area came from Bartlett (1932). He carried out the well known "war of the ghosts" experiment where people read an unusual ghost story and were later asked to recall it. By and large what the subjects recalled was not the actual story in detail but a more predictable "usual" version of the story. In other words they recalled what they had expected the story to be. Based on this and other findings, Bartlett put forward the notion of *schemas*. Schemas are types of knowledge structures through which we interact with the environment. They enable us to process information efficiently, but at the same time restrict us by hindering our ability to appraise entirely new and unexpected events. After Bartlett, researchers working within the information processing paradigm looked at memory encoding as a series of sequential processes. In the 1950's a large body of research on the limitations of the perceptual system was done thanks to the development of the tachistoscope. This "New Look" movement established the notion of "perceptual defense," meaning that people will "block out" information they do not want to perceive, because it is self threatening or highly emotionally arousing (Bruner, 1957). In a typical experiment from this era, various nonverbal symbols were shown to Jewish and non-Jewish subjects for very brief periods of time using the tachistoscope. There was no significant difference between subject groups for recognition of items with one major exception: The non-Jewish subjects successfully recognized a swastika amongst other symbols; the Jewish subjects did not. This typical finding supported the idea of *perceptual* defense; the experiment showed how the subjects blocked out the highly arousing stimulus. Although the New Look movement generated a plethora of interesting research findings, its general approach was too simplistic (Erdelyi, 1974) and after the 50s, interest waned.

This is not the place to review all the theoretical approaches to the concept of "control." The concepts of Miller, Galanter & Pribram (1960) or Powers (1973) may however help to clarify the complex task of action and perception control.

## DEFENSIVE REGULATORY ACTIVITY: WHY IT IS NECESSARY AND HOW IT IS DONE

In our terminology, a person may *cope* with stressor events of external origin or *defend* against excessive arousal of internal origin. Thus, *coping manoeuvres* handle external crises imposed by stressful events. *Defensive manoeuvres* handle internal crises. Adaptive defenses can create a useful "time-out" for the restauration of internal equilibrium. Maladaptive defenses lead to a temporary "time-out" which is problematic because of the excessive and prolonged denial of serious personal implications of the stressors.

Control processes regulate preconscious information processing and action planning. We propose that automatic controls can be implemented and altered by either conscious or unconscious intentions or by both. We assume that control processes are implemented by implicit anticipations of possible future outcomes of information processing. Irrational ideas and actions are therefore not viewed as mere breakdown products of impaired brain functions, they are sometimes the result of purposive and restitutive constructive processes. The outcomes of defensive control processes are neither always maladaptive nor always adaptive. Periods of faith and hope, stemming from fantasy compensation for threats and losses can prevent breakdowns due to fatigue and dispair. Avoidance can be followed by purposive confrontations, conflict can be reduced in a dose-by-dose manner.

## STRATEGIES THAT PEOPLE USE TO REGAIN THEIR SENSE OF SELF-CONTROL AND EMOTIONAL STABILITY

We propose three main levels of control that influence how representations are processed. The way crucial information is processed has implications for emotional reactions. In a new model of fear extinction, Le Doux (1996) has proposed a theory that the inhibition of the fear response is not an extinction of the learned stimulus but a control process. According to Le Doux, emotional responses are blocked by nuclei of the amygdala, which have strong connections to the prefrontal cortex. Thus, the memory is still in the "brain" and the extinction is achieved by pathway inhibition or interruption. What is important is the notion that activated structures may be used to inhibit emotional responses, which nevertheless remain represented in the system.

Schemas (or cognitive maps), often organize different parallel processes (such as appraisals and revisions of information on the same topic) at the same time. Conscious representation can be regarded as the output of several parallel channels, formed into a composite (Znoj, 1992; Rumelhart & McClelland, 1986). A supraordinate operation combines subordinate sets of information (like nodes forming clusters). The choices involved in this fitting process form a pathway (chreode), which results in a working model organizing a current state of mind. Organizing schemas influence the changing strengths of associational linkages and, at higher levels, these are often schemas of the self and others. These organizing schemas also include scripts (how to do things), roles, and value schemas. Person schemas include transactional sequences that can fulfill wishful and defensive aims and avoid feared consequences.

Our position can be summarized by the statement that consciousness is a possible output of the information processing system; likewise, an emotional response is the product of processed information. Control processes are guided by the anticipation of outcomes varying from desired to dreaded states of mind (compare with positive and negative schemata in the terminology of Grawe and coworkers, e.g., Grawe, Grawe-Gerber, Heiniger, Ambühl, & Caspar, 1996). In this sense, defensive controls are part of a motivational matrix.

Some controls alter the content. Other control processes alter the form. Still other controls can alter person schemas.

In the following classification scheme, we differentiate between processes that control which contents will become conscious, processes that control the form of the conscious representation, and processes that control the organziation of schema activation (Horowitz, Znoj, & Stinson, 1996).

The classification scheme consists of various types of control processes, which hinder emotional arousal from reaching a certain level. They are divided into three main categories (control of content, control of form, control of person schemas, and role relationship models) each with its three different types of outcome (adaptive, maladaptive, and dysregulation).

## Controlling Contents

The contents of focal awareness or the plans for communicative expressions can be selected by control processes that shift attention from one topic to another or from one set of concepts to the next. Control processes can change the relevance of concepts to the self and by doing so change the following sequence of concepts. They can also alter the threshold for disengaging attention from a topic.

Adaptively, *shifting the focus of attention from one topic to another* can reduce emotion and prevent a person from entering into a dreaded state of mind. Maladaptively, extended forgetting or denial of a stressful topic can lead to the failure of the coping process.

Concepts are potential ideas about a topic and the sequencing of concepts in cognition can lead to clarity or confusion. *Altering the next concept* can change the emotional valence and direction of a narrative.

A chain of concepts may lead to a solution and can be followed by a second chain of concepts. Weighting the relative importance of such chains to the self may lead to better solutions (see Damasio, 1994). *Altering the importance of a chain of concepts* will affect choices; the significance of a chain of concepts can be exaggerated or minimized, leading either to rational evaluations or irrationally varying meanings.

One can also *declare a topic concluded* before a solution has been reached. Thus, a problematic topic, with its emotional conflicts, is interrupted and personal dilemmas remain unresolved.

## Controlling the Form of Conscious Thought

Emotion can be controlled by altering forms of awareness. Such processes include the alteration of representation, time span, logic level, level of action planning, and arousal level.

A topic of thought might be mainly represented in words, images, or in somatic enactions. Normally, meaning is transferred between the modes. The isolation of meaning in one mode, especially in the lexical mode, can reduce emotion. Often, there is even contradictory meaning between modes, e.g., smiling when telling a sad story. *Switching modes of representation* can help reduce emotional reaction.

Time spans can be set to limit an associational search for information, they may include or exclude the future. The remote or recent past as well as the near or distant future can be specifically focused on in setting an attentional frame. Focusing consciousness on the immediate future can be a help in planning action without being overwhelmed by emotions. *Altering the time span* can therefore be a strategy for emotional control.

People shift the rules of thought from rational problem solving to broad, creative, and even illogical associations. A strategy to decrease emotional reaction is to focus on small, even irrelevant details of a memory, or to switch to very general issues. Preoccupation with cleaning the car or daydreaming of a heroic future can reduce emotion concerning a likely future earthquake. *Altering the logic level* not only influences thought but also emotional reactions.

The focus of attention can change from contemplating art or music to immediate action, for example when climbing a difficult rock or playing football. Control processes can alter a setpoint for the degree of thought and the degree of concomitant motor activity. When used defensively, a person can act too impulsively instead of thinking, or ruminate constantly without taking action (see also Kuhl—latest development). *Changing the level of action* planning is also a strategy for emotional inhibition.

Sometimes, people seek stimuli (so called "sensation seekers"), they may take drugs, try to meditate, and choose calming activities. *Changing the level of activity and arousal* can be deliberately used to avoid serious issues. Both thrills and lethargy can reduce emotional threat.

## Controlling Person and Value Schemas

Emotions can be changed or reduced by altering how the self and others are viewed. Processes that control schema activation can be divided into processes affecting schemas of the self, schemas of other persons, role-relationship models, value schemas and executive-agency schemas.

Alterations in schemas of the self and others can directly and indirectly alter the emotions that accompany a state of mind. One can reverse the roles for the self and others; for example, instead of experiencing fear, a person can get angry enough to make somebody else anxious. By *altering the roles of the self and others*, one can escape from a dreaded state of fear to a stronger position, where one threatens another; in one state, the self is perceived as a victim, the other as an aggressor; in the altered state, the self becomes the aggressor and the other the victim. In the case of a loss, a person may perceive the other in too favourable a way, in order to reduce feelings of guilt.

Role relationship models are internal maps and scripts for social transaction. In any relationship, there are different role relationship models. Some may be desired, some feared, and some may be compromises. For example, the dilemma between the excitement of intimacy and the feared pain of rejection can be reduced by a shift into the compromised view that the relationship is just a game without deeper meaning, as if only playing with possibilities before going on with life.

People always judge actions by value schemas. For example, to make a career at the firm can be of high priority. If one fails, one might change the value system by judging a possible career as morally damaging, thus saving oneself from feelings of remorse. One can even perceive deceit as a good strategy, if it is necessary for a good purpose. *Altering value schemas* often helps to reduce or change emotional reactions that may hinder planned actions.

Executive agency designates the person or persons believed to be in charge of forming plans and prompting action. In everyday life, the "I" as a sense of identity may be the executive agent. The "I" can be changed into a "we" signifying the family or a relevant group. *Shifts in executive agency* may reduce feelings of guilt or enhance feelings of power, as in the case of the "royal we."

The proposed classification of emotion regulation has evolved through efforts in both qualitative research with careful case studies of patients undergoing psychotherapy for stress response syndromes (Horowitz, Znoj, & Stinson, 1996; Horowitz, 1986; Horowitz, Fridhandler, & Stinson, 1991) and quantitative research with studies on instruments registering verbal expression (Horowitz, Stinson, Curtis, Ewert, Redington et al., 1993; Horowitz, Milbrath, Jordan, Stinson, Ewert et al., 1994). For the operationalization of the proposed defensive control theory of emotion regulation, we focussed on reportable strategies and observable outcomes of such mental operations.

The following section summarizes the results obtained with a self-report measure (Znoj, Horowitz, Maercker, & Bonanno, 1998) and with a recently developed observer measure.

## STUDIES WITH THE SENSE OF
## SELF-CONTROL QUESTIONNAIRE

The Sense of Self-Control Questionnaire was recently developed at the Langley Porter Psychiatric Institute at UCSF. First, studies were conducted with a sampe of people who had lost a spouse and with a college student sample. In formulating the items, we followed the theory of defensive control processes. We focused on the outcomes of emotion control and differentiated between adaptive and maladaptive outcomes of regulatory activity within the three postulated levels; content, form, and person schemas and values.

We included the Sense of Self-Control measure in a questionnaire study with undergraduates. The main goal of this study was to establish the reliability of the new measure. At the same time, we also included several coping measures (e.g., Antonovsky's Sense of Coherence, 1987), an anxiety scale and a life-event questionnaire. It turned out that the students had suffered only a few serious life-events and that the main goal of this study—to examine the link between serious life-events and various coping strategies—was not feasible.

At approximately the same time, we also included the Sense of Self-Control measure in a two-year follow-up study within the spousal bereavement project (Horowitz, Siegel, Holen, & Bonanno, 1997) conducted at that time. Two years post-loss, about 50% of the bereaved participants remained in the study. We found no statistical differences between the remaining participants and the ones who dropped out on any of the demographic or other variables.

Internal and external validity of the Sense of Self-Control measure showed good psychometric properties and good stability over time. The distinction between adaptive and maladaptive ways of regulating emotion was empirically validated with adaptive strategies showing high cohesion with adaptive personality traits (Clark, 1993), sense of coherence (Antonovsky, 1993), and general well-being (Horowitz, Sonneborn, Sugahara, & Maercker, 1996), whereas maladaptive strategies were related to experiencing anxiety (Beck, 1988), psychological symptoms (Derogatis, 1977), maladaptive personality traits (Clark, 1993), and neurotic style (Costa & McCrae, 1985). These relations were true for the bereaved as well as for the student group (Znoj, Horowitz, Maercker, & Bonanno, 1998).

On the one side we had a group with almost no serious life-events, consisting of highly educated, well organized, young, and healthy students; on the other a group of middle-aged bereaved persons who had lost their spouses. The fact that these two groups were comparable in terms of economic and educational background set the stage for a comparison between the two samples.

The main quest of the comparison was to test a proposition derived from findings in bereavement literature, namely that the experience of loss can buffer against future losses and stressors (Stroebe & Stroebe, 1993; Vachon, Rogers, Lyall, Lancee, Sheldon, & Freeman, 1982), the opposing view being that disruptive life-events have an additive and impairing effect (e.g., Holmes & Rahe, 1967).

TABLE 16.2
Mean (and Standard Deviations) score on SSC-items between the student sample and the 25 months post-loss bereavement group.

| SSC Items | M (and SD) for group | | F | ETA$^2$ | Post hoc |
|---|---|---|---|---|---|
|  | Student (1) n=159 | Bereaved (2) n=51 |  |  |  |
| Adaptive items: |  |  |  |  |  |
| bringing up stressful topic | 2.98 (.76) | 3.14 (.69) | 1.70 | .01 |  |
| expressing strong feelings clearly | 2.97 (.93) | 3.31 (.68) | 5.81* | .03 | B > S |
| talking in depth about emotions | 2.99 (.92) | 3.29 (.81) | 4.54* | .02 | B > S |
| working hard but also getting rest | 2.43 (.94) | 3.06 (.90) | 17.24*** | .08 | B > S |
| let go | 2.55 (.93) | 3.08 (.82) | 12.95*** | .06 | B > S |
| having strengths and weaknesses | 3.21 (.76) | 3.49 (.54) | 5.82* | .03 | B > S |
| maintaining equal relationships | 3.03 (.87) | 3.24 (.76) | 2.22 | .01 |  |
| having good self-esteem |  |  |  |  |  |
| caring for self and others | 3.08 (.87) | 3.24 (.84) | 1.33 | .01 |  |
|  | 3.24 (.77) | 3.25 (.74) | .01 | .00 |  |
| disagreeing without disrupting | 3.38 (.70) | 3.43 (.57) | .25 | .01 |  |

TABLE 16.2 continued

| SSC Items | M (and SD) for group | | F | ETA$^2$ | Post hoc |
| | Student (1) n=159 | Bereaved (2) n=51 | | | |
|---|---|---|---|---|---|
| *Maladaptive items:* | | | | | |
| joking about hard to handle topics | 2.65 (1.01) | 1.94 (.97) | 19.36*** | .09 | S > B |
| emotionally overreacting | 2.48 (1.04) | 2.12 (1.05) | 4.64* | .02 | S > B |
| getting fed up and leaving | 2.30 (1.00) | 1.69 (.86) | 15.36*** | .07 | S > B |
| using distractions | | | | | |
| becoming confused | 2.55 (.97) | 2.18 (1.01) | 5.55* | .03 | S > B |
| jumbling time | 2.20 (.99) | 1.63 (.75) | 14.15*** | .06 | S > B |
| moving restlessly | 1.97 (.89) | 1.41 (.67) | 17.41*** | .08 | S > B |
| constantly monitoring | 2.30 (.91) | 1.84 (.88) | 9.68** | .04 | S > B |
| expressing too hastily | 2.81 (.90) | 2.00 (.92) | 30.45*** | .13 | S > B |
| misperceiving / misunderstanding | 2.48 (.88) | 2.10 (.73) | 7.72** | .04 | S > B |
| | 2.16 (.78) | 1.78 (.61) | 9.98** | .05 | S > B |
| concern with other's feelings | | | | | |
| avoiding social situations | 2.96 (.94) | 2.75 (.82) | 2.07 | .01 | |
| blaming others | 2.91 (.90) | 2.41 (1.00) | 11.35*** | .05 | S > B |
| ending relationship | | | | | |
| | 1.84 (.89) | 1.33 (.62) | 14.21*** | .06 | S > B |
| | 1.93 (1.03) | 1.59 (.78) | 4.79* | .02 | S > B |

*Note:* SSC: S = Student Sample, 2 cases missing; B = Bereaved Group, 3 cases missing
* p < .05 (2-tailed)
** p < .01 (2-tailed)
*** p < .001 (2-tailed)

When we performed a Principal Component Analysis, we found factor solutions that seemed structurally similar for both groups. We tested the structural equality of a two factor model with a structural equation model with unequal factor correlations (Bentler, 1989). The result indicated that the structure of the questionnaire could be maintained in the two highly different populations. We then compared the levels of the reported strategies for emotional regulation in the two samples. The result of this analysis supported the future losses theory, as the bereaved had higher levels of adaptive strategies and lower levels of maladaptive strategies for dealing with unwanted emotions.

What was really striking was the finding that the students had higher levels on all the items—there was not a single exception—that had been constructed as maladaptive strategies for coping with strong feelings. Students indicated that they would leave a group of people when angered and to avoid painful memories. They used more distractions than the bereaved; they indicated to end relationships to avoid feelings of humiliation; they would monitor themselves and others when overwhelmed with unwanted feelings and—compared to the bereaved—they indicated to express too hastily whatever comes up in those moments. A complete overview is given in Table 16.2.

There are two possible explanations for this result: One explanation follows the idea of a life-long development of defense and coping. This idea, probably most clearly formulated by Vaillant (1993) states that with age a person becomes more adaptive, more gentle, and more wise (see also Brandtstädter & Baltes-Gotz, 1990; Baltes & Smith, 1990). The explanation of a life-long development does not exclude the explanation that we favor: It is not the fact of simply becoming older that makes people wise and more adaptive when coping with stressors but the stressors themselves trigger a learning process that buffers against future stressors. There is only scarce empirical evidence that such learning occurs. Stroebe et al. (1993) quote literature that indicates that previous losses can ease the course of future losses. Kobasa's work on hardiness (Kobasa, 1982) also suggests that life-events might buffer the reaction to future stressors. It is not clear what makes us cope better with distress. Our explanation would be that we learn to use more adaptive regulatory strategies because the maladaptive ones cause symptoms and problems when we use them too much.

Although we favor this interpretation, more work has to be done before we can safely exclude alternative explanations.

Recently, one of the authors (Znoj, 1996), used a translated form of the Sense of Self-Control Questionnaire to study the use of emotion regulation strategies in a group of outpatients in the psychotherapy center of the psychological institute at the University of Bern. The psychometric properties are comparable to the original version used in the two mentioned studies. In this study we were interested in the relation of emotion regulation to reported symptomatic distress levels at pre-treatment. The results indicated that the highest level of experienced emotion (anger and anxiety) and the use of adaptive emotion regulation strategies explain 37% of the total variance of the Derogatis (1977) general symptom index

(Znoj, 1997) in patients who seek psychotherapy. It seems that not only avoidance or inhibition of information (Hayes, Wilson, Gifford, Follette, & Strosahl, 1996) play a major role in the development of symptoms and experience of distress but also the way people deal with their emotions. Although maladaptive regulations have been shown to correlate with distress (the first two studies), here it is the use of *adaptive* strategies in combination with the experienced level of negative emotion (anger and anxiety) which provides the most adequate model of experienced distress.

Hodel (Hodel & Brenner, 1996) has developed a therapeutic approach to dealing directly with such emotion regulation strategies, though the focus lies more in teaching schizophrenics and other seriously disturbed patients how to interpret emotional signals, both from social and body cues.

Dealing directly with emotions may not always be appropriate and there are many findings in the coping literature (e.g., Folkman, Lazarus, Gruen, & De-Longis, 1986) that relate emotion focused coping strategies to problematic states and even serious health complications. The main reason for these statements might be that focusing on emotion and emotional response does not alter the circumstances that lead to the necessity for coping with a situation. Sometimes, however, it is not possible to cope with a situation in a task-oriented manner. At the beginning of this section, we mentioned post-traumatic stress disorder as the main motive to develop a classification of emotion control strategies. In general, situations that cause a prolonged mismatch between expected and experienced reality can lead to a problematic adaptation process, mainly due to emotional pangs and the necessity to avoid, or dampen, these inner stressors.

The focus of existing coping measures is mainly on rational information processing, be that constructive thinking (Epstein & Meier, 1989), task orientation, or problem orientation (Endler & Parker, 1994; Folkman & Lazarus, 1988; Carver, Scheier, & Weintraub, 1989; mindfulness (Langer, 1992), or sense of coherence (Antonovsky, 1987). Only recently has there been a notion that the experience of arousal itself could have adaptive value (Dienstbier, 1989). In our view, not just the arousal itself is important, but how we deal with it. This needs no conscious effort, it seems that inhibitory functions are inherent to the emotion system (Le Doux, 1996; Ekman & Davidson, 1994), and work towards controlling intensity.

## CONCLUSION

Research on the regulation of emotion is a fairly new discipline (Ekman & Davidson, 1994) and our understanding is therefore still limited. Here, we have proposed a classification system that allows the delineation of certain strategies that are reportable and can be accessed by awareness. Emotions certainly have the function of alarming, focusing, and directing attention, decisions, and action (Damasio,1994). Without variation in emotional experience, our lives would be colorless and empty. Well-being is a balanced state, a sign of a system that can fully and reliably react to environmental tasks, and in that sense, well-being might also be a coherent state. Emotions and the experience of emotions may be a prime indicator of what is going on, inside and outside of what we call our body.

The control and regulation of potentially disruptive perceptions or unintegrated information is an often neglected perspective both in terms of research and in terms of application in prevention and therapy. In contrast, cognitive strategies such as perceived control over the situation are already established factors in trauma research (e.g., Ehlers, Clark, & Winton, 1997). A sense of autonomy during the traumatic event predicts better outcome in terms of symptomatology, even when the actual situation does not change. A sense that life is meaningful and manageable is inversely related to symptoms (Maercker, 1997). However, social support seems to be more effective in preventing onset of PTSD when the focus is on emotional experience rather than instrumental help (Schützwohl & Maercker, 1997). The research of Pennebaker et al., (1989) showed that talking about the trauma not only enhances subjective well-being but also reduces doctoral visits. Regulation of affect is presumably a very important factor to overcome traumatic experience. In our work, we focus on strategies that people report on how they try to control perception and representation of traumatic content. These often automated strategies are shaped by experience and may help to cope better with future threats and losses.

## REFERENCES

Allport, G. W. (1964). The open system in personality theory. In H. H. Ruitenbeck & E. P. Dutton (Eds.), *Varieties of personality theory*, New York.

Antonovsky, A. (1987). *Unraveling the mystery of health.* San Francisco: Jossey-Bass.

Antonovsky, A. (1990). Pathways leading to successful coping and health. In M. Rosenbaum (ed.), *Learned resourcefulness: On coping skills, self-control, and adaptive behavior. Springer series on behavior therapy and behavioral medicine, Vol. 24,* 31–63. New York: Springer.

Antonovsky, A. (1993). The structure and properties of the sense of coherence scale. *Social Science & Medicine, 36 (6),* 725–733.

Baltes, P. B., & Smith, J. (1990). Toward a psychology of wisdom and its ontogenesis. In J. Sternberg (ed.), *Wisdom: Its nature, origins, and development,* 87-120. New York: Cambridge University Press.

Bartlett, F. C. (1932/1977). *Remembering. A study in experimental and social psychology.* Cambridge: Cambridge University Press.

Beck, A. T., Epstein, N., Brown, G., & Steer, R. A. (1988). An inventory for measuring clinical anxiety: Psychometric properties. *Journal of Consulting and Clinical Psychology, 56(6),* 893–897.

Bentler, P. M. (1989). *EQS Structural Equations Program Manual.,* Encino, CA: Multivariate Software.

Brandtstaedter, J., & Baltes-Gotz, B. (1990). Personal control over development and quality of life perspectives in adulthood. In P. B. Baltes & M. M. Baltes (Eds.), *Successful aging: Perspectives from the behavioral sciences,* 197–224. Cambridge, MA: Cambridge University Press.

Bruner, J. (1957). On perceptual readyness. *Psychological Review, 64(2),* 123–152.

Cartwright , D., & Harary, F. (1956). Structural balance: A generalization of Heider's theory. *Psychological Review, 63,* 277–293.

Carver, C. S., Scheier, M. F., & Weintraub, J. K. (1989). Assessing Coping Strategies: A Theoretically Based Approach. *Journal of Personality and Social Psychology, 56(2),* 267–283.

Clark, L. A. (1993). *SNAP. Schedule for nonadaptive and adaptive personality. Manual for administration, scoring, and interpretation.* Minneapolis: University of Minnesota Press.

Costa, & McCrae. (1985). *The NEO personality inventory.* Manual: Psychological Assessment Resources.

Damasio, A. R. (1994). *Descarte's error. Emotion, Reason, and the human brain.* New York: Avon Books.

Derogatis, C. R. (1977). *SCL-90, Administration, Scoring, and Procedures. Manual 1 for the R(evised) version and other instruments of the Psychopathology Rating Scale Series.* Baltimore: John Hopkins University School of Medicine.

Dienstbier, R. A. (1989). Arousal and physiological toughness: Implications for mental and physical health. *Psychological Review, 96(1),* 84–100.

Ehlers, A., Clark, D. M., & Winton, E. (1997 in press). Predicting response to exposure treatment in PTSD: The role of mental defeat and alienation. *Journal of Traumatic Stress.*

Ekman, P., & Davidson, R. (Eds.). (1994). *The nature of emotion.* New York: Oxford University Press.

Endler, N. S., & Parker, J. D. A. (1994). Assessment of multidimensional coping: Task, emotion, and avoidance strategies. *Psychological Assessment, 6(1),* 50–60.

Epstein, S. (1991). The self-concept, the traumatic neurosis, and the structure of personality. In D. Ozer (ed.), *Perspectives in Personality, Vol. 3,* 63–98. London: Jessica Kingsley.

Epstein, S., & Meier, P. (1989). Constructive thinking: A broad coping variable with specific components. *Journal of Personality and Social Psychology, 57(2),* 332–350.

Erdely, M. H. (1974). A new look at the New Look: Perceptual defense and vigilance. *Psychological Review, 81,* 1–25.

Festinger, L. (1957). *A theory of cognitive dissonance.* Stanford: Stanford University Press.

Folkman, S., & Lazarus, R. S. (1988). The Relationship Between Coping and Emotion: Implications for Theory and Research. *Society of Scientific Medicine, 26(3),* 309–317.

Folkman, S., Lazarus, R. S., Gruen, R., & DeLongis, A. (1986). Appraisal, coping, health status, and psychological symptoms. *Journal of Personal and Social Psychology, 50,* 571–579.

Freud, A. (1936). *The ego and the mechanisms of defense.* New York: International Universities Press.

Grawe, K. (1998). *Psychologische Therapie.* Göttingen: Hogrefe

Grawe, K., Grawe-Gerber, M., Heiniger, B., Ambühl, H., & Caspar, F. (1996). Schematheoretische Fallkonzeption und Therapieplanung—Eine Anleitung für Therapeuten. In F. Caspar (Ed.), *Psychotherapeutische Problemanalyse,* 189–224. Tübingen: dgvt-Verlag.

Hayes, S. C., Wilson, K., G., Gifford, E., V., Follette, V., M., & Strohsal, K. (1996). Experiential avoidance and behavioral disorders: A functional dimensional approach to diagnosis and treatment. *Journal of Consulting and Clinical Psychology, 64(6),* 1152–1168.

Heider, F. (1946). Attitudes and cognitive organization. *Journal of Psychology, 21,* 107–112.

Hodel, B., & Brenner, H. D. (1996). Ein Trainingsprogramm zur Bewältigung von maladaptiven Emotionen bei Schizophren Erkrankten. *Nervenarzt, 67,* 564–571.

Holmes, T. H., & Rahe, R. H. (1967). The social readjustment scale. *Journal of Psychosomatic Research, 11,* 213–218.

Horowitz, M., Sonneborn, D., Sugahara, C., & Maercker, A. (1996). Self-regard: A new measure. *American Journal of Psychiatry, 153(3),* 382–385.

Horowitz, M. J. (1986). *Stress response syndromes.* (2nd ed.). New York: Aronson.

Horowitz, M. J. (1991). Emotionality and Schematic Control Processes. In M. J. Horowitz (Ed.), *Person Schemas and Maladaptive Interpersonal Patterns,* 413–423. Chicago: University of Chicago Press.

Horowitz, M. J., Bonnano, G., A., & Holen, A. (1993). Pathological grief: Diagnosis and explanation. *Psychosomatic Medicine, 55,* 260–273.

Horowitz, M. J., Milbrath, C., Jordan, D. S., Stinson, C. H., Ewert, M., Redington, D. J., Fridhandler, B., Reidbord, S. P., Hartley, D. (1994) Expressive and defensive behavior during discourse on unresolved topics: A single case study. *Journal of Personality, 62 (4),* 527–563.

Horowitz, M. J., Siegel, B., Holen, A., & Bonanno, G. A. (1997). Diagnostic criteria for complicated grief disorder. *American Journal of Psychiatry, 154 (7),* 904–910.

Horowitz, M. J., Stinson, C., Curtis, D., Ewert, M., Redington, D., Singer, J., Bucci, W., Mergenthaler, E., Milbrath, C., & Hartley, D. (1993). Topics and Signs: Defensive Control of Emotional Expression. *Journal of Consulting and Clinical Psychology, 61(3),* 421–430.

Horowitz, M. J., Stinson, C. H., & Fridhandler, B. (1991). Person schemas and emotion. *Journal of the American Psychoanalytic Association, 39(Suppl.),* 173–208.

Horowitz, M. J., Znoj, H., & Stinson, C. (1996). Defensive control processes for coping with excessively emotional states of mind. In M. Zeidner & N. Endler (eds.), *Handbook of Coping: Theory, Research, Applications,* 532–553. New York: Wiley.

Kessler, R. C., Sonnega, A., Bromet, E., Hughes, M., & Nelson, C. B. (1995). Posttraumatic stress disorder in the National Comorbidity Survey. *Archives of General Psychiatry, 52,* 1048–1060.

Kobasa, S. C., Maddi, S. R., & Kahn, S. (1982). Hardiness and Health: A Prospective Study. *Journal of Personality & Social Psychology, 42(1),* 168–177.

Langer, E. J. (1992). Matters of mind: Mindfulnbess/mindlessness in perspective. *Consciousness and Cognition, 1,* 289–305.

LeDoux, J. (1996). *The emotional brain.* New York: Simon and Schuster.

Lewin, K. (1935). *A dynamic theory of personality.* New York: McGraw Hill.

Maercker, A. (Ed.). (1997). *Therapie der posttraumatischen Belastungsstörungen.* Berlin: Springer.

Miller, G. A., Galanter, E., & Pribram, K. H. (1960/1973). *Plans and the structure of behavior dt.: Strategien des Handlens. Pläne und Strukturen des Verhaltens.* Stuttgart: Klett.

Moos, R. H., & Schaefer, J. A. (Eds.). (1986). *Coping with life criss. An integrated approach.* New York: Plenum.

Parker, J. D., & Endler, N. S. (1996). Coping and defense: A historical overview, *Handbook of Coping. Theory, research, applications,* 3–23. In M. Zeidner & N. S. Endler (eds.), *Handbook of coping: Theory, research, applications,* New York: John Wiley.

Peak, H. (1958). Psychological structure and psychological activity. *Psychological Review, 65(6),* 325–347.

Pennebaker, J., Kiecolt-Glaser, J., & Glaser, R. (1988). Disclosure of traumas and immune function: Health implications for psychotherapy. *Journal of Consulting and Clinical Psychology, 56,* 239–245.

Pennebaker, J. W. (1989). Confession, inhibition, and disease. In L. Berkowitz (ed.), *Advances in experimental social psychology,* Vol. 22, 211–244. New York: Academic.

Pennebaker, J. W. (1993). Putting stress into words: Health, linguistic, and therapeutic implications. *Behaviour Research & Therapy, 31(6),* 539–548.

Powers, W. T. (1973). *Behavior: The Control of Perception.* Chicago: Aldine.

Rumelhart, D. E., & McClelland, J. L. (1986). *Parallel distributed processing I&II.* Cambridge: MIT Press.

Schnyder, U., Valach, L., & Hofer, D. (1996). Trauma-related disorders in Psychiatrists' and General Practioners private practice in Switzerland. *Journal of Traumatic Stress, 9(3),* 631–641.

Schützwohl, M., & Maercker, A. (1997). Social support and coping as predictors of PTSD thirty years after traumatization. In A. Maercker, M. Schützwohl, & Z. Solomon (Eds.), *Posttraumatic stress disorder: A life-span perspective.* Seattle: Hogrefe & Huber.

Stanton, A. L., Danoff-Burg, S., Cameron, C. L., & Ellis, A. P. (1994). Coping through emotional approach: Problems of conceptualizaton and confounding. *Journal of Personality & Social Psychology, 66(2),* 350–362.

Stroebe, M. S., Stroebe, W., & Hansson, R. O. (Eds.). (1993). *Handbook of bereavement: Theory, research, and intervention.* New York: Cambridge University Press.

Stroebe, W., & Stroebe, M. S. (1993). Determinants of adjustment to bereavement in younger widows and widowers. In M. S. Stroebe, W. Stroebe, & R. O. Hansson (Eds.), *Handbook of bereavement: Theory, research, and intervention.,* 208-226. Cambridge: Cambridge University Press.

Thagard, P. (1989). Explanatory coherence. *Behavioral and Brain Sciences, 12,* 435–502.

Vachon, M. L. S., Rogers, J., Lyall, W. A. L., Lancee, W. J., Sheldon, A. R., & Freeman, S. J. J. (1982). Predictors and correlates of adaptation to conjugal bereavement. *American Journal of Psychiatry, 139,* 998–1002.

Vaillant, G. E. (1993). *The wisdom of the ego.* Cambridge: Harvard University Press.

Zeidner, M., & Endler, N. S. (Eds.). (1996). *Handbook of Coping: Theory, research, applications.* New York: Wiley.

Zeidner, M., & Saklovske, D. (1996). Adaptive and Maladaptive Coping. In M. Zeidner & N. S. Endler (Eds.), *Handbook of coping: Theory, research, applications,* 505–531. New York: Wiley.

Znoj, H. (1997). *Strategien im Umgang mit Trauergefühlen.* Paper presented at the 10. Kongress der Schweizerischen Gesellschaft für Psychologie, Basel.

Znoj, H., Horowitz, M., Maercker, A., & Bonanno, G. (1998 in press). Emotional Regulation: The Sense of Self-Control Questionnaire. *Psychosomatic Medicine.*

Znoj, H.-J. (1992). *Veränderung durch Psychotherapie. Ein Modell des therapeutischen Interaktions-Prozesses.* Unpublished Dissertation, Universität Bern.

# 17

# Self-Regulation and Rumination:
# Negative Affect and Impaired Self-Accessibility

*Julius Kuhl*
*Nicola Baumann*

## INTRODUCTION

Since the beginnings of psychology as an experimental science, attempts to investigate phenomena described in terms of *self-regulation, volition, will-power* or *ego-strength* have been confronted with considerable difficulties. Ach (1910) , interested in introspections associated with the *primary act of will*, tried to develop experimental techniques for a *functional analysis* of the accompanying mechanisms. Despite these early attempts, personality approaches to self-regulation have widely relied on global self-report assessments of self-regulatory competence (e.g., Bandura, 1982). In cognitive psychology, experimental approaches to the functional analysis of *controlled versus automatic processing* (Shiffrin & Schneider, 1977) or *executive control* (Baddeley, 1996; Norman & Shallice, 1986) have been developed. Unfortunately, these methods are of limited use for personality research because cognitive approaches do not cover personality processes presumably supported by volitional mechanisms such as resistance to temptation, delay of gratification, self-control of motivational states (Mischel & Mischel, 1983), self-monitoring and self-management (Kanfer & Schefft, 1988) or action control (Kuhl, 1981, 1984). Common to many recent approaches to the study of volition is a shift from global concepts toward attempts to decompose the functional constituents of self-regulation (Allport, Styles & Hsieh, 1994; Kuhl, 1984; Stuss, Shallice, Alexander & Picton, 1995). Validation of a recently developed self-report instrument decomposing self-regulatory competence into 30 functional mechanisms showed a remarkable convergence between subjective and objective indicators of self-regulatory functions (Kuhl & Fuhrmann, in press). Replacing one global index of volitional competence by specific indices of various functional components can help improve practical attempts to develop better procedures for training and psychological intervention (Fuhrmann & Kuhl, in press).

Most scales of the *Volitional Components Inventory* (VCI) developed by Kuhl & Fuhrmann (in press) do not ask for direct judgments of volitional competencies. Instead the instrument addresses many indirect concomitants of self-regulatory processing that are accessible to conscious awareness. In this chapter, we focus on one of these introspectively accessible concomitants of self-regulatory competence, namely *uncontrollable rumination*. From its beginnings in the late seventies, our work on individual differences in rumination has been based on an effort to understand self-regulation (Kuhl, 1981, 1984). Daydreaming and rumination per se can be controllable or uncontrollable (Klinger, 1981; Klinger & Murphy, 1994; Martin & Tesser, 1989):

Volitional attempts to disengage from ruminative thinking and focus on a task or pursue a goal are successful in the former case but unsuccessful in the latter. The personality construct of state versus action orientation assessed by the *Action Control Scale* (ACS) is closely associated with a tendency to have *uncontrollable* ruminations and intrusions, especially after being exposed to aversive events (Kuhl & Beckmann, 1994a). Each item of a subscale of the ACS called *preoccupation* describes an aversive experience (e.g., having dropped a valuable vase) and offers a state-oriented and an action-oriented response alternative (e.g., "not being able to concentrate on anything else for quite a while" versus "putting the experience out of my mind quickly").

Presumably, this scale assesses the ability to volitionally control perseveration of negative affect and intrusive thoughts elicited by it (*preoccupation* vs. disengagement). Another ACS-scale assesses the ability to volitionally mobilize the energy necessary to make decisions and initiate intended actions (i.e., *hesitation* vs. initiative).

From a functional perspective, at least three types of rumination can be distinguished. The first two types are based on *implicit* attempts to control intrusive thoughts and feelings, whereas the third is based on explicit attempts. Implicit attempts are characterized either by active efforts to engage in a task at hand without conscious attempts to suppress task-irrelevant intrusions (Wegner, 1994) or by unconscious ("automatic") mechanisms of selective inattention to unwanted contents (Blum & Barbour, 1979). In the first case, control of thought is mediated by implicit mechanisms because it is a by-product of an active process directed at the control of *intended* action rather than at suppression of non-intended thoughts. The second case also involves *implicit* control of thought because it is mediated by *automatic* mechanisms of repression in terms of selective inattention to anxiety-linked stimuli (Blum & Barbour, 1979), rather than conscious attempts toward suppression of unwanted thought.

Recent advances in understanding the mechanisms underlying the construct of action versus state orientation suggest that the two types of unwanted thought, which can be attributed to *inhibition of implicit* mechanisms of control, are associated with the two main components of state orientation: the hesitating and preoccupation components (Kuhl & Fuhrmann, in press). The *hesitating and undecisive* type of state orientation is expected to be associated with uncontrollable intrusions because the individual's ability to initiate *wanted* activities is inhibited in these individuals. In this case, the individual should retain the capacity to perceive that the intrusive thoughts are unwanted and incongruent with self-related concerns *(informed self-incongruence).* That is, if intrusive thoughts are attributable to an individual's inability to volitionally concentrate on the task at hand, he or she can perfectly well acknowledge the unwantedness of those task-irrelevant intrusions.

On the other hand, the *preoccupation* component of state orientation is expected to be associated with uncontrollable intrusions that are not perceived as unwanted. The paradoxical dissociation between uncontrollability and unwantedness is expected in this case because the experience of "wantedness" requires access to an implicit self-representational system that, according to our theory (see below), is inhibited during states of preoccupation. Inhibited access to implicit self-representations both impairs the ability of that system to inhibit intrusions *and* disables the individual to perceive those intrusions as unwanted. To the extent that an individual loses access to the *implicit self*, this system cannot do what it normally does, which is automatically to inhibit emotions and thoughts that are not compatible with current self-representations (i.e., with what a person *wants*). That is, without knowing what one wants there is no criterion against which to assess and inhibit "unwanted" thoughts. Inhibited access to implicit self-representations can therefore be expected to impair *awareness of the unwantedness* of intrusive thoughts *(uninformed self-incongruence).* For example, inhibited access to implicit self-representations renders it difficult to decide whether thoughts and feelings aroused at a particular moment are compatible with self-interests, whether they are wanted, and whether they are relevant to one's self-esteem. In this chapter, we discuss theory and evidence related to these two forms of *implicit or automatic* control of unwanted thoughts and feelings.

Since the two types of rumination we focus on are attributable to failures of *implicit* control mechanisms for thought, they can be distinguished from the explicit form of rumination control that is associated with continuous attempts to actively and consciously *suppress* intrusive thoughts. The differences between the three types of rumination are also reflected in their quite divergent pathological correlates: The extreme forms of informed and uninformed rumination can be related to dejected and agitated forms of depression (Kuhl & Kazén, 1994b) whereas obsessive-compulsive disorders are interpreted as extreme forms of suppressive rumination. According to recent theory and evidence, people ironically lose control over intrusive thoughts the more they *consciously* try to control them (Wegner, 1994). This mechanism explains why people who compulsively try to suppress intrusive thoughts may paradoxically suffer from intensive bouts of rumination. Patients suffering from obsessive thinking typically try to suppress unpleasant thoughts and associate feelings of guilt and responsibility with these thoughts (Salkovskis, 1989).

In contrast, *state-oriented rumination* (mediated by a failure of one of the two implicit mechanisms mentioned) is not necessarily associated with these attributes of obsessive thinking (unless it coincides with an obsessive-compulsive condition).

Wegner's theory focuses on the *processes that cause* the resurgence of suppressed thoughts. Similarly, our work on state orientation has focused on the processes underlying self-incongruent rumination that is not necessarily associated with suppressive attempts. In addition, research on state orientation has focused on questions concerning the distal antecedents and consequences of state orientation: What are the mechanisms underlying spontaneously occurring ruminations in everyday life (i.e., even when one does not consciously try to suppress them)? What are the proximal and distal antecedents of individual differences in the tendency to have frequent uncontrollable ruminations (i.e., ruminative state orientation)? What are the proximal and distal *effects* of uncontrollable ruminations and the processes associated with them?

Many answers to these questions have been summarized in a recent book (Kuhl & Beckmann, 1994a). Compared to action-oriented participants, state-oriented participants who report having perseverating and uncontrollable thoughts after aversive experiences (as assessed by the Disengagement versus Preoccupation subscale of the ACS: Kuhl, 1985, 1994a), show more signs of *alienation* (e.g., failures to switch from boring to attractive activities, inconsistent preference judgments, etc. (Guevara, 1994; Kuhl & Beckmann, 1994b), they more often misperceive assigned unattractive activities as self-chosen or self-compatible (Kuhl & Kazén, 1994a), and they show more rigidity as assessed by "shift costs" in an alternation task (Kuhl & Fuhrmann, in press). This research and the theory of volition developed on the basis of it lead to one important conclusion concerning the functional basis of uncontrollable rumination: There are functionally different forms of rumination, some of which are related to separable impairments of self-regulatory functions.

Specifically, the two forms of rumination based on impairments of *implicit* mechanisms of control can be attributed to inhibition of volitional functions (i.e., impaired initiative and impaired activation of self-representations, respectively), whereas the third form of rumination can be explained in terms of *excessive* volitional control (i.e., deliberate suppression of unwanted thoughts). According to the basic idea of our approach, the more precisely we can describe the properties of volitional functions and their impairments, the better we will be able to understand rumination and several related phenomena, such as alienation, self-infiltration (mistaking introjected self-alien goals for self-compatible ones) and compulsive perseveration (rigid adherence to goals and behaviors even when they become unrealistic or inadequate). For this reason, we provide a brief summary of our theory of volition, and the theory of personality in which it is embedded (Kuhl, 1994b, 1997).

## A THEORY OF PERSONALITY AND VOLITION (PSI-THEORY)

Theoretically, *self-regulation* can be described as one particular mode for centrally coordinating psychological subsystems (i.e., subsystems that control motivation, emotion, arousal, attention, and cognitive contents). This self-regulatory mode of central coordination prepares and adjusts psychological states across these subsystems in an effort to make internal and external behavior as compatible as possible with the organism's self-representations (i.e., with implicit, holistic representations of a variety of needs, emotions, preferences, and beliefs that constitute the "self"). When an intended activity is perceived as compatible with the self, overall self-compatibility can be enhanced by increasing one's motivation (*Motivation Control*: e.g., focusing on pleasant aspects of the activity), by enhancing one's positive mood *(Emotion Control)*, by heightening one's arousal and interest related to the task *(Control of Arousal, or "Temperament")*, and so forth.

A second mode of central coordination is called *self-control*. Whereas self-regulation is a *self-maintenance* mode, self-control focuses on self-disciplined *goal-maintenance*. It does this by modifying psychological states (e.g., motivation, emotion, arousal, attention, cognitions) so as to maintain the goal pursuit and attain the goal—even if this requires transient or permanent suppression of implicit needs, values, and other self-aspects (e.g., reducing attention to stimuli that distract from the current goal, suppressing interfering needs, etc.).

## Volition And Its Inhibition

Ideally, the two modes of central (volitional) coordination cooperate: All subsystems are coordinated in a way that both self-compatibility of goals and operations are maintained *(self-maintenance)* and simultaneously goals are shielded against interfering distractors and temptations *(goal-maintenance)*. Unfortunately, self-maintenance and goal maintenance are often incompatible: Pursuing achievement goals often requires the suppression of many self-related concerns (i.e., self-control). A woman who pursues her career goals may believe that she has to suppress some of her needs and preferences (e.g., spending more time with her family, reading her favorite novels, etc.). Conversely, self-actualization often requires giving up certain goals: For example, being more in touch with and realizing more of one's needs, values, or other aspects of one's self-identity, may require giving up high-level career goals.

When one of the two volitional modes permanently exceeds a critical intensity, their balanced synergism can turn into an opposing antagonism: The consequence is excessive self-indulgence or overcontrol, depending on which volitional mode becomes dominant. According to the theory, overcontrol occurs when the goal-maintenance mode *(self-control)* dominates at the expense of the self-maintenance mode *(self-regulation)*. Overcontrol is characterized by (a) chronic suppression[1] of self-representations, and (b) self-motivation through anticipation

---

[1]The term *suppression* does not always denote conscious and deliberate control: The inhibition of self-representations supposedly associated with self-control and the preoccupation form of state orientation are not necessarily associated with conscious efforts toward suppression comparable to those that we associate with compulsive attempts to suppress ruminative thinking.

of negative consequences of insufficient self-discipline (rigid duty, "inner dictatorship"). State orientation can be explained in terms of inhibition of self-regulatory and/or self-control functions when an organism is exposed to stressful events. Two types of stressful circumstances can be distinguished: Stress can result from (a) a high load or demand on cognitive resources (e.g., pursuing *difficult* goals), or (b) threatening circumstances. In the first case, that is when an organism faces a difficult situation, it can be adaptive to inhibit premature action, for example in order to engage in problem-solving or to wait for help. This form of volitional inhibition can be regarded as the adaptive side of the hesitation component of state orientation, which is associated with *reduced positive affect* (Kuhl, 1997). Depression can be interpreted in this context in terms of an exaggerated form of this adaptive mechanism, which normally enables the organism to delay gratification, avoid premature action, and engage in problem-solving activity.

In *threatening situations*, the second type of volitional inhibition can be adaptive: Inhibiting access to implicit self-representations through high levels of *negative affect* increases attention to unexpected and unwanted information, prepares the organism for flight, should it become necessary, and increases its openness to external control of behavior (e.g., being guided by external warning signals or by helpful others). Within this theoretical context, rumination can be regarded as an indicator of adaptive attempts to cope with environmental stress by reducing volitional control of action and increasing the system's sensitivity to external cues and guides to behavior. A recent model of rumination (Martin and Stoner, 1996) attributes intrusive thoughts to frustration of goal-striving: Whenever an individual is hindered in his or her attempts to approach a goal, ruminative thoughts are generated. A similar assumption has been proposed earlier on the basis of an elaborated theory of motivation (Klinger, 1977, 1990). This assumption is compatible with our modelling of the first type of rumination associated with *informed self-incongruence* and *hesitation* (i.e., inhibition of the performance of intended actions). The goal-frustration model does not, however, cover the second type of rumination attributed to impaired self-accessibility and the *preoccupation* form of state orientation (i.e., uninformed self-incongruence): According to this concept, *any type of conflict* between integrated self-representations and specific activated cognitive contents can elicit ruminative activity, irrespective of whether or not goal pursuits are inhibited (Kuhl & Beckmann, 1994b). An additional difference between the current account and the goal-frustration model should be noted: Despite the fact that inhibition of an intended action (i.e., hesitation) includes goal frustration, it is not confined to this case: The capacity to enact intentions can be reduced even if no goal pursuit is frustrated. As a result, the hesitation hypothesis predicts that uncontrollable intrusions may occur even in the absence of concrete frustrations of goal-directed activity, provided that the conditions that produce hesitation are present (e.g. reduced positive affect, high task difficulty, frustration of a need).

## PSI-Theory

The types of rumination related to volitional inhibition (i.e., hesitation vs. preoccupation) are derived from a theory of personality that can be applied to a diversity of phenomena. The theory spells out the modulatory impact of basic affects on the activation of two high-level and two low-level cognitive systems. Uncontrollable rumination can be directly related to a predominance of low-level over high-level (i.e., volitional) processes (Beckmann, in press; Kuhl & Beckmann, 1994b): Thoughts or emotions related to an unpleasant event perseverate on an elementary level of processing because their top-down modulation by goal- or self-representations is inhibited *(volitional inhibition)*: When exposed to aversive events, state-oriented people cannot exert top-down control on their thoughts and feelings according to their current goals and self-representations.[2] Considerable progress in understanding the antecedents, the functional basis, and the effects of these processes could be made by analyzing the functional characteristics of the high- and low-level processes involved, the interactions among them, and their interrelations with affective states (figure 17.1).

The two high-level functions or systems supporting goal-maintenance and self-maintenance, respectively, can be described in terms of two cognitive macro-systems: (a) goal-oriented, analytical *thinking*, which heavily relies on sequential verbal processing and an *explicit memory for intended actions* (often related to "left hemispheric" processing), and (b) Holistic *feeling* can be modeled by parallel-distributed networks (often related to right hemispheric processing), and relates to an implicit representational (high-level) system providing *integrated knowledge* about the self and the environment. The many functional differences between Thinking and Feeling have been described in C. G. Jungs (1936) theory as well as in more recent approaches (e.g., Epstein, 1994; Kuhl, 1983a; Paivio, 1983). It should be noted that holistic Feeling, in addition to its implicit format of cognitive representations (cf. Berry & Dienes, 1993; Goschke, in press; Reber, 1993), has much closer ties to physiological concomitants of emotions than left hemispheric processing (Kuhl, 1997; Wittling, 1990). The cognitive characteristics of Feeling can be described in terms of parallel activation of broad and remote *contexts* of meanings, remote action alternatives, an *extended network of relevant self-aspects* and other background information associated with verbal messages, goals, and self-representations currently processed by the organism (cf. Baars, 1988; Beeman et al., 1994; Nakagawa, 1991).

---

[2]It might appear contradictory to assume that ruminative *thoughts* are associated with an *inhibition* of higher order processes such as thinking: The paradox is resolved when one notes that Thinking is a highly organized form of having thoughts (goal-oriented, sequential-analytic, action-oriented) whereas ruminative thoughts are not integrated in a functional network consisting of planning, problem-solving, and operational subsystems (Kuhl & Goschke, 1994a; see also Klinger's distinction between thinking and rumination: Klinger, 1971).

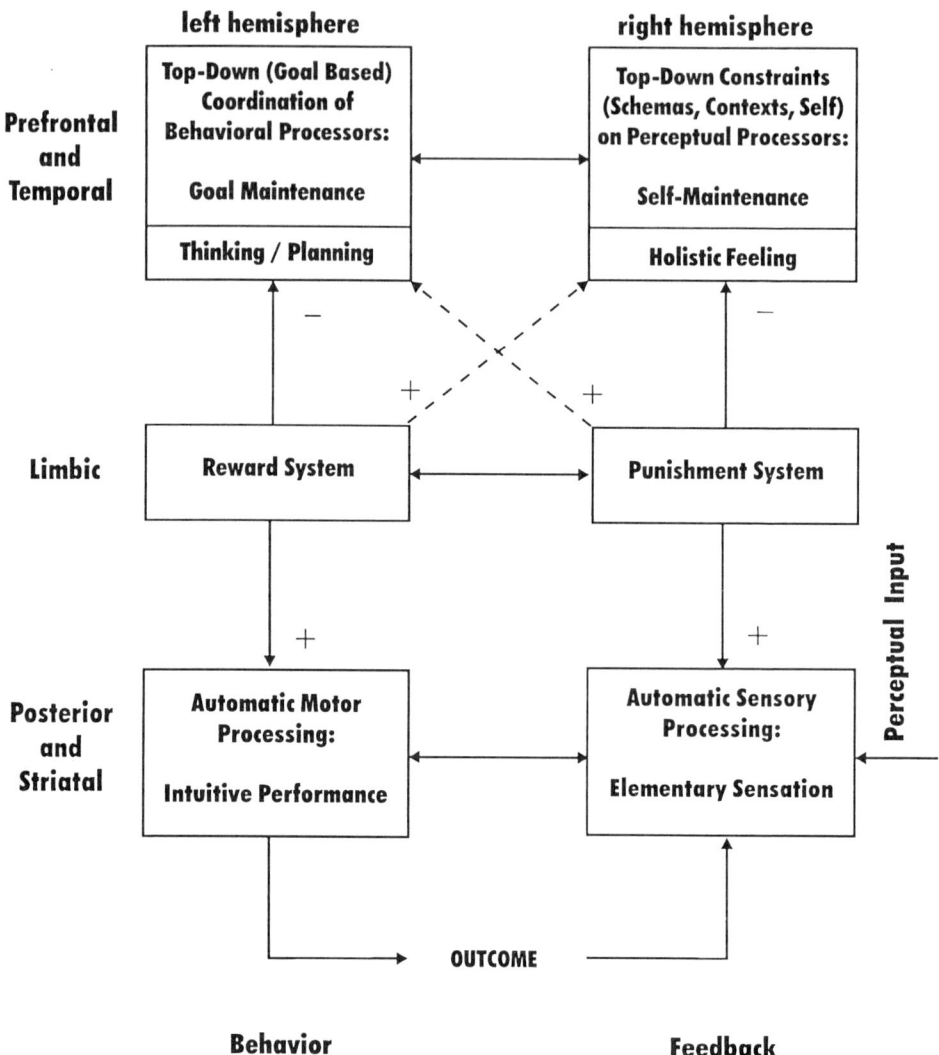

FIG. 17.1. Outline of the Theory of Personality-Systems Interactions (PSI-theory).

In addition to the two high-level functions (i.e., Thinking and Feeling), PSI-theory specifies functional properties of two low-level functions or systems, namely elementary *Sensation* and *Intuitive Performance* (figure 17.1). The latter contains all behavioral programs that can be performed "intuitively," that is, without (or with little) high-level support. Examples are well-practiced behavioral routines, verbal representations of such routines as instructions and social norms, but also pre-wired response schemas such as innate flight responses. In contrast to the action-oriented functions of Thinking and Intuitive Performance, the functions of Sensation and Feeling refer to perceptual and experiential rather than planning and action-oriented processing. Whereas Sensation includes elementary perceptual objects, Feeling encompasses highly integrated, holistic aggregations of many elementary sensations such as perceptions, needs, preferences, and so on. It should be noted that the description of the low-level system called *elementary sensation* is based on a rather broad concept of "object" perception: Any entity (e.g., a visual object, a sequence of tones, an emotion, a semantic category) that can be explicitly identified and *recognized* (i.e., matched with a previously perceived sensation) is called an object. The high-level system called Feeling is described in terms of integrated representations consisting of a variety of objects and relations among them. According to PSI-theory, these "cognitive-emotional maps" or "landscapes" are too complex to be explicitly identified, recognized, or verbalized.

Access to holistic representations is essential to self-maintenance: Holistic cognitive "landscapes" of preferences, needs, beliefs, norms, etc. enable the organism to construe behavioral options that satisfy multiple constraints defined by the needs, preferences and other self-aspects integrated in the active cognitive landscape. Losing access to such integrated represensations results in behavior that satisfies *fragments* of the self only (e.g., a specific Sensation of an isolated need ignoring other self-aspects). This part of the theory offers a mechanism for explaining extrinsically motivated behavior: Loss of intrinsic interest in an ongoing activity, typically observed when individuals focus too much on extrinsic incentives or are controlled by external pressures (Deci & Ryan, 1991), can be attributed to inhibited access to integrated self-representations, resulting in behaviors that are instigated by fragmented representations of isolated needs (i.e., by sensations provided by the low-level object recognition system) rather than by high-level, integrated self-representations.

Perhaps the most crucial assumption of the theory of Personality-Systems-Interactions (PSI-theory) concerns the interaction between the four cognitive macrosystems (i.e., Thinking, Feeling, Sensation, and Intuitive Performance), on the one hand, and motivational and emotional systems on the other. Enhanced positive affect (or an increased activation of the reward system) dampens Thinking and Planning systems and facilitates systems supporting Intuitive Performance (figure 17.1). The plausibility of this *First Affect–Cognition Modulation Hypothesis* can be derived from the assumption that positive affect indicates a situation in which goals can be reached easily, that is, without substantial planning and volitional effort, simply by activating available behavioral routines (Intuitive Performance). Formal statements of similar hypotheses (Kuhl, 1983a; Isen, 1984) have been corroborated by many empirical results (Abele-Brehm, 1995; Fiedler & Forgas, 1988; Isen, 1987; Schwarz, 1990).

PSI-theory contains a *Second Affect-Cognition Modulation Hypothesis*. It states that negative affect dampens the accessibility of holistic Feeling and Self-maintenance systems and facilitates elementary Sensations and attentional orienting to novel stimuli (figure 17.1). The latter is assumed to be part of the network of subsystems supporting elementary Sensation across various modalities. To the extent that ruminative state orientation is associated with an increased sensitivity of the punishment system (i.e., a disposition to experience intense and perseverating negative affect when exposed to aversive events), we can attribute alienation and self-infiltration effects observed in state-oriented participants (Kuhl & Beckmann, 1994b; Kuhl & Kazén, 1994a) to the inhibition of Feeling and self-representations postulated by the Second Modulation Hypothesis: As pointed out earlier, inhibited access to integrated self-representations amounts to not knowing, or not *feeling* what one wants, which in turn disables the mechanisms that would otherwise automatically inhibit intrusions incompatible with what the individual momentarily wants. One advantage of this account is its global parsimony: PSI-theory explains uncontrollable rumination on the basis of the same mechanism that can also explain alienation, self-infiltration, and other symptoms of volitional inhibition (Kuhl & Beckmann, 1994a).

## FURTHER APPLICATIONS TO RUMINATION

Returning to our central question concerning the mechanisms, antecedents and effects of rumination, we can now see uncontrollable rumination in a broader context. As pointed out, the same mechanisms can be applied to explain rumination and many other phenomena such as alienation and self-infiltration: Each of these phenomena can be attributed to reduced accessibility of holistic Feeling and self-representations in participants having (a) a disposition toward strong negative affect when exposed to aversive events, plus (b) a disposition toward inhibiting high-level volitional functions under such circumstances (i.e., state-oriented individuals). As a result of reduced participation by the self-system, the self cannot exert top-down inhibition (figure 17.1) of unwanted, "self-alien" thoughts (rumination), it cannot mediate consistent judgments of one's preferences or self-consistent behavior (alienation) because reliable access to self-representation of one's preferences is impaired. In addition, the self-system is not accessible when it is needed for identifying the self-alien status of goals imposed by others. As a result, it was postulated and found that state-oriented individuals have an increased tendency toward *self-infiltration* in terms of misperceiving assigned (self-alien) activities as self-chosen (Kuhl & Kazén, 1994a).

A second advantage of discussing rumination within the broader context of PSI-theory is that antecedents of state-oriented rumination can be specified, especially for the subtype associated with misinformed self-incongruence: According to PSI-theory, rumination, alienation, and self-infiltration, should occur when perseverating negative affect is activated on the basis of a personal disposition (i.e., ruminative state orientation) and situational arousal of negative affect. For relaxed conditions that arouse positive affect, the theory predicts increased access to self-representations, facilitated performance and a lack of alienation and self-in-filtration, even for state-oriented participants. This prediction has been corroborated by recent findings demonstrating superior performance of state-oriented participants, even at complex tasks, when they were allowed to work in a relaxed situation without time-pressure or external pressures that would arouse ego-threatening concerns (Menec, 1995).

The third advantage of looking at rumination from the perspective of PSI-theory relates to *consequences* of ruminative state orientation. Although this aspect will not be elaborated in this paper, it may be interesting to note that many results  have been obtained confirming theoretically expected effects of ruminative state orientation on functional helplessness (Brunstein & Olbrich, 1985; Kuhl, 1981), resistance to temptation and other volitional abilities (Kuhl & Fuhrmann, in press), on procrastination and prospective memory (Beswick & Man, 1994; Goschke & Kuhl, 1993; Kuhl, 1982; Kuhl & Goschke, 1994b), decision-making (Dibbelt & Kuhl, 1994; Kuhl & Beckmann, 1983; Stiensmeier-Pelster, 1994), scholastic achievement (Boekaerts, 1994; Bossong, 1994), on depression (Kuhl & Helle, 1986; Kuhl & Kazén, 1994b) and other psycho-pathological disorders (Hautzinger, 1994), and on performance and event-related brain potentials obtained from top-ranking athletes (Haschke, Tennigkeit & Kuhl, 1994; Roth & Strang, 1994).

## EMPIRICAL RESULTS ON RUMINATION

### Evidence For Increased Rumination In State-Oriented Participants

Although a tendency toward having uncontrollable rumination is already indicated by the face and content validity of the ACS, independent evidence for such a tendency has also been obtained. In an earlier study, state-oriented participants reported significantly more thoughts concerning an unsolvable training task than action-oriented participants did, even when participants were trying to focus on a new task (Kuhl, 1983b, p. 290f.). These results were replicated in a helplessness study by Kuhl & Weiss (1994; Kuhl, 1983b, p. 294). A remarkable demonstration of perseverating rumination was found at the end of the first study mentioned: Compared to action-oriented participants, state-oriented participants reported significantly more frequent thoughts about the first (unsolvable) task, even after having worked for more than 45 minutes on a variety of solvable tasks (including many tasks they succeeded on).

## Elaborating The Mechanisms Underlying Rumination

The mechanism presumably causing uncontrollable rumination according to PSI-Theory can now be elaborated in more detail. The basic mechanism can be described in terms of *involuntary attention* to conflict-arousing emotional information. Attentional orienting towards incongruent, emotional or conflict-arousing information cannot easily be suppressed by conscious effort (Berlyne, 1960; Wegner, 1994). This mechanism should work equally in action- and state-oriented participants and it should be related to each of the three forms of rumination described earlier: When exposed to or reminded of an emotionally arousing event, both action- and state-oriented individuals should experience intrusive rumination as long as it is not necessary to control them (i.e., as long as no task is introduced that requires full attention). However, action-oriented participants should have fewer uncontrollable ruminations than state-oriented participants do in situations in which uncontrollable ruminations interfere with optimal task performance. Presumably, the difference between the two groups is a relative rather than an absolute one: Action-oriented participants are better able to control intense emotions than state-oriented participants are. When the intensity of emotions associated with a particular thought exceeds a critical threshold, action-oriented participants are expected to have uncontrollable ruminations as well. Consequently, when asked to report examples of uncontrollable ruminations from their lives both groups should be able to retrieve such experiences.

According to PSI-theory, an additional difference between the two groups concerns the degree of self-involvement when having intrusions. To the extent that state-oriented participants[3] have reduced access to self-representations when exposed to aversive events, they should have problems differentiating intrusive thoughts from non-intrusive ones in all attributes related to the self.

Specifically, an increased access to self-representations should enable action-oriented more than state-oriented individuals to perceive intrusive thoughts as potentially self-relevant (i.e., threatening to one's self-esteem) and less "wanted". The results from a recent experiment (Baumann, 1993) confirm this expectation (table 17.1). In this study, participants were asked to list intrusive and non-intrusive thoughts from their everyday experience. The uncontrollability of intrusive thoughts was emphasized. The results confirm the expectation that both action- and state-oriented participants are able to report uncontrollable and unpleasant intrusive thoughts (table 17.1) and that state-oriented participants are not able to perceive intrusive thoughts to be associated with more relevance to self-esteem, less self-involvement, and less intendedness, than non-intrusive thoughts (table 17.1). How can this paradoxical finding be explained? Why is it that state-oriented participants perceive intrusive thoughts as less controllable than non-

---

[3]In the remainder of this chapter, we focus on the preoccupation type of state orientation associated with increased punishment sensitivity and reduced access to self-representations when exposed to stress, according to PSI-theory.

intrusive ones, but do not rate intrusive thoughts as more threatening to their self-esteem and (as a result) less intended (more "unwanted") than non-intrusive ones?

TABLE 17.1

Mean ratings of intrusive and non-intrusive words for action- and state-oriented participants (n = 20).

| Ratings | | Word Type | |
|---|---|---|---|
| | | intrusive | non-intrusive |
| Uncontrollability | | | |
| | action | 5.93 | 3.64* |
| | state | 5.93 | 3.66* |
| Pleasantness | | | |
| | action | −1.77 | 2.11* |
| | state | −1.02 | 1.35* |
| Involvement | | | |
| | action | 4.61 | 6.08* |
| | state | 5.60 | 6.14 n.s. |
| Intendedness | | | |
| | action | 3.54 | 6.00* |
| | state | 4.87 | 5.44 n.s. |
| Relevance to self-esteem | | | |
| | action | 7.37 | 5.87* |
| | state | 6.09 | 6.33 n.s. |

*Note:* * indicates a significant within-row paired comparison ($p < .05$).

According to PSI-theory, judgments of self-involvement, intendedness, and self-relevance require access to self-representations, which state-oriented individuals tend to lose when exposed to aversive thoughts or events. On the basis of this "self-inhibition" (i.e., inhibited access to self-representations), we can explain the results reported earlier that state-oriented participants have more problems in suppressing ruminative thinking if it is in conflict with top-down operating representations of their current self-based concerns: Supposedly, state-oriented participants' ruminations are more perseverative than action-oriented participants' intrusions—even when the "self" is trying to ignore task-irrelevant intrusions—because action-oriented people have better access to self-representations that help terminate unwanted (i.e., non-self) ruminations through automatic, top-down inhibitory mechanisms.

## Alienation And Self-Infiltration

Extending the framework of rumination research to include phenomena such as alienation and self-infiltration has the advantage of attaining a parsimonious explanation for several phenomena rather than formulating separate models for each phenomenon under investigation. If the *perseverating* form of rumination is caused by reduced access to self-representations, we can explain why people reporting perseverating ruminations after being exposed to aversive events (i.e., state-oriented individuals) also show signs of alienation (e.g., unreliable access to their preferences: Kuhl & Beckmann, 1994b), and self-infiltration (e.g., false self-ascriptions of assigned activities: Kuhl & Kazén, 1994a): Common to all these phenomena is an impaired ability to "read" self-representations (i.e., form analytical representations of holistic self-representations) or perform activities consistent with them. When participants lose access to their implicit self-representations, they not only have difficulties controlling intrusive thoughts, but they also tend to mistake activities that had been assigned to them by the experimenter as self-chosen (Kuhl & Kazén, 1994a).

In a recent experiment, we obtained additional evidence for a common mechanism of both this self-infiltration effect (i.e., false self-ascription of assigned activities) and perseverative rumination: In the first part of the experiment, participants role-played "a working day of a secretary". They were asked to choose several activities from a list of things to be done (e.g., seal letters, make phone calls etc.). Subsequently, the experimenter taking the role of the "boss" assigned several activities to the participants. Later, each activity from that list was presented on the computer screen and the participant had to decide whether it was a self-chosen or an assigned activity. In the second part of the experiment, participants read a boring text presented on the screen. They were instructed to press a key whenever they had an irrelevant, intrusive thought. As expected there was a significant correlation ($r = .59$) between the number of false self-ascriptions during the activity classification task and the number of intrusions reported during reading. However, this correlation occurred only in a group of participants that had been exposed to a negative mood induction procedure (Baumann, 1997). In two groups in which a positive or a neutral mood was induced, the respective correlations were even negative (-.15, for positive, and -.32, for neutral mood conditions). State-oriented participants' tendency to accept and perform more assigned unattractive activities than action-oriented participants usually do (Kuhl & Beckmann, 1994b; Kuhl & Kazén, 1994a) was associated in this experiment with a higher proportion of intrusions during text reading, intrusions that were related to assigned rather than unchosen (i.e., neither self-chosen nor chosen by the experimenter), unattractive activities.

## Helplessness: An Example Of Effects Of State-Oriented Rumination

In several studies of helplessness induced by failure experiences, generalized performance deficits following induced failure were not attributable to motivational deficits or reduced self-efficacy beliefs as commonly assumed (e.g., Bandura, 1982; Seligman, 1975), but to interference from uncontrollable rumination about failure, its causes, and its emotional consequences (cf. Brunstein & Olbrich, 1985; Diener & Dweck, 1978; Kuhl, 1983b, p. 294; Kuhl & Weiss, 1994). An earlier study (Kuhl, 1981) had shown that, despite impaired performance after failing on an unsolvable task, state-oriented participants did not generalize their reduced expectancies of control to the subsequent task and they even reported increased effort rather than the reduced effort predicted by traditional helplessness theory (Hiroto & Seligman, 1975).

The debilitating effect of rumination on performance is of practical importance because it suggests limitations of the traditional explanation and treatment of helplessnes-related disorders such as depression and many others (Hautzinger, 1994): Encouraging patients to develop positive cognitive schemas, benign attributions, or optimistic control beliefs (Abramson, Seligman & Teasdale, 1978; Beck, 1967) is often not sufficient and it can even backfire: When patients are confronted again with their functional (volitional) deficits, positive expectations induced in therapy may plunge them into feelings of helplessness that are even deeper than the original ones. Although functionally oriented procedures for training self-regulatory skills are available (e.g., Kanfer & Schefft, 1988), and although several studies have disconfirmed cognitive explanations of helplessness based on reduced control beliefs (Danker-Brown & Baucom, 1982; Lewinsohn, Steinmetz, Larson & Franklin, 1981), cognitive approaches have demonstrated a surprising degree of resistance to assimilating this evidence.

## EEG Correlates Of Volitional Inhibition

Further evidence for the claim that impaired performance after failure is attributable to functional rather than motivational deficits comes from research using electroencephalographic methods. The various functions associated with volition (i.e., central coordination in terms of self-regulation and/or self-control) are supported by a large system of neural networks in the frontal part of the brain (Fuster, 1989; Luria, 1973; Shallice, 1988; Stuss & Benson, 1984). If performance deficits in helplessness are, in fact, attributable to an *inability* to avoid task-irrelevant intrusions, that is, if those performance deficits are attributable to an inhibition of volitional functions (such as planning, goal-maintenance, impulse control, self-motivation, self-determination, etc.), intrusive material should be accompanied by inhibitory brain potentials at electrodes placed over prefrontal sites of the scalp. We found support for this hypothesis in several studies examining slow brain potentials at 19 sites across the scalp when participants were exposed to neutral and intrusive words that they had generated before the experiment (Rosahl, Tennigkeit, Kuhl & Haschke, 1993; Haschke & Kuhl, 1994).

## Antecedents Of Rumination

Many experiments reported here and elsewhere (Kuhl & Beckmann, 1994a) provided evidence for antecedents of perseverating rumination and other consequences of state orientation. State-oriented participants (of the preoccupation type) have debilitating and perseverating ruminations only when they are confronted with aversive events, when a negative mood is induced or pressure is exerted (e.g., time-pressure or an ego-involving instruction). These findings are consistent with the theoretical claim that inhibition of Feeling and holistic self-representations is mediated by a tonic increase in the activation of the punishment system (figure 17.1).

Our results support this claim. Recall that the negative correlation between the number of intrusions during text reading and the number of false self-ascriptions of assigned activities occurred in the negative mood condition only (Baumann, 1997). The higher incidence of intrusions related to assigned activities during text reading occurred for *unattractive* activities only (supposedly activating the punishment system). Under relaxed conditions, that is, when the punishment system is not aroused, state-oriented participants should have unobstructed access to their self-representations (figure 17.1). As a result, they are not expected to engage in more unwanted (i.e., self-unintended) rumination than action-oriented participants do. Consistent with this implication of PSI-theory, Klinger & Murphy found an equal amount of "rumination" in action- and state-oriented participants' daydreams. Likewise, Beckmann (1994) found no differences in the amount of ruminative thought between action- and state-oriented participants during a break between two parts of an experiment, that did not induce negative mood.

In recent experiments, we found that state-oriented participants show an increased rate of false self-ascriptions only when they feel sad. When they rated their mood as not sad or even relaxed, they showed even less false self-ascriptions than action-oriented participants did (Baumann, 1997; Kuhl, Baumann, Fuhrmann & Kazén, 1995). Similarly, we found in a recent study that state-oriented participants showed positive ("inhibitory") DC-shifts in pre-frontal brain potentials only after being exposed to negative words (e.g., murder, shame). Even brief exposures to positive words (e.g., good luck, success) produced a reversal in slow potential shifts: After positive words, state-oriented subjects showed *facilitatory* (i.e., negative) potential shifts at frontal electrodes (Kuhl, Schapkin & Gusew, 1994). Could it be that state-oriented participants even have increased access to their self-representations and self-regulatory skills when they feel good? Recent results confirm this conclusion: When state-oriented participants were given an opportunity to work under relaxed conditions (e.g., an accepting atmosphere without time-pressure or exaggerated ego-involvement), they outperformed action-oriented participants, even at a complex text comprehension task (Menec,

1995). We believe that these findings expose a strong bias in industrialized societies to focus on how people function under stress. To the extent that psychologists are interested in the full story, they might want to focus more on how
people react under friendly conditions.

## PRACTICAL IMPLICATIONS

The ability to discriminate intendedness and other self-related aspects between
intrusive and non-intrusive thoughts can be used as a simple method for assessing individual differences in basic affective dispositions (e.g., low positive versus
high negative emotionality) and volitional styles related to such differences:
Simply asking people about the "wantedness" of their task-irrelevant intrusions
may give a hint as to the mode of volition  they prefer. People leaning toward
self-control, or even overcontrol in terms of high goal maintenance and reduced
self-awareness and self-determination, may be identified by the fact that they do
not perceive task-irrelevant (uncontrollable) intrusions as unwanted. In other
words, people who claim that they "want" to perseverate when having uncontrollable ruminations even when they acknowledge the interfering effects of those
ruminations have an increased risk of developing overcontrol, according to theory
and data presented in this chapter and elsewhere: Both uninformed rumination and
a tendency toward overcontrol has been observed within the same group of individuals, i.e., participants scoring high on the preoccupation scale of state orientation (Kuhl & Fuhrmann, in press). Uninformed rumination as indicated by a
failure to acknowledge the unwantedness of interfering intrusions can be more
practical than other methods in applied settings such as educational contexts or in
psychotherapy because it can be regarded as a *consciously accessible* concomitant
of processes that are less easily available in conscious awareness (e.g., negative
emotionality, inhibited access to self-representations, overcontrol, etc.).

Obviously, more research is needed to delineate the merits and limitations of
informed versus uninformed rumination as a marker of volitional styles. The
practical significance of searching for such markers can be illustrated by the following example from a recent series of studies (Fuhrmann & Kuhl, in press).
According to this research, the degree of self-accessibility seems to be a determinant of the extent to which positive emotional conditions facilitate or debilitate
volitional efficiency as assessed by the proportion of intended behaviors actually
enacted. The study disconfirmed the general notion that positive affect and self-
reward always facilitates volitional efficiency. Participants who applied a self-
reward strategy during an intervention program aiming at an improvement of
dietary behaviors enacted more of their intentions (e.g., eat less french fries) if
they leaned toward self-regulation rather than self-control styles as defined above.
However, participants scoring high on scales assessing self-control or overcontrol
enacted *less* intended behaviors in a self-reward compared to a self-punishment
condition. Apparently, training and therapy based on positive reward can have
deleterious effects on goal-maintenance and volitional efficiency, at least in the

short run, in people leaning toward self-control or overcontrol, whereas aversive incentives may even facilitate the enactment of intended behavior in this group.

PSI-theory offers a common mechanism to explain both the fact that people leaning toward self-control and the preoccupation type of state orientation have difficulties to perceive self-incongruent and interfering intrusions as unwanted and the finding that goal attainment is facilitated by self-punishment strategies in this group: Extended periods of inhibited access to self-representations that are associated with negative emotionality (according to the Second Modulation Assumption of PSI-theory) should interfere with the *integration of goals* into the self-system. The reason for this application of the theory is obvious: Integration of new information into a specific memory system cannot take place unless the system in question is *activated*. As a result of inhibited activation of the self, this system has a reduced capacity for supporting goals, e.g., by suppressing goal-irrelevant intrusions and by facilitating goal-relevant behavior. People who have a reduced ability to integrate new goals into their self-system should find it easier to stick to an explicit goal when the self-system is inhibited as a result of negative emotionality or self-punishment strategies. This sort of volitional facilitation through negative affect can be explained because facilitated access to the self-system is likely to activate goal-irrelevant tendiencies in these people.

## CONCLUSION

It can be concluded from our analysis that a functional account of rumination may lead to distinctions, even among different types of rumination that appear rather similar from a phenomenological point of view. Specifically, two types of rumination can be distinguished that relate to informed vs. uninformed self-incongruence (or "unwantedness") of task-irrelevant intrusions. To the extent that these two types of rumination depend on different affective conditions (i.e., low positive affect vs. high negative affect, respectively), they can be applied to the assessment of different types of self-regulation associated with the two affective systems, according to the findings cited (Kuhl & Fuhrmann, in press). It may be further concluded, that people leaning toward overcontrol (a) may be identified on the basis of uninformed self-incongruence of task-irrelevant intrusions, and (b) cannot learn to take advantage of the positive effects of self-reward over self-punishment strategies until they develop the ability to integrate explicit goals into their implicit self-representations.

## REFERENCES

Abele-Brehm, A. (1995). *Stimmung und Leistung.* Göttingen: Hogrefe.
Abramson, L. Y., Seligman, M. E. P., & Teasdale, J. D. (1978). Learned helplessness in humans: Critique and reformulation. *Journal of Abnormal Psychology, 87,* 49–79.
Ach, N. (1910). *Über den Willensakt und das Temperament.* Leipzig: Quelle & Meyer.

Allport, D. A., Styles, E. A. & Hsieh, S. (1994). Shifting attentional set: Exploring the dynamic control of tasks. C. Umilta & M. Moscowitch (Eds.), *Attention and Performance XV* (pp. 421–452). Cambridge, MA: MIT Press.

Baars, B. J. (1988). *A cognitive theory of consciousness.* Cambridge, MA: Cambridge University Press.

Baddeley, A. (1996). Exploring the central executive. *The Quarterly Journal of Experimental Psychology, 49,* 5–28.

Bandura, A. (1982). Self-efficacy mechanism in human agency. *American Psychologist, 37,* 122–147.

Baumann, N. (1993). *Volitionale Vermittlung differentieller Zugriffszeiten auf persönlich intrusive versus nicht-intrusive Wörter bei Lage- und Handlungsorientierten.* [Volitional mediation of differential retrieval latencies for intrusive and non-intrusive words in state versus action-oriented participants]. Unpublished diploma thesis. University of Osnabrück.

Baumann, N. (1997). *Emotion, Introjektion und Persönlichkeit* [Emotion, introjection and personality]. Unpublished manuscript. University of Osnabrück.

Beck, A. T. (1967). *Depression: Causes and treatment.* Philadelphia, PA: University of Pennsylvania Press.

Beckmann, J. (1994). Ruminative thought and the deactivation of an intention. *Motivation and Emotion, 18,* 317–334.

Beckmann, J. (in press). *Handlungskontrolle und Leistung* (Action control and performance). Göttingen: Hogrefe.

Beeman, M., Friedman, R. B., Grafman, J., Perez, E., Diamond, S. & Lindsay, M. B. (1994). Summation priming and coarse coding in the right hemisphere. *Journal of Cognitive Neuroscience, 6,* 26–45.

Berlyne, D. E. (1960). *Conflict, arousal, and curiosity.* New York: McGraw-Hill.

Berry, D. C. & Dienes, Z. (1993). *Implicit learning: Theoretical and empirical issues.* Hillsdale, NJ: Lawrence Erlbaum Associates.

Beswick, G., & Man, L. (1994). State orientation and procrastination. In J. Kuhl & J. Beckmann (Eds.), *Volition and personality: Action versus state orientation* (pp. 391–396). Göttingen, Seattle: Hogrefe.

Blum, G. S. & Barbour, J. S. (1979). Selective inattention to anxiety-linked stimuli. *Journal of Experimental Psychology: General, 108,* 182–224.

Boekaerts, M. (1994). Action control: How relevant is it for classroom learning? In J. Kuhl & J. Beckmann (Eds.), *Volition and personality: Action versus state orientation* (pp. 427435). Göttingen, Seattle: Hogrefe.

Bossong, A. (1994). Scholastic stressors and achievement-related anxiety. In J. Kuhl & J. Beckmann (Eds.), *Volition and personality: Action versus state orientation.* Götingen, Seattle: Hogrefe.

Brunstein, J. C., & Olbrich, E. (1985). Personal helplessness and action control: An analysis of achievement-related cognitions, self-assessments, and performance. *Journal of Personality and Social Psychology, 48,* 1540–1551.

Danker-Brown, P. & Baucom, D. H. (1982). Cognitive influences on the development of learned helplessness. *Journal of Personality and Social Psychology, 43,* 793–801.

Deci, E. L., & Ryan, R. M. (1991). A motivational approach to self: Integration in personality. In E. Dienstbier (Ed.), *Nebraska Symposium on Motivation* 1990 (pp. 237–288).

Dibbelt, S. & Kuhl, J. (1994). Volitional processes in decision-making: Personality and situtional determinants (pp. 177–194). In J. Kuhl & J. Beckmann (Eds.), *Volition and personality: Action versus state orientation.* Seattle/Göttingen: Hogrefe.

Diener, C. I., & Dweck, C. S. (1978). Analysis of learned helplessness: Continuous changes in performance, strategy, and achievement cognitions following failure. *Journal of Personality and Social Psychology, 36*, 451–462.

Epstein, S. (1994). Integration of the cognitive and the psychodynamic unconscious. *American Psychologist, 49*, 709–724.

Fiedler, K. & Forgas, J. (Eds.) (1988). *Affect, cognition and social behavior.* Seattle/Göttingen: Hogrefe.

Fuhrmann, A. & Kuhl, J. (in press). Maintaining a healthy diet: Effects of personality and self-reward versus self-punishment on commitment to and enactment of self-chosen and assighned goals. *Psychology and Health.*

Fuster, J. M. (1989). *The prefrontal cortex.* 2nd ed. New York: Raven Press.

Goschke, T. (in press). Implicit learning and unconscious knowledge: Mental representation, computational mechanisms, and brain structures. In K. Lamberts & D. Shanks (Eds.), *Knowledge, concepts and categories.* London: University College of London Press.

Goschke, T., & Kuhl, J. (1993). The representation of intentions: Persisting activation in memory. *Journal of Experimental Psychology: Learning, Memory, and Cognition, 19*, 1211–1226.

Guevara, M. L. (1994). *Alienation und Selbstkontrolle: Das Ignorieren eigener Gefühle.* (Alienation and self-control: Ignoring one's preferences). Unpublished dissertation: University of Osnabrück.

Haschke, R., & Kuhl, J. (1994). Action control and slow potential shifts. *Proceedings of the 41st International Congress of Aviation and Space Medicine* (pp. 207–211). Bologna: Monduzzi.

Haschke, R., Tennigkeit, M., & Kuhl, J. (1994). Personality and task-related slow potential shifts: The role of test anxiety and action vs. state orientation in top-ranking soccer players' coping with failure. In J. Kuhl & J. Beckmann (Eds.), *Volition and personality: Action versus state orientation* (pp. 475–483). Göttingen, Seattle: Hogrefe.

Hautzinger, M. (1994). Action control in the context of psychopathological disorders. In J. Kuhl & J. Beckmann (Eds.), *Volition and personality: Action versus state orientation* (pp. 209–216). Göttingen/Seattle: Hogrefe.

Hiroto, D. W., & Seligman, M. E. P. (1975). Generality of learned helplessness in man. *Journal of Personality and Social Psychology, 31*, 311–327.

Isen, A. M. (1984). Toward understanding the role of affect in cognition. In R. S. Wyer, Jr. & T. K. Srull (Eds.), *Handbook of social cognition* (Vol. 3, pp. 179–236). Hillsdale, NJ: Lawrence Erlbaum Associates.

Isen, A. M. (1987). Positive affect, cognitive processes, and social behavior. In L. Berkowitz (Ed.), *Advances in experimental social psychology* (Vol. 20, pp. 203–253). New York: Academic Press.

Jung, C. G. (1936/1990). *Typologie.* München: dtv.

Kanfer, F. H., & Schefft, B. K. (1988). *Guiding the process of therapeutic change.* Champaign, IL: Research Press.

Klinger, E. (1971). *Structure and functions of fantasy.* New York: Wiley.

Klinger, E. (1977). *Meaning and void: Inner experience and the incentives in people's lives.* Minneapolis: University of Minnesota Press.

Klinger, E. (1981). The central place of imagery in human functioning. In E. Klinger (Ed.), *Imagery: Concepts, results and applications* (Vol 2, pp. 3–16). New York: Plenum.

Klinger, E. (1990). *Daydreaming.* Los Angeles: Tarcher/Putnam.

Klinger, E. & Murphy, M. D. (1994). Action orientation and personality: Some evidence on the construct validity of the Action Control Scale. In J. Kuhl & J. Beckmann (Eds.), *Volition and personality: Action versus state orientation* (pp. 79–92). Göttingen, Seattle: Hogrefe.

Kuhl, J. (1981). Motivational and functional helplessness: The moderating effect of state vs. action orientation. *Journal of Personality and Social Psychology, 40,* 155–170.

Kuhl, J. (1982). Handlungskontrolle als metakognitver Vermittler zwischen Intention und Handeln: Freizeitaktivitäten bei Hauptschülern. *Zeitschrift für Entwicklungspsychologie und Pädagogische Psychologie, 14,* 141–148.

Kuhl, J. (1983a). Emotion, Kognition und Motivation: II. Die funktionale Bedeutung der Emotionen für das problemlösende Denken und für das konkrete Handeln. *Sprache & Kognition, 4,* 228–253.

Kuhl, J. (1983b). *Motivation, Konflikt und Handlungskontrolle* (Motivation, conflict and action control). Heidelberg: Springer.

Kuhl, J. (1984). Volitional aspects of achievement motivation and learned helplessness: Toward a comprehensive theory of action-control. In B.A. Maher (Ed.), *Progress in Experimental Personality Research* (Vol. 13., pp. 99–171). New York: Academic Press.

Kuhl, J. (1985). Volitional mediators of cognitive-behavior consistency: Self-regulatory processes and actions versus state orientation. In: J. Kuhl & J. Beckmann (Eds.), *Action control: From cognition to behavior.* (pp. 101–128). Heidelberg, New York: Springer.

Kuhl, J. (1994a). Action versus state orientation: Psychometric properties of the Action-Contol-Scale (ACS-90). In J. Kuhl & J. Beckmann (Eds.), *Action control: From cognition to behavior.* Göttingen/Toronto: Hogrefe.

Kuhl, J. (1994b). Motivation and Volition. In G. d'Ydevalle, Bertelson & Eelen (Eds.), *International perspectives on psychological science* (Vol. 2); (pp. 311–340). Hillsdale, NJ: Lawrence Erlbaum Associates.

Kuhl, J. (1997). *Personality and volition: Centrally organized patterns of affect-cognition interactions.* Manuscript. University of Osnabrück.

Kuhl, J., Baumann, N., Fuhrmann, A., & Kazén, M. (1995). Messung und Analyse von Selbstdiskriminationsdefiziten [Assessment and analysis of self-discrimination deficits]. Unpublished research report. University of Osnabrück.

Kuhl, J., & Beckmann, J. (1983). Handlungskontrolle und Umfang der Informationsverarbeitung: Wahl einer vereinfachten (nicht-optimalen) Entscheidungsregel zugunsten rascher Handlungsbereitschaft. *Zeitschrift für Sozialpsychologie, 2,* 1–27.

Kuhl, J., & Beckmann, J. (1994a). *Volition and personality: Action versus state orientation.* Göttingen/Seattle: Hogrefe.

Kuhl, J., & Beckmann, J. (1994b). Alienation: Ignoring one's preferences. In J. Kuhl & J. Beckmann (Eds.), *Volition and personality: Action versus state orientation* (pp. 375–390). Göttingen/Seattle: Hogrefe.

Kuhl, J. & Fuhrmann, A. (in press). Decomposing self-regulation and self-control: The volitional components checklist. In J. Heckhausen & C. Dweck (Eds.), *Life span perspectives on motivation and control.* Mahwah, NJ: Lawrence Erlbaum Associates.

Kuhl, J. & Goschke, T. (1994a). A theory of action control: Mental subsystems, modes of control, and volitional conflict-resolution strategies. In J. Kuhl & J. Beckmann (Eds.), *Volition and personality: Action versus state orientation* (pp. 93–124). Göttingen/Seattle: Hogrefe.

Kuhl, J., & Goschke, T. (1994b). State orientation and the activation and retrieval of intentions in memory. In J. Kuhl & J. Beckmann (Eds.), *Volition and personality: Action versus state orientation* (pp. 93–124). Göttingen/Seattle: Hogrefe.

Kuhl, J., & Helle, P. (1986). Motivational and volitional determinants of depression: The degenerated-intention hypothesis. *Journal of Abnormal Psychology, 95,* 247–251.

Kuhl, J., & Kazén, M. (1994a). Self-discrimination and memory: State orientation and false self-ascription of assigned activities. *Journal of Personality and Social Psychology, 66,* 1103–1115.

Kuhl, J., & Kazén, M. (1994b). Volitional aspects of depression: State orientation and self-discrimination. In J. Kuhl & J. Beckmann Eds.), *Volition and personality: Action versus state orientation* (pp. 297–315). Göttingen/Seattle: Hogrefe.

Kuhl, J., Schapkin, S. & Gusew, A. (1994). *A theory of volitional inhibition and an empirical test: Individual differences in the topography of ERP patterns for action- versus state-oriented processing of emotional words.* Manuscript. University of Osnabrück.

Kuhl, J. & Weiss, M. (1994). Performance deficits following uncontrollable failure: Impaired action control or global attributions and generalized expectancy deficits? In J. Kuhl & J. Beckmann (Eds.), *Volition and personality: Action versus state orientation* (pp. 317–328). Göttingen/Seattle: Hogrefe.

Lewinsohn, P. M., Steinmetz, J. L., Larson, D. W. & Franklin, J. (1981). Depression-related cognitions: Antecedent or consequence? *Journal of Abnormal Psychology, 90,* 213–219.

Luria, A. R. (1973). *The working brain.* New York: Penguin.

Martin, L. L. & Tesser, A. (1989). Toward a motivational and structural theory of ruminative thought. In J. S. Uleman & J. A. Bargh (Eds.), *Unintended thought* (pp.306–326). New York: Guilford.

Martin, L. L. & Stoner, P. (1996). Mood as Input: What we think about how we feel determines how we think. In L. L. Martin & A. Tesser (Eds.), *Striving and feeling: Interactions among goals, affect, and self-regulation* (pp. 279-301). Mahwah, NJ: Lawrence Erlbaum Associates.

Menec, V. H. (1995). *Volition and motivation: The effect of distracting learning conditions on students differing in action control and perceived control.* Dissertation. University of Manitoba.

Mischel, H. N. & Mischel, W. (1983). The development of children´s knowledge of self-control strategies. *Child Development, 54,* 603–619.

Nakagawa, A. (1991). Role of anterior and posterior attention networks in hemisphere asymmetries during lexical decisions. *Journal of Cognitive Neuroscience, 3,* 313–321.

Norman, D. A., & Shallice, T. (1986). Attention to action: willed and automatic control of behavior. In R. J. Davidson, G. E. Schwartz & D. Shapiro (Eds.), *Consciousness and self-regulation: Advances in research* (Vol. 4, pp.1–18). New York: Plenum.

Paivio, A. (1983). The empirical case for dual coding. In H. Yuille (Ed.), *Imagery, memory, and cognition* (pp. 397–332). Hillsdale, NJ: Lawrence Erlbaum Associates.

Reber, A. S. (1993). *Implicit learning and tacit knowledge: An essay on the cognitive unconscious.* Oxford: Oxford University Press.

Rosahl, S. K., Tennigkeit, M., Kuhl, J., & Haschke, R. (1993). Handlungskontrolle und langsame Hirnpotentiale: Untersuchungen zum Einfluß subjektiv kritischer Wörter (Erste Ergebnisse). *Zeitschrift für Medizinische Psychologie, 2,* 1–8.

Roth, K. & Strang, H. (1994). Action versus state orientation and the control of tactical decisions in sports. In J. Kuhl & J. Beckmann (Eds.), *Volition and personality: Action versus state orientation* (pp. 467–474). Göttingen/Seattle: Hogrefe.

Salkovskis, P. M. (1989). Cognitive-behavioral factors and the persistence of intrusive thoughts in obsessive-compulsive disorders. *Behaviour Research and Therapy, 27,* 677–682.

Schwarz, N. (1990). Feelings as information: Informational and motivational functions of affective states. In R. M. Sorrentino & E. T. Higgins (Eds.), *Handbook of motivation and cognition: Foundations of social behavior* (Vol. 2, pp. 527–561). New York: Guilford Press.

Seligman, M. E. P. (1975). *Helplessness: On depression, development, and death.* San Francisco: Freeman.

Shallice, T. (1988). *From neuropsychology to mental structure.* Cambridge, MA: Cambridge University Press.

Shiffrin, R. M & Schneider, W. (1977). Controlled and automatic human information processing: II. Perceptual learning, automatic attending, and a general theory. *Psychological Review, 84,* 127–190.

Stiensmeier-Pelster, J. (1994). Choice of decision-making strategies and action versus state orientation. In J. Kuhl & J. Beckmann (Eds.), *Volition and personality: Action versus state orientation* (pp. 167–176). Göttingen/Seattle: Hogrefe.

Stuss, D. T., & Benson, D. F. (1984). Neuropsychological studies of the frontal lobes. *Psychological Bulletin, 95,* 3–28.

Stuss, D. T., Shallice, T., Alexander, M. P., & Picton, T. W. (1995). A multidisciplinary approach to anterior attentional functions. In J. Grafman, K. J. Holyoak & F. Boller (Eds.), *Annals of the New York Academy of Sciences, 769,* 191–211.

Wegner, D. M. (1994). Ironic processes of mental control. *Journal of Personality and Social Psychology, 101 (1),* 34–52.

Wittling, W. (1990). Psychophysiological correlates of human brain asymmetry: Blood pressure changes during lateralized presentation of an emotionally laden film. *Neuropsychologia, 28,* 457–470.

# 18

# The Concept of Control: A Key Concept in Understanding and Overcoming Barriers to Responsible Environmental Behavior[1]

*Ursula Peter*

*Ruth Kaufmann-Hayoz*

## INTRODUCTION

Control beliefs about environmental impacts of human action have been shown to be an important determinant of individuals' readiness to adopt responsible environmental behaviors. However, due to the specific character of environmental impacts as mostly unintended and indirect consequences of collective action, it is very difficult for individuals to develop strong and differentiated control beliefs in this domain. Therefore, although a majority of people express strong environmental concern, they often feel helpless regarding the effects of their personal behavior. In this chapter, the relevance of different aspects of control, as well as of development and change of control beliefs for environmental behavior, is examined.

## ENVIRONMENTAL ISSUES AND ACTION PROBLEMS

Changes in the natural environment of humans which are undesired or threatening and which are induced by human action are usually called "environmental issues." The anthropogenic emission of greenhouse gases, for example, such as $CO_2$ and methane enhance the natural greenhouse effect. This causes an increase of global mean temperatures, which may eventually have a number of effects on the climate and the biosphere. These direct and indirect consequences of human actions most often occur as unintended side effects of individual or collective action. The challenge for mankind consists in developing new ways of living and acting which are not associated with so many undesired environmental impacts. There is an increasing awareness among researchers in environmental sciences that—if science is to contribute substantially to the solution of environmental issues—the "human dimen-

[1]We thank our colleagues Susanne Bruppacher, Wolfgang Gessner, and Silvia Ulli-Beer for their critical reading of the manuscript and their most helpful comments.

sions" of these issues need to be studied much more intensively than has been the case up to now (Kaufmann-Hayoz & Di Giulio 1996; Kaufmann-Hayoz 1997; Jochimsen 1996; CASS/Proclim, 1997; WBGU, 1996). This means that the social sciences and humanities such as psychology, economics, political sciences, or history, which traditionally have been studying various aspects of individual, collective, and societal human acting, should get involved in environmental research and especially in research on sustainable development.

From the point of view of psychology which focusses on individual behavior and actions, an important question to be asked is the following: *Why is it so difficult to arrive at effective changes of individual environmentally relevant behavior?* In a research project that was part of the multidisciplinary Swiss Priority Program "Environment,"[2] it has been stated that *essential preconditions for adequate goal-directed behavior and behavior change are typically missing in environmentally relevant situations of acting* (Gessner & Kaufmann-Hayoz, 1995; Kaufmann-Hayoz, 1996; Kaufmann-Hayoz et al., 1996). In this view the missing preconditions constitute the major *action problems*, or *barriers to environmentally responsible behavior*, which are to be analyzed. They inhibit behavior changes and thus lead to the retention of environmentally destructive ways of acting. Although the analysis focusses on individual behavior, it would be simplistic to consider people as completely independent individuals and to look for the key to the solution of environmental problems in the psychological domain only (Stern, 1995). Obviously, social relations, power structures, economic constraints and incentives, physical and organizational characteristics of infrastructures, and legal norms, constrain individual behavior. Interacting with psychological determinants in a strict sense, these frame conditions may function as barriers to behavior change in response to the recognition of environmental issues (Gessner, 1996).

Twelve classes of action problems, or "barriers," have been defined. Some of them refer to psychological factors such as specific aspects of perception, motivation, or information processing in the context of environmental issues; whereas others refer to societal factors that contribute in important ways to the frame conditions of individual environmental action. The twelve classes of problems are the following (see Gessner & Kaufmann-Hayoz 1995; Flury 1997):

1. Problems related to *norms and values* (e.g., lack of accepted and socially shared norms and values with respect to the environment);
2. Problems related to *emotional control and motivation* (e.g., unstable motives and resistance to change);
3. Problems related to *perception* (e.g., insufficient ability to perceive environmental change);
4. Problems related to *cognitive processes* (e.g., inadequate processing of information about environmental changes and their causes);

[2]"Intervention models for the development of responsible environmental behavior," project no. 5001-35276 of the Swiss National Science Foundation.

5. Problems related to *complex, dynamic systems* (e.g., insufficient ability to deal with non-linear relations);
6. Problems related to the *control of action* (e.g., inadequate control beliefs);
7. Problems related to *aggregation and collectivity* (e.g., social dilemmata);
8. Problems related to socio-cultural structures of *knowledge production and reproduction* (e.g., absence of coherent environmental education);
9. Problems related to *social and economic policies* (e.g., externalization of environmental costs);
10. Problems related to *technical infrastructures and instrumental arrangements* (e.g., spatial separation of places for different daily activities);
11. Problems related to *legal norms and enforcement* (e.g., inadequate regulations concerning high risk technologies);
12. Problems related to *political decision making and administrative frame-work* (e.g., inadequate coping with slow changes and long-term impacts).

In this chapter we analyze some of the problems related to the *control of action.* We review several well-studied aspects of control and control beliefs and examine their relevance and significance for the problem of responsible environmental behavior. We do this mostly by giving examples from everyday life. The empirical testing of the hypotheses that can be derived from this analysis has yet to be done. However, Jaeggi et al. (1996; also Tanner, in press, 1998) have shown that control beliefs with respect to the environmental impacts of personal behavior have an indirect effect on responsible environmental behavior: In combination with a general awareness of environmental issues, they are important determinants of a sense of commitment and personal responsibility, which seems to be a major psychological precondition for responsible environmental acting.

## THE SIGNIFICANCE OF CONTROL BELIEFS FOR RESPONSIBLE ENVIRONMENTAL BEHAVIOR

### Domain Specificity Of Control Beliefs

Personal control is domain-specific, it can be learned, and it is tied to concrete actions (Flammer, 1990, p.22).[3] Individuals have varying amounts of experience in different life domains, so that they have specific control beliefs only in some domains but not in others. Flammer et al. (1987) found control beliefs of Swiss adolescents to be quite different in different life domains. Control beliefs are not necessarily developed in all life domains, but they exist at least in those domains in which one gains considerable experience (Flammer, 1995b). Children develop subtly differentiated beliefs about their level of achievement in different subjects in school. Through extensive experience they learn what they can achieve: by their grades, and by their

---

[3] Many of the basic ideas and findings on control are cited from Flammer 1990. We indicate the pages where the concepts are discussed and further literature is mentioned.

teachers' remarks they get detailed feedback on their achievement. In this way, children develop precise control beliefs on their personal achievement at school.

For the domains of school (having personal influence on the curriculum) and of environmental issues it was found that the majority of adolescents was convinced to have little personal control (Flammer, 1996). Since domain-specific experience is probably the most important precondition for the development of control beliefs (Flammer 1995b), this is not surprising, since there are very little opportunities to gain knowledge about one's environmental "competences." Most of the time there is no feedback or very indirect and delayed feedback on positive as well as negative environmental impacts of personal actions. This is especially true for new or alternative types of environmentally more responsible behaviors.

If one has no specific control belief about a new behavior, one can transfer control beliefs about similar situations to the new situation. But sometimes people cannot think of similar experiences or they do not recognize them as being relevant (Flammer, 1990, p. 261). Social learning theory assumes that generalized expectan-cies are transferred to situations with a similar structure (Krampen, 1989). Such generalization is most probable in clear and assessable situations. In new, ambiguous situations which are hard to grasp, it is often difficult to find similarities with anything familiar. This is often the case in the domain of environmentally relevant behavior, because many situations seem to be ambiguous: If even experts do not agree whether or not collecting waste aluminum in private households for recycling makes sense, should I collect used aluminium foil at home, or not?

Generalizing across different situations may be just about as complex as generalizing across different cultures: If you emigrate to a foreign country, you cannot necessarily transfer your experiences from home to a situation which seems similar in the new country. These difficulties are due to cultural differences: A certain behavior which was perfectly adequate at home may be quite inadequate in the new culture.

Remembering similar situations can spark off typical kinds of feelings. A presentiment of joy, sadness, or anger can be evoked by certain tasks (Flammer, 1990, p. 267). Such emotional conditions can have a crucial influence: If I know I will get angry in a certain situation, this will influence my decisions. Also, an individual may see certain elements in a situation which are not really there but are activated by remembering a similar situation (Flammer, 1990, p. 268). Thus, certain experiences may make one think that responsible environmental behavior generally takes extra time and energy. One might not check if this holds true for a specific behavior: Travelling by public transportation will not always cost me extra time and energy, although this is a responsible environmental behavior. Also, if I do not try, I cannot make the experience that commuting by train with good connecting schedules may be much more relaxing and less dangerous than travelling by car.

## Development And Change Of Control Beliefs

Personal experience is the most important source of information for the development and change of control beliefs (Flammer, 1990, p. 219). The more personal experience one has in a specific life domain, the more subtly differentiated the corresponding control belief will be. For example, if I often travel by bicycle, I will know better and better, with growing experience, how much time I will need, how hard it will be, if I enjoy it, etc. I will develop a precise notion of when I want to use my bicycle, and when I do not.

In studies on control beliefs, subjects were asked why they believed to be able or unable to reach certain goals. Besides personal characteristics, they said that experience counts most. Subjects were more certain of control beliefs in domains where they had gained concrete experience (Flammer, 1995b). However, in the domain of new, responsible environmental behaviors, people lack personal experience. We assume that control beliefs are absent or not adequately differentiated in this domain. Thus a crucial prerequisite for choosing responsible environmental behavior is missing.

The more subjectively important a certain domain of action is, the more influence personal experience has on control beliefs (Flammer, 1990, p. 219). People want to have control especially in those domains which are important to them. In subjectively unimportant domains, individuals probably don't strive for personal control. For example, if eating organically grown food isn't important to me, I will hardly worry about the kind of food I buy. I will not try to control having a good supply of organic food products. Individuals who don't consider environmental issues as being important will not try out new, environmentally more responsible, behaviors. They will not try to have as much control as possible in this domain.

Besides personal experience, assumptions about causality are also essential for the development of control beliefs. It is assumed that causal attributions are permanently—but unconciously—made and that they play an important role for understanding the world, for emotional reactions to events and for planning actions (Krampen, 1989). Assumptions about causality can be a stimulus for deciding to do something or not to do it (Flammer, 1990, p. 31). If I don't assume that exaust gas contributes to global warming, I will not see any reason to refrain from driving my car. With respect to most environmental changes, causes are not visible or otherwise perceivable. I cannot *see* with my own eyes if exaust gas is a cause of global warming, so I must make an assumption. If I hear the statement that exaust gas is one of the main causes of global warming, then I must *assume* whether it is true or false.

Correct assumptions about causality are optimal for planning actions. But what happens if wrong assumptions are made? So-called *attribution errors* are a well-known field of research. The following are specific tendencies which distort assumptions about causality.

*Attribution Styles.* Many people tend to explain different types of events in a similar way (Flammer, 1990, p. 74). They make similar assumptions about different events regarding their personal control: That they have personal control or not (internality), that it will stay that way or change (stability), and that it applies to one or to several life domains (globality). If I assume that I have little or no influence on the local supply of organic food products, I may make the same assumption with respect to air pollution, without further examining the issue. This means that I would not be able to perceive my own potential influence in some other domains.

***Restriction Principle.*** Attributions are generally made as economically as possible. If there is a satisfying explanation for an event (which may be too simple, or even false), there is no need to search for further explanations (Flammer, 1990, p. 223). If I assume that global warming is a strictly natural phenomenon, I will not consider the fact that exaust gas from my car will also contribute to global warming.

***Proportionality Principle.*** It is often assumed that cause and effect are proportional: Strong effects are presumed to have strong causes. But with respect to environmental changes, small causes can have far-reaching effects (Flammer, 1990, p. 47): The decimation of a *tiny* insect which is a pest for food crops, can have *great* consequences for the ecosystem because one of the elements is removed and the natural balance is disturbed.

***Fundamental Attribution Error.*** One often attributes one's own actions to the situation, but the actions of others to their person (Flammer, 1990, p. 51): If *I* use my car to quickly buy food just before the store closes, I tell myself that I'm in a hurry. If *my neighbor* does the same thing, I assume they are too lazy to use their bicycle.

In summary, we can say that several conditions must be fulfilled in order to develop subtly differentiated control beliefs in a specific life domain:

- a sufficient amount of concrete and personal experience must be gained;
- the particular life domain must be important to the person;
- one must be willing to change one's opinion through new experiences;
- one must make correct causal attributions.

Consequently, if control beliefs are to be developed in the environmental domain, the following demands must be made:

- more opportunities for gaining personal experience in responsible environmental behavior must be made available;
- responsible environmental behavior must become subjectively important to individuals;
- opportunities for gaining new experiences must be made attractive;
- correct (causal) information about environmental issues must be communicated in an effective way.

## High Levels Of Control Beliefs

Control is not simply either internal or external. It is therefore important to find out *how much* control people think they have in general and in particular life domains.

We are interested in the significance of high or low levels of control beliefs for responsible environmental behavior.

Several traditionally important values in our western culture are clearly tied to control beliefs. For example, the biblical imperative to subjugate the earth is pushed so far today that the very existence of life on earth is endangered (Flammer, 1995a)[4]. In our culture, control is highly valued and seems indispensable for a happy life. Practically undisputable fundamental values such as autonomy, individual emancipation, responsibility, or working and achievement ethics require a feeling of strong personal control (Flammer 1995c). Having little personal control is associated with giving in, giving up, or making compromises and hardly seems desirable in our culture.

A cultural comparison of Germany and Japan shows differences in the way children are brought up and in the significance of control (Flammer, 1990, p. 159). In Germany, individualism is highly valued in education. Children are brought up to be independent and assertive individuals, which requires strong personal control. In Japan, group orientation has priority. Mothers bring their children up to be good members of society and to be resilient. Individuals can only be harmoniously integrated into a group if they are willing to share or delegate control in certain cases.

Therefore, the significance of personal control seems to be culture-specific. In our western culture, a high level of personal control is desirable. What are the implications of strong personal control for individual behavior, specifically for responsible environmental behavior? Based on specific findings, we make the following presumptions:

- Because having strong personal control is so important in our culture, it is not astonishing that people want to acquire as much control as their neighbors (Flammer, 1990, p. 168). This can be a reason for excessive consumption: Some goods are not purchased because they are necessary, but for other reasons, e.g., just to show that one can afford as much as everybody else (Lange, 1997). This can unduly strain natural resources.
- Compared to depressive subjects, non-depressive subjects were found to overestimate their level of personal control. This seems to be a healthy form of optimism (Flammer, 1990, p. 99). Most people believe that their situation will improve in the future, that it will improve more than other people's situation, and that undesirable events will affect themselves less than other people (Flammer, 1995b). Such control illusions could mislead people to believe that an ecologically harmful situation will not affect them personally or that it will

---

[4] However, some authors state that this biblical imperative has been misinterpreted. Modern theological research has found that in the context of the Hebrew language of that time, the imperative means to be responsible, and to take care of creation rather than dominate it (Klopfenstein, 1996; Link, 1991). Also, Gardner & Stern (1996) report inconsistent results about the relationship between Judeo-Christian affiliation, belief in the literal truth of the Bible, and environmental concern.

improve by itself, without them having to make a personal effort. This would lead to passive behavior without perceiving the necessity of a personal contribution in favor of the environment.

- Grob (1991) found that levels of control beliefs in various domains were negatively correlated with responsible environmental behavior. The hypothesis that people with a generally high level of control beliefs will engage in more responsible environmental behavior could not be confirmed. If we overestimate our personal control, we may take risks for which we cannot take responsibility (Flammer, 1990, p. 141). People with a high level of control beliefs are willing to take more and higher risks which can have long-term consequences (Flammer, 1995b). This could lead to careless environmental behavior. Obviously, a generally high level of control beliefs is not sufficient for choosing responsible environmental behavior. Presumably, corresponding environmental values are also required.

- Optimism combined with environmental values can lead to more *collective* responsible environmental behavior. Individuals will not so easily be discouraged because their *individual* effort leads to very small effects. A study by Market Street Research (1995) showed that successful promoters of the GAP Program were enthusiastic and not easily discouraged by failure. They were convinced they could win new members for GAP teams.

## Low Levels Of Control Beliefs, Missing Or Restricted Control

Personal control can be *restricted* in different ways. Other people, institutions, authorities, society, politics or laws of nature can have a share in control (Flammer et al., 1987). In many domains of everyday life, individuals experience a loss of control in our bureaucratized society. Smaller and assessable fields of life seem desirable (Flammer, 1990, p. 169). If I intend to introduce recycling bins in my neighborhood, I will be more likely to succeed if I know exactly where to get information in my community than if I am sent from one office to the other.

Under favorable circumstances, individuals can attain more control (Lüthi et al., 1989). The division of labor leads to a low level of personal control at work. Many people try to attain more personal control by planting their own vegetables, sewing their own clothes, etc.

In many domains, it is not possible to have exclusive personal control. Individuals *share* control with others (Flammer, 1990, p. 83). This is typically the case with most environmental changes: I cannot exclusively control the amount of CFC that is emitted into the atmosphere. I can decide not to use any products containing these substances, but this will only have a minimal effect unless everybody else does so, too.

In the case of mutually shared control, a goal can be reached only if the entire group strives for it. This is especially problematic concerning responsible environmental behavior (commons dilemma, free-rider problem; see Frey & Bohnet, 1996; Ostrom, 1990; Keohane & Ostrom, 1995). Only if every individual has a feeling of belonging to a group which strives for common environmental goals, the group will be able to attain the desired control. In this respect, cultural comparisons can yield useful information. In cultures where integration of individuals into the group is more important than individualism and independence (e.g., in Japan), common group goals might be more easily reached. Today's western culture, in which individualism, independence and the ability to assert oneself are fundamental values, could learn from traditional or eastern cultures. In group-oriented cultures, there may be better conditions for mutually taking responsibility than in individual-oriented cultures.

For challenges which can only be met in a joint effort, it is extremely important how people perceive the role of others (Flammer, 1990, p. 267). People who repeatedly experience that others make no effort to achieve a common goal will start thinking that their own effort is futile: If I use water very sparingly in my household but I constantly notice that other families waste fresh water, I can easily come to the conclusion that my personal effort to save water is pointless. In such situations, a change towards successful common control is more likely if one has personal contact with the others who are also in control. Discussing something with friends is easier than contacting an anonymous institution (Lüthi et al., 1989): I would probably rather try to convince my friends not to waste water than go to the waterworks and suggest they run a campaign for saving water. On the other hand, going to the waterworks would probably have a greater effect, and a study by Market Street Research (1995), found that some people would rather choose such a strategy than participate in an EcoTeam Program, where individual participants are exposed to social control by other team members.

Having a free choice is highly valued, it is generally preferred to forced choice. How do people react when they feel restricted in their control? Flammer (1990, p. 154) mentions four possible ways of reacting:

- Reactance: investing more energy or extraordinary means to assert personal control;
- Indirect control: trying to reach a goal through others who have control;
- Secondary control: if it's impossible to change a situation according to their own needs, people try to change themselves or their demands in order to be satisfied with the situation;
- Renounced control / loss of control: the individual gives up personal efforts to exert control and feels helpless.

If attempts at attaining control are unsuccessful, people's first reaction is reactance or trying to attain indirect control. If these strategies are not successful and further attempts at attaining personal control seem hopeless, then secondary control becomes relevant. Only if this fails, too, loss of control or renounced control is admitted (Flammer, 1990, p. 154).

*Reactance in the Domain of Responsible Environmental Behavior.*
Reactance in the domain of responsible environmental behavior is mainly to be expected when personal freedom is restricted by new regulations and laws. New laws
which protect the environment but limit people's free choice of action, are not readily
accepted by everyone. Reactance can be expressed by different forms of behavior.
For example, objects or activities can become more attractive when free access to
them is limited (Flammer, 1990, p. 128). If people learn that cars with twelve-
cylinder motors will no longer be permitted next year, then some customers will
decide to buy such a car before the deadline. Some of them had originally intended to
buy a new car later on, or to buy a car of a lower class.

If personal freedom is just restricted but not totally limited, people have the tendency to choose exactly those alternatives which are endangered. By concentration
and extra effort, they try to reach the obstructed goal. If a popular seminar at the
university is only offered to a limited number of students, possibly even more students will sign up for it. If a particular type of action is actually obstructed, people
like to find a symbolic alternative in order to feel they still have a free choice (Flammer, 1990, p. 128). If water-skiing was no longer permitted on Swiss lakes, some of
the people might start flying gliders, parachuting, or riding motorcycles as an alternative. Limiting freedom can also lead to aggression (Flammer, 1990, p. 128). If an
area which has been a hangout for adolescents for a long time is suddenly barricaded
by a fence, they often react with aggression and destroy the obstacle.

People are more likely to show reactance if they expect to have a free choice in a
particular situation and their freedom is unexpectedly limited (Flammer, 1990, p.
129). In our democratic society, the great importance of having as much personal
freedom as possible makes the enforcement of regulations which call for restrictions
for the good of the environment difficult. Concluding from the examples stated
above, it is clear that it's not at all easy to work out new environmental regulations
without evoking reactance in the public. It would probably be easier to introduce
restrictions on a step by step basis and then gradually become more restrictive than to
suddenly introduce severe restrictions. Restrictions are more likely to be accepted if
citizens are prepared for them and they are not confronted with such situations too
suddenly and unexpectedly.

*Indirect Control in the Domain of Responsible Environmental Be-
havior.* Instead of showing reactance, people can also try to exert indirect control if
personal control is restricted. Maybe they know somebody who can reach a certain
goal for them. A child who wants to make a personal contribution to the recycling of
waste paper could ask her teacher to talk about the subject in class. In this way, she
could indirectly exert influence through her teacher, so that the entire class would
learn about the issue and participate in the project. In politics, groups with specific
interests can increase their influence by lobbying.

With the means of indirect control, more potential types of action can be carried
out than alone. With the help of the right partners, one can achieve many things
which one would not be capable of doing alone. We think it is important to make

people aware that they are capable of many responsible environmental actions if they cooperate with others. Using social networks could possibly allow a surprising amount of new options for responsible environmental behavior. People are more likely to take their own initiative if they learn of the potential success of group actions, for example by news about successful groups. In fact, Diekmann & Franzen (1996), have shown that living in integrated social networks, e.g., neighborhood networks, is positively related to environmental behavior. Also, Fuhrer et al. (1995), found that such information was most effective when communicated face to face, which shows the importance of personal contact.

*Secondary Control in the Domain of Responsible Environmental Behavior.* If an obstructed goal cannot be reached by reactance or indirect control, then secondary control becomes relevant. Individuals must constantly try to adapt to the environment in a satisfying way. If problems are perceived to be unsolvable, it is important to change oneself or one's demands in order to be able to accept the situation. This can lead to passive, cautious, or submissive behavior (Flammer, 1990, p. 148). Doing nothing, contemplative thinking, detachment, indifference, or thinking of worse situations are typical behaviors.

Secondary control can be expressed in diverse ways. For instance, being disappointed by not having personal control can be avoided by not having high expectations. Individuals who fear personal failure and are low on self-confidence often choose this strategy. They don't allow themselves any hopes which could lead to disappointment (Flammer, 1990, p. 145).

If one knows that one has no control, one can still nourish the illusion of control. Many people think luck is on their side. Also, predictability could lead to control illusions. Subjects felt electric shocks were less stressful if they were announced in advance, even though they could not be avoided (Flammer, 1990, p. 108). If I know about specific risks of some action for the environment or if I can predict them, I will probably perceive them as being less harmful.

Personal demands can be reinterpreted so that they are fulfilled by the situation (Flammer 1990, p.145). If I live in an appartment which does not correspond to my ideals at all, I can lower my demands so that I am still satisfied. With respect to environmental issues, such reinterpretations can be dangerous: If people who are exposed to loud noise, polluted air, etc., lower their demands for a healthy environment, they are less likely to stand up for their rights. Maybe this view offers an interpretation of the findings by Diekmann & Franzen (1996): Although people in the French- and Italian-speaking parts of Switzerland generally feel *more personally affected* by environmental changes, they express *less environmetal concern and action* than people in the German-speaking areas.

*Renounced Control / Loss of Control in the Domain of Responsible Environmental Behavior.* Helplessness is the belief that one's own behavior has no influence on subsequent events. People who permanently fail in their attempts at gaining control experience helplessness (Seligman, 1975). If I intend to change my diet to strictly organic food, I will feel helpless if I find out that there is no sufficient supply available after I have visited every store in the area.

According to Seligman (1975), the state of helplessness has cognitive, emotional, and motivational consequences:

- **Cognitive consequences:** the experience of helplessness can hinder people from perceiving remaining or new possibilities of control.
- **Emotional consequences:** the belief that an unpleasant event is uncontrollable can lead to fear, resignation or even to depression.
- **Motivational consequences:** people who feel helpless usually do not think it is worth trying to change the situation. In such a passive state, new experiences can hardly be made. New experience of personal control becomes very unlikely.

These consequences clearly make it difficult for people to change their state of helplessness and to begin striving for more control. In order to participate more in responsible environmental behavior, renounced or lost control must be restored to individuals. Then, they might have the courage to become more active and to use their full potential for the benefit of the environment. This could be promoted by making people familiar with the following points:

1. A lack of personal control is not simply due to *myself*; certain types of *situations* typically lead to the feeling of helplessness. Knowing this, individuals will more likely consider it possible to attain stronger personal control.
2. In situations in which I have little influence alone, *cooperation* with others can lead to success. A group of people sharing the same goal can successfully exert mutually shared control.
3. I can increase my own influence on environmental issues if I participate in *group actions*. There are many examples of successful environmental group actions, which should be communicated to a larger community.
4. Successful group actions concerning responsible environmental behavior can lead to more self-confidence and courage for individuals and to the empowerment of groups. On this basis, more individual and group *commitment* for the benefit of the environment can arise.

## CONCLUSION

Nozick (1993) has proposed that the description of a well-defined intellectual problem should consist of five elements: description of the goal, description of the initial state, description of the admissible operations, description of constraints, and description of the outcome as final state. Action problems may be described by using a similar, slightly adapted schema consisting of eight elements (Gessner & Kaufmann, 1995). An action problem is defined by identifying a discrepancy between an undesired actual state and a desired goal, with respect to essential preconditions for individual behavior change towards environmentally more responsible behavior. The problem of restricted and shared control and of undifferentiated or inadequate control beliefs in the environmental domain may be described—as a way of summing up the above analysis—in the following way:

## Goal
Subtly differentiated control beliefs are developed in the domain of responsible environmental behavior. Individuals know which types of responsible environmental behavior they are able to perform, and what their effects are, they think of suitable behaviors in relevant situations and decide to carry them out. Individuals attain strong personal control which they deliberately exert to the benefit of the environment, based on environment-friendly attitudes.

## Actual state
*Mutually shared control:* Concerning environmental actions, individuals typically share control with others. In such situations, cooperation with others is necessary to be able to reach a common goal.

*Restricted control:* Many decisions that have far-reaching environmental consequences (e.g., in energy production and in the economic domain), are beyond the influence of individuals.

*Lack of differentiated control beliefs:* For many responsible environmental behaviors, people lack differentiated control beliefs, because they lack sufficient personal experience. Therefore, they have no precise notion about whether or not they will be able to perform specific behaviors, and what the environmental (and other) effects of different behaviors are.

*Ambiguous situations:* Inconsistent information on specific issues makes the development of differentiated control beliefs more difficult.

*Subjective importance:* If responsible environmental behavior is not relevant to individuals, they will not strive for strong control in this domain.

*False causal attributions:* Wrong assumptions on the causality of environmental problems can lead to incorrect ideas about possible solutions.

## Resources for solutions
In order to develop differentiated control beliefs, there should be more opportunities for gaining personal experience in responsible environmental behavior. Personal competences and strong confidence in personal control should be developed. Smaller, assessable life domains are desirable so that a greater amount of control is available to each individual. Common answers must be found for environmental issues, so that people cooperate and use their mutually shared control in favor of the environment. Correct information is necessary to be able to decide if technical solutions are adequate to solve a particular problem or if changes in behavior are needed. Some goals which would be inaccessible alone can be reached through indirect control by addressing the right partners.

## Transformation potentials

*Education:* The development of differentiated control beliefs in the domain of responsible environmental behavior can be fostered by specific action- oriented continuing education in families, at school, at work, by media campaigns or advertisements, in clubs, etc.

*Feedback:* Direct and clear feedback on individual consumption that is easy to interprete. For example, in appartment buildings, heating bills should be calculated on the basis of individual consumption.

*More personal control:* By participation in community affairs, a larger number of people can share control. Renounced or lost control can be restored to many individuals.

*Intermediate goals:* Breaking down complex goals for solving environmental problems into several partial goals makes them more easily accessible. Every successful step can strengthen personal control beliefs.

*Generalization of control beliefs:* The experience of being successful in a certain type of environmental action can lead to the expectation of personal control for other new environmental actions, too.

## Constraints

*More personal control:* Increasing personal control is difficult or sometimes impossible in complex modern societies with a high level of division of labor.

*Feedback:* In certain domains, only long-term feedback is possible. Without feedback, the development of differentiated control beliefs is more difficult.

*Common goals:* Personal interests (e.g., short-term profit, laziness, conserving present power or privileges) hinder commitment to common goals, so that mutually shared control is not readily employed for the good of the environment.

*False causal attributions:* False information on the causes of environmental problems or a lack of concensus among experts can make it difficult to orient oneself and form differentiated control beliefs.

## Outcome

In the domain of responsible environmental behavior, people develop subtly differentiated control beliefs which they employ for the benefit of the environment. Protecting the environment is a fundamental value which leads individuals to decisions in favor of the natural environment. It is a matter of course to consider negative consequences for the environment and to avoid them. Individuals are aware of their full potential of responsible environmental behavior, and such behaviors are regularly carried out.

## Side effects

*Helplessness and reactance:* Individuals stop feeling helpless about environmental problems because they are convinced they have personal control and adequate forms of action. Instead of reactance, difficult situations will stimulate personal commitment and courage to overcome difficulties.

*Relationship with nature:* Being occupied with responsible environmental behavior and its consequences can lead to a better relationship of humans with nature.

*Responsibility:* Strengthening personal control and employing it for the good of the environment can lead to individuals taking on more responsibility and delegating less problems to others.

## Costs
Costs are expected for (continuing) education, media campaigns, advertisements, and for measures or devices for feedback at home and at work.

## REFERENCES

Bruppacher, S., & Peter, U. (1997). *Bedingungen und Restriktionen der Entwicklung von Umweltbewusstein und umweltverantwortlichem Handeln. Probleme der Wissens- und Wertvermittlung, insbesondere bei Kindern und Jugendlichen.* Lizentiatsarbeit. Bern: Institut für Psychologie.

CASS/Proclim. (1997): *Visionen der Forschenden. Forschung zu Nachhaltigkeit und Globalem Wandel—Wissenschaftspolitische Visionen der Schweizer Forschenden.* Bern: Konferenz der Schweizerischen Wissenschaftlichen Akademien und ProClim.

Diekmann, A., & Franzen, A. (1996). Einsicht in ökologische Zusammenhänge und Umweltverhalten. In Kaufmann-Hayoz, R. & Di Giulio, A. (Ed.): *Umweltproblem Mensch.* Bern: Haupt, 135–157.

Flammer, A. (1990). *Erfahrung der eigenen Wirksamkeit. Einführung in die Psychologie der Kontrollmeinung.* Bern: Huber.

Flammer, A., Grob, A., & Lüthi, R. (1987). *Kontrollattributionen bei Jugendlichen.* Forschungsbericht 1987-4. Universität Bern: Psychologisches Institut.

Flammer, A. (1995a). Possum, ergo sum—nequeo, ergo sum qui sum. In Oosterwegel, A. & Wicklund, R. (Eds.): *The self in European and North-American culture: Development and Processes* (pp. 333–349). Amsterdam: Klüwer.

Flammer, A. (1995b). Developmental analysis of control beliefs. In Bandura, A. (Ed.): *Self-efficacy in changing societies* (pp. 69–113). New York: Cambridge University Press.

Flammer, A. (1995c). Kontrolle, Sicherheit und Selbstwert in der menschlichen Entwicklung. In: Edelstein, W. (Hrsg.): *Entwicklungskrisen kompetent meistern* (pp. 35–42). Heidelberg: Asanger.

Flammer, A. (1996). Das kompetente Selbst und seine Entwicklung. *Vierteljahresschrift für Heilpädagogik und ihre Nachbarwissenschaften, 65,* 266–279.

Flury, M. (1997). *Preconditions for sustainable resource management.* Paper contributed to workshop PPE/Project Group CONTICI, July 8–9 in Berne, Switzerland.

Frey, B. S., & Bohnet, I. (1996). Tragik der Allmende. Einsicht, Perversion und Überwindung. In: Diekmann, A. & Jäger, C. C. (Ed.): *Umweltsoziologie. Kölner Zeitschrift für Soziologie und Sozialpsychologie, Sonderheft 36,* 292–306.

Fuhrer, U., Kaiser, F. G., Seiler, I., & Maggi, M. (1995). From social representations to environmental concern. The influence of face-to-face versus mediated communication. In Fuhrer, U. (Ed.): *Ökologisches Handeln als sozialer Prozess.* Basel: Birkhäuser, 61–76.

Gessner, W. (1996). Der lange Arm des Fortschritts. In Kaufmann-Hayoz, R. & Di Giulio, A. (Ed.): *Umweltproblem Mensch.* Bern: Haupt, 263–299.

Gessner, W., & Kaufmann-Hayoz, R. (1995). Die Kluft zwischen Wollen und Können. In Fuhrer, U. (Ed.): *Ökologisches Handeln als sozialer Prozess*. Basel: Birkhäuser, 11–25.

Grob, A. (1991). *Meinung, Verhalten, Umwelt. Ein psychologisches Ursachennetz-Modell umweltgerechten Verhaltens*. Bern: Lang.

Jaeggi, C., Tanner, C., Foppa, K., & Arnold, S. (1996). Was uns vom umweltverantwortlichen Handeln abhält. In Kaufmann-Hayoz, R. & Di Giulio, A. (Eds.): *Umweltproblem Mensch*. Bern: Haupt, 181–196.

Jochimsen, M. (1996). *Research and Monitoring of Climate and Global Change in Switzerland. Part III—Human Dimensions of Global Environmental Change*. Bern: ProClim.

Kaufmann-Hayoz, R. (1996). Förderung umweltverantwortlichen Handelns—Versuch einer Synthese. In Kaufmann-Hayoz, R. & Di Giulio, A. (Eds.): *Umweltproblem Mensch*. Bern: Haupt, 509–536.

Kaufmann-Hayoz, R. (Ed.) (1997). Proceedings des Symposiums "Umweltverantwort-liches Handeln" vom 4.–6./7.9.1996 in Bern. *Allgemeine Ökologie zur Diskussion gestellt, Nr. 3/1 bis 3/4*. Universität Bern: IKAÖ.

Kaufmann-Hayoz, R., & Di Giulio (Eds.) (1996). *Umweltproblem Mensch. Humanwissenschaftliche Zugänge zu umweltverantwortlichem Handeln*. Bern: Haupt.

Kaufmann-Hayoz, R., Häuselmann, C., & Gessner, W. (1996). 'Eco-Design'—die wahrnehmungspsychologische Erweiterung eines technischen Konzepts. In Lesch, W. (Ed.): *Naturbilder*. Basel: Birkhäuser, 71–93.

Keohane, R. O., & Ostrom, E. (1995). *Local commons and global interdependence. Heterogeneity and cooperation in two domains*. London: Sage.

Klopfenstein, M. (1997). *Der Mensch—das verantwortliche Geschöpf in der Schöpfungsgemeinschaft*. Der Bund, 26. 10., 1996. Bern.

Krampen, G. (1989). Diagnostik von Attributionen und Kontrollüberzeugungen. Theorien, Geschichte, Probleme. In Krampen, G. (Ed.): *Diagnostik von Attributionen und Kontrollüberzeugungen*. Göttingen: Hogrefe, 3–19.

Lange, E. (1997). *Konsumorientierungen und Umweltbewusstsein von Jugendlichen*. Vortrag am Symposium "Jugend und Umwelt" vom 15./16.9., 1997 in Bern, Schweiz.

Link, C. (1991). Schöpfung. Schöpfungstheologie angesichts der Herausforderungen des 20. Jahrhunderts. *Handbuch systematischer Theologie, Bd. 7/2*. Gütersloh: Gerd Mohn.

Lüthi, R., Grob, A., & Flammer, A. (1989). Differenzierte Erfassung bereichsspezifischer Kontollmeinungen bei Jugendlichen. In Krampen, G. (Ed.): *Diagnostik von Attributionen und Kontrollüberzeugungen*. Göttingen: Hogrefe, S. 134–145.

Market Street Research (1995). *Assessing the market potential of the household ecoteam program*. Northampton, MA: Market Street Research, Inc.

Nozick, R. (1993). *The nature of rationality*. Princeton: Princeton University Press.

Ostrom, E. (1990). *Governing the commons. The evolution of institutions for collective action. Political economy of institutions and decisions*. Cambridge, MA: Cambridge University Press.

Seligman, M. E. P. (1975). *Helplessness. On depression, development and death*. San Francisco: W. H. Freeman.

Stern, P. (1995). Understanding and changing environmentally destructive behavior. In Fuhrer, U. (Ed.): *Ökologisches Handeln als sozialer Prozess*. Basel: Birkhäuser, 89–96.

Tanner, C. (1997). *Constraints of environmental behavior*. Manuscript under review.

WBGU (1996). *Welt im Wandel. Herausforderung für die deutsche Wissenschaft. Jahresgutachten 1996 des Wissenschaftlichen Beirats der Bundesregierung, Globale Umweltveränderung*. Berlin: Springer.

# V

# Developmental Perspectives: Stability and Change

# 19

# Dynamics of Perceived Control Across Adolescence and Adulthood[1]

*Alexander Grob*

## INTRODUCTION

In this chapter, perceived control is conceptualized as the agentic representation that persons construct for themselves. Three questions were addressed. The first investigates to what extent perceived control is specific to particular domains, the second, how many dimensions are involved in perceived control, and the third deals with the dynamics between the components of perceived control and their effects on subjective well-being. These questions were investigated in three studies with a total sample size of more than 8,000 participants, including a longitudinal study across adolescence, a cross-sectional study across the life-span, and a cross-sectional study across 14 socio-cultural contexts. Hence we think that the conclusions drawn from this research on the dynamics of perceived control are generalizeable across both adolescence and adulthood as well as across socio-cultural contexts. We found that the various situations representing the participants' life context can be represented by three major domains, the personal, the interpersonal, and the societal domain. Confirmatory factor analyses revealed in each study a two-factor structure of perceived control. We called these two components control expectancy and control appraisal. These two components in both life domains showed stability across individual development, consistent mean-level changes across different age-cohorts, and they were important predictors of the participants' subjective well-being. Overall, these results foster theoretical evidence that perceived control is multidimensional and domain-specific, and that perceived control is an important predictor of psychosocial functioning. Before presenting the relevant results, we refer to a few more theoretical considerations about the dynamics of perceived control in human life.

[1]This manuscript was written while I stayed as guest researcher at the University of Illinois at Urbana/Champaign by a grant of the Swiss National Science Foundation (11-45780.95). I thank the colleagues who contributed to the research reported in this chapter, most prominently my mentor, August Flammer. Furthermore I thank Michael D. Robinson for his valuable editorial help.

The interest in the notion of agency has a long history in philosophy and religion (Fend, 1998). Its success as an empirical construct can be traced to Julian Rotter's publication in 1966 entitled "Generalized expectancies for internal versus external control of reinforcement." Rotter was interested in the extent to which people believe that they are able, through their actions, to obtain desired outcomes, particulary the extent to which they see control as located internally (they can exert much influence) or externally (they can exert only a little influence). Rotter's paper seized the imagination of psychologists, with a consequent outpouring of theoretical studies, empirical findings, and an ever widening variety of scales. As might be expected after more than three decades, a number of psychologists are taking stock, asking what has been learned, and what the next steps are (Bandura, 1997). A central proposition in this research tradition is that people strive to exercise control over the events that affect their lives (Flammer, 1990; Seligman, 1975; White, 1959), and so it is self-evident that a key question is the relative extent of this influence. By exerting influence over the flow of positively and negatively reinforcing events, people maximise their utility (Headey & Wearing, 1992).

Utility depends not only whether events are positive or negative in their consequences, but also on the *degree* to which such events influence people's lives. It is often assumed that the importance of an event for a person can be ignored, a view that implicitly assumes that the importance of an event or domain and its perceived controllability will not vary independently of one another.

An overview of previous work on perceived control has been provided by a number of writers (see among others Bandura, 1997; Flammer, 1995; Furnham & Steele, 1993; Rotter, 1990; Skinner, 1996; Strickland, 1989). In summary, these reviews identify two questions as fundamental: First, to what extent is perceived control general or specific to particular domains, and, second, is perceived control a one- ore two-factor construct. If latter is the case, control expectancy, i.e. whether an individual can make an event happen, and control appraisal, i.e., how important is the event to the individual, may be separable components.

Before looking at these issues in more detail, it is important to clarify the aspect of control that are discussed in this chapter. We investigate control belief or perceived control, i.e., the subjective agentic representation of, or belief about one's capability of exercising control (Flammer, 1990). In order to believe in one's own control or in one's own non-control, people must typically be aware of their own former successes or failures. Although most control beliefs are rooted in personal control experiences, some may also originate from other people's feedback. Still another (relatively rare) possibility stems from the observation of comparable others (Bandura, 1977; Flammer & Grob, 1994). However, there is no doubt that perceived control does not always exactly represent actual control, i.e. the level to which a person or a system regulates the process itself. Many studies have shown that people generally overestimate their control competencies (Alloy & Abramson, 1982; Langer, 1975; Taylor & Brown, 1988).

## THE SPECIFICITY VERSUS GENERALITY
## OF PERCEIVED CONTROL

Perceived control concerns people's perception of their control in particular situations. However, perceived control is a concept, usually defined, like intelligence, as dispositional both in terms of stability over time and relative generalizeability over domains (Nowicki & Strickland, 1973; Phares, 1976). In practice, though, locus of control has been treated more or less as domain specific, with only the number of domains and their extent being a matter for argument (Krampen, 1989).

The opposite view, that locus of control develops only as a result of experience, and depends on what particular experiences people have, would hold that locus of control is primarily situation specific, and reflects the acquisition of competence in these specific situations. This view, deriving from learning theory, allows the possibility of generalisation, but it implies that an analysis of control in a wide range of situations would yield a multi-factor rather than a few or one-factor solution (Mielke, 1982; Paulhus & Christie, 1981; Skinner, 1996).

The literature that speaks to this question concludes that at the very least, the number of persons involved in the control behavior context is important. The kind and possibility of effective control behavior varies as a function of this dimension (Flammer, Grob & Lüthi, 1989; Flammer, Züblin & Grob, 1988; Schneewind, 1995).

Therefore it is crucial to investigate perceived control in different life situations which—among other characteristics—differ in the number of persons possibly sharing control over the outcome of a specific event. It is apparent that the occurance of specific events differ tremendously with respect to the number of individual, social and physical conditions that are involved. For example, the number of people who collaborate for a clean environment, or the number of people who have to share control during a space mission, is enormous. However, each person's relative control in his or her domain is crucial for the success of the whole undertaking. Therefore each person contributes to a certain degree—even though it might be minimal—to the occurance of a particular event, and indeed has personal control. However, there are other events, for example writing scientific articles or doing playing sports, in which the amount of personal control is actually much greater. Hence, we assume that the level of personal control varies at least as a function of the number of persons contributing towards a specific outcome, the degree of required collaboration among these persons, and as a function of the physical conditions. We expect *a priori* three domains in which the levels of perceived control differ importantly. These domains are the *personal*, the *interpersonal*, and the *societal* domain.

## THE DIMENSIONALITY OF PERCEIVED CONTROL

In extending Rotter's (1966, 1990) single factor concept of locus of control, perceived control has been understood as a composite of contingency beliefs and competence beliefs (Flammer, 1990; Weisz & Stipek, 1982), or outcome expectancy and efficacy expectancy (Bandura 1977, 1986), or means-ends beliefs and agency beliefs (Chapman, Skinner & Baltes, 1990; Skinner, Chapman & Baltes, 1988). Both components together make up what we call *control expectancy*. The above mentioned frameworks share in common an emphasis on the cognitive component of perceived control. The relevance, however, of an action for the person has been largely neglected.

We think that it is worthwhile to consider in addition to the expectancy component the importance to the person of the domains in which perceived control can operate. This dimension has rarely been studied, although it seems evident that it is important. Not being in control of subjectively *important* events certainly affects one's life more than not being in control of subjectively *unimportant* events (Abramson, Seligman & Teasdale, 1978). The literature on hopelessness and on depression has shown that helplessness alone might not be psychically detrimental as long as one's stake is not vital (Barber & Winefeld, 1987; Miller & Norman, 1979).

Why then is the importance dimension so often ignored in research about the consequences of perceived control and non-control? There might be two reasons, one methodological and one substantial. The methodological reason has to do with the effort of most researchers to investigate control mechanisms only in areas that are self-evidently important, like proving to be intelligent, being a good problem-solver, making money, etc. Thus, if the importance variable is basically held constant there is nothing to be learned about this variable. The second reason has to do with the fact that perceived control is more or less correlated with the importance one attributes to the respective domain and the control expectancy in this domain. Subjective importance of control can be operationalized in several ways, e.g., by having the individual rates (a) the subjective importance of a given domain or events, or (b) the subjective importance of the relative personal control. Following Lazarus' (1966; Lazarus & Folkman, 1984) general framework, we use *control appraisal*, the second component of perceived control, as a general term to reflect the process of the assessment of importance.

## PERCEIVED CONTROL AND SUBJECTIVE WELL-BEING

Understanding humans as active and constructive beings, and believing that people are instrumental in their own development (Lerner, 1982) we think that actions themselves and their cognitive antecedents affect people's subjective well-being. In addition to the biological, economic, cultural, social and biographical conditions, we assume in line with many other theorists that especially cognitive-evaluative processes affect subjective well-being. This process is characterized by an overall calculation between demands and resources on individual, social, and societal levels. The purpose of this evaluative process is to better understand the actual situation, and its role in the co-determination of subjective well-being.

Most of the relevant stress literature focused on stress either under a behavioral-physiological perspective (Selye, 1982) or under a psycho-dynamic perspective (Freud, 1986; Haan, 1977). A far-reaching approach was proposed by Lazarus and his colleagues (1966; Lazarus & Launier, 1978; Lazarus & Folkman, 1984, 1987). Under this perspective, stress is defined in the person-environment transaction. Psychological stress occurs if a person perceives him- or herself in danger because the demands with which he or she is confronted overstep his or her coping capacities. Lazarus and his colleagues differentiate two processes: Cognitive appraisal, and coping behavior. Of major interest for our purpose are the concepts of primary and secondary appraisal. The first refers to the evaluation of an event as being challenging or threatening, and the second refers to, among other things, the evaluation of whether the stressor is perceived as controllable or not. Both processes affect directly and conjointly people's well-being. The fact that a person concludes that something important is at stake, and that this situation or event is personally controllable, leads a person to perceive the same situation as being more of a challenge than a threat. In addition, the person experiences less stress and a higher level of subjective well-being. In this example, the fact that one feels in control leads to a positive reappraisal of the situation.

These considerations concerning the person–enviornment–transaction are in accordance with many theories of well-being. Theories of subjective well-being span—by and large—two basic approaches: cognitive-oriented and affect-oriented. Cognitive-oriented theories generally maintain that deficits in meeting one's needs lead to ill-being and that positive discrepancies between perceived reality and personal aspirations lead to well-being (Brickman, Coates, & Janoff-Bulman, 1978; Duncan, 1975; Headey & Wearing, 1992; Michalos, 1985; Wills, 1981). From this viewpoint, people compare an actual situation with an intended, expected, or ideal situation. Accurate appraisals and positive discrepancies between actual and intended states are evaluated favorably, and lead to satisfaction (Cantril, 1965). Affect-oriented theories of well-being suggest that satisfaction is enhanced by short-term positive experiences or reducing aversive states (for overviews, see Diener, 1984, 1994). From this perspective, well-being reflects the feelings people experience during their everyday lives (Bradburn, 1969; Diener & Larson, 1993).

In our studies, we operationalized well-being as a positive attitude toward life, a generally positive sense of self-esteem, an enjoyment of life, and very low levels of depressed mood (Grob, 1995a; Grob, Lüthi, Kaiser, Flammer, Mackinnon & Wearing, 1991). Given that these aspects of well-being are influenced by cognitive- and affect-related processes (Diener, 1984), they are enhanced when numerous antecedents are successfully managed (Evans, 1994). Some of these antecedents include: (a) a stable historical, cultural, and social context (Bronfenbrenner, 1986); (b) accomplishing well-defined normative and age-specific developmental tasks (Havighurst, 1948); (c) accomplishing desired non-normative developmental tasks (Grob, 1991a); (d) having meaningful life goals and future perspectives (Brunstein, 1993; Emmons, 1992; Nurmi, 1992); and especially, (e) having the personal conviction that one is in control in important life domains (Bandura, 1997; Flammer, 1995; Seligman, 1975).

## EMPIRICAL EVIDENCE

In the following section we will show empirical evidence for the three general assumptions outlined in the previous section, i.e., that perceived control is best described by control expectancy and control appraisal, that perceived control operates in three domains, and that perceived control is an important predictor of subjective well-being. Since the studies to which we refer are already published, we only briefly report their methodology.

### Perceived Control: Control Expectancy and Control Apparaisal

*Adolescence.* In the *Berne longitudinal study on adolescence* (Flammer et al., 1989), 4,201 adolescents between 14 and 20 years of age completed questionnaires either once, twice, or three times with a two year time lag. The adolescents were drawn from the Swiss schooling and apprenticeship system and were assessed in class rooms during regular school hours; female and male adolescents were equally represented. Half of the participants lived in urban and suburban areas, and half in rural areas. Among other questionnaires, the adolescents were asked to fill out a questionnaire about perceived control ("Berne questionnaire on adolescents' perception of control;" Lüthi, Grob & Flammer, 1989). This questionnaire differentiates eleven aspects of control in nine situations. For the purpose of the ongoing argumentation, we included seven aspects of control per situation. The nine everyday situations represented three life domains, i.e., the personal, the interpersonal, and the societal. The personal domain comprised four situations. For example personal domain comprised four situations, i.e., personal appearance, future working place, personality development, and pocket money; the interpersonal domain was composed of two situations, namely conflict with parents and intimate friendship. Finally, the societal domain contained three situations, i.e., natural environment (demise of forests), subject matters, and local politics (initiation of a youth meeting place). Each situation contained a short description. For example "physical appearance" was described in the following terms: "You are standing in front of a mirror and are looking at yourself, your eyes, your face, your hair, your entire body. Perhaps, you think you are good-looking, perhaps you think you are not".

After the presentation of each of the situations the participants had to answer a series of questions concerning different aspects of control: (a) *present control belief I* ("Do you think that you can influence X"), (b) *present control belief II*

("Indicate to what extent you can influence X"), (c) *future control belief* ("Indicate to what extent you will be able to influence X in three to five years"), (d) *share of control* of different control instances ("Who or what has a share in the influence on X"), (e) *importance of control* ("How important is it to you to be able to influence X?"), (f) *striving for control* ("Do you try to get more influence over X?"), and (g) *importance of the situation* ("How important is X to you?").

To assess whether perceived control can be regarded as consisting of two components, confirmatory factor analyses were conducted with the same seven items in each of the nine situations using LISREL (Jöreskog & Sörbom, 1989). All analyses were carried out in the same manner: *First*, a one-factor model, wherein it was assumed that all seven variables measure a single construct—global domain specific perceived control—was fitted to the data. *Second*, a two-factor model was fitted to the data with two components—*control expectancy* (the former four above mentioned questions: present control belief I and II, future control belief, share of control) and *control appraisal* (the later three above mentioned questions: importance of control, striving for control, importance of the situation). The indices of the nine pairs of models were compared to one another. In addition, the large sample was randomly divided into smaller subsamples in order to enlarge the power of the tests.

The indices for each of the 18 confirmatory factor analyses showed unequivocally that the two-factor solution provided a superior fit to the data than did the one-factor solution (i.e., in terms of chi-square/degree of freedom ratios; Goodness-of-Fit indices, and root-mean-square residuals; details in Grob, Flammer & Wearing, 1995). Overall, these analyses gave empirical evidence that perceived control is composed of two factors: control expectancy and control appraisal. Furthermore, the result was replicated with two randomly selected subsamples in each of nine different situations; this indicates that the two factor structure of control holds across very different life situations.

Using the data from the *longitudinal sample* of the Berne adolescence study we tested whether the two-factor pattern of perceived control is generalizable not only across different life domains, but also across individuals over time. We assumed that perceived control is constituted by control expectancy and control appraisal, and that there is a correlation between the two components at each measurement point. The new assumption that we tested with the longitudinal sample concerned the stability of the factor pattern, particularly predicting that the two perceived control components at a later time would be best predicted by the two perceived control components at a former time.

The nine situation specific matrices were submitted to LISREL analyses with the above mentioned restrictions. Again, our expectations were largely confirmed. The variance explained by each control expectancy component varied from 4% (subject matters) to 19% (personal appearance) from time 1 to time 2, and jumped to 10% (conflict with parents) to 24% (for personal appearance) from time 2 to time 3. The stability coefficients for control appraisal were higher than those for the control expectancy component; the former mentioned averaged about .40, whereas the latter averaged about .50, each over a two-year period. Overall, the results of the longitudinal sample confirmed that perceived control is composed of two components. Furthermore, we showed that the two-factor solution was stable over two longitudinal intervals. Again, these results were replicated in each of nine different situations and indicate that the two component structure of control is generalizeable across development.

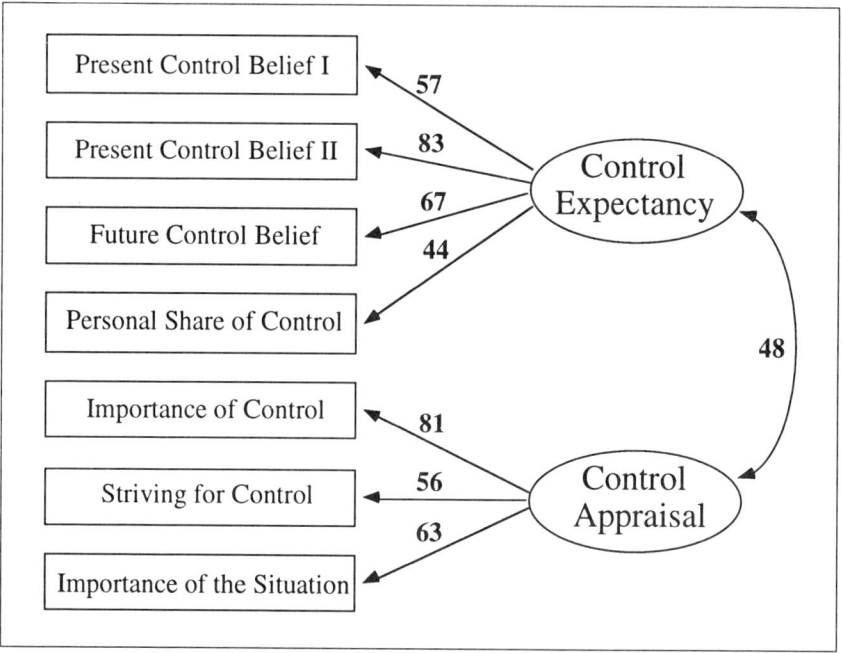

FIG. 19.1. Two components of perceived control: Control expectancy and control appraisal, their relation, and indicators.

*Life Span.* So far, we established a distinct two component pattern of perceived control across adolescence and different life situations. However, one might wonder whether this pattern holds across the life span. One would anticipate a similar correlation pattern under the assumption that the individual difference relations reflect the normative psychological interrelations among the control constructs across the life span. For this purpose data from the *Berne longitudinal study on adolescence* (Flammer et al., 1989) and a study of *adults' control attributions and attitudes toward the environment* (Grob, 1991b; 1995b) were combined with a total sample size of 1631 participants. The age of the participants ranged between 14 and 89 years. To test the age related trends, the sample was divided into twelve age cohorts, each presented with the same life situations (personal appearance, handling a conflict with the partner, spouse or parents, and natural environmental problem). The data were submitted to MACS procedures with LISREL analyses (Little, 1997).

The life-span data showed that the latent correlations among the control constructs were indeed statistically the same, both across the three life situations and across the twelve age cohorts (Grob, Little & Wanner, 1998). This outcome indicates that the correlational structure among the control constructs is generalizable across the three life situations *and* the twelve age cohorts. Control expectancy and control appraisal overlapped approximately 18 % within each domain. Notably, the identical nature of the structure among the control constructs within each domain and across each age-cohort highlights the robust nature of the psychological meaning of these constructs across the life span.

*Socio-Cultural Context.* The next question was whether we would find this same pattern of perceived control across different socio-cultural contexts. We tested this assumption with 3,844 adolescents from 14 different socio-cultural contexts in eastern Europe, western Europe, and the US (Grob, Little, Wanner, Wearing & Euronet (1996). Fifty-two percent of the subjects were female students. The mean age of the sample was 14 years, 10 months. Depending on the students' respective educational systems, the younger participants were randomly drawn from either elementary, junior, middle, or senior high schools, and the older participants were drawn from senior high schools or vocational training schools. The socioeconomic profiles of each sample were comparable (for more details about the sample see Alsaker, Flanagan & Csapó, 1998). As in the former studies, the perceived control items came from the "Berne questionnaire on adolescents' perception of control" (Lüthi et al., 1989). However, only three life situations were assessed in the Euronet protocol (personality development, work place, and school matters). Also in this study we used the items *present control belief, future control belief* and *share of control* to measure control ecpectancy, and the items *importance of control, striving for control* and *importance of the situation* to measure control, appraisal. As in the analyses mentioned above, the data were submitted to MACS procedures with LISREL analyses.

Our model was overwhelmingly confirmed: The expected indicator-to-latent-factor model fit the data in each of the 14 socio-cultural contexts and the equality constrained model did not decrease the goodness of fit indices. Furthermore, in each of the 14 socio-cultural contexts the correlation between control expectancy and control appraisal could be constrained to $r = .44$. The dominant outcome was that the individual-difference relations among the two constructs in each of the 14 sociocultural settings was the same. Overall, we have strong evidence that there is a cross-nationally generalizable two factorial pattern of perceived control, i.e., control expectancy and control appraisal, and that this relation is robust across socio-cultural contexts.

## Domain Specificity Of Perceived Control

In each of the three studies we attempted to reduce the number of situations to a reasonable higher order cluster. We assumed that the level of perceived control varies as a function of the number of persons involved in a specific outcome, and this difference would manifest itself across personal, interpersonal, and societal domains.

In the *Berne longitudinal study on adolescence* the participants were given nine everyday situations representing these three life domains. The analyses, however, indicated that only two domains could be empirically discerned (Grob et al., 1995). The everyday situations covering the personal and interpersonal domain loaded into one domain (personal appearance, future working place, personality development, pocket money, conflict with parents and intimate friendship), but the societal domain emerged separately (natural environment, subject matters, local politics). However, it is noteworthy that the methodology for testing the independence of the domains was not as strong as in the following analyses in which we employed confirmatory factor analyses.

The *life-span* study included only three everyday situations, i.e. personal appearance (for the personal domain), handling a conflict with the partner or parents (interpersonal domain), and problems with the natural environment (societal domain). A high degree of discrimination emerged among the three domains. In particular, the perceived control constructs in the societal domain and the same constructs in the personal domain showed no overlap. The constructs showed low, but positive correlations between the societal and social domains (median $r$ = .06), and between the social and personal domains (median $r$ = .12). These low correlations of the control constructs across the three life domains provide evidence for the domain specificity of psychological control. Also, the systematic differences in the between-domain correlations suggest that the social domain shares some commonality with both personal and societal issues, but that personal and societal issues are quite independent domains.

## Trajectories Of Perceived Control

So far, we have shown that control expectancy and control appraisal are different facets of perceived control, and that they operate in three domains, i.e., the personal, the interpersonal, and the societal domain. However, we have not discussed age- and culture-related mean level trajectories. We address these interesting issues in the next section.

*Adolescence.* In the *Berne study on adolescence* the participants were questioned three times over a four year period. The results indicated that over this time period (1986 to 1990) the adolescents' control expectancy increased, whereas control appraisal stayed the same.[2] The time effect did not interact with the adolescents' gender or age. Under a perspective that investigates how social change affects people's representation of their life, this result is very important. Given the limited space, we do not discuss this finding in this chapter.

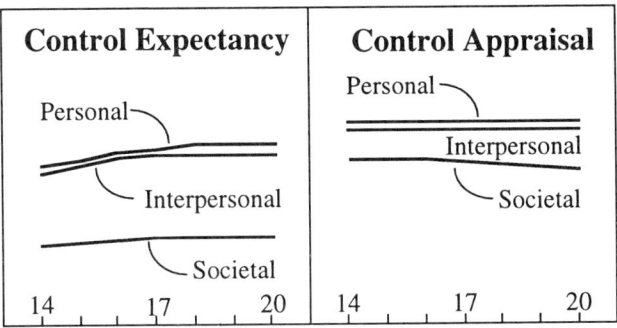

FIG. 19.2. Developmental trajectories of control appraisal and control expectancy across the three life domains during adolescence.

Figure 19.2 depicts the results of two factorial ANOVAs (age and sex), on the domain specific control expectancy and control appraisal measures. *Control expectancy* increased steadily from age 14 through age 17 and remainded at a high level until age 20 in both of two domains, the personal and the interpersonal, respectively. The level of expected control in these two domains was importantly higher than the level of expected control in the societal domain. In addition, age did not vary with control expectancy in the societal domain. Interestingly, female adolescents expected higher levels of personal control in societal matters than male adolescents did. The pattern for *control appraisal* was different from that of control expectancy. Each of the three domains was rated as more important by female adolescents than by male adolescents. Again the societal domain was appraised as being less important than the other two domains. In addition, the importance of control appraisal decreased with the adolescents' age in the societal domain, but not in the personal and interpersonal domains.[3]

---

[2] Control expectancy in the personal domain $F(2,5425) = 23.8$; in the interpersonal domain $F_{(2,5417)} = 29.9$; in the societal domain $F(2,5408) = 73.7$; all $ps < .001$.

[3] We report the significant effects (all $ps < .001$) of two-factorial ANOVAs with the factors age (14 through 20 years), sex and their interaction. Control expectancy (CE) in the personal domain (PD): age ($F_{(6,5451)} = 23.5$); CE in the interpersonal domain (ID): age ($F_{(6,5443)} = 11.0$); CE in the societal domain (SD): gender $F_{(1,5408)} = 29.5$; Control appraisal (CA) in PD: gender $F_{(1,5451)} = 19.3$; and CA in

*Life Span.* Consistent with our expectations, the control expectancy and control appraisal assessed across the three life domains showed substantially different life-span trajectories. Across the life span, the control expectancy in the personal and social domains was rated higher than in the societal domain. Although the slopes for the personal and social domains did not differ, the intercept did. The paths showed an increase from adolescence to about the third life decade, followed by a decrease into old age, with some slowing after around age 60. The trend for societal-environmental concerns, in contrast, showed a steadily linear decrease, and, in terms of absolute levels, was rated quite low across each age-cohort.

The trends for control appraisal differed substantially from those of control expectancy. The social and societal domains were rated as more important than the personal domain. Social relations were viewed as equally important across the life span, while the importance of societal concerns increased, surpassing the importance of the social domain around age 55. In contrast to the social and societal domains, the trajectory for the personal domain showed a pronounced decrease from adolescence to about age 65, followed by a general stability into old age.

*Socio-Cultural Context.* Mean level trajectories were also examined across socio-cultural contexts. It is noteworthy that none of the mean-level differences were related to measurement artefacts or to differential mental representations of perceived control (details see Grob et al., 1996). Instead, there are valid differences because of the measurement equivalence and the similar correlational structure among the constructs. At a general level, we found that the eastern countries had higher values of control expectancy and control appraisal than the western countries. In terms of the national context patterns, the French adolescents and French-speaking Swiss adolescents were consistently lower than their western peers in perceived control, and the Hungarian adolescents were consistently lower than their eastern peers on the perceived control dimensions. On the other hand, the American adolescents were consistently higher than both their western European and eastern European compatriots on control expectancy, and the Russian adolescents were among the highest in control expectancy and control appraisal. Despite the interesting national patterns, the most striking result concerns the fact that adolescents from eastern countries reported higher levels of perceived control than their western peers.

## Perceived Control And Subjective Well-Being

We hypothesized that a positive sense of control fosters people's self-esteem and satisfaction. Therefore, we split the participants in the Berne adolescent study

---

ID: gender $F_{(1,5445)} = 103.7$; CA in SD: age ($F_{(6,5438)} = 4.9$, gender ($F_{(1,5438)} = 87.2$).

into low and high control expectancy group. The adolescents with high levels of control expectancy indeed reported higher levels of positive attitude toward life, higher levels of self-esteem and joy in life, and lower levels of depressed mood, than did adolescents with low levels of control expectancy (Grob, 1997).

In the cross-national study we conducted a regression analyses in which the background variables were entered first, followed by the agentic variables (see Grob, Stetsenko, Sabtier, Botcheva, & Macek, 1998). Controlling for the adolescents' age, gender, and cultural background, as well as level of strain, and emotion- and problem-oriented coping, control expectancy contributed significantly to an increase in the explanation of adolescents' subjective well-being. On the disattenuated correlational level, control expectancy correlated with positive attitudes in all contexts at $r = .35$, whereas the correlation between control expectancy and self-esteem was significantly higher in the eastern contexts ($r = .44$) than in the western contexts ($r = .35$) (see Grob et al., 1996). Overall, we found strong evidence that perceived control is indeed an important predictor for subjective well-being.

However, the pattern becomes more complex if we refer to the longitudinal sample. Figure 19.3 depicts the result on satisfaction, control expectancy and control appraisal in each of the three waves (1986, 1988, 1990). Satisfaction was measured with positive attitudes toward life, self-esteem, lack of depressive mood, and joy in life (Grob et al., 1991). In the following analyses, control expectancy and control appraisal were sampled from the personal domain. The model indicates that each of the three constructs is stable across time (standaradized mean $\beta = .53$ for satisfaction, $\beta = .64$ for control expectancy and $\beta = .54$ for control appraisal). However, the predictive constellation of the concepts across time (for example, control expectancy at time 1 —> satisfaction at time 2, or control appraisal at time 1 —> control expectancy at time 2) was consistently negative. This result is even more convincing, given that the paths between time 2 and time 3 were constrained to the same levels as the same paths between time 1 and time 2 without a loss of fit (Grob, 1995c). Finally, the same negative paths were replicated with two more two-wave longitudinal samples (Grob et al., 1995). Nevertheless, these robust findings were not expected, and therefore need some *post hoc* interpretation.

Under a cross-sectional perspective, the results indicate that a positive sense of control leads to well-being. However, the longitudinal data did not confirm this result. Referring to the literature that has shown that people in general overestimate their control competencies (Alloy & Abramson, 1982; Taylor & Brown, 1988), one might assume that the adolescents in our study overestimated their control competencies. It is noteworthy that this fact is not detrimental per se. If, however, the adolescents were not able to justify their level of control expectancy across the two year period, this fact might have a negative impact on their well-being. This particular interpretation highlights the functionality of control illusions. Taylor and Brown (1988, 1994; for a recent critique see Block & Colvin, 1994; Colvin & Block, 1994) argued that positive illusions foster well-being in each case, whereas Baumeister (1989) argued for optimal levels of illusion. Interpreting our results in this light, it might be that control optimism becomes dysfunctional if the adolescents were not able to actualize their high level of perceived personal control in everyday experiences. This hypothesis assumes that unjustified levels of control might be disadvantageous for future well-being. However, it is evident that in this particular question further research is needed.

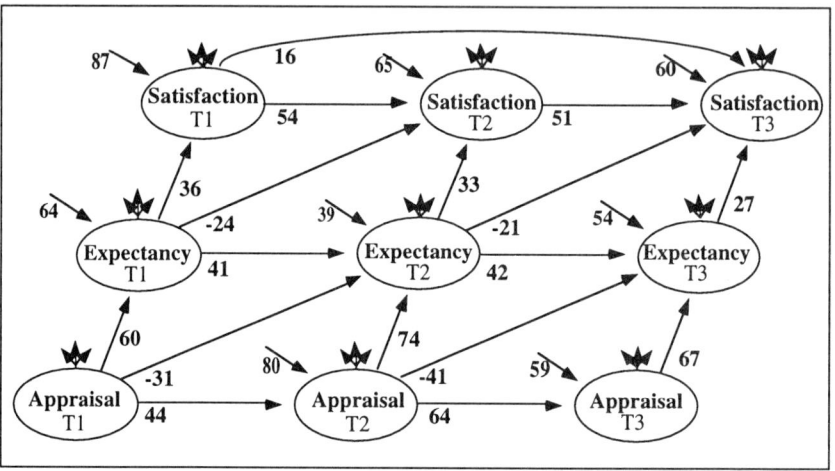

FIG. 19.3. Satisfaction, control expectancy and control appraisal across adolescence [N = 392; $\chi^2$ (df =310) = 461.1; Goodness-of-Fit = .91 (adjusted GFI = .90); RMSR < .05; the measurement model is not depicted in this figure].

## CONCLUSION

Broadly speaking, a number of important points can be derived from our studies. The points differ with regard to their significance for research. While the first two conclusions are intended to be implemented as standards in control research, the following two deal with open questions. The final conclusion is a meta-level comment on perceived control in the late 20th century.

First, perceived control is a multidimension construct. We could identify two components of perceived control: control expectancy and control appraisal. The correlational structure of these components was stable across three life domains, across the life span, and across different socio-cultural contexts. This finding highlights on one side the robustness of the interrelations between control expectancy and control appraisal, and on the other side the importance of the motivational component of perceived control. Specifically, the expectancy component refers to generalized cognitive estimates of the amount of control one possesses, whereas the appraisal component refers to the valuation or perceived importance of the situation at stake. These two features of the perceived control system are in accordance with well-known expectancy–value theories (e.g., Weiner, 1992). For that reason, we think it is worthwhile to include both components of perceived control in future control research.

Second, the constructs' low correlations across the three life domains highlights the distinctive, domain-specific nature of perceived control. The differentiation between different domains certainly depends on the domains that are under study. This is why such studies never can definitely answer the question of how many and what kind of domains have to be distinguished. However, the three dimensions that came out of our studies represent fundamental divisions. The distinctive feature of our division is the number and kind of people having a share in perceived control. We conclude that perceived control is domain specific and that control research should take this fact seriously into account.

Third, although the relation of control expectancy and control appraisal are consistent across life domains, age-cohorts, and different socio-cultural contexts, their mean-level trajectories are quite variable. Pronounced differences emerged for control expectancy. Adolescents and adults at all ages reported low amounts of control expectancy for societal concerns and this relative lack of control expectancy decreased steadily with age. On the other hand, the expectation of attaining one's goals in the social and personal domains was quite high. Although the three life domains were quite distinctive and heterogeneous, they were appraised as being important across the life span. However, beginning with young adulthood, the importance of social and societal matters was greater than the importance of personal matters. We think that these various life-span patterns are interpretable with regard to three superordinate approaches (details in Grob et al., 1998), i.e., (a) bio-physical aging processes, (b) meeting culturally shared developmental tasks and life cycles (Havighurst, 1948; Erikson, 1959), and (c) the selection, optimization, and compensation of different life task across the life span (Baltes, 1987). A challenge for future research and theorizing will be to focus on specific predictions regarding how, why, and when certain control expectancies in specific life domains increase while others decrease, and still others remain stable. In this regard, measures of life experiences, bio-physical level, and personal resources would help to guide such multiply specific hypotheses.

Fourth, regarding the correlational pattern between subjective well-being and perceived control, control appraisal had a low relationship with well-being, whereas control expectancy had a considerably higher relationship. These correlational pattern were nearly identical across the socio-cultural settings. The positive direction of the correlations between well-being and perceived control supports the idea that people who believe they are able to exert influence over the flow of events also show higher levels of self-esteem and perceive their world in a more positive light. This system of relations is consistent with a causal model in which control expectancy is an important self-regulatory component of one's well-being. However, the modest levels of this relationship indicate that these components of the self-system are not locked together in a fixed system. Instead, the antecedents of well-being and perceived control may encompass different features of people's social psychological world, and the nature of this system of relations remains an open question for future research. For example, to what degree is perceived control a moderator, rather than a direction contributor, to well-being? Also, is it true that high levels of perceived control can have a detrimental impact on people's well-being, and, if so, under what circumstances?

The fifth conclusion concerns the meaning of control in people's lives at the end of the twentieth century at large. Our data showed that adolescents from eastern European countries believed themselves to have more control than their western peers. We assume that the objective degree of freedom were the same in both countries. However, compared to the west, the perception of control in the east might indeed have increased since the Iron Curtain disappeared. It might also be that the situation did not change for the best at once, and therefore it is also plausible that adolescents living in eastern contexts anticipated an even better future. Although these interpretations are preliminary, they represent important directions for future research. Adolescents from two very distinct macrosocial contexts report high levels of personal control, and the adaptive psychological interface among these aspects of personal control and well-being appear to be robust in the face of sociopolitical fluctuations in both socio-cultural environments. Furthermore, similarily high levels of perceived control were found across the life span.

Hence one might relate these findings to the *Zeitgeist*. At the end of the twentieth century people live in a world where most events are expected to be caused by personal agency and competence: A person is what she or he personally does. This contemporary understanding of how the world functions is largely shared cross-contextually and across the life span. It appears to us that high levels of perceived control are not only descriptive of individuals, but also descriptive of modern societies. There might be even a societal pressure for having high levels of personal control. If this account has some accuracy, the study of individual perceived control also tells us about society at large.

# REFERENCES

Abramson, L. Y., Seligman, M. E. P., & Teasdale, J. D. (1978). Learned helplessness in humans: Critique and reformulation. *Journal of Abnormal Psychology*, *87*, 49–74.

Alloy, L. B., & Abramson, L. Y. (1982). Learned helplessness, depression, and the illusion of control. *Journal of Personality and Social Psychology*, *42*, 1114–1126.

Alsaker, F. D., Flanagan, C., & Csapó, B. (1998). The issues of sampling in cross-national / cross-cultural research. In F. D. Alsaker, & A. Flammer (Eds.), *The adolescent experience: European and American adolescents in the 1990s*. Hillsdale, NJ: Lawrence Erlbaum Associates.

Baltes, P. B. (1987). Theoretical propositions of life span developmental psychology: On the dynamics between growth and decline. *Developmental Psychology*, *23*, 611–626.

Bandura, A. (1977). Self-efficacy: Toward a unifying theory of behavioral change. *Psychological Review*, *84*, 191–215.

Bandura, A. (1986). *Social foundations of thought and action: A social cognitive theory*. Englewood Cliffs, NJ: Prentice Hall.

Bandura, A. (1997). *Self-efficacy. The exercise of control*. New York, NY: Freeman.

Barber, J. G., & Winefeld, A. H. (1987). Three accounts of learned helplessness effects. *Genetic, Social and General Monographs*, *112*, 143–163.

Baumeister, R. F. (1989). The optimal margin of illusion. *Journal of Social and Clinical Psychology*, *8*, 176–189.

Block, J., & Colvin, C. R. (1994). Positive illusions and well-being revisited: separating fiction from fact. *Psychological Bulletin*, *116*, 28.

Bradburn, N. M. (1969). *The structure of psychological well-being*. Chicago: Aldine.

Brickman, P., Coates, D., & Janoff-Bulman, R. (1978). Lottery winners and accident victims: Is happiness relative? *Journal of Personality and Social Psychology*, *36*, 917–927.

Bronfenbrenner, U. (1986). Ecology of the family as a context for human development: research perspectives. *Developmental Psychology*, *22*, 723–742.

Brunstein, J. C. (1993). Personal goals and subjective well-being: A longitudinal study. *Journal of Personality and Social Psychology*, *65*, 1061–1070.

Cantril, H. (1965). *The pattern of human concerns*. New Brunswick, NJ: Rutgers University Press.

Chapman, M., Skinner, E. A., & Baltes, P. B. (1990). Interpreting correlations between children's perceived control and cognitive performance: Control, agency, and means-ends beliefs? *Developmental Psychology*, *26*, 246–253.

Colvin, C. R., & Block, J. (1994). Do positive illusions foster mental health? An examination of the Taylor and Brown formulation. *Psychological Bulletin*, *116*, 3–20.

Diener, E. (1984). Subjective well-being. *Psychological Bulletin*, *95*, 542–575.

Diener, E. (1994). Assessing subjective well-being: Progress and opportunities. *Social Indicators Research*, *31*, 103–157.

Diener, E., & Larson, R. J. (1993). The experience of emotional well-being. In M. Lewis & J. M. Haviland (Eds.), *Handbook of Emotions* (pp. 405–415). New York: Guilford.

Duncan, O. D. (1975). Does money buy satisfaction? *Social Indicators Research*, *2*, 267–274.

Emmons, R. A. (1992). Abstract versus concrete goals: Personal striving level, physical illness, and psychological well-being. *Journal of Personality and Social Psychology*, *62*, 292–300.

Evans, D. R. (1994). Enhancing quality of life in the population at large. *Social Indicators Research*, *33*, 47-88.

Erikson, E. H. (1959). Identity and the life cycle. *Psychological Issues*, *1*, 50-100.

Fend, H. (1998). The cultural scripts of control and individualization: Consequences for growing up during adolescence in modern societies. In W. J. Perrig, & A. Grob (Eds.), *Control of human behavior, mental processes, and consciousness*. New York: Lawrence Erlbaum Associates.

Flammer, A. (1990). *Erfahrung der eigenen Wirksamkeit* [Experiencing one's own efficacy]. Bern: Huber.

Flammer, A. (1995). Developmental analysis of control beliefs. In A. Bandura (Ed.), *Self-efficacy in changing societies* (pp. 69–113). New York: Cambridge University Press.

Flammer, A., & Grob, A. (1994). Kontrollmeinungen, ihre Begründungen und Autobiographie [Control beliefs, their justification, and autobiographical memory]. *Zeitschrift für Experimentelle und Angewandte Psychologie, 41*, 17–38.

Flammer, A., Grob, A., & Lüthi, R. (1989). Swiss adolescents' attribution of control. In J. P. Forgas, & J. M. Innes (Eds.), *Recent advances in social psychology: An international perspective* (pp. 81–94). North-Holland: Elsevier Science Publishers.

Flammer, A., Züblin, C., & Grob, A. (1988). Sekundäre Kontrolle bei Jugendlichen [Secondary control in adolescents]. *Zeitschrift für Entwicklungspsychologie und Pädagogische Psychologie, 20*, 239–262.

Freud, A. (1936). *Das Ich und die Abwehrmechanismen* [Ego and defense mechanisms]. Wien: Internationaler Psychoanalytischer Verlag.

Furnham, A., & Steele, H. (1993). Measuring locus of control: A critique of general, children's, helath, and work-related locus of control questionnaires. *British Journal of Psychology, 84*, 443–479.

Grob, A. (1991a). Der Einfluss bedeutsamer Lebensereignisse auf das Wohlbefinden und auf bereichsspezifische Kontrollmeinungen von Jugendlichen [The impact of significant life events on subjective well-being and domain specific control attributions]. *Schweizerische Zeitschrift für Psychologie, 50*, 48–63.

Grob, A. (1991b). *Meinung—Verhalten—Umwelt. Ein psychologisches Ursachennetz-Modell umweltgerechten Verhaltens* [Belief—behavior—environment: A causal network model of environment appropriate behavior]. Bern: Lang.

Grob, A. (1995a). Subjective well-being and significant life events across the life span. *Swiss Journal of Psychology, 54*, 3–18.

Grob, A. (1995b). A structural model of environmental attitudes and behaviour. *Journal of Environmental Psychology, 15*, 209–220.

Grob, A. (1995c). Two Components of Perceived Control: Expectancy and Appraisal. Symposium. VIIth European Conference on Developmental Psychology. Krakow, Poland.

Grob, A. (1997). Entwicklung und Regulation des Wohlbefindens [Development and regulation of subjective well-being]. Habilitationsschrift. Faculty of Philosophy and Humanities. University of Berne, Switzerland.

Grob, A., Flammer, A., & Wearing A. J. (1995). Adolescents' perceived control: Domain specificity, expectancy, and appraisal. *Journal of Adolescence, 18*, 403–425.

Grob, A., Little, T. D., Wanner, B., Wearing, A. J., & Euronet (1996). Adolescents' well-being and perceived control across fourteen sociocultural contexts. *Journal of Personality and Social Psychology, 71*, 785–795.

Grob, A., Little, T. D., & Wanner, B. (1998). Control judgements across the life span. Manuscript under review.

Grob, A., Lüthi, R., Kaiser, F. G., Flammer, A., Mackinnon, A., & Wearing, A. J. (1991). Berner Fragebogen zum Wohlbefinden Jugendlicher (BFW); [Berne questionnaire on subjective well-being (BSW-Y)]. *Diagnostica, 37*, 66–75.

Grob, A., Stesenko, A., Sabatier, C., Botcheva, L., & Macek, P. (1998). A model of adolescents' well-being in different social contexts. In F. D. Alsaker, & A. Flammer (Eds.), *The adolescent experience: European and American adolescents in the 1990s*. Hillsdale, NJ: Lawrence Erlbaum Associates.

Haan, N. (1977). *Coping and defending—Processes of self-environment Organization*. New York: Academic Press.

Havighurst, R. J. (1948). *Developmental tasks and education*. New York: McKay.
Headey, B., & Wearing, A.J. (1992). *Understanding happiness: A theory of subjective well-being*. Melbourne: Longman Cheshire.
Jöreskog, K. G., & Sörbom, D. (1989). *LISREL 7: A guide to the program and applications*. Chicago, IL: SPSS.
Krampen, G. (1989). Mehrdimensionale Erfassung generalisierter und bereichsspezifischer Kontrollüberzeugungen [Multidimensional assessment of generalized and domain specific locus of control]. In G. Krampen (Ed.), *Diagnostik von Attributionen und Kontrollüberzeugungen*. (pp. 100–106). Göttingen: Hogrefe.
Langer, E. J. (1975). The illusion of control. *Journal of Personality and Social Psychology, 32*, 311–328.
Lazarus, R. S. (1966). *Psychological stress and the coping process*. New York: McGraw-Hill.
Lazarus, R. S., & Folkman, S. (1984). *Stress, appraisal, and coping*. New York: Springer.
Lazarus, R. S., & Folkman, S. (1987). Transactional theory and research on emotion and coping. *European Journal of Personality, 1*, 141–170.
Lazarus, R. S., Launier, R (1978). Stress-related transactions between person and environment. In L. Pervin, & M. Lewis (Eds.), *Perspectives in international psychology* (p. 287–327). New York: Plenum.
Lerner, R. M. (1982). Children and adolescents as producers of their own development. *Developmental Review, 2*, 342–370.
Little, T. D. (1997). Mean and covariance structures (MACS) analyses of cross-cultural data: Practical and theoretical issues. *Multivariate Behavioral Research, 32*, 53–76.
Lüthi, R., Grob, A., & Flammer, A. (1989). Differenzierte Erfassung bereichsspezifischer Kontrollmeinungen bei Jugendlichen [Assessment of domain specific control beliefs in adolescence]. In G. Krampen (Ed.), *Diagnostik von Attributionen und Kontrollüberzeugungen* [Assessment of attributions and control beliefs]; (pp. 134-145). Göttingen: Hogrefe.
Michalos, A. C. (1985). Multiple discrepancy theory. *Social Indicators Research, 16*, 347–413.
Mielke, R. (1982). *Interne/externe Kontollüberzeugung* [Internal/external locus of control]. Bern: Huber.
Miller, I. W., & Norman, W. H. (1979). Learned helplessness in humans: A review and attribution-theory model. *Psychological Bulletin, 86*, 93–118.
Nowicki, S., & Strickland, P. R. (1973). A locus of control scale for children. *Journal of Consulting Psychology, 141*, 277–286.
Nurmi, J-E. (1992). Age differences in adult life goals, concerns, and their temporal extension: A life course approach to future-oriented motivation. *International Journal of Behavioral Development, 15*, 487–508.
Paulhus, D., & Christie, R. (1981). Spheres of control: An interactionistic approach to assessment of perceived control. In H. M. Lefcourt (Ed.), *Research with the locus of control construct, vol. 1* (pp. 161–188). New York: Academic Press.
Phares, E. J. (1976). *Locus of control in personality*. Morristown, NJ: General Learning Press.
Rotter, J. B. (1966). Generalized expectancies for internal versus external control of reinforcement. *Psychological Monographs, 80*, no. 609.
Rotter, J. B. (1990). Internal versus external locus of control of reinforcement. *American Psychologist, 45*, 489–493.

Schneewind, K. A. (1995). Impact of family processes on control beliefs. In A. Bandura (Ed.), *Self-efficacy in changing societies* (pp. 114–148). New York: Cambridge University Press.

Seligman, M. E. P. (1975). *Helplessness.* San Francisco: Freeman.

Selye, H. (1982). History and present status of the stress concept. In L. Goldberger, & S. Breznitz (Eds.), *Handbook of stress. Theoretical and clinical Aspects* (pp. 7–20). New York: The Free Press.

Skinner, E. A. (1996). A guide to constructs of control. *Journal of Personality and Social Psychology, 71,* 549–570.

Skinner, E. A., Chapman, M., & Baltes, P. B. (1988). Control, means-ens, and agency-beliefs: A new conceptualization and its measurement during childhood. *Journal of Personality and Social Psychology, 54,* 117–133.

Strickland, B. R. (1989). Internal-external control expectancies: From contingency to creativity. *American Psychologist, 44,* 1–12.

Taylor, S. E., & Brown, J. D. (1988). Illusion and well-being: A social-psychological perspective on mental health. *Psychological Bulletin, 103,* 193–210.

Taylor, S. E., & Brown, J. D. (1994). Positive illusions and well-being revisited: separating fact from fiction. *Psychological Bulletin, 116,* 21–27.

Weiner, B. (1992). *Human Motivation.* Newbury Park, CA: Sage.

Weisz, J. R., & Stipek, D. J. (1982). Competence, contingency and the development of perceived control. *Human Development, 25,* 250–281.

White, R. W. (1959). Motivation reconsidered: The concept of competence. *Psychological Review, 66,* 297–333.

Wills, T. A. (1981). Downward comparison principles in social psychology. *Psychological Bulletin, 90,* 245–271.

# 20

# The Development of a Depressive Personality Orientation: The Role of the Individual[1]

*Françoise D. Alsaker*

## INTRODUCTION

Adolescence is often reported as an important period of life regarding the development of depressive symptoms and disorders. In fact, there is broad evidence indicating that the prevalence of depression increases dramatically during adolescence (e.g., Harrington, 1993; Merikangas & Angst, 1995; Rutter, 1986). Furthermore, longitudinal studies have shown that depressive symptoms are not a transient phenomenon linked only to the adolescent period; depressed adolescents are at an increased risk for later depression disorder, as compared to nondepressed adolescents (Harrington, 1993; Merikangas & Angst, 1995). Given the importance of the adolescent period for depression and the shaping of individual developmental pathways, the adolescent age group will receive particular attention, even if the processes discussed in the present chapter are not specific for adolescence.

Findings on the long-lasting character of depressive symptoms converge with the fact that depressiveness is often regarded as a personality characteristic. Depression is, actually, to be found among the facets of neuroticism in the Big Five model of personality (e.g. McCrae & Costa, 1995). Also, the findings from a recent study addressing the utility of the five-factor model in descriptions of children and adolescents (van Lieshout & Haselager, 1994) gives support to the hypothesis that a depressive orientation can reliably be observed in children and adolescents as well as in adults. The authors analyzed the California Child Q-Set (J. H. Block & J. Block, 1980) which is considered a well-established personality inventory for children and adolescents. They found the first five factors to be clearly identifiable as the Big Five personality factors. But most interestingly, they found "Emotional (In)Stability" to come out as one of the two most robust

[1]The present paper was written during a stay as a visiting professor at the University of Bologna, Italy. I am deeply indebted to Dr. Giusy Speltini, who demonstrated the proverbial hospitality of the Italians in all its possible forms.

factors (the other one being agreeableness). Emotional Instability corresponds to Neuroticism in other classifications and a look at the items comprised in this factor shows striking similarities with items from instruments tapping depression (child lacks self-reliance and self-assertiveness, ruminates and worries, feels unworthy, feels guilty, is indecisive, and cries easily, (e.g., Costello & Angold, 1988; Kazdin & Petti, 1982; Kovacs, 1980, 1981; Roberts, Lewinsohn, & Seeley, 1991).

At this point, a depressive orientation should be differentiated from a depressive disorder. An individual with a high score on the depressive facet of any personality inventory is not necessarily clinically depressed. He or she, however, is a person who shows some symptoms associated with a depressive disorder, such as depressive thoughts and feelings. Moreover, we may expect a person with a depressive personality orientation to be likely to react with depressive symptoms in adverse situations. Therefore, we may conceive of depressive symptoms as manifestations of an underlying personality orientation and we may at the same time conceive of a stable depressive orientation as the result of depressive episodes.

While much theoretical and empirical research has been devoted to the possible antecedents of depressive disorders and orientations, the mechanisms behind the maintenance of depressive thoughts and feelings are not well established. The fact that depressive symptomatology is conceived of as a personality characteristic by some authors does not explain how it becomes a stable component of an individual's personality, but it allows to consider more general models of personality development to search for plausible explanations.

In this chapter, I propose that the individual plays a major role in the consolidation of depressive symptoms and thus in the development of a depressive personality orientation. The role of the individual will be addressed in terms of self-representations and behavior. Self-representations are considered to be active in processing information and organizing experiences. They help us make predictions and at the same time they are a central element of depression, specifically in terms of negative self-evaluation. Self-evaluation is a pervasive component of self-representations, and as stated by Lapsley and Quintana (1985) the process of self-evaluation seems to be initiated whenever a dimension of the self is the focus of self-directed attention. Depressive episodes may be triggered by a wide range of factors which themselves are thought to influence self-representations. Once an individual's self-representations are motivated by such factors and biased by depressive cognitions, they are assumed to influence the individual's intake and processing of new information and his or her behavior. In other words, I want to look into how the cognitive and behavioral patterns usually associated with depression may reinforce the psychological state and finally usher in a resistent personality orientation. Such a depressive personality orientation is in turn expected to play a crucial role in the construction of the individual's life course.

Most definitions of development converge in referring to change (Lerner, 1986). In a recent formulation of a holistic model of personality development

Magnusson and Törestad (1993) stated for example, that "development, in its most general form, refers to any process of progressive change" (p. 428). Therefore, lack of change has usually been regarded as less interesting in developmental research. Traditionally, development has also had positive connotations, such as purposefulness, enhancement, or improvement. However, some of the most central issues addressed in personality development today are not necessarily concerned with age-related or positive changes (Alsaker, 1992). Interest in elderly people and life-span psychology has brought new dimensions in the concept of development. One of these dimensions is that "development is conceived of not as a monolithic process of progression and growth, but as an ongoing changing, and interacting system of *gains and losses*" (Marsiske, Lang, Baltes, & Baltes, 1995, p. 37). Also, a greater emphasis on person-oriented approaches (e.g., Magnusson & Bergman, 1988)—in contrast to variable oriented approaches—has contributed to considering individual life trajectories as a core concern of developmental psychology. Life trajectories are necessarily characterized by gains and losses and by change as well as by stability/consistency.

Depressive symptomatology is usually found to be associated with impairment on many levels of psychological adjustment and consequences are expected as to the general developmental pathway of an individual and his/her adult life. Merikangas and Angst (1995), for example, mention the interruption of the completion of developmental tasks in the educational, social, and psychological spheres as one of the major consequences of depression in adolescence. This chapter addresses the issue of how a depressive personality orientation, which clearly involves losses, can be maintained in spite of the fact that most psychological theories assume that individuals have a hedonistic orientation and are inclined to think in positive terms about themselves (Epstein, 1973) and their compentences (Flammer, 1995).

The idea that children and adolescents produce their own development (Lerner, 1982) has become increasingly prevalent in the last decades. Studies with infants have provided evidence that human beings from the very first moment of life are active—and not only reactive—participants of the complex social world in which they are born (Papousek & Papousek, 1979; Stern, 1985; Trevarthen, 1985). That is, individuals, through qualities such as their sensitivity to stimuli or their responsiveness, play an active role, at least in the development of their relational world, throughout the life span (Hartup, 1980; Rutter, 1979). Research on temperament has also shown that children's characteristics influence their responses to a variety of stress situations (Rutter, 1990).

Focusing on relational factors Cummings and Cicchetti (1990) have proposed to conceive of the development of depression in terms of potentiating and protective factors instead of causes. This perspective fits well with the general field of research, and it implicitly also leaves some space for individual factors.

In the following, I first present different approaches to depression succinctly and discuss to what extent these approaches and related empirical findings can contribute to an understanding of the process underlying the maintenance of depressive symptoms and how much the individual can be considered as active in this process. Second, the role of self-representations and self-evaluation will be discussed. And, finally, I will turn to the role of behavior.

## APPROACHES TO DEPRESSION

In the following discussion, we should keep in mind first that co-occurrence does not mean causality, even if it may suggest it, and second, that co-occurent variables and consequences of depression may be even more central than causes of depression in explaining how depressive symptoms are maintained. Genetic, social, and cognitive approaches will be discussed.

### Genetic Factors

One possible explanation for the onset and maintenance of depressive symptoms could be a strong genetic predisposition. Whereas epidemiological and family studies have provided evidence of a genetic predisposition in a substantial proportion of patients with a major depressive disorder (Cytrin, McKnew, Zahn-Waxler, & Gershon, 1986), the genetic factor has proved to be far less important in unipolar than in bipolar depression (Merikangas & Angst, 1995). That is, neither the onset nor the maintenance of depressive symptoms can be explained by heritability to any large extent. This leads to the supposition that cognitive (attributions and interpretations), social, and individual factors may play an even greater role in the development and maintenance of less severe depressive symptoms or a depressive orientation.

### Social Relationships

The major models of childhood depression are clearly based on social environmental influences (see Kashani et al., 1981, for an overview). Studies on child-rearing practices have shown that proneness to depression is associated with practices that combine elements of rejection, inconsistent expression of affection, and strict control (McCranie & Bass, 1984). Other studies have shown that both authoritarian and permissive practices seem to be associated with the development of depression in adolescence (Kandel & Davies, 1982), whereas limit-setting itself is not (Puig-Antich et al., 1985). Strict control as well as indifference typically convey to the child or the adolescent a feeling that he/she is considered incompetent and invaluable by significant others (Emde, Harmon, & Good, 1986). These attributes are, in turn, often considered crucial features of depressive thoughts.

Furthermore, depression is usually found to be associated with impaired interpersonal relationships (Harrington, 1993). However, whereas poor parental relationships have primarily been examined as risk factors, poor peer relationships have often been understood as a consequence of depression. Given the importance of peers in adolescence, poor peer relationships ought to be considered powerful risk factors of depressive problems as well. This is especially true of problems such as rejection by peers or victimization that have been shown to correlate with self-derogation and depression (Alsaker & Olweus, 1992a; Kupersmidt & Patterson, 1991; Olweus, 1993). That is, depressed adolescents are likely to have experienced rejection in relationships that were important to them.

Bowlby (1969) and Stern (1985) have claimed that the young child, through his or her interaction with others, constructs mental representations of the self and of others (called, respectively, "working models" and "representations of interactions generalized"). Actually, the two sets of representations, constructed on the basis of experiences within the same relationships, are assumed to develop in close complementarity (Bretherton, 1987). A consequence of the complementarity of the models is that children experiencing rejection from their caregivers, for example, will be likely to construct working models of a worthless self. Therefore, we may expect individuals with such experiences of rejection to have developed negative working models of others and of themselves.

On the basis of the model presented by Stern (1985), I would like to argue that extensive exposure to a certain type of experience may cause an overconsolidation of self-perceptions, that is of the generalized representations of interactions in Stern's terms, and thus make them difficult to change, even in the presence of clear changes in the social environment. This may be particularly true when the repeated interactions with others trigger intense emotional self-experiences, such as feelings of helplessness, worthlessness, mental pain or shame. This would be typical of self-experiences of rejected or victimized children.

Several authors (Adams & Adams, 1991; Patteron & Capaldi, 1990) have proposed to place a greater emphasis on the role of social skills in depressed adolescents. These authors have proposed to see poor social competence as an antecedent of depression. However, we might also reverse the arguments and propose that recurrent negative experiences, and the depressive state itself, can lead to a deterioration of competences in the social realm. It is noteworthy here that impairment in relationships with family and peers is frequently found to be a consequence of depression, leading to a lack of social support that itself may generate a negative feedback loop in which the consequence of depression may actually serve to maintain the depressive episode (Merikangas & Angst, 1995).

Alsaker and Flammer (1996), conducted a series of analyses on Swiss and Norwegian adolescents who scored high (the highest 10% for each gender in each sample) on a short depression inventory aimed at tapping depressive orientation, rather than clinical depression. In comparison to their nondepressed peers, depressed adolescents reported to be isolated (rejected) by peers, they reported more negative events related to peers, they scored higher on feelings of alienation in groups of peers, and lower on beliefs about their ability to resolve conflicts with friends. Interestingly, they did not differ from other adolescents in terms of having a best friend, or as to the quality of their relationship with their best friends. This differentiation of findings as to their reports on peer relations supports the assumption that the adolescents did not only report isolation because of a depressive perception of social relationships. Had this been the case, then they would also have been likely to report that they had no friend, or that the quality of the friendship was not as good as those of non-depressed adolescents. In sum, depressed adolescents might feel well in dyads but they might avoid larger peer groups and therefore also be more likely to be isolated at school.

Controlling for self-reported isolation in a following set of analyses did not change the results as to reports of peer-related hassles, feelings of alienation, and control beliefs, indicating that depression might have an effect on certain types of social activities and social perceptions, independent of poor peer experiences.

In sum, being victimized, rejected, or ignored by others (peers or family) conveys a sense of worthlessness—even of non-existence—and of incompentence. Furthermore, the depressed adolescent, whether he/she has experienced rejection or not, is likely to interpret social situations in negative ways and subsequently to create an environment which is conducive to the development of vicious circles of depression.

## Depression and Causal Explanations

Seligman (1975) proposed learned helplessness as a model of depression. The model, however, proved to be unable to explain the chronicity of depression and the poor self-esteem of depressed individuals. Therefore, it was reformulated giving attributions a central role (Abramson, Seligman, & Teasdale, 1978). According to the reformulation "individuals who have an explanatory style that invokes internal, stable, and global causes for bad events tend to become depressed when bad events occur" (Peterson & Seligman, 1984, p. 347). The belief that the cause of a bad event is stable should explain the chronicity of feelings of helplessness and depression following bad events as well as the expectation that this will not differ in the future. Reviewing a broad range of studies, Peterson and Seligman (1984) have provided evidence that depressive symptoms are in fact associated with internal, stable and global explanations for bad events, in undergraduate students, in adults, in lower-class women, in children, and in depressed patients. Furthermore, a depressive explanatory style at a given point in time seems to predict depressive symptoms six months later over and above the level of depression at the first assessment (Seligman et al., 1984). Also Nolen-Hoeksema (1983, cited in Peterson & Seligman, 1984), found nondepressed children with a depressive explanatory style to be likely to be depressed three months later, whereas this was not the case for children without a depressive explanatory style.

Reviewing studies on attribution, Harrington (1993) came to the conclusion that there were strong developmental trends that could explain the increased rates of depressive symptoms in adolescence. However, there has been some discussion as to the extent to which the attributional style should be considered an antecedent of depression, or rather a consequence (Harrington, 1993). Still, empirical studies give support to the hypothesis that a depressive explanatory style can play an important role in the maintenance of symptoms, independent of what came first: depression or the attributional style. An individual who blames themselves for negative events (internal attributions) is likely to develop a feeling of incompetence, worthlessness, and consequently a rather poor self-esteem, which is considered a central feature in depression (e.g., Beck, 1967; Becker, 1979). Independent of the stability of the negative events in themselves, individuals with a depressive explanatory style expect the causes of such events also to remain stable. That is, they have no confidence that they could change anything concerning the occurence of bad events, even if they attribute the causes of these events to internal factors. This model fosters our understanding of how the vicious relational circles addressed in the previous section can evolve. A depressed adolescent is already more likely than others to feel rejected (independent of the "cause" of his or her depressive state) and explains the experienced rejection in internal stable terms. On such a basis this adolescent has no reason to believe that a relationship could be rewarding at any point. When we, in addition, bear in mind that the depressive explanatory style also includes a global element, we can only wonder how such an adolescent could be motivated to engage in any kind of peer relationship?

## Depression And Cognitive Biases

Beck (1967) has proposed that the cognitive components of depression are central, resulting in other disturbances. Negative self-evaluations are considered one of the primary features of depression in this tradition (Kuiper, Derry, & MacDonald, 1982). The depressed patients usually perceive themselves as incompetent, or lacking qualities most people would have, which corresponds to personal helplessness in another terminology (e.g., Weisz, Weiss, Wasserman, & Rintoul, 1987). Another central attribute of depressed individuals is that they blame themselves. These disturbed attitudes toward the self correspond well with the consequences of the depressive attributional style described in the previous section. In Beck's tradition, they are thought to result from a biased information processing. Beck (1976) proposed that automatic processes determine to a large extent the way we interpret experiences. This fits with the recent developments in the area of the self (the self as an organization of knowledge, Greenwald & Pratkanis, 1984), and especially with the concept of the self-schema presented by Markus (1977). Actually, experimental studies have shown that depressed patients reported significantly more adjectives with a depressed self-referenced content than adjectives with a nondepressed self-referenced content. Furthermore, the self-reference bias only helped them recall depressive adjectives, whereas nondepressed individuals usually recalled more positive self-referent adjectives (Kuiper, MacDonald, & Derry, 1983).

Also studies including children and adolescents have documented the association between negative self-referenced biases and depression, demonstrating for example that the cognitions of depressed school children were characterized by more negative self-evaluations than those of nondepressed peers (Kendall, Stark, & Adam, 1990; Harrington, 1993).

The approaches discussed above all converge in at least one point: They consider self-evaluation (and the resulting self-esteem, or lack of such) to be a central element in depression. In the next section the role of the individual in the development of his/her own depressive orientation will be addressed with a special focus on self-evaluation.

## The Role Of The Individual: Self-Evaluation

As part of a "construction system" of personality, global self-evaluations are expected to have a certain degree of stability (in an absolute sense), helping us to organize our experiences in a meaningful way. On the other hand, under normal circumstances, they are also assumed to continue to develop and change with new experiences across the lifespan.

Epstein (1985) suggested that the essence of a person's personality is "the implicit theory of the self and the world that the person constructs" (p. 283). In a first paper (Epstein, 1973) he emphasized the attributes that a person's self-theory has in common with scientific theories. Of interest in our context is what he called extensivity: Good theories, he said, become more differentiated and extensive with the input of new data, and so would good self-theories, too. Other attributes that characterize good self-theories and may be relevant in the present investigation were empirical validity, internal consistency, and usefulness.

But, because the self-system is assumed to help us make sense, to organize experiences in an efficient way, and to aim at consistency between self-representations (Epstein, 1973), it is also supposed to be active in the possible distortion of so-called "disturbing" information, that is in Markus' (1977) terms counterschematic information. This is what happens in the case of a depressive orientation. As Bretherton (1987) stated, "some distortion of incoming information in the service of adaptive simplification is normal and unavoidable" (p. 1068). In fact, realistic self-perceptions are not necessarily assumed to be the most functional ones (Cairns & Cairns, 1988). However, when the selection is based on defensive exclusion of information in response to mental pain, for example, the model is not only useless, it becomes maladaptive, and as proposed by Bretherton (1987), it will interfere with effective coping and with optimal development. Also, as noted by Markus (1977), the stronger the self-schemata, the greater the tendency to make inferences from minimal and fragmentary data. That is, a depressive individual with a depressive attributional style and a well-established set of negative self-evaluations including representations of rejection by others, may interpret the lack of explicit social approaches from the side of peers as rejection and a confirmation of his/her worthlessness. Such interpretations occur automatically and even if they are not based on facts, they serve to further consolidate the existing self-representations.

In this context, it is worth noting that Bowlby (1969), and Tulving (1983) have emphasized the fact that personally experienced events or episodes are stored in episodic memory, whereas generalizations based on such events and thus, also knowledge about the self, in terms of concepts, rules etc., are assumed to be stored in semantic memory. This distinction is important because, as stated by Tulving, access to semantic memory tends to be automatic, but that access requires conscious effort in episodic memory. Furthermore, semantically stored information about the self need not be consistent with episodically stored information. Becker (1979) noted, for example, that the low self-esteem of some depressed subjects operated across situations and independent of identifiable events. Defensive exclusion of information may also interfere with the retrieval of information in episodic memory and therefore, models based on defensiveness are assumed to be rather difficult to change.

Negative self-evaluations have been shown to be fairly stable during adolescence and to become increasingly stable with age in this period of life (Alsaker & Olweus, 1992b). This gives support to the hypothesis that, in general, with increasing age, a gradual consolidation of the personality structures occurs, and that a certain set of experiences will have less impact on an individual's domain-specific structures, the higher their degree of consolidation.

Although evaluative constructs have generally been intentionally omitted from personality descriptive systems, some researchers, using not only descriptive, but also evaluative lexical terms have identified two additional factors to the Big Five, positive valence and negative valence (McCrae & Costa, 1995). Positive valence could be defined as a dimension of self-appraisal close to self-esteem, they say, whereas negative valence would correspond to the opposite. Negative valence has been demonstrated to correlate positively with the depression facet of neuroticism and negatively with aggreeability. The latter result would indicate that individuals who are likely to evaluate themselves negatively are less aggreeable, i.e., more difficult partners in social contexts.

The key figure in Stern's (1985) theory regarding early relationships is the "self-regulating other." The self-regulating other may be any person who interacts with the infant in a way that triggers or arouses different states in the infant. These other-regulated states lead to experiences which are associated with the self, and called self-experiences. Such states may be excitation, arousal, emotions, attention etc. These are mostly states that could not have been experienced by the infant alone. Relationships are central to individuals during their entire lives. What Stern described as important elements of early relationships is also valuable in later relationships. Especially the suggestion that some emotions that are central to self-representations can only be experienced in interaction with others is important to our discussion. Depressed individuals may, actually, have less opportunity for such experiences, and experiences of shared affects, either because they give wrong signals to others, withdraw, or are not able to interpret the situation adequately.

In summary, the cognitive bias toward negative self-evaluation in depressive subjects (Beck, 1967) can be understood as a stable self-maintaining feature of the personality. In maintaining themselves, the negative self-perceptions will not only maintain, or foster, individuals' proneness to depressive thoughts and feelings, but they will possibly also make it difficult for them to obtain gratifications in interpersonal relationships (see also Becker, 1979). The next question to be addressed is the role of behavior in the maintenance of a depressive orientation.

## THE ROLE OF THE INDIVIDUAL: BEHAVIOR AND CHOICES

Rutter (1990) has drawn our attention to the early studies of Murphy (1962, cited in Rutter, 1990) on mastery, who already emphasized the active role of the individual. Resilience was not just a matter of constitutional strength or weakness; it was also a reflection of *what one did* about the difficulties one encounters. Harrington (1993) stated that depressed people *do not engage* in forms of behavior that lead to pleasant consequences. As argued above, depressed subjects are less likely to have contact with other people and so they become even less likely to experience positive social reinforcement.

Furthermore, negative cognitive schemata may be active in the selection of experiences that reinforce the individual's negative view of her/himself and others. In other words, poor peer relationships may lead to depressive cognitions, but depressive cognitions may lead to negative perceptions of relationships, and elicit *behavior* that may be detrimental to the formation of positive relationships.

The role of behavior in the interplay between individual and environment has been neglected in psychological research. Most theory and research has focussed on explanations of individual differences in behavior and, as stated by Bandura (1978) most models have been unidirectional, conceiving of behavior as a function of individual and environmental factors. In his model of reciprocal determinism, Bandura (1978) conceives of behavior, individual, and environmental factors as influencing each other. Through their characteristics and their behavior, individuals typically activate different environmental reactions and "people do not simply react mechanically to situational influences—they actively process and transform them" (p. 351).

Thus, through their actions individuals determine the nature of their experiences, at least to a certain extent (Bandura, 1978). What happens to depressed subjects? As could be expected from their negative self-evaluations and their low beliefs in their competences, they are reported to be *less active* than others. This, however, has only been described in clinically depressed subjects (Harrington, 1993).

In an earlier section, results were presented (Alsaker & Flammer, 1996) which indicated that depressed adolescents experienced to be isolated more often than their peers, and that they did not feel well in groups of peers. What about their behavior? Using the same data set and examining adolescents' time-use, Alsaker and Flammer (1996) and Alsaker (1998) found depressed adolescents to participate less than their peers in typical social activities, such as going to the cinema with friends. Furthermore, even if there were cultural differences as to the frequency of performing such activities (Norwegians were less engaged in social activities than their Swiss peers), in both countries depressed adolescents differed from their nondepressed peers. Depressed adolescents went less often to restaurants or sports arrangements and they trained less often in sports clubs. However, they were not passive, they did train, but they did it preferably alone. Also depressed adolescents watched more television than their peers during week-ends, they read more, and reported "doing nothing"more often.

These findings give support to hypotheses stating that depressed adolescents are socially less integrated than others. They also show that depressed adolescents do not only *interpret* their environment in a depressive manner, they actually also *act* in ways that are apt to maintain their depressive orientation.

Bandura (1978) wrote that "when belief differs from actuality behavior is weakly influenced by its actual consequences until more realistic expectations are developed through repeated experience" (p. 356). Also the idea of the individual producing "information-generating experiences" is central to the model of reciprocal determinism. Depressed adolescents do not produce "nothing". They produce situations that are probably rewarding to them, at least in terms of avoiding situations that would be experienced negatively. But doing so, depressive adolescents prevent themselves from experiencing any social reward, or any shared experience with others.

## CONCLUSION

The starting point for this chapter was the puzzling finding that depressive cognitions and disorders are stable constructs although people generally aim at maximizing pleasure and minimizing pain, and at enhancing their self-esteem. The issue was addressed of how much the individual could be seen as an agent in the development and maintenance of such a personality orientation.

The approaches and findings selected have provided much evidence for the role of the individual in this process. However, the question arises whether an adolescent can be called the *agent* of his or her own personality development when self-perceptions, self-evaluations, and self-schemata appear to be the motor of the process. Self-evaluations that seem to be central to the consolidation process are most often the result of automatic or subconscious processes that can hardly be considered deliberate actions. Actually, a change in this process presupposes intensive work with one's cognitions and interpretations combined with repeated positive experiences. Therefore, even if the individual becomes aware of the unadequateness of her/his self-representations, he or she may not be able to change them without help from a therapist. When it comes to behavioral components, the vicious circle becomes evident. Depressed adolescents may in fact protect themselves (they are less integrated than others and possibly actively rejected by others), through withdrawal. However, their withdrawal may primarily be a consequence of their biased perceptions. So or so, a spontaneous change in behavior seems extremely unprobable. On the basis of the analysis presented in this chapter, it seems reasonable to conclude that depressed individuals do regulate their behavior, but that they do so more in terms of minimization of pain than in maximization of pleasure.

## REFERENCES

Abramson, L. Y., Seligman, M. E. P, & Teasdale, J. D. (1978). Learned helplessness in humans: Critique and reformulation. *Journal of Abnormal Psychology*, *87*, 49–74.

Adams, M., & Adams, J. (1991). Life events, depression, and perceived problem solving alternatives in adolescents. *Journal of Child Psychology and Psychiatry*, *32*, 811–820.

Alsaker, F. D. (1998). Individual life-style and societal impact on time-use: The case of adolescents with problem behavior. In F. D. Alsaker & R. Larson, *Time-use at the crossroad between individual and societal priorities*. Symposium presented at the Biennial Meetings of the Society for Research on Adolescence, San Diego, USA, February 1998.

Alsaker, F. D., & Flammer, A. (1996). *Social relationships and depression in adolescents: Social causation and social selection*. Paper presented at the Biennial Meetings of the Society for Research on Adolescence, Boston.

Alsaker, F. D., & Olweus, D. (1992a). *Parental relationships, peer relationships, and the development of depressive tendencies in adolescence*. Paper presented at the Biennial Meetings of the Society for Research on Adolescence, Washington DC.

Alsaker, F. D., & Olweus, D. (1992b). Stability of self-evaluations in early adolescence. A cohort longitudinal study. *Journal of Research on Adolescence*, *2*, 123–145.

Beck, A. T. (1976). *Cognitive therapy and the emotional disorders*. New York: International Universities Press.

Beck, A. T. (1967). *Depression: Clinical, experimental, and theoretical aspects*. New York: Hoeber.

Becker, J. (1979). Vulnerable self-esteem as a predisposing factor in depressive disorders. In R. A. Depue (Ed.), *The psychobiology of the depressive disorders: Implications for the effects of stress* , (pp. 317–334). New York: Academic Press.

Block, J. H., & Block, J. (1980). The role of ego-control and ego-resiliency in the organization of behavior. In W. A. Collins (Ed.), *Development of cognition, affect, and social relations* , (pp. 30–101). Hillsdale, NJ: Lawrence Erlbaum Associates.

Bowlby, J. (1969). *Attachment and loss: Vol.1. Attachment*. New York: Basic Books.

Bretherton, I. (1987). New perspectives on attachment relations: Security, communication, and internal working models. In J. D. Osofsky (Ed.), *Handbook of infant development*. New York: Wiley.

Cairns, R. B., & Cairns, D. D. (1988). The sociogenesis of self-concepts. In N. Bolger, A. Caspi, G. Downey, & M. Moorehouse (Eds.), *Persons in context.Developmental processes*. Cambridge, MA: Cambridge University Press.

Costello, E. J., & Angold, A. (1988). Scales to assess child and adolescent depression: Checklists, screens, and nets. *Journal of American Academic Child and Adolescence Psychiatry*, *27*, 726–737.

Cummings, E. M., & Cicchetti, D. (1990). Toward a transactional model of relations between attachment and depression. In M. T. Greenberg, D. Cicchetti, & E. M.

Cummings (Eds.), *Attachment in the preschool years: Theory, research, and intervention* , (pp. 339–372). Chicago: Univesity of Chicago Press.

Cytrin, L., McKnew, D. H., ZahnŒWaxler, C., & Gershon, E. S. (1986). Developmental issues in risk research: The offspring of affectively ill parents. In M.Rutter, C.E.Izard, & P.B.Read (Eds.), *Depression in young people*, (pp. 163–188). New York: The Guilford Press.

Emde, R. N., Harmon, R. J., & Good, W. V. (1986). Depressive feelings in children: A transactional model for research. In M. Rutter, C. E. Izard, & P. B. Read (Eds.), *Depression in young people. Developmental and clinical perspectives* , (pp. 491–519). New York: Guilford Press.

Epstein, S. (1973). The self-concept revisited, or a theory of a theory. *American Psychologist, 28*, 404–416.

Epstein, S. (1985). The implications of cognitive-experiential self-theory for research in social psychology and personality. *Journal for the Theory of Social Behavior, 15*, 283–310.

Flammer, A. (1995). Developmental analysis of control beliefs. In A. Bandura (Ed.), *Self-efficacy in changing societies*, (pp. 69–113). Cambridge: Cambridge University Press.

Greenwald, A. G., & Pratkanis, A. R. (1984). The self. In R. S. Wyer, & T. K. Srull (Eds.), *The handbook of social cognition* (Vol. 3). Hilldale, NJ: Lawrence Erlbaum Associates.

Harrington, R. (1993). *Depressive disorder in childhood and adolescence.* Chichester: Wiley.

Hartup, W. W. (1980). Family relations and peer relations: Two social worlds. In M. Rutter (Ed.), *Scientific Foundations of Developmental Psychiatry* , (pp. 280–292). London: Heinemann.

Kandel, D. B., & Davies, M. (1982). Epidemiology of depressive mood in adolescents. *Archives of General Psychiatry, 39*, 1205–1212.

Kashani, J. H., Husain, A., Shekim, W. O., Hodges.K, K., Cytryn, L., & McKnew, D. H. (1981). Current perspectives on childhood depression: An overview. *American Journal of Psychiatry, 138*, 143–153.

Kazdin, A. E., & Petti, T. A. (1982). Self-Report and interview measures of childhood and adolescent depression. *Journal of Child Psychological Psychiatry, 23*, 437–457.

Kovacs, M. (1980/81). Rating scales to assess depression in school-aged children. *Acta paedopsychiatria, 46*, 305–315.

Kuiper, N. A., Derry, P. A., & MacDonald, M. R. (1982). Self-reference and person perception in depression: A social cognition perspective. In G. Weary, & H. L. Mirels (Eds.), *Integrations of clinical and social psychology.* New York: Oxford University Press.

Kuiper, N. A., MacDonald, M. R., & Derry, P. A. (1983). Parameters of a depressive self-schema. In J. Suls, & A. Greenwald (Eds.), *Psychological perspectives on the self* (Vol. 2). Hillsdale, NJ: Lawrence Erlbaum Associates.

Kupersmidt, J. B., & Patterson, C. J. (1991). Childhood peer rejection, aggresion, withdrawal, and perceived competence as predictors of self-reported behavior problems in preadolescence. *Journal of Abnormal Child Psychology, 19*, 427–449.

Lapsley, D. K., & Quintana, S. M. (1985). Integrative themes in social and developmental theories of self. In J. Pryor, & J. Day (Eds.), *The Development of social cognition.* (pp. 153–176). New York: Springer.

Lerner, R. M. (1982). Children and adolescents as producers of their own development. *Developmental Review, 2*, 342–370.

358                                                                          ALSAKER

Magnusson, D., & Bergman, L. R. (1988). Individual and variable-based approaches to longitudinal research on early risk factors. In M. Rutter (Ed.), *Studies of psychological risk: The power of longitudinal data* , (pp. 45–61). Cambridge: Cambridge University Press.

Markus, H. (1977). Self-schemata and processing information about the self. *Journal of Personality and Social Psychology, 35*, 63–78.

Marsiske, M., Lang, F. R., Baltes, P. B., & Baltes, M. M. (1995). Selective optimization with compensation: Life-span perspectives on sucessful human development. In R. A. Dixon, & L. Bäckman (Eds.), *Compensating for psychological deficits and declines: Managing losses and promoting gains* , (pp. 35–79). Mahwah, NJ: Lawrence Erlbaum Associates.

McCrae, R. R., & Costa, P. T. (1995). Positive and negative valence within the five-factor model. *Journal of Research in Personality, 29*, 443–460.

McCranie, E. W., & Bass, J. D. (1984). Childhood family antecedents of dependency and self-criticism: Implications for depression. *Journal of Abnormal Psychology, 93*, 3–8.

Merikangas, K. R., & Angst, J. (1995). The challenge of depressive disorders in adolescence. In M. Rutter (Ed.), *Psychosocial disturbances in young people: Challenges for prevention*. New York: Cambridge University Press.

Olweus, D. (1993). Victimization by peers: Antecedents and long-term outcomes. In K. H. Rubin, & J. B. Asendorpf (Eds.), *Social withdrawal, inhibition, and shyness in childhood* , (pp. 315–342). Hillsdale, NJ: Lawrence Erlbaum Associates.

Papousek, H., & Papousek, M. (1979). Early ontogeny of human social interaction: Its biological roots and social dimensions. In M. Von Cranach, K. Foppa, W. Lepenies, & D. Ploog (Eds.), *Human ethology: Claims and limits of a new discipline*. Cambridge, MA: Cambridge University Press.

Patterson, G. R., & Capaldi, D. M. (1990). A mediational model for boys' depressed mood. In J. E. Rolf, A. Masten, D. Cicchetti, K. Neucherterlein, & S. Weintraub (Eds.), *Risk and protective factors in the development of psychopathology*, (pp. 141–163). Cambridge, MA: Cambridge University Press.

Peterson, C., & Seligman, M. E. P. (1984). Causal explanations as a risk factor for depression: theory & evidence. *Psychological Review, 91*, 367–374.

Puig-Antich, J., Lukens, E., Davies, M., Goetz, D., Brennan-Quattrock, J., & Todak, G. (1985). Psychosocial functioning in prepubertal major depressive disorders. I. Interpersonal relationships during the depressive episode. *Archives of General Psychiatry, 42*, 500–507.

Roberts, R. E., Lewinsohn, P. M., & Seeley, J. R. (1991). Screening for adolescent depression: A comparison of depression scales. *American Academy of Child & Adolescent Psychiatry, 30*, 58–66.

Rutter, M. (1986). The developmental psychopathology of depression: Issues and perspectives. In M. Rutter, C. E. Izard, & P. B. Read (Eds.), *Depression in young people. Developmental and clinical perspectives*, (pp. 3–30). New York: The Guilford Press.

Rutter, M. (1979). Maternal deprivation. 1972-1978: New findings, new concepts, new approaches. *Child Development, 50*, 285–305.

Rutter, M. (1990). Psychosocial resilience and protective mechanisms. In J. Rolf, A. S. Masten, D. Cicchetti, K. H. Nuechterlein, & S. Weintraub (Eds.), *Risk and protective factors in the development of psychopathology*, (pp. 181–214). New York: Cambridge University Press.

Seligman, M. E. P. (1975). Helplessness. On depression, development and death. San Fransisco: W. H. Freeman & Co.

Seligman, M. E. P., Peterson, C., Kaslow, N. J., Tannenbaum, R. L., Alloy, L. B., & Abramson, L. Y. (1984). Explanatory style and depressive symptoms among children. *Journal of Abnormal Psychology*, *93*, 235–238.

Stern, D. N. (1985). *The interpersonal world of the infant. A view from psychoanalysis and developmental psychology.* New York: Basic Books.

Trevarthen, C. (1985). Facial expressions of emotion in mother-infant interaction. *Human Neurobiology*, *4*, 21–32.

Tulving, E. (1983). *Elements of episodic memory.* New York: Oxford University Press.

van Lieshout, C. F., & Haselager, G. J. (1994). The big five personality factors in q-sort descriptions of children and adolescents. In C. F. Halverson Jr., G. A. Kohnstamm, & R. P. Martin (Eds.), *The developing structure of temperament and personality from infancy to adulthood*, (pp. 293–318). Hillsdale, NJ: Lawrence Erlbaum Associates.

Weisz, J. R., Weiss, B., Wasserman, A. A., & Rintoul, B. (1987). Control related beliefs and depression among clinic-referred children and adolescents. *Journal of Abnormal Psychology*, *96*, 58–63.

# 21

# Control of Action and Interaction: Perceiving and Producing Effects in Action and Interaction with Objects[1]

*Liselotte van Leeuwen*

*Franz Kaufmann*

*Daniel Walther*


## INTRODUCTION

Flammer (1995) rises the question of how a personal agency or causal schema emerges in relation to a perceptual causal schema in development. The personal causal schema is assumed to facilitate the control of one's own action, i.e. the production of causal events. The perceptual causal schema is described as related to events in the environment which are observed but not affected by a child's action. Flammer (1995) asks if those schemata emerge in a certain sequence or if one is accommodated into the other. In the following we will argue for the interwoven development of the perceptual and the personal agency schema from birth. Results from research in early event perception and action will illustrate our point of view. Data from object-centered mother–child interaction will be used to show how mothers focus on both the perceptual schema and the personal agency schema in order to facilitate action with objects and interaction. Consequences of the chosen viewpoint for clinical intervention, as well as for toy design, will be discussed.

## THEORETICAL ARGUMENTS

The ability to cause effects or to perform goal directed actions is directly related to the ability to perceive effects in event structures. Michotte & Thinès (1963/ 1991), in their concept of phenomenal causality, stress that the perception of causal relations forms the basis for our understanding of events which we observe as well as of those which we produce. "It is hardly necessary to stress that

[1]The project presented was supported by grant no. 11114-042349 of the Swiss National Science Foundation.

causal relations are essential to our knowledge of the world, since they seem to provide valid explanations of the changes that occur both around and inside us. Moreover, they allow us both to predict the occurrence of certain events and ultimately to control or adapt to them" (Michotte et al., 1963/1991, p. 66). Flammer (1995) describes the ontogenetic construction of control beliefs. He distinguishes between contingency beliefs which address the "probability with which a certain action will lead to a certain outcome" and competence beliefs which "refer to the ability to produce these actions oneself" (p. 69). The two types of beliefs correspond to the prediction of observed and produced phenomenal causality respectively.

Meltzoff (1990, 1993) argues that infants from birth on are able to make a difference between people and things. Meltzoff and Moore (1989), introducing the concept of active intermodal matching (AIM), tried to describe the infants' ability to apprehend the equivalence between acts seen and acts done. The specific attention infants show for actions of other people is explained by the match between their own proprioceptive abilities and actions which are performed by others. Shared action capacities are assumed to be the *psychological bridge* between infants and adults from birth on (Meltzoff, 1993). Actions of other people inform the infant about events he or she can potentially produce.

Michotte & Thinès (1963/1991), describe the dynamic structure of events in the environment which provide the basis for the perception and production of causal events. Meltzoff points to the role of shared action capacities of humans which allow the infant to learn how to control her own action. The concept of Ecological Realism (Gibson, 1979) combines both views by focusing on the complementary relationship between organism and environment. Information about events in the environment as well as about the organism is perceived continuously. Perception from the very first moment seems to be directed towards the detection of invariance in event structures. Control of action happens by complementary relating both types of events. Within Ecological Realism, one would argue that the ability to perceive structural and transformational invariance is what enables an organism to perceive causality and cause effects. Predicting an event outcome is based on the transformational invariance of the event. This holds for events observed as well as for events produced.

Within the concept Perception is studied in terms of what information a certain environment offers an individual organism for action. The environment is described as scaled to the body, i.e., as a function of the body. What is perceived are action possibilities or affordances.

Action is studied in terms of action capacities or effectivities. The focus of research is how the specific action capacities of an organism can be related to certain environmental conditions. The organism is described as scaled to the environment, i.e., as function of the environment. Action capacities are described with respect to the environment in terms of effectivities.

In the following section we try to illustrate the argument of an interwoven development of the ability to perceive and produce phenomenal causality. First we report some examples of research which show that both the perception of causality and the control of action with respect to objects emerges in parallel. Secondly, results from object-centered mother-child interaction will show how mothers provide their children from early on with both, information about causal events in the environment and information about how to produce causal events.

## EMPIRICAL DATA

### Early Event Perception And Actions With Objects

In the following we will explore three types of event perception including objects.

**Type 1:** The observation of events in the physical environment

**Type 2:** The observation of events with objects caused by other human actors

**Type 3:** The observation of self produced events, i.e. actions with objects

*Type 1: Observation of Events in the Physical Environment.* The ability to predict event outcomes, like the reappearance of an object after it moved behind a screen, was shown to be present at 3 to 4 months (e.g., Gibson & Spelke, 1983; Ashmead, Davis-De Ford, Whalen & Odow, 1991; and Arterberry, 1993).

The perception of causal event structures in infancy was studied using mechanical interaction of objects. Habituation times for physical events which obey the laws of Newtonian physiscs were compared to events in which those laws were seemingly denied (Baillargeon 1993; Leslie, 1982, 1984; Leslie & Keeble, 1987; Cohen & Oakes, 1993; and Sitskoorn & Smitsman, 1995). An example from Sitskoorn & Smitsman (1995), is the comparison between an event in which a big cube moves downwards to a smaller open box and rests on top of it with an event where the same cube disappears magically in that smaller box. If the habituation times for the miraculous event were longer than for the lawful event it was concluded that infants make a difference between logically expected and unexpected events. A basic assumption for this research was that information for causality is specified in visual information and therefore directly accessible for the perceiver. The ability to perceive dynamic relations between objects seems to emerge around 9 months of age. At the same age infants start to produce those events, i.e., incorporate relationships between objects in their actions, like putting a smaller cup into a bigger one (see e.g. Schaffer, 1984).

*Type 2: Observation of Events with Objects Caused by Other Human Actors.* Meltzoff (1995), conducted experiments in which 18-month-old children's ability to perceive intentions of human actors with respect to objects was tested. Children's performance of certain actions with objects was measured after they observed another person performing them more or less completely. Four different ways of demonstration by another person were used: The demonstrator performed a certain action on an object (e.g., pulling apart a dumbbell); the demonstrator tried but did not succeed to perform a certain action with an object; the adult did not demonstrate actions; the demonstrator performed other than the target acts on the objects. The results suggest that children at 18 months of age can understand the intended acts of adults even when the adult does not fulfill his intention.

Rochat (1991), asked 3-, 4-, and 5-year-olds when another person would be able to touch a moving object. Children in these age groups were surprisingly accurate in their judgments concerning the other person.

*Type 3: Self-Produced Events, i.e. Actions with Objects.* Research shows that from birth on information about the environment and about the own body is complementary related in perception-action cycles (Gibson, 1988; Adolph, Eppler & Gibson, 1993). The attention to new and complex events seems to guide the discovery of control. The recognition of information about possibilities to control the own body and about controlling objects in the environment seems to emerge in parallel. Van der Meer (1991) demonstrates the emergence of arm movement control in the first two months. She describes how infants discover the contingency between the visual and the proprioceptive event of their own arm movements.

The earliest instance of actions with objects is grasping. Von Hofsten (1982), showed that neonates direct their arm movements towards moving objects. From 3 months on adjustments to distance, object size, shape and orientation were found (Corbetta and Thelen, 1992; von Hofsten & Ronnqvist, 1988). For an overview see Adolph, Eppler & Gibson (1993).

The perception of contingency between body movement and events in the environment was shown by Watson's (1966) famous experiment where 2- to 3-month-olds control a mobile attached to their foot. Dunham & Dunham (1990) demonstrated 3-month-olds' control of a light by eye movements. In both cases it seems that changes in the environment attract attention. Subsequently, the resemblance between the proprioceptive information about the movement to the environmental change is detected, which in turn reinforces the action and facilitates control.

## EARLY OBJECT-CENTERED
## MOTHER-CHILD INTERACTION

Van Leeuwen, Kaufmann-Hayoz, Kaufmann, & Walther (1994) observed 50 mother–child dyads repetitively during 10 minutes of free-play. The four times of observation were chosen according to dramatic changes in the child's action repertoire (see Table 21.1).

*TABLE 21.1*
*Required criteria to be fulfilled for the free-play sessions at 3, 7, 16 and 30 months of age.*

| Average age | Required action capacities |
|---|---|
| 3 months | making eye contact with and smile at mother, following moving objects |
| 7 months | sitting free, grasping and holding objects, shaking and bouncing them, and changing objects from one hand to the other |
| 16 months | walking free |
| 30 months | 2–word sentences |

We described the quality of actions both partners initiated with objects. Actions with objects were discriminated in terms of the uniqueness of an action for a certain object compared to others. Actions which are more unique for an object are more likely to produce new and complex events. They also are more likely to open up new possibilities for action to the child than actions which can be performed with a lot of different objects. Uniqueness of an action with a certain object was defined as follows:

**Specific** actions are actions which can be performed with less than three out of the 10 objects presented (e.g., rolling a ball).

**Medium specific** actions can be performed with more than 7 out of the 10 objects presented (e.g., grasping a ball).

**Unspecific** actions are not directed towards a certain object (e.g., pointing to a basket with several toys in it).

The results demonstrate that infants' actions with objects are directed towards producing new and complex events in which they are the cause for the emerging effect.

Figure 21.1 shows dramatic changes in both, absolute and relative amount of specific and medium specific actions during early development. With increasing action capacities children perform more and more actions which are unique for a certain object. Children's potential to produce, i.e., control events involving material objects increases (t-tests for paired samples showed significant differences between all age groups at the .01 or .000 level for medium specific and specific actions). The absolute and relative number of actions which can be performed with the majority of available objects (medium specific actions) decreases between 7 to 30 months of age. The results confirm our assumption that age related changes in action capacities lead to an increased production and control of complex events which are unique for certain objects.

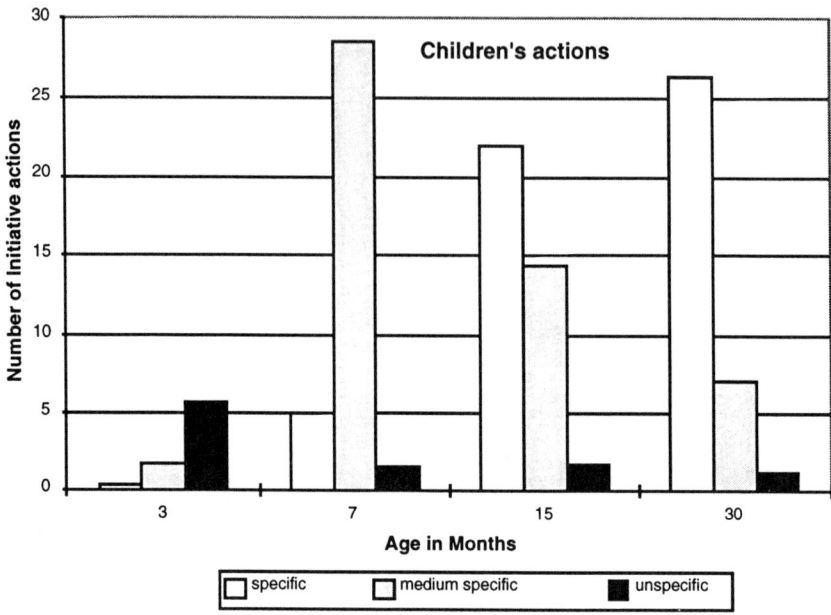

*FIG. 21.1: Averaged frequency of children's actions with objects according to their object specificity (specific, medium specific and unspecific) at 3, 7, 15, 30 and 48 months of age.*

The average number of medium specific actions increases heavily from 3 to 7 months. Babies at this age are known to apply, according to their action capacities, a limited number of manipulative actions to a wide range of objects. Grasping, fingering and mouthing are the actions which were performed mostly with the available objects. These actions provide information about the distinct properties of objects. Different effects can be caused by applying the same action to different objects. In terms of sustained attention, e.g., 7 month olds clearly prefer a rustling bag over a foam object. Both objects can be grasped, fingered and shaken easily. They differ with respect to the complexity of events caused by those actions. All actions performed with the rustling bag produce a complex visual-tactile-auditive event whereas with the foam object there is no sound produced and the visual–tactile events emerging are far less complex.

At 16 months of age activities which involve locomotion are preferred. The new action capacity of walking incorporates a high potential for creating new and complex events. Driving, sitting on and pushing a toy engine or moving up and down stairs in different ways are preferred activities. An increasing number of different actions are applied to one and the same object.

At 30 months of age children combine actions they performed earlier in isolation. An often observed example is to carry a toy-engine up some stairs or loading it with other objects. New information emerges about how different object properties can be combined with each other. At the same moment the limits of available action capacities are explored, e.g. by walking up stairs while holding a big object.

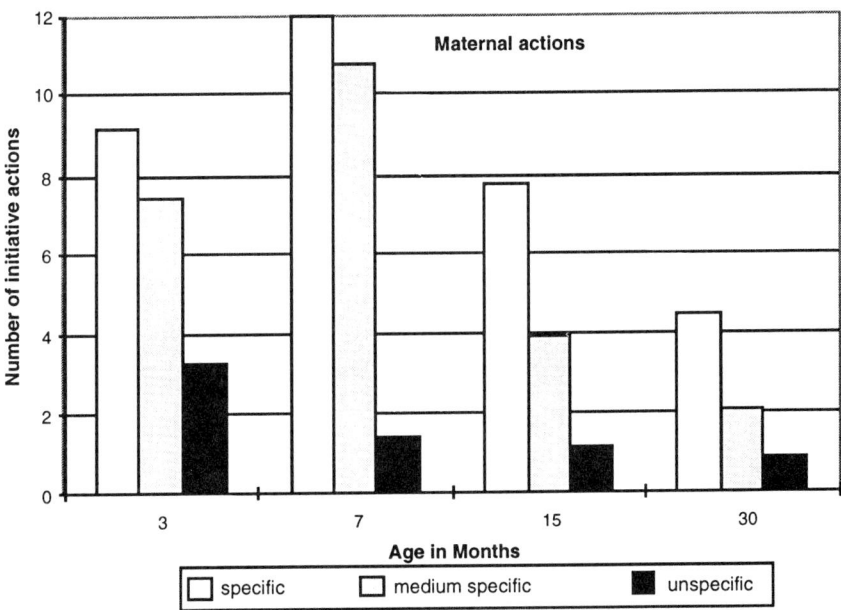

FIG. 21.2. Averaged frequency of mother's actions with objects according to their object specificity (specific, medium specific, and unspecific) at 3, 7, 15 and 30 months of age.

## OBJECT-CENTERED MOTHER–CHILD INTERACTION

The influence of adults' actions with objects on infants' actions with objects was shown e.g., by Lockman and McHale (1989). They found that 8- and 10-month-old infants manipulating objects showed more frequent use of object-appropriate actions, more fingering behavior, and more focused exploration when joined by their mothers, compared to exploring alone. Hofsten and Siddiqui (1994), showed that mother's modeling of certain object-specific actions leads, for some objects, to increased performance of those actions by 6-to 12-month-old infants. These results suggest that information provided by others has an influence on infants' actions on objects. A mother's object manipulation highlights certain object properties as well as related action possibilities in a consistent and appropriate manner. Actions of others disambiguate an object with respect to its potential for action.

As described earlier, infants' attention is directed towards new and complex events to be observed as well as to be produced by own actions. For object-centered mother-child interaction we would accordingly expect that mothers, in order to focus the baby's attention, try to provide them with new and complex events to be observed as well as to be performed.

Figure 21.2 shows the uniqueness of actions with objects mothers perform in the free-play situation at all ages. At 3 and 7 months mothers actions are about equally distributed over specific and medium specific actions (a t-test for paired samples provides no significant difference between both types of actions at 3 and 7 months). Mothers focus their actions on both providing new and complex events and on facilitating children's actions with objects. Specific actions reflect the tendency to provide the children with new and complex events which focus the infant's attention and potentially involve them in object-centered action and/or interaction. The relatively high amount of medium specific actions at 3 months is due to actions like bringing an object within sight of the infant, and in a few cases, to offering the objects for grasping. At 7 months, objects are often offered for grasping or placed in front of the child after a unique action had been performed with the object. Since bringing objects within reach is no longer necessary for their accessibility to the walking child, the relative amount of medium specific actions decreases from 16 months of age. Maternal control of children's actions with objects changes according to the available action capacities, i.e., the infant's capacity to control actions with objects. Accordingly, the amount of medium specific actions is significantly lower than that of specific actions from 16 months on.

In object-centered interaction control is shared between the partners. One way to analyze the distribution of control between mother and child in the free play situation is the degree in which the partners determine the situation by performing initiative actions with objects. With initiative actions objects and actions with them are chosen which are independent of already ongoing actions with objects by the partner. Reactive actions are related to the partners ongoing verbal or non-verbal actions with objects.

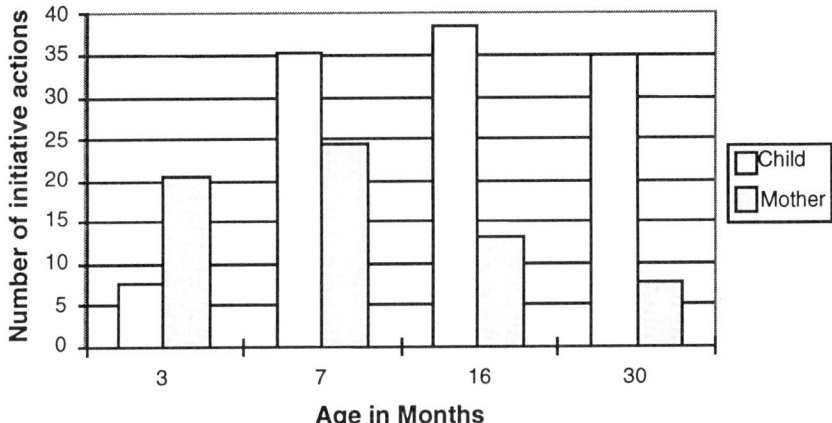

*FIG. 21.3. Averaged number of initiative actions with objects for 50 mother–child dyads at 3, 7, 16 and 30 months of age.*

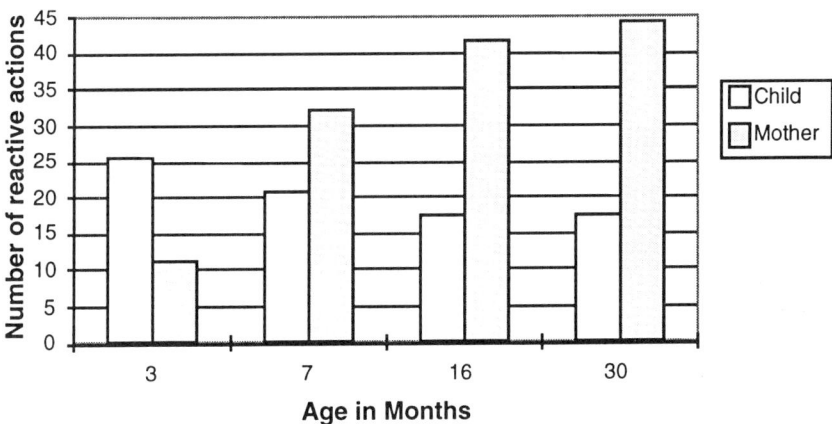

*FIG. 21.4. Averaged number of reactive actions with objects for 50 mother-child dyads at 3, 7, 16 and 30 months of age.*

Initiative actions with objects allow partners to determine the potential for action and interaction with objects. Figure 21.3 shows a change in relative amount of initiative actions over age. With increasing action capacities infants control more and more the content of the free play situation. Complementary, mothers become more and more reactive (see figure 21.4). They tune their own actions increasingly to the objects the child has chosen instead of making new objects available. With their initiatives mothers expand the action possibilities of their children according to the available action capacities. With 3-month-olds, mothers control almost completely what objects are involved and in what way. Infants mainly observe their mothers' actions with objects. But note that even at this age babies are able to integrate offered information about objects in their own actions when mothers meet the constraints of their action capacities. This was the case if the mother placed a light wooden rattle in the baby's hand, who finally grasped it.

At 7 months when grasping objects is easy to perform, the majority of initiative actions with objects is already performed by the child. Mothers bring new objects within reach for the baby and demonstrate how to use them. At 16 and 30 months of age mothers' initiatives with objects become more and more verbal. Mothers direct the attention of their children to certain objects or actions with them. They usually don't bring objects within reach anymore. The ability to walk expands the physical action radius of the child to the entire room. Mothers' initiatives are clearly tuned to this new ability. At 30 months, initiatives of mothers often include the combination of different objects. This also mirrors a newly emerged way of acting with objects by the child.

In object-centered mother–child interaction, mothers provide the child with information about possible ways to relate to objects. There are principally two ways of controlling an organism-environment relationship. There is the possibility to either change the environmental conditions according to the own action capacities or to adapt the own action capacities to the environmental conditions. Accordingly, when mothers support their infants in achieving a certain goal, they have the choice to focus their help on either the effectivities or the available affordances for the child. If a 7-month-old reaches for an out of reach toy the mother can either move the object within reach or change the infant's position with respect to the toy. In the first case she changes the affordance of the toy by making it reachable for the child and in the latter case she adapts the infant's effectivities to the toy by, e.g., changing the baby's posture.

From the free play situation we selected those episodes in which mothers help their children after an unsuccessful attempt to perform a certain action with an object. We observed whether mothers change the environmental conditions with respect to the child or adapt the child's effectivities with respect to the desired object.

Figure 21.5 shows that both ways of controlling the child-environment relationship are used at all ages. An analysis of variance showed significant effects of both age and kind of maternal control. The increase of affordance-directed control reflects the increasing action capacities of the child with respect to the available objects.

At 3 months, mothers direct their help according to the baby's gaze. Often the baby's posture is changed in order to make it easier for her to observe the actions with objects her mother performs. As the infant looks towards a mobile the mother will often carry her very near to it in order to make it easier to look. Mothers also try to fit the hand around a rattle as the infant tries to grasp.

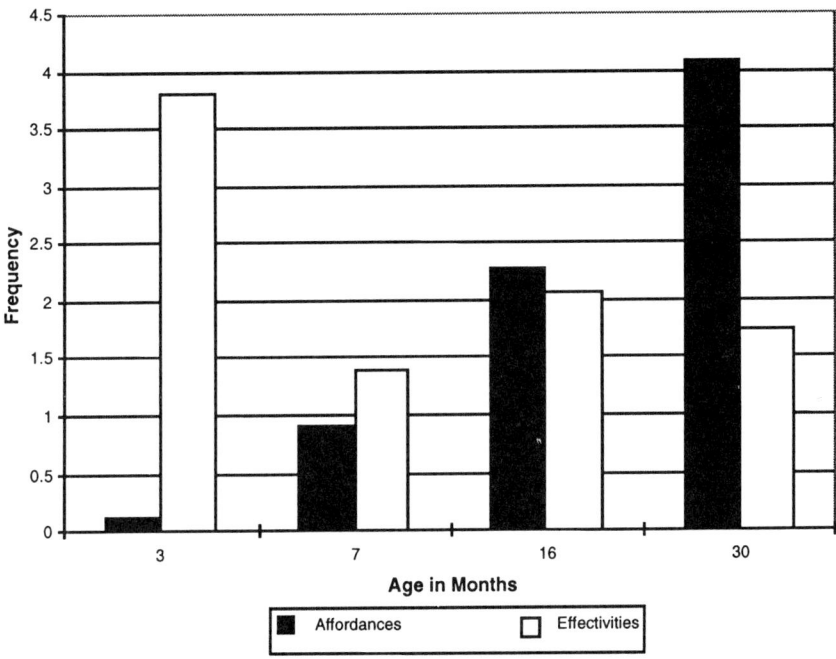

*FIG. 21.5. Averaged frequency of supportive actions of mothers as directed to affordances or effectivities of the child for 50 mother-child dyads at 3, 7, 16 and 30 months of age.*

At 7 and 16 months, mothers focus control on both affordances and effectivities (according to a t-test for paired samples, there is no significant difference between the number of affordance- respectively effectivity-directed control at 7 and 16 months). At 7 months, mothers change the posture of the baby in order to allow reaching and grasping. They aso bring objects within reach as the baby tries but can't actually reach an object. At 16 months mothers focus their help on the effectivities as they facilitate locomotion by supporting the baby walking, or placing her on the toy engine. They focus on affordances if they put the receiver of a toy telephone to the child's ear, or put a string to pull a toy in the child's hand.

At 30 months, mothers focus their control mainly on affordances by in-structing verbally about how to relate objects to each other. They tell the child, e.g., that she needs to use a small object to put in a cable train if the object the child tries to fit in is too big. They focus on effectivities, e.g., as they tell or show how to hold a handle.

The results shown favor a view in which the ability to perceive and produce causal events emerge complementarily related to each other. In the following, some consequences of this view for clinical intervention methods, as well as for toy design, will be suggested.

## CONCLUSION

Flammer (1995), addresses the question of how the development of a personal agency schema is related to the development of the perceptual causal schema. Theoretical as well as empirical arguments were presented which favor a view in which the development of a personal causal schema and a perceptual causal schema occurs as an interwoven process. One focus of future research should be to investigate the interrelatednes of both processes directly on a micro level.

Two research strategies should be integrated. One is the study of perceptual development as a function of emerging motor control and the other is the study of motor control as a function of perceptual changes in development. Complementing the results of both strategies will allow to describe the dynamics of the relationship between perception and action. This results are of vital interest for practical work from clinical psychology to the design of early learning tools. Early development of perception and action can be supported in two ways. One is by focusing on biomechanical aspects of action, and the other is by supporting the perception of action possibilities. The following two examples illustrate the practical relevance of the question pointed out by Flammer (1995). The first example, from a clinical context, shows how a video intervention can help to increase parent's control in interaction with their children by changing the perception of action possibilities in a situation. The second example concerning toy design shows how the early experience of control can be supported by design which takes in account and challenges both, perceptual as well as motor capacities at a certain age.

Parents of ADHD children often report a loss of control in interaction with their children. In certain situations it seems nearly impossible to predict the child's behavior on the basis of parental offers or requests. Van Leeuwen, Kaufmann & Walther (1997) developed a video-intervention method in which object-centered mother-child interaction episodes are used to discover possibilities for parental control. In order to analyze interaction episodes, actions with objects of both partners are compared. From an Ecological Realism perspective interaction takes place if the changes in the environment caused by one partner are perceived as action possibilities by the other. In order to control interaction with objects, adults have to meet the constraints for perception and action of the children in the given situation. Information for both affordances and effectivities is needed in order to increase control of interaction. With the video intervention we tried to increase the parent's sensitivity to action relevant information. Inefficient interaction episodes were analyzed with respect to the sufficiency of the information for action given to the child. Children seem to ignore parental offers including objects if the required action capacities are not available to the child (e.g., not being able to turn a handle;

the offered action includes too many sub-actions to be controlled by the child (e.g., 'Play bowling' instead of 'There are pins you can place...');

the child is occupied by another action.

After becoming aware of the criteria, parents clearly experience an increase in control of object-centered interaction.

Flammer (1995) points out that results from early contingency learning have important implications for caregivers and toy design. As described above, in performing actions with objects control can be arrived by either adjusting the environment to the available action capacities or by adapting the action capacities to a given environment. Toys can be designed so that information emerges mainly about affordances or about effectivities. The rapid change of action capacities in the first year of life provides a very concrete and rich source for toy design. Since, e.g., at 7 months a limited number of actions can be performed, a toy should maximize the information about the environment that can be arrived by those actions. In case of fingering, e.g., a toy which includes different textures, softness, and sound potential would focus the infant on potential action possibilities and encourage searching for more diversity in the environment. Complementary, at this age a toy could challenge early motor control by adding constraints for action, e.g., for sitting, which invite the child to apply control in different ways, i.e., expand the action repertoire.

The emergence of new and complex events drives action from the earliest age on. The results presented from literature imply that for toy design it is important to give babies the possibility to cause complex and diverse events with their limited action capacities. In order to do this, a careful analysis of available action capacities at different ages is needed. Only a very limited number of infants' action capacities are really addressed by current toy characteristics.

The facilitating role of adults for learning control of actions with objects should be addressed by toy designers. Toys for young children are often designed for solitary play. Since the development of interaction takes place by relating actions in the physical world, toys could be designed to support this process. Specific demands for toys can be formulated which facilitate interaction at early ages. Toys can be designed so that adults, by using them, can challenge emerging action capacities like walking. Toys facilitate interaction if they contain a maximum number of shared affordances for adult and child, and affordances which exist only for child or adult, but combined allow for shared action. The design of toy objects can support and expand possibilities for early control of action and interaction.

374 VAN LEEUWEN, KAUFMANN, WALTHER

## REFERENCES

Adolph, K. E., Gibson, E. J., & Eppler, M. A.(1990). Perceiving affordances of slopes: The ups and downs of toddlers' locomotion (Tech. report no. 16). Atlanta, GA: Emory University, Emory cognition project.

Arterberry, M. E. (1993). Development of spatiotemporal integration in infancy. *Infant behavior and Development, 3,* 343–363.

Ashmead, D. H., Davis-De Ford, L., Whalen, I., & Odom, R. D. (1991). Sound localization and sensitivity to interaural time differences in human infants. *Child development, 6,* 1211–1226.

Baillargeon, R. (1993) The object concept revisited: New directions in the investigation of infants' physical knowledge. In: C.E. Granrud (Ed.), *Visual perception and cognition in infancy* (pp.265–313). Hillsdale, NJ: Lawrence Erlbaum Associates.

Cohen, L. & Oakes, L.M. (1993). How infants perceive a simple causal event. *Developmental Psychology, 29,* 421–433.

Corbetta, D. & Thelen, E. (1992). Bimanual reaching in 5- to 8-month-olds: Task effects and neuromotor mechanisms. In P. Rochat (Chair), *New directions in the study of infant reaching.* Symposium conducted at the meeting of the International Conference on Infant Studies, Miami.

Dunham, P. & Dunham, F. (1990). Effects of mother-infant social interactions on infants' subsequent contingency task performance: *Child Development, 61,* 785–793.

Flammer, A. (1995): Developmental analysis of control beliefs. In A. Bandura (Ed.), *Self-efficacy in changing societies.* New York: Cambridge University Press, pp. 69–113.

Gibson, E. J. & Spelke, E. (1983). The development of perception. *In P.Mussen (Ed.), Handbook of Child Development, Vol.III.* New York: Wiley.

Gibson, E. J. (1988). Exploratory behavior in the development of perceiving, acting and the acquiring of knowledge. *Annual Review in Psychology, 39,* 1–41.

Gibson, J.J. (1979). *The ecological approach to visual perception.* Boston: Houghton Mifflin.

Hofsten, C. von (1982). Eye-hand coordination in newborns. Developmental Psychology, 18, 450-461.

Hofsten, C. von, & Rönnqvist, L. (1988). Preparation for grasping an object: A developmental study. *Journal for Experimental Psychology: Human Perception and Performance, 14,* 610–621.

Hofsten, C. von & Siddiqui, A. (1993). Using the mother's actions as a reference for object exploration in 6- and 12-month-old infants: *British Journal of Developmental Psychology, 11,* 61–74.

Leslie, A. M. (1984). Spatiotemporal continuity and the perception of causality in infants. *Perception,13,* 287–305.

Leslie & Keeble (1987). Do six-month-olds perceive causality? *Cognition, 25,* 265–288.

Lockman, J. J., McHale, J. P. (1989). Object manipulation in infancy: developmental and contextual determinants. In J. J. Lockman & N. L. Hazen (Eds.), *Action in a social context: Perspectives on early development* (129-172). New York: Plenum.

Meltzoff, A.N. (1995). Understanding the intentions of others: Re-enactment of intended acts by 18-month-old children. *Developmental Psychology,* 31, 838–850.

Meltzoff, A. N. (1993). The centrality of motor coordination and proprioception in social and cognitive development: From shared actions to shared minds. In G. J. P. Savelsberg (Ed.), *The development of coordination in infancy.* Amsterdam: Elsevier Science Publisher.

Meltzoff, A. N. (1990). Foundations for developing a concept of self: The role of imitation in relating self to other and the value of social mirroring, social modeling, and self-practice in infancy. In: D. Cicchetti & M. Beeghly (Eds.), *The self in transition: infancy to childhood.* Chicago: University of Chicago Press.

Meltzoff, A. N., & Moore, M. K.(1989). Imitation in new-born infants: Exploring the range of gestures imitated and the underlying mechanisms. *Developmental Psychology, 25,* 954–962.

Michotte, A. & Thinès, G. (1963/1991). Perceived causality. In G. Thinès & A. Costall (eds.), *Michotte's experimental phenomenology of perception.* Hillsdale, NJ: Lawrence Erlbaum Associates, 66–86.

Rochat, P. (1991). *Perceiving and representing what is reachable for self and for others in 3-to 6-year-old children.* Paper presented at the meeting of the International Society for Ecological Psychology, Hartford, CT.

Schaffer, H. R. (1984). *The child's entry into a social world.* London: Academic Press.

Sitskoorn, M. M., & Smitsman, A. W. (1995). Infants' perception of dynamic relations between objects: Passing through or support? *Developmental Psychology, 31,* 437–447.

Van Leeuwen, L., Kaufmann, F. & Walther, D. (1997). *Video Intervention in ADHD children.* Internal report, Department of Pediatrics, University of Berne.

Van Leeuwen, L., Kaufmann-Hayoz, R., Kaufmann, F. & Walther, D. (1994). *Actions of others as sources of information about objects.* Paper presented at the European Workshop on Event Perception and Action, Borken-Hoxfeld, 1994

Van der Meer, A. L. H. (1991). Arm movements in the neonate: establishing a frame of reference for reaching. In: P. J. Beek, R. J. Bootsma, & P. C.W. van Wieringen (Eds.), *Posters presented at the 6th international conference on event perception and action.* Amsterdam: Rodopi.

Watson, J. S. (1966). The development and generalization of "contingency awareness" in early infancy: Some hypotheses. *Merrill-Palmer Quarterly, 12,* 123–135.

# 22

# The Development of Internal versus External Control Beliefs in Developmentally Relevant Contexts of Children's and Adolescents' Lifeworlds

*Wolfgang Edelstein*

*Matthias Grundmann*

*Alexandra Mies*

## INTRODUCTION

Much has been written about internal vs. external control in children and adolescents since Rotter's monograph was published in 1954, but few publications are concerned with domain-specific aspects of control beliefs. Flammer (1990) is an exception. While in earlier work control theorists (e.g. Rotter, 1982; Crandall et al., 1965) assumed that control beliefs are stable personality dispositions, in more recent studies a trajectory towards internality has been postulated. For theoretical reasons and due to findings since the 1980ies increasing attention has been given to the development of control beliefs within important domains in children's lives (Flammer, 1990, Lüthi, Grob & Flammer, 1989). This research perspective is grounded in the assumption that developmental trajectories in different domains may diverge, given the different experiences of children and adolescents. Among these domains are settings for interactions with significant others such as parents, friends, and classmates, sometimes located in specific contexts (e.g., school, Oettingen & Little, 1993). In contrast with Rotter's assumption that internal vs. external control beliefs represent generalized control expectancies, Lüthi, Grob & Flammer (1989) postulated that individual control beliefs should be conceptualized as domain specific expectancies which may differ from one situation to the next. Accordingly, control beliefs do not represent stable dispositions of individuals but self-schemes which rest on specific and subjectively relevant experiences.

One reason for divergent findings about domain-specific control beliefs may be inadequate measurement with tests that are not tailored to the task. Relatively low reliabilities have been reported in most studies, especially with children.

Krampen (1979), has argued that low reliability is due to the inappropriateness of the locus of control items for children because their cognitions of the self and the environment remain unstable. However, although in most studies internal consistency and split-half reliability are low, this does not mean that at early ages control beliefs do not obtain, as Grob, Wicki and Flammer (1997) have noted. The assumption of generalized control ignores that the construct of control may refer to domain specific meanings and that domain specificity may precede the development of generalized locus of control. Thus, domain specific control beliefs may be more marked in childhood than in adolescence and adulthood.

Although many researchers have studied the development of control beliefs, most understood development merely in terms of the influence of antecendent conditions, either exerted by significant others or by specific agencies (Krampen, 1982). Others neglected the developmental perspective altogether (Rotter, 1954; Levenson, 1972). Moreover there is little agreement about the putative trajectories of control beliefs across the life-span (Skinner & Chapman, 1987). Piaget and Inhelder (1975), postulated that internal control will decrease with increasing age because younger children tend to overestimate their own role in producing events (magico-phenomenalism), but begin to recognize the limitations of their efforts and abilities when they grow older. Few researchers followed Piaget's lead and reconstructed the developmental aspects of control beliefs. Most control theorists (Bialer, 1961; Lefcourt, 1976; Nowicki & Strickland, 1973), disagreed with Piaget's theoretical perspective and assumed that children will, with age, experience increasing empowerment in important life-domains. Other control theorists reported no consistent developmental trends in their studies (Crandall, Katkovsky, & Crandall, 1965). Skinner and Chapman (1987), were able to account for these seemingly contradictory findings: They found that various control scales included a variety of internal and external causes, such as effort or luck that were salient at different ages while some only refer to children´s beliefs about control over academic outcomes that evidence little change across development.

Chapman and Skinner's findings highlight the role of both age- and domain specific experience for the development of children's control beliefs. Different domains and experiences of children´s and adolescent's lifeworlds have different implications for the development of individual competencies or control beliefs. Wicki, Reber, Flammer and Grob (1994) showed that children are more deeply involved in the processes of acquisition of concepts, skills, competencies, and social networks than adults (for the domains of friendship, see Selman, 1980; Damon, 1984; Keller, 1996). Moreover, some combinations of persons and situations may affect children's self-efficacy beliefs and thus foster the development of a sense of internal control. Contexts or relationships may actively influence individuals' sense of control throughout the entire span of development (e.g. friendship); other contexts may exert only temporary influence (e.g., parents; teachers, school, Oettingen & Little, 1993). Equality based friendship and peer relations as well as authority-dominated interactions with parents or other family members may influence the development of control beliefs, but contribute differentially to the outcome. Younger children confront important life events in developmentally relevant contexts on the basis of limited cognitive or socio-cognitive competence which may also vary between domains (Keller, 1996). Thus it appears important to adopt an ontogenetic viewpoint and take age-specific cognitive and interactive action potentials of children, adolescents and adults into account. Flammer's (1990) model describes variations of control beliefs as a function of lifeworld experiences and specific developmental tasks at different ages and in different domains of development. Flammer assumed that domain specific control beliefs at an earlier age are moulded, in the course of development, into more generalized beliefs. This view fits with empirical findings that generalized control beliefs can be reliably measured only after age 12 (Krampen, 1997).

A review of the literature shows that most studies of locus of control in childhood and adolescence refer to a generalized control beliefs construct. The Nowicki and Strickland Locus of Control Scale was adapted from a scale originally developed for adults (Krampen, 1997), and thus implied a general construct modeled on experience with adults. The psychometric properties of the scale, not unexpectedly, led to the conclusion that the construct of control could not be validated for children and needed reformulation to accommodate the developmental characteristics of children and adolescents. This conclusion and the concomitant assumption that domain specific experience plays a major role in the constitution and growth of control beliefs, call for qualitative analyses of item-specific distributions and longitudinal patterns in children and adolescents. Surprisingly, no analysis of this type has been reported in the literature.

The study reported below purports to tie together various aspects that have remained unconnected in previous research. We recognize that different individuals are exposed to different experiences in different domains of interpersonal interaction that have differential impact on the development of the system of control beliefs. We assume that the development of control beliefs will cover developmental trajectories that depend on distinctions between various lifeworlds and contexts. Our analysis will examine domain specific variations of control beliefs in the course of development from childhood to adolescence. A comparison with generalized control beliefs will help interpret the meaning of major lifeworld domains for the development of external and internal locus of control. Besides the methodological issues dealt with in most studies in this field we will focus on certain ontogenetic and sociogenetic conclusions derived from our findings. In sum, we conceptualize control beliefs as depending on the subjective competencies and experiences that children and adolescents are exposed to in different domains.

In the present study, therefore, the development of control beliefs is followed across a set of contexts. It is hypothesized that development will vary across domains, depending on children's typical lifeworld experiences. Lifeworld-specific subjective competencies (Wicki et al., 1994) may promote domain-

specific development towards internality, or lead to domain-specific predominance of an external orientation, and preclude the generalization of one or the
other orientation.

## METHOD

Our analysis is part of a longitudinal study of "Individual Development and
Social Structure," conducted at the Max Planck Institute for Human Development and Education (see Edelstein, Keller & Schröder, 1990). The development
of internal and external control beliefs was investigated longitudinally with a
slightly modified version of the Nowicki & Strickland's Locus of control Scale
for children (CNS-IE, 1973). A sample of 121 children from Reykjavík (Iceland)
—rather equally distributed across the two sexes and six social classes—was
assessed at ages 9, 12 and 15 years. The children were asked to answer the di-
chotomous (internal–external) control items of the one-dimensional scale. A
classification of these items showed 34 of 53 items to have longitudinally identical semantic structure (see table 22.1). The remaining items were discarded, as
they had different meanings for different ages. All longitudinal items were coded
in the direction of externality: thus, lower scale values represent higher internality values. The aggregate scores show significant development from external to
internal locus of control between ages 9, 12 and 15. This is in agreement with
findings from other studies.

The longitudinal items were analyzed in a twofold manner. First we reproduced the generalized locus of control scale as described in previous research
(e.g., Bialer, 1961; Nowicki & Strickland, 1973). The low to moderate reliability
coefficients of this scale (see appendix; table 22.A2), ranging from Cronbachs a
= .50 at age 9, a = .60 at age 12, and a = .71 at age 15, correspond to the results
of other studies (Krampen, 1997).

*TABLE 22.1*
*Psychometric characteristics of the generalized locus of control-scale*

| LOC | Number of cases | Number of items | Cronbachs Alpha | Cronbachs Alpha (stand.) |
|-----|-----|-----|-----|-----|
| 9 | 94 | 34 | 0.50 | 0.49 |
| 12 | 74 | 34 | 0.60 | 0.64 |
| 15 | 93 | 34 | 0.71 | 0.72 |

The generalized control belief scale is used as a baseline for comparison with
the developmental courses of subscales that refer to specific lifeworld domains.
In order to analyze the interaction between domains and the development of
control, five important domains of the lifeworld of children and adolescents were

identified on the basis of the different themes that are addressed in the CNS-IE: (a) parent–child-interaction or interaction with family members, (b) relationships with friends and nonfriends, (c) interactions with other important roles and persons, (d) intellectual achievement situations, and (e) actions of the self. The reason for selecting these domains cannot be presented here (see Mies, 1997). Various relevant domains for control beliefs are not represented by the longitudinal items of the CNS-IE. Examples are health, work, and leisure. In contrast to most earlier studies on domain specific control beliefs, in this study the domains were not derived statistically, but were based on content or socio-cognitive considerations. For reasons of space, data will only be reported for two of the five domains: relationship with friends and nonfriends, and intellectual achievement situations. The following reasons led to the choice of these two exemplary domains: Intellectual achievement is a traditional domain of control theory representing a set of standardized cultural norms of action involving attributions of control and responsibility. Relationships with friends represent a central domain of social cognitive competence, while control over peers depends, in part at least, on cognitive development. Thus this domain is an obvious candidate for in-depth investigation.

TABLE 22.2
*Descriptive characteristics of the generalized locus of control-scale*

| LOC | N | Mean | Std dev | Range |
|-----|-----|-------|---------|-------------|
| 9   | 105 | 0.460 | 0.108   | 0.088-0.735 |
| 12  | 110 | 0.373 | 0.108   | 0.118-0.588 |
| 15  | 106 | 0.275 | 0.115   | 0.029-0.676 |

A pattern analysis was done for each item of each domain to ascertain the developmental importance of the domain specific control beliefs. This provided a window to observe whether control beliefs develop towards internality, whether indeed they exhibit any systematic pattern of development. Thus external-to-internal, internal-to-external, stable internal, stable external, and a mixed pattern of development were identified. This overall pattern of variations differs substantively from the pattern of generalized development towards internal locus of control, which has been identified in the literature.

**RESULTS**

First the longitudinal development of the generalized locus of control scale was investigated. A trajectory was established with significant age differences between all three measurement points (see figure 22.1, and table 22.2): This finding is consistent with the literature (Flammer, 1990). The development of generalized control beliefs shows the following significant trend: Older children and adolescents responded more internally than younger children. The mean of the first measurement (9 years), is .46 (std. .11). At the age of 12 years, the mean has decreased to .37 (std. .11). At the age of 15 years, the mean is .28 (std. .12). Note that the data are scored for externality, so that lower numbers indicate higher internality values. The differences between the means are significant. But because of insufficient internal consistency the analysis does not truly confirm a directed developmental change. Even though the psychometric properties of the scale confirm its reliability, inconsistency highlights heterogeneous item–structures. Single items may measure different domains that generate heterogeneity.

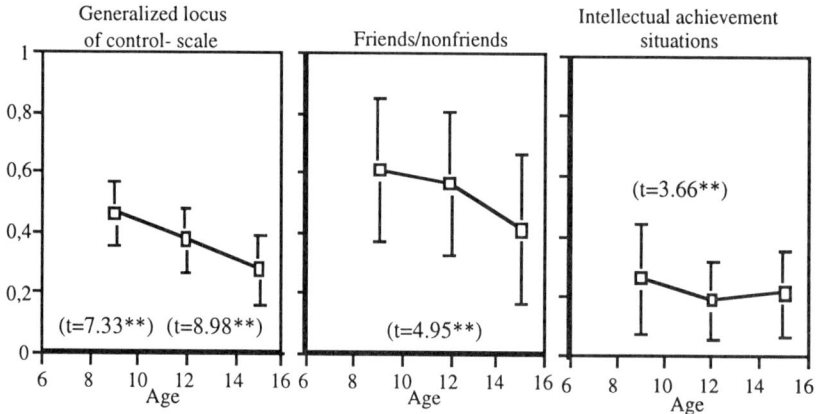

FIG. 22.1. Longitudinal development of generalized and domain-specific control beliefs

Comparing the generalized scale with the distribution and the longitudinal patterns of domain specific items we find marked differences. In the domain of friendship no significant development towards internality is found between age 9 and age 12. An important increase of internality only emerges between age 12 and age 15. While younger children have more restricted competencies when interacting with friends, older children or adolescents recognize their increased skills and competencies in interaction with their peers. The distribution in the domain of intellectual achievement situations is very different. Between ages 9 and 15, children tend to answer the items in this domain more internally than the generalized scale indicates. In this domain the most significant change from external to internal control beliefs occurs between ages 9 and 12. At age 9, children have already developed rather internal control beliefs concerning achievement situations (e.g., in school)—and hardly differ from the internal orientation achieved by older children. Apparently the younger subjects believe more strongly in their competencies at school than in their ability to exert influence on friends or enemies. These items may represent the degree to which children and adolescents have internalized social norms or standards, or certain claims that specific environments (such as schools) place on them. The longitudinal trajectories of the three other domains, parent–child-interaction; interaction with other important roles and persons; and actions of the self also evidence significant development toward internality with increasing age.

The contradiction between the developmental structure of the generalized scale and the different domains strengthens the assumption of domain specific developmental paths. In fact, contradictory development can also be a cause of the low internal consistency of the scale as described by Krampen (1997). The heterogeneity of the scale may derive from differential item–structures.

Supposedly every single item measures different domains which are accountable for the heterogeneity of the scale. These psychometric arguments are confirmed by the variance in the answers to the domain specific items as shown in the figures above. It is true that the distribution of the means indicates development from external to internal locus of control. But the variance in the age-specific measures calls for a more precise method for describing the developmental patterns for each subject in the study. The method used here permits to explore the individual developmental pattern of each item subgroup in view of individual domain-specific differences in a longitudinal perspective. As mentioned earlier, the following types of trajectories were found: two patterns of directed development, two stable patterns, and one mixed pattern. Four of the five patterns appear compatible with the different theoretical considerations discussed earlier: The development from external to internal is consistent with the developmental theory locus of control, as formulated by numerous researchers (Bialer, 1961; Nowicki & Strickland, 1973). The stable patterns are consistent with the early control theories, defining control beliefs as stable personality dispositions (e.g., Rotter 1982). Contrary to a dispositional perspective but consistent with Piaget's (1975) arguments is the development from internal to external locus of control. The mixed pattern, which is defined by children who change their modes of attribution between the measurement points, contradicts all theoretical points of view that have been advanced in the discussion.

At the item level, however, the picture is more complex. On the basis of the individual pattern analysis of all items of the domain–specific subgroups a classification system was derived which makes it possible to describe every pattern in a longitudinal perspective as either indicating development or stability (no change) of control beliefs (see tables 22.3 and 22.4).

A view of the developmental patterns within the two domains under study provides an impression of the domain specificity of locus of control in childhood and adolescence (see the appendix). The results of the pattern analyses show that some developmental trajectories deviate from the pattern of increasing internality by age suggested by the generalized locus of control scale. On the item level it is obvious that locus of control for these lifeworld domains is a far cry from a clear case. Patterns differ between different domains. In the case of the friendship domain, the moderate percentages of the external–internal pattern contradict the theoretical assumptions. The typical pattern showing increase of internality in most subjects emerged only in item 17 ("Do you feel you have a lot of choice in deciding who your friends are?"). For all other items patterns are found that do not clearly indicate development. Other items represent stable internal or stable external patterns. This is particularly visible in the high percentages of children who fit the mixed pattern. Surprisingly between 10% and 20% of the children change the direction of a friendship-related sense of control across the three measurement points in a nonexpectable way (mixed pattern). A striking frequency pattern is evidenced by item 11 ("Most of the time do you find it hard to change a friend's mind?"). Most subjects' responses to this item fall into a stable external pattern. Empirically, the implication appears clear: Mostly friends will not change their mind in response to pressure or persuasion from the actor. The logical implication is less clear: are friends considered internally driven resisters to persuasion, and does that conviction leave the actor with an "external" belief? Such findings make a heterogeneous interpretation of the items appear plausible.

Moreover, item responses appear highly situation specific. In fact, item 17 and item 18 ("Do you feel that when a kid your age decides to hit you, there's little you can do to stop him or her?") refer to concrete actions such as deciding who is your friend, or the possibility of preventing being hurt. For these items that indicate high internal control, we find high percentages of patterns with stable or increasingly internal patterns. This differs from the item response patterns representing actor's influence on others, such as changing the friend's opinion (item 11, discussed earlier) which evidence a high percentage in the stable external group. This is not surprising considering that children may experience significant others at this age as an external influence *per se*.

TABLE 22.3
*Frequencies of the friends/nonfriends item group (%)*

| Item | external-internal (1) | stable internal (2) | internal-external (3) | stable external (4) | mixed pattern (5) | n |
|------|-----|-----|-----|-----|-----|-----|
| 11 | 27.8 | 5.2 | 17.5 | 36.1 | 13.4 | 24 |
| 17 | 46.4 | 16.8 | 6.3 | 13.7 | 16.8 | 26 |
| 18 | 35.7 | 32.7 | 12.2 | 6.1 | 13.3 | 23 |
| 24 | 20.6 | 15.5 | 16.5 | 21.6 | 25.8 | 24 |
| 25 | 33.7 | 11.2 | 15.3 | 28.6 | 11.2 | 23 |

For the domain of "intellectual achievement situations," the pattern structure was more unified than for the friendship domain. The greater part of the items show a pattern of stable internality. Except for item 4 which refers to recognition for hard work, all items in this domain evidence remarkably high percentages in the stable internal and the increasingly internal patterns. Thus, most children make the experience that intellectual achievement can be influenced by one's own actions, a view which is consistent with the cultural norm in Western societies. However, item 4 ("Most of the time do you feel that getting good grades means a great deal to you?") does not correspond to these experiences. In more than 70% of the cases the answers to this item follow an increasingly external or stable external pattern. The item thus indicates what the child expects from significant others and perhaps the experience that the desire for recognition does not as such imply that recognition comes easily.

TABLE 22.4
*Frequencies of the intellectual achievement situations-subgroup (%)*

| Item | External-Internal (1) | Stable Internal (2) | Internal-External (3) | Stable External (4) | Mixed Pattern (5) | n |
|------|------|------|------|------|------|------|
| 4 | 10.4 | 8.2 | 30.9 | 39.2 | 11.3 | 24 |
| 6 | 15.8 | 71.6 | 2.1 | 1.1 | 9.5 | 26 |
| 15 | 21.2 | 48.5 | 16.2 | 6.1 | 8.1 | 22 |
| 30 | 9.2 | 83.7 | 5.1 | - | 2.0 | 23 |
| 32 | 18.3 | 69.9 | 7.5 | - | 4.3 | 28 |
| 34 | 18.2 | 74.7 | - | - | 7.1 | 22 |

## CONCLUSION

Before discussing the results, the prevailing theoretical views of the development of control beliefs can be summarized as follows: While some control theorists (e.g., Rotter, 1982; Crandall et al., 1965) assumed that control beliefs are stable personality dispositions, others postulated a trajectory towards either internality with increasing age, or towards externality (Piaget, 1975). Skinner and Chapman succeeded in reconciling these views developmentally. A small number of theorists have shown interest in the development of control beliefs within different domains of relevance for children and adolescents (Flammer, 1990; Lüthi, Grob & Flammer, 1989). This perspective is grounded in the assumption that developmental trajectories in different domains may diverge given different experiences of children and adolescents. Such important domains represent typical experiences of interaction with significant others, such as parents, friends, and peers in specific contexts such as the school (Oettingen & Little, 1993).

Within the limits of this paper only two contrastive domain analyses could be conducted in some depth. Multiple contrasts would have needed a much more extensive treatment, considering that individual item trajectories constitute an integral part of these structural analyses (see Mies, 1997).

The present study was mainly concerned with the longitudinal development of control beliefs within circumscribed contexts or domains of experience. The results of our analyses cast doubt on the developmental model of increasing internality. It appears more reasonable to assume that the development of individual control beliefs proceeds in domain specific ways, based on exposure to different experiences, and depending on individual life course patterns. It is important to investigate both intraindividual and interindividual variance. Future studies may profitably attend to the question whether individuals construct similar beliefs across a number of domains because of shared experiences or similar circumstances. On the other hand, individuals may develop dissimilar control beliefs in different domains, and thus show dissimilarity rather than similarity in the individual patterning of control beliefs across important lifeworld domains.

Three interrelated points of view have dominated the analyses presented above: (a) adequate developmental models for control beliefs are needed; (b) control beliefs develop specific to context or domain; and (c) control beliefs develop as a function of individual experience. Both aggregate development across domain specific item configurations and item specific trajectories may disclose meaningful patterns of development. Thus, even individual items may indicate relevant experientially-based trajectories. Intraindividual differences will disclose relevant differences in constitutive experience. Interindividual differences presumably reflect different experiences of different groups due to varying patterns of socialization and dominant norms of interaction.

Future studies should focus on other domains of relevance for the development and socialization of control beliefs in children, adolescents, and adults. However, it should be noted that only longitudinal studies yield the basic information needed to assess differences in the developmental trajectories of control that represent the variation of typical experiences mirrored by these patterns. Little attended domains of interest are those of health (Schwarzer, 1992), and leisure (Hoff, 1992). Finally, it is important to pay attention to cultural variations (Essau & Trommsdorff, 1995; Oerter & Oerter, 1995), since culture is likely to be a major influence on the development of control beliefs. It is clear that understanding internality and externality presupposes an understanding of the ways in which different cultures define agency (Triandis, 1990; Trommsdorff, 1995).

## REFERENCES

Bialer, I. (1961). Conceptualization of success and failure in mentally retarded and normal children. *Journal of Personality*, 29, 303–320.

Crandall, V. C., Katkovsky, W. & Crandall, V. J. (1965). Children's beliefs in their own control of reinforcements in intellectual-academic achievement situations. *Child Development*, 36, 91–109

Damon, W. (1984). *Die soziale Welt des Kindes*. Frankfurt/M.: Suhrkamp.

Edelstein, W., Keller, M. & Schröder, E. (1990). Child development and social structure: A longitudinal study of individual differences. In: Baltes, P. B., Featherman, D. L. & Lerner, R.M. (Eds.), *Life-Span Development and Behavior*, 151–185.

Essau, C. A. & Trommsdorff, G. (1995). Kontrollorientierung von Jugendlichen in individualistischen und gruppenorientierten Kulturen. In: Trommsdorff, G. (Ed.), *Kindheit und Jugend in verschiedenen Kulturen* (S. 211–224). Bern: Huber.

Flammer, A. (1990). *Erfahrung der eigenen Wirksamkeit.* Bern: Huber.

Grob, A., Wicki, W. & Flammer, A. (1997). Kann mangelnde Konsistenz systematische Befunde beeinträchtigen? *Zeitschrift für Entwicklungspsychologie und Pädagogische Psychologie*, Band XXIX, Heft 2, 129–132.

Hoff, E.-H. (1992). *Arbeit, Freizeit und Persönlichkeit.* Heidelberg: Asanger.

Krampen, G. (1979). Differenzierungen des Konstrukts der Kontrollüberzeugungen: Deutsche Bearbeitung und Anwendung der IPC-Skalen. *Zeitschrift für experimentelle und angewandte Psychologie*, 26, 573–595.

Krampen, G. (1982). Familiäre und schulische Entwicklungsbedingungen von Kontrollüberzeugungen. *Schweizerische Zeitschrift für Psychologie*, 41, 16–35.

Krampen, G. (1997). Interne Konsistenz der Kinder oder der Forscher bei der Erfassung von Kontrollüberzeugungen und Attributionsstilen von Kindern? *Zeitschrift für Entwicklungspsychologie und Pädagogische Psychologie*, Band XXIX, Heft 2, 119–128.

Keller, M. (1996). *Moralische Sensibilität: Entwicklung in Freundschaft und Familie.* Weinheim: Psychologie Verlags Union.

Lefcourt, H. M. (1976). *Locus of control: Current trends in theory and research.* Hillsdale, NJ: Lawrence Earlbaum Associates.

Levenson, H. (1972). Distinctions within the concept of internal-external control: Development of a new scale. *Proceedings of the 80th Annual Convention of the APA*, 7, 261–262.

Lüthi, R., Grob, A. & Flammer, A. (1989). Differenzierte Erfassung bereichsspezifischer Kontrollmeinungen bei Jugendlichen. In: Krampen, G. (Hrsg.), Diagnostik von Attributionen und Kontrollüberzeugungen (S.134–144). Göttingen: Hogrefe.

Mies, A. (1997). *Longitudinale Entwicklungsmuster internaler und externaler Kontrollüberzeugungen bei isländischen Kindern.* Unpublished master thesis. Berlin: Max Planck Institute for Human Development and Education.

Nowicki, S. & Strickland, B. R. (1973). A locus of control scale for children. *Journal of Consulting and Clinical Psychology*, 40,148–154.

Oerter, R. & Oerter, R. (1995). Zur Konzeption der autonomen Identität in östlichen und westlichen Kulturen. In: Trommsdorff, G. (Ed.), *Kindheit und Jugend in verschiedenen Kulturen* (S.153–173). Bern: Huber.

Oettingen, G. & Little, T. D. (1993). Intelligenz und Selbstwirksamkeitsurteile bei Ost- und Westberliner Schulkindern. *Zeitschrift für Sozialpsychologie*, 24, 186–197.

Piaget , J. (1975). *The child's conception of the world.* Totowa, NJ: Littlefield-Adams.

Piaget, J. & Inhelder, B. (1975). The origin of the idea of chance in children. New York: Norton (original work published in 1951).

Rotter, J. B. (1954). *Social learning and clinical psychology.* Englewood Cliffs, N.J.: Prentice-Hall.

Rotter, J. B. (1982). Generalized expectancies for internal versus external control of reinforcement. In: *The development and application of social learning theory.* Selected papers. Praeger, 169–214, (originally in: Psychological Monographs: General and Applied, 1966, 80).

Schwarzer, R. (1992). *Psychologie des Gesundheitsverhaltens.* Göttingen: Hogrefe.

Schwarzer, R. (1993). *Streß, Angst und Handlungsregulation.* Stuttgart: Kohlhammer.

Selman, R. L. (1980). *The growth of interpersonal understanding.* New York: Academic Press.

Skinner, E.A. & Chapman, M. (1987). Resolution of a developmental paradox: How can perceived internality increase, decrease, and remain the same across middle childhood? *Developmental Psychology,* Vol. 23, 1, 44–48.

Triandis, H. C. (1990). Cross-cultural studies of individualism and collectivism. In J. J. Berman (Ed.), Nebraska Symposium on Motivation: 1989, Vol. 37, Cross-cultural perspectives (pp. 41–133). Lincoln, NE: University of Nebraska Press.

Trommsdorff, G. (Ed.); (1995). *Kindheit und Jugend in verschiedenen Kulturen.* Bern: Huber.

Wicki, W., Reber, R., Flammer, A. & Grob, A. (1994). Begründung der Kontrollmeinung bei Kindern und Jugendlichen. *Zeitschrift für Entwicklungspsychologie und Pädagogische Psychologie,* Band XXVI, Heft 3, 241–261.

## APPENDIX

*TABLE 22.A1*

*Longitudinal items of the Locus of Control scale for children (CNS-IE) by Domains 1-5\* (items from domains analysed in this chapter in **bold print**)*

| Item | | Domain |
|---|---|---|
| 1. | Do you believe that most problems will solve themselves if you just don't fool with them? | 5 |
| 2. | Do you believe that you can stop catching a cold? | 5 |
| 3. | Are some kids just born lucky? | 3 |
| **4.** | **Most of the time do you feel that getting good grades means agreat deal to you?** | **4** |
| 5. | Are you often blamed for things that just aren't your fault? | 3 |
| **6.** | **Do you feel that most of the time it doesn't pay to try hard because things never turn out right anyway?** | **4** |
| 7. | Do you feel that if things start out well in the morning that it's going to be a good day no matter what you do? | 5 |
| 8. | Do you feel that most of the time parents listen to what their children have to say? | 1 |
| 9. | Do you believe that wishing can make good things happen? | 5 |

*TABLE 22.A1 (continued)*

| Item | | Domain |
|------|------|--------|
| 10. | When you get punished does it usually seem its for no good reason at all? | 3 |
| **11.** | **Most of the time do you find it hard to change a friend's (mind) opinion?** | **2** |
| 12. | Do you feel that it's nearly impossible to change your parent's mind about anything? | 1 |
| 13. | Do you believe that your parents should allow you to make most of your own decisions? | 1 |
| 14. | Do you feel that when you do something wrong there's very little you can do to make it right? | 5 |
| **15.** | **Do you believe that most kids are just born good at sports?** | |
| 16. | Do you feel that one the best ways to handle most problems is just not to think about them? | 5 |
| **17.** | **Do you feel that you have a lot of choice in deciding who your friends are?** | **2** |
| **18.** | **Do you feel that when a kid your age decides to hit you, there's little you can do to stop them?** | **2** |
| 19. | Will your parents usually help you if you ask them to? | 1 |
| 20. | Have you felt that when people were mean to you it was usually for no reason at all? | 3 |
| 21. | Most of the time, do you feel that you can change what might happen tomorrow by what you do today? | 5 |
| 22. | Do you think that kids can get their own way if they just keep trying? | 3 |
| 23. | Most of the time do you find it useless to try to get your own way at home? | 1 |
| **24.** | **Do you feel that when somebody your age wants to be your enemy there's little you can do to change matters?** | **2** |
| **25.** | **Do you feel that it's easy to get friends to do what you want them to?** | **2** |

*TABLE 22.A1 (continued)*

| Item | | Domain |
|---|---|---|
| 26. | Do you feel that when someone doesn't like you there's little you can do about it? | 3 |
| 27. | Are you the kind of person who believes that planning ahead makes things turn out better? | 5 |
| 28. | Most of the time, do you feel that you have little to say about what your family decides to do? | 1 |
| 29. | Do you think it's better to be smart than to be lucky? | 5 |
| **30.** | **Do you often feel that whether you do your home-work has much to do with what kind of grades you get?** | 4 |
| 31. | Do you believe that whether or not people like you depends on how you act? | 3 |
| **32.** | **Do you feel that when good things happen they happen because of hard work?** | 4 |
| 33. | Do you feel that you have little to say about what you get to eat at home? | 1 |
| **34.** | **Do you usually feel that it's almost useless to try in school because most other chilfren are just plain smarter than you are?** | 4 |

\* Domains:

1 = parent-child-interaction
2 = relationships with friends and nonfriends
3 = interaction with other important roles and persons
4 = intellectual achievement situation
5 = actions of the self

# 23

# School-Related Self-Efficacy Among Adolescents from Former East and West Germany: Age Trends, Association with School Performance, and Family Correlates[1]

*Rainer K. Silbereisen*
*Margit Wiesner*

## INTRODUCTION

German unification in 1991, and subsequent ongoing sociopolitical transformations, have provided unique opportunities for research on human development. Several research programs on children and adolescents in post-unification Germany have already reported results (for an overview see Hormuth et al., 1996). They share an interest in aspects of human development which seem to be particularly relevant for success under the new social and political conditions of life. Presumably it is fair to say that a basic distinction between the two former countries was the role people attributed to the state, as compared to the role they attributed to themselves. Until recently it was still true that one third in the West, but two thirds in the East held the belief that the government, rather than the citizens themselves should be responsible for welfare, particularly concerning issues such as employment, housing, or retirement (Zapf, 1996).

A psychological variable related to such differences in belief systems is self-efficacy, that is, "beliefs in one's capabilities to organize and execute the courses of action required to manage prospective situations" (Bandura, 1995, p. 2). Given the fact that life and development implies normative and non-normative challenges, many of which overtax established routines and require new efforts in resolving them, a healthy degree of overestimating one's control over such issues

---

[1] We are grateful for the support received from the German Research Council (Si 296/14-1, 2, 3, 4, 5; Principal Investigator: Rainer K. Silbereisen). Special thanks go to the colleagues of our research consortium at the University of Siegen (Principal Investigator: Juergen Zinnecker), and Bamberg (Principal Investigator: Laszlo Vaskovics). We want to thank all the young people and their families who participated in the studies.

of development is functional. Otherwise people would feel insecure vis-a-vis the tasks in navigating a period of life such as adolescence.

Following an approach introduced by Havinghurst (1952), adolescence is characterized by a number of prominent tasks, such as the development of romantic relationships or the exploration of occupational opportunities. Although such new domains of behavior are associated with societal expectations with regard to their accomplishment, they resemble more complex, ill-defined problem solving tasks than clearly described pathways into adulthood (Cantor, 1994). Confronted with such challenges, individuals can rely on a small number of general purpose capabilities which make a basic difference in how they approach the problem. Among such capabilities the following figure prominently; construction competencies which ease gathering and processing of information about the tasks (Clausen, 1991); ego resilience as a resource which allows to cope with unavoidable frustrations (Shedler & Block, 1990); and, most importantly, self-efficacy.

According to Bandura (1995), the role of self-efficacy is manifold. Resolving any of the developmental tasks requires the exploration of future time perspectives with regard to goals and means to accomplish them (Nurmi, 1993). Further, success will not be achieved without tenacity in pursuing such goals over extended periods of time. A high level of self-efficacy is also important in enabling adolescents to trust in their capability to achieve, and thus overcome, ill-defined or even threatening developmental challenges.

Identifying and pursuing goals is one thing—searching for, or shaping the right kind of supportive contexts is another. Adolescents influence their development by choosing and forming environments, from discotheques to shopping malls, conducive for the challenges ahead (Silbereisen, Noack & von Eye, 1992). Again, self-efficacy is important to enable adolescents to utilize opportunities offered in the contexts, rather than to shy away from the effort which may be required for beneficial (or risky) development.

The modal level of self-efficacy held in a population is likely to reflect opportunities and necessities within the given cultural context. Furthermore, such contexts many differ in the domains where self-controlled actions and decision-making is possible or mandatory. Concerning the negotiation of developmental tasks during adolescence, for instance, former East and West Germany differed in part as far as the amount of individual options is concerned. Finding an occupation after school is a case in point. In the past, there was a remarkable degree of planning by state authorities in former East Germany, which resulted in assigning opportunities for vocational training based on extra-personal conditions, such as demand from the state-run industries (Heinz, 1996; Silbereisen, Vondracek & Berg, 1997). In spite of raising unemployment, the situation concerning control over such developmental tasks improved after unification.

With regard to the past, however, at least in some domains, assuming lower levels of self-efficacy among the young in the East, as compared to the West, seems plausible. Indeed, a series of studies on children's self-efficacy in West and East Berlin samples, gathered soon after unification, revealed differences as expected. Oettingen, Little, Lindenberger, and Baltes (1994), studied school students in grades 2 to 6 and, among other measures, administered a questionnaire on self-efficacy beliefs, covering the dimensions of effort, ability, luck, and teacher support (Skinner, Chapman, & Baltes, 1988). Self-efficacy was understood as children's belief that they have access to, can use, or can implement specific means relevant for school performance. Two results stood out. First, school-related self-efficacy was lower among East Berlin students than was common among their West Berlin age-mates, and second, the correlation between self-efficacy and performance (grades), was higher in the East.

The results were interpreted with regard to differences in the dimensionality of the school curriculum and the manner of performance feedback. Teachers in East Berlin uniformly organized daily activities for all children in a rather standardized way which was not particularly geared to the specific learning needs of the individual student. Moreover, feedback concerning school performance was given in a public and direct way, with the aim of establishing early a realistic self-evaluation. In both regards, teachers from West Berlin were known to show contrasting classroom behaviors, namely, less standardized instruction and more supportive feedback in private. These proximal differences were thought to dampen East Berliners' self-efficacy beliefs, and, at the same time, to increase the correlation with their actual performance.

Taking this interpretation as valid, in further longitudinal research, Little, Lopez, Oettingen, and Baltes (1997) expected that the introduction of the western school system in 1992 would result in a lower correlation between self-efficacy and performance, thus resembling the degree of correspondence found previously in the West. In contrast, as the level of school-related self-efficacy is likely to rest on accumulated experiences of success and failure over an extended period of time, no immediate trend towards the level of the West Berlin sample was expected when comparing data gathered in 1993 (the year after the change of the school system), with those collected one and two years earlier. Both expectations were confirmed.

This provocative research had to rely on rather small samples which cannot deemed representative for Germany. In the following, we take advantage of samples from our own research program on being adolescent in Germany soon after unification. An overview of the results on social and personality development as well as on major contexts of adolescent activities is given in a recent book edited by Zinnecker and Silbereisen (1996). Among many other aspects self-efficacy beliefs were also part of the agenda.

## AIMS

The first aim of the present three-year longitudinal study reported in this chapter is directly related to these earlier studies. Utilizing large stratified samples of 10- to 13-year-olds, originally investigated in 1993 in both former parts of Germany, we wanted to find out whether school-related self-efficacy shows similar levels in both parts of the country. Gathered for the first time one year later than the data reported on by Oettingen et al. (1994), and Little et al. (1997), the prediction based on their earlier research was that the samples should reveal no difference between the regions. This should be so because the school-related proximal processes (curriculum, feedback) are presumed to be more or less identical given the common school system. The second aim refers to the association between school-related self-efficacy and school performance. Again, given the common-alties in the school system in 1993, there is no reason to expect that this association would differ along the former political divide.

However, concerning both aims, some qualification, referring to the situation of young people and their teachers in 1993 and the following years, should be noted. The majority of teachers in East Germany were educated in the old system of teaching, and thus when the curriculum changed in 1992 needed re-training through workshops parallel to their normal duties. Although we have no actual assessments, it is quite likely that issues such as individualized instruction and private feedback were quite salient, and consequently showed up in subsequent teaching behavior. Furthermore, given the heightened appreciation of self-determined behavior under the new social and political circumstances, it is also possible that students received more positive feedback for their own actions in general. It may even be that the adaptation of teachers and students to the new rules lead to, what in research on acculturation among immigrants is called "overshooting" (Triandis et al., 1986), that is, a somewhat exaggerated taking over of the new modes of thinking and behaving, resulting in conditions more favorable for higher school-related self-efficacy than in the West.

Given the opportunity provided by a large sample, we also wanted to analyze differences in self-efficacy with regard to gender, age, and school track. Gender differences are known to exist primarily in self-efficacy related to occupational development (Hackett, 1995), but it is unlikely, that this would also apply to school-related self-efficacy in the age group we studied. In line with previous research, we also did not expect age-related differences in school-related self-efficacy (Skinner & Convell, 1986), but predicted higher efficacy among college-bound students as compared to those attending vocational and other tracks (Flammer, Grob, & Lüthi, 1987; 1989).

The third aim of the present study refers to a relatively underinvestigated topic in research on self-efficacy and related concepts. We are interested in the familial experiences which account for individual differences in level and/or change of school-related efficacy. According to Schneewind (1995), there is surprisingly little research on how self-efficacy beliefs become socialized within the family context. As a matter of fact, the scarcity of research lead him to collate all studies which were related to control and self-efficacy in a more general sense. As far as parental influences are concerned, a few distinct dimensions seem to play a role. One is the consistent responsiveness to children's behavior (Skinner, 1986) and parents' relating to them in an emotionally supportive way

(Krampen, 1989). A second dimension pertains to the granting of autonomy and independence (Gordon, Nowicki, & Wichern, 1981). Finally, control and self-efficacy seem to profit from family environments which provide stimulation (Schneewind, 1989), such as greater variety of shared recreational and cultural activities, and more extended contacts outside of the family. The latter is obviously reminiscent of the notion of social capital as promoted by Coleman (1988). Although the above research does not refer to school-related self-efficacy, it seems reasonable to assume that higher levels of emotional sensitivity, stimulating social and cultural experiences, and autonomy granting correspond to higher self-efficacy. It should be acknowledged, however, that the measures available to us do not cover the full meaning of these dimensions.

In addition, parental involvement in school was deemed important in the present study. Parents who monitor their children's progress, help with homework, and take part in school affairs are known to have academically better performing children, and school involvement rather leads to than stems from school success (Steinberg, Lamborn, Dornbusch, & Darling, 1992). Moreover, according to the same study, school involvement seems to mediate the effect of achievement promoting parenting behaviors. In line with Bandura (1995), parenting behaviors are likely to provide mastery experiences, offer successful social models, and may reduce stress. Consequently, parents's interest in academic activities should also enhance school-related self-efficacy.

Recent research on parental support behaviors and school involvement has demonstrated their equal importance across numerous ecological niches (formed by ethnicity, education, family structure, etc.), and thus we did not consider differences between East and West in the predicted associations with school-related efficacy (Steinberg, 1992; Bogenschneider, 1997).

In summary, first, in comparing early adolescents who were born and raised in the former East and West Germany, we expected no differences in the level of school-related self-efficacy. Additional predictions referred to the absence of gender differences and age trends, and to differences between school tracks, with college-bound tracks revealing higher levels. Second, no differences were expected across the political regions concerning the correspondence between self-efficacy and performance in school. Third, it was expected that different trajectories of self-efficacy across time can be distinguished by parental behaviors. More specifically, high or increasing levels of school-related efficacy were hypothesized to correspond to higher levels of parental support and sensitivity.

## METHOD

### Sample

Out of 722 students in the age range of 10 to 13 years, raised in the eastern or the western part of Germany, the 247 who had taken part in all three annual waves of assessment, starting in 1993, were selected. As shown in Table 1, about two third were from the West, and one third from the East. The male to female ratio was 40:60, higher than in the population. Students following college-bound tracks amounted to slightly more than 50% (as tracking had not yet occurred for the youngest students, in this case, their intended track was used). The original sample was stratified according to political region (former East Germany oversampled), gender, school track, and community size. Trained interviewers contacted 5 to 7 adolescents each, observing the quota criteria provided, and conducted the interviews at the family home. Parental consent was mandatory. The data gathering was organized by a commercial survey institute, based on the materials provided by the research group.

Compared to the composition of the sample at Wave 1 there was attrition across waves. Respective analyses revealed significant ($p < .01$) differences between stayers and students who did not take part in all three waves with regard to age, gender, and region. In contrast, no significant differences were found concerning the target, school-related self-efficacy, and all other variables which were utilized as predictors in distinguishing self-efficacy trajectories across time.

TABLE 23.1
*Sample Broken Down by Political Region, Gender, Age and School Track*

| | Male | Female | Non-college bound school track | College-bound school track |
|---|---|---|---|---|
| East | 38 | 51 | 36 | 53 |
| | (15,4%) | (20,6%) | (14,6%) | (21,5%) |
| West | 59 | 99 | 71 | 87 |
| | (23,9%) | (40,1%) | (28,7%) | (35,2%) |
| Total | 97 | 150 | 107 | 140 |
| | (39,3%) | (60,7%) | (43,3%) | (56,7%) |

| | 10 yrs | 11 yrs | 12 yrs | 13 yrs | Total |
|---|---|---|---|---|---|
| East | 27 | 8 | 31 | 23 | 89 |
| | (10,9%) | (3,2%) | (12,6%) | (9,3%) | (36%) |
| West | 34 | 41 | 41 | 42 | 158 |
| | (13,8%) | (16,6%) | (16,6%) | (17,0%) | (64%) |
| Total | 61 | 49 | 72 | 65 | 247 |
| | (24,7%) | (19,8%) | (29,2%) | (26,3%) | (100%) |

## Measures

School-related efficacy was assessed using selected items from a questionnaire published by Schwarzer (1986). According to him this scale correlates positively with self-esteem and negatively with school-related helplessness and achievement anxiety. Due to space limitations, only 10 out of originally 13 items were included in the interview materials.

By running a series of nested measurement models utilizing structural equation modeling (AMOS 3.6, Arbuckle, 1997) it was examined whether school-related self-efficacy was assessed in an equivalent way between contexts and across periods of time. Equivalence was tested by constraining factors loadings, stability coefficients, and other relevant indices to be equal. In sum, the results revealed that the factor structure of school-related self-efficacy can be treated as equivalent across both time and political region. Also, the stability coefficients, ranging from .24 to .41 in the total sample, showed neither a significant difference between waves in the whole sample nor between political regions. In all cases the goodness-of-fit of the estimated models was adequate and the chi-square difference between the initial models and the more constrained models was non-significant. Based on these analyses, only the seven items with substantial factor loadings (t-values greater than 2) were used in forming the self-efficacy composite scale (e.g., If I work hard in school, everything works accordingly to plan). The response scale ranged from 1 (does not apply) to 4 (applies fully). The internal consistencies for each wave ranged between .80 and .82.

As comparisons will be made with the earlier studies by Oettingen (Oettingen et al., 1994; Little et al., 1997), it is important to characterize school-related self-efficacy, as used here, in relation to their assessment instrument, the CAMI (Skinner, Chapman, & Baltes, 1988). Means-ends beliefs (is a given means useful in producing a given outcome?) and control expectancies (can one produce a given outcome?) as tapped in the CAMI were not gathered in our study. Rather, we concentrated on what they called agency (does one possess a given outcome-relevant mean?). Compared to the CAMI, all seven items stressed the availability of enough effort to achieve school-related success, disregarding ability, luck and teacher support, which were also tapped in the Skinner et al. measure.

The aspects of parent–adolescent interaction addressed in the hypotheses were assessed at the first wave, tapping the six dimensions of monitoring, school involvement, sensitivity, advice, strictness in discipline, and shared cultural activities. The items were answered by the adolescents. A confirmatory factor analysis was conducted on the six measures. The fit was adequate. Thus, monitoring (Jugendwerk der Deutschen Shell, 1992) was assessed by two items (e.g., Do you tell your parents where you spend your time after school?; 1 = never, to 4 = always; $r = .62, p < .001$).

School involvement (Jugendwerk der Deutschen Shell, 1992), encompassed parental supervision of school achievement (e.g., My parents pay attention to the school grades which I bring home; 1 = does not apply, to 4 = applies fully; Cronbach's alpha = .64). Sensitivity (Jugendwerk der Deutschen Shell, 1992; Schneewind et al., 1985a; 1985b), referred to parental sensitivity of their childrens´ moods and troubles (e.g., My parents notice immediately that I am anxious about something; 1 = does not apply, to 4 = applies fully; Cronbach´s alpha = .66). Advice (Projektgruppe Bildungsmoratorium Siegen, 1994) was assessed by two items (e.g., My parents help me when I have personal problems; 1 = never, to 4 = regularly; $r = .31, p < .001$). The measure of strictness in discipline (Schneewind et al., 1985a; 1985b) was obtained by three items (e.g., When my parents decided that I am not allowed to do something, they stick to it and don't change their mind afterwards; 1 = does not apply to 4 = applies fully; Cronbach's alpha = .55). Finally, shared cultural activities (Jugendwerk der Deutschen Shell, 1992) assessed whether the family was conducive to joint cultural activities (e.g., We are playing music together; 1 = does not apply, to 4 = applies fully; Cronbach's alpha = .69). In all cases composite mean scales were used.

## RESULTS

The results are presented in three sections. Corresponding to the three aims, we begin with the question whether indeed students from East and West show similar levels of school-related self-efficacy.

### Mean Level Differences In School-Related Self-Efficacy Across Contexts

In order to test this prediction, a repeated measures ANOVA was computed with self-efficacy as dependent variable, and Region and Wave as factors. The effect of Wave was not significant ($F = 1.23; df = 2$), nor was there a significant interaction between Wave and Region ($F = 2.14; df = 2$). Thus, at least in the age range studied, there was no change in the mean levels of school-related self-efficacy. In contrast, the samples from former East and West Germany differed significantly ($F = 5.23; df = 1; p < .05; eta^2 = .02$). As shown in Table 23.2, the mean levels in the East region were somewhat higher than in the West. Note that this result does not disagree with the interpretations offered by Oettingen and colleagues, but conforms even better with our view on the situation of teachers and school students in the East. At any rate, in line with predictions, self-efficacy was not lower in the East.

TABLE 23.2
Means and Standard Deviations (in parentheses) of School-related Self-efficacy over Three Measurement Waves

|  | East | | West | |
|---|---|---|---|---|
|  | Non college-bound school tracks | College-bound school track | Non college-bound school tracks | College-bound school track |
| School-related self-efficacy, 1993 | 3.32 (.49) | 3.42 (.43) | 3.14 (.47) | 3.27 (.46) |
| School-related self-efficacy, 1994 | 3.19 (.63) | 3.34 (.45) | 3.16 (.46) | 3.33 (.43) |
| School-related self-efficacy, 1995 | 3.39 (.45) | 3.24 (.40) | 3.11 (.49) | 3.24 (.44) |

Separate repeated measures ANOVAs were computed with Gender and Wave, Age group and Wave, and School track and Wave. The results did not reveal significant gender ($F = 1.18$; $df = 1$), or age group effects ($F = 1.23$; $df = 3$). Concerning differences between school tracks, it was found that students who pursued a college-bound track reported higher levels of self-efficacy than their agemates attending the other tracks ($F = 6.21$; $df = 1$; $p < .05$, $eta^2 = .02$).

In summary, samples born and raised in former East and West Germany differed in favor of higher mean levels held by adolescents from the East. As this result corresponds to our view on the role of the new circumstances at the schools in former East Germany (e.g., more individualized feedback), the relationship between self-efficacy and school performance could also be closer than found by the previous research.

**Trajectories Of School-Related Self-Efficacy And Their Relationship With School Performance**

In analyzing the relationship of school-related self-efficacy with performance (grades), a pattern approach was pursued (Cairns, Cairns, Rodkin, & Xie, in press). More specifically, we were interested in the number of prototypical trajectories across time in self-efficacy, and whether they were reflected in a corre-

sponding course of performance. Following the established approach in identifying trajectories, in a preliminary step the three-wave self-efficacy data were
subjected to a cluster analysis (k-means; SPSS 6.0, Norusis, 1993). Based on
cluster size and interpretability, a three-cluster solution was chosen. The means
representing this solution are depicted in figure 23.1.

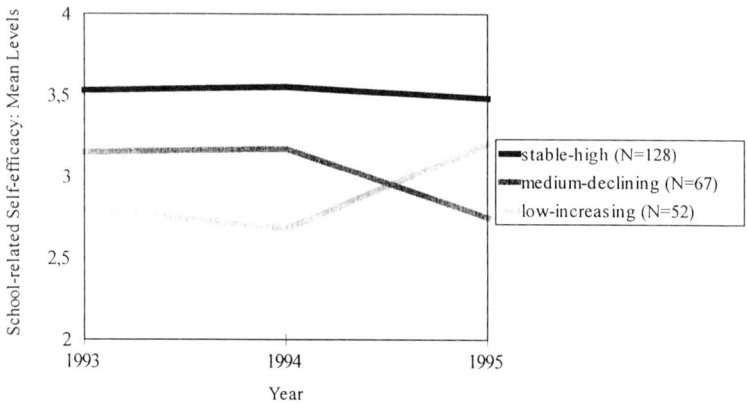

*FIG. 23.1. Trajectories of School-related Self-efficacy, 1993-1995.*

The *stable-high* cluster (*n* = 128) showed high levels of self-efficacy across
all three waves. The *increasing* cluster (*n* = 52) started out with the lowest mean
of all clusters, but approached a medium level subsequent to Wave 2. The *declining* cluster (*n* = .67), in contrast, began with a medium level of self-efficacy
but approached the low origin of the second cluster subsequent to Wave 2. The
clusters did not differ according to age group and gender, and the share of students from the East and West was also alike. The stable-high cluster, however,
had a relatively higher portion of college-bound students.

In order to gain insight into the relationship with grades, a repeated measures
ANOVA was computed with Cluster and Wave as factors and grades as dependent variable. School grades, which can range between 1 and 6, with 1 being the
best grade, were reported by the students for Mathematics and German. The
mean was used in the analyses. The main effect of Cluster was significant ($F$ =
13.47, $df$ = 2, $p$ < .001; $eta^2$ = .10) and also it´s interaction with Wave ($F$ = 5.23,
$df$ = 4; $p$ < .001; $eta^2$ = .04). The mean grades are shown in figure 23.2. They
reveal a differential trend in grades among the clusters.

As can be seen, the trend towards lower grades (see figure 23.2) is the same
for the stable-high and the declining trajectory in school-related self-efficacy,
albeit at clearly different levels (significant single comparison). Students of the

stable-high cluster had better grades than their age-mates from the declining cluster. The increasing cluster, which was characterized by the lowest self-efficacy of all clusters, initially had the lowest grades but improved parallel to the gain in self-efficacy subsequent to Wave 2 (significant single comparisons).

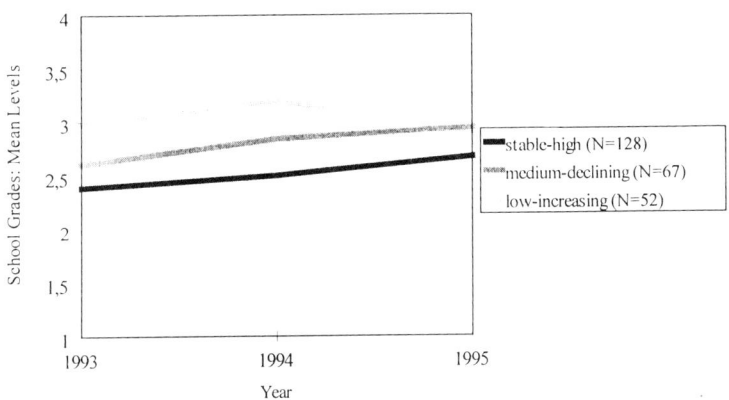

*FIG. 23.2. School Grades by Trajectories of School-related Self-efficacy.*

In summary, there seems to be a degree of correspondence between the trajectories of school-related self-efficacy across time and students' school performance. As Oettingen and her colleagues reported the association between self-efficacy and grades in terms of correlation coefficients, in addition the equivalent analyses were conducted with the present data. The correlation averaged across waves was -.42 for the West and -.41 ($p$ <.01) for the East. Thus, as expected, there was no significant difference between the two former parts of Germany. Moreover, the magnitude of the correlation was lower than reported by Oettingen et al. (1994) and corresponded to the levels known from the U.S. literature (Little, Oettingen, Stetsenko, & Baltes, 1995).

In two additional ANOVAs, with Age group and Wave, and Region and Wave as factors, we confirmed the well-known fact that grades become worse across time ($F = 12.76$, $df = 2$; $p < .001$; $eta^2 = .05$) and among older compared to younger age groups ($F = 5.08$, $df = 3$; $p < .01$; $eta^2 = .06$). In other words, either individual performances declined, or, more likely, the standards used in grading became stricter with students' age. We also found significantly better grades among the sample from East Germany ($F = 23.36$, $df = 1$; $p < .001$; $eta^2 = .09$). This result is in line with previous research (Kornadt, 1996).

## Trajectories Of School-Related Self-Efficacy And Distinguishing Family Experiences

After gaining some insight into school performance, deemed to be influenced by the self-efficacy trajectories, the question of whether the trajectories can be distinguished by students' experiences with parental behaviors, i.e., the third aim of the present research, can be addressed. Following the model of other research conducted in the pattern approach mode (Cairns et al., in press; Brooks-Gunn, 1995), discriminant analysis was used (Norusis, 1993, SPSS 6.0) to identify dimensions of parental behaviors which best distinguish the three trajectories of school-related self-efficacy. Monitoring, school involvement, sensitivity, advice, strictness in discipline, and shared cultural activities at Wave 1 were used as variables in this analysis. Two discriminant functions were maintained (only the first one was marginally significant, $p < .10$) and utilized in the interpretation.

In table 23.3 the structure matrix is given. It shows the correlations between the variables and the discriminant functions. As can be seen, parental monitoring is highly correlated with both functions, whereas strictness in discipline shows no substantial correlation on either discriminant function. Common for the pattern of correlations on the first function are the relevance of a high level of parental support, shared parent–child activities, and school involvement. In contrast, beyond monitoring the second function is primarily characterized by a high correlation with parental sensitivity to adolescents' needs. As monitoring actually indicates children's deliberate sharing of intimate information with their parents, it makes sense that this variable correlates with both functions.

*TABLE 23.3*
*Correlations of Predictors with Discriminant Functions*

|  | *Discriminant Functions* | |
| --- | --- | --- |
| *Predictors* | 1 | 2 |
| Monitoring | .65 | .64 |
| School involvement | .51 | .14 |
| Sensitivity | -.11 | .64 |
| Advice | .49 | .07 |
| Strictness in discipline | .26 | .26 |
| Shared cultural activities | .53 | -.23 |
| Canonical R | .23+ | .18 |

+ p < .10

The centroids of the three clusters on the discriminant functions do not differ a great deal (and consequently, the rate of correct classifications was only 41%, about 10% higher than expected by chance), but nevertheless the differences are quite instructive. The adolescents belonging to the cluster representing those who gained in self-efficacy revealed lower support and involvement than the stable-high and the declining clusters. Both clusters representing change in self-efficacy differed from the stable-high on the second discriminant function. The latter group of adolescents revealed higher levels of parental sensitivity. In other words, those reporting consistently high school-related self-efficacy were better off in terms of parental school involvement and support, and also experienced more sensitivity from parents. This result matches the predictions mentioned at the beginning of this chapter. In addition, the pattern approach helped us to learn about parental behaviors that correspond to increase and decline in school-related self-efficacy.

## CONCLUSION

In 1993, two years after the political unification of Germany, we began a multi-theme survey on development in early adolescence in the new Germany. Among many other topics covered, there were also assessments of school-related self-efficacy, utilizing an abridged version of a questionnaire introduced by Schwarzer (1986). The data were gathered annually for two additional waves. Adolescence is characterized by new challenges, such as the development of romanctic relationships or the exploration of occupational opportunities. As these challenges resemble complex, ill-defined problem solving tasks, self-efficacy is important as a general purpose resource which empowers individuals to pursue the new goals with endeavour, and trust in one's success (Bandura, 1995; Silbereisen, 1996).

The first and second aims for the present chapter were to analyze whether mean levels would differ, and whether the relationship with school performance would be equally high in the East and the West. Such data would allow comparisons with results found by Little et al. (1997) in their 1993 follow-up of Berlin samples, which they had first investigated in 1990/91. Whereas at the earlier time the self-efficacy mean was lower and its relationship with performance higher in the East, the trend after unification was toward the level of self-efficacy and association with performance known from the West. However, as the level of self-efficacy is the result of accumulated school experiences, this aspect was understood as taking more time to resemble western standards, thus maintaining lower self-efficacy in the East. If we assume Little et al.'s results and interpretation to be valid, our data gathered in 1993 and the following years should reveal a further trend in the direction pointed out by these authors, that is, both level and association with performance of school-related self-efficacy should no longer differ between the two parts of the country. This we found, except that the mean levels of school-related self-efficacy were even higher in the Eastern sam-

ple. Expressed by correlation coefficients, the degree of association was around -
.40 (negative sign due to the fact that better grades are indexed by smaller numbers, 1 being the best grade). This resembles the U.S. data reported by Little et
al. (1995), but is much lower than the association they found with their Berlin
samples.

The third aim of the present chapter was to investigate some facets of the
parent–adolescent interaction as markers of self-efficacy trajectories across time.
Using cluster analysis, a stable-high, an increasing, and a declining trajectory
were distinguished. The increasing cluster was characterized by the lowest score
on a first discriminant function which represents parental school involvement
and support behaviors. The stable-high cluster differed from the two other clusters by the highest score on a second discriminant function, which indicates
differences in parents' emotional sensitivity. In other words, adolescents who
enjoyed high parental school involvement and support behaviors, and also experienced sensitivity with regard to their feelings, preferably belonged to the stable-
high self-efficacy trajectory.

Before discussing these results, we have to give a number of caveats. First,
our data cannot strictly confirm or disconfirm the findings by Oettingen et al.
(1994), and Little et al. (1997). This is due to the fact that our sample ranged
from ages 10 to 13 at the first wave of measurements, whereas their first wave
encompassed grades 2 to 6 (roughly corresponding to ages 8 to 12). Further, the
measure we used was limited to beliefs concerning one's own efforts in school,
whereas Oettingen and colleagues used a scale comprising several aspects, including effort, ability, luck and the availability of teacher support. However, in
favor of the present study is the larger and more diversified sample used (Oettingen et al., 1994, tested students from two schools each in East and West Berlin).
Whereas in the Berlin study, data was collected from students in classrooms
(thus, data are actually clustered), the adolescents of the present study were interviewed at home. Second, all interpretations rest on assumptions concerning
proximal processes, such as the actual teacher–student interaction, which were
not measured. In this regard, however, the situation is not different from the one
which lead Little et al. (1997) to their understanding of the diminishing differences between East and West Berlin students. In agreement with their findings,
there was a clear indication that school-related self-efficacy and school performance corresponded in both regions alike.

In contrast to the expectation of diminishing differences between political regions as indicated by Little et al. (1997), the mean score of the Eastern sample
was even higher. In order to make sense of this result, it is tempting to use the
explanation in terms of the proximal processes discussed by Oettingen et al.
(1994), and to combine this with plausible assumptions about the results of
teacher re-training after unification. More specifically, it is conceivable that the
teachers in the East not only refrained from public performance feedback, but
also were more supportive than in the past, and that there may have been a shift
towards a higher importance of mastery, as compared to performance goals in

general. All three behaviors are known to enhance school-related self-efficacy (Bandura, 1995), and it is more than likely that workshops and other training opportunities for teachers stressed such issues. As comparable efforts were not common among teachers in the West, at least not on such a scale, the differences we found may indeed be rooted in the higher salience of such aspects of teaching among Eastern teachers.

As already mentioned, we have no data on the actual behavior of the teachers in class. There is evidence, however, that teachers in general enjoyed the changes in the curriculum which took place after 1992. Silbernagel, Hoppe, and Rolff (1994) reported higher satisfaction compared to pre-unification times with the new freedom concerning the choice of subjects and the adaptation to students' needs. Kornadt (1996) admits the paucity of research on the degree to which the former teacher-centered, highly standardized style of instruction (Döbert, 1995) was indeed replaced by a stronger emphasis on students' exploration-oriented learning, but sees no indication to the contrary. Concerning the change from public evaluation to personal feed-back, according to Döbert (1995), teachers seem to have had no difficulties at all.

In addition to changes in classroom behaviors, other factors may have played a role. One has to bear in mind that school was not the only context where the particular East German style of standardized instructions and feedback was held in high regard. Extracurricular activities, organized by the party-controlled youth organization, followed the same track, but this influence broke away after unification (Trommsdorff & Chakarat, 1996). Moreover, in actuality, the entire meso-system comprising school, youth organization, work place, and family was changed, with the new school curricula being confined to teaching rather than socialization in broader sense, as was common during East German times (Silbereisen, in press). Thus, our results are likely to be influenced by a multifacetted change of contexts conducive for self-efficacy.

A more trivial interpretation could refer to the result that grades in the East on average were somewhat better than in the West. This could in itself be an explanation for the higher mean self-efficacy in the East. As teachers during times before unification were held responsible for student´ failure, more lenient grading was common (Kornadt, 1996). In order to find out whether such effects could have had an impact, all analyzes were computed again utilizing a standardization of grades at the grand mean for East and West. Using this information as covariate in the ANOVAs, the significant difference between the regions in school-related self-efficacy was still found, and the correlations with school performance were virtually unchanged. Thus, the higher self-efficacy means in the East are not a simple reflection of better grades, which would potentially induce more positively biased beliefs in one's efficacy.

It should be mentioned that recent investigations concerning other aspects of control beliefs also showed no differences between samples from the two political regions around the time of our research. Sydow, Wagner, Jülisch, and Kauf (in press) assessed students' belief in their control over future-time events, including activities in school (grades 8, 10, and 12), drawn from 10 schools each in East and West Berlin. No differences between the regions were found in 1993, nor in the two consecutive years. Thus, it may well be that the differences Oettingen et al. (1994) reported no longer apply, concerning not only school-related self-efficacy, but also other aspects of control.

The present study also contributes to a better understanding of family correlates of school-related self-efficacy. Our results on the role of parental school involvement and joint cultural activities match well with earlier studies on the importance of a stimulating family environment (Nowicki & Schneewind, 1982; Schneewind, 1989). The other aspect, the interpersonal sensitivity which distinguished the stable-high cluster from the other two, also is in line with previous research. Krampen (1989), for instance, found more internal control orientations among adolescents whose parents treated them in a warm, and emotionally supportive way. It should be noted, however, that these studies did not deal with self-efficacy in the specific sense investigated here. This is also true for a 16-year longitudinal study on general self-efficacy reported by Schneewind (1995). Beyond gender-specific antecedents in the realm of achievement-related demands (school-involvement, as gathered in the present study, would fall into this category), he found a small but consistent relationship between young adults' general efficacy beliefs and their perceptions of their families, gathered during late childhood and early adolescence, as providing stimulating interpersonal and cultural environments.

In other words, variety of experiences and responsiveness toward feelings seem to have concurrent, as well as long-term, effects on various aspects of control beliefs. The results of our study fit into this general picture, adding information on a specific aspect of school-related self-efficacy, and its change across time. The pattern approach (Cairns et al., in press) utilized in distinguishing different trajectories did not lend itself to an analysis of the mutual longitudinal effects of school performance and family environment on change in self-efficacy. This remains a task for future analyses.

In a nutshell, in this chapter we have shown that individual differences in school-related self-efficacy trajectories across early adolescence can be tied to parent-child interaction at home, as well as to achievement in school. The presumed mediating experiences, such as parental involvement in school matters and styles of classroom instruction, would certainly require further investigation. Moreover, it would be important to learn more about the role of school-related self-efficacy in the establishment of an overall sense of one's causative capabilities. The present data set offers rich research opportunities that we will explore in the future.

## REFERENCES

Arbuckle, J. L. (1997). *Amos Users' Guide, Version 3.6.* Chicago: Small Waters Corporation.

Bandura, A. (1995). Exercise of personal and collective efficacy in changing societies. In A. Bandura (Ed.), *Self-efficacy in changing societies* (pp. 1–45). Cambridge, MA: Cambridge University Press.

Bogenschneider, K. (1997). Parental involvement in adolescent schooling: A proximal process with transcontextual validity. *Journal of Marriage and the Family, 59,* 718–733.

Brooks-Gunn, J. (1995). Children in families in communities: Risk and intervention in the Bronfenbrenner tradition. In P. Moen, G. H. Elder, & K. Luscher (Eds.), *Examining lives in context: Perspectives on the ecology of human development* (pp. 467–519). Washington, DC: American Psychological Association

Cairns, R. B., Cairns, B. D., Rodkin, P., & Xie, H. (in press). New directions in developmental research: Models and methods. In R. Jessor (Ed.), *New perspectives on adolescent Risk behavior.*Cambridge, MA: Cambridge University Press.

Cantor, N. (1994). Life task problem solving: Situational affordances and personal needs. *Personality and Social Psychology Bulletin, 20,* 235–243.

Clausen, J. S. (1991). Adolescent competence and the shaping of the life course. *American Journal of Sociology, 96,* 805–842.

Coleman, J. (1988). Social capital in the creation of human capital. *American Journal of Sociology, 94,* 95–120.

Döbert, H. (1995). *Curricula in der Schule: DDR und ostdeutsche Bundesländer* [School curricula: GDR and eastern federal states]. Köln, Weimar, Wien: Böhlau Verlag.

Flammer, A., Grob, A., & Lüthi, R. (1987). Einfluss und Partizipation (Influence and participation). *Schweizerische Zeitschrift für Psychologie, 46,* 237–249.

Flammer, A., Grob, A., & Lüthi, R. (1989). Swiss adolescents' attribution of control. In J. P. Forgas, & J. M. Innes (Eds.), *Recent advances in social psychology: An international perspective* (pp. 81–94). North Holland: Elsevier Science Publishers.

Gordon, D. A., Nowicki, S., & Wichern, F. (1981). Observed maternal and child behaviors in a dependency-producing task as a function of children's locus of control orientation. *Merrill-Palmer Quarterly, 27,* 43–71.

Havighurst, R. J. (1952). *Developmental tasks and education (2nd ed.).* New York: Plenum.

Heinz, W. R. (1996). Berufsverläufe im Transformationsprozeß (Career trajectories during the sociopolitical transformation). In S. E. Hormuth, W. R. Heinz, H.-J. Kornadt, H. Sydow, & G. Trommsdorff (Eds.). *Individuelle Entwicklung, Bildung und Berufsverläufe* (pp. 273–329). Opladen: Leske & Budrich.

Hormuth, S. E., Heinz, W. R., Kornadt, H.-J., Sydow, H., & Trommsdorff, G. (1996). *Individuelle Entwicklung, Bildung und Berufsverläufe* (Individual development, education, and occupational careers). Opladen: Leske & Budrich.

Jugendwerk der Deutschen Shell (Hg.) (1992). *Jugend '92* (Youth '92) (Bd. 1–4). Opladen: Leske & Budrich.

Krampen, G. (1982). Schulische und familiäre Entwicklungsbedingungen von Kontrollüberzeugungen (School and familial antecedents for the development of control beliefs). *Schweizerische Zeitschrift für Psychologie und ihre Anwendungen, 41,* 16–35.

Kornadt, J.-J. (1996). Erziehung und Bildung im Transformationsprozeß (Socialization and education during the sociopolitical transformation). In S. E. Hormuth, W. R. Heinz, H.-J. Kornadt, H. Sydow, & G. Trommsdorff (Eds.), *Individuelle Entwicklung, Bildung und Berufsverläufe* (pp. 203–271). Opladen: Leske & Budrich.

Little, T. D., Oettingen, G., Stetsenko, A., & Baltes, P. B. (1995). Children's action-control beliefs about school performance: How do American children compare with German and Russian children? *Journal of Personality and Social Psychology, 69,* 686–700.

Little, T. D., Lopez, D. F., Oettingen, G., & Baltes, P. B. (1997). *A comparative-longitudinal study of action-control beliefs and school performance: On the role of context.* Unpublished Manuscript.

Norusis, M. J. (1993). *SPSS for Windows base system user's guide release 6.0.* Chicago: SPSS Inc.

Nurmi, J.-E. (1993). Adolescent development in an age-graded context: The role of personal beliefs, goals and strategies in the tackling of developmental tasks and standards. *International Journal of Behavioral Development, 16,* 169–190.

Oettingen, G., Little, T. D., Lindenberger, U., & Baltes, P. B. (1994). Causality, agency, and control beliefs in East versus West Berlin children: A natural experiment on the role of context. *Journal of Personality and Social Psychology, 66,* 579–595.

Projektgruppe Bildungsmoratorium Siegen (1994). *Kindersurvey 1993. Grundauszählung und Skalen* [Children's survey: Descriptive statistics and scales]. Siegen: Gesamthochschule Siegen.

Schneewind, K. A., Beckmann, M., & Hecht-Jackel, A. (1985a). *Das ES-Testsystem. Testmanual* (The ES-Testing System). Forschungsberichte aus dem Institutsbereich Persönlichkeitspsychologie und Psychodiagnostik der Universität München. München: Universität München.

Schneewind, K. A., Beckmann, M., & Hecht-Jackel, A. (1985b). *Das ET-Testsystem. Testmanual* (The ET-Testing System). Forschungsberichte aus dem Institutsbereich Persönlichkeitspsychologie und Psychodiagnostik der Universität München. München: Universität München.

Schneewind, K. A. (1989). Eindimensionale Skalen zur Erfassung von Kontrollüberzeugungen bei Erwachsenen und Kindern (Unidimensional scales for assessing control beliefs in adults and children). In G. Krampen (Ed.), *Diagnostik von Attributionen und Kontrollüberzeugungen* (pp. 80–92). Göttingen: Hogrefe.

Schneewind, K. A. (1995). Impact of family processes on control beliefs. In A. Bandura (Ed.) (1995). *Self-efficacy in changing societies* (pp. 114–148). Cambridge: Cambridge University Press.

Schwarzer, R. (Hg.) (1986). *Skalen zur Befindlichkeit und Persönlichkeit* (Scales for the assessment of mood and personality). Forschungsbericht 5 der FU Berlin, Institut für Psychologie, Abt. Pädagogische Psychologie. Berlin: Freie Universität Berlin.

Shedler, J., & Block, J. (1990). Adolescent drug use and psychological health: A longitudinal inquiry. *American Psychologist, 45,* 612–630.

Silbereisen, R. K., Noack, P., & von Eye, A. (1992). Adolescents' development of romantic friendship and change in favorite leisure contexts. *Journal of Adolescent Research, 7,* 80–93.

Silbereisen, R. K. (1996). Jugendliche als Gestalter ihrer Entwicklung: Konzepte und Forschungsbeispiele (Adolescents as shapers of their development: Concepts and research). In R. Schumann-Hengsteler, & H. M. Trautner (Eds.), *Entwicklung im Jugendalter* (pp. 1–18). Göttingen: Hogrefe.

Silbereisen, R. K., Vondracek, F. W., & Berg, L. A. (1997). Differential timing of initial vocational choice: The influence of early childhood family relocation and parental support behaviors in two cultures. *Journal of Vocational Behavior, 50,* 41–59.

Silbereisen, R. K. (in press). Viel erreicht, noch mehr zu bewältigen: Zum Bericht der KSPW über individuelle Entwicklung, Bildung und Berufsverläufe. *Berliner Journal für Soziologie.*

Silbernagel, P., Hoppe, R., & Rolff, H. G. (1994). Die autonome Schule: Freiraum für Reformen oder mangelnde Selbstverwaltung? (Autonomous schools: Leeway for reforms or lack of self-government?) In: *Bildung zwischen Finanznöten und neuen Aufgaben* (pp.16-22). Frankfurt: Verband der Schulbuchverlage.

Skinner, E. A. (1986). The origins of young children's perceived control: Mother contingent and sensitive behavior. *International Journal of Behavioral Development, 9*, 359–382.
Skinner, E. A., Chapman, M., & Baltes, P. B. (1988). Children's beliefs about control, means-ends, and agency: Developmental differences during middle childhood. *International Journal of Behavioral Development, 11*, 369–388.
Steinberg, L., Lamborn, S. D., Dornbusch, S. M., & Darling, N. (1992). Impact of parenting practices on adolescent achievemant: Authoritative parenting, school involvement, and encouragement to succeed. *Child Development, 63*, 1266–1281.
Sydow, H., Wagner, C., Jülisch, B.-R., & Kauf, H. (in press). Future oriented control and subjective well-being of students in East- and West-Berlin. In R. K. Silbereisen, & A. von Eye (Eds.), *Growing up in times of social change.* Berlin: de Gruyter.
Triandis, H. C., Kashima, Y., Shimada, E., & Villareal, M. (1986). Acculturation indices as a means of confirming cultural differences. *International Journal of Psychology, 21*, 43–70.
Trommsdorff, G., & Chakkarath, P. (1996). Kindheit im Transformationsprozeß. [Childhood during the sociopolitical transformation]. In S. E. Hormuth, W. R. Heinz, H.-J. Kornadt, H. Sydow, & G. Trommsdorff (Eds.). *Individuelle Entwicklung, Bildung und Berufsverläufe* (pp. 15–78). Opladen: Leske & Budrich.
Zapf, W. (1996). Zwei Geschwindigkeiten in Ost- und Westdeutschland (Two speeds in East and West Germany). In M. Diewald, & A. U. Mayer (Eds.), *Zwischenbilanz der Wiedervereinigung. Strukturwandel und Mobilität im Transformationsprozeß* (pp. 317–328). Opladen: Leske & Budrich.
Zinnecker, J. & Silbereisen, R. K. (1996). *Kindheit in Deutschland* (Childhood in Germany). Weinheim: Juventa.

# 24

# Control Beliefs, Health, and
# Well-Being in Elderly

*Pasqualina Perrig-Chiello*

## INTRODUCTION

Health and control are central issues in the life of elderly. It has been suggested that control beliefs may influence physical and psychological well-being, and health, and that the strength of the relationship between control and health is positively age correlated. It is indeed the case that with advancing years, people are increasingly challenged by internal and external changes, which may threaten the sense of control they have over life in general and over health in particular. Older people undergo physiological and physical changes which may be perceived and interpreted as uncontrollable stressors. In addition, changes in the social network (losses) and the confrontation with the pertinacious ageism in our society could contribute to an increase in physical and psychological vulnerability and feelings of helplessness/loss of control in the elderly.

A review of the literature reveals a considerable research tradition dealing with age-correlated changes in control beliefs and their relationship to well-being and health. Even though empirical psychology began to deal with the concept of control in the late 1960's (in gerontological research more than one decade later), it arose earlier in humanistic psychology. Rogers' view of fully functioning persons stresses that they have an internal locus of evaluation which allows them to define their own personal standards independently of external social influences (Rogers, 1961).

The gerontologist Bernice Neugarten (1968) in the same tradition as Rogers, defines ageing as a process of interiorisation. A characteristic feature of this interiorisation process is that the ageing person tends to question external norms governing everyday life and adapt them to their own requirements. Jahoda (1958) also emphasised autonomy (defined as self-determination, independence, regulation of behavior from within) as the main criterion for physical and psychological well-being, and health in the elderly. This life goal, often referred to as *environmental mastery,* consists of choosing and creating environments which fit with one's physical and psychic possibilities, which consequently allows a active participation. In addition, Loevinger's theory of ego development proposed autonomy and self-determination as the main developmental goals (Loevinger,

1976). Whether elderly people can integrate and cope with the increasing internal (psycho-physiological) and external (social) restrictions of ageing, depends—according to Erikson (Erikson, Erikson and Kivnick, 1986)—on their ability to withdraw deliberately and consciously and to exert control and influence from distance.

Even though these growth-oriented approaches are highly valuable—in a theoretical and practical sense—they have had hardly any influence on the empirical research on ageing until a decade ago (Baltes and Baltes, 1986; Ryff, 1989; Flammer, 1990).

## HEALTH CONTROL BELIEFS IN ELDERLY

Within the last decade a growing number of papers have been published concerning the relationship between biological and social age-correlated changes, and perceived and real (actual) control (Rodin and Timko, 1992; Heckhausen and Schulz, 1995). In the majority of the studies, control beliefs were measured in general terms, without referring to specific life topics. Different studies have, however, suggested the necessity for domain specific differentiation (Lachman, 1986; Beisecker, 1988). It has been shown that control beliefs do not become more external in general with advanced age. An increase of externality (and a decrease of internality) seems to be highly domain specific. Nurmi et al (1992) found that although health related beliefs become more external with age, beliefs about goals concerning e.g., family and occupation did not change.

The focus on health related control beliefs in the elderly raises several questions:

- how consistent is the phenomenon that health control beliefs become more external with age, what does it mean, and what consequences does it have on well-being in general?
- Do people with more external health control beliefs suffer more ill health, and do they feel more unwell and helpless than those with predominantly internal health control beliefs?

If we refer to correlational studies to answer these questions we cannot get a reliable answer as the results are remarkably inconsistent. Positive correlations between internality and good health ratings are reported by Mancini (1981) and Brothen and Detzner (1983). Baltes, Wahl and Schmid-Furstoss (1990), also found positive correlations between personal control and functional health. A study carried out by Robinson-Whelen and Storand (1992) also suggests a positive relationship between negative health ratings and less desire for behavioural involvement in the health care process. However, studies conducted by Hunter, Linn and Harris (1981), Ziegler and Reid (1983) as well as by Brown and Granick (1983) yielded inconsistent results regarding the relationship between locus of control and health ratings.

In our opinion, these inconsistent findings may result from the very divergent operationalisation of the concept "health" (it includes very global self-ratings as well as objective health parameters). It is thus difficult to draw valid conclusions form the reported correlational data. Because correlational studies cannot be used to test causal hypotheses, we have to rely on experimental intervention studies to gain a better understanding of the relationship between control beliefs and health. A considerable number of clinical intervention studies were performed by different research teams (Reich and Zautra, 1989, 1991), which suggested that experimentally induced loss of control is associated with negative health ratings. Schulz and Brenner (1977) as well as Krantz and Schulz (1980), hypothesised that increasing control (predictability) over a new environment for the elderly just entering a long-term care facility/institution (e.g., a hospital, a nursing home, etc.), would counteract the psychological and physical problems typically associated with relocation. In Krantz and Schulz's study (1980), a replication of a study by Langer and Rodin (1976), people recently admitted to a nursing home were randomly assigned to a experimental group (participants received control-relevant information about the new environment, which enhanced the predictability of their institutions) or to a control group (irrelevant control condition, which did not help make the environment more predictable). After the intervention (post-test measurements two weeks and two months after respectively) participants who received control-relevant information were more likely than the control group participants to rate their health more optimistically. In addition, they were judged by nurses as healthier, more satisfied, and more enterprising. Rodin (1986) suggests that already the perceived control over the decision to relocate to an institution exerts an important influence on health outcomes: having control was a better predictor of ultimate return home than coping style, self concept, or severity of illness during hospitalization.

However, even though experimental studies are more consistent than the correlational ones regarding the positive relationship between control and health, here too we find divergent results. In a replication of the Schulz investigation (1976; increase in feelings of control as a result of visits of undergraduate students to nursing home patients) Hautzinger and Bommer (1992) found that a greater degree of control possibility and predictability over social contacts did not result in more positive physical and psychological well-being. Reich and Zautra (1989) who conducted an intervention study similar to that of Schulz (1976) and Langer and Rodin (1976), found a significant improvement in psychological well-being, but the effects were only short-term.

Despite some divergent results, the majority of (control) intervention research strongly suggests that increased control has a beneficial effect on physical and psychological well-being. However, most of these studies do not specify which mechanisms are responsible for the obtained effects/changes. Intervening variables such as physiological adaptations and cognitive processes, as well as external/environmental variables, may explain the relationship between control beliefs and changes in physical and psychological functioning.

## Physiological Mechanisms

Perceived control can activate a wide range of physiological mechanisms that mediate human health and disease. For example, the relationship between control and immune function can play a dramatic role in the health of the elderly. On the one hand because psychosocial stressors that have been shown to affect immunity, are more common in elderly—on the other hand, because the immune system itself becomes less effective with advancing age (Palmblad, 1981; Siskind, 1981; Bandura, 1992). These facts strongly suggest that the relationship between lack of control and suppression of the immune system and its consequences on well-being and health are much stronger in the elderly than in younger people (Rodin and Timko, 1992).

## Psychological Mechanisms

Perception of control may operate as a major determinant that regulates human cognition, motivation, and emotion, which are crucial for expectation beliefs and actions concerning prevention and remediation of health problems. Some evidence exists, which suggests that the tendency for individuals with lower perceived control to show less health-protective attitudes increases with age, because physical decline is frequently viewed as an unalterable part of the ageing process (Rodin, 1987). Different studies have suggested that people with higher perceived control take greater responsibility for their health than those with lower perceived control. That means, that the internals show a greater willingness to seek and adopt information concerning their health problems than externals even though both groups highly valued health (Wallston and Wallston, 1982; Lohaus, Gaidatzi and Hagenbrock, 1988). In addition, different intervention studies reported that internals showed dietary and medication compliance and knew more about their condition that externals (Dishman, Ickes and Morgan, 1980; Frey and Maas, 1985).

Elderly people are more likely than younger subjects to attribute physical symptoms produced by an illness to their age, coping by accepting or minimising the symptoms, therefore neglecting the optimal selection of remediation or therapy (Leventhal and Prohaska, 1986). Health problems may be underattributed to situational factors such as the number of environmental and stress-inducing events (Rodin and Timko, 1992).

Cognitive reappraisal and selection mechanisms of course interact strongly with external variables (environmental). This can be illustrated by studies performed in institutionalised settings.

## Environmental Influence

The higher occurrence of contacts with the medical care system as well as hospitalisations (as a result of the higher amount of multimorbidity, s. Perrig-Chiello, 1997) in the elderly may lower perceived control. Health professionals obviously prefer the more manageable and adjusted patients (Timko and Rodin, 1985). This fact allows the conclusion to be drawn, that internal control is not a desirable attribute of elderly persons, and that instead external control beliefs (powerful others, social externalty) are reinforced.

This phenomenon, mostly observed in institutionalised settings, has been described by Wahl and Baltes (1992) as the dependency-support-pattern, which fosters helplessness at the cost of autonomy/health. This pattern is of crucial importance in institutionalised settings because dependency represents the best way for old people to gain attention and social contact—apparently independent of type of institution, length of institutionalisation, gender, or health status. Based on their own research findings, Felton and Kahana (1974) as well as Cicirelli (1987) come to the conclusion, that external control beliefs (powerful others) are more beneficial to psychological well-being than internal ones for institutionalised elderly people.

## HEALTH CONTROL BELIEFS REVISITED: A CRITICAL INTERIM STATEMENT

The majority of the studies on health control beliefs, especially intervention studies, show significant relationships between health control beliefs and physical well-being and health for elderly people. It is important to note that inconsistencies still exist which suggest the need for further methodological and differential considerations in this research field:

1. Methodological considerations: Operationalisations of the concept "health" are very divergent, in the most cases they refer to subjective health. An explicit (and transparent) differentiation between subjective health ratings and objective health (medical indicators) and the inclusion of both measures in studying the relationship of control beliefs and health and physical well-being is thus a major priority.
2. Differential considerations: We still do not know much about developmental changes in health control beliefs at different phases of old, and oldest age. Elderly people are usually referred to as an homogeneous group, even though gerontological research has always stressed the huge individual differences among elderly, and that clearly individuals' preferences for control will vary widely (Rodin and Timko, 1992). Differential aspects, especially gender differences, were seldom taken into consideration in studies on control in general, and on health control beliefs in particular.

This contribution wants to show data from an interdisciplinary longitudinal ageing study (Perrig-Chiello et al., 1996; Perrig-Chiello, 1997), which allows us to perform:

- a descriptive analysis of age- and time-correlated changes in health control beliefs of different cohorts of elderly people by taking into account gender as a differential aspect;
- group comparisons between objectively and subjectively healthy or sick people and their health control beliefs.

## CONTROL BELIEFS, HEALTH, AND WELL-BEING IN ELDERLY: AN EMPIRICAL STUDY

### Methods

*Participants.* The data presented here were collected through the Basle Longitudinal Project (Inter-Disciplinary Study on Ageing, IDA) with status measurements in 1993 and 1995 (Perrig-Chiello et al., 1996). Participants were 442 community elderly, 309 men, 133 women, aged 65 - 94 years (mean age: 74,95 years). These participants were selected by chance from a sample of retired workers and employees from major chemical companies (N = 3768).

*Variables.* *1. Health control beliefs.* Despite the fact that control beliefs are thought to have an important impact on health and well-being in the elderly, no domain-specific test-instruments normed for old and very old people exist. We therefore constructed a short questionnaire based on the three-dimensional locus-of-control model following Levenson (1974). The test is comprised of six items (statements), two on internality (e.g., physical diseases in old age can be prevented by a healthy life style), two on social externality (e.g., physical diseases in old age cannot be avoided by regular medical visits), and two on fatalistic externality (e.g., physical diseases are part of the destiny of old people). Respondents rate each item on a 3-point scale (3 = I agree, 2 = I'm not sure, 1 = I disagree). This instrument meets all psychometric standards; stability, validity (for more details see Perrig-Chiello, 1995).

*2. Objective health.* Objective health was opertionalized through 20 medical parameters. The sum of the pathological values represents the "objective health index". The 20 indicators were:

Systolic and diastolic blood pressure (standing and seating), pulse, serum cholesterol, serum iron, blood sugar, haemoglobin, MCV (mean cell volume), HDL (high density lipoprotein), triglycerides, leukocytes, thrombocytes, electrocardiogram (rhythm, blocks, ischemy, necroses, hypertrophy, digitalis).

*3. Subjective health.* Subjective health was operationalized as follows:

(a) Subjective health rating (3-point scale: 1 = very good, 3 = very bad health), and (b) Sum of subjective health complaints (perceived physical discomforts): A list of 12 defined frequent health complaints, plus two open categories, was presented to participants; yes/no-responses.

## Results And Discussion

*Health Control Beliefs, Age, and Gender.* Our results reveal that chance health control beliefs are the most frequent in elderly (mean 1993/1995 = 5,38), followed by the internal (mean 1993/1995 = 4,93) and the powerful others ones (mean 1993/1995 = 4,12) (see figure 24.1).

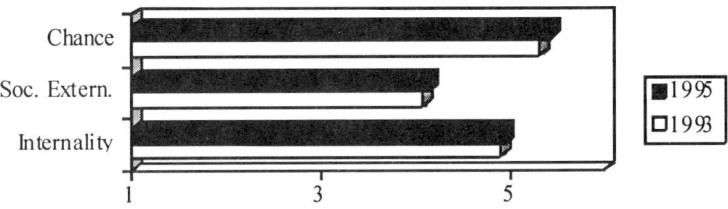

*FIG. 24.1. Health control beliefs, 1993 and 1995.*

We calculated 3-factorial ANOVAs to test a possible dependency of the IPC-dimensions on age, gender, and time (longitudinal comparison: 1993 and 1995). There was no significant age-effect for internality (F = 1,40(3,337), p = .24). Main effects were however found for powerful others and chance, which means an age-correlated increase for powerful others (F = 3,67(3,337), p = .01) and for chance (F = 6,27(3,341), p = < .0001).

Gender effects were found for internality (F= 10,09(1,337), p = < .0001), and for powerful others (F= 5,22(1,337), p = .02): Women showed significantly lower internality and powerful others scores than men.

No significant main effects were observed for the time-factor, besides a tendential increase for fatalistic control beliefs (F= 2,56(1,341), p = .11). There were no significant interactions within these factors.

We can thus conclude that "destiny" plays a dominant role in the elderly's self-appraisal of health, the importance of which increases significantly with age, along with beliefs in powerful-others. In contrast, internal control beliefs seem to be age-resistant. At a first glance this result may astonish, since in the literature —unlike our results—it has been usually reported that an age-correlated increase in external health control beliefs is accompanied by a decrease in internal ones (Beisecker, 1988; Keller et al, 1989). A possible explanation could be, that our averagely healthy population shares the conviction—based on their life-long experience and on their rather optimistic attitude toward life—that on the one hand destiny/faith (whatever this might mean for individuals) is an important determinant of health in old age and that therefore one has to rely more and more on powerful others with advancing age. On the other hand, they have a consolidated experience of not giving up personal responsibility. On the contrary: Exactly because increasing age is associated with more diseases and frailty, one has to encounter them actively, if necessary by activating the help of powerful others (such as doctors, nurses, relatives, etc.). This attitude seems to be rather time-resistant. Our data show further clear gender effects. As in other studies (Ryff, 1989) we found significantly lower internality-scores in women.

Reasons can be sought in the gender-specific socialisation of women. This socialisation is thought to cause women to tend to react with helplessness in demanding or stressful settings (Golombok and Fivush, 1994). Such an attitude could also be responsible for the fact that they do not believe as strongly in the help of powerful others as men do, and that they accept age-correlated health problems as they are, namely, as an inherent reality of ageing.

## Objective And Subjective Health Status, Control Beliefs, And Health Relevant Behavior

The data presented so far refer to an "average, healthy aged" population. But what should we expect if we look at "objectively sick/healthy" and "subjectively sick/healthy" people? Do they differ from each other concerning control beliefs and health relevant behavior?

We divided our sample (N = 442) into three groups taking their objective health status as the criterion and compared them with regard to their health control beliefs: Healthy people (n = 43; no objective diseases), moderately healthy people (n = 296; 1 - 5 objective diseases), rather sick people (n = 57; 5 - 9 objective diseases).

The results show that the three groups did not differ from each other concerning health control beliefs: internality ($F = .778(2,394)$, p = n.s.), social externality ($F = .243(2,394)$, p = n.s.), and fatalistic externality ($F = 1,05(2,394)$, p = n.s.).

We get a rather different situation when the analogous comparison with subjective health self-appraisal (physical complaints) is performed: Healthy people (n = 111; no complaints), moderately healthy people (n = 296; 1 - 5 complaints), rather sick people (n = 57; 5 - 9 complaints). Those reporting the most symptoms (subjectively sick) have significantly lower internality scores than the moderately sick ones (p = .006) and the healthy ones (p = .004) (main effect: $F = 4,707(2,438)$, p = .009) (see figure 24.2).

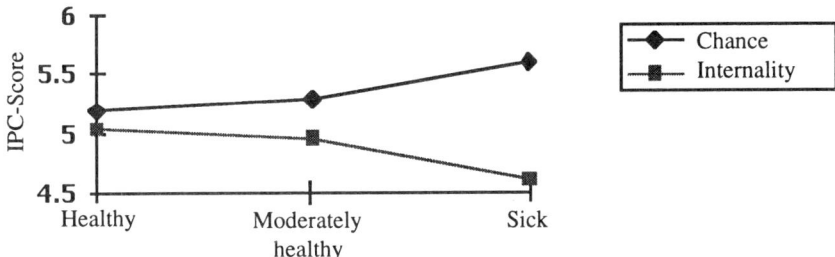

*FIG. 24.2. Internality and chance health control beliefs of subjectively sick, moderately sick and healthy elderly people.*

These lower internality scores are associated with higher scores in chance control beliefs (fatalistic externality) in subjectively sick people (main effect: $F = 5,038(2,439)$, $p = .006$, see figure 24.2). Subjectively sick people have significantly higher chance control beliefs than subjectively healthy ones ($p = .002$) or moderately healthy ones ($p = .009$). Pessimistic subjective health self appraisals are not only associated with lower internality and higher chance control beliefs but also with a specific health-relevant behavior. Results from an ANOVA with the factors "objectively sick" and "subjectively sick" show that subjectively sick people engage significantly less in sports ($F = 7,24(2,431)$, $p = .008$) and consume significantly more psychiatric medication ($F = 4,541(2,433)$, $p = .011$).

These results demonstrate the remarkable power of subjective health appraisals: It is not the fact of how objectively sick a person is, which determines the strength of belief in destiny/faith, rather how strongly she or he feels sick.

## CONCLUSION

The main purpose of this paper was to examine the extent of health control beliefs in different age cohorts of elderly people by taking into account differential aspects such as gender. We were further interested in the relationship between health control beliefs and objective and subjective health.

Our data demonstrate the importance of chance control beliefs followed by the ones of internality and of social externality over all age cohorts. We thus can conclude that "destiny" plays a dominant role in the elderly's health appraisal. At the same time one has to note that no age-correlated decrease of internality could be observed. That means that even though "destiny" is an important issue in the elderly's health control beliefs this doesn't mean that they give up control with age.

According to other authors (Heckhausen and Schulz, 1995), it can be concluded that internal control (primary control) remains stable well into old age, whereas an age-correlated increase of externality (social and fatalistic externality) can be observed. By assuming that externality is roughly equivalent to secondary control (activation of powerful others to maintain physical well-being), then our data provide evidence that elderly people increasingly use secondary control strategies to cope with the inevitable physiological decline and associated functional disabilities of ageing to maintain their relatively stable perception of primary control.

Our data show further strong gender effects in internality and social externality: Women have significantly lower internality and powerful others scores than men. It is known from the literature that women generally show lower internality beliefs than men (Ryff, 1989). Reasons are sought in the gender-specific socialisation of women. Women are encouraged throughout their life course to be comfortable with many experiences of dependency (empathy, social intimacy, perspective taking, etc., Harris and Miller, 1989). Male socialisation however involves some powerful inhibitors to dependence. Dependency (or "to be without control over one's own environment"), is de-emphasised in male socialisation, it is discouraged and even prohibited (Harris and Miller, 1989, 298). Thus having control over one's own environment might have highest priority for balancing well-being in men but not necessarily in women, who may rather prefer good social relationships instead of autonomy and control.

Interestingly enough the women in our sample rely less on powerful others than men do. This result can be explained by the fact that if women do not give such high priority to maintain primary control, they consequently do not need to engage as much in secondary control strategies (beliefs in powerful others), since for them the lower (primary) control is not threatening and not so crucial for balancing their physical well-being as it is for men. In fact we have to add here that the women in our sample did not differ significantly from men in terms of their subjective health self-appraisal and their physical complaints (Perrig-Chiello, 1997).

Finally, our data impressively demonstrate the strong impact subjective health self-evaluations/ratings have on health control beliefs in contrast to objective health parameters. Subjective health appraisals and subjective health complaints deserve to be taken seriously as diagnostic devices and not be depreciated as subjective and therefore of minor value. In this sense we consent to Idler's statement: "There is certainly merit in the view that what people say about their health bears listening to." (Idler, 1992,51)

## REFERENCES

Bandura, A. (1992). *Exercise of personal agency through the self-efficacy mechanism.* In R. Schwarzer (Ed.) Self-efficacy: Thought control of action. Washington: Hemi-sphere.

Baltes, M. M., Baltes, P. B. (Eds); (1986). *The Psychology of Control and Ageing.* Hillsdale, NJ: Lawrence Erlbaum Associates.

Baltes, M. M., Wahl, H. W. & Schmid-Furstoss, U. (1990). The daily life of elderly Germans: Activity patterns, personal control, and functional health. *Journal of Gerontology: Psychological Sciences, 45, 4,* 173–179.

Beisecker, A. E. (1988). Ageing and the desire for information and input in medical *decisions. Gerontologist, 28,* 330–335.

Brothen, T. & Detzner, D. (1983). Perceived health and locus of control in the aged. *Perceptual and Motor Skills, 56,* 946.

Brown, B. R. & Granick, S. (1983). Cognitive and psychosocial differences between I and E locus of control aged persons. *Experimental Aging Research, 9,* 107–110.

Cicirelli, V. G. (1987). Locus of control and patient role adjustment of the elderly in acute-care hospitals. *Psychology and Aging, 2, 2,*138–143.

Dishman, R. K., Ickes, W. & Morgan, W. P. (1980). Self-motivation and adherence to habitual physical activity. *Journal of Applied Social Psychology, 10,* 115–132.

Erikson, E. H., Erikson, J. M., Kivnick, H. Q.(1986). *Vital involvement in old age.* New York: Norton.

Felton, B. & Kahana, E. (1974). Adjustment and situationally bound locus of control among institutionalised aged. *Journal of Gerontology,29,* 295–301.

Flammer, A. (1990). *Erfahrung der eigenen Wirksamkeit. Einführung in die Psychologie der Kontrollmeinung.* Bern: Huber.

Frey, D. & Maas, A. (1985). Persönlichkeit und Krankheit und Gesundheit. In Th. Herrmann & E. D. Lantermann (Hrsg). *Persönlichkeit. Ein Handbuch in Schlüsselbegriffen.* München: Urban & Schwarzenberg.

Golombok, S. & Fivush, R. (1994). *Gender development.* New York: Cambridge University Press.

Harris, A. & Miller, N. (1989). *The implication of gender and speech for the experience of control in ageing.* In P. S. Fry (Ed) Psychological perspectives of helplessness and control in the elderly. (pp. 291–219). Amsterdam: North-Holland.

Hautzinger, M. & Bommer, M. (1992). Die Auswirkungen von Kontrolle und Vorhersagbarkeit auf das Befinden älterer Menschen - eine Replikation. *Schweizerische Zeitschrift für Psychologie, 51, 3,* 191–198.

Heckhausen, J. & Schulz, R. (1995). A life-span theory of control. *Psychological Review, 102, 2,* 284–304.

Hunter, K. I., Linn, M. W. & Harris, R. (1981–82). Characteristics of high and low self-esteem in the elderly. *International Journal of Ageing and Human Development, 14,* 117–126.

Idler, E. L. (1992). *Self-assessed health and mortality: A review of studies.* In S. Maes, H. Leventhal & M. Johnston: *International Review of Health Psychology.* Chichester: Wiley.

Jahoda, M. (1958). *Current concepts of positive mental health.* New York: Basic Books.

Keller, M. L., Leventhal, H. & Prohaska, T. R. (1989). Beliefs about ageing and illness in a community sample. *Research in Nursing and Health, 12,* 247–255.

Krantz, D. S. & Schulz, R. (1980). Personal control and health: Some applications to crisis of middle and old age. In A. Baum & J. E. Singer (Eds). *Advances in environmental psychology.* (Vol. 2, pp. 23–57). New York: Academic Press.

Lachman, M. E. (1986). Locus of control in ageing research. *Psychology and Aging,1,*34–40.

Langer, F. & Rodin, J. (1976). The effects of choice and enhanced personal responsibility: A field experiment in an institutional setting. *Journal of Personality and Social Psychology, 34,* 191–198.

Levenson, H. (1974). Activism and powerful others: Distinction within the concept of internal-external control. *Journal of Personality Assessment,38,* 377–383.

Leventhal, E. A. & Prohaska, T. R. (1986). Age, symptom interpretation, and health behaviour. *Journal of the American Geriatrics Society, 34,* 185–191.

Loevinger, J. (1976). *Ego development.* San Francisco: Jossey-Bass.

Lohaus, A. (1992). Kontrollüberzeugungen zu Gesundheit und Krankheit. *Zeitschrift für Klinische Psychologie, XXI, 1,* 76–87.

Lohaus, A. & Schmitt, G. M. (1989). *Fragebogen zur Erhebung von Kontrollüberzeugungen zu Krankheit und Gesundheit.* Göttingen: Hogrefe.

Mancini, J.A. (1981/82). Effects of health and income on control orientation and life satisfaction among aged public housing residents. *International Journal of Ageing and Human Development, 12,* 215–220.

Neugarten, B. L. (1968). The awareness of middle age. In B. L. Neugarten (Ed). *Middle age and ageing* (pp. 93–98). Chicago: University of Chicago Press.

Nurmi, J.E., Pulliainen, H. & Salmela-Aro,K. (1992). Age differences in adults' control beliefs related to life goals and concerns. *Psychology and Ageing, 7, 2,* 194–196.

Palmblad, J. (1981). Stress and immunologic competence: Studies in man. In R. Ader (Ed). *Psychoneuroimmunology* (pp. 229–257). New York: Academic Press.

Perrig-Chiello, P. (1995). Wohlbefinden, Kontrolle und Autonomie im Alter. Ein diagnostisches Inventar. *Schweizerischer Nationalfonds, NFP 32-Bulletin "Alter", Nr. 3,* 8–14.

Perrig-Chiello, P., Perrig, W. J., Stähelin, H. B., Krebs, E. & Ehrsam, R. (1996). Autonomie, Wohlbefinden und Gesundheit im Alter: Eine interdisziplinäre Altersstudie (IDA). *Zeitschrift für Gerontologie und Geriatrie, 29,* 95-109.

Perrig-Chiello, P. (1997). Ressourcen des Wohlbefindens im Alter. Weinheim: Juventa.

Reich, J. W. & Zautra, A. J. (1989). A perceived control intervention for atrisk older adults. *Psychology and Aging, 4, 4,* 415–424.

Robinson-Whelen, S. & Storandt, M. (1992). Factoral structure of two health belief measures among older adults. *Psychology and Aging, 7, 2,* 209–213.

Rodin, J. (1986). Ageing and health: Effects of the sense of control. *Science, 233,* 1271–1276.

Rodin, J. (1987). Personal control through the life course. In R. P. Abeles (Ed). *Life-span perspectives and social psychology* (pp. 103–120). Hillsdale, NJ: Lawrence Erlbaum Associates.

Rodin, J. & Timko, C. (1992). Sense of control, ageing and health. In M. G. Ory, R. P. Abeles, P. D. Lipman (Eds). *Ageing, health and behaviour.* Newbury Park: Sage.

Rogers, C. R. (1961). *On becoming a person.* Boston: Houghton Mifflin.

Ryff, C. D. (1989). Happiness is everything, or is it? Explorations on the meaning of psychological well-being. *Journal of Personality and Social Psychology, 57, 6,* 1069–1081.

Schulz, R. (1976). Effects of control and predictability on the physical and psychological well-being of the institutionalised aged. *Journal of Personality and Social Psychology, 33,* 563–573.

Schulz, R. & Brenner, G. (1977). Relocation of the aged: A review and theoretical analysis. *Journal of Gerontology, 32,* 323–333.

Siskind, G. (1981). Immunological aspects of ageing: An overview. In R. T. Schinke (Ed). *Biological mechanisms of ageing* (NIH Publ. Nr. 81-2194, pp. 455–466). Bethesda, MD: Nat. Institute of Health.

Timko, C. & Rodin, J. (1985). Staff-patient relationships in nursing homes: Sources or conflict and rehabilitation potential. *Rehabilitation Psychology, 30,* 93–108.

Wahl, H. W. & Baltes, M. M. (1992). Die Mikroökologie alter Menschen: Forderung nach Autonomie und Sicherheit. In C. Petzold & H.G. Petzold (Hrsg.) *Lebenswelten alter Menschen.* Hannover: Vincentz Verlag.

Wallston, K. A. & Wallston, B. S. (1982). Who is responsible for your health? The construct of health locus of control. In G. Sanders & J. Suls (Eds). *Social Psychology of health and illness* (pp 65–95). Hillsdale, NJ: Lawrence Erlbaum Associates.

Ziegler, M. & Reid, D. W. (1983). Correlates of changes in desired control scores and in life satisfaction scores among elderly persons. *International Journal of aging and Human Development, 2,* 135–146.

# VI

# Socialization, Systems, and Culture

# 25

# Do I Choose? Attribution and Control in Students of a Technical School[1]

*Claude Albert Kaiser*
*Anne-Nelly Perret-Clermont*
*Jean-François Perret*

## INTRODUCTION

Our age is marked by the idea of change. Reference is often made to the technological, economic, and social mutations that industrialized nations are undergoing. There is question of establishing new production methods which are more competitive and offer greater flexibility. This will have an impact on the evolution and complexity of knowledge that people need to acquire. The new challenge for education is providing interactive, individualized training, centered not only on the learning of contents, but also on the acquisition of skills. Changes in the meaning and value attributed to work are also at issue. It is hoped that people's increased participation in their own training will bring about a new relationship to work.

In a sense, the ideal individual is considered to be one who knows what they want, who is able to project themselves into the future, anticipating their actions; in short, an individual who makes choices and is not governed only by circumstances. Learning by repetition and conditioning are replaced by creativity, innovation, and a spirit of initiative. Discourses of order are giving way to discourses of autonomy and performance (Ehrenberg, 1992).

This new emphasis on the role of personal action and the individual's control over his own environment is an issue that relates to an important field of study in psychology, attribution of causality. We will briefly recall of some of the principles and findings of research in this domain, and present some results that

---

[1]This work was financed by the Swiss Foundation for Scientific Research (National Program no. 33, project no. 4033-035846, A.-N. Perret-Clermont, R. Bachmann and L.-O. Pochon). We thank our colleague Danièle Golay Schilter for her active contribution to the survey, and Felice Carugati of the University of Bologna for his precious suggestions.

427

indicate the important role people play in determining what happens to them. We will discuss these issues in relation to education in a professional technical school in which we carried out a study. We will try to highlight discrepancies that can exist between discourse and reality. Although the documents issued by the official professional associations that we consulted place considerable emphasis on the importance of fostering student autonomy and skills in communicating, the results of our study show that the students enrolled in the technical school tended to place value on traditional learning methods based on imitation and rehearsal. What then becomes of the role ascribed to the agent in making choices?

Globally speaking, the students in our study preferred to maintain that their professional choices were dictated by personal characteristics rather than circumstances. This seemed to suggest that they placed value on explanations of their own behavior in which they play an active role, and that they know these values are in line with the spirit of our time. However, we found that the intensity with which these views were expressed depends on the status of the program in which the students are enrolled. Thus, the students in the higher status program showed a more voluntarist position than the other students. Do these differences reflect stable or invariant personality traits, or are they elicited by the social and institutional context?

Although we recognize that our results do not provide a decisive answer to this question, they do bring forth the complexity of the problem, in particular with respect to the different levels of analysis and explanation involved in accounting for the emphasis placed on the role of the actor in determining events and outcomes.

## RESEARCH ON ATTRIBUTION

Making predictions and having control over one's environment, involve separating out that which is due to chance and that which results from stable effects. The process of explaining the causes of events has been the focus of two main fields of research in psychology. The first, generally subsumed by the term "attribution of causality," stems from the work of Heider (1958), and later of Jones and Davis (1965), and Kelly (1967). Its aim is to gain an understanding of how people make inferences about their behavior. The second field concerns "locus of control" (LOC); it is interested in people's generalized expectancies for internal versus external control of reinforcement (Rotter, 1966). In the first field, the focus is on people's explanations of behavior, whereas in the second it is people's expectations about the control they have over the reinforcements they receive, and this within a differential perspective, leading to the design of tests for measuring individual differences in perception of control. Admittedly, it is not always easy to draw this distinction, especially in the case of studies that bear upon the reasons people invoke to explain their success or failure (see Weiner, 1979, 1986).

As various authors have pointed out (Apfelbaum & Herzlich, 1970, 1971; Hewstone & Jaspars, 1982; Deschamps, 1983), in both fields the theoretical explanations of inference processes usually do not take into account the role of social factors and relations between groups. Studies on causal attribution quickly led to the finding that individuals do not conduct themselves altogether rationally, tending to make internal attributions related to personality factors, rather than external attributions involving circumstances (see Jones, Davis, & Gergen, 1961; Steiner & Field, 1960; Jones & Harris, 1967). This so called "fundamental attribution error" (Ross, 1977), was considered to show that individuals can be characterized by stable traits that lead to specific biases in their explanations of behavior.

However, later studies, in which social factors were taken into account, concluded that the attribution error does not manifest itself in a regular fashion, that it depends importantly on the type of interaction between individuals and between groups, as well as on the status attributed to them (see Deschamps & Clémence, 1990). The tendency to overestimate dispositional factors in explanations of behavior is particularly characteristic of disadvantaged individuals and groups in situations characterized by an asymmetry of status (Thibaut & Riecken, 1955). It has also been shown that subjects modulate their causal attributions in order to preserve their social identity, accentuating their personal merits, or those of the group to which they belong, when engaged in a socially valued enterprise (Taylor & Jaggi, 1974; Deaux & Emswiller, 1974).

Whereas many studies point to the necessity of taking social factors into account, it seems that matters present themselves differently for locus of control (LOC). This field of work, as already stated above, is affiliated with differential psychology since it is concerned with the determination and measurement of differences between individuals regarding causal explanation. Although this approach is more descriptive than explanatory, it provides useful leads for carrying out interventions in institutional settings. As Dubois (1994) points out, the findings that individuals with the highest internality scores on the locus of control scales are more successful in their studies (see Findley & Cooper, 1983), and that internality scores correlate positively with professional success (see Eichler, 1980), lead to questions about the nature of the relation between success and belief in internal control. It appears that correlation between intellectual abilities (as measured by tests) and responses on locus of control scales is weak (Dubois, 1994). If internal attributers succeed better, even though they are not necessarily more intelligent, we need to find out which contextual factors work to their advantage. Py and Somat (1991) have shown that school children with the highest scores for internality are judged more favorably by their teachers from an emotional standpoint. Thus, it is possible that internal attributers benefit from some sort of "Pygmalion effect" (Rosenthal & Jacobson, 1968).

Also close to the locus of control approach is research on "control belief" *(Kontrollmeinung),* which bears on people's subjective representation of their ability to exert control (Flammer, Grob & Lüthi, 1989; Flammer, 1992, 1994).

This work shows in particular that control beliefs are constructed during onto-genesis, that they affect self-esteem, and that there are cultural variations in feel-ing of being in control.

This last point brings us back to the question of the meanings associated with the concept of fundamental attribution error. The cultural differences in control belief evidenced by the work of Flammer and his collaborators, as well as Beauvois' theoretical analysis using the concept of "norm of internality" (Beau-vois, 1984) suggest that the overestimation of the importance of dispositional factors in explanations of social behavior is in actual fact a socially learned norm: subjects recognize that people place value on explanations of psychological events in which there is emphasis on the actor as a causal factor. Hence, Dubois (1988a) shows that minor variations in task instruction are sufficient to provoke a change in attribution. For instance, a self-valuing instruction results in an increase of internality scores, whereas a self-devaluing instruction results in de-crease of these scores.

The institutional context also seems to play a role. Le Poultier (1986), work-ing in an education center, and Dubois (1988b) working in the context of a train-ing program for hospital staff, both observed an increase in internality scores between the beginning and the end of the program.

Social status also modulates interpretations of behavior since people from so-cially disfavored classes tend to be significantly less internal with respect to matters of control over reinforcements than members of upper classes (Claus, 1981). Similar effects were obtained in research conducted in schools and voca-tional training, but this time in relation to students' status within the institution (Doise, Meyer & Perret-Clermont, 1976; Bell & Perret-Clermont, 1984; Bell, Perret-Clermont & Baker, 1989; Clémence, Deschamps & Roux, 1986; Kaiser, 1997).

All the studies we have mentioned underline the important role of social and cultural factors in people's explanations of behavior and reinforcement, and in the degree to which they overestimate dispositional factors.

## STUDENTS' REPRESENTATIONS OF THEIR VOCATIONAL TRAINING: A STUDY IN A TECHNICAL SCHOOL

The rapid transformation of techniques and knowledge, as well as an incessant need to increase productivity, have profoundly modified the current demands placed on technical professions. Flexibility and innovation of production systems are becoming viewed more and more as a guarantee for competitiveness.

Gaining knowledge of the full range of new technologies, and acquiring total mastery in using them, seems to be an unrealistic educational goal. A global understanding of production procedures mobilizes students' cognitive and social capacities. Furthermore, what is learned during initial training risks becoming obsolete very quickly. Consequently, it has been suggested that initial vocational training should focus on fostering a state of mind that allows for continual revision and questioning of what is learned during professional life, and that it should encourage the future professionals to play an active, autonomous role in their own education, viewed as a continuous process.

We think that a different relation to knowledge would to be established. Rather than transmitting traditional techniques in an authoritative, planned fashion, one has to equip students with general skills that allow them to move their way around actively in a continually changing and ever more complex landscape of knowledge and know-how (Golay Schilter, 1995).

What might such general skills be? They should of course comprise expert knowledge and practices, but also general problem-solving skills, which often call for an ability to manage social relationships and communication methods effectively, and to consider others as opportunities for learning rather than as models to imitate. There are connections to be drawn between the focus on autonomy and personal initiative and the previously mentioned studies on causal attribution and internal versus external locus of control.

For our present purposes, the main question is whether students really feel that they play an active role in their studies or training, which seems to be the wish of the people in charge of the professional schools. Furthermore, are there differences according to the students' membership to the different professional categories within the institution, when certain categories enjoy a higher status than others?

Our survey, using a questionnaire, was carried out in a technical school which trains practitioners in mechanics and electronics to a national certificate level (Certificat Fédéral de Capacité) and technicians to a post certificate level (post-CFC). Students were questioned about the reasons for their vocational choices, their feelings of control over their environment, their implicit representations of the learning process, as well as their ways of interpreting success and failure at school (see Kaiser, Perret-Clermont, Perret & Golay Schilter, 1997). There were 129 students present on the day of the survey, 43 practitioners in mechanics, 38 in electronics and 37 technicians. The mean age of the participants, all males, was 19.

## REASONS FOR VOCATIONAL CHOICES

One part of the questionnaire was aimed at determining the main dimensions that underlie students' choice of vocation. The participants were presented with a set of twenty-one reasons from which they had to choose the seven reasons that best reflected their own situation and the seven questions that did so least. Their response were analyzed by performing a cluster analysis on response patterns of conjointly rejected or accepted reasons. The principle groupings evidenced by this analysis are presented in a synthetic form in table 25.1.

TABLE 25.1

*Principal groupings resulting from a cluster analysis on the reasons for choice of vocation*

| External reasons, focused mainly on circumstances | Internal reasons focused mainly on personal characteristics |
|---|---|
| It's what I was advised | It fits with my personality |
| It corresponds to my parents' wishes | I like to work independently, the way I want |
| It was closest to home | It allows me to learn a trade |
| It bored me the least | It allows me to do further training afterwards |
| My schooling doesn't leave me any choice | It will give me access to jobs of the future |
| It allows me to meet people | I just like it |
| I like teamwork | It is a profession in which you constantly learn new things |
| It will give me access to higher positions | It is a profession in which there are always new challenges |
| I can find work more easily | I like anything that's technical |
| I can get a well-paid job | I like finding solutions to problems |
| | I like to build objects, to make things |

A first main subdivision was found between reasons referring mainly to circumstances and reasons involving personality or own interests. The reasons of the first category could be further subdivided to distinguish reasons involving the advice of others and school performance from reasons related to job prospects and pay. The reasons involving more personal characteristics could also be subdivided: reasons involving personality traits and reasons referring to personal interests or the career perspectives that the profession has to offer.

To evaluate the weight of the different categories of reasons indicated by the cluster analysis, we compared the frequency of "positive" and "negative" choices within each category, depending on whether subjects chose a reason as being most or least in line with their own. For all participants combined, internal reasons were chosen "positively" more frequently than "negatively" ($p < .01$). In contrast, external reasons were more often rejected than accepted. ($p < .01$).

However, these general trends fluctuated according to the sub-samples. Thus, internal reasons, chosen "positively" by all students, were favored more by technicians than practitioners in mechanics and in electronics ($p < .03$). Reciprocally, external reasons were refused more often by technicians than practitioners in mechanics and in electronics ($p < .02$).

Probably for reasons of social desirability, the majority of students chose items that indicate they made choices based on personal will. Internality, a norm which is valued by society and favors individual autonomy, was clearly acknowledged by the majority of the participants of our study. Nevertheless, adherence to this norm varied according to the subsamples: internal factors were chosen positively less often by practitioners in mechanics and electronics than by technicians.

## CONTROL BELIEFS

The different types of logic with respect to vocational choices, as evidenced by our study, can be related to students' views on educational situations. Here, our goal was to investigate the degree of control subjects believed they had on their immediate or future environment. Since, as we saw above, practitioners in mechanics and electronics were less inclined to evoke internal reasons for choice of vocation than technicians, we hypothesized that they would also feel less in control of their environment.

Using items from a questionnaire elaborated by Flammer for doing research on control beliefs (see Grob, Bodmer & Flammer, 1993; Flammer, 1994), the participants in our study were requested to imagine three situations. The first concerned a situation of finding a job, the second learning in school settings, and the third general modes of conduct in everyday life. In each case, participants had to estimate the influence they would have over the situation, both at present and in three or four years' time.

Globally, control was judged to be lowest for the school situation, followed by finding a job, and then by general situations of personal life, in which control was perceived to be highest. These estimations of control were generally shared by all the participants, and did not vary significantly according to present and future situations.

Thus, contrary to our predictions, we did not observe differences in perception of control between the subgroups of our sample. What was even more surprising, however, was that students considered control to be lowest for the school learning situation, a result that was also obtained in a study by Flammer, Grob and Lüthi (1989). This certainly does not seem congruent with the educational goals of autonomy and active participation desired by the school authorities.

## SUCCESS AND FAILURE IN SCHOOL

Another means of evaluating the participants' representations regarding their feelings of control over their environment consisted in analyzing the reasons they gave for success and failure in school. Previous studies on causes of success and failure show that there is a general tendency to attribute success to factors within the subject's control, such as invested effort. In contrast, failure is more often seen to be the result of uncontrollable factors, such as insufficient capacities (Luginbuhl, Crowe & Kahan, 1990; Rotter, 1966; Weiner, 1979, 1986). The same trends were observed by Perret (1981) and Goslin (1992), and discussed by

Carugati & Selleri (1996) in relation to teachers' explanations of the mediocre results obtained by students.

Our questionnaire presented two sets of reasons, one for success in school and the other for failure. Students had to choose the three reasons that corresponded most closely to themselves. Each set comprised the same types of explanations, which were adjusted to match the case of failure or success. The explanations presented concerned the degree of interest in the subject matter, the quality of the explanations given by teachers, the amount of effort invested in learning, the level of course requirements, the fact of having a feel for the subject matter, the atmosphere in the classroom, chance and luck, receiving help from a fellow student, and the appeal of the teacher.

In the case of success, the three most commonly chosen reasons were directly related to the contents being taught, namely interest in the subject matter, the quality of explanations provided, and the amount of effort invested. These choices contrasted with reasons which were more closely related to situational factors than course content, namely the role of chance, help from a peer, or having a good relationship with the teacher. The attitudes toward success were shared by all the students; we did not obtain any significant differences between the subgroups of the sample. It should be noted, however, that of the three most chosen reasons, only invested effort was directly controllable by the subject.

For failure in school we obtained very similar response patterns. Lack of effort insufficient explanation, and too little interest for the subject matter were considered to be the main reasons for failure. This time, however, we obtained differences between the choices of the technicians and the practitioners in mechanics and electronics. The technicians seemed to attribute more responsibility to themselves (lack of effort) in a situation of failure than did practitioners in mechanics and electronics ($p < .01$). Furthermore, having a good relationship with the teacher seemed to be more important for the practitioners in mechanics and electronics than for the technicians ($p < .01$).

On the whole, success and failure were attributed to factors related to the course contents. Although effort, a controllable factor, was given greatest importance for explaining success, and especially failure, it rests that the other two reasons—quality of explanations and interest in subject matter—are not directly in the learner's control: it is easier to make more effort than to change the teacher's contribution, or the nature of the subject matter. Finally, the appeal of the teacher, a more or less uncontrollable factor, seemed to be relatively more important for mechanics than practitioners in electronics.

## IMPLICIT REPRESENTATIONS OF LEARNING METHODS

Although educational institutions have objectives of transmitting knowledge and techniques, instilling modes of reasoning, or even social norms, they also aim to foster a certain state of mind that one might qualify as creative, communicative, critical and constructive. These objectives reflect two different conceptions of the learner: in one he is a passive receiver, in the other an active agent. Consequently, in order to reach these goals, educational institutions should not only be places where knowledge is transmitted but also environments for gaining experience in applying acquired knowledge, as a preparation for future vocational activities.

Now, the question is whether a single didactic approach is suitable for both the acquisition of knowledge and the gaining of practice? In this connection, research indicates that cognitive acquisitions are related to the social conditions that prevail in the educational situations (see for example: Perret-Clermont et al., 1984; Monteil, 1989; Perret-Clermont & Schubauer-Leoni, 1989). Practice in implementing these cognitive acquisitions are dependent on the social conditions in the situations that are encountered later on (Nicolet, 1995; Perret-Clermont et al. 1994, 1997; Perret-Clermont & Schubauer-Leoni, 1981; Perret-Clermont, Schubauer-Leoni, & Trognon, 1992).

Whereas it is possible to transmit knowledge and skills, or standard problem solving strategies, the student's appropriation of these competencies does not necessarily occur through a transmission process. Didactic situations in which there is a relationship of dependence between "he who does not know" and "he who does " favor the idea of learning as a process of mere reproduction of knowledge and modes of thought. In contrast, didactic situations based on interdependence between teachers, students and subject matter tend to favor the construction of more personalized concepts.

To study students' implicit representations of learning methods we designed questions that referred to three models of learning. The first model is that of learning through direct experience and reproduction of responses leading to favorable consequences. This is the so called model of "operant conditioning," in which responses are learned by reinforcement, and repetition plays an essential role. The second model is that of learning through observation of people performing correctly. What the learner acquires is inferred from the behavior of the model, who serves as a guide for behavior. A third model is one in which learning results from socio-cognitive conflict (Doise, Mugny, & Perret-Clermont, 1975; Perret-Clermont, 1979/1996; Doise & Mugny, 1981; Perret-Clermont & Nicolet, 1986). This model does not emphasize the selection and reinforcement of desirable responses, nor the mere transmission of knowledge; it focuses on situations that allow the active construction of responses and knowledge. The term socio-cognitive conflict refers to situations in which there is cognitive conflict between different ways of conceptualizing or solving problems, and social conflict arising from the relationship between actors. The subject's cognitive constructions are thus seen to be the result of coordination between the subject's own view points and those of others, and integration of the social relations between individuals or groups (De Paolis, Doise & Mugny, 1987; Carugati & Gilly, 1993).

The students were asked questions about the activities that should be undertaken or the attitudes that should be adopted when one encounters difficulties in a theoretical course. The purpose of our analysis was threefold: to examine the students' response patterns and extract the dimensions, or factors, that organize their representations of the learning process (using a principal components factor analysis); to determine which categories of items (activities, attitudes) were judged to be most efficient (by analyzing the mean scores of groups of items corresponding to each dimension); and finally, to analyze the positions of the three subgroups of students with respect to each dimensions (by comparison of the mean factor scores for each subgroup of students).

## IN CASE OF DIFFICULTIES

When asked about the most efficient measures for dealing with difficulties in a theoretical course, the students gave answers indicating the presence of four main dimensions, as revealed by the factor analysis. The first dimension grouped items that corresponded to the model of learning through repetition and copying of correct examples; the items that loaded this factor were doing extra exercises, revising the basic notions, and repeating the activity to be learned several times over. The second dimension was more interactional, relating to communication with peers. Items that loaded this factor were asking explanation from a class-mate, and working with a classmate who is successful or experiencing similar difficulties. The third dimension might be interpreted as a factor of decentering, since it grouped activities that are related or similar to the target activity, relaxing, and saying to oneself that sooner or later one will catch on. The fourth dimension was organized around the idea of confrontation with a correct model, like the first dimension, but this time in the form of a request directed at the teacher. Thus, contrary to the second factor, which involved interaction in a symmetrical relationship, the fourth factor involved asymmetrical relations, being loaded by items such as watching teachers perform a demonstration, or asking them for explanations.

When the items corresponding to each factor were grouped together, the ones referring to confrontation with a correct model (factor 1) were judged to be the most efficient. They were followed by the items of factor 4, involving requests directed at the teachers. And, next in line, we found items referring to confrontation with peers and decentering activities.

Comparison of the mean factor scores of the three sub-group of students showed that the technicians tended to place more emphasis on learning through repetition and confrontation with a correct model than the students in the other vocational groups ($p < .01$).

We also asked students about the most efficient means for dealing with learning difficulties in practical work, as opposed to difficulties in theoretical courses. For these questions we did not obtain any clear trends. The technicians, as well as the practitioners in mechanics and electronics, believed that everything was important: imitation, repetition, and asking the teacher were all judged to be suitable strategies. Only one item was clearly rejected: asking support from a classmate who is experiencing similar difficulties.

This last finding might seem surprising, given that interaction between "novices" in a symmetrical relationship has specific beneficial effects due to the decentering they induce, as numerous studies have shown. What accounts for the fact that equal importance was given to all courses of action? Perhaps school ideology is less prominent in the realm of practical courses (although students did believe in the need for an asymmetrical relation with an "expert") since practical knowledge and skills are not easily put into words and transmitted by discourse. Another interpretation might be that students realize teachers need to constantly update themselves with respect to the rapid evolution of professional knowledge and tools, and that therefore, they cannot rely on copying others who may also experience difficulties with the task.

## CONCLUSION

The results of our survey underline the great complexity of apprehending the meaning of the emphasis placed on people's active participation. When we examined students' reasons for choosing their professional training, the criteria referring to personal motivations were chosen most frequently than those pertaining to context. This tendency was comparatively stronger in students enrolled in the more highly valued training program. If this means that students with superior status are more "internal," we need to find out why. Do these students share specific personality traits, or are their responses determined by the context? Another possibility is that they have come to realize the importance of playing an active role as consequence of their experiences during the educational settings provided by their school. Flammer (1990) has shown, for instance, that feelings of control are increased through direct confrontation with reality in concrete situations.

A partial answer is provided by the results obtained for the control belief scales in our questionnaire. Contrary to expectations, students enrolled in the three training programs did not differ in feelings of control. On the other hand, we found that it was precisely in the domain of school education that the participants perceived their own influence to be weakest. This result is interesting on several counts. It shows the impact institutional settings have on the perception of control. It may be an effect that works against the development of an increased participation of students in the management of their own learning. Finally, it evidences the discrepancies that can exist between the intentions proclaimed by the people in charge of training program and the attitudes of the students.

As to implicit representations concerning ways of learning and factors that explain success and failure, we found that students' responses reflected a very traditional view. Among the reasons chosen most frequently for explaining success or failure, some are under the students' control, such as personal effort. Such reasons were chosen more frequently by the students enrolled in the more highly estimated program. But we also obtained high frequencies for reasons that are mostly beyond personal control, such as the explanations given by the teacher and interest in the subject matter. Finally, our analysis of students' ideas about the effectiveness of different ways of learning showed a preference for traditional approaches based on imitation, repetition and confrontation with a correct model. This effect was strongest in the student enrolled in the more prestigious program for technicians, and with respect to learning contexts that are held in greatest esteem by society, namely theoretical courses.

The participants in our study who evidenced the greatest degree of internality—the ones following the more esteemed program—were also the ones who seemed to adhere most strongly to traditional conceptions of learning, conceptions that probably continue to be the main reference for teachers when it comes to educational practices, in spite of the fact that their discourse proclaims autonomy and active participation. Consequently, and following mechanisms of construction of social identity concepts (Turner, 1982), students with the highest status adhere to the group they desire to become part of, attributing to themselves the characteristics of this group, which are perceived in a stereotypical manner.

The means by which professional insertion is carried out induces specific representational frameworks in students (Doise, Meyer & Perret-Clermont, 1976). According to Beauvois (1994), internality is in fact a norm propagated by socially favored groups. Does our study then confirm previous findings that subjects' expression of attitudes of internality, or even the degree of perceived control over choices, are not reflections of invariant personality traits, but the consequence of the subjects' experiences in different situations as well as the social status they possess at a given time?

No doubt, we still need to arrive at a better articulation, on a theoretical plane, of the different explanations for the value placed on control, and of the determinants of choice and internality, in particular from a social standpoint. According to Doise (1982) it is useful to distinguish four levels of explanation of social phenomena: an intra-individual level that concerns the subject's personal psychological organization; an inter-individual level that refers to processes of interactions between individuals; an inter-group level in which interactions between individuals are explained in terms of membership to social categories; and finally an ideological level that bears upon people's belief systems and representations.

We cannot limit ourselves to an intra-individual level to account for the observed preference for internality in explanations of behavior since this preference does not seem to reflect invariant characteristic of personality, but derives from social processes that apparently make this type of a response "adequate". We need to go beyond this level of explanation by referring to variables that take into account the interactions between individual and groups, and thereby apprehend the nature of the supposed adequacy of internality. At this level of analysis, internality appears to be a socially desirable value, which is expressed most frequently by privileged individuals. These persons have succeeded from the point of view of the model advocated by the institution, and therefore reproduce its ideological views, in particular with respect to the causality of success in school.

Few theories discuss the issue in terms of ideology. Dubois (1994), defends the idea that the preference for internality is characteristic of liberal societies since it allows for evaluation on according to individual criteria. The privileged classes and individuals of society place greater emphasis on internality because it is a good way of justifying their advantaged position. Dubois' ideas go in the direction of Papastamou's work (1986) on "psychologization" which show that the establishment of causal connections between psychological characteristics and social behaviors has important social implications. For example, it accounts for ideological mechanisms of resistance to social change, in which social differences between groups or individuals are taken to be the result of stable, unalterable psychological traits or variables.

If Papastamou's theory is correct, then one might predict that the particular attention given by schools to the psychological characteristics of students actually works toward conservation of traditional functioning in schools. But technical schools, as the one in our study, wish to open their doors to new objectives such as student autonomy and team work. Consequently, the schools, with all its actors, including directors, teachers, and students, should not be interested exclusively in the characteristics of the learners, such as level of competence, motivations, and internality. They should pay far more attention to the characteristics of inter-individual, ideological, and institutional functioning, and look at aspects such as the implicit and explicit didactic "contracts," hierarchical organization, and value systems. They should examine not only their own representations and discourse, but also the concrete effects of the working conditions—such as available space, equipment, methods, and scheduling—on the educational practices of teachers and students. This is the focus of some of the other parts of our study (Golay Schilter, 1997; Golay Schilter et al., 1997, in press; Perret, 1997). Preliminary results reveal contradictions between what students said (or have learned to say) and what actually happened in class. For instance, technical students trying to carry out a practical task imposed by the teacher constantly sought help or support from classmates, and the presence of a third party elicited decentering responses favorable to success in the task. Situations of learning through simple repetition and imitation seemed to be rare.

## REFERENCES

Apfelbaum, E., & Herzlich, C. (1970–1971). La théorie de l'attribution en psychologie sociale. *Bulletin de Psychologie, 24,* 961–976.

Beauvois, J.-L. (1984). *La psychologie quotidienne.* Paris: Presses Universitaires de France.

Bell, N., & Perret-Clermont, A. N. (1984). Répercussions psychosociologiques de l'échec et de la sélection scolaire. *Cahiers de Psychologie de l'Université de Neuchâtel, 22.*

Bell, N., Perret-Clermont, A.-N., & Baker, N. (1989). La perception de la causalité sous-jacente à l'insertion scolaire chez des élèves en fin de scolarité obligatoire. *Revue Suisse de Psychologie, 48,* 190–198.

Carugati, F., & Gilly, M. (1993). The multiple sides of the same tool: cognitive development as a matter of social contruction of meaning. In: F. Carugati & M. Gilly (eds.), Everyday life, social meanings and cognitive functioning. *European Journal of Psychology of Education (special issue), 8, 4,* 345–353.

Carugati, F., & Selleri, P. (1996). *Psicologia sociale dell'educazione.* Bologna: Il Mulino.

Claus, D.B. (1981). *Toward the Soul: An enquiry into the meaning of psyche before Plato.* London: Academic Press.

Clémence, A., Deschamps, J.-C., & Roux, P. (1986). La perception de l'entrée en apprentissage. *L'Orientation Scolaire et Professionnelle, 15,* 311–330.

Deaux, K., & Emswiller, T. (1974). Explanations of successful performance on sex-linked tasks: what is skill for the male is luck for the female. *Journal of Personality and Social Psychology, 29,* 80–85.

De Paolis, P., Doise, W. & Mugny, G. (1987). Social marking in cognitive operations. In W. Doise & S. Moscovici (eds.), *Current Issues in European Social Psychology (Vol. 2).* Cambridge, MA: Cambridge University Press.

Deschamps, J-C. (1983). Social attribution. In J. Jaspars, F. Fincham & M. Hewstone (Eds.), *Attribution theory, essays and experiments.* London: Academic Press.

Deschamps, J-C., & Clémence, A. (1990). L'explication quotidienne. Cousset/Fribourg (Switzerland): DelVal.

Doise, W. (1982). *L'explication en psychologie sociale.* Paris: Presses Universitaires de France.

Doise, W., & Mugny, G. (1981). *Le développement social de l'intelligence.* Paris: Inter-Editions.

Doise, W., Meyer, G., & Perret-Clermont, A.-N. (1976). Etude psychosociologique des représentations des élèves en fin de scolarité obligatoire. *Cahiers de la section des sciences de l'éducation, 2.* Genève: Université de Genève.

Doise, W., Mugny, G., & Perret-Clermont, A. N. (1975). Social interaction and the development of cognitive operations. *European Journal of Social Psychology, 53,* 367–383.

Dubois, N. (1988a). The norm of internality: social valorization of behavior and reinforcements in young people. *Journal of Social Psychology, 128,* 431–439.

Dubois, N (1988b). Formation d'adultes et acquisition de la norme d'internalité. *International Review of Applied Psychology, 37,* 213–225.

Dubois, N. (1994). *La norme d'internalité et le libéralisme.* Grenoble: Presses Universitaires de Grenoble.

Ehrenberg, A. (1992). *Le culte de la performance.* Paris: Calmann-Lévy.

Eichler, V. L. (1980). Locus of control and occupational structure. *Psychological Reports, 46,* 957–958.

Findley, M. J., & Cooper, H. M. (1983). Locus of control and academic achievement. A literature review. *Journal of Personality and Social Psychology, 44,* 419–427.

Flammer, A. (1990). *Erfahrung der eigenen Wirksamkeit.* Bern, Stuttgart: Hans Huber.

Flammer, A. (1992). Secondary control in an individual-centered and in a group-centered culture. In W. Meeus, M. de Goede, W. Kox & H. Hurrelmann (Eds.), *Adolescence, careers and cultures.* Berlin: Walter de Gruyter.

Flammer, A. (1994). Developmental analysis of control beliefs. In A. Bandura (Ed.), *Self efficacy in changing societies.* New York: Cambridge University Press.

Flammer, A., Grob, A., & Lüthi, R. (1989). Swiss adolescents' attribution of control. In J. P. Forgas & J. M. Innes (Eds.), *Recent advances in social psychology: An international perspective.* North Holland: Elsevier Science Publishers.

Golay Schilter, D. (1995). Regards sur l'organisation et les enjeux de l'enseignement à l'Ecole Technique de Sainte-Croix. *Document de recherche, No 4.* Neuchâtel: Université de Neuchâtel- Séminaire de psychologie.

Golay Schilter, D. (1997). Apprendre la fabrication assistée par ordinateur: Sens, enjeux et rapport aux outils. *Document de recherche, No 13.* Neuchâtel: Université de Neuchâtel- Séminaire de psychologie.

Golay Schilter, D., Perret, J.-F., & Perret-Clermont, A.-N. (in press). Socio-cognitive interactions in a computerised industrial task: Are they productive for learning? In K. Littleton & P. Light (eds).

Golay Schilter, D., Perret-Clermont, A.-N., Perret, J.-F., De Guglielmo, F., & Chavey, J.-P. (1997). Aux prises avec l'informatique industrielle: collaboration et démarches de travail chez des élèves techniciens. *Document de recherche, No 7.* Neuchâtel: Université de Neuchâtel- Séminaire de psychologie.

Gosling, P. (1992). Les attributions de la réussite et de l'échec par les enseignants; justification pédagogique ou justification d'évaluation? *International Review of Social Psychology, 5, 2,* 73–86.

Grob, A., Bodmer, N., & Flammer, A. (1993). *Living conditions and the development of adolescents in Europe: The case of Switzerland.* Research Reports. Berne: Department of psychology.

Heider, F. (1958). *The psychology of interpersonal relations.* New York: Wiley.

Hewstone, M., & Jaspars, J. (1982). Intergroup relations and attribution processes. In H. Tajfel (Ed.), *Social identity and intergroup relations.* Cambridge, MA: University Press.

Jones, E. E., & Davis, K. E. (1965). From acts to dispostions: the attribution process in person perception. In L. Berkowitz (Ed.), *Advances in experimental social psychology (Vol. 2).* New York: Academic Press.

Jones, E. E., Davis, K. E., & Gergen, K. J. (1961). Role playing variations and their informational value for person perception. *Journal of Abnormal and Social Psychology, 63,* 302–310.

Jones, E.E., & Harris, V.A. (1967). The attribution of attitudes. *Journal of Experimental Social Psychology, 3,* 1–24.

Kaiser, C. (1997). *Education des choix.* Genève: Centre de recherches psychopédagogiques du Département de l'instruction publique du canton de Genève.

Kaiser, C., Perret-Clermont, A.-N., Perret, J.-F., & Golay-Schilter, D. (1997). Apprendre un métier technique aujourd'hui: Représentations des apprenants. *Document de recherche, No 10.* Neuchâtel: Université de Neuchâtel- Séminaire de psychologie.

Kelley, H. H. (1967). Attribution theory in social psychology. In L. Levine (Ed.), *Nebraska symposium on motivation, 15.* Lincoln, NE: University of Nebraska Press.

Le Poultier, F. (1986). *Travail social, inadaptation sociale et processus cognitifs.* Paris: Presses Universitaires de France.

Liginbuhl, J. E. R, Crowe, D. H., & Kahan, J. P. (1990). Causal attribution for success and failure. *Journal of Personality and Social Psychology, 31,* 86–93.

Monteil, J.-M. (1989). *Eduquer et former. Perspectives psycho-sociales.* Grenoble: Presses Universitaires de Grenoble.

Nicolet, M. (1995). *Dynamiques relationnelles et processus cognitifs : Etude du marquage social chez des enfants de 5 à 9 ans.* Lausanne, Paris: Delachaux et Niestlé.

Papastamou, S. (1986). *La psychologisation.* Thèse pour le Doctorat d'Etat. Paris: Ecole des Hautes Etudes en Sciences Sociales.

Perret, J.-F. (1981) A quoi les difficultés d'apprentissage en mathématiques sont-elles attribuées? *Document de recherche, No 81.07.* Neuchâtel: Institut romand de recherche et de documentation pédagogique.

Perret, J.-F, Perret-Clermont, A.-N., & Golay Schilter, D. (1997). Interactions entre maître et élèves en cours de travaux pratiques. *Document de recherche, No 6*. Neuchâtel: Université de Neuchâtel- Séminaire de psychologie.

Perret-Clermont, A. N. (1979, 1996). *La construction de l'intelligence dans l'interaction sociale*. Berne: Peter Lang (English version: *Social interaction and cognitive development in children*. London & New-York: Academic Press, 1980).

Perret-Clermont, A. N., Brun, J., Saada, E. H., & Schubauer-Leoni, M. L. (1984). Learning : a social actualization and reconstruction. In H. Tajfel (Ed.), *The social dimension*. Cambridge: Cambridge University Press.

Perret-Clermont, A. N., Grossen, M., Iannaccone, A., & Liengme Bessire, M. J. (1994). Social comparison of expertise: interactional patterns and dynamics of instruction. In H. C. Foot et al. (Eds.), *Group and interactive learning*, 471–476. Southampton, Boston: Computational Mechanics Publications.

Perret-Clermont, A. N., Marro Clément, P., Grossen, M., & Trognon, A. (1997). *The peer as teacher or interlocutor: An experimental and interlocutory analysis*. Symposium on social interactions and cognitive development. European Conference of Developmental Psychology. Rennes, France.

Perret-Clermont, A.-N., & Nicolet, M. (Eds.). (1986). *Interagir et connaître*. Cousset/ Fribourg (Switzerland): Del Val.

Perret-Clermont, A.-N., & Schubauer-Leoni, M.-L. (1981). Conflict and cooperation as opportunities for learning. In P. Robinsons (Ed.), *Communication in development*, 203–233. London: Academic Press.

Perret-Clermont, A. N., & Schubauer-Leoni, M. L. (1989). Social factors in learning and instruction: Towards an integrative perspective. *International Journal of Educational Research, 13, 6*.

Perret-Clermont, A. N., Schubauer-Leoni, M. L., & Trognon, A. (1992). L'extorsion des réponses en situation asymétrique.*Verbum, 1-2*, 3–32.

Py, J., & Somat, A. (1991). Normativité, conformité et clairvoyance: leurs effets sur le jugement évaluatif dans un contexte scolaire. In J.-L. Beauvois, R.V. Joule & J.-M. Monteil (Eds.), *Perspectives cognitives et conduites sociales (Vol. 3)*, (pp.167–193). Cousset/Fribourg (Switzerland): Del Val.

Rosenthal, R., & Jacobson, L. (1968). *Pygmalion in the classroom: Teachers expectation and pupils' intellectual development*. New York: Holt, Rinehart & Winston.

Ross, L. (1977). The intuitive psychologist and his shortcoming. In L. Berkowitz (Ed.), *Advances in experimental social psychology (Vol. 10)*, 173–220. New York: Academic Press.

Rotter, J. B. (1966). Generalized expectancies for internal versus external control of reinforcement. *Psychological Monographs, 80, 1, no. 609*.

Steiner, I. D., & Field, W. L. (1960). Role assignment and interpersonal influence. *Journal of Abnormal and Social Psychology, 61*, 239–246.

Taylor, D. M., & Jaggi, V. (1974). Ethnocentrism and causal attribution in a South Indian context. *Journal of Cross-Cultural Psychology, 5*, 162–171.

Thibault, J. W., & Riecken, H. W. (1955). Some determinants and consequences of the perception of social causality. *Journal of Personality, 24*, 113–133.

Turner, J. C. (1982). Towards a cognitive redefinition of the social group. In H. Tajfel (Ed.), *Social Identity and Intergroup Relations*. Cambridge: Cambridge University Press.

Weiner, B. (1979). A theory of motivation for some classroom experiences. *Journal of Educational Psychology, 71*, 3–25.

Weiner, B. (1986). *An attributional theory of motivation and emotion*. New York: Springer.

# 26

# Social Influence and Control Beliefs in Identity Threatening Contexts[1]

*Juan Manuel Falomir*

*Gabriel Mugny*

*Alain Quiamzade*

*Fabrizio Butera*

## INTRODUCTION

Control beliefs are regarded as primary in determining people's decisions to act. They are important for at least two reasons (*cf.* Flammer, 1995). First, they are prerequisites for the planning, initiation and regulation of goal-oriented actions. If people believe they have power to produce results, i.e., beliefs about control over actions and outcomes, they will attempt to make things happen. Second, control beliefs are part of the self-concept, and they largely determine feelings of self-esteem, causing such emotional states as pride, shame, or depression. This chapter focuses on this second aspect of control beliefs and particularly on how losses and gains in beliefs about behavioral control are related to identity threat and this affects social influence processes.

### Lack Of Control As A Threat To Identity

In individualistic cultures autonomy and individual freedom are two of the most important values for the self (Beauvois, 1994; Dumont, 1987). Therefore, the perception of personal control is one of the most significant aspects of an individual's self-perception. People derive a major part of their self-esteem from the control they believe themselves to have through, for example, being autonomous in the presence of others. Control beliefs about self-attitudes and behaviors determine self-representations and cognitive and behavioral adjustment (*cf.* Langer & Rodin, 1976; Seligman, 1975). Indeed, both people's beliefs about lack of control and their attributions of their own behavior to external causes, i.e., beliefs in external control over own behavior, can be regarded as threats to identity.

---

[1]This research program was supported by the Fonds National de la Recherche Scientifique, Switzerland.

Individuals can therefore cope with this threat by initiating actions that restore their autonomy and freedom.

External causes of behavior can be various and individual reactions to these threats can also be different. According to the smoking behavior literature, perceptions of two external factors seem to play a major part in controlling smokers' behavior. The first of these is their attribution concerning smoking addiction (i.e., nicotine dependence). On the one hand, addiction is taken to be an obstacle for smokers who may want to give up smoking, since they accept a lack of control and this justifies not implementing any action (self-inefficacy beliefs). For instance, smokers characterised by high attribution of addiction and thus perceived lack of control over their own behavior have little confidence in their ability to change their behavior without professional help (Eiser & Gossop, 1979), and make less effort to give up smoking (e.g., Eiser, Sutton & Wober, 1977). On the other hand, smokers can react to the loss of control arising from addiction and can try to restore their feelings of control. Indeed, escaping from addiction is regarded, together with avoiding physical health consequences, as one of the most important motives for giving up smoking (Lesourne, 1984).

The second external determinant of beliefs concerning lack of behavioral control is social influence. Despite the fact that psychological adjustments to external factors which threaten the individual's autonomy and freedom can occur (e.g., Janoff-Bulman & Schwartzberg, 1991; Seligman, 1975), a reactive response can also be expected when this threat is associated with a source of influence. If people believe they are controlled by external sources of influence, they will react to these sources in such a way as to restore their freedom (Apter, 1983; Brehm & Brehm, 1981). One notable example is smokers' reactions to social pressures to smoke (from peers, tobacco companies) which threaten their feelings of autonomy and freedom. One way to cope with this threat is to deny it has any influence on their own behavior. For instance, young smokers appear to attribute their behavior to the intrinsic benefits of smoking itself rather than to external pressure (Eiser, Morgan & Gammage, 1987), and smokers in general seem not to recognize the influence of tobacco advertising (cf. Becoña, 1995).

Another way smokers could cope with this threat would be to give up smoking. This idea is supported by a body of research on social influence in which smokers are confronted with an argued case against tobacco use (cf. Pérez & Mugny, 1992; Falomir, Mugny & Pérez, 1999). The anti-smoking text describes smokers as individuals dependent on an artificial need to smoke, manipulated by advertising, and serving the interest of the tobacco industry. Results reveal that under appropriate experimental conditions, a text arguing for external causes of smoking behavior can lead smokers to strengthen their intention to give up smoking.

Belief in external control of smoking behavior may thus be considered as a form of threat which can lead smokers to stop smoking. Indeed, one assumption of influence campaigns might be that if smokers became aware of the negative outcomes of smoking (e.g., that multinational companies control their own behavior) this would cause them to give up smoking. In effect, when an anti-tobacco message stresses the external causes of smoking behavior one way to cope with this threat to identity is to accept the anti-smoking point of view, which means the smokers acknowledging the criticism of their own identity. If this provides the necessary encouragement to adopt a more autonomous identity, stopping smoking would in this case be an effective *individual mobility* strategy (*cf.* Tajfel & Turner, 1986) for managing the threat to identity.

However, social psychology has shown that certain kinds of behavior often do not relate to beliefs or attitudes (*cf.* Terry & Hogg, 1999). From the point of view of social influence, this observation brings us back to the fact that an attempt to influence beliefs does not necessarily involve a change in the corresponding behaviors. The possibility to be considered here is that the social context in which the influence attempts occur affects the relationship between attitudes or beliefs and behaviors (Falomir et al., 1999), i.e., aspects of the social context in which anti-smoking campaigns take place can cause smokers to act against threatening beliefs in ways that have repercussions for behavior. More concretely, we will examine what kinds of influence settings allow beliefs about external behavioral control to determine behavioral intentions.

## Identity Threat And Social Influence

When do factors that question the identity of smokers fail to induce them to change? The existence of a threat to identity (e.g., the belief that thoughts and actions are subject to external control), effectively adds two elements to the process of influence. First, targets will have heightened defensive motivation, processing information in such a way as to allow protection of their threatened identity. Nevertheless, this defensive motivation can result either in the inhibition of change in behavior (e.g., a strategy of collective action) or in the facilitation of change (e.g., a strategy of individual mobility). Second, the targets may relate the content of the threat to salient features of the social relationship (Falomir et al., 1999; Falomir, Mugny, Sanchez-Mazas, Pérez & Carrasco, in press). Influence at the level of behavior will consequently be obstructed by the fact that the smoker responds in terms of a *conflict of identity*, a response to the enhanced salience of the relational context characterized by smokers' restoration of their identity as smokers.

This socio-relational approach to resolving the conflict determines the disposition to defend identity, and at the same time preserves initial attitudes and behaviors. Because giving up smoking can be represented as yielding in the social relationship and as being forced to acknowledge the identity threat, the general hypothesis is that the resistance induced by such a conflict of identity does not allow the operation of any influence on intention to give up smoking. Given that this conflict involves interpreting the identity threat in relation to salient elements of the social influence relationship, such a resolution will depend on the presence and the salience of these elements of the social relationship. The nature of this conflict will then be determined by an influence relationship in which the targets perceive no control over their own thoughts and behavior which are instead perceived to be caused by the source. In this socio-relational elaboration of the identity threat (i.e., external or source-related elaboration of the conflict), the influence source will be seen as the real cause of the threat to identity. When the influence relationship itself is made salient, the processing of information will be biased by the targets' desire to defend their own beliefs and values (*cf.* Chaiken, Giner-Sorolla & Chen, 1996; McGuire & Papageorgis, 1961). Rather than accepting the source's external imposition, the targets will then be more reluctant to process the content of the source's message in an objective manner and may fail to draw any implications for their own behavior.

One aspect of the social relationship which possibly activates an identity conflict is the salience of the link that targets can make between the threat to their identity and the influence attempt itself. The salience of this link can enhance a belief in external control by an influence source, thus leading targets to elaborate an identity conflict. This should be particularly likely to occur when the influence source has high social status (e.g., expert or competent sources, or those with a certain power of decision over the individuals concerned). It has been shown that when confronted by a high status source (e.g., experts, majorities)—rather than a low status source (e.g., non-experts, minorities)—individuals are more prone to focus predominantly on social comparison (Moscovici, 1980; Guillon & Personnaz, 1983) and perceived persuasive constraint (Falomir et al., 1999; in press). Therefore, it could be argued that high status sources are more likely to activate a belief in external control over people's thoughts and behaviors, inducing an external elaboration of the identity threat.

This point can be illustrated by a study in which smokers had to describe the first five ideas which came into their minds with respect to an anti-tobacco text they had just read (Falomir, Mugny & Pérez, 1996). For each idea, they were asked to assess, in percentage terms, the extent to which (a) they had thought of this before (an idea pre-dating the text), (b) it had been directly suggested by the text (idea derived from the text), and (c) the idea had come to them at that moment (self-generated idea). The three percentages had to total to one hundred.

The results revealed an interaction between the status of the source and the origin of the ideas. First of all, degree of novelty (extent to which ideas were seen as self-generated) did not differ as a function of the status of the source and was the smallest category of responses. Depending on the source, however, the prominence of the message in the conflict varied significantly. Ideas were regarded as mainly originating from the text when stemming from a high status source as opposed to a low status source. In contrast, ideas were perceived by the smokers as having an origin predating their reading of the text when the source of the text had a low status. Thus, smokers' responses to the conflict appeared to be more closely associated with the influence relationship when the source had high status while this response was dissociated from the influence relation when the source had low status.

These results suggest that exposure to a low status source spontaneously activates an internal elaboration of the conflict which dissociates message content from the influence relationship. Conversely, the high status source spontaneously activates an external—i.e., socio-relational—elaboration of the conflict associating message content with the influence relationship itself (i.e., an identity conflict).

## Internal Laboration Of The Conflict And The Illusion Of Control

The above discussion might be taken to imply that high status sources could never induce any kind of influence because of the external elaboration of the conflict they activate. A way of avoiding the activation of such a conflict of identity is to allow targets to respond to the identity threat without relating this threat to features of the influence context. This, for example, would be the case if, when confronted with a high status influence source, a target is able to assert his autonomy and independence. Such a self-affirmation process (Steele, 1988) would reduce the persuasive constraint otherwise associated with an asymmetric influence relationship.

Research on anti-tobacco influence has supported this idea. In one study (Pérez, Falomir & Mugny, 1995), smokers were exposed to the same anti-smoking message as used in the Falomir et al. Study (1996), attributed either to a source with a high status (a group of university professors) or to one of low status (a minority group). During the experimental session, they either did or did not have the opportunity to smoke. The main measure concerned the change in personal intention to give up smoking. The results revealed an interaction between the two variables, confirming that when faced with a high status source the intention of smokers to give up smoking increased if they had the opportunity to smoke. This effect was specific to a high status source; when the source had low status the act of smoking had a negative effect on change. As shown in a replication (Falomir et al., 1996), among the subjects who had the option of smoking, those who took advantage of this option changed, as predicted, more when the source had high status than when the source had low status; the subsequent intentions of those who chose not to smoke under these conditions did not differ as a function of source status.

The results support the idea that individuals placed in a situation involving an identity threat need some positive way of adjusting to the influence relationship if they are to be able to work out their own personal intention to act. Indeed, smoking represents a positive expression of the smokers' independence in the face of a high status source. And it was this "illusion of control" over their own behavior, manipulated in the experiment by allowing the smokers to smoke and so redress the balance of this otherwise unequal influence relationship, which resulted in the increased influence on their intention to quit smoking.

These results reflect a method of working out the conflict which is employed when a source has high status. The expert source may, in contrast to a non-expert source, produce an increase in agreement with its claims (as in Falomir et al., 1996) but not necessarily an increase in the intention to give up smoking. Indeed, when confronted with high status sources, self-affirmation contributed to a conflict resolved by an identity change (i.e., individual mobility). When the influence context excludes a positive response to this asymmetric relation of influence, which in the present case is so when subjects do not smoke, the persuasive constraint associated with the source is found to lead to the defensive attitude characteristic of identity conflict (i.e., excluding any change in the direction of the source).

Another way to cope with the identity conflict produced by confrontation with high status sources is through an internal elaboration (i.e., non source-related elaboration). It would then be predicted that the influence of high status sources will decrease when conflict is worked out in an external or source-related elaboration. Hence, if smokers can resolve the threat to their identity without being led to relate this threat to the influence attempt itself, influence should increase. Such a way of elaborating the divergence, a characteristic effect of low status sources (see, Pérez & Mugny, 1990a; Pérez, Papastamou & Mugny, 1995), apparently provides the needed illusion of control over the influence relationship, and might also facilitate the influence of high status sources. In this latter case, the identity conflict should not be activated. Although it has been confirmed experimentally that external elaboration of the conflict is a spontaneous influence process with high status sources (Falomir et al., 1996), no study has directly manipulated the internal (target-related) versus external (source-related) options for elaborating conflict. A recent study which explores this possibility will now be presented.

## AN EXPERIMENTAL ILLUSTRATION

In this experiment, subjects (all "regular" smokers) began by indicating the extent to which they had internalised an identity threat, measured as the degree to which they attributed control of smoking behavior to an external, social source. They were then exposed to a strongly argued case against tobacco use attributed to a high status source (a group of university professors). This text emphasized external causes of smoking behavior, describing the smoker as dependent on an artificially created need to smoke, manipulated by advertising, and serving the interest of the tobacco industry (cf. Pérez & Mugny, 1990b). Subjects were asked next to choose (from a list of arguments extracted from the text they just had read) that disturbed them the most, and to indicate, in one condition, which arguments had already occurred to them before reading the text (self-related elaboration), or, in the other condition, which came to their mind because of the anti-tobacco text (source-related elaboration). The main influence measure was the intention to give up smoking.

The principal hypothesis was that smokers with strong beliefs in external control of smoking behavior, i.e., smokers with a high internalized threat to their autonomy and freedom, can be influenced by an anti-tobacco appeal only when elaboration is internal (i.e., smoker-related); it will show a decrease of influence when elaboration is external (i.e., source-related).

## Method

A sample of 127 individuals completed the questionnaire, of whom 110 (65 women and 45 men, 18- to 64-years-old, with a mean age of 29.59, $SD$ = 11.85), satisfied minimal criteria for being classified as smokers: they had smoked for at least a year (mean 11 years and a half, $SD$ = 10.31), smoked at least five cigarettes a day (average consumption was 18.46 cigarettes a day, $SD$ = 11.75), and had not expressed in the pretest an extreme intention to give up smoking. Subjects were allowed to smoke.

*Pretest.* After having answered questions about various biographical details and their smoking habits, subjects were asked to indicate whether they intended to give up smoking soon (1 = no, 7 = yes; the mean response on this measure in the pre-test was 3.39). Among other scales measuring social representations of tobacco, the questionnaire included a scale assessing attribution of responsibility for smoking behavior: "Are. . . (persons, groups, or institutions) responsible for encouraging people to smoke?" (1 = not at all, 7 = totally; *cf.* Echebarria, Fernandez & Gonzalez, 1994). An index of beliefs about *external control of smoking behavior* was obtained by computing the answers to four items concerning multinational enterprise interest, government policy, advertising and socio-economical factors (Cronbach's alpha: .70). [2]

*Status of the Source and Anti-Smoking Message.* The anti-smoking text was presented next (*cf.* Pérez & Mugny, 1990b), and attributed in all conditions to a high status source (a group of university professors in political economy). The message basically stressed that smokers are manipulated by publicity and by the economic interests of tobacco companies. The following extracts are illustrative: "Smokers do not smoke because of a natural need for tobacco. They smoke because a false need has been created in them;" "The smoker purely and simply enters into the game of the tobacco industry and advertising, and ends up being a veritable accomplice;" "The smoker's freedom is an illusion. It is obvious that smoking is nothing but entry into the mesh of a vicious circle of production-marketing-consumption."

---

[2] A factor analysis on all questions was performed. In the context of the present chapter, we are only considering the factor which includes these four causal explanations for smoking.

*Self-related Versus Source-Related Elaboration of Anti-To-bacco Arguments.* After reading the message, subjects were presented with eleven arguments extracted from the anti-tobacco message and were asked to indicate the five arguments that disturbed them the most as smokers. From these five disturbing arguments, they had then to identify either (depending on the experimental condition) the four they thought they already had most in mind before reading the text (arguments preceding the text) or the four which the anti-tobacco text had put most into their minds (arguments derived directly from the text). It was anticipated that subjects in the first condition would be led to elaborate the anti-tobacco arguments internally (self-related elaboration) when the latter would be induced to elaborate the anti-tobacco arguments externally (source-related elaboration).

*Post-test.* The post-test included the same measure of intention to give up smoking as in the pre-test. The analysis was carried out on the post-test scores after they were adjusted to make allowance for the corresponding pre-test scores. A question measuring degree of agreement with the anti-tobacco text was also introduced. Finally, the post-test included questions to check the experimental manipulation together with further questions that will not be analysed here.

## Results

*Self-Related Versus Source-Related Elaboration.* During the post-test subjects were asked to indicate the degree to which reading the text made them think about its arguments (1 = not at all, 7 = totally). Analysis of variance revealed that subjects were more likely to concede that reading the text made them think about these arguments when elaboration was source-related ($M = 4.22$) than when elaboration was self-related ($M = 3.45$; $F(1,108) = 4.94$, p < .03). Subjects were also more likely to agree that the reasons that caused them to smoke were represented in the text if the elaboration was source-related ($M = 2.70$) than if the elaboration was self-related ($M = 2.23$, $F(1,108) = 3.51$, $p < .07$). The manipulation of this variable seems, therefore, to have functioned as expected.

*Belief in External Control of Smoking Behavior.* Analyses of correlations showed that the more strongly subjects believed (at the pretest stage) in external control of smoking behavior the more they believed that the people most at risk to become smokers are smokers' own children ($r(110) = .22$, $p < .02$), people in contact with smokers ($r(110) = .20$, $p < .04$), and insecure people ($r(110) = .29$, $p < .002$). Belief in external control was also related to belief that school ($r(110) = .25$, $p < .007$), social customs ($r(110) = .17$, $p < .07$), and social models (music stars, movie stars, etc.; $r(110) = .31$, $p < .001$), induce people to smoke. Thus, beliefs about external control of smoking behavior were related to beliefs that smokers have no control over their behavior and are influenced by social factors.

*Influence Measures.* Hierarchical regression analyses were performed. The first examined the effect of believing that smoking behavior is externally controlled (7 = totally) on intention to give up smoking (7 = yes; $M$ = 3.12, $SD$ = 1.29), a second examined the effect of the experimental variable (1 = self-related elaboration and 2 = source-related elaboration), and the final analysis examined the interactive effect between these two variables (multiplicative term). The full factorial model accounts significantly for influence ($R^2$ = .081, $F(3,106)$ = 3.12, $p < .03$). A belief in external control does not contribute to explanation of intention ($F(1,108)$ = 0.00, n.s.), neither does the kind of elaboration increase the variance explained ($DR^2$ =.001, $DF(2,107)$ = 0.16, n.s.), but the interaction term accounts for a significant increment in variance explained ($DR^2$ = .079, $DF(3,106)$ = 9.18, $p < .004$; see figure 26.1). As predicted, belief in external control is positively related to the intention to give up smoking when arguments elaboration is self-related ($b$ = .28, $t$ = 2.11, $p < .04$), and negatively when arguments elaboration is source-related ($b$ = -.28, $t$ = 2.17, $p < .04$).

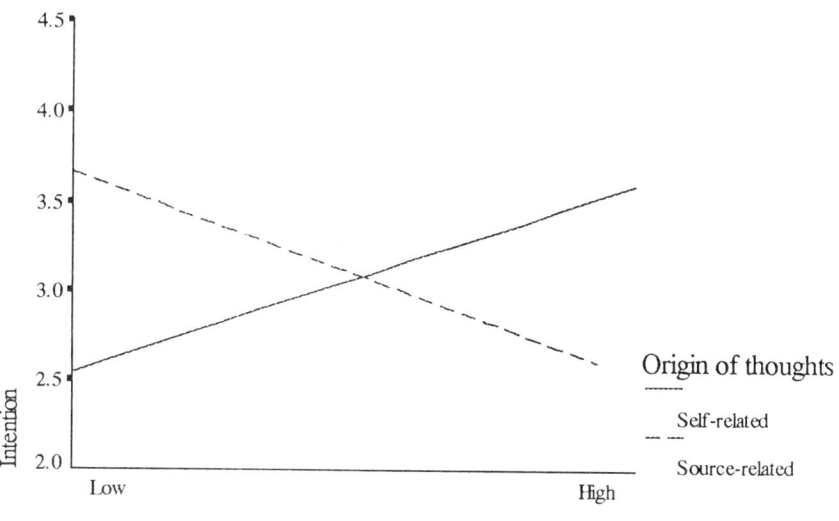

FIG. 26.1. *Intention to give up smoking (predicted values, a greater value corresponds to a positive influence of the source, e.g., 7 = yes)*

*Complementary Analyses.* During both pretest and posttest, subject indicated to what extent they would describe smokers as addicted to tobacco (1 = not at all, 7 = totally). An index of change (difference between posttest and pretest judgments) was computed. Correlational analyses between this index and prior beliefs about external control of smoking behavior shows that when the origin of thoughts was self-generated, high levels of beliefs in external behavioral control were related to a strengthening of the belief that smokers are tobacco addicted ($r(52) = .29$, $p < .03$). Thus, an internal elaboration of the threat allows consideration of more alternative sources of threat and smokers can confront the threat in an objective manner. Conversely, when the origin of the thoughts was perceived to be the source, higher levels of belief in external behavioral control were related to a decrease in belief that smokers are addicted to tobacco ($r(57) = -.38$, $p < .003$, $z = 3.59$, $p < .01$). Therefore, an external elaboration of the threat to identity prevents smokers with higher external beliefs of control from recognizing external sources of control over their own behavior.

Thus, threatening smokers' identity (i.e., inducing a high perception of external control of smoking behavior) reduces their intention to give up smoking when this threat is interpreted in relation to an influence attempt, but increases it when it is elaborated without external reference to the source, that is, when it is elaborated in a self-related or internal way. This effect supports the idea that smokers who have internalised the identity threat are reluctant to accept it in an asymmetrical influence relationship, and elaborate an identity conflict (*cf.* Falomir et al., 1999). Because of the persuasive constraint of the source, smokers will deal with this situation as a socio-relational conflict, and will be motivated to defend their identity as smokers, i.e., not to quit tobacco consumption. Conversely, an internal elaboration provides the best conditions for meeting a threat to identity and translating it into behavior. Indeed, because the source is not psychologically salient, intention to give up smoking carries with it no implication of yielding to the source. Content-related conflict is dissociated from relational concerns and smokers can feel free to decide to give up.

The opposite pattern of results emerged for smokers who were less inclined to believe in the external control of smoking behavior—i.e., smokers with a low internalised identity threat. Since these smokers are reluctant to accept such an anti-tobacco point of view, they have not, themselves, generated any reasons to change, and an internal source of conflict is not sufficient to influence their intentions to give up or to continue smoking. Here, influence needs an external source of conflict to disrupt smokers, and only a source-related elaboration forces smokers to consider external causes of smoking behavior. Prior belief in low external control seems to allow smokers to feel free in the influence setting, and external conflict elaboration can result in a greater influence on intention to quit smoking. Confirming this idea, smokers who believed least in external control of behavior were also less likely to view the text as imposing a particular point of view than smokers who believed most strongly in external control. Such a result suggests that a prior rejection of external control prevents the activation of an identity conflict (Snyder & Wicklund, 1976).

## CONCLUSION

It has been proposed that the social context (namely the influence relationship) within which campaigns of persuasion operate, includes both factors facilitating the translation of attitudes and beliefs into behavior and factors counteracting this translation. To illustrate this idea, it has been argued that the beliefs about external causes of tobacco consumption introduce a threat to the identity of smokers which can be translated into intention to give up smoking. Despite the fact that this threatening belief is intended to encourage smokers to seek out a more valued behavior and identity (i.e., behavior that is not externally controlled), an external elaboration of the threat, i.e., a source-related elaboration of threatening factors, can motivate them to defend their identity as smokers, and to persevere with their smoking.

The kinds of high status sources that are most frequently associated with anti-smoking campaigns (e.g., experts) can be regarded as encouraging an interpretation of the threat as an identity conflict. In effect, the elaboration of such an identity conflict prevents internalization of the anti-smoking perspective at the level of action; i.e., it prevents smokers from deciding for themselves to stop smoking. When identity threat is internalized, smokers' loss of control in the influence process motivates them to defend their identity as smokers.

A conflict of identity will be less likely to arise here if smokers can preserve their autonomy and independence within the influence relationship or if the influence source does not impose any persuasive constraint. This will be the case when the source has a low status (Falomir et al., 1999) or, as the experimental illustration has confirmed, when confronted with a high status source if the smokers can elaborate threatening factors in an internal way, i.e., by feeling themselves to be the only source of the process of change. In effect, the emergence of a conflict of identity is less likely here to the extent that the identity of smokers is guaranteed in the influence relationship with a high status source, either because such a relationship is not salient or the smoker is focused on an internally originated process of influence.

Persuasive campaigns seem, so far, to have involved trying to convince people (or to impose on them), what they have to do and introducing legislation which will lead them to do it. However, the validity of a point of view is not inherent solely in the facts on which it draws, and the relations individuals maintain with other social actors (e.g., sources of influence) affects the validity they accord to opposing points of view and the way they treat them. In effect, even though the credibility or power of influence sources can reinforce the validity of their claims, this is not always the case, and the way in which they try to impose it is one of the most important determinants of the observed influence.

The results reported in this chapter are more in accord with the notion that high status sources may in practice need to negotiate the conflict they create (e.g., Moscovici, 1985). The contemporary cultural values of autonomy and freedom should encourage such a consideration among those involved in the practices of persuasion or influence. Moreover, such negotiation would be particularly recommended when the social context is of a kind which involves a threat to the identity of targets. Targets who have internalized the identity threat would be motivated not to reconsider it within the influence relationship, and substantially diminished influence could then result. Persuasive campaigns which give the targets control over the process of influence and decision would seem more efficacious. Under these conditions, people do not need pressure to accept the new information supplied by the influence source, but a comfortable relationship that is not threatening to identity. In this case, persuasive campaigns using high status sources can improve their impact by allowing the targets to feel autonomous (Falomir et al., 1996) or, as has been demonstrated here, by increasing the target's illusion of control over the influence process itself.

## REFERENCES

Apter, M. J. (1983). Negativism and the sense of identity. In G. M. Breakwell (Ed.), *Threatened identities*. New York: Wiley.

Beauvois, J. L. (1994). *Traité de la servitude liberale : une analyse de la soumission*. Paris: Dunod.

Becoña, E. (1995). *Evaluación de la eficacia de las acciones emprendidas por la Consellería de Sanidade e Servicios Sociales en el Día Mundial sin Tabaco (31 de Mayo) del año 1995*. Consellería de Sanidade e Servicios Sociales (Dirección Xeral de Organización Sanitaria) and Universidade de Santiago de Compostela.

Brehm, S. S. & Brehm, J. W. (1981). *Psychological reactance: a theory of freedom and control*. San Diego: Academic Press.

Chaiken, S., Giner-Sorolla, R. & Chen, S. (1996). Beyond accuracy: defense and impression motives in heuristic and systematic information processing. In P. M. Gollwitzer & J. A. Bargh (Eds.), *The psychology of action: linking motivation and cognition to behavior*. New York: Guilford Press.

Dumont, L. (1987). *Ensayos sobre el individualismo: una perspectiva antropológica sobre la ideología moderna*. Madrid: Alianza.

Echebarría, A., Fernandez, E. & Gonzalez, J. L. (1994). Social representations and intergroup conflicts: who's smoking here? *European Journal of Social Psychology, 24,* 339–355.

Eiser, J. R. & Gossop, M. R. (1979). 'Hooked' or 'sick:' addicts' perceptions of their addiction, *Addictive Behaviors, 4,* 185–191.

Eiser, J. R., Morgan, M. & Gammage, P. (1987). Belief correlated of perceived addiction in young smokers. *European Journal of Psychology of Education, 2 (4),* 375–385.

Eiser, J. R., Sutton, S. R. & Wober, M. (1977). Smokers, non-smokers and the attribution of addiction. British *Journal of Social and Clinical Psychology,* 16, 4, 329–336.

Falomir, J. M., Mugny, G. & Pérez, J. A. (1996). Social Influence and threat to identity: Does the fight against tobacco use require a ban on smoking? *International Review of Social Psychology, 2,* 95–108.

Falomir, J. M., Mugny, G. & Pérez, J. A. (1999). Social influence and identity conflict. In D. Terry & M. Hogg (Eds.), *Attitudes, behavior, and social context : The role of norms and group membership*. London: Lawrence Erlbaum Associates.

Falomir, J. M., Mugny, G., Sanchez-Mazas, M., Pérez, J. A. & Carrasco, F. (in press). Influence et conflit d'identité: de la conformité à l'intériorisation. In J.L. Beauvois, R. V. Joule & J. M. Monteil (Eds.), *Perspectives cognitives et conduites sociales* (vol. VI). Neuchâtel: Delachaux & Niestlé.

Flammer, A. (1995). Developmental analysis of control beliefs. In A. Bandura (Ed.), *Self-efficacy in changing societies*. New York: Cambridge University Press.

Guillon, M. & Personnaz, B. (1983). Analyse de la dynamique des représentations au cours d'une interaction d'influence avec une minorité et une majorité. *Cahiers de Psychologie Cognitive*, 3, 65–87.

Janoff-Bulman, R. & Schwartzberg, S. (1991). Toward a general model of personal change. In C. R. Snyder & D. R. Forsyth (Eds.), *Handbook of Social and Clinical Psychology: The Health Perspective*. New York: Pergamon Press.

Langer, E. J. & Rodin, J. (1976). The effects of choices and enhanced personal responsibility for the aged. *Journal of Personality and Social Psychology*, 34, 191–198.

Lesourne, O. (1984). *Le grand fumeur et sa passion*. Paris: PUF.

McGuire, W. J. & Papageorgis, D. (1961). The relative efficacy of various types of prior belief-defense in producing immunity against persuasion. *Journal of Abnormal and Social Psychology*, 62, 327–337.

Moscovici, S. (1980). Toward a theory of conversion behavior. In L. Berkowitz (Ed.), *Advances in experimental social psychology* (vol. 13). New York: Academic Press.

Moscovici, S. (1985). Innovation and minority influence. In S. Moscovici, G. Mugny & E.Van Avermaet (Eds.), *Perspectives on minority influence*. Cambridge, MA: Cambridge University Press.

Pérez, J. A., Falomir, J. M. & Mugny, G. (1995). Internalisation of conflict and attitude change. *European Journal of Social Psychology*, 25, 117–124.

Perez, J. A. & Mugny, G. (1990a). Minority influence, manifest discrimination and latent influence. In D. Abrams & M. A. Hogg (Eds.), *Social identity theory: constructive and critical advances*. London: Harverster Wheatsheaf.

Pérez, J. A. & Mugny, G. (1990b). Changement d'attitude, crédibilité et influence minoritaire: interdépendance et indépendance de la comparaison sociale. *Revue Suisse de Psychologie*, 49, 3, 150–158.

Pérez, J. A. & Mugny, G. (1992). Social impact of experts and minorities, and smoking cessation. In M. von Cranach, W. Doise & G. Mugny, (Eds.), *Social representations and the social bases of knowledge*. Lewinston, NY: Hogrefe & Huber.

Pérez, J. A., Papastamou, S. & Mugny, G. (1995). 'Zeitgeist' and minority influence-where is the causality: A comment on Clark (1990). *European Journal of Social Psychology*, 25, 703–710.

Seligman, M. E. P. (1975). *Helpiness*. San Francisco: Freeman, 1975.

Snyder, M. & Wicklund, R. A. (1976). Prior exercise of freedom and reactance. *Journal of Experimental Social Psychology*, 12, 120–130.

Steele, C. M. (1988). The psychology of self-affirmation: sustaining the integrity of the self. In M. P. Zanna (Ed.), *Advances in experimental social psychology* (vol. 21). San Diego: Academic Press.

Tajfel, H. & Turner, J. C. (1986). The social identity theory of intergroup behavior. In S. Worchel & W. G. Austin (Eds.), *Psychology of intergroup relations*. Chicago: Nelson-Hall.

Terry, D. & Hogg, M. (1999); (Eds.). *Attitudes, behavior, and social context: The role of norms and group membership*. London: Lawrence Erlbaum Associates.

# 27

# Adolescents as Agents in the Promotion of their Positive Development: The Role of Youth Actions in Effective Programs[1]

*Richard M. Lerner*
*Catherine E. Barton*

## INTRODUCTION

Adolescence has been described as a transition period, one involving multiple dimensions of change in individuals and between individuals and their contexts (Lerner, 1987, 1995). These changing relations involve the actions of the adolescent on the context and, of course, the actions of the context on the adolescent. In other words, adolescents' actions are influences on, as well as are influenced by, the context of human development. In so affecting their context and thus shaping a source of behavioral change, adolescents are producers of their own development (Brandtstädter, 1998; Flammer, 1995; Gottlieb, Wahlsten, & Lickliter, 1998; Lerner, 1982; Lerner & Busch-Rossnagel, 1981). They are agents in their development; they exert control over the course of their lives. This relational influence of adolescents on their development constitutes the basic process of development in this period of life, and indeed, across life.

This relational and agentic process involves *circular functions* in ontogeny (Schneirla, 1957). The individual's embeddedness in his or her context involves influencing the way the context influences (feeds back to) him or her. Through this circular process, then, an individual's control over his or her development occurs via a self-stimulative function wherein the young person's actions constitutes a "third source" of development (Gottlieb et al., 1998; Lerner, 1976, 1986; Schneirla, 1957), one distinct from influences associated with either "nature," or "nurture" alone. The individual is thus (always at least partially), "in control" of the source of his or her development; through the influences he or she has on the context, the feedback that occurs through this influence, and the resulting deve-

---

[1]The preparation of this chapter was supported in part by a grant from the W. T. Grant Foundation. The authors thank Mary E. Walsh and Anne Norris for their comments about the manuscript.

lopment that arise, the individual shapes the setting that shapes him or her (Lerner & Lerner, 1989).

This process underlies both positive and negative outcomes during adolescence (Lerner, 1984, 1993a, 1993b, 1995). Theory and contemporary research suggest that both outcomes are possible (Lerner, 1995; Lerner & Galambos, 1997). As such, from the standpoint of applying developmental science to promote positive youth development, systematic interventions should be devised to direct the agency (control) of adolescents toward circular functions promoting healthy outcomes (*cf.* Lerner, 1995; Lerner, et al., 1994). In other words, such interventions, which may be understood as youth development programs, must capitalize on the individual control "function" of the developmental process to foster person–context relations that are linked to desired ontogenetic change. For instance, programs that enhance the capacity of adolescents to shape and/or otherwise meet the behavioral demands of significant others (e.g., parents, peers, teachers) of their context—that is, to create a "goodness of fit" between person and context (Lerner & Lerner, 1983)—are associated with good adjustment in this period of life (Lerner & Lerner, 1987).

Accordingly, youth development programs that inculcate or enhance such control (agency) among adolescents should, from this theoretical perspective, and do, from an empirical perspective (Dryfoos, 1990; Hamburg, 1992; Lerner, 1995; Little, 1993), increase the likelihood of positive youth development. At this juncture in the history of the world the need for such increments in vital. While it is certainly the case that the adolescent transition *can* be positive, within both Western and developing nations, contemporary challenges to the health, positive development, and—most basically—the survival of youth, occur in regard to problems of poor nutrition, drug and alcohol abuse, unsafe sex, violence, school failure, underachievement, school dropout, crime, teenage pregnancy and parenting, lack of job preparedness, and challenges to health (e.g., lack of immunizations, inadequate screening for disabilities, insufficient prenatal care, and lack of sufficient infant and childhood medical services). The sequelae of persistent and pervasive poverty; and feelings of despair and hopelessness pervade the lives of youth, whose parents have lived in poverty and see themselves as having little opportunity to do better, that is, to have a life marked by societal respect, achievement, and opportunity (Carnegie Corporation of New York, 1995; Center for the Study of Social Policy, 1995; Children's Defense Fund, 1996; di Mauro, 1995; Dryfoos, 1990; Grob, Flammer, Kaiser, & Lüthi, 1989; Hamburg, 1992; Huston, 1991; Huston, McHoyd, & Coll, 1994; Johnston, O'Malley, & Bachman, 1996; Lerner, 1993a, 1993b, 1995; Little, 1993; McKinney, Abrams, Terry, & Lerner, 1994; Schorr, 1988; Smith, 1994; United States Department of Health and Human Services, 1996; Wilson, 1987; World Health Organization, 1986, 1993).

Moreover, in today's world 90% of the individuals who are born will live beyond infancy and grow into adulthood (International Youth Foundation [IYF], 1995). Yet, over 90% of all human service programs and resources are directed toward the first five years of life or, alternatively, to early adulthood (IYF, 1995). Despite a disproportional omission of resources directed towards them, children and adolescents between age 5- and 20-years-old face numerous developmental and ecological challenges, both generic to this period of life and specific to the particular historical, geopolitical, and socioecological niche within which they are developing (Feldman & Elliott, 1990; Grob et al., 1989; Flammer, 1995; Hamburg, 1992; Lerner, 1995; Lerner, Ostrom, & Freel, 1997; Magnusson, 1988, 1995; Silberson & Todt, 1994; Schulenberg, Maggs, & Hurrelman, 1997; Stattin & Magnusson, 1990).

With limited financial support and fewer effective, appropriately scaled and sustained programs for them, these young people have an already problematic period of life exacerbated by a lack of adequate attention by the world's youth-serving professionals. In order to ensure and maximize the probability of healthy and positive development among adolescents, the attention of policy makers and program professionals should be focused on youth development; more specifically, their attention should be linked to contemporary scientific understanding of the individual and contextual changes involved in promoting positive youth development (Pittman, 1996; Pittman & Irby, 1996).

We believe that the theoretical approach to developmental science that we have outlined above captures the complexities of the systems of influence on development and allows knowledge to be forwarded about how to effectively promote the positive development of adolescents through building programs that involve circular functions. That is, this approach—developmental contextualism (Lerner, 1991; 1996; 1998)—by stressing the dynamic relationships between the adolescent and the changing context suggests that research, and the policies and programs derived from it, should take an integrative, individual agency-promoting, person-context perspective in order to promote positive development.

Indeed, we believe that principles of positive programs that have been identified by several scholars (e.g., Dryfoos, 1990; Hamburg, 1992; Lerner, 1995; Little, 1993; Schorr, 1988) are consistent with the ideas found in developmental contextualism. As such, these principles of effective youth programming suggest specific public policy initiatives that may be pursued to ensure that actions effective to promote positive development are sustained (Lerner, 1995). Accordingly, in this chapter we will: (a) summarize key features of developmental contextualism, and (b) describe features of effective youth programs and the role of youth action and control processes.

## KEY FEATURES OF DEVELOPMENTAL CONTEXTUALISM

Developmental contextualism (Lerner, 1986; 1991; 1995; 1998) is a perspective about human development that takes an integrative approach to the multiple levels of organization presumed to comprise the nature of human life; that is, "fused" (Tobach & Greenberg, 1984), and changing relations among biological, psychological, and social contextual levels comprise the process of developmental change. Rather than approach variables from these levels of analysis in either a reductionistic or in a parallel-processing way, the developmental contextual view rests on the idea that variables from these levels of analysis are dynamically interactive—they are reciprocally influential over the course of human ontogeny.

From this perspective, humans are both products and producers of their own development (Lerner, 1982; Lerner & Busch-Rossnagel, 1981), and the development of action (Brandtstädter, 1998) and of individual efficacy, control, and control beliefs (Flammer, 1995; Flammer & Grob, 1994; Flammer & Rheindorf, 1991; Flammer & Scheuber-Sahli, 1995; Grob, Flammer & Wearing, 1995; Grob et al., 1989; Held & Hein, 1963; Wicki, Reber, Flammer, & Grob, 1994) become critical foci of developmental analysis. In other words, the development of action and of individual efficacy, control, and control beliefs involve circular functions between the adolescent and his or her context, and constitute the key, relational process linking the developing person to the other levels of his or her context.

## Circular Functions and Bidirectional Socialization

To illustrate, reciprocal adolescent–parent relations involve youth stimulating differential reactions in their parents, reactions based on the individual characteristics of the adolescent, e.g., in regard to his or her temperament of physical attractiveness (Lerner & Lerner, 1989); these reactions provide the basis of feedback to the adolescent, that is, return stimulation which influences him or her further individual development. These circular functions underscore the point that adolescents are producers of their own development and that people's relations to their context involve bidirectional exchanges (Lerner, 1982; Lerner & Busch-Rossnagel, 1981). The parent shapes the adolescent, but part of what determines the way in which that parent does this is the youth.

Adolescents shape their parents—as adults, as spouses, and of course, as parents per se—and in doing so help organize feedback to themselves, feedback that contributes further to their individuality, thus starting the circular function over again. Characteristics of behavioral or personality individuality allow the young person to contribute to this circular function. However, this idea of circular function needs to be extended; that is, in and of itself the notion is mute regarding specific characteristics of the feedback (e.g., its positive or negative valance) an adolescent will receive as a consequence of his or her individuality. In other words, to account for the specific character of adolescent–context relations the circular functions model needs to be supplemented; that is, the contribution of the *goodness of fit model*.

## The Goodness of Fit Model

Just as an adolescent brings his or her characteristics of individuality to a particular social setting, there are demands placed on the adolescent by virtue of the social and physical components of the setting (Lerner & Lerner, 1989). These demands may take the form of: (a) attitudes, values, or stereotypes that are held by others in the context regarding the person's attributes (either his or her physical or behavioral characteristics); (b) the attributes (usually behavioral), of others in the context with whom the youth must coordinate, or fit, his or her attributes (also, in this case, usually behavioral) for adaptive interactions to exist; or, (c) the physical characteristics of a setting (e.g., the presence or absence of access ramps for the motorically handicapped) which require the adolescent to possess certain attributes (again, usually behavioral abilities) for the most efficient interaction within the setting to occur.

The adolescent's individuality, in differentially meeting these demands, provides a basis for the specific feedback he or she gets from the socializing environment. For example, considering the demand "domain" of attitude, values, or stereotypes, teachers and parents may have relatively individual and distinct expectations about behaviors desired of their students and adolescents, respectively. Teachers may want students who show little distractibility, but parents might desire their children to be moderately distractible, for example, when they want their children to move from watching television, to dinner, or to bed. Youth whose behavioral individuality was either generally distractible or generally not distractible would thus differentially meet the demands of these two contexts. Problems of adjustment to school or to home might develop as a consequence of a child's lack of match (or goodness of fit) in either or both settings (Lerner & Lerner, 1989). In turn, interventions aimed at ameliorating or preventing such problems should focus on enhancing the fit—on improving the adolescent–context *relation*—and not on either the adolescent of the context alone (Howard, Alten, Walsh & Lerner, in press).

The importance of such an approach to intervention is underscored by the research of Thomas and Chess (1977, 1980, 1981) and Lerner and Lerner (1983, 1989). These researchers have found that if a youth's characteristics of individuality provide a goodness of fit (or match) with demands of a particular setting, adaptive outcomes will accrue in that setting. Those children whose characteristics match most of the settings they exist in receive supportive or positive feedback from the context, and show evidence of the most adaptive behavioral development. These findings lend support to the idea of using developmental contextualism as a frame for youth programs.

## Implications of Developmental Contextualism for Youth Interventions

As illustrated by processes involved in bidirectional socialization and in the goodness of fit model, person–context relationships involve circular functions between individuals and their social networks, as well as the community, societal, cultural, and historical levels of organization, where individuals and networks are embedded. Given that the multiple levels of change involved in person–context relations may involve individuals at any point in their lives—whether they are infants or young children, on the one hand, or adults (acting in roles such as parents, spouses, or teachers) on the other, it is possible to see why a developmental contextual perspective provides a useful frame for studying development and for planning person–context relational interventions across the life span. In essence, individual control/action processes involving (a) individuality (diversity); (b) change, involving both the individual and the context; and, as a consequence, (c) further individuality, are the essential features of human development within developmental contextualism.

The variation in settings within which people live means that studying development in a standard (e.g., in an experimenter-controlled) environment, does not provide information pertinent to the actual (ecologically valid) developing relations between individually distinct people and their specific contexts (e.g., their particular families, schools, or communities). This point underscores the need to conduct research in real-world settings, and leads to the idea that policies and programs constitute natural experiments, i.e., planned interventions for people and institutions; the evaluation of such activities becomes a central focus in the developmental contextual research agenda. That is, research in human development that is concerned with one or even a few instances of individual and contextual diversity cannot be assumed to be useful for understanding the life course of all people. To understand, then, how variation in person–context relations is associated with differences in the outcomes of development, theoretically predicted changes in these relations must be introduced into the actual ecology of people's development, and appraised for their efficacy in influencing changes in developmental trajectories. In effect, these planned changes constitute developmental interventions; depending on the levels of organization at which they are aimed they may be understood as policies or programs (Lerner, et. al., 1994).

In this view, then, policy and program endeavors do not constitute secondary work, or derivative applications, conducted after research evidence has been complied. To the contrary, policy development and implementation, and program design and delivery, become integral components of this vision for research; the evaluation component of such policy and intervention work provides critical feedback about the adequacy of the conceptual frame from which this research agenda should derive. This conception of the integration of multidisciplinary research endeavors centrally aimed at diversity and context, with policies, programs, and evaluations, is illustrated in figure 27.1.

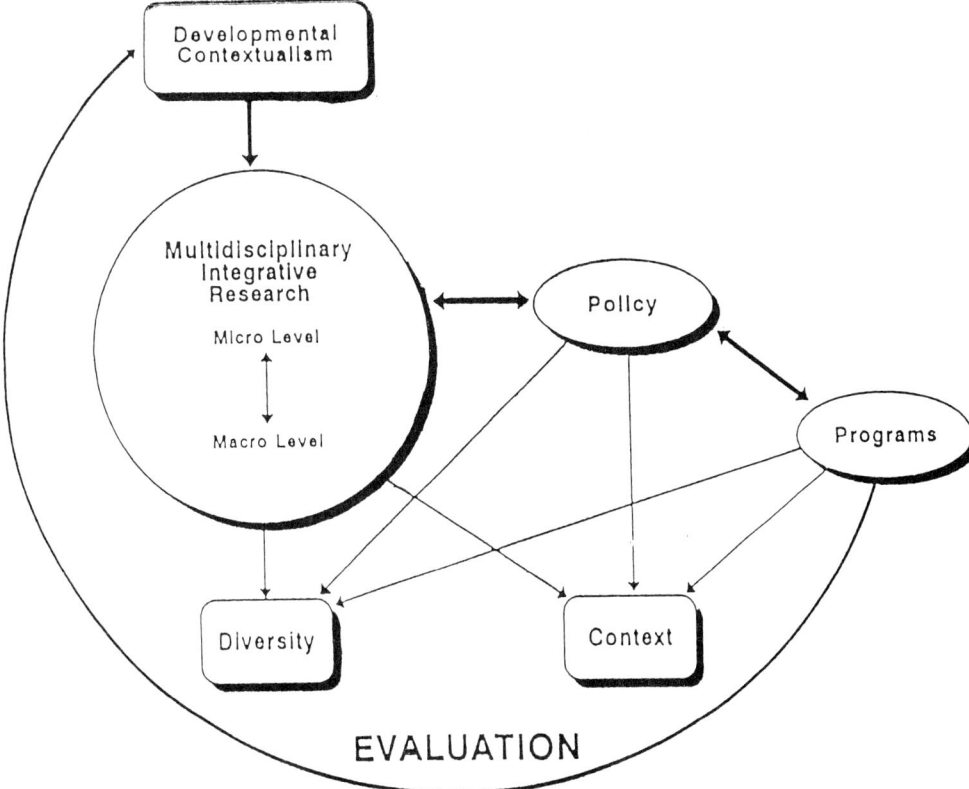

FIG. 27.1. A developmental contextual model of the integration of multilevel, multidisciplinary research aimed at diversity and context, with policies, programs, and evaluations.

## FEATURES OF EFFECTIVE YOUTH PROGRAMS: THE ROLE OF YOUTH ACTIONS

Developmental contextualism stresses that diversity and context should be the focus of both research and intervention efforts. Consistent with these foci, Dryfoos (1990) notes that a primary feature of successful programs is *intensive and individualized attention to the participants in the program*, a stress consonant with the core role of individuality and of action in development brought to the fore by the notion of circular functions. Each adolescent brings his or her characteristics of individuality to a particular social setting, and, in return, each social setting presents unique demands on the adolescent. Effective youth programs involve creating a fit between the person and the context domains of the individuality; they rest on creating opportunities for adolescents to influence their context in manners that elicit feedback promoting positive developmental outcomes (Howard, Alten, Walsh, & Lerner, in press; Lerner, Walsh, & Howard, 1998). Thus, an emphasis on the diversity and individuality of the youth in a program is key to the success of the intervention. This diversity includes race, ethnicity, culture, physical ability status, and—as Hamburg (1992) emphasizes—the developmental level of the people in the program. Similarly, Little (1993), in formulating the 17 criteria used by the International Youth Foundation (IYF) to identify successful youth programs, also stresses that the activities of good programs are developmentally appropriate.

Moreover, Hamburg (1992) notes that in successful programs any incentives used for program participation must be relevant to the individual features of the lives of the youth. This is another key instance of diversity, then: Knowledge of the individual's specific motivations, interests, aspirations, beliefs, and needs will be critical if incentives are to be effective (e.g., see Flammer, 1995; Flammer & Grob, 1994; Flammer & Rheindorf, 1991; Flammer & Scheuber-Sahli, 1995; Grob, Flammer & Wearing, 1995; Grob et. al., 1989; Wicki, Reber, Flammer, & Grob, 1994). In a similar vein, Schorr (1988) stresses that successful prevention programs design their services to be *responsive to the individual needs of the people most at risk*. In addition, she notes that to create programming that is sensitive to these significant problems of the individual requires establishing a non-bureaucratic "program culture," one that is "user friendly," and continues to evolve to be increasingly responsive to the individual needs of the people the program is attempting to serve.

Hamburg (1992) also stresses the importance of user friendliness. He indicates that successful programs have social rules and behavioral expectations that are clear to, and respected by, youth; when these characteristics are present, the programs provide youth with a predictable environment. Moreover, stressing the need for the individual to be an active agent in the program, a key point emphasized within developmental contextualism, Hamburg (1992) notes that successful programs promote active youth participation and provide the opportunity to learn new skills.

Moreover, Schorr (1988) emphasizes such focus on the individual allows a program to have, at its core, a preventive orientation. That is, through a focus on the individual and his or her distinctive needs, a program may be able to strengthen and empower the person for long-term, healthy development (Little, 1993). Similarly, Dryfoos (1990) emphasizes that successful programs incorporate early identification and intervention; such program components serve to enhance individual capacities; they have a better chance to avoid the actualization of risk, and thus the need to have to rely on ameliorative interventions to reduce the already crystallized presence of problematic behaviors.

Furthermore, Dryfoos (1990), Schorr (1988), and Hamburg (1992) emphasize that the focus on the individual must occur within a program structure that *integrates* key features of the context within which the individual is embedded. For instance, Hamburg (1992) notes that successful programs promote relationships among multiple supports in the youth's context. Little (1993) agrees with this view. Among the 17 criteria the IYF uses to identify successful programs is the idea that an effective program meaningfully involves parents, extended family, and/or other "significant adults." Similarly, Dryfoos (1990) indicates that successful prevention programs for adolescents involve the four social institutions essential to development during this period: The family, the peer group, the work place, and the school.

In short, then, interventions aimed at promoting the positive development of youth should focus on enhancing the fit—on improving the quality of the interaction between the adolescent and his or her context—and not on the adolescent or the context alone (Howard, Alten, Walsh & Lerner, in press; Lerner, Walsh & Howard, 1998). In other words, in order to be effective, prevention program for adolescents must enhance the fit between their actions on, and the actions of, several key features of their context.

1. *A youth's parents*, due to the continued salience of the family for healthy development in the adolescent period (Allison & Lerner, 1993); that is, there are several features of family life that foster healthy development—not only in adolescence but, as well, during childhood. Hamburg (1992) has identified several of these features of the family. Among these are: An intact, cohesive, and dependable nuclear family; a parent–child relationship marked by love and nurturance; an experienced parent who enjoys raising his or her child, who can cope with the stresses of childrearing, and who enjoys teaching his or her child; social support provided by the extended family; and the provision to the child of predictable adult behavior and a family context that inculcates in the child a vision of a positive adult future.

2. *A youth's peers in the program*, due to the increased salience of the peer group during this period of life (Lerner, 1988) and because peers have credibility with other adolescents (Hamburg, 1992); thus, even with many of the most difficult problems of adolescence (e.g., drug use, unprotected sex), well trained peers can help other youths build skills to resist engagement in risk behaviors, and in turn, to pursue healthier behavioral options (Hamburg, 1992). Moreover, when peer involvement takes the form of a tutor–tutee relationship, there are often personal, social, and academic benefits for both youths (Hamburg, 1992).

3. *The world of work*, due to (a) the increased presence of the workplace as part of the ecology of contemporary adolescents' lives (e.g., about 60% of all adolescents enrolled full-time in high school also work part-time; Steinberg, 1983); and (b) the fact that unless intervention programs during adolescence are linked to a successful transition to adult life—which centrally involves engagement in productive and socially useful employment —any positive developments produced by the programs will be wasted. In this regard Hamburg (1992, p. 332) notes that preparation for work is a

key component of a multi-faceted set of skills needed by adolescents in order for them to become successful citizens of the modern world.
4. *The role of schools as an institutional locus for successful prevention programs.* In regard to the school as a key social institution involved in successful prevention programs, Dryfoos (1990) first indicates that such programs involve community-wide, multi-agency collaborative—and integrated—approaches, that is, approaches where agency or program "turf" is ceded for the benefit of providing a comprehensive and integrated focus on the totality of the individual and his or her context—and not on artificially segmented portions of his or her individual and/or social functioning (Dry-foos, 1994).

Hamburg (1992) places similar stress on the importance of integrated and comprehensive services. Moreover, Schorr (1988) also indicates that successful prevention programs involve integration—of children within the family and, as well, in "families" within their communities. Moreover, Schorr also notes that such programs must be comprehensive; in addition, however, because of the need to attend to the individual, and to what may be his or her changing needs over the course of participation in the program, programs need to be intensive (i.e., long-term), flexible, and responsive. Tharinger et al., (1996) and Holtzman (1997) have described schools as one of the few stable institutions serving the entire community, thus making these institutions an appropriate locus for the community-collaborative programs for which we are calling.

For schools to collaborate, however, there will need to be a redefinition of the mission of schools—one that is changed from a strict focus on education to one committed to the holistic education and development of the child (Holtzman, 1997; Illbach, Cobb, & Joseph, 1997; Tharinger, et al. 1996). The challenges that youth today face to health, positive development, and survival are influencing, and are influenced by, performance in school (Illbach, Cobb, & Joseph, 1997; Short & Talley, 1997). Schools cannot afford to avoid joining forces with the community to address these issues and taking an active role in the collaborative effort—expanding the mission of schools to address these characteristics as they influence and are influenced by education (Brabeck, Walsh, Kenny, & Comilang, 1997; Lerner, 1993; Talley & Short, 1996).

Thus, Dryfoos (1990), Hamburg (1992), and Schorr (1988) indicate that programs should not promote and, by implication, policies should not mandate (or perhaps even allow) the separate focus on mental health, public health, social service, and educational issues. Rather, programs (and policies) should promote an integrated, "case management" approach to services. Similarly, one of the criteria used by the IYF to identify successful programs is that the features or components of a program must be appropriate in multiple contexts; they must promote *cross-setting continuity* (Little, 1993). Thus, to Little (1993), such a program would be coordinated, as appropriate, with the services of other child and adolescent programs.

In essence, then, such integrated approaches will emphasize the specific needs of the individuals and contexts served by the program, and will avoid the personal and familial fragmentation that may accompany being embedded in a system wherein one is compelled to "be served" by several disconnected agencies and programs. In addition, such integration will save money; it will avoid the creation of "million dollar families," that is, families who are "served" by several disconnected programs (Lerner, 1995). When this collaboration occurs between the school and the youth- and family-serving agencies and programs within the community in which the school is embedded, an integrated and comprehensive community-wide system is established. Dryfoos (1994, 1995) terms this entity a "full-service school." It is important to note that, in addition to being embedded within community-wide, multi-agency integrated structures, such as full-service schools, successful programs have several other distinctive features.

## The Importance of Training

Dryfoos (1990), Schorr (1988), and Little (1993) stress that training in the features of the program and in social skills are among the most important of these features. Often, the personnel delivering a program are not experienced in the substance of the program or are nor familiar with the principles of human development that pertain to the children, youth, and families participating in the program. Thus, Little (1993) stresses that successful programs include initial training, plus follow-up training and support for project staff and other participants as needed. Moreover, a youth may not have the skills needed to fit the demands of complex and perhaps contradictory social settings (e.g., ones where the demands of peers and adults differ); in turn, program personnel may not possess the particular social skills requisite for interacting effectively with the children, and/or families participating in a program. The need for social skills training will be increased if program personnel are not from the same socioeconomic, cultural, racial, or ethnic backgrounds as are the program participants.

Hence, successful programs include arrangements for training of the substance of a program, for education about the developmental and cultural characteristics of the program participants, and for building *culturally competent* social skills (Dryfoos, 1990; Schorr, 1988). Indeed, Little (1993) notes that, in successful programs, the content, strategy, and leadership of the program are appropriate to the culture of the community. Accordingly, with provisions for the inculcation of culturally appropriate knowledge and skills, programs thereby support the establishment of trusting and meaningful relationships among program personnel and participants (Schorr, 1988).

In addition, in order to be successful in continuing a program over time, personnel must have, or be trained to possess, the ability to develop a feasible plan to become self-sustaining in financial support, in facilities and materials, in leadership, and in continuing to address identified needs (Little, 1993). Moreover, according to the IYF, programs that have staff trained in this way, standardly include as part of the functioning of the organization planning, monitoring, evaluation, and feedback (Little, 1993). Furthermore, successful programs are those that, to the greatest extent possible, include the youth participants not only in these organizational activities but also in the implementation of, and dissemination about, the program (Little, 1993).

Finally, successful training involves interprofessional and collaborative experiences (Castro, 1994). In order to promote the integrated services we are calling for, professionals need to be skilled in methods to effectively communicate and collaborate with other professions (Winitzky, Sheridan, Crow, Welch, & Kennedy, 1995). If professionals are trained to collaborate with one another, such interprofessional training should provide a depth and breadth of understanding of a youth, the complex issues that he or she presents, and multiple perspectives and viewpoints in order to intervene in a child's life in an effective, appropriate way (Castro, 1994; Winitzky et al., 1995). In this manner, successful training involves interprofessional and collaborative experiences.

## Building a Caring Community

Finally, Dryfoos (1990), Schorr (1988), and Little (1993) stress that effective programs, while they may be primarily located in schools, need to also be situated in the community more pervasively. That is, children and adolescents are not always in schools: They spend time on the streets of their neighborhoods, in other youth-serving institutions (e.g., 4-H clubs), "hanging out" at malls or at friends' homes, or just being by themselves (Carnegie Corporation of New York, 1992). These contexts must not become "cracks" through which our youth fall. Communities must provide continuity of programming efforts that extend to all portions of neighborhoods, and community members must ensure that all youth in need of a program have access to it (Hamburg, 1992). For instance, the IYF notes that successful programs are built on a community approach that includes: (a) Involving multiple sectors of the community; (b) being responsive to locally identified needs; and (c) a process for building thorough community/neighborhood participation (Little, 1993). In short, the community must ensure that, no matter where a child or adolescent goes in the community, he or she is supported and protected.

Thus, programs that are focused in schools must also be embedded thoroughly in the complete fabric of the community. Adults must adopt the ethos—once prevalent in communities but, now, more difficult to find—that *all children* in the community are *their children*. We must take the responsibility, and give each other the right, to prevent youth risk behaviors whenever and wherever we see them. If we "turn our backs" on our youth, if we do not work to extend the meaning and intent of effective, school-based programs to the entire community, and build a seamless social support net for our youth, then not only "their children," but "our children," and indeed all of us, will suffer in numerous and historically unprecedented ways.

The importance, then, of Schorr's (1988) idea, that effective programs see children as part of families, and both as part of the community, seems clear. Similarly, the truth of the now often-cited African proverb, that it takes an entire village to raise a child, has never appeared more certain. It will take the efforts of every citizen in a community to protect adequately their youth and, in turn, to increase to the level of absolute certainty the chance of every member of the younger generation to maximize his or her potential for healthy and productive development.

## CONCLUSION

We may capitalize on the contributions of youth to their own development by focusing on the individually-based control/action processes involved in circular functions in youth development. Such processes involve multiple characteristics of the young person; for instance, his or her developmental level, knowledge of risk taking, intrapersonal resources (e.g., self esteem, self competence, control beliefs, and values), and interpersonal management skills (e.g., being able to engage useful social support and prosocial behaviors from peers); successful risk prevention programs may be developed through an emphasis on such control/action processes (Flammer, 1995; Flammer & Grob, 1994; Flammer & Rheindorf, 1991; Flammer & Scheuber-Sahli, 1995; Grob, Flammer & Wearing, 1995; Grob et al., 1989; Levitt, Selman, & Richmond, 1991; Wicki, Reber, Flammer, & Grob, 1994).

However, these programs do more than focus on diminishing risk. The sort of programs we are describing emphasize the strengths and assets of young people, that is, their capacities for acting to influence their own positive development and their possession of attributes—protective factors—that keep them moving forward on a positive developmental path. Protective factors—individual attributes, such as self esteem, religious values and knowledge, skills, and motivation to do well; and contextual attributes, such as the experience of having authoritative parents and a socially supportive, prosocial peer group—have been identified as integral in the healthy development of young people (e.g., Brown & Rife, 1991; Feldman, Rosenthal, Brown, & Canning, 1995; Jessor, Van Den Bos, Vanderryn, & Costa, 1995; Stiffman, Chueh, & Earls, 1992).

In essence, then, there are multiple features of person and context that should be combined to design and deliver a successful program preventing the actualization of risk in adolescence. Building on the lifespan general processes of person–context relations involved in circular functions, and the specific developmental characteristics of the adolescent period that involves identity, family, peer, and institutional (e.g., school and work) contextual levels, these programs, when also attuned to the specific characteristics and needs of the youth and their setting, will help them not just avoid the development of risk behaviors. In addition, positive youth development may be promoted.

In short, we may be optimistic about the likely success of programs if we design and deliver them in the context of keeping in mind that no single, isolated effort is apt to succeed, given that risk behaviors are interrelated and influenced by a host of individual and contextual factors. Thus, a coordinated set of community-based programs, aimed at creating or enhancing "fit" between individuals and their contexts, is required for success; these programs should begin as early as possible and should be maintained for as many of the adolescent years as feasible. No one effort, even a comprehensive one, can continue to prevent the appearance of risk across all of this period.

Clearly, then, means may be found to design and deliver programs that will help prevent, among the proportion of youth at risk for the development of major instances of problem behaviors, the development of such an undesirable status. Perhaps more significant means exist for not just keeping youth from following a course of negative behaviors. Our knowledge of design criteria for effective youth programs serves also as a guide for devising means to capitalize on the potentials and strengths of all youth, their families, and communities, and through meeting their developmental needs, promote their positive development.

However, if the knowledge we have about how to promote positive development is to reach the maximum number of youth possible, we need to marshal the resources of society in the service of designing programs consistent with our vision for young people. To attain this end, scholars of youth development must engage public policy and policymakers in support of effective programs for youth (Lerner, 1995; Lipsitz, 1991; Hamburg & Takanishi, 1996).

The stress on individuality within developmental contextualism leads to a key implication for youth policy, one that returns to the point that the scholarship promoted by this perspective involves a merger of both basic and applied science. Developmental contextualism conceives of evaluation as providing information both about policy and program efficacy, and about how the course of human development can be enhanced through policies and programs (Lerner et al., 1997; Ostrom, Lerner, & Freel, 1995). Thus, evaluation is also a means to empower program participants and to enhance their capacities to engage in actions (i.e., program design, delivery, and evaluation) that promote the use of *participatory-normative evaluation procedures* (Weiss & Greene, 1992). Such evaluations will increase understanding of the lives developing within the context of the policies and programs one is implementing and, simultaneously, will inculcate greater capacities and further empower youths, families, and communities involved in the programs being evaluated. Simply, evaluation may be a key means to promote the ability of youth to take actions that enhance programs linked to their positive development. Such evaluation is, then, a vehicle for capitalizing on the ability of youth to act to promote their own development.

In short, we know how to design effective programs. Our task now is to formulate a set of social rules—policies—that will enable our values about youth to be translated into effective actions, ones that are appropriately scaled, sustained, and empowering of the actions and development of the individuals involved in them.

## REFERENCES

Allison, K. W., & Lerner, R. M. (1993). Integrating research, policy, and programs for adolescents and their families. In R. M. Lerner (Ed.), *Early adolescence: Perspectives on research, policy, and intervention* (pp. 17–23). Hillsdale, NJ: Lawrence Erlbaum Associates.
Brabeck, M., Walsh, M. E., Kenny, M., & Comilang, K. (1997). Interprofessional collaboration for children and families: Opportunities for counseling psychology in the 21st century, *The Counseling Psychologist, 25(4)*, 615–636.
Brandtstäder, J. (1998). Action perspectives on human development. In R. M. Lerner (Ed.), *Theoretical models of human development* (pp. 807–864). Volume 1 of the *Handbook of Child Psychology* (5th ed.), Editor-in-Chief: William Damon. New York: Wiley.
Brown, C. S., & Rife, J. C. (1991). Social, personality, and gender differences in at-risk and not-at-risk sixth-grade students. *Journal of Early Adolescence, 11*, 482–495.
Carnegie Corporation of New York (1995). *Great Transitions: Preparing Adolescents for a New Century.* Carnegie Council on Adolescent Development.
Carnegie Corporation of New York. (1992). *A matter of time: Risk and opportunity in the nonschool hours.* Carnegie Council on Adolescent Development.
Castro, R. M. (1994). Education for interprofessional practice. In R. M. Castro & M. Julia (Eds.), *Interprofessional care and collaborative practice.* Pacific Grove, CA: Brooks-Cole.
Center for the Study of Social Policy (1995). *Kids count data book.* Washington, DC: Author.
Chess, S., & Thomas, A. (1984). *The origins and evolution of behavior disorders: Infancy to early adult life.* New York: Brunner/Mazel.
Children's Defense Fund (1996). *The state of America's children yearbook.* Washington, DC: Author.
di Mauro, D. (1995). *Sexuality research in the United States: An assessment of social and behavioral sciences.* New York: The Social Science Research Council.
Dryfoos, J. G. (1990). *Adolescents at risk: Prevalence and prevention.* New York: Oxford University.
Dryfoos, J. G. (1994). *Full service schools: A revolution in health and social services for children, youth and families.* San Francisco: Jossey-Bass.
Dryfoos, J. G. (1995). Full service schools: Revolution or fad? *Journal of Research on Adolescence, 5*, 147–172.
Feldman, S., & Elliott, G. (1990). *At the threshold: The developmental adolescent.* Cambridge, MA: Harvard University Press.
Feldman, S. S., Rosenthal, D. R., Brown, N. L., & Canning, R. D. (1995). Predicting sexual experience in adolescent boys from peer rejection and acceptance during childhood. *Journal of Research on Adolescence, 5(4)*, 387–412.
Flammer, A. (1995). Developmental analysis of control beliefs. In A. Bandura (Ed.), Self-efficacy in changing societies. New York, NY: Cambridge University Press.
Flammer, A., & Grob, A. (1994). Control beliefs: Their justification and autobiographical recollections. *Zeitschrift für Experiementelle und Angewandte Psychologie, 41(1)*, 17–38.
Flammer, A. & Rheindorf, E. (1991). Control beliefs and selective recall from autobiography. *Archives de Psychologie, 59(229)*, 125–142.

Flammer, A., & Scheuber-Sahli, E. (1995). Selective recall as intervention to modify control beliefs in an academic achievement setting. *Schweizerische Zeitschrift für Psychologie, 54(1),* 50–56.

Gottlieb, P., Wahlsten, D., & Lickliter, R. (1998). The significance of biology for human development: A developmental psychobiological systems view. In R. M. Lerner (Ed.), *Theoretical models of human development* (pp. 233–274). Volume 1 of the *Handbook of Child Psychology* (5th ed.), Editor-in-Chief: William Damon. New York; Wiley.

Grob, A., Flammer, A., Kaiser, F. G., & Lüthi, R. (1989). Subjective well-being and control in delinquent and nondelinquent youths. *Schweizerische Zeitschrift für Psychologie, 48(2),* 75–85.

Grob, A,. Flammer, A., & Wearing, A. J. (1995). Adolescents' perceived control: Domain specificity, expectations, and appraisal. *Journal of Adolescence, 18(4),* 403–435.

Hamburg, D. A. (1992). *Today's children: Creating a future for a generation in crisis.* New York: Time Books.

Hamburg, D. A., & Takanishi R. (1996). Great transitions: Preparing American youth for the 21st century—the role of research. *Journal of Research on Adolescence, 6,* 379–396.

Held, R., and Hein, A. V. (1963). Movement-produced stimulation in the development of visually guided behavior. *Journal of Comparative and Physiological Psychology, 56,* 872–876.

Holtzman, W. H. (1997). Community psychology and full-service school in different cultures. *American Psychologist, 52(4),* 381–389.

Howard, K., Barton, C. E., Walsh, M. E., & Lerner, R. M. (in press). Social and contextual issues in interventions with children and families. In T. Ollendick and S. Russ (Eds.), *Handbook of psychotherapies with children and families.* New York: Plenum.

Huston, A. C. (Ed.). (1991). *Children in poverty: Child development and public policy.* Cambridge, MA: Cambridge University Press.

Huston, A. C., McLoyd, V. C., & Garcia Coll, C. T. (1994). Children and poverty: Issues in contemporary research. *Child Development, 65,* 275–282.

Illbach, R. J., Cobb, C. T., & Joseph, H. M. (Eds.); (1997). *Integrated Services for Children and Families: Opportunities for Psychological Practice.* Washington, DC: American Psychological Association.

International Youth Foundation (1995). *Annual Report.* Baltimore: Author.

Jessor, R., Van Den Bos, J., Vanderryn, J., & Costa, F. M. (1995). Protective factors in adolescent problem behavior: Moderator effects and developmental change. *Developmental Psychology, 31(6),* 923–933.

Johnston, L., O'Malley, R. A., & Bachman, J. G. (1996). *National survey results on drug use from the monitoring the future study, 1975-1994.* Vol. II: College students and young adults. Washington, DC: National Institute on Drug Abuse.

Lerner, J. V., & Lerner, R. M. (1983). Temperament and adaptation across life: Theoretical and empirical issues. In P. B. Baltes & O. G. Brim, Jr. (Eds.), *Life-span development and behavior* (vol. 5., pp. 197-230). New York: Academic Press.

Lerner, J. V., & Lerner, R. M. (1989). Introduction: Longitudinal analyses of biological, psychological, and social interactions across the transitions of early adolescence. *Journal of Early Adolescence, 9,* 175–180.

Lerner, R. M. (1976). *Concepts and theories of human development.* Reading, MA: Addison-Wesley.

Lerner, R. M. (1982). Children and adolescents as producers of their own development. *Developmental Review, 2,* 342–370.

Lerner, R. M. (1984). *On the nature of human plasticity*. New York: Cambridge University Press.

Lerner, R. M. (1986). *Concepts and theories of human development* (2nd ed.). New York: Random House.

Lerner, R. M. (1987). A life-span perspective for early adolescence. In R. M. Lerner & T. T. Foch (Eds.), *Biological-psychosocial interactions in early adolescence* (pp. 9-34). Hillsdale, NJ: Lawrence Erlbaum Associates.

Lerner, R. M. (1988). Early adolescent transitions: The lore and laws of adolescence. in M. D. Levine & E. R. McArarney (Eds.), *Early adolescent transitions* (pp. 1-21). Lexington, MA: D.C. Health.

Lerner, R. M. (1991). Changing organism-context relations as the basic process of development: A developmental-contextual perspective. *Developmental Psychology, 27*, 27-32.

Lerner, R. M. (1993a). Investment in youth: The role of home economics in enhancing the life chances of America's children. *AHEA Monograph Series, 1*, 5-34.

Lerner, R. M. (1993b). Early adolescence: Toward an agenda for the integration of research, policy, and intervention. In R. M. Lerner (Ed.), *Early adolescence: Perspectives on research, policy, and intervention* (pp. 1-13). Hillsdale, NJ: Lawrence Erlbaum Associates.

Lerner, R. M. (1995). *America's youth in crisis: Challenges and options for programs and policies*. Thousand Oaks, CA: Sage.

Lerner, R. M. (1996). Relative plasticity, integration, temporality, and diversity in human development: A developmental contextual perspective about theory, process, and method. *Developmental Psychology, 32(4)*, 781-786.

Lerner, R. M. (Ed.). (1998). *Theoretical models of human development* (pp. 1-24). Volume 1 of the *Handbook of Child Psychology* (5th ed.), Editor-in-Chief: William Damon. New York: Wiley.

Lerner, R. M. (in press). Diversity and context in research, policy, and programs for children and adolescence: A developmental contextual perspective. In M. B. Spencer & G. K. Brookins (Eds.), *Ethnicity & diversity: Minorities no more*. Hillsdale, NJ: Lawrence Erlbaum Associates.

Lerner, R. M., & Busch-Rossnagel, N. A. (Eds.). (1982). *Individuals as producers of their own development: A life-span perspective*. New York: Academic Press.

Lerner, R. M. & Galambos, N. (1997). Adolescent development: Challenges and opportunities for research, programs, and policies. In J. T. Spence (Ed.), *Annual Review of Psychology* (Vol. 49, pp. 413-460). Palo Alto, CA: Annual Review Inc.

Lerner, R. M., Miller, J. R., Knott, J. H., Corey, K. E., Bynum, T. S., Hoopfer, L.C., McKinney, M. H., Abrams, L. A., Hula, R. C., & Terry, P. A. (1994). Integrating scholarship and outreach in human development research, policy, and service: A developmental perspective. In D. L. Featherman, R. M. Lerner, & M. Perlmutter (Eds.), *Life-span development and behavior, 12* (pp. 249-273). Hillsdale, NJ: Lawrence Erlbaum Associates.

Lerner, R. M., Ostrom, C. W., & Freel, M. A. (1997). Preventing health compromising behaviors among youth and promoting their positive development: A developmental-contextual perspective. In J. Schulenberg, J. L. Maggs, & K. Hurrelman (Eds.), *Health risks and developmental transitions during adolescence* (pp. 498-521). New York: Cambridge University Press.

Lerner, R. M & Spanier, G. B. (1980). A dynamic interactional view of child and family development. In R. M. Lerner & G. B. Spanier (Eds.), *Child influences on marital and family: A life-span perspective* (pp. 1-20). New York: Academic Press.

Lerner, R. M., Walsh, M. E., & Howard, K. (1998). Person-context relations as the bases for risk and resiliency in child and adolescent development: A developmental contextual perspective. In T. Ollendick (Ed.), *Comprehensive clinical psychology. Vol. 5: Children and Adolescents: Clinical formulation and treatment (pp. 1–24).* New York: Elsevier Science Publishers.

Levitt, M. A., Selman, R. L., & Richmond, J. B. (1991). The psychosocial foundations of early adolescents' high-risk behavior: Implications for research and practice. *Journal of Research on Adolescence, 1,* 349–378.

Lipsitz, J. (1991). Public policy and young adolescents: A 1990s context for researchers. *Journal of Early Adolescence, 11,* 40.

Little, R. R. (1993, March). *What's working for today's youth: The issues, the programs, and the learnings.* Paper presented at an ICYF Fellows Colloquium, Michigan State University, East Landsing, MI.

Magnusson, D. (1988). Individual development from an interactional perspective. In D. Magnusson (Ed.), *Paths through life* (vol. 1, pp. 3–31). Hillsdale, NJ: Lawrence Erlbaum Associates.

Magnusson, D. (1995). Individual development: A holistic integrated model. In P. Moen, G. H. Edler Jr., & K. Luscher (Eds.), *Examining lives in context: Perspectives on the ecology of human development* (pp. 19–60). Washington, DC: American Psychological Association.

McKinney, M., Abrams, L. A., Terry, P. A., & Lerner, R. M. (1994). Child development research and the poor children of America: A call for a developmental contextual approach to research and outreach. *Family and Consumer Sciences Research Journal, 23,* 26–42.

Ostrom, C. W., Lerner, R. A., & Freel. M. A. (1995). Building the capacity of youth through university/community collaborations: The Development-In-Context Evaluation (DICE) model. *Journal for Research on Adolescence 10(4),* 427–448.

Pittman, K. J. (1996). Community, youth, development: Three goals in search of connection. *New Designs for Youth Development,* Winter, 1996.

Pittman, K. J., & Irby, M. (1996). *Promoting life skills for youth: Beyond indicators for survival and problem prevention.* Baltimore: International Youth Foundation.

Schneirla, T. C. (1965). Interrelationships of the innate and the acquired in instinctive behavior. In P. P. Grasse (Ed.), *L'instinct dans le conportement des animaux et de l'homme* (pp. 387–452). Paris: Mason et Cie.

Schorr, L. B. (1988). *Within our reach: Breaking the cycle of disadvantage.* New York: Doubleday.

Schulenberg, J., Maggs, J. L., & Hurrelmann, K. (Eds.); (1997), *Health risks and developmental transitions during adolescence.* New York: Cambridge University Press.

Short, R. J., & Talley, R. C. (1997). Rethinking psychology and the schools: Implications of recent national policy, *American Psychologist, 52(3),* 234–240.

Silberson, R. & Todt, E. (Eds.); (1994). *Adolescence in context: the interplay of family, school, peers, and work in adjustment.* New York: Springer.

Smith, T. M. (1994). Adolescent pregnancy. In R. J. Simeonsson (Ed.), *Risk, resilience and prevention: Promoting the well-being of all children.* Baltimore: Paul H. Brookes Publishing.

Stattin, H., & Magnusson, D. (1990). *Pubertal maturation in female development.* Hillsdale, NJ: Lawrence Erlbaum Associates.

Steinberg, L. (1983). The varieties and effects of work during adolescence. In M. Lamb, A. Brown, B. Rogoff (Eds.), *Advances in developmental psychology* (vol. 3, pp. 1–37). Hillsdale, NJ: Lawrence Erlbaum Associates.

Stiffman, A. R., Chueh, H., & Earls, F. (1992). Predictive modeling of change in depressive disorder and counts of depressive symptoms in urban youths. *Journal of Research on Adolescence, 2(4)*. 295–316.

Talley, R. C., & Short, R. J. (1996). Social reforms and the future of school practice: Implications for American psychology, *Professional Psychology: Research and Practice, 27(1)*, 5–13.

Tharinger, D. J., Lambert, N. M., Bricklin, P. M., Feshbach, N., Johnson, N. F., Oakland, T. D., Paster, V. S., & Sanchez, W. (1996). Educational reform: Challenges for psychology and psychologists, *Professional Psychology: Research and Practice, 27(1)*, 24–33.

Thomas, A., & Chess, S. (1977). *Temperament and development*. New York: Brunner/Mazel.

Thomas, A., & Chess, S. (1980). *The dynamics of psychological development*. New York: Brunner/Mazel.

Thomas, A., & Chess, S. (1981). The role of temperament in the contributions of individuals to their development. In R. M. Lerner & N. A. Busch-Rossnagel (Eds.), *Individuals as producers of their own development: A life-span perspective*. New York: Academic Press.

Tobach, E., & Greenberg, G. (1984). The significance of T. C. Schneirla's contribution to the concept of levels of integration. In G. Greenberg & E. Tobach (Eds.), *Behavioral evolution and integrative levels* (pp. 1–7). Hillsdale, NJ: Lawrence Erlbaum Associates.

United States Department of Health and Human Services (1996). *Trends in the well-being of America's children and youth: 1996*. Washington, DC: Department on Health and Human Services, Office of the Secretary for Planning and Evaluation.

Weiss, H. B., & Green, J. C. (1992). An empowerment partnership for family support and education programs and evaluations. *Family Science Review, 5*, 131–148.

Wicki, W. Reber, R., Flammer, A., & Grob, A. (1994). Justification of control beliefs in children and adolescents. *Zeitschrift für Entwicklungspsychologie und Pädagogische Psychologie, 26(3)*, 241–261.

Wilson, W. J. (1987). *The truly disadvantaged: The inner city, the underclass, and public policy*. Chicago: University of Chicago.

Winitzky, N., Sheridan, S., Crow, N., Welch, M., & Kennedy, C. (1995). Interdisciplinary collaboration: Variations on a theme. *Journal of Teacher Education, 46(2)*, 109–119.

World Health Organization (1986). WHO study group on young people and "Health for all by the year 2000." In *Young people's health: A challenge for society* (Technical Report Series, no. 731). Geneva: World Health Organization.

World Health Organization (1993). *The health of young people: A challenge and a promise*. Geneva: World Health Organization.

# 28

# Social Control, Perceived Control, and the Family[1]

*Werner Wicki*

## INTRODUCTION

The focus of this article is on how control processes affect family functioning, particularly parenting behaviors. The influences of both social control and perceived control are considered, assuming that a better understanding of the joint impact of these factors is necessary. This is illustrated regarding effective family support programs in the final section.

## SOCIAL CONTROL AND THE FAMILY

Social control is genuinely a sociological construct that has been most fully articulated by Hirschi (1969). Briefly, this theory refers to the occurrence of delinquency, assuming that respective tendencies are rather "natural," and that the individual is less likely to act delinquently if his or her bonds to significant others (e.g., parents, friends, neighbors, siblings, teachers) and his or her commitment to conventional social order (e.g., school, occupation) as well as the belief in shared (common) values, are strong, and vice versa. This theoretical framework has been supported by a number of recent studies. For example, Junger, Terlouw, and Van der Heiden (1995) demonstrated the impact of social control (including the control exerted through the parents) on delinquency and accidents in a large Dutch sample (N = 2918) of 12- to 24-year-olds, and Le Blanc (1994) demonstrated the influences of both family and school control variables on criminal activities in adolescence and young adulthood among 458 boys. Among girls, high social control, exerted through the parents, predicts a later (compared to earlier) onset of first sexual intercourse (Crockett, Bingham, Chopak, & Vicary, 1996). In addition, drug consumption and school failure of adolescents proved to be associated with a lack of social control (e.g., Marcos & Bahr, 1995; Simons, Whitbeck, Conger, and Conger, 1991). So far, the application of social control theory was mostly limited to problem behaviors of children and adoles-

[1]I am grateful to Françoise D. Alsaker, Adrian Bangerter, and Ursula Peter for their comments on an earlier draft of this article.

cents, largely neglecting further domains of human development and the impact of social control on *parents'* behaviors.

The inclusion of such relations is an obvious advantage of the ecological approach in *developmental psychology*. It is nearly 20 years ago that this approach emerged as an important perspective (*cf.* Bronfenbrenner, 1979), and that Cochran and Brassard (1979) pointed out the relevance of parents' personal social network regarding their offsprings' development. In their instructive review, the authors detailed several pathways of network influences, mainly distinguishing direct influences which are "transmitted through the range and variety of persons with whom the child has contact on a recurring basis" (p. 602), and indirect influences on the child mediated "through the kinds of influences the network members have upon the parents themselves as developing individuals" (p. 602).

Although Cochran and Brassard (1979) did not explicitly point to the social control concept they considered some pathways of influences that are of interest in this context. *First*, they assumed that parents' access to emotional and material assistance from the social network is an important resource that exerts (mainly) positive effects on parenting behaviors (e.g., Holtzman & Gilbert, 1987; Jennings, Stagg, & Connors, 1991), especially among single, disadvantaged, or distressed parents (e.g., Alwin, Converse & Martin, 1985; Colletta, 1979; Tietjen, 1985; Weinraub & Wolf, 1983). Obviously, the parents' access to such resources depends on the mere presence *and* the quality of the relations (or "bonds") to significant others, like kins, neighbors, and friends. Thus, isolated, distressed families are not only assumed to suffer from deficient assistence, but also, as predicted by social control theory, to be more susceptible to inadequate or even illegal parenting "styles" like beating their children, and maltreatment, resulting in negative developmental outcomes. *Second*, as already outlined by Cochran and Brassard (1979), members of the personal network influence the parents' actual child-rearing performance through encouraging or discouraging particular behaviors. This kind of control can be exerted very subtly, for example, the mother's sister raising an eyebrow when witnessing the mother beating her child, or very strongly, for example, telling a neighbor that she (should not) hit her baby. With such interactions in mind, it seems quite reasonable that the strength of social bonds as outlined by Hirschi (1969) affects the behavior of individuals because of anticipated concerns or concrete experiences regarding social sanctions. More specifically, besides the fact that social bonds to significant others are important sources of assistance, the same significant others are also sources of social control. In other words, anonymous neighbors or relatives, to whom the parents have no contact cannot exert any effective social control.

Although these theoretical considerations seem rather convincing, at least one empirical problem connected to the theory has rarely been addressed and is not resolved till today. I mean the construct of the "isolated family." As indicated by the network and social support literature, the size of the personal network and the number of contacts have only a small positive impact regarding individual or family functioning in general (in fact, social bonds also exert detrimental effects, cf. Rook, 1992), while perceived support emerges as a more important factor (e.g., Lairaiter & Baumann, 1992; Thoits, 1992; Weinraub & Wolf, 1983). Isolation is often conceptualized as a continuum ranging from maximum integration, which is assumed to be optimal, to complete isolation as the negative end of the scale. I consider this view inaccurate, and prefer to assume a *critical level of integration* differing from family to family depending on several factors, for example, on intrafamilial resources (Riley & Eckenrode, 1986). While exceeding the critical level is not assumed to further improve family functioning, it is likely that falling short of the critical level leads to a significant detriment of family functioning.[2] The Berne transition to parenthood study (Wicki, 1997, in press; Wicki, Dumont, & Signer-Fischer, 1995) addressed some network issues including the number of self-reported contacts of both parents, in addition to family resources, social support, well-being, parental coping, and childrearing behaviors. In the following, I present some cross-sectional data to illustrate the impact of the social isolation phenomenon in Swiss first-time parents. I refer to the 1993 questionnaire data of the first group, which were collected among 189 mothers and 177 fathers, when their first child was aged between two- and six-months-old. Regarding the frequency of contacts with acquaintances and friends (telephone contacts were also included), we found a linear correlation with perceived social support ($r = .28$, $p < .001$) among mothers, while the remaining associations, for example, with partner conflicts, perceived cohesion, parental coping, child-rearing or well-being, were weak ($r < .18$) among both parents (all analyses were performed separately for mothers and fathers). As expected, most of the parents had rather frequent contacts with their friends, ranging from weekly to daily. However, we identified a very small group of 7 mothers and 7 fathers reporting that their contacts with friends only happen monthly or even less frequently. I compared these "isolated" mothers and fathers with the remaining sub-samples by means of Mann-Whitney U tests. This procedure revealed a more comprehensive pattern of findings: Among mothers, the isolated group reported more perceived conflicts with the partner ($z = 2.5$, $p < .05$) and tended to be more prone to worries and depressed mood ($z = 1.91$, $p = .056$) than the mothers with more contacts to friends, while isolated fathers perceived less social support ($z = 2.4$, $p < .05$) and reported less sensitivity with respect to the baby (for example, less cuddling behaviors, $z = 2.6$, $p < .01$), than the fathers with more contacts to friends did. Of course, this analysis is not conclusive regarding causes and effects. In addition, other factors, such as personality, could also explain at least some associations. From the perspective of social control theory, the result concerning fathers' reduced sensitivity is most interesting. Probably, a lack of contacts with friends could imply relatively rare contacts with other families which, in turn,

---

[2]A further empirical problem of some studies is merely adding up "significant" neighbors or relatives because of the vagueness of the term "significant." For example, consider the case that *one* significant neighbor or relative assists more reliably and more often than *two* significant neighbors or relatives do together.

would not be able to correct or sanction inadequate behaviors. In addition, they would fail to serve as models helping the father to adopt more adequate child-rearing behaviors. The modeling pathway, of course, has mostly been pronounced in the social learning framework (Bandura, 1986).

Additional factors that should be included when considering the "isolated" family and social control are neighborhood characteristics and poverty. As in other respects of family development, the case of child maltreatment is very revealing in this respect (e.g., Belsky, 1984). Although child maltreatment is influenced through a variety of factors (e.g., Belsky, 1993), the significance of neighborhood characteristics and poverty have repeatedly been emphasized in favor of a better understanding (and more effective prevention) of this phenomenon (e.g., Steinberg, Catalano, and Dooley, 1981; Garbarino & Kostelny, 1992). Analyzing census and administrative agency data of 177 census tracts in Cleveland, Ohio, a recent study showed that child maltreatment rates were much higher in neighborhoods characterized by impoverishment (Coulton, Korbin, Su, & Chow, 1995). More specifically, as pointed out by these authors, "areas with the highest maltreatment rates were those with the intertwined conditions of poverty, unemployment, female-headed households, racial segregation, abandoned housing, and population loss" (p. 1271).

Instability of neighborhood (measured through the proportion of households that had moved) was also related to higher child maltreatment rates. Almost the same factors that predicted child maltreatment were also capable of predicting the rates of drug trafficking, violent crime, juvenile delinquency, teenage child-bearing, and low birth weight. Although these results confirm the control theoretical framework, the process of how poor neighborhood conditions and poverty produce poor parenting and poor developmental outcomes remains unexplained. A number of recent studies discerned the significance of intrafamily variables as mediators, or at least as moderators, of poverty and neighborhood conditions. For example, Sampson and Laub (1994) showed that family processes (i.e., parental–child attachment, maternal supervision, harsh discipline) largely mediated the effects of the structural context (i.e., family poverty, resident mobility, and others) on delinquency. In the same vein, Conger, Ge, Elder, Lorenz, and Simons (1994), demonstrated that the effects of economic pressure on adolescents' internalizing or externalizing symptoms were completely mediated by their parents' depression, marital conflicts, parent hostility, and parent–adolescent financial conflict. As far as the development of offspring is concerned, the mediating model seems empirically proved. Regarding the parents' behaviors, the empirical findings mentioned above predominantly point to direct environmental effects. However, as assumed when considering the results with respect to social isolation, parents' personal resources could play an important role by interacting with environmental conditions. This issue is addressed in the next section.

## PERCEIVED CONTROL AND THE FAMILY

In contrast to social control, *perceived control*, or *perceived self-efficacy*, is a genuine psychological construct referring to the personal "beliefs in one's capabilities to organize and execute the course of action required to manage prospective situations" (Bandura, 1995, p. 2). The view that such beliefs regulate human psychological functioning, health, and well-being throughout the life span is widely accepted (e.g., Bandura, Cioffi, Taylor, & Brouillard, 1988; Bandura, Taylor, Williams, Mefford, & Barchas, 1985; Cozzarelli, 1993; Flammer, 1990, 1995; Major, Cozzarelli, Sciacchitano, Cooper, Testa, & Mueller, 1990; Schwarzer & Fuchs, 1995). Besides the fact that the family is one of the main contexts where control beliefs develop (Schneewind, 1995), the functioning of the family itsself is assumed to be influenced by the family members' perceived control. In the following, the focus is on the pathways of such influences, mainly considering the effects of parents' perceived control on parenting behaviors and related issues, and therefore continues the discussion on the sources of adequate family functioning.

*Parenting* is widely recognized as a major, long-term task including very different behaviors, such as responsive caregiving (Bornstein, 1995), from the very beginning, which subsequently becomes more and more substituted through understanding, monitoring, guiding, teaching, and supporting the child, while fostering the child's self-management and social responsibility, and facilitating positive relationships with siblings, peers, relatives, teachers, etc. (Collins, Harris, & Susman, 1995). Most parents probably agree on the statement that the parenting task is one of the most complex and most challenging of adulthood. But they also easily confirm that the gratification of being a parent is often undermined by conflictual interactions between parents and children (e.g., Lee & Bates, 1985), requesting strategies to control negative emotions (Dix, 1991). Parenting rarely produces visible short-term results, and rewards are often completely missing. In summary, experiences of contingency and efficacy are rare, and therefore, the *belief* in parenting efficacy as a protective resource against emotional strain (e.g., Cutrona & Troutman, 1986) is not easily developed and maintained. In addition, parenting activities,e.g., helping the child with their schoolwork, playing with them or telling them riddles or stories, are not socially gratified since this is unpaid labor, commonly considered *unqualified* (Ochel, 1989). Regarding parenting in this context, the significance of the marital relationship and of social support become obvious (Belsky, 1981, 1984). In the Berne study of the transition to parenthood, parental coping, measured as perceived capability to manage the everyday tasks of parenting, was strongly dependent on the perceived amount of family conflicts, family cohesion, and support from the spouse (Wicki, in press, a). LISREL analyses prospectively demonstrated that less conflicts, high cohesion, and strong emotional support from the spouse predicted better parental coping in both mothers and fathers. In the Berne study we did not assess the beliefs in one's parenting capabilities but the perceptions based on the actual respective behaviors. Although these constructs are different, social learning and control theory would predict that perceived experiences lead to respective beliefs (Bandura, 1986; Flammer, 1990). These considerations are in line with the results of Cutrona and Troutman (1986), who identified parental self-efficacy as a mediator between supportive interpersonal relationships and maternal postpartum depression, which in turn increases the risk for insufficient parenting (Field, 1995).

Several explanations have been proposed with respect to the positive effects of parental efficacy beliefs. Bugental and Cortez (1988) referred to the role of physiological reactivity when facing a difficult child. They found that physiological reactivity was lower among more efficacious adults compared with less efficacious adults. Bugental, Blue, & Cruzcosa (1989) stressed the impact of inadequate attributions about the controllability of negative caregiving outcomes, which were related to risk for abusive caregiving. Examples for inadequate attributions are general beliefs that the child's disobedience is due to negative intentions and dispositions (instead of also referring to external causes), or that the child fully understands and has control over his negative behavior (Dix, 1991). As extensively outlined by Dix (1991), parenting involves emotional, motivational, and cognitive processes that guide specific behaviors. For example, skillful parenting includes adequate age-related expectations, empathic understanding and guidance of the child, warm, affective communications, and other important aspects. Of course, control beliefs do not cause such processes and actions, but they mediate them, because they help to maintain positive behaviors despite troublesome experiences and emotional strain (Teti & Gelfand, 1991).

## ON THE INTERFACE OF SOCIAL AND PERCEIVED CONTROL IN THE FAMILY CONTEXT— CONCLUSIONS AND PRACTICAL IMPLICATIONS

Recently, Bandura (1995) proposed that parental self-efficacy is a more important resource for parents living under disadvantaged conditions where little social resources are available, e.g., among single parents or parents living in impoverished neighborhoods. This notion refers to the possibility that a personal resource like perceived control could be more important when facing a lack of social resources. Researchers have been more concerned about the distressing effects of social support (besides the positive ones) resulting from the demand to reciprocate received support, since this is more easily done by resourceful individuals than by those who are already overwhelmed facing their own strains, and who do not perceive any opportunity to commit themselves to the concerns of significant others (e.g., Riley & Eckenrode, 1986). Bandura's notion constitutes a reversal of such findings by emphasizing that the worse the social conditions are, the more important it is to maintain parental self-efficacy. This assumption implies an interaction between social conditions and perceived control.

With regard to support programs, it follows that providing instrumental support to distressed families can be problematic if parental self-efficacy beliefs are undermined at the same time. Thus, support programs should attempt to improve the families' ability to *solve their problems themselves*, and act more effectively on behalf of their children. Schorr's (1991) review stressed the role of professionals in successful programs who

> are perceived by those they serve as people they can *trust*, people who *care* about them and *respect* them. Virtually without exceptions, leaders of successful programs emphasize the importance of relationships. They know that *how* services are provided is as important as *what* is provided. (p. 268)

As already discussed above, positive relationships are more likely to exert social control. However, this does not mean that family programs should focus exclusively on intrapsychic processes and parent education, in contrast, they should focus on environmental difficulties, like poor housing conditions or unemployment (McLoyd & Wilson, 1991).

In fact, programs aimed to improve families' housing conditions deserve much more attention in the future than they had in the past, since they focus on environmental factors and on family functioning at the same time. Strong efforts should be undertaken to create safe and stimulating homes and neighborhoods that afford children's social play and explorative behaviors (David & Weinstein, 1987; Moore, 1990). For example, new apartment house construction could include specific common rooms to meet children's and adolescents' specific needs for joint activities (Lang, Mengering, & Harloff, 1988). Again, this is a matter of the interface of social and perceived control.

## REFERENCES

Alwin, D. F., Converse, P. E., & Martin, S. S. (1985). Living arrangements and social integration. *Journal of Marriage and the Family, 47,* 319–334.

Bandura, A. (1986). *Social foundations of thought and actions: A social cognitive theory.* Englewood Cliffs, NJ: Prentice-Hall.

Bandura, A. (1995). Exercise of personal and collective self-efficacy in changing societies. In A. Bandura (Ed.), *Self-efficacy in Changing Societies* (pp. 1–45). Cambridge, MA: Cambridge University Press.

Bandura, A., Cioffi, D., Taylor, C. B., & Brouillard, M. E. (1988). Perceived self-efficacy for coping with cognitive stressors and opiod activation. *Journal of Personality and Social Psychology, 55,* 479–488.

Bandura, A., Taylor, C. B., Williams, S. L., Mefford, I. N., & Barchas, J. D. (1985). Catecholamine secretion as a function of perceived coping self-efficacy. *Journal of Consulting and Clinical Psychology, 53,* 404–414.

Belsky, J. (1981). Early human experience: a family perspective. *Developmental Psychology, 17,* 3–23.

Belsky, J. (1984). The determinants of parenting: A process model. *Child Development, 55,* 83–96.

Belsky, J. (1993). Etiology of child maltreatment: A developmental-ecological analysis. *Psychological Bulletin, 114,* 413–434.

Bornstein, M. H. (1995). Parenting infants. In M. H. Bornstein (Ed.), *Handbook of parenting.* Volume 1. Children and parenting (pp. 3-39). Mahwah, NJ: Lawrence Erlbaum Associates.

Bronfenbrenner, U. (1981). *The ecology of human development.* Cambridge, MA: Harvard University Press.

Bugental, D. B., & Cortez, V. L. (1988). Physiological reactivity to responsive and unresponsive children as moderated by perceived control. *Child Development, 59,* 686–693.

Bugental, D. B., Blue, J., & Cruzcosa, M. (1989). Perceived control over caregiving outcomes. *Developmental Psychology, 25,* 532–539.

Cochran, M. M., & Brassard, J. A. (1979). Child development and personal social networks. *Child Development, 50,* 601–616.

Colletta, N. D. (1979). Support systems after divorce: Incidence and impact. *Journal of Marriage and the Family, 41,* 837–846.

Collins, W. A., Harris, M. L., Susman, A. (1995). Parenting during middle childhood. In M. H. Bornstein (Ed.), *Handbook of parenting.* Volume 1. Children and parenting (pp. 65–89). Mahwah, NJ: Lawrence Erlbaum Associates.

Conger, R. D., Ge, X., Elder Jr., G. H., Lorenz, F. O., & Simons, R. L. (1994). Economic stress, coercive family process, and developmental problems of adolescents. *Child Development, 65,* 541–561.

Coulton, C. J., Korbin, J. E., Su, M., & Chow, J. (1995). Community level factors and child maltreatment rates. *Child Development, 66,* 1262–1276.

Cowan, C. P., & Cowan, P. A. (1992). *When partners become parents.* The big life change for couples. Basic Books.

Cozzarelli, C. (1993). Personality and self-efficacy as predictors of coping with abortion. *Journal of Personality and Social Psychology, 65,* 1224–1236.

Cutrona, C. E., & Troutman, B. R. (1986). Social support, infant temperament, and parenting self-efficacy: A mediational model of postpartum depression. *Child Development, 57,* 1507–1518.

Crockett, L. J., Bingham, C. R., Chopak, J. S., & Vicary, J. R. (1996). Timing of first sexual intercourse: The role of social control, social learning, and problem behavior. *Journal of Youth and Adolescence, 25,* 89–111.

David, T. G., & Weinstein, C. S. (1987). The built environment and children's development. In C. S. Weinstein & T. G. David (Eds.), *Spaces for children* (pp. 3–18). New York: Plenum.

Dix, T. (1991). The affective organization of parenting: Adaptive and maladaptive processes. *Psychological Bulletin, 110,* 3-25.

Field, T. (1995). Psychologically depressed parents. In M. H. Bornstein (Ed.), *Handbook of parenting.* Volume 4. Applied and practical parenting (pp. 85–99). Mahwah, NJ: Lawrence Erlbaum Associates.

Flammer, A. (1990). *Erfahrung der eigenen Wirksamkeit* [Experiencing one's own efficacy]. Bern: Huber.

Flammer, A. (1995). Developmental analysis of control beliefs. In A. Bandura (Ed.), *Self-efficacy in Changing Societies* (pp. 69–113). Cambridge, MA: Cambridge University Press.

Garbarino, J., & Kostelny, K. (1992). Child maltreatment as a community problem. *Abuse & neglect, 16,* 455–464.

Hirschi, T. (1969). *Causes of Delinquency.* Berkeley, CA: University of California Press.

Holtzman, E. H., & Gilbert, L. A. (1987). Social support networks for parenting and psychological well-being among dual-earner Mexican-American families. *Journal of Community Psychology, 15,* 176–186.

Jennings, K. D., Stagg, V., & Connors, R. E. (1991). Social networks and mothers' interactions with their preschool children. *Child Development, 62,* 966–978.

Junger, M., Terlouw, G. J., & Van der Heijden, P. G. M. (1995). Crime, accidents, and social control. *Criminal Behavior and Mental Health, 5,* 386–410.

Laireiter, A., & Baumann, U. (1992). Network structures and support functions—theoretical and empirical analyses. In H. O. F. Veiel & U. Baumann (Eds.), *The meaning and measurement of social support* (pp. 33–55). New York: Hemisphere.

Lang, H.-P., Mengering, F., & Harloff, H.-J. (1988). Zur Sozialwirksamkeit gebauter Umwelt. Eine empirische Studie zum Nachbarschaftsverhalten in einer Neubausiedlung (On the social effects of the built environment. An empirical study on the neighborhood interactions in a new apartment house). *Zeitschrift für Sozialpsychologie, 19,* 63–72.

Le Blanc, M. (1994). Family, school, delinquency and criminality, the predictive power of an elaborated social control theory for males. *Criminal Behavior and Mental Health, 4,* 101–117.

Lee, C. L., & Bates, J. E. (1985). Mother-child interaction at age two years and perceived difficult temperament. *Child Development, 56,* 1314–1325.

Major, B., Cozzarelli, C., Sciacchitano, A. M., Cooper, M. L., Testa, M., & Mueller, P. M. (1990). Perceived social support, self-efficacy and adjustment to abortion. *Journal of Personality and Social Psychology, 59,* 452–463.

Marcos, A. C., & Bahr, S. J. (1995). Drug progression model: A social control test. *International Journal of the Addictions, 30,* 1383–1405.

McLoyd, V. C., & Wilson, L. (1991). The strain of living poor: Parenting, social support, and child mental health. In A.C. Huston (Ed.), *Children in poverty. Child development and public policy* (pp. 105–135). Cambridge, MA: Cambridge University Press.

Moore, R.C. (1990). *Childhood's domain—play and place in child development.* Berkeley, CA: MIG Communications.

Ochel, A. (1989). *Hausfrauenarbeit. Eine qualitative Studie über Alltagsbelastungen und Bewältigungsstrategien von Hausfrauen* (Housewives' work. A qualitative study on everyday strains and coping strategies in housewives). München: Profil.

Riley, D., & Eckenrode, J. (1986). Social ties: Subgroup differences in costs and benefits. *Journal of Personality and Social Psychology, 51,* 770–778.

Rook, K. S. (1992). Detrimental aspects of social relationships: Taking stock of an emerging literature. In H. O. F. Veiel & U. Baumann (Eds.), *The meaning and measurement of social support* (pp. 157–169). New York: Hemisphere.

Sampson, R. J., & Laub, J. H. (1994). Urban poverty and the family context of delinquency: A new look at structure and process in a classic study. *Child Development,* *65,* 523–540.

Schneewind, K. A. (1995). Impact of family processes on control beliefs. In A. Bandura (Ed.), *Self-efficacy in Changing Societies* (pp. 114–148). Cambridge, MA: Cambridge University Press.

Schorr, L. B. (1991). Effective programs for children growing up in concentrated poverty. In A. C. Huston (Ed.), *Children in poverty. Child development and public policy* (pp. 260–281). Cambridge, MA: Cambridge University Press.

Schwarzer, R., & Fuchs, R. (1995). Changing risk behaviors and adopting health behaviors: The role of self-efficacy beliefs. In A. Bandura (Ed.), *Self-efficacy in Changing Societies* (pp. 259–288). Cambridge, MA: Cambridge University Press.

Simons, R. L., Whitbeck, L. B., Conger, R. D., & Conger, K. J. (1991). Parenting factors, social skills, and value commitments as precursors to school failure, involvement with deviant peers, and delinquent behavior. *Journal of Youth and Adolescence, 20,* 645–664.

Steinberg, L., Catalano, R., & Dooley, D. (1981). Economic antecedents of child abuse and neglect. *Child Development, 52,* 975–985.

Teti, D. M., & Gelfand, D. M. (1991). Behavioral competence among mothers of infants in the first year: The mediational role of maternal self-efficacy. *Child Development, 62,* 918–929.

Thoits, P. A. (1992). Social support functions and network structures: A supplemental view. In H. O. F. Veiel & U. Baumann (Eds.), *The meaning and measurement of social support* (pp. 57–62). New York: Hemisphere.

Tietjen, A. M. (1985). The social networks and social support of married and single mothers in Sweden. *Journal of Marriage and the Family, 47,* 489–496.

Weinraub, M., & Wolf, B. M. (1983). Effects of stress and social supports on mother-child interactions in single- and two-parent families. *Child Development, 54,* 1297–1311.

Wicki, W. (1997). *Übergänge im Leben der Familie* (Transitions in the family context). Bern: Huber.

Wicki, W. (in press). The impact of family resources and satisfaction with division of labor on coping and worries after the birth of the first child. *International Journal of Behavioral Development.*

Wicki, W., Dumont, J., & Signer-Fischer, S. (1995). Funktion und Nutzung sozialer, familialer und personaler Ressourcen beim Übergang zur Elternschaft (Function and use of social, family, and personal resources during the transition to parenthood. Technical report.). Forschungsbericht Nr. 1995-4, aus dem Institut für Psychologie der Universität Bern.

# The Cultural Scripts of Control and Individualization: Consequences for Growing Up During Adolescence in Modern Societies

*Helmut Fend*

## INTRODUCTION

The lifespan of every individual is a unique intersection of biological forces, sociocultural opportunity structures and idiosyncratic individual efforts. This truism, well known since Pestalozzi's essay *Nachforschungen* (Pestalozzi, 1938), has been scientifically substantiated in the last hundred years by showing the interaction of biology and culture in human development. The individual person comes into this equation via the concept of action and control. While the biology of human beings is rooted in the evolution of the human species, the sociocultural opportunity structures evolve from human actions and traditions.

In this chapter, I bring together literature substantiating the thesis that the history of Western civilization can be described *as a path from fate to control*. The evolution of the cultural script of control contains the opportunity structures for growing up in modern societies. In a second line of argument I will outline the implications of this modern script of life for the context of development in adolescence. This will figure as the background for the analysis of differential reactions of modern age cohorts to their conditions of life. These reactions are considered to be different in terms of representing pathways to risk or success, thereby representing losers and winners of modern opportunities for self-fulfillment.

## RATIONALITY AND CONTROL

The main reference for the analysis of the evolution of Western civilizations and their being based on the principle of control and rationality is, of course, Max Weber and his investigations into the *sociology of religion* (1920, 1921)

According to Weber, the origins of the culture of Western societies are rooted in religious conceptions of life and man. What is special about the occidental script can only be seen by comparing it with different scripts in different religions. The question there is why here do we find science in the empirical sense, based on technology as a rational way of organizing life.

Weber's great discovery boils down to abstracting two dimensions to locate different approaches to life, resulting from different religions. The first one is the dimension of *control*. In facing hardship, obstacles, desires, and temptations one can react in two different ways: Actively coping with them, striving for fulfillment and satisfaction, or in trying to deny them, to make them ineffective. The other dimension refers to the basic attitude toward the world: to consider it as inherently good or bad, positive or negative.

| | | *Path to salvation* | |
| --- | --- | --- | --- |
| | | *active (asceticism)* | *passive (mysticism)* |
| *Attitude toward the world as a whole* | *Rejection of the world:*<br>*– Driven by conscience*<br>*– Salvation oriented religions* | World control<br><br>Judaism<br>Christianity | Retreat from the world<br><br>Hinduism |
| | *World affirmation:*<br>*– Cosmological-metaphysical world view* | World adaptation<br><br>Confucianism | World contemplation<br><br>Greek metaphysic |

FIG. 29.1. World religions and their implications for control

Against this background, what's the difference between Christianity and other world religions? They represent different ways of regulating life and specific attitudes toward the world.

For Christianity, the world is sinful, and man and his world are out of order. The underlying principle, therefore, is denial of the factual world. However, passive acceptance does not proceed from this. Rather, reshaping this world and reshaping one's self via asceticism leads to salvation.

On the other hand, Hinduism recommends retreat from the world and not world control as a formula against a negative view of this world. In Confucianism and in Greek metaphysics, a more positive estimation of the world comes through. Man only needs to develop an adequate attitude toward this world, and adapt to its circumstances actively. Unlike passivity resulting from rejection and denial of the world in Buddhism and Hinduism, Western man has the mandate to actively govern the world and an obligation to methodically attain self-perfection in this life as a prerequisite for eternal holiness.

Against the background of Christianity, man's striving to attain personal perfection is linked to actively changing the world. Neither passive acceptance nor passive enjoyment are permitted him, rather he is tasked with sanctifying the world. This obligation to actively shape the world gave birth to science. However, its birth had many other roots. The legacy of the ancient period is just as important as the Renaissance which placed man at the center of attention. The Enlightenment, as well as empirical science, can be linked to it. The fundamental result of these "spiritual inventions" was that it led to a strengthening of confidence in the abilities of man to think for himself and to the empirical discovery of the laws of reality. The rational-mathematical method of thinking was of critical importance to the process of generalization of experimental studies. The search for basic laws in nature, even in the universe, that characterizes Western thinking began in ancient times, and was primarily centered around the search for laws governing the motion of stars. An aspect that is taken completely for granted by us today had gained the upper hand, namely the source of knowledge: our own observation and tested experience. Galileo represented the conflict that this provoked between authoritative pronouncement by the church and scientific observation that could be tested. That man's thought could rely on himself and on his observation and not on authority and the pronouncements of others: this epistemological position was the breakthrough made during the Enlightenment. It was generalized into a view of man according to which rational man became the center of truth and responsibility. Kant's famous formula of the Enlightenment as the "exit from self-imposed ignorance" is among the key tenants in the history of Western thought. From the stance of the researching and experimenting man, there developed the natural sciences and technology that have contributed so much to the active control of relationships in life in current civilization. However, this rationalism soon gained a universal character. It also played a role in the shaping of political relationships, in the Just Government of the French and American Revolutions and in the social movements of the 19th century.

All of these, and many other currents too numerous to mention here, have contributed to the development of the cultural code of rationality. It is supposed to lead mankind out of uncertainty, mythological thinking, and superstition. It is the origin of personal responsibility, the mandate to control one's desires and impulses, and the mandate for discipline on the way to worldly perfection. It is the background for the development of enormous amounts of knowledge, of techniques and practices for shaping the world. The concept of control is unthinkable without these traditions and accomplishments.

Personal responsibility in actively coping with one's life is the core of the resulting script of life. Today, it is stripped of its religious origin, whereby this attitude was closely tied to the concept of man acting on behalf of God by executing His will in the world. Rationality and a disciplined way of life, a view of the world directed towards the active control of external conditions, are now positions typical of the Western world. Modern sciences represent the most visible route toward control of the world, which itself has moved over three routes to these current *ways of living*:

1. Control over nature in the sense of manipulating laws for the purpose of achieving desired effects is embedded in our artificial world, aptly called "Leonardo-World"—thus signifying by reference to Leonardo da Vinci an environment, created by man, based on rational insights.
2. Control over one's self in the sense of a disciplined life-style, represents the secular form of transforming the sinful man into a purified human being, acting responsibly and ethically.
3. Control over one's fellow man is the most complicated route toward a rationalization of life. It is embedded in the evolution of laws and jurisdiction and in the evolution of legitimate power.

This development, which, since Weber, has been labeled *rationality* has far-reaching consequences for the conditions of growing up. The more control a human being attains over his environment, the more he himself, as the responsible actor, becomes the center of attention. The more oriented towards the here and now man's interpretation of the world becomes, the less possible it is to think in terms of fulfillment in life after death, and all the more important does it become that *this one life, for which one is personally responsible, will be successful*.

Contemporary theories of "modernity" (see for example Kohli, 1985; Kohli, 1989) label this process of change, which leads to this program of personal development, *individualization*. This concept refers to a development in the history of civilization which has reached a climax in the last few decades and as a result of which the individual has become the central and responsible agency in the shaping of his or her own life. What the individual ultimately wants to achieve in his or her life becomes the central point of reference in the planning and the exercise of responsibility. Assuming a normative allocation of responsibility, whether one succeeds or does not succeed, depends in large measure on the individual themself. Modern man, therefore, is caught between the achievement of control over one's life and the assignment of personal responsibility.

This normative code of being responsible for one's own life and in control of shaping it only had a chance to find acceptance because changes in objective opportunity structures, and the technologies to control it, made it functional to adopt the new lifestyle. Developments in the science of medicine, which made life more secure, as well as developments of democratic political systems and a market economy, have made control possible since they have extended personal choices.

## LONG WAVES OF DEVELOPMENT: FROM TRADITIONAL SOCIETY TO THE MODERN SCRIPT OF CONTROL AND SOCIAL OPPORTUNITY STRUCTURES

The attitudes toward life are embedded in the conditions for survival, which in the last two hundred years, have changed dramatically. The change is commonly labelled as a path from traditional to modern societies.

A vivid picture of traditional life-circumstances is revealed in parish registries dating from the 17th to the 19th century. From these documents it becomes evident how people were continuously threatened by hunger, war, and death during their entire lifetime. Imhof (1988) has analyzed these registries. He provides the following picture:

> Far into the nineteenth century death was highly probable in all phases of life. Fifty percent of newborn children did not live to experience adult life. War, famine, and hunger were omnipresent causes of the decimation of the population. Today, for the majority of the population, death occurs late in life after a long phase characterized by a high degree of security.

Due to a historically unique health care, life has become highly predictable and therefore, subject to planning. In addition, the process of secularization has rendered the consolatory promise of personal fulfillment in eternal life incredible, fulfillment during earthly life attainable, and the goal to pursue.

As has been well documented, the scientific, economic, and social conditions for a predictable life-course began to change in the second half of the 19th century. This may also be the reason why historians like Jacques Le Goff see modern man emerge not earlier than *the end of the 19th century*. At this time, man got control of his life in the modern sense. It became plannable, calculable, and secure (Fritz-Vannahme, 1991, p. 52). Up to this point, the world of Central Europe had been dominated by constant threats to life, by famine, war, and poverty.

The surface phenomena of this social change in living conditions are well known: increasing urbanization, a decrease in child mortality, and connected with this, an increase in life expectancy, expansion of the educational system, development of the welfare state, etc. These developments accompany the basic change in the attitude toward the world from accepting life as fate to controlling life.

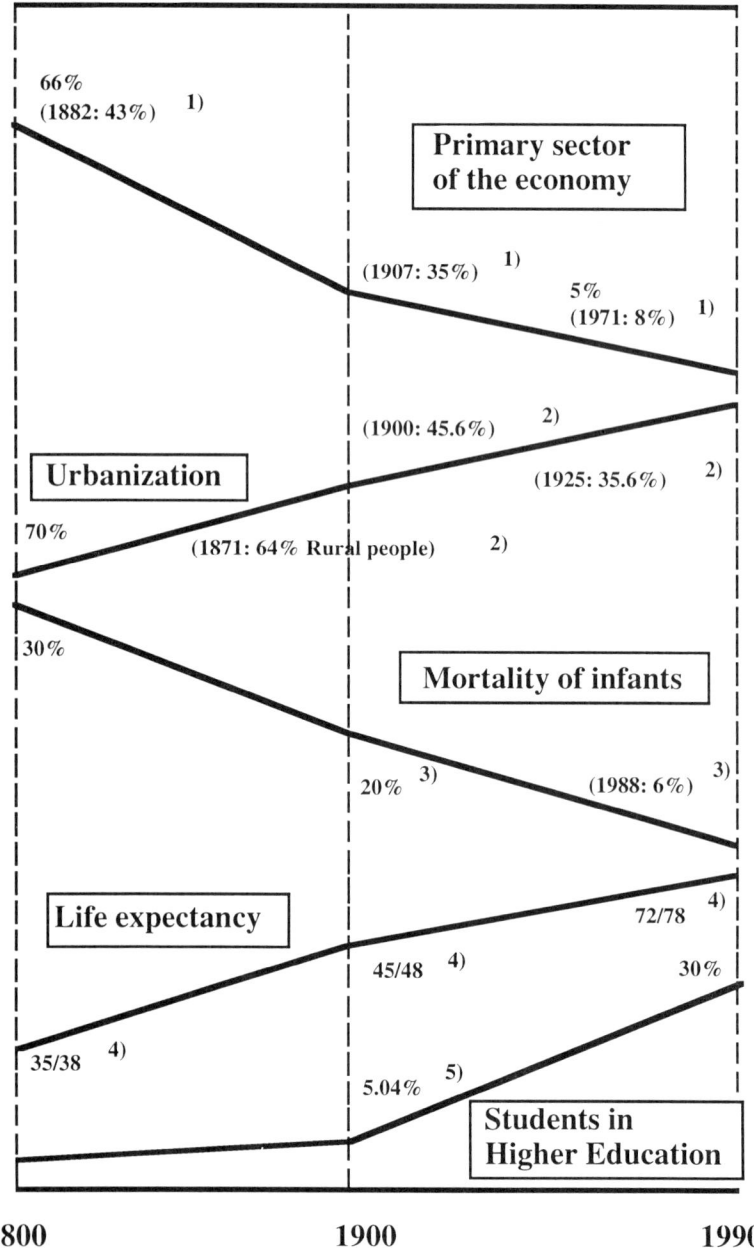

*FIG. 29.2. Socio-economic change, relevant for a life-style of control.*

| | Pre-Modern | Modern |
|---|---|---|
| *Duration of adolescence as a life phase* | Short; biological onset of adolescence between age 15 and 18; early entry into the workforce | Long; biological onset between age 11 and 14; depending on length of training; entry into working life between age 17 and age 30 |
| *Socialization contexts* | Age heterogenous groups; close work relationships between generations | Growing up in age-homogenous groups; peer-groups and small families |
| *Aims of upbringing* | Industry, modesty, frugality; values: strength of character; agreement with views and attitudes of parents, taking one's place in the given social and attitudinal system; moral integrity | Diverse competencies; achievement, qualifications, flexibility; having one's own opinion: ability to act on one's own initiative, and to be responsible for shaping one's own life; best possible realization of individual potential |
| *Methods of upbringing* | Upbringing by means of sanctions in enforcing conformity; participating in small communities and in extended family upbringing with the necessities of life | Methodically arranged experiences; systematic training; upbringing by negotiation and by the exchange or the withdrawal of emotions |
| *System of social control* | Clear authority relations in family, the church, and the school | "Authority," based on the quality of personal relationships; instrumental control in market-relationships |
| *Models for successful and unsuccessful lives* | Preoccupation with life after death; earthly life of modesty and integrity | Self-fulfilment in the sense of an attractive and successful life |

FIG. 29.3. Adolescence as a distinct life span in traditional and modern societies.

## TRADITIONAL AND MODERN SCRIPTS FOR
## ADOLESCENCE: PERSONAL PROJECTS AND CONTROL

The socio-historical changes which were described above have led to a restructuring of the course of life. (Kohli, 1985). Planable phases of *preparation for an occupation, working life,* and *retirement* became a reality. Adolescence as a distinct life span emerged in the last century, as a consequence of changes in the economic sector and as a consequence of attendant changes in the educational system. The prolongment of adolescence through the extension of the period required for professional training is the most important aspect of the institutionalization of adolescence. Today, adolescents experience a period in their lives where their main task is cognitive training, and to determine for their own personal life what they think they are and what they would like to be in the future.

If we were to attempt a typological comparison between the pre-modern and the modern contextual living conditions of adolescents, it might be represented as in figure 29.3.

As figure 29.3 suggests, the transition to modernity is characterized by a profound emancipation of the individual from local, familial, and religious bonds. The spread of paid labor, the abolition of legal restrictions with regard to marriage, the institutionalization of basic civil rights, and the expansion of the educational system contributed to this process. These socio-historical developments opened a wide array for *individual decision making.* It is during adolescence that the individual in modern society is for the first time in his life confronted with diverse options. They constitute a developmental program, which is translated into *age-specific developmental tasks,* such as finding a profession, choosing a marriage partner, choosing a lifestyle, developing a basic intellectual orientation, coping with partial separation from parents, forming intimate relationships with members of the opposite sex. It is not the adolescent's ability to conform to external demands and circumstances which is the primary developmental task, but rather his or her *ability to make good decisions.*

To discover *what one is,* and *what one would like to be* in this world, has become the central task of adolescence, and it is in this process that adolescents first begin to detach themselves from the authority structures of their childhood. This attainment of independence means that external controls weaken and new internal models of behavioral control must be acquired. They have to result from individual aims and norms targeted at idealized new modes of existence. It is in this way that they experience the "script of life in modern societies" (Buchmann, 1989): Fulfillment in an occupation, security in love relationships, and excitement in leisure time. To achieve this, they have to be, above all, in control of their lives and their circumstances.

## THE IMMEDIATE PAST IN EUROPE: THE ACCELERATED PROCESS OF MODERNIZATION

There are many indications that the modern project of rationality and control has experienced an accelerated development in the last 40 years, from 1950 to 1990. Sociologists speak of a second push toward individualization. Therefore, in the second part of this essay, I will concentrate on patterns of social change in the last 40 years and outline the consequences for social constraints and opportunities, for new chances and new dangers in the life span of adolescence, especially for the issue of control.

The data are representative for Central Europe (Fend, 1988; Fleiner-Gerster, Gilliand & Lüscher, 1991), especially for German-speaking areas. In spite of these regional restrictions, we can observe similar changes in all industrialized Western societies.

### Society as a Context for Development in the Last Forty Years

It is well documented that in the last forty years we have witnessed many changes in society. The rise in the standards of living in Western societies is impressive. It can be seen in the equipment with TV, cars, telephones, and so on. They point toward a fundamental change in communication patterns *making residential factors and geographical distances less important.* This should be of even greater importance for rural areas and for the maintenance of family-relationships in the light of mobility and migration.

The expansion of the educational system, and the rise of the welfare state are as well known as the better living conditions. Scientific developments are of great importance, especially those in the communication sector, but also in the medical sector. The greatest change in youth behavior might well be caused by the *development of contraceptives*, which make the process of conception, pregnancy, and child-birth controllable.

The technological and economic changes are accompanied by a shift of cultural values to an enormous extent. They are pinpointed by the dramatic *reduction in church affiliation*, the *changed attitudes toward sexuality*, and the *new work ethic* in which a balance between leisuretime and commitment to work is aspired to (Fend, 1988).

On the whole, social change unmistakably indicates an increase in chances and burdens of individual responsibility.

## The Family: Decline in Good Parenting
## or Change in Locus of Responsibility?

The picture represented by socio-historical changes in the family is thoroughly ambivalent. There are many indications of a new ideal type of a modern family. It suggests that the old authoritarian structures within the family have diminished, and that we can see a change from the *family based on the principle of command to the family based on principles of negotiation* (Van der Linden, 1991). During adolescence, there is indeed a lot to be negotiated, for the traditional age-related norms with regard to what is "normal," what is "early," and what is "late" have collapsed. Values such as obedience and conformity have lost ground in the face of the overriding importance of independence and intellectual ability.

Children play an important role in the "Life-Project" of parents, they are no longer economic factors but part of a fulfilled life of the parents themselves. They no longer need children as economic security for old age. Therefore, the quality of the parent-child relationship has changed dramatically from a authority based one-sided flow of information and support to a relationship of mutuality and equality. Today, *parents learn more from their children* and adolescents than in earlier times. The old authority conflicts between the generations centred around sexuality and ideological debates have become less dramatic (Wagner-Winterhager, 1990). The relationships between parents and their children are acquiring a value in themselves, whereby the quality of these relationships must be cultivated and the maintenance of an enduring relationship from parents to children becomes a normative task for parents (Smollar & Youniss, 1988).

But the indicators of social change within families in the last few decades (for a summary, see Fend, 1988) do not only point to supportive family structures. In the last few years the frequency of differences of opinion in families and the intensity of conflict within the family have both increased. More children show resistance especially in puberty and report that they sometimes even shouted at their parents.

For the same period, there are various hints that, with greater emotional intensity, *the internal stability of the family has decreased*—after a highly stable phase of family life in the sixties. The number of dissatisfied marriage partners has increased, especially the number of dissatisfied women. Compared with other European countries, Germany, with 300 divorced marriages in every 1000, occupies a middle position, comparable with countries like Belgium, Holland, Switzerland and Austria. Distinctly higher divorce rates (over 400 in 1000 marriages) can be found in Denmark, Sweden and England (Hess, 1992).

Overall, changes in the family *enhance* the conscious focus on the *individuality* of children and adolescents and at the same time *diminish security* as to the predictability of social relationships.

## Changes in the School System:
### The Exclusive Value of Individual Achievements

Parallel to the changes in the family we have to mention changes in the school system. In the last few decades, school has become the prime social context for more adolescents for longer periods of time and has, at the same time, become a central agency in planning future life courses for opening up or blocking opportunities. Via the selection process into different educational tracks the educational system regulates access to opportunities for continuing education or employment. Therefore, it has an *increased instrumental significance*. At the same time it has lost ground in the *transmission of values* and as an agent of *moral upbringing* (Leschinsky, 1990).

School culture has conspicuously changed parallel to the stronger *instrumental* attitude toward school on the part of the pupils (Allerbeck & Hoag, 1985; Schröder, 1994). On the other hand, there is now *less social distance* between teachers and pupil, causing problems of discipline. Pupils' demands for personal treatment have become greater (Fend, 1994). Hence there is a peculiar tension between the greater instrumental relevance of the school, and increased student demands for personal relationships and individual treatment.

The expansion of schooling has had a central consequence, which is unanimously confirmed by all socio-historical investigations: The *increase in the importance of the peer group*. In the early 60s, only 16% of adolescents between 16 and 18 were firmly involved in cliques, in the eighties, about 57% reported being firmly integrated in cliques (Allerbeck & Hoag, 1985). Hence, there has been an increase in the significance of the peer context as a socializing agency in adolescence. Thereby, the educational system functions as a facilitating context, breeding resistance toward learning inside its own breast.

On the whole, we are left puzzled about the mainstream of change in schools. On the one hand, achievement orientation is firmly ingrained in the fabric of the modern school. On the other hand, social attachments and narcistic motives grow and flourish within this chilly achievement climate.

## COPING AND DEFENSE IN ADOLESCENT COHORTS

In the course of social change during the last forty years adolescents have received mixed messages what they ought to do and what their lives will be. At the same time, they lived with quite varied opportunity structures.

How did adolescents utilize new opportunities and cope with dangers in growing up in a modern age? Are there relevant socio-historical data, which reveal how adolescents responded to new exigencies of life and agencies of socialization (Rutter, 1980)? Is more affluence accompanied by more well-being and satisfaction, feelings of control and optimistic life-projects?

## Values

Compared with other countries, Germany is in unique situation if one wants to reconstruct social change in behavior, attitudes and values of different generations after World War Two. The so called Shell-studies offer a somewhat difficult but rare database (Jugendwerk der Deutschen Shell, 1977; Jugendwerk der Deutschen Shell, 1981; Jugendwerk der Deutschen Shell, 1985; Jugendwerk der Deutschen Shell, 1992; Jugendwerk der Deutschen Shell, 1997). Even more sophisticated replication studies provide us with additional information about social change in the behavior of young people (Allerbeck & Hoag, 1985; Mansel, 1995; Schröder, 1995).

Looking at cohorts from the fifties to the nineties well-known change-patterns can be validated in several cultural domains. In many investigations the decline in young people's *links with the church* is well documented. At the same time, *sexual norms* have changed drastically. Positive attitudes toward the *legitimacy of premarital intercourse* have increased conspicuously. In general there has been a liberalization of sexual norms in the direction of everything being allowed as long as love is involved. The pattern "fall in love—get engaged—get married" has been replaced by the different pattern "get to know someone—move in with him or her—split up—move in with someone else—perhaps have children—marry" (Nave-Herz, 1994).

These normative changes have not remained without consequences. This becomes clear in investigations which are concerned with the changes in sexual *behavior* themselves. They all show that, in the last twenty years, we have experienced a shift of about three years as far as the age of first sexual experience is concerned. What 19- to 20-year-old's experienced twenty years ago, is today experienced by 15- to 16-year-old's (Clement, 1986; Ludwig Boltzmann Institut für Gesundheitspsychologie der Frau, 1990/91; Neubauer, 1990; Schmid-Tannwald & Urdze, 1983).

The change in the work-ethic is more complicated (Klages, 1984; Noelle-Neumann, 1985; Noelle-Neumann & Piel, 1983). Work remains to occupy a central position in biographical planning strategies of adolescents. Nevertheless, the value attributed to work has changed. On the one hand younger generations expect that work should provide *more opportunities for self-realization*, on the other hand, a greater *equilibrium between work and leisure* is desired. The "readiness to make sacrifices" and to accept things as they are have both diminished, while expectations with regard to self-realization have increased. Young people are less willing to accommodate to given circumstances. Compared with secondary control, primary control is clearly preferred (Flammer, 1990; Flammer, 1993; Flammer, Züblin & Grob, 1988).

If one examines the attitudes toward life of the younger generation we can easily isolate the most important aspects which guide adolescents. They desire a fulfilled life with many friends and, if possible, a steady relationship with a partner of the opposite sex. They desire a job which, above all, should provide security and make it possible for them to make full use of their abilities. Money itself is not as important but there should be enough of it to satisfy the requirements of a lifestyle oriented towards the active exploitation of leisure time. So they long on the one hand for personal integrity, psycho-social health and wholeness, for personal growth and personal freedom, on the other hand, they look for security in intimate relationships and being at home in small social groups. Between these longings for freedom and connectedness, there is inevitably tension.

There is no doubt that the social changes in the structure of the adolescent's life-space favor patterns of personality which are functional for new forms of leading a happy and successful life. This "new personality" is characterized by *flexible internal control systems* which are rooted in a stable ego-ideal and *high resiliency*. Insofar as external control has diminished, internal regulations have become more important. They have to be built up in childhood and adolescence.

## THE PARADOX: RISING WELFARE AND DECLINING SATISFACTION

Very often, we see paradoxical effects between the changing opportunity structures for growing up in adolescence and their subjective representations in different cohorts. Better living conditions are not automatically accompanied by more satisfaction, less problem behavior and optimistic attitudes toward life.

One explanation could run as follows: In times of affluence, as they could be experienced from the sixties to the eighties, questions of primary control regarding a safe economic underpinning for occupational placement fade to the background of thinking. Longings for connectedness and attachment, wholeness and self-acceptance become the focus of attention. But primary control in the domains of social relationships and narcistic satisfaction is very difficult. If young generations invest mainly in these unstructured battle-fields of gains and losses, feelings of helplessness and being a victim increase in probability. These phenomena might explain the unexpected rise in psychosocial problems and risk behavior of adolescents in times of rising standards of living, welfare and economic opportunities. This explanation is part of a more encompassing perspective, described below.

## CONCLUSION

To explain changing generational outlooks, it is evidently necessary to place them in a broad context of social change from pre-modern to modern societies. I have characterized these process as one from fate to control. In closing, I want to come back to this concept to sharpen the picture of changes in growing up today.

The central message to every child and adolescent in the modern age is that he must make as much as possible out of himself and his life. In the process of secularization focusing life toward hell and heaven has vanished. Behavior is not primarily regulated anymore by the consequences for an afterlife but tuned toward the preconditions for earthly fulfillment. A "good life" manifests itself in the spheres of beauty and physical appearance, in exciting experiences, in being loved, achieving recognition and influence, and in models of success and afflu-ence. The consumer aspect, as Bell (1976) critically noted, has clearly entered the foreground. Productive work plays an instrumental background role. Neverthe-less, the modern script of life is one of individual responsibility for one's destiny, is one of personal control and active planing. These standards are universal, the opportunities diversified.

Not all adolescents can cope equally well with the high demands of modern civi-lizations which favor attractive, intelligent, highly flexible, socially secure, and self-confidant personalities. The natural endowments of different individuals, especially the inherited level of intelligence, the physical appearance and tem-perament can put children and adolescents at risk. The economic, social and cul-tural resources of the social class in which one grows up, represent additional factors, which influence the chances for realizing modern aspirations.

Discrepancies between induced aspirations and limited opportunities for meet-ing them are endemic in modern experiences of growing up. Especially in times of economic recession and unemployment, there is a hiatus between economic resources and the goods and services offered in the market. Since the analysis by Merton (1957) we are familiar with the problem which results from the conflict between internalized values and aims and the lack of opportunities for their ful-fillment. The feeling of exclusion and of being "robbed" are coped with in vari-ous ways ranging from self-destructiveness to delinquency, whereby the desired goods are acquired "illegally." Modern society is no longer a society of modesty and frugality. It induces potentially more and more aspirations than should be fulfilled and more demands than should be met.

Against this background Klaus Wahl speaks of the "modernization trap" (1989). By this he refers to the phenomena that in modern times the myth of happiness in a loving marriage and family harmony are universally induced ex-pectations. In the media, attractive people are portrayed as self-confident and autonomous and experiencing self-realization in their job. To live up to these dreams is, however, not equally attainable for all. Some fall short of fulfillment totally. These discrepancies figure high as causes for the pathologies of human beings in modern times, especially those of *self-destruction* and those of outward *attack*.

The *"Modern World"* thus encloses an *"Environment of Growing Up"*. Its most essential characteristic is the included *teleology for becoming a successful and worthy person*. It contains messages and imperatives for the basic attitude toward life: "Make the best of yourself! Enjoy life! Be affluent, important, and attractive!"

This developmental program is ingrained in the highly differentiated social contexts like the family, the school, the peer group and the media outside school. These environments both *translate* and *modify* the central developmental program. The family represents the perspective of the best possible development of *children as a whole*. The school has specialized on the best possible development of the *achievement potential*. The peer group is oriented toward the *negotiation of social attractiveness* and *of equality*. The media transport messages about the *"successful and good life"*.

Groups of winners and losers of the internalization of these aspirations emerge already in childhood and especially in adolescence. To follow their traces, age-cohorts have to be split at least by gender, race and educational level. For instance, the cultural script for adolescent girls is mainly restricted toward "being attractive and nice," of evoking attention. Critics speak of the imprinting of passivity and losing voice and stamina.

These problems as many others can fruitfully be formulated in questions of primary and secondary control, as Flammer pointed out (Flammer, 1990; Flammer, 1993; Flammer et al., 1988). A well-known process may illustrate the way to follow. In modern society, the transition from childhood to adolescence represents for different subgroups differences in the timing of leaving a sheltered childhood. Dreams and realities in occupational choice, in physical attraction and social relatedness begin to clash differently in different subgroups. But all subgroups encounter the same cultural message of omnipotent primary control, making secondary control to a painful process of adaptation to the inevitable. Therefore, adolescence is characterized by the evolvement of a subgroup-specific mix of control strategies. Future research should address this problem, thereby taking into account differences in modalities of handling control-problems. They can be worked on on a imaginary level or on a real-life level. Illusions of control are inevitably connected with blocked avenues of primary control. Therefore, in analyzing growing up during adolescence in modern society it is equally important to concentrate on control in everyday coping and to take into account the dreams and fantasies of the "good life." There interplay constitute the special phenomenologies of being adolescent.

502                                                                FEND

## REFERENCES

Allerbeck, K., & Hoag, W. (1985). *Jugend ohne Zukunft?* München: Piper.
Bell, D. (1976). *The cultural contradictions of capitalism.* (second ed.). London: Heinemann.
Buchmann, M. (1989). *The script of life in modern society. Entry into adulthood in a changing world.* Chicago: Chicago University Press.
Clement, U. (1986). *Sexualität im sozialen Wandel. Eine empirische Vergleichsstudie an Studenten 1966 und 1981.* Stuttgart: Enke.
Conze, W. (1976). Sozialgeschichte 1800–1850. In H. Aubin & W. Zorn (Eds.), *Handbuch der deutschen Wirtschafts und Sozialgeschichte,* (vol. 2, pp. 426–494). Stuttgart: Klett.
Fend, H. (1988). *Sozialgeschichte des Aufwachsens.* Frankfurt: Suhrkamp.
Fend, H. (1994). *Sozialer Wandel, Lehrerleitbilder und Lehreraus- und -fortbildung.* Soest: Landesinstitut für Schule und Weiterbildung.
Flammer, A. (1990). *Erfahrung der eigenen Wirksamkeit. Einführung in die Psychologie der Kontrollmeinung.* Bern: Huber.
Flammer, A. (1993). *Development of Control Beliefs: A stage theory outline.* Paper presented at the VIth European Conference on Developmental Psychology, Bonn.
Flammer, A., Züblin, C., & Grob, A. (1988). Sekundäre Kontrolle bei Jugendlichen. *Zeitschrift für Entwicklungspsychologie und Pädagogische Psychologie, 20(3),* 239–262.
Fleiner-Gerster, T., Gilliand, P., & Lüscher, K. (Eds.); (1991). *Familien in der Schweiz.* Freiburg: Universitätsverlag Freiburg.
Fritz-Vannahme, J. (1991). Die Erfindung der Seele. Ein ZEIT-Gespräch mit dem französischen Historiker Jacques Le Goff. *Die Zeit(16),* 52.
Hess, L. E. (1992). *Changing Familiy Patters in Western Europe: Opportunity and Risk Factors for Adolescent Development.* Unpublished paper.
Imhof, A. E. (1988). *Die Lebenszeit. Vom aufgeschobenen Tod und von der Kunst des Lebens.* München: Beck.
Jugendwerk der Deutschen Shell (Ed.); (1977). *Jugend zwischen 13 und 24. Vergleich über 20 Jahre.* Bielefeld.
Jugendwerk der Deutschen Shell (Ed.); (1981). *Jugend 81. Lebensentwürfe, Alltags-Kulturen, Zukunftsbilder.* Hamburg: Rowohlt.
Jugendwerk der Deutschen Shell (1985). *Jugendliche und Erwachsene 1985. Generationen im Vergleich.* Leverkusen: Leske & Budrich.
Jugendwerk der Deutschen Shell (Ed.); (1992). *Jugend '92.* Opladen: Leske & Budrich.
Jugendwerk der Deutschen Shell (Ed.); (1997). *Jugend '97.* (vol. 12). Opladen: Leske & Budrich.
Klages, H. (1984). *Wertorientierungen im Wandel.* Frankfurt: Campus.
Kohli, M. (1985). Die Institutionalisierung des Lebenslaufes. Historische Befunde und theoretische Argumente. *Zeitschrift für Soziologie und Sozialpsychologie, 37(1),* 1–29.
Kohli, M. (1989). Institutionalisierung und Individualisierung der Erwerbsbiographie. In D. Brock (Ed.), *Subjektivität im gesellschaftlichen Wandel,* (pp. 249–278). München: DJV-Verlag.
Leschinsky, A. (1990). Schultheorie und Schulverfassung. *Deutsche Schule, 82(4),* 390–407.
Ludwig Boltzmann Institut für Gesundheitspsychologie der Frau. (1990/91). *Internationale Studie Jugendsexualität und AIDS 1990/91.* Wien.
Mansel, J. (1995). Quantiative Entwicklung von Gewalthandlungen Jugendlicher und ihrer offiziellen Registrierung. Ansätze schulischer Prävention zwischen An-

spruch und Wirklichkeit. *Zeitschrift für Sozialisationsforschung und Erziehungssoziologie, 15(2),* 101–121.

Merton, R. K. (1957). Social structure and anomie. In R. K. Merton (Ed.), *Social theory and social structure,* (pp. 131–194). New York: Free Press.

Nave-Herz, R. (1994). *Familie heute. Wandel der Familienstrukturen und Folgen für die Erziehung.* Darmstadt: Wissenschaftliche Buchgemeinschaft.

Neubauer, G. (1990). *Jugendphase und Sexualität. Eine empirische Ueberprüfung eines sozialisationstheoretischen Modells.* Stuttgart: Enke Verlag.

Nipperdey, T. (1990). *Deutsche Geschichte 1866–1918. Erster Band: Arbeitswelt und Bürgergeist.* München: C. H. Beck.

Noelle-Neumann, E. (1985). Die altmodischen Tugenden sind es, die den Meinungsführer machen. Ein Wertewandel in die falsche Richtung. *Schulintern* (1).

Noelle-Neumann, E., & Piel, E. (Eds.). (1983). *Eine Generation später. Bundesrepublik Deutschland 1953–1979.* München: K. G. Saur.

Pestalozzi, J. H. (1938). Meine Nachforschungen über den Gang der Natur in der Entwicklung des Menschengeschlechtes. In J. H. Pestalozzi (Ed.), *Sämtliche Werke* (vol. 9).

Rutter, M. (1980). *Changing Youth in a Changing Society.* Cambridge, MA: Harvard University Press.

Schmid-Tannwald, I., & Urdze, A. (1983). *Sexualität und Kontrazeption aus der Sicht der Jugendlichen und ihrer Eltern. (Schriftenreihe des Bundesministeriums für Jugend, Familie und Gesundheit. Bd. 132).* Stuttgart: Kohlhammer.

Schröder, H. (1994). *Jugend und Modernisierung: Strukturwandel der Jugendphase und Statuspassagen auf dem Weg zum Erwachsensein.* Bielefeld.

Schröder, H. (1995). *Jugend und Modernisierung. Strukturwandel der Jugendphase und Statsupassagen auf dem Weg zum Erwachsensein.* Weinheim: Juventa Verlag.

Smollar, J., & Youniss, J. (1988). Adolescents Interpersonal Relationships in Social Context. In T. J. Berndt & G. W. Ladd (Eds.), *Peer Relationships in Child Development,* (pp. 300–316). New York: Wiley.

Van der Linden, F. J. (1991). *Adolescent Lifeworlds. Theoretical and empirical considerations in socialization processes of Dutch Youth.* Amsterdam: Swets & Zeitlinger.

Wagner-Winterhager, L. (1990). Jugendliche Ablösungsprozesse im Wandel des Generationenverhältnisses: Auswirkungen auf die Schule. *Deutsche Schule, 82,* 452–465.

Wahl, K. (1989). *Die Modernisierungsfalle.* Frankfurt am Main: Suhrkamp.

Weber, M. (1920). *Gesammelte Aufsätze zur Religionssoziologie.* (9. Aufl. ed.). (vol. Band I). Tübingen: J. C. B. Mohr (Paul Siebeck).

Weber, M. (1921). *Gesammelte Aufsätze zur Religionssoziologie.* (7. Aufl. ed.). (vol. Band II). Tübingen: J. C. B. Mohr (Paul Siebeck).

# 30

# Domain-Specific Control Beliefs in Literacy and Numeracy vs. Actual Performance Among Adults[1]

*François Stoll*
*Philipp Notter*

## INTRODUCTION

The present contribution investigates the relationship between skill beliefs as domain specific control beliefs and actual performance on the basis of the Swiss results in the International Adult Literacy Survey (IALS; OECD & Statistics Canada, 1995). It discusses the great differences observed between subjective skill beliefs and objective performance scores. It tries to show, that the measurement of skill beliefs has an important function in surveys that measure competences. According to Flammer (1994)

> trust in one's own control or in one's own self-efficacy fulfills an important function in human life. It allows not only appropriate plans for and the execution of behavior but also provides a crucial basis of self-acceptance and self-esteem (p. 18).

In the behavioral areas of reading and arithmetic, that were evaluated in the International Adult Literacy Study, the term skill fits more aptly than control. And in fact, "The concept of control is closely related to the concept of skill. The practice of control requires corresponding skills. If one skill alone is critical, then the terms *control* and *skill* cover the same thing. Thus, skills are prerequisites for control" (Flammer 1990, 21). From this, it follows that one's skill belief is a component of one's control belief.

It is important to look at the function of skill belief in the context of the present investigation. Most studies of control belief focus on the implications of control belief at the individual level. In this study, in contrast, the main interest

---

[1] A first version of this contribution was edited by Katja Herz. The paper was translated by Ellen Russon.

505

is at the population level—population in the statistical as well as conventional sense. Skill beliefs or in this context self-evaluation can have three functions in this study: First, as an economical proxy measure for direct skill assessment, second, as a validation of reference criteria established by experts, and third, as a measure for possible demands for further education in a specific area, as a skill belief neither too low nor too high can be considered a prerequisite for one's readiness to improve one's skill. The present contribution investigates how good self evaluation of skills can fulfill the first two functions in the context of the IALS survey. The underlying problem here is a general problem in the study of control or skill beliefs: What do subjective skill beliefs mean on an objective level and how can a qualitative self-rating of skills be mapped on an objective measure of skills?

## THE IALS PROJECT AND THE MAIN FINDINGS ON SKILL BELIEFS

Close collaboration between seven governments and three international organizations produced the first survey to find out how well people in different countries perform reading tasks that are relevant to their daily lives and to performance on the job (OECD, 1995). The results, which indicate that there is a serious literacy deficit, should help governments understand the problem and devise effective solutions.

Canada, Germany, the Netherlands, Poland, Sweden, Switzerland, and the United States participated in the first round of the International Adult Literacy Survey (IALS), in which a representative sample of people aged 16–65 were successively interviewed and tested in their homes (N in Switzerland = 2,828).

Apart from questions on their personal background the subjects in this investigation were requested to evaluate themselves in terms of their abilities in reading and arithmetic. Subsequently, they were asked to complete a number of reading and arithmetic tasks. The introductory interview contained the following questions, which will serve to operationalize skill beliefs on reading and arithmetic:

* How would you rate your reading skills in French/German for your main job?
* How would you rate your mathematical skills for your main job?
* How would you rate your reading skills in French/German needed in daily life?
* How would you rate your mathematical skills needed in daily life?

Answers: excellent – good – moderate – poor

TABLE 30.1
Skill belief in the Swiss sample (values in percent).

|  | excellent % | good % | moderate % | poor % |
|---|---|---|---|---|
| reading skills at work | 64 | 29 | 5 | 2 |
| in daily life | 65 | 27 | 6 | 2 |
| arithmetic skills at work | 56 | 35 | 8 | 1 |
| in daily life | 57 | 32 | 9 | 1 |

The primary reasons for including these questions on self-assessment of literacy skills in the questionnaire was to verify promising results in a preceding Canadian literacy survey (Statistics Canada, 1991) that showed self-assessment to be a rather good proxy measure of literacy (Centre for educational research and innovation (CERI, 1992).

The results in table 30.1 show that of the participants in the study, 55% to 65% rated their competence in reading and arithmetic as "excellent," while only 1% to 2% rated their abilities as "poor" (table 30.1). What does this self-rating of skills tell us? How does it relate to an objective measure of reading and arithmetic performance?

## SKILL BELIEF IN RELATION TO PERFORMANCE

Actual Performance in reading and arithmetic presents a completely different picture than skill belief, at least if one considers the criteria established by experts in terms of the literacy requirements of the world of work and everyday life. In IALS respondents were given practical tasks requiring literacy skills ranging from understanding instructions on a medicine bottle to finding precise information in a newspaper, to assimilating information from a personnel office memo. Three types of literacy were tested:

- Prose literacy, measuring ability to understand and use information in a text. (In this paper performance of this type will be used as an indicator for *reading literacy*.)
- Document literacy, measuring ability to process information in everyday materials such as tables, schedules and maps. (Performance of this type will not be used in the following because it correlates highly [.92] with the prose scale for the Swiss sample.)
- Quantitative literacy, measuring ability to identify and perform arithmetic operations that arise in everyday reading situations. (In this paper we will call performance of this type *numeracy* or *arithmetic*.)

508                                                    STOLL AND NOTTER

The results on the three types of literacy were expressed on three IRT scales, with scores ranging from 0 to 500, with a mean of about 270 scores, and a standard deviation of about 60 scores.[2] These scales have been divided into five levels of literacy based on the difficulty and cognitive demand of typical test tasks. Literacy level 1 being a level that is deemed definitively not sufficient for life in modern society and level 4 and 5 being excellent levels of literacy. The cutpoint for these levels has been empirically determined based on a model of document and text difficulties developed by Kirsch and Mosenthal, 1992 (Kirsch, 1995).

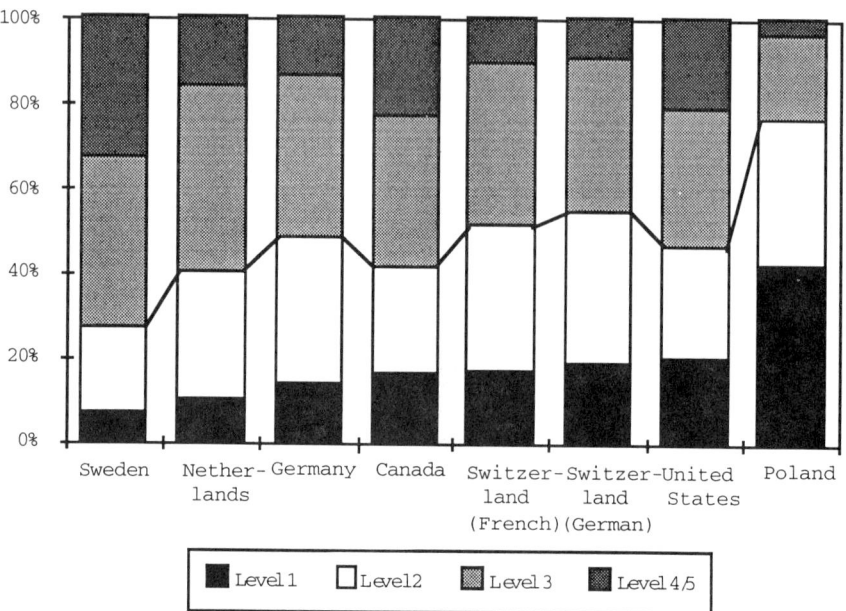

*FIG. 30.1. Distribution of literacy levels prose scale.*

The results for prose literacy in figure 30.1 show that a disturbing proportion of adults in all countries examined have low literacy skills. The results for the other two scales are quite similar and therefore not shown here. For the German- and French-speaking parts of Switzerland it was found that in prose reading approximately 18% of the adults, and in arithmetic, approximately 13%, perform at

---

[2] In the first study with a similar design, the Young Adult Literacy Survey (Kirsch & Jungeblut, 1986) the scale had a mean of 250 and a standard deviation of 50 scores. Through successive linking of the scales in the following U.S. studies (Kirsch, I. S., Jungeblut, A. & Campbell, A., 1992; Kirsch, Jungeblut, Jenkins & Kolstad, 1993) and through linkage of the IALS scales to the American National Adult Literacy Survey scales (Kirsch, Jungeblut, Jenkins & Kolstad, 1993) the means in the different IALS scales are about 270 scores and the standard deviations about 60 scores.

level 1 only, in the view of the experts, a clearly unsatisfactory basic qualification in reading and arithmetic. If we compare these percentages to the 1% or 2%, who consider their skills as poor, one sees a great gap between skill beliefs and actual performance. If one looks also at level 2, a level still considered unsatisfactory by the experts, between 40% to 50% of the adults in Switzerland perform at level 2 or lower, but only 7% to 10% consider their skills in reading or arithmetic as moderate or poor.

Although the distribution of participants' skill belief and their performance as judged by the experts are widely different, one has to bear in mind that this is not a direct comparison of subjective skill beliefs and objective performance scores. It is actually a *comparison* of skill beliefs and an *interpretation* of the objective scale by experts, expressed in levels of literacy. The objective performance scale as such does not tell us very much, as most skills can reasonably be measured in such a way as to yield a normal distribution of scores.

Between the objective scores of performance and the skill beliefs there are very clear relations, which show without doubt that participants' self evaluations were not unfounded. Those subjects who rated themselves better also achieved better mean scores than those participants who rated themselves poorer as shown in figure 30.2. It is just that performance achieved does mostly not measure up to the level of performance as defined by the experts corresponding to the skill beliefs. In figure 2 only skill belief for reading on the job are shown, as skill belief for reading on the job and in daily life were practically identical. In figure 30.2 the vertical lines at scores 225, 275 and 325 indicate the critical scores between levels 1, 2, 3, and 4, respectively, in the performance scales. Because the percentage who rated their skills as poor is very low, they are grouped in figure 30.2 and subsequently together with those who rated their skills as moderate.

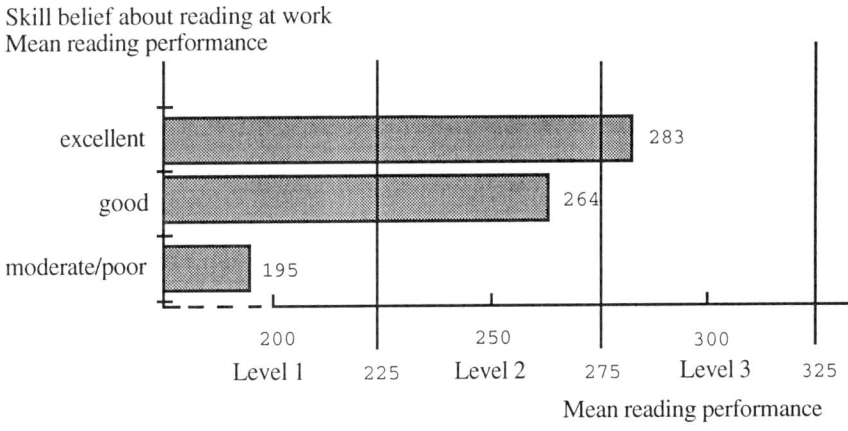

Skill belief about reading at work
Mean reading performance

excellent ............ 283
good ............ 264
moderate/poor ... 195

200   Level 1   225   Level 2   275   Level 3   325
300
Mean reading performance

*FIG. 30.2. The relation between skill belief about reading at work and mean reading performance.*

The following relations also support the assumption that the skill belief of the subjects has some legitimation.

*Gender:* Women showed slightly better performance on the prose literacy scale than men, while men's scores on numeracy were higher than those of women (OECD, 1995, 1983). This is also the case also when we control for level of education (OECD, 1997, figure 30.1).

In skill belief, very little differences are found between women and men, but their direction is the same as the small differences in performance: for women, 67% rate their reading skills as excellent versus 62% percent for men. Likewise, 59% of the men rate their numeracy skills as excellent versus 52% of the women.

*Level of education.* The higher the level of schooling of a participant, the higher both their average performance and their skill belief. Here again, skill belief and performance correspond in direction.

*Age.* There is an inconsistent finding with reference to age. In Switzerland, as in the other countries, performance tends to decrease with increasing age (OECD, 1995, 1981). The opposite is true of skill belief. The percentage of very high skill belief is particularly high in the group 46 to 55 years of age (70%). The high self-evaluation, which is true of all age groups, is thus even more marked in older age groups. And with this, the difference between skill belief and performance becomes even greater.

## SEEKING TO EXPLAIN THE FINDINGS

Very high (and often unrealistically optimistic) skill beliefs have been found for the most varied areas of competence. Investigations which have demonstrated this phenomenon include the abilities and achievements of driving skill (Groeger & Grande, 1996), athletic competence (Dunning, Meyerowitz & Holzberg, 1989), school achievement (Mabe & West, 1982) and performance on the job (Meyer, 1980; Moser, Donat, Schuler, Funke, & Roloff, 1994). Cross (1977) even found that 94% of college professors report that their performance is above average. Imagine how very below-average the performance of the remaining 6% would have to be! The authors of such studies usually describe the reasons for such distortion as "self-serving" (Dunning et al., 1989) or "self-preserving" (Groeger & Grande, 1996). In view of the extent of distortion in our study, however, we can no longer speak of self-preserving exaggeration; the degree of distortion seems to border on the ridiculous. But this would be going too far, as the answers of thousands of subjects in several industrialized countries must be approached seriously. Moreover, we must not ignore the fact that the experts, in order to evaluate performance in reading and writing, and subjects, in order to rate their own performance *prior to* performing the reading and arithmetic tasks, must in all probability have used very different reference points or experiences.

How did the experts evaluate the reading performance? The method used by the experts was, on the one hand, content-analysis, whereby the choice of items included certain everyday subjects and previously defined cognitive operations and familiar types of text; on the other hand, experts' procedure to classify test tasks and subjects was based upon item response theory, in order to assure comparability of the results for different languages (OECD, 1995; Kirsch & Mosenthal, 1990). Because the experts used distances between the competence levels corresponding to a fixed score interval on a scale defined by mean and standard deviation, their evaluations automatically resulted in a corresponding distribution of competence levels in the international population. Such a distribution does not, however, tell us anything about the critical competence level which would be required in this area for appropriate control. To find this, experts can merely base themselves upon the face-validity of the test tasks used. So the experts interpretation of the objective scale is as much open to questions as the subjective skill beliefs.

How did the subjects evaluate their reading ability? In order to rate their abilities, subjects most probably fall back upon their experience in everyday life. It is very likely that they experience their own reading ability at work and in daily life as relatively satisfactory. In contrast to the researchers, subjects would not likely compare themselves to the anonymous average population, nor would it occur to them, when making a rating of their competence, to think of the type of text with which they are seldom confronted or which they can easily avoid. Therefore, as they form an opinion of their skills based on their experience, their skill belief is correspondingly high. On the other hand, this experience of the subjects can serve us to make an economical estimate of how high reading skills must be to be more or less adequate in our society.

To verify these assumptions, we can utilize information from the IALS study found in the responses to the questions on the frequency of reading certain types of texts at work and on any limitations experienced in job opportunities. The questions on the frequency of reading tasks at work may be seen as a subjectively experienced feature of the work place. Although only frequency and not difficulty of the texts is considered, these items serve as a rudimentary measure of the demands of a particular work place on reading competency. Out of the frequency of reading various types of text at work, a reading frequency scale was formed, and quartiles were established on the basis of the distribution in the total sample. Figure 30.3 shows the relation among reading skill belief, reading competence and reading frequency quartile. It appears that there is a relation between skill belief and both measured performance and demands of the work place, as expressed by reading frequency. Subjects who express a low skill belief are found mainly in competence level 1. Of these, 32% rate their reading ability as moderate or poor. In terms of work place reading demands, it can be seen that persons with low skill belief work mostly in jobs which have low reading demands. It is conceivable that particularly with low competence, skill belief will worsen with increasing demands, as abilities would be called into question again and again. This is, however, not shown in our data. In part, this could be due to the very limited operationalization of the demand level of the work place, but in the main

512                                                      STOLL AND NOTTER

the reason is most probable that one's "current" job is, after all, the result of years or decades of selection and socialization processes (see Semmer & Schallberger, 1996). This means that for most subjects, their skill belief is not simply based upon the reading demands at work, and success or failure at meeting them, but rather that competence and skill belief themselves have perhaps determined their job type and level and thus the demands that are encountered. This could also explain, why skill beliefs increase with age, even though performance decreases, as the probability of an adequate match between skills and skill beliefs of the individual and skill demands of the job increases with time.

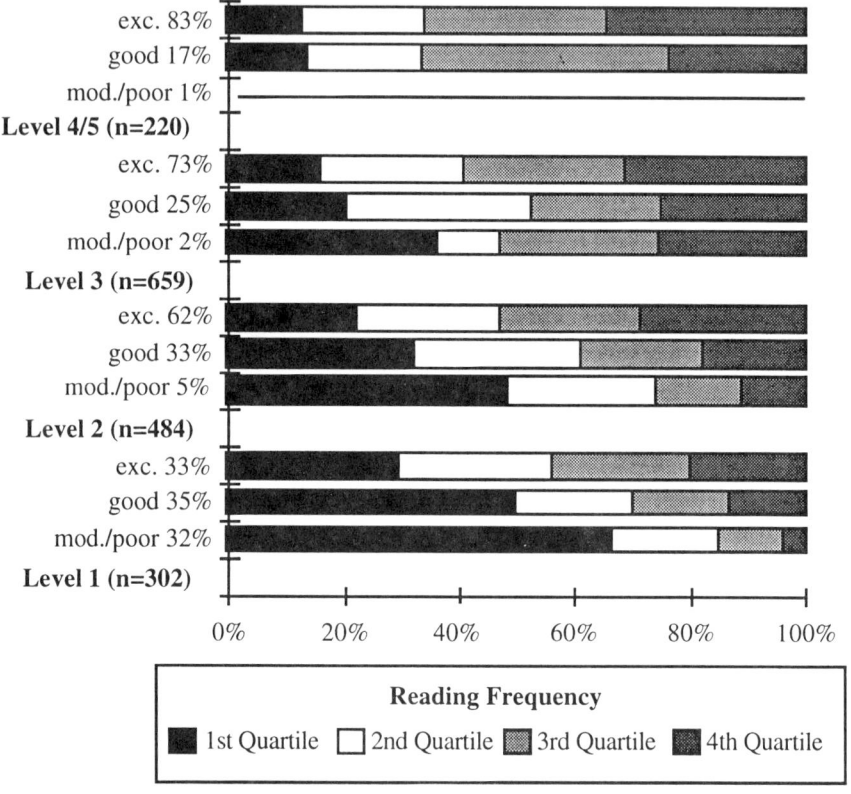

FIG. 30.3. Self-rating, reading frequency, and reading performance (prose).

Similar results are yielded by the questions regarding limitations in one's work career due to the competences in reading and arithmetic. Assuming content validity of the reading and arithmetic tests, we would expect persons showing competences at levels 1 and 2 to have experienced considerable limitations of job opportunities. The following questions tapped limitations experienced by the subjects:

To what extent do your reading skills in German/French limit your job opportunities—for example, advancement or getting another job?
To what extent do your mathematical skills limit your job opportunities—for
example, advancement or getting another job?

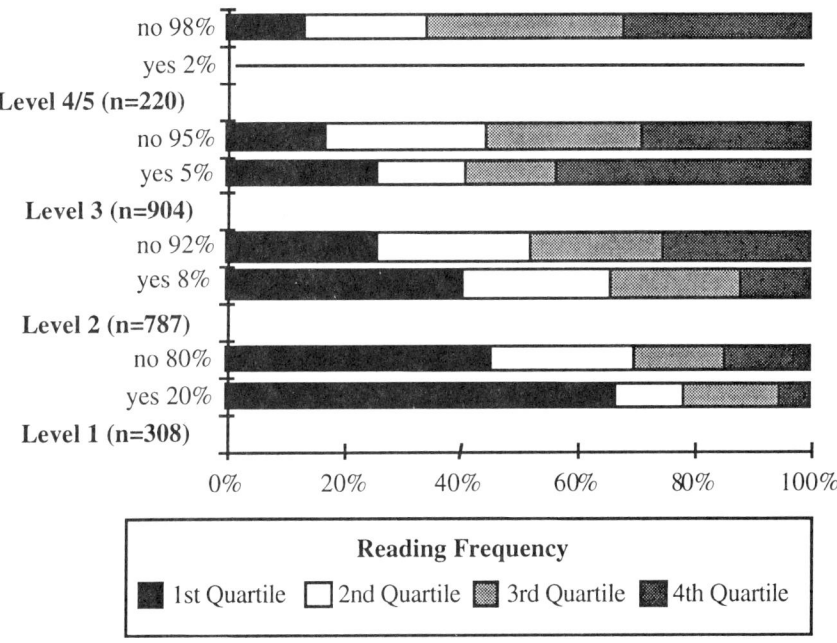

*FIG. 30.4. Perceived job limitations, reading frequency, and reading performance (prose).*

The extent of limitation experienced (and admitted to) is very low. With regard to competence in both reading and arithmetic, 92% of the subjects report
that they do not experience any limitation due to insufficient competence in these
areas. Figure 30.4 shows the relation among limitations experienced, reading
competence, and reading frequency at work. The same main relations are found as
with self-ratings of reading competence. Again, it is mainly subjects with a
reading competence level of 1 who report that their job opportunities are limited
by their reading skills (20%).
In general, however, competence self-ratings are probably in part determined
by the very fact that subjects have not experienced limitations of their job opportunities caused by their levels of reading competency.
To summarize, firstly the findings above confirm the assumption that subjects orient themselves at their daily life when self-evaluating their skills. Secondly, the great difference between competence levels 1 and 2—both in self-rating
and in experienced limitation of job opportunities—suggests that the borderline

between satisfactory and insufficient competence in reading and arithmetic in our society lies between these two levels. This stands in contrast to the opinion of the experts, who set the cut-off point between levels 2 and 3 (OECD & Statistics Canada, 1995). "Satisfactory" competence is to be understood here as that level below which reading and arithmetic skills will lead to problems in everyday life and not in any sense as the desirable level of competence. Actually already the mere figures derived from the interpretation of the scale by the experts provoke some questions. To maintain that for instance 40% to 50% of the Swiss population have insufficient skills in reading or arithmetic for their daily live is a daring contention. Are they unhappy? Are they poor? Apparently they mostly live a decent live and don't seem to be hampered by their *insufficient literacy skills*. Of course in the perspective of the economical and technical development the experts may be right, that people with such levels of literacy skills will increasingly encounter problems in their daily life.

A possible limitation of these findings could result from a social desirability effect. There are some indications of this when subjects who speak German or French (Swiss languages) are compared to subjects who speak a foreign language. We assume that it is easier for a foreign-language speaking person to admit having reading problems in German or French than for a native speaker of French or German. The expectation that a French or German native speaker can read French or German texts is self-understood, while foreign-language speakers may more readily admit to have difficulties in this area.

*TABLE 30.2*
*Skill belief for reading ability (in daily life) in French or German*
*by foreign-language speakers and French/German speakers.*

|  | Foreign-language speakers, Level 1 | French- and German speakers, Level 1 | Other Levels |
|---|---|---|---|
| excellent | 12% | 51% | 70% |
| good | 29% | 36% | 26% |
| moderate | 36% | 12% | 4% |
| poor | 23% | 1% | 0% |
| Total percent | 100% | 100% | 100% |
| Total number | 162 | 222 | 2121 |

There is indeed a great difference between foreign-language speakers and French, respectively German native speakers at the lowest literacy level 1 with regard to their skill belief as shown in table 30.2. Of the foreign-language speakers at the lowest literacy level, 60% rate their reading abilities as moderate to poor in contrast to 13% of French/German speakers with the same literacy level. These findings support the hypothesis that in stated skill beliefs about reading there is also a social desirability effect at work.

## CONCLUSION

We have seen that skill belief, despite a massive ceiling-effect, demonstrates meaningful, performance-oriented tendencies. In the sense of criterion or construct validity, this confirms the significance of skill belief. But why are the evaluations by the researchers so very much lower than the self-evaluations of a representative sample of people living in Switzerland—and, by the way, in other industrialized countries? As mentioned, subjects in the study and the experts probably utilize very different reference points in their evaluations of reading ability. While subjects base their skill belief on their experience in everyday life and on the job, experts base their evaluations upon an analysis of the test tasks, the distribution of competence in the population and the face-validity of the tasks. This demands a closer look.

Flammer and Grob (1994) mentioned three sources of the phenomenon of unrealistically optimistic self-ratings: "This unfavorable discrepancy between reality and conviction may have various causes: (a) Persons having less control belief tend to selectively perceive failure more than success. (b) Depending on their previous experience, people evaluate the same experiences as either successes or failures. (c) People tend to remember those personal experiences which correspond to their current control beliefs." (p. 18). In our case, all of these three possibilities may play a part in the findings. There are many adults in our society whose mastery of reading and arithmetic is poorer than required by the curriculum of the public schools, but they often develop a number of subtle strategies which allow them to avoid failure in these areas—through imitation, listening, smiling helplessness or forced division of labor (a calendar recently quoted that "He who cannot read dictates"). Through avoidance of difficult tasks in reading or arithmetic, a person may achieve a feeling of success in other tasks, and it is on this that their high self-ratings base. People do not compare their abilities, like the educational specialists, with the total population, but rather only in terms of the demands they take on and master. Apart from these strategies of the individuals to avoid reading failures there are probably also strategies of the society or parts of the society to avoid communication failures caused by poor reading competence. In Swiss economy for instance, in certain branches the majority of workers are foreigners often from different nations, so in these branches communication cannot rely on the written word. These social strategies reinforce the individual strategies. After all the "new" fact of poor reading competences of large proportion of the population may be not so new on the work-place.

The effect of social desirability lends additional reinforcement. It is certainly particularly difficult to admit—to oneself and to others (in this case unknown strangers)—that one can read and do arithmetic only moderately to poorly. An adult is simply supposed to be able to read "well" or "excellently." The differentiation between foreign-language speakers and French/German speakers gave indications of this phenomenon. Foreign-language speakers in the lowest reading level rate their own abilities so much worse and in the same time more realistic than do French or German speakers. This difference in competence self-ratings may also be connected to the fact that foreign-language speakers are much more conscious of the language of the country, and thus of reading problems. This would in turn be related to the fact that French or German speakers develop more strategies in order to avoid failure in the area of reading, while foreign-language speakers may endure failure without serious threats to their self-esteem.

But there is something else. The scale of multiple choices from poor to excellent may be insufficiently or merely idiosyncratically anchored through the specifications at work and in daily life. Subjects need not remember what it was like to fill in their last tax return according to the instructions, to read the most recent voting issues or to understand the manual that came with their coffee machine on monthly servicing. Questions of this type pertain to concrete experiences and yield more concrete, case-specific evaluations of one's own abilities.

Accordingly, questions on skill belief should a) not leave too much room open for interpretation, but refer to concrete activities, and b) avoid expressions which are obviously threatening to self-esteem (such as "I rate my reading ability as poor").

In spite of these difficulties with self-ratings, there are reasons of some weight for continuing to use self-evaluations. Reading competence is self-understood in industrialized countries—almost as much so as the ability to walk. It would not be surprising if many more than 90% of the active population were to rate their walking ability as good to excellent. However, it would be possible to develop an objective walking scale, taking into account speed and endurance for example, on which the population would show a normal distribution, but this scale would hardly be the appropriate means of judging the every day competence of the population. On the other hand, to develop a criterion-oriented test, the criterion would have to be known. The attempt to determine, objectively and empirically, the societal demands on reading competence—not for one specific group, but for the entire population—would be a difficult undertaking indeed. On this background, self-ratings present an inadequate, but economical and rational alternative, even though it is not a good proxy measure of literacy it self. Furthermore, one must remember that experts themselves usually are "experts" in the ability they are to evaluate, and that this has an effect not only on their own skill belief, but also on the expectations on competence they hold for others. The only control of this "expert effect" can be objective competence measurements on the one hand and subjective skill belief on the other. Subjective skill beliefs and the interpretation of objective scores by experts may be seen as necessary upper and lower bounds of confidence or uncertainty.

## REFERENCES

Centre for educational research and innovation (CERI) (Ed.). (1992). *Adult illiteracy and economic performance*. Paris: OECD.

Cross, P. (1997). Not can but will college teaching be improved. *New directions for higher education*, 17, 1–15.

Dunning, D., Meyerowitz, J. & Holzberg, A. (1989). Ambiguity and self-evaluation: The role of idiosyncratic trait definitions in self-serving assessments of ability. *Journal of Personality and Social Psychology, 57,* 1082–1090.

Flammer, A. & Grob, A. (1994). Kontrollmeinungen, ihre Begründungen und autobiographisches Erinnern. *Zeitschrift für experimentelle und angewandte Psychologie, 41,* 17–38.

Flammer, A. (1990). *Erfahrung der eigenen Wirksamkeit. Einführung in die Psychologie der Kontrollmeinung.* Bern: Huber.

Groeger, J. A. & Grande, G. E. (1996) Self-preserving assessment of skill? *British Journal of Psychology, 87,* 61–79.

Kirsch, I. S. (1995). Literacy performance on three scales: definitions and results. In OECD & Statistics Canada (Eds.), *Literacy, economy and society* (pp. 27–53). Paris: OECD.

Kirsch, I. S. & Jungeblut, A. (1986). *Literacy: profiles of America's young adults.* Princeton, N. J.: National Assessment of Educational Progress.

Kirsch, I. S., Jungeblut, A. & Campbell, A. (1992). *Beyond the school doors: The literacy needs of job seekers served by the U. S. Departement of Labor.* Washington, D. C.: U. S. Departement of Labor.

Kirsch, I. S., Jungeblut, A., Jenkins, L. & Kolstad (1993). *Adult literacy in America: A first look at the results of the National Adult Literacy Survey.* Washington, D.C.: National Center for Education Statistics, U. S. Departement of Education.

Kirsch, I. S. & Mosenthal, P. B. (1990). Exploring document literacy: Variables underlying the performance of young adults. *Reading Research Quarterly, XXV,* (1), 5–30.

Meyer, H. H. (1980). Self-appraisal of job performance. *Personnel Psychology, 33,* 291–295.

Moser, K. Donat, M., Schuler, H. Funke, U. & Roloff, K. (1994). Validität der Selbstbeur-teilung beruflicher Leistung: eine Untersuchung im Bereich industrieller Forschung und Entwicklung. *Zeitschrift für experimentelle und angewandte Psychologie, 3,* 473–479.

OECD & Statistics Canada (eds.). (1995). *Literacy, economy and society. Results of the first International Adult Literacy Survey.* Paris: OECD.

OECD & Statistics Canada (eds.) (1997). *Literacy skills for the knowledge society. Further results from the International Adult Literacy Survey.* Paris: OECD.

Semmer, N. & Schallberger, U. (1996). Selection, socialisation, and mutual adaptions: Resolving discrepancies between people and work. *Applied Psychology: An International Review, 45 (3),* 263–288.

# 31

# Using Employee Opinion Surveys to Identify Control Mechanisms in Organizations[1]

*Peter M. Hart*

*Alexander J. Wearing*

## INTRODUCTION

Although control is a central concept in the study of human factors, and an important variable in the investigation of individual differences, it has been largely ignored in the field of organisational behavior. One reason for this apparent disregard may be that few usable models are readily available that indicate how control structures may be measured and implemented. The goal of this chapter is to show (a) how data from employee opinion surveys (EOSs) can be used to develop a model of the operation of an organisation that (b) indicates which control procedures or managerial interventions are likely to be effective in changing the level and/or quality of the output of that organization. Accordingly, we work through three concrete examples that illustrate the 'nuts and bolts' issues involved in constructing specific models of organisations that indicate what interventions are likely to be effective in managing their 'bottom line' variables.

### Control: An Invisible Presence

Control is woven into every moment that we live, and and is part of each action that we take. We are cybernetic beings, and so control is a fundamental and continuing component of our lives, both as managers of organisations and as individuals. Despite its pervasiveness, however, textbooks of organisational behaviour usually include only scattered references to control.

Although the word itself may make only cameo appearances, related notions play a significant role in the study of organisations. Terms like *development*, *change*, and *transformation* are central in texts of organisational behaviour. Each depends upon the ability to exert control. Why might it be that the presence of control is invisible? One reason may be that our 'working model' of the world is

[1]This research was supported by a National Health and Medical Research Council Public Health Fellowship (Grant No. 954208). The authors made an equal contribution to this chapter, and the order of authorship was determined alphabetically.

an equilibrium one; things should stay as they are unless an external disturbance upsets them.

Consider the task facing the manager of an organisation. A significant part of it is either to deal with events and interventions that threaten the performance and stability of the organisation, or to create interventions that will lift performance to a higher level while maintaining its stability. The term *control*, on the other hand, connotes continuous change and thus continuous regulation.

Continuous regulation creates a problem for a manager in that the application of control implies both precise measurement and quantitative relationships between the variables in the system. In the study of organisations, one often finds careful measurement of the attributes of an organisation, but the descriptions of relationships between concepts and variables are usually only qualitative.

## The Managers' Models:
## From The Intuitive To The Explicit

Given that managers need to control their organisational environment, every manager needs a model of the causal relationships that link the variables in the system for which he or she is responsible. Without this model, it is difficult to understand and deal effectively with change. Currently, the causal models that are commomly used derive from the 'mental models' of consultants and managers These are usually based upon some combination of organisational and human resource management theory, knowledge of the company and its particular situation, their own experience, and their preferred methods of operating. Whatever the virtues of these mental models of how an organisation works (and for the perceptive and experienced these models may be largely accurate), they are still intuitive, not quantitatively precise, and probably difficult to communicate to others except in a very general sense. Moreover, intuitive models can rarely account for the full complexity of organisational systems, particularly when looking at the causes and consequences of change in a single variable that is embedded within a large system of other variables. Models abound, see for example Howard & Associates (1994), that attempt to represent dynamic relationships, but in general they do so in an abstract, non-quantitative way so that the reader is left with a schematic representation that provides only limited policy guidance. In sum, more precise quantitative models (a) provide a means for explicitly testing competing causal hypotheses, (b) control for the effects of extraneous variables, (c) facilitate the forecasting and cost benefits analyses that should guide organisational change, and (d) provide a means for understanding the complexity of change and its consequences. We present such quantitative procedures below.

## Organizations Need both State and Change Information

Organizational effectiveness is determined in large part by the quality of managerial decision making, and this in turn depends upon the information provided to the decision makers. We may distinguish two kinds of information. The first kind is about the *state* of an organisation, sometimes called structural, or static information. Organization charts, balance sheets, perceived quality of management, information about stocks, or levels of stress and morale are examples of static information. While useful in providing information about a single variable in isolation from all other variables, this type of information tells us nothing about the relationships between the variables and, more importantly, whether or not these relationships can be considered as causal. To formulate policy, or exercise effective control, it is important to understand the causal relationships between the variables. For example, although it is useful to know how satisfied employees are with different aspects of management, it is much more useful to know how changes in various aspects of management are related to change in different aspects of employee or company performance.

Thus the second kind of information is about processes of *change*, or dynamic information. Examples are graphs of weekly sales as a function of advertising expenditure plotted over a quarter. Because managers need to understand change, dynamic information is fundamentally important to them. They need to know how change in one variable results in changes in other variables, indeed, how change in one part of the system causes changes in the rest of the system.

## DETERMINING CAUSAL STRUCTURE: SOME WORKED EXAMPLES

To illustrate the importance for policy and strategic decision-making of knowing how different variables are related to one another, we shall present three worked examples. The purpose of this nuts and bolts approach is to make the practical utility of so-called *causal modeling* clear to those readers who are involved in issues of organisational control, but are not familiar with structural equation modeling. From the outset, we should clarify our use of the term *causal*. In most situations, employee opinion surveys provide only a snapshot of the organisation. This is because they provide information that has been collected at a single point in time. Accordingly, it is only possible to use this information to develop and test theoretical causal models; models that are consistent with a causal theory about how the organisation functions. To examine actual causation, it is necessary to analyse information that has been collected on two or more different occasions (e.g., Kessler & Greenberg, 1981; Magnusson, Bergman, Rudinger, & Torestad, 1991; Menard, 1991).

## EXAMPLE 1: DETERMINING THE JOB SATISFACTION OF POLICE OFFICERS

We begin with a simple example taken from a project designed to investigate the determinants of the job satisfaction among police officers. This project was concerned with understanding how police officers' personality characteristics (neuroticism and extraversion) and coping styles (problem and emotion focused coping), as well as their positive and negative work experiences (police hassles and uplifts), contribute to job satisfaction. Data were obtained from 330 police officers, and the sampling procedure has been described elsewhere (Hart, Wearing & Headey, 1993; 1995).

## Correlational Analysis

The simplest way in which to look at the relationships between these seven variables is with a correlation matrix (see table 31.1). Although these correlation coefficients provide us with information about the *direction* (positive or negative) and *strength* of the relationship between any two variables, they do not tell us how the system of variables operates as a whole. The correlation between any two variables may to be due to their 'natural' or 'true' relationship, but may also be due to their joint dependence on other variables. For example, the correlation of -.25 between Emotion-Focused Coping and Job Satisfaction is statistically significant, and suggests that these two variables are inversely related; the more police officers use emotion-focused coping, the less their job satisfaction (or vice versa). As shown below, however, this relationship is spurious because it is due to the effects of other variables. There is no direct relationship between Emotion-Focused Coping and Job Satisfaction; the correlation merely reflects their joint dependence on other variables such as Neuroticism.

*TABLE 31.1*

*Pearson product-moment correlation matrix showing the relationships between personality, coping, work experiences, and job satisfaction among police officers.*

| Variable | | 1 | 2 | 3 | 4 | 5 | 6 | 7 |
|---|---|---|---|---|---|---|---|---|
| 1. | Job satisfaction | 1.00 | | | | | | |
| 2. | Police hassles | -.47 | 1.00 | | | | | |
| 3. | Police uplifts | .38 | .03 | 1.00 | | | | |
| 4. | Emotion focused coping | -.25 | .37 | .11 | 1.00 | | | |
| 5. | Problem focused coping | .02 | .22 | .33 | .46 | 1.00 | | |
| 6. | Neuroticism | -.37 | .36 | -.07 | .37 | .05 | 1.00 | |
| 7. | Extraversion | .22 | -.03 | .23 | .07 | .25 | -.24 | 1.00 |

*Note.* $N = 261$. Correlations are significantly different from zero at the .05 level if the absolute value of the correlation is greater than .12.

## Multiple Regression Analysis

Multiple regression analysis (given certain assumptions) informs us about the unique relationship between each predictor variable (e.g., police hassles) and the dependent variable, in this case job satisfaction. The standardized beta coefficients derived from this analysis also enable us to determine the relative importance of the different predictors. For example, police hassles with a beta of -.39 is a stronger predictor of job satisfaction than is neuroticism with a beta of -.15. The analysis reported in table 31.2 suggests that police hassles is the strongest determinant of job satisfaction, followed by police uplifts and neuroticism. The nonsignificant beta coefficients for emotion-focused coping, extraversion and problem-focused coping suggest that these variables contribute neither positively nor negatively to job satisfaction, once the other predictors have been taken into account.

*Table 31.2*
*Multiple regression analysis showing the unique contribution*
*made to job satisfaction.*

| Variable | | Beta | *p* |
|---|---|---|---|
| 1. | Police hassles | -.39 | < .001 |
| 2. | Police uplifts | .36 | < .001 |
| 3. | Neuroticism | -.15 | < .01 |
| 4. | Emotion-focused coping | -.11 | > .05 |
| 5. | Extraversion | .10 | > .05 |
| 6. | Problem-focused coping | .02 | > .05 |

*Note.* N = 261. The beta coefficients indicate the relative strength of the relationships between each predictor and job satisfaction (the larger the absolute value, the stronger the relationship). The *p* value indicates whether the relationship is significantly different from zero (values > .05 are not statistically significant from zero).

***Policy Implications of the Regression Analysis.*** From a policy or control point of view, it could be concluded from these findings that police administrators need to reduce the negative aspects (police hassles) and increase the positive aspects (police uplifts) of police work in order to improve job satisfaction. When considering the relationship between neuroticism and job satisfaction, one might conclude that those high in neuroticism, which is a tendency to focus on the negative aspects of oneself and the environment, should be screened out during recruitment.

There are three further policy implications that flow from these findings. First, the influence of neuroticism is weak when compared to the influence of police work experiences. This may lead to the conclusion that it is more important to try to change the police work environment than the personal attributes of police officers. Second, extraversion, which is marked by the tendency to be sociable and display interpersonal warmth, was not related to job satisfaction. Consequently, it seems that for job satisfaction it does not matter whether or not police are high or low in extraversion. Third, neither of the two coping styles was significantly related to job satisfaction. This suggests, from a normative perspective, that teaching coping skills to police officers will not increase job satisfaction.

*Limitations of Multiple Regression Analysis.* Multiple regression, however, may be too simple a model. It assumes that there are only two stages in the causal process; a set of input or predictor variables (in this case six) and a single outcome or dependent variable. It is possible, however, that there may be *multiple* stages in the causal process.

## Structural Equation Modeling

Structural equation modeling enables us to examine the entire pattern of *direct* and *indirect* relationships between variables which reflect the causal operations within the system (e.g., Cuttance & Ecob,1987; Hayduk, 1987; Loehlin, 1992; Marcoulides & Schumacker, 1996a; 1996b). As noted earlier, it is not possible to infer causality unequivocally from one wave of data. It is possible, however, to use a single wave of data to develop and test usable models that represent a causal theory. The structural equation model shown in figure 31.1 is based on the same data that gave rise to tables 31.1 and 31.2.

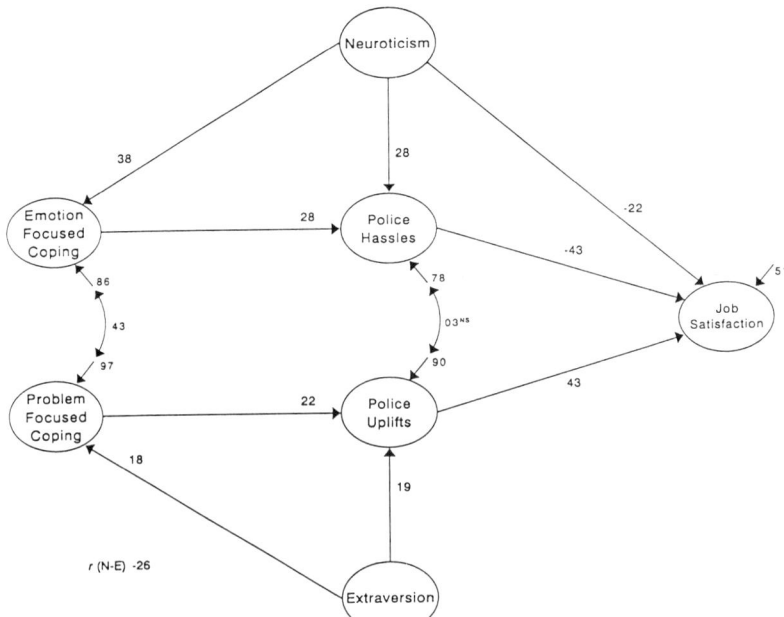

*FIG. 31.1. Theoretical causal model showing the relationship between seven variables assessed in an employee opinion survey completed by 330 police officers (goodness-of-fit statitics: root-mean-square residual = .05; relative noncentrality index = .96).*

***Structural Models.*** The structural equation modelling procedure relates the latent variables or constructs (see the discussion of measurement models below) to one another, as shown in figure 31.1. The relations shown in a structural equation model are not emprically derived, but must be specified according to some underlying theory. It is not possible, as in a multiple regression analysis, to merely include a set of predictor variables and allow the statistical procedure to determine what is important. A theoretical model must be specified first, and this model is then tested to see whether it is consistent with the data. In some circumstances, several theoretical models may be consistent with the data (see below for discussion on how to choose between competing models). The theoretical basis for the model shown in figure 31.1 is reported in Hart, Wearing and Headey (1995).

The relationships between the latent constructs in a structural equation model can either be *correlational* or *causal*. A correlation is depicted by a double headed arrow. For example, figure 31.1 shows that there is a .43 correlation between emotion-focused coping and problem-focused coping, once the effects of personality (neuroticism and extroversion) have been taken into account. Likewise, the model shows that there is a nonsignificant correlation of .03 between police hassles and police uplifts, once personality and coping have been taken into account. These correlations are interpreted in a similar way to the correlations shown in table 31.1.

***Causal Relationships.*** A causal relationship is depicted by a single headed arrow which joins two latent constructs. The arrow also indicates the direction of causation. The numbers associated with these arrows are standardised beta coefficients and, therefore show the strength of the relationship between the two variables, and the strength of this relationship can be compared directly with the strength of other relationships. For example, the -.22 coefficient between neuroticism and job satisfaction suggests that a unit (100%) increase in neuroticism will lead to a .22 (or 22%) decrease in job satisfaction.

Likewise, a unit (100%) increase in police hassles will lead to a .43 (43%) decrease in job satisfaction, and a unit increase in police uplifts will lead to a .43 (43%) increase in job satisfaction. As suggested by the multiple regression analysis, this model shows that police hassles and police uplifts have much stronger direct effects on job satisfaction than does neuroticism.

***Direct and Indirect Causal Effects.*** From the causal relationships specified in a model it is possible to establish direct and indirect effects. Direct effects are simply shown by the individual arrows in the diagram. For example, the direct effect of neuroticism on emotion-focused coping is .38. It can also be seen that there are three direct effects on job satisfaction; from neuroticism (-.22), police hassles (-.43) and police uplifts (.43). These three direct effects are the same as those suggested by the multiple regression analyses (see table 31.2). However, two points are worthy of note. First, the effects are larger in figure

31.1. This is because the modelling procedure takes the measurement error into account. Second, the model shows that there is a complex pattern of relationships between the six predictors of job satisfaction that was not revealed by the multiple regression analysis.

*Residual Variance.* One purpose of structural equation modeling is to determine how much of the variation in a dependent variable is explained by a set of predictor variables. Although this is similar to one of the purposes of multiple regression analysis, structural equation modeling allows for the possibility that *all variables* can have causal antecedents and so be treated as separate dependent variables. In other words, a policy maker can determine, for example, how much variation is explained in emotion-focused coping (14%), police hassles (22%) and job satisfaction (49%) by the system of variables depicted in figure 31.2. The amount of unexplained variance is shown in the diagram by a single headed arrow that is connected to only one variable. For example, the unexplained variance in job satisfaction is .51 and, therefore, the explained variance is .49 or 49%. Consequently, it may be concluded that there are other causes of job satisfaction which have not been measured. Moreover, it may be that these unknown causes, once identified, are more policy amenable.

*Policy and Control Implications: A Comparison of Structural Equation Modeling and Multiple Regression Analysis.* Examination of the direct and indirect effects depicted in figure 31.1 shows that all the variables are important, and that some of the conclusions we drew from the multiple regression analysis (see table 31.2) were incorrect. For example, from this analysis it can be seen that coping styles are important in determining police hassles and uplifts. It would therefore be appropriate to focus on improving police officers' coping styles in order to improve their work experiences and, ultimately, their job satisfaction; a conclusion that was contra-indicated by the multiple regression analysis.

Furthermore, it was concluded from the multiple regression analysis that neuroticism played a minor role in determining job satisfaction when compared to the influence of police hassles and police uplifts. It can be seen from figure 31.1, however, that neuroticism is causally related to emotion-focused coping and police hassles, as well as to job satisfaction. This means that neuroticism has both direct and indirect effects on job satisfaction; a finding that was obscured in the multiple regression analysis. The strength of these indirect effects can be calculated by multiplying the relevant direct effects. For example, the indirect effect of neuroticism on job satisfaction through police hassles is .28 x -.43 = -.12. Likewise the indirect effect of neuroticism on job satisfaction through emotion-focused coping and police hassles is .38 x .28 x -.43 = -.05. Adding the direct and indirect effects shows that the total effect of neuroticism on job satisfaction is -.39; providing a quite different picture from that suggested by the multiple regression analysis or examination of the direct effects alone.

In the following examples we will illustrate the use of structural equation modelling by demonstrating its application to employee opinion surveys (EOSs) that were conducted in two multinational organisatons. Many organisations now conduct EOSs as a matter of routine, so it may be possible for readers to apply these examples to their own situations.

## EXAMPLE 2: DETERMINING CAUSAL STRUCTURE IN EMPLOYEE'S OPINIONS ABOUT A TELECOMMUNICATIONS COMPANY

Employee opinion surveys (EOSs) are widely used to 'take the temperature' of organizations (Kraut, 1996). They not only provide an assessment of how positively or negatively employees feel about their organization, but they also indicate the extent to which employees believe that their supervisors and management are performing satisfactorily. In addition they provide information about the level of commitment, the perceived adequacy of physical conditions and the effectiveness of the organization, and so on. This information may be of diagnostic significance in that it identifies 'hot spots' or areas that are in need of managerial attention. It also provides an indication of how well employees understand and are committed to the aims, priorities, and performance of the organization.

To exercise control, however, requires that we not only know the state of the organisation, but we also know what factors are causing these states to change. The data for this example are drawn from a survey of 3,822 staff of a telecommunications company. The major goal of these analyses was to identify one or more causal models that fitted (i.e., were consistent with) the data.

**Measurement Models**

Most EOS variables, such as Job Satisfaction, are measured with a set of survey items. Although items may differ from one another in terms of their particular semantic content, it is assumed that they measure the same underlying or latent construct. The measurement model in structural equation analysis relates survey items or scales to the latent constructs (variables in the model) which the items or scales are thought to approximate, much as in factor analysis where several items may load on a single underlying construct. Survey items and scales contain, to varying degrees, measurement error and unique variance. One of the benefits of structural equation modeling is its ability to account for this measurement error and unique variance; something that is not possible with traditional procedures such as multiple regression analysis. This does not solve the problems associated with poor measurement or purely defined concepts, but it does enable us to estimate more accurately the true effects of one variable on another. This is important when selecting variables as foci for intervention and for accurately forecasting the effects of change in these variables. Simple bivariate correlations and beta coefficients derived from multiple regression analyses are generally biased

downwards because of measurement error. It is important for the successful application of structural equation modeling, however, that the concepts are clearly
defined, measured well, and differentiated both theoretically and statistically from
other concepts.

*Table 31.3*
*Description and reliability of the 14 variables used in the*
*structural equation analyses report for example 2.*

| Variable | Description | a |
|---|---|---|
| *Multiple Item Scales* | | |
| Appraisal | Knowing how one's job is evaluated, and a belief that it is evaluated fairly. | .71 |
| Company reputation | A belief that the company is highly regarded by competitors, customers, employees, and the general public. | .76 |
| Customer orientation | Being responsive to customer requirements and expectations. | .69 |
| Efficiency | Working in a department which is well managed, organized, and efficient. | .81 |
| Job satisfaction | The extent to which employees are satisfied with their work relationships, opportunities for growth, and benefits. | .89 |
| Loyalty | Feeling that one is part of the organization, as well as believing that the company operates with integrity and values ist employees. | .77 |
| Management | Management which is seen to be caring, competent, fair, and open, as well as being respected and trusted by employees. | .86 |
| Pay | A sense of being paid fairly, when compared to colleagues and other companies. | .82 |
| Self worth | A belief that one's job is important and worthwhile, as well as achieving a sense of accomplishment and positive attitude toward work. | .85 |
| Supervision | A belief that supervisors are fair, and actively | .77 |

*Table 31.3 (continued)*

| Variable | Description | a |
|---|---|---|
| | facilitate the involvement of staff. | |
| *Single Item Scales* | | |
| Company Satisfaction | The extent to which the company is either the best or worst to work for, when compared to other companies. | |
| Intention to leave | The extent to which employees are seriously considering leaving the company. | |
| People | The extent to which employees get along well with their colleagues. | |
| Work pressure | The extent to which employees feel bothered by excessive pressure in their work. | |

*Note.* For the purpose of the structural equation analyses, it was assumed that the reliability of the single item scales was .85

As the focus of this chapter is on using causal models to control or steer organizations, we will not discuss this issue further except to say that exploratory and confirmatory factor analyses of the EOS yielded 10 reliable scales which were then used for modelling (i.e., structural equation analysis). Additionally, 4 single item scales were included in the structural equation analysis, because these items measured important constructs that were of relevance to the organisation. The variables assessed by the 14 scales are briefly described in table 31.3. The coefficients alpha for the multiple item scales are also shown.

**Structural Models**

As in figure 31.1, these models are presented as path diagrams which show the theoretical causal relationships between the variables. The coefficients have been standardised so that they indicate how much change could be expected. A positive integer suggests that an increase in the predictor variable will cause an increase in the outcome variable, whereas a negative interger suggests that an increase in the predictor variable will cause a decrease in the outcome variable.

As noted in example 1, the indirect effects of one variable on another can also be determined. The direct and indirect effects are additive, so it is possible to ascertain the total effect of one variable on another. In this manner, it is possible to identify key causal variables, as well as their antecedents and consequences. The structural equation model shown in figure 31.2 is based on the data obtained from employees in the telecommunications company. This model was developed

ment. In our experience, it is unusual to correctly specify, in the first instance, a model involving this many variables that is consistent with the data.

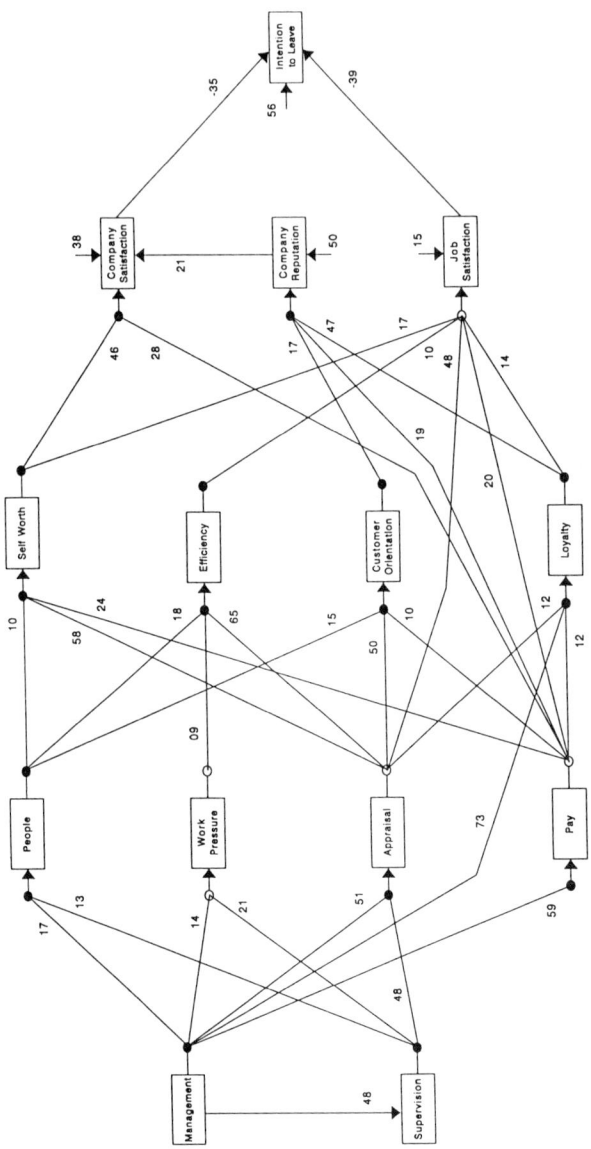

FIG. 31.2. *Theoretical causal model showing the relationship between 14 varia-bles assessed in an employee opinion survey completed by 3,822 telecommunica-tions workers (goodness-of-fit statistics: root-mean-square residual = .03; relative noncentrality index = .97).*

*Using These Results, or What Does This Model Tell Us that Could Not Otherwise Have Been Known.* These results provide information about how to control the system of variables. Management is the cornerstone of the system, and is related, either directly or indirectly, to all other variables. Consequently, by following the various paths it is possible to estimate the likely changes throughout the system if there was a 10% improvement in management. For example, a 10% improvement in management would lead to a 6% improvement in loyalty, a 4.9% improvement in customer orientation, but only a 1.4% improvement in work pressure. Likewise, a 10% improvement in appraisal will lead to a 4.1% improvement in job satisfaction, whereas a 10% improvement in work pressure will lead to a mere 0.5% increase in job satisfaction.

*Even More Information: A Second Model.* The model shown in figure 31.2 assumes that there are five stages in the causal process. It is possible, however, to take the analyses a step further and investigate the causal relationships between all 14 variables. For example, the third stage in figure 31.5 includes the variables self-worth, efficiency, customer orientation, and loyalty. It was assumed, for the purpose of exposition, that no causal relationships exist between these variables. Since this assumption was unlikely to be correct, we developed a model which took into account the possible causal relationships between all variables. This model is quite complex, and cannot easily be represented diagrammatically. Figure 31.3 shows the causal relationships between the four variables at stage 3 of the model shown in figure 31.2.

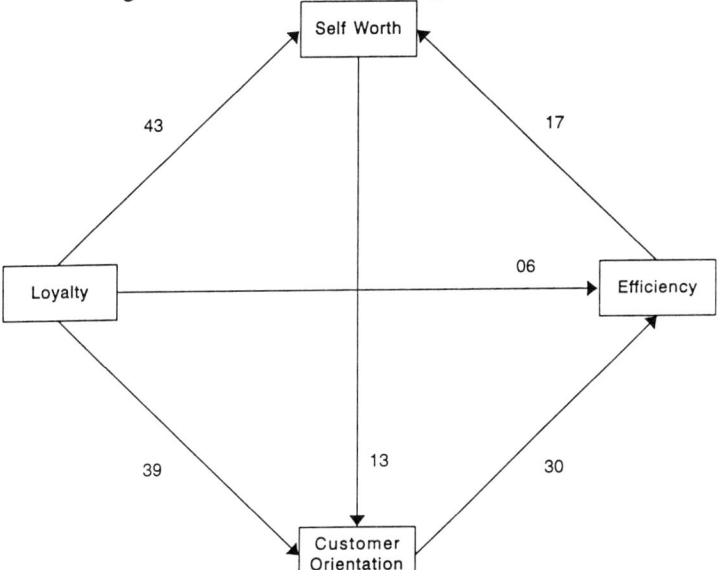

*FIG. 31.3. Theoretical causal model showing the relationship between four of the variables in figure 31.2.*

It can be seen from figure 31.3 that important relationships exist between these four variables. In order of importance, loyalty is causally antecedent to self-worth (beta = .43), customer orientation (beta = .39), and efficiency (beta = .06). Self-worth is causally antecedent to customer orientation which, in turn, is causally related to efficiency. Efficiency is also related to self-worth, suggesting that these three variables form a cyclic feedback system.

More importantly, having an understanding of these relationships adds to the interpretation of figure 31.2 and, therefore, increases the policy options that are available. For example, figure 31.2 suggests that self-worth is not related to company reputation; so changing employees' sense of self-worth will not lead to an improvement in the level of perceived company reputation. While it is true that there is no direct relationship between self-worth and company reputation, the more complex analysis shown in figure 31.3 shows that self-worth is *indirectly* related to company reputation through customer orientation. In a similar vein, this analysis shows that customer orientation is indirectly related to job satisfaction through efficiency and self-worth, even though there is no direct relationship between them.

Two benefits flow from this more complex analysis. First, it provides more options for controlling the system. For example, customer orientation can be enhanced by improving employees' sense of self-worth and loyalty; options that were not apparent from figure 31.2. Secondly, the flow-on effects of change in one part of the system can be more accurately estimated. This information is useful when assessing the cost/benefits of different policy options. For example, a 10% improvement in loyalty will have a much greater effect on company satisfaction in light of figure 31.3. According to figure 31.3, a 10% change in loyalty would result in a 1% improvement in company satisfaction. When the causal relationships shown in figure 31.3 are also taken into account, a 10% improvement in loyalty would result in a 3% improvement in company satisfaction.

*What Model is Correct and How Can One Know?* It is not straightforward, particularly when using cross-sectional data, to determine which model is the correct one. With cross-sectional data it is not possible to separate with certainty causal from spurious effects; this would require at least two waves of data in the case of uni-directional causal relationships, and at least three waves of data in the case of reciprocal (two-way) causal relationships (e.g., Headey, Veenhoven & Wearing, 1991). In these ambiguous cases, theoretical and practical criteria have to be used to choose the *best* or most appropriate model. This can be done by asking the following questions: (a) Does the model accord with theoretical knowledge? (b) Is it consistent with previous research findings? (c) Can the model be replicated with different data sets? (d) Does the model make sense to those who know the organisation? (e) Do predictions made on the basis of the model hold true? The more of these questions which can be answered affirmatively, the more confidence one can have in the model.

## EXAMPLE 3: DETERMINING CAUSAL STRUCTURE IN EMPLOYEE'S OPINIONS ABOUT AN INTERNATIONAL AIRLINE

In this example we consider the following question: What are the causes and consequences of quality management? This question was examined with data obtained through an employee opinion survey that was completed by 14,028 employees of an international airline. To maintain confidentiality, we will refer to the airline as International Airlines.

### Answering Dynamic Questions: Psychometric Prerequisites

As noted above, it is important that the variables are well measured. When using EOS's to develop and test causal models, a high degree of precision is needed in the measurement of theoretical constructs so that fine grain distinctions between the variables can be made with confidence. For example, we might be interested in two separate questions about goals: (a) what determines employees' beliefs that they can set their own goals (goal setting); and, (b) what contributes to an employees' understanding of how their jobs contribute to departmental or corporate goals (goal contribution). In order to answer these two questions, we must be confident that appropriate items in the EOS measure as separable constructs the two variables of goal Setting and goal contribution. We must be confident that the items measuring these two variables are not assessing the same thing.

*Identifying the Best Measures.* The first stage of any analysis must be concerned with identifying the best measures. In our experience, the theoretical structure of an employee opinion survey is not always supported by the data. Although a survey might be designed to measure certain constructs that are of interest to an organisation, in reality, the data may show that the items cohere in a way that is quite different. For example, items that were designed to measure a single construct reflecting management processes may in fact assess a number of distinct, but related constructs (e.g., communication, participative decision-making, role clarification, and supportive leadership). Accordingly, it is important to determine the structure and quality of the survey instrument.

In this example, 8 psychometrically adequate scales were constructed from 21 items. Sixteen further items were retained as single item scales because of their conceptual importance. Although 14 of the single item scales could be combined to form two higher-order constructs reflecting management performance (9 items) and corporate performance (5 items), for the purpose of these analyses, we were more concerned about understanding the individual contribution made by each of the items. Of course, if we were interested in a more global question about the relation between these two different aspects of performance, it may have been appropriate to use the aggregated scales. Table 31.4 provides a brief description of the 24 multiple and single item scales that were used in the structural equation analysis. The coefficients alpha for the multiple item scales are also shown.

*TABLE 31.4*
*Description and reliability of the 24 variables used*
*in the structural equation analyses reported for example 3.*

| Variable | Description | a |
|---|---|---|
| *Multiple Item Scales* | | |
| Customer orientation | The extent to which staff believe that their department actively seeks to understand and be responsive to customer needs. | .86 |
| External reputation | The extent to which staff believe that International Airlines is highly regarded by its customers and the general public. | .78 |
| Goal contribution | The extent to which staff feel they understand how their jobs contribute to departmental and corporate goals. | .79 |
| Goal setting | The extent to which staff believe that there is an effective process for setting their own and their work group's goals. | .91 |
| Goal understanding | The extent to which staff feel that they understand their department's goals, and how they will be achieved. | .87 |
| Quality improvement | The extent to which staff believe that International Airlines is doing a good job in implementing quality improvement initiatives, and providing the necessary resources, tools, and training to achieve quality improvement. | .84 |
| Staff commitment | The extent to which staff are proud to work for International Airlines, feel that they would like to stay with International Airlines for the foreseeable future, and believe that International Airlines has a brighter future than most other airlines. | .69 |
| Staff feel valued | The extent to which staff feel that they are treated as individuals, as well as with respect and fairness. | .84 |

*TABLE 31.4 (continued)*

| Variable | Description | a |
|---|---|---|
| *Single Item Scales (management performance)* | | |
| Allowing initiative | The extent to which staff believe that management allow staff to use their own initiative. | |
| Communicating business | The extent to which staff believe management regularly communicate business. | |
| Consistency | The extent to which staff believe management show consistency in dealing with employees. | |
| Continuous Improvement | The extent to which staff believe management encourage continuous improvement. | |
| Giving honest feedback | The extent to which staff believe management provide honest feedback. | |
| Listening | The extent to which staff believe management listen to staff. | |
| Management performance | The extent to which staff believe they are managed well. | |
| Managing change | The extent to which staff believe management manage change well. | |
| Trusting staff | The extent to which staff believe management trust staff. | |
| *Single Item Scales (corporate performance)* | | |
| Customer responsiveness | The extent to which staff believe that International Airlines is meeting its goal of being responsive to customers. | |
| Financial performance | The extent to which staff believe that International Airlines is meeting its goal of delivering a strong and consistent financial performance. | |
| Industry best | The extent to which staff believe that International Airlines is the best and most successful company in the industry. | |

*TABLE 31.4 (continued)*

| Variable | Description | a |
|---|---|---|
| Superior service and value | The extent to which staff believe that International Airlines is meeting its goal of providing superior service and value for money. | |
| Work environment | The extent to which staff believe that International Airlines is meeting its goal of sustaining a work environment that attracts, retains, and develops committed employees. | |
| *Single Item Scales (other)* | | |
| Company satisfaction | The extent to which staff are satisfied with International Airlines as a company to work for. | |
| Global job satisfaction | The extent to which staff are satisfied with their jobs overall. | |

*Note.* For the purpose of the structural equation analyses, it was assumed that the reliability of the single item scales was .85.

## Estimating the Structural Equation Models

To reiterate, when causal models are based on cross-sectional data, the models provide only one of several plausible explanations of the data. Although it is difficult, when a large system of variables is under investigation, to develop multiple causal models that are both theoretically and empirically sound, it is still possible that more than one model of equal merit exists. In some cases, for example, the model will fit the data equally as well when nothing more that the direction of the relationship (arrow) linking two variables is reversed (e.g., Mac-Callum, Wegener, Uchino, & Fabrigar, 1993). Nevertheless, in practice it is difficult to get a model that fits the data well when there are many variables in the system. Figure 31.4 shows a model that takes into account the possible causal relationships between the 24 variables that were examined in this analysis.

Figure 31.4 shows that there are essentially two causal paths that run throught the 24 variables; one leading to external reputation, and the other leading to staff commitment. We will look first at the path leading to external reputation. It can be seen from this model that management's emphasis on continuous improvement leads to goal understanding and quality improvement. In turn, quality improvement contributes to the four corporate goals included in this model. These four corporate goals contribute to staff perceptions about International Airlines being the industry's best airline. Finally, staff perception about the extent to which International Airlines is the industry's best airline, and the extent to which they believe that International Airlines is meeting its goal of providing superior service and value, both contribute directly to staff's perception about how International Airlines is viewed by its customers and the general public. Consequently, this part of the model suggests that *management emphasis should be placed on continuous improvement in order for staff to feel positive about International Airlines performance and reputation outside of the company.*

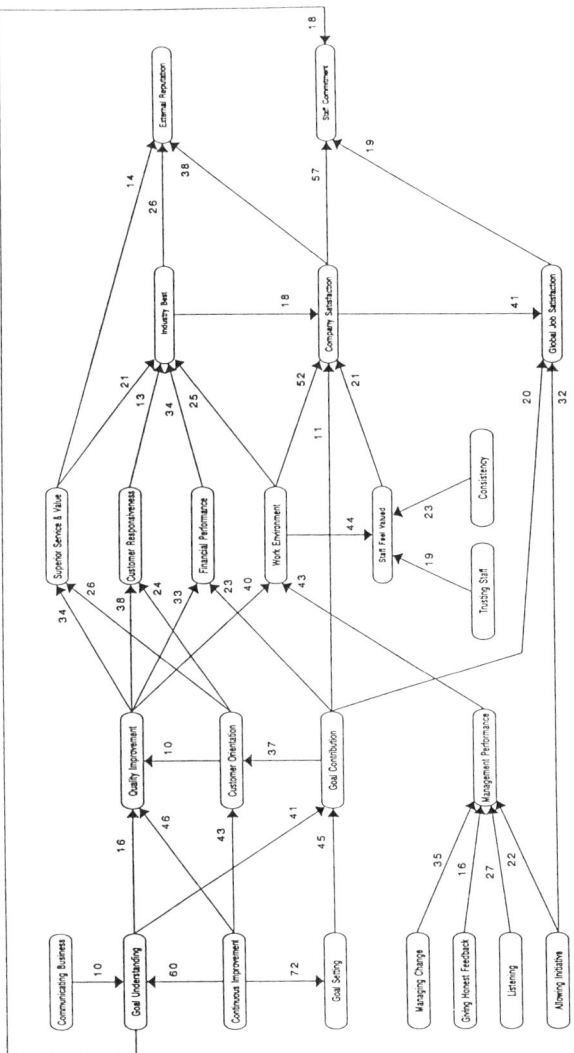

FIG. 31.4. *Theoretical causal model showing the relationship between 24 variables assessed in an employee opinion survey completed by 14,028 airline workers (goodness-of-fit statitics: root-mean-square residual = .02; relative noncentrality index = 1.00).*

Figure 31.4 also shows the main components that contribute to staff commitment. It can be seen that the four dimensions of management contribute to staff perceptions about management performance. In turn this contributes to the extent to which staff believe International Airlines is meeting the goal of providing a positive work environment. Meeting the goal of providing a positive work environment contributes to staff feeling that they are valued and determines the extent to which they are satisfied with International Airlines as a company to work for. Moreover, company satisfaction contributes to global job satisfaction, and both company satisfaction and global job satisfaction determine the levels of staff commitment. In essence, this part of the model suggests that *management performance, and meeting the goal of establishing a positive work environment are important in determining staff commitment.*

It can be seen from the full model that there is some overlap between the two main causal paths. For example, goal contribution and company satisfaction contribute to both paths. Consequently, although the two main causal paths can be considered as separate, there are some connections which bring them together as an integrated system. It should also be noted that these models are based on the perceptions of staff, and may or may not reflect the objective reality about the link between job satisfaction and company performance.

Figure 31.4 shows that the interrelationships are complex, requiring many causal links to be taken into account as policy measures are developed. A careful study will show that many causal variables are important, depending upon the outcome desired. Nevertheless, the 42 paths shown in this model represent only 15.2% of the total possible paths (based on 24 variables), which demonstrates the capability of such modeling to reduce the complexity of EOS data to a manageable level. Moreover, this reduction has been achieved and we are still able to explain 98% of all covariation in this system of 24 variables (the root-mean-square residual was .02).

Again, it is possible that other models fit the data equally well. It is important to test all plausible alternatives before using the results of a particular model. Many alternatives are usually examined during the model development phase. Since managers, who are the users of the information derived from the analyses, are likely to have strong views about how their organizations work, it is important to examine the models generated by these views. In this manner, it is possible to use the modeling procedure to test the competing views of different managers. We have found this to be a powerful technique that can assist managers to understand how their organisations may actually function.

## CONCLUSION

The three examples show different models. We have not discussed the many technical issues involved in developing such models, nor have we drawn out all the policy and control implications of these analyses. Our intention was to provide enough detail to show how this modelling technology can assist the development of multifactorial control strategies. Moreover, it indicates those control activities that are likely to be effective as well as those which are not, and suggests the priority that should be assigned to each of the effective control strategies. Although this type of analysis should not be seen as the *holy grail* of employee opinion surveys, it does provide a rich source of information about how an organisation functions. When used to supplement the static information that is typically derived from an employee opinion survey, the results of these analyses can provide a powerful decision aide that enables managers to gain a clearer undestanding of the control mechanisms operating within their organizations.

## REFERENCES

Cuttance, P. & Ecob, R. (Eds) (1987). *Structural Modeling by Example, Applications in Educational, Sociological and Behavioral Research.* New York: Cambridge.

Hart, P. M. (1994) Teacher quality of work life: Integrating work experience, psychological distress and morale. *Journal of Occupational and Organizational Psychology, 67,* 109–132.

Hart, P. M., Wearing, A. J. & Headey, B. (1993). Assessing police work experiences: development of the Police Daily Hassles and Uplifts Scales. *Journal of Criminal Justice, 21,* 553–572.

Hart, P. M., Wearing, A. J. & Headey, B. (1995). Police stress and well-being: integrating personality, coping and daily work experiences. *Journal of Occupational and Organizational Psychology, 68,* 133–156.

Hayduk, L. A. (1987). *Structural Equation Modeling with LISREL: Essentials and Advances.* Baltimore, MA: John Hopkins University.

Headey, B., Veenhoven, R., & Wearing, A. J. (1991). Top-down versus bottom-up theories of subjective well-being. *Social Indicators Research, 24,* 81–100.

Howard, A., & Associates (1994) *Diagnosis For Organisational Change.* New York: Guilford Press.

Kessler, C. & Greenberg, D. F. (1981). *Linear Panel Analysis: Models of Quantitative Change.* New York: Academic Press.

Kraut, A. (Ed); (1996) *Organisational Surveys.* San Francisco: Jossey-Bass.

Loehlin, J. C. (1992). *Latent Variable Models: An Introduction To Factor, Path, And Structural Analysis (2nd Ed.).* Hilldsdale, NJ: Lawrence Erlbaum Associates.

Magnusson, D., Bergman, L. R., Rudinger, G., & Torestad, B. (1991). *Problems and Methods in Longitudinal Research: Stability and Change.* Cambridge: Cambridge University Press.

Marcoulides, G. A, & Schumacker, R. A. (1996a) *A Beginner's Guide To Structural Equation Modeling.* Mahwah, NJ: Lawrence Erlbaum Associates.

Marcoulides, G. A, & Schumacker, R. A. (Eds) (1996b). *Advanced Structural Equation Modeling.* Mahwah, NJ: Lawrence Erlbaum Associates.

MacCallum, R. C., Wegener, D. T., Uchino, B. N. & Fabrigar, L. R. (1993). The problem of equivalent models in applications of covariance structure analysis. *Psychological Bulletin, 114,* 185–199.

Menard, S. (1991). *Longitudinal Research.* (Sage University Paper Series on Quantitative Applications in the Social Sciences, No. 07-076). Newbury Park, CA: Sage.

# 32

# Self-Efficacy and the School System[1]

## Fritz Oser

## THE SCHOOL AS A PLACE WHERE SELF-EFFICACY IS UNDERMINED

August Flammer (1990, pp. 144 ff), in his important book on control belief, analyses in detail the concept of secondary control and its meaning with respect to different comparable theories. In general, secondary control means the following: If a person feels unable to change the world according to his or her own wishes, then that person examines the possibility to change himself/herself or to adapt the wishes in question to the given state of affairs. Of course, there are many forms of secondary control, and Flammer thinks that the transformation from primary to secondary control should clearly be distinguished from learned helplessness. What we find less in his book is the application of secondary control to one of the most powerful systems in our culture, namely the school. How does the school as a system develop self efficacy on the one hand and secondary control on the other? What does it mean for a child to feel helpless with respect to that system? What kinds of experiences lead most children to view the system as something in regard to they have absolutely no influence and no control—that is our hypothesis—so that secondary control is the only remaining possibility?

Most research on school quality clarifies nothing regarding that aspect, and even from analyses of the school climate and the respective factors (e.g., Dreesmann 1982, Eder 1996) little can be learned about the control students have of the system. Mortimore (1997), in his excellent review on findings concerning school effectiveness, points out that good effectiveness is primarily due to "differences in the way schools were managed and in the quality of teaching and learning" (p. 4).

But a closer look at the variables shows that no such thing as control over the system was included. It is a general phenomenon that humans feel without power and helpless when confronting institutions and their behavior. Sometimes the institution can indeed be effective, and still its members have no influence on it. The individual then can turn to an orienting interaction (Rusch 1996), ie. try to

---

[1]This contribution refers closly to the following article: F. Oser, Selbstwirksamkeit und Bildungsinstitution. In W. Edelstein (Ed.) *Entwicklungskrisen kompetent meistern.* Heidelberg: Asanger, 1995, pp. 63–73.

understand how his or her own intentions, goals, activities, and their desired results could be achieved within the system, but nothing remains except secondary control, the adaptation to the system. Many economic enterprises may serve as good examples for such a situation: the more employees are driven to work hard without critical reflection, the more the management is satisfied—success is defined solely by output numbers. Insecurity and lack of control are the best predictors for submission. With respect to decision making structures, schools resemble economic enterprises, and whereas autopoesis (Luhmann 1986) exists at the higher echelons, one hardly can clearly claim that all other persons concerned have a similar say in processes of delimitation and equilibration. In some social systems most members profit from the structures without being aware of those structures. In other social systems the relationship between the system and the individuals is consciously hidden by the management in order not to upset the *status quo*. This is one way of external control for obtaining blind obedience from the employees—especially in a period of unemployment. Elsewhere I call this the tyranny of the status quo of a system (Oser 1995 p. 63).

Children and adolescents do not see the school as a place over which they have any control. They see it as an alien system which they enter and exit as if it were a tunnel. And even entering and exiting are regulated by the school itself. Their need for (partial) control is not considered, even less its granting envisaged. The possible spaces for students' action and their resources for developing strategies are minimal and restricted, so that the system is never endangered. Illich (1972) spoke about a vicious circle in that students and parents believe the more that they need control the more schools exercise control. That is why he recommended to abolish schools, to "deschool" society.

However, if children and adolescents are not merely required to function, but can co-determine and co-implement what goes on in their school or class as (partial) system, and have their say in elaborating or changing rules, norms and standards, then they can learn much about social regulations, democracy, communication processes, secret interactions in the class, implicit moral rules, etc. Similarly, if teachers have the possibility to change the way the school operates, then they experience something concerning the responsibility to create an optimal learning environment for children and adolescents. School autonomy then means that initiatives within the system get attention and lead to debates. That in turn could improve school quality.

But we observe the curious phenomenon that the tyranny of the status quo in the school has to do with the fact that those who decide and exert control are not, or only partially, part of the system. That may be a reason for the weakness and helplessness—i.e., the lack of self-efficacy—vis-à-vis the effects of the system already mentioned.

At this point I would like to sketch three examples of helplessness and lack of self-efficacy, in which individuals function as parts of the system without being able to influence the system. Bandura & Schunk (1981) opine that considerations regarding self-efficacy beliefs occur mostly under conditions of insecurity, ambiguity, unfamiliarity and/or stress; they are not so usual in conditions of routine activities or everyday behavior. Hence, questioning self-efficacy becomes possible when achieving task objectives becomes difficult, when action space is restricted. Focusing again on the school, then the difficulties come to mind which arise in the context of acting, learning, and processing knowledge on the part of the students, this in regard to (a) teacher education, (b) instruc-tional practice, and (c) meaning making. An example will be presented for each.

## AN EARLY START OF TRAINING TO BECOME A FAILURE

The first example is about teacher education. As part of her study course, a female teacher student has to give an exercise lesson. She fails to match most standards. The subject matter is badly organized, and class discipline is lacking (students ridicule each other, deride those who want to say something, laugh endlessly, edge each other on, the noise level becomes unacceptable). After the class an evaluation by the faculty member and the practice teacher follows; in the discussion, the teacher student states that she did not know what she could have done differently. The lecturer explains how she could have structured the subject matter differently according to the principle of functional rhythm, and how she should have interrupted her class and started an urgent discussion of the bursts of laughter when those occurred, making it quite clear in the process how outraged she was. The teacher student leaves with a feeling of dissatisfaction about herself and her teaching abilities. She resolves to perform better next time; however, this next time will only be two month later, just before her next practice period. That class is again a failure! Her feeling of professional self-efficacy starts to be demolished.

Such anecdotal cases permit to put the right questions, but not to draw generalizations. One question is why the student could not have given her next lesson immediately after, and again, and again, until her main problems were ameliorated at the levels of competence and performance. The structure of teacher education usually does not permit that (at least not in Switzerland), because the students are not given access to an expert teacher, but are being allocated fixed class periods. Teacher students learn early on that the chances are high to fail. On account of the difficulties and problems associated with the didactic, organizational, person-related and social aspects of their actions, students have little opportunity to experience success *early* on in their education. The issue is not whether they acquire an unadequate feeling of self-efficacy, but whether they form a feeling of self-inefficacy because of a lack of understanding of learning processes on the part of the institution and those who are in charge.

To that a complication related to the inner workings of science is added. Novice teachers start from the belief that to be successful means that *they* carry on class (a) effectively, (b) meaningfully, and (c) in a positive climate. Their yardstick for professional efficacy has to do with their own person, not with the efficacy of the students' learning process. One can see that from two empirical indications which shed light on important aspects on their understanding of self-efficacy. First, Janssen (1987, p. 14) reports that two years after the end of their education the mind of young teachers is occupied to the tune of 50% by the subject matter to be taught, 45% by their own behavior, and only about 5% by the students and their learning. Second, in the course of our study on teachers' professional morality, we have interviewed 60 teachers about their notion of ethos (Oser et al., 1991). As a first reaction they all said something like, "Ethos means that *I* as the teacher engage myself, that *I* am responsible, that *I* prepare myself well, that *I* take care of school matters, that *I* . . ., that *I* . . ." Only two teachers answered immediately, "Ethos means to care that *students* engage themselves, that *students* take responsibility, that *students* achieve objectives, that *students* take care of school matters, etc." In the first set of quotes, self-efficacy has the wrong objective. We call this phenomenon *structurally controlled inefficacy*.

These quotes make clear that the measure for teachers' effectiveness is to be searched for and found in the students' behavior. However good or bad a teacher is in presenting course material, in the use of teaching methods, in structuring lessons, his superiors, his educators, and he or she himself or herself should measure efficacy with reference to students' acts, operations, experimenting, prosocial behavior, cooperation, etc. However, that is usually not the way it happens, neither structurally nor issue-related. The more teachers have problems, the more they are fed with information and recommendations about themselves, about their behavior and actions. Not the interaction with the students is being thematized, but their "right" or "wrong" behavior.

## BURNOUT: RIGIDITY OF ANY SECURITY MEASURES

A second example: Teachers who feel tied up by their own school system all to often burn out. In practice, teachers often want to change formal aspects of their lectures and teaching techniques. Exemplar changes encompass things such as double lectures, team teaching, and interdisciplinary collaboration with others but also school celebrations and artistic enterprises that cover the entire school. However, such changes usually fail since the school's regulatory system does not allow for it. Schedules must be met, students from different classes cannot exchange ideas as it may cause unwanted disturbances, and artistic enterprises of entire schools are not considered as part of the curriculum by the department of education and, hence, they are seen as superfluous.

When reliable, engaged, and committed model employees all of a sudden reveal symptoms such as mental fatigue, stubbornness, and negativistic attitudes and when they get cynical, tired at work as well as depressive they have to be called, according to Freudenberger (1974), burned out. "Burnout results from a continued, repeated emotional stress in combination with intensive care for others" (Kramis-Aebischer 1994, p. 36, translated by the author). Two scales can be used to measure burnout: the *Maslach-Burnout-Inventory* (MBI), which assesses mental fatigue, depersonalization, and dissatisfaction with one's own achievement; and the *Tedium Measure* (TM), which assesses weariness.

Burisch (1989, p. 1, translated by the author) gives another description of the very same syndrome:

> Burnout refers to the young teacher who seemed turned old after a single year at school. She is usually so exhausted after school that she falls asleep immediately. Then, at night, she has to prepare the next day's classes. Asked for it, she describes herself as follows: 'I never thought of becoming as bitter as some of my older colleagues that quickly. A teacher who shouts at students and enforces order by disciplinary measures such as extra work. Meanwhile, however, I succeed in getting things done my way. The sole purpose of teaching are grades anyway.'

For this particular teacher, both the small scale system, the classroom, as well as the large scale system, the school itself, are totally out of control.

## BLOCKED INITIATIVE

Students powerlessness is a third example: Occasionally, a school system enforces unfair rules just to suppress or discredit some students, leaving fellow students without any possibility to interfere with it. In a high school, for instance, 17 year-old students intended to organize artistic performances, plays, concerts, and readings of poetry. The teachers' council, however, turned these plans down without any justification. The students were "requested to do as their teachers said". Understandably, students became frustrated and they were left without any commitment to their school. Frustration, in this case, can be seen as a result of negative expectancies. The teachers' council suggested basically that students "won't achieve anything anyway." Such a withdrawal of teachers' "trust in advance," their preliminary confidence in their students' ability made these students withdraw from being engaged in school activities as well.

Advance confidence in one's ability is, evidently, a major precondition to experience self-efficacy. Forced helplessness, in opposition, may be responsible for increased school violence. Students' academic self-esteem depends more heavily on success based on effort and on self-efficacy beliefs than on goal achievement (*cf.* Baumert 1993). Moreover, youths high in separation as well as in loss anxiety are low in self-esteem compared to youths low in these two anxieties (*cf.* Schellhas 1994). All these findings refer to reasons for a loss in collective self-efficacy beliefs caused by a schooling system that turns people helpless: While people need their schools they cannot affect or modify it. Learned or forced helplessness implies both a loss in primary control—people change their environment—and in secondary control—people modify themselves to balance personal needs and environmental possibilities (*cf.* Flammer, 1990)—in a system that people cannot leave at their own discretion.

What is the common issue of all three examples? All three settings describe people, evidently, as tied up to a system. They differ, however, in what lack of control the teacher student (first example), the teacher (second example), or the high school students (third example) experience. Obviously though, people feel helpless facing a monolithic system. Since people outside the school system are hardly affected schools turn their participants helpless. We call this phenomenon forced helplessness or institutional ineffectiveness. Currently, the catholic church may be seen as one of the most prominent examples for this situation: Religious people get stuck between their inability to modify the church and their unwillingness to adapt to its antique structures. A predicament that leaves them with only one solution, to abandon (disappointedly) their parishes.

## SELF-EFFICACY TOWARD A SYSTEM: THE JUST COMMUNITY APPROACH

In educational terms, the analysis so far leads to very dissatisfying results. Schools *should* be organized in a way that allows for changes in children's and adolescents' belief that systems are not movable, cannot be influenced, do not permit participation. I remember my first month as a student of the University of Zurich. I had the feeling that no one ever had dared to question or even shaken this hard and powerful structure. In 1996, Luhmann describes the school children as people who need their minor possibilities to make jokes and tease teachers in order to tolerate the structural coercion exerted by the school, and he speaks about the necessity of school reforms as functional adaptations of the system (pp. 45/46). Given that the purpose of schooling is not only knowledge transmission but also the development of personal and social competences, the system's rigidity and lack of flexibility weakens the system itself.

In the following paragraph, I would like to describe how children and adolescents can enhance their influence on the system through collective participation in a Just Community school. A result of this influence is the growth of self-efficacy belief toward the system school. This system itself becomes a means for this growth, and problems in the functioning of the system are seen as occasions for deliberate attempts to change the system from an inside-perspective. Our example is taken from the Just Community approach as practiced in two Swiss schools. One characteristic of this type of inner school reform is its participatory and democratic structure: Rules and regulations regarding interpersonal issues are jointly decided upon; student initiatives are explicit enabled. Assemblies of all school members take place regularly and can be called in when needed in order to solve a conflict.

For these "town meetings," all teachers and students come together in the big gymnasium for 1 or 2 hours. They discuss points at issue, consider conflict solutions or generalized rules and decide upon their implementation. Those points at issue can be, e.g., how to deal with the problem of frequent thefts in school, what to do in order to reduce violence among students during the break, which rules help to keep the corridors and walls clean, how to establish and organize a self-governed kiosk that could provide students with healthy snacks for the break, how to realize an open day for the parents or a school celebration. Although from the students' perspective the material results are of a high importance, educationally they are not. The major educational criterion is what learning processes are rendered possible. The experience of a public deliberation that includes reasoning and listening to others' arguments, the common search for solutions, the experience that responsibility taking is meant serious and that rule enforcement is a matter of everyone in the school community (after everyone had a say in deciding upon those rules)—all this is conducive to social and moral learning and—evidently—to self-efficacy. Furthermore, all these processes in themselves are moral acts. The serve to pursue a common good, to establish an atmosphere of fairness, respect, and care. Conceptually, they are based on a notion of process morality in assuming that the solutions are as moral as the procedures leading to those solutions and that moral procedures require a balancing between the moral needs and claims of the persons involved, independent of the question of whether they are framed in terms of justice, care, or truthfulness/integrity.

To date, the Just Community approach to democratic schooling has been implemented in a number variations, following Kohlberg's suggestion not to adopt but rather to adapt the basic ideas to the diversity of local settings (cf. Kohlberg 1986, Oser & Althof 1992, Power et al. 1989, Korte 1987, Solomon et al. 1989, Mosher 1979, 1990, Wassermann 1980, Lind 1993, Schreiner 1987, 1989, Leschinsky 1987 etc.)

Let us have a look at some selected results. A first example refers to the teachers in a Just Community elementary school (figure 32.1): Compared to a similar control school, the overall picture of results shows a grown professional self-efficacy. These teachers would significantly more often choose their profession again (if they had to decide anew), have more feelings of success and pleasure in teaching; finally the are motivated more to improve their professional competences.

Below, some results regarding parents' experiences in a second Just Community school are reported. The parents are pretty convinced that their voices are heard and respected, in that sense they believe to have more control over the school. Furthermore, they have the impression that their children developed a higher self efficacy belief through participation in decision making of the whole school.

The following items (from Althof's, 1998, parent survey) reflect parents' efficacy beliefs (questionnaire items with four point scale):

- We parents feel as partners of the teachers in the education of our child ($X$ = 3.09)
- The teachers are happy about the help of the parents concerning the organization of special subject-matter ($X$ = 2.85)

- The schools has become more opened up; communication between teachers and parents has improved ($X = 2.77$)
- My child works in a more purposeful manner ($X = 2.68$)
- My child has more confidence in his or her own abilities ($X = 2.64$)

## Identification with Profession

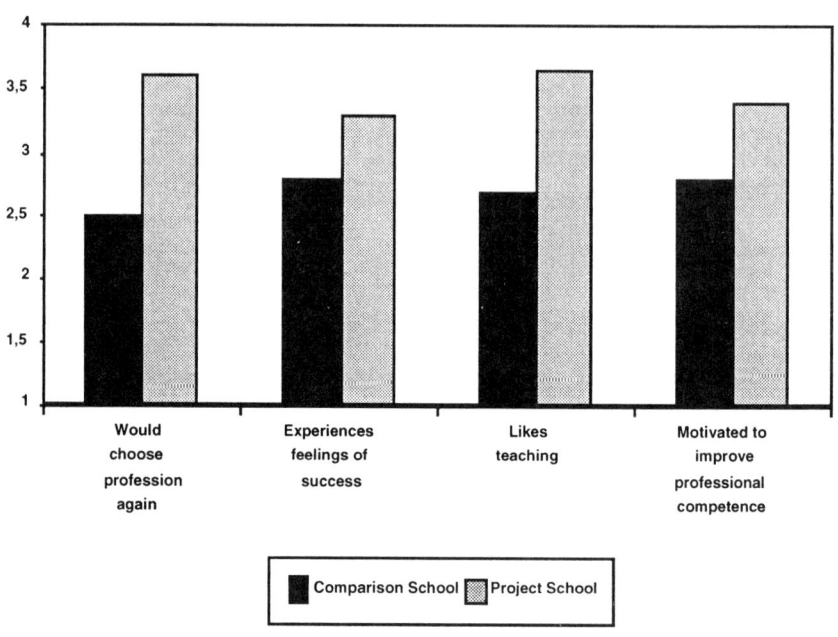

FIG. 32.1. Identification of teachers with their profession (from Althof, 1998).

Other questions only allowed for a "yes" or "no" answer. The following items refer to changes during the past school year that the parents observed in their children's social attitudes and behaviors.

- My child wants to be more included in family decision and rule making (Yes: 73.8%, No: 26.2%)
- My child has more self confidence in tackling difficult tasks (Yes: 67.7%; No: 32.3%)

Several scales of the student questionnaire can also be easily related to issues of self esteem and self efficacy. Data indicate that participating in the variety of Just Community activities helps children to develop self confidence. Figure 32.2 is an example: Before the start of the Just Community program, boys showed a significantly lower academic self esteem than girls; one year later, this difference has completely disappeared.

## Academic Self-Esteem

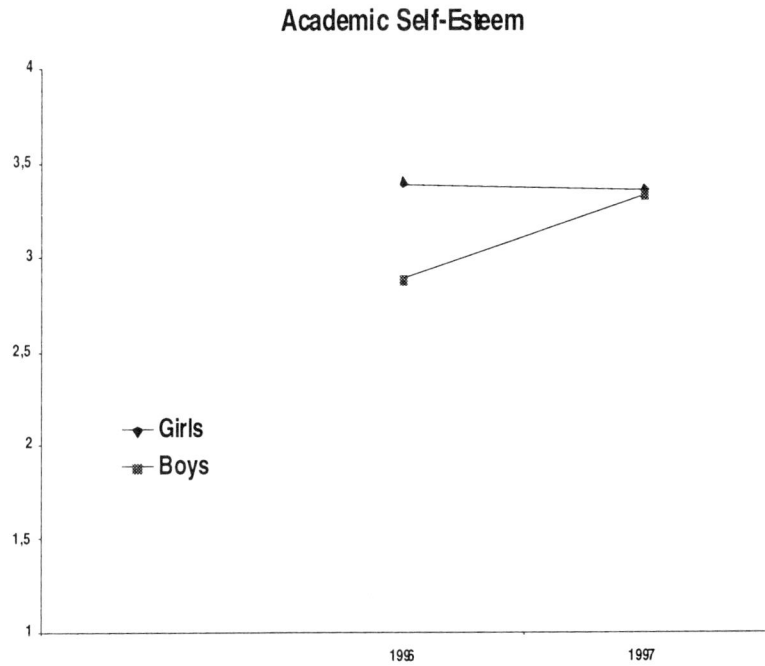

*FIG. 32.2. Academic self esteem (sample item: I think I am a good student).*

In general, we can say that the Just Community model influence the behavior of the students significantly. In a number of program schools the students exhibited a higher level of moral judgment and a higher level of community values after a relatively short time. They showed more helping behavior, more prosocial behavior, less offensive behavior, and a higher level of identification with the norms and rules voted on. This last point is particularly important. If, for instance, the rule of helping each other becomes of central importance, students have the feeling that they can influence the whole system by putting this rule into practice. If a strict rule of not using drugs is central, students believe that they have consciously achieved something that affects everyone. This is to say that people participating in a Just Community experience a higher level of self-efficacy within the system. They tend to view the school as *their* school, they emphasize community norms and believe that they can change things.

The fundamental principle at work here can be generalized as follows: When teachers and students can structure their day, plan with colleagues in a team and create a school culture within their school, they experience a sense of freedom from the typical *Procrustean bed* that occupies most schools. Teachers have the feeling that they are effective and this gives them a professional sense of well-being. Students are "co-effective." Such participation occurs in the sense of a gradually unfolding autonomy in the school, whereby the distribution of decision-making competence is shifted to new coordinates and is no longer simply a transmission of power from the administration to the principals. The same thing holds for teacher training: Experts should have the possibility to work coordinately and cooperatively in order to more quickly fulfill educational needs and to build up confidence in their professional and collective self-efficacy. Instead, however, one finds increasingly phenomena such as the following (Strittmatter, 1986, pp. 8–12, and Biener, 1988):

- Teachers get sick more frequently than, e.g., administrators or self-employed;
- teachers have a distinctly shorter life span compared to employees at a similar level of competence;
- teachers have a higher risk of heart disease.
- Similarly, teachers complain more frequently of nervousness, sleep disturbances, constipation, emotional disturbances and mood swings;
- Noticeable is the high number of cases of exhaustion and hypertension.

What are the prerequisites of a democratic educational system that lead to higher self-efficacy?

## PREREQUISITES FOR A GROUNDED SELF-EFFICACY

Within the framework of our research project on professional morality, we have defined forms of decision-making in conflict situations occurring in educational and classroom situations. They are as follows: avoidance (responsibility is perceived but not accepted); delegation (responsibility is perceived and transferred to some kind of authority); unilateral decision-making (responsibility is spontaneously assumed and the problem immediately resolved); discourse I position (thinking and discussion occur based on the assumption that everyone is able to understand everyone else's reasoning); and discourse II position (where decisions are also made cooperatively). Two facts should be mentioned here:

- A high level of discourse preference is related to the success of systemic effect, e.g., in the area of expertise. It seems that the conditions of the discourse have a mediating effect for the prognosis of successful ethos (measured by student statements).
- Initially, we hypothesized that the largest positive relationship between the decision-making type and the various variables for effect would be found among the teachers who preferred unilateral decision making (as

estimated by students). However, this hypothesis did not prove true. With one exception (the variable "comfort"), we discovered that the positive relationships emerged between the student variables on the one hand and the student preference for either extreme of professional moral decision-making on the other; in other words, either for avoidance or complete discourse. Students prefer teachers who either allow everyone to participate, or who tend to refrain from any kind of intervention.

All these results lead us to the question of collective self-efficacy and confidence among teachers and students. The above results show that group decision-making does not cause chaos or reduced achievement. Rather, it leads to an identification with the system and its goals and standards. Co-determination and decision-making, however much effort they require, are the source of collective confidence and self-efficacy because individuals believe through this process that it is possible to have an effect on the system of which they are a part. That is the reason why the type of school reform that is mandated from the outside cannot be successful. We know little about the peripheral conditions of collective self-efficacy today. We have only information about the conditions under which individual students can not experience self-efficacy—for example, norm-based (instead of criteria-based) grading (one-third of the students); lack of short- and long-term planning with students (weekly plan); lack of self-reflection on the learning process and the lack of assuming responsibility for it (metacognition); induction of learning anxiety and absence of independence; not entrusting students with checking their own work, etc. All of these are areas where a lot of research data is available, but the political conditions for collective change are hardly fulfilled.

Social efficacy is left out of more or less every social curriculum. The secondary school curriculum has barely addressed in a systematic fashion how, for instance, things such as cultural awareness, social awareness, emotional skills, perspective taking skills, negotiation skills, love values (to express, identify and discuss the feelings associated with the inherent desire to be close and commended to others), or freedom values (Selman, 1994) are learned. Similarly, the analysis of mistakes in the classroom has barely been looked at in terms of increasing individual social efficacy.

The model of the Just Community that we have discussed above, makes it possible for professionals and students to assail the system so that they can create something new from within. Schools have become a cold, self-fulfilling, rule-bound domain instead of a pedagogical area of influence. The direct withdrawal of control increasingly narrows the possiblities for cooperative work in institutions. The end effect is a withdrawal of interest in the school system and its structure on the part of the teachers and students. Schools become merely 'shopping malls' for information, and the vigour that comes from people creating and recreating systems from the inside out disappears.

# REFERENCES

Baumert, J. (1993). *Lernstrategien, motivationale Orientierung und Selbstwirksamkeits-überzeugung im Kontext schulischen Lernens. Unterrichtswissenschaft, 21(4)*, S. 327–354.

Biener, K. (1988). *Stress. Epidemologie und Prävention*. Bern: Huber.

Burisch, M. (1989). *Das Burnout-Syndrom. Theorie der inneren Erschöpfung*. Berlin u.a.: Springer.

Dreesmann H. (1982). *Unterrichtsklima. Wie Schüler den Unterricht wahrnehmen. Ein Beitrag zur "Ökologie des Lernens"*. Weinheim: Beltz Verlag.

Eder F. (1996). *Schul- und Klassenklima. Ausprägung, Determinanten und Wirkungen des Klimas an höheren Schulen*. Innsbruck: Studienverlag.

Flammer, A. (1990). *Erfahrung der eigenen Wirksamkeit. Einführung in die Psychologie der Kontrollmeinung*. Stuttgart: Huber.

Freudenberger, H. J. (1974). Staff burn-out. *Journal of Social Issues, 30(1)*, 159–165.

Illich, I. (2nd ed., 1972). *Entschulung der Gesellschaft*. München: Kösel-Verlag.

Janssen, S. (1987). *What are beginning teachers concerned about?* Paper read at the first Joint Conference of the "Arbeitsgruppe für Empirische Pädagogische Forschung" and the "Onderzoeksthemagroep Onderwijsleerprocessen", Düsseldorf, April 6–7, 1987.

Kohlberg, L. (1986). Der "Just Community"–Ansatz der Moralerziehung in Theorie und Praxis. In: F. Oser, R. Fatke & O. Höffe (Hrsg.), *Transformation und Entwicklung. Grundlagen der Moralerziehung*. Frankfurt/M.: Suhrkamp, S. 21–55.

Korte, M. (1987). *Die Entwicklung der moralischen Atmosphäre in einem Jugendwohnheim: Eine Interventionsstudie*. Frankfurt/M.: Lang.

Kramis-Aebischer, K. (1995). *Bstress, Belastungen und Belastungsverarbeitung im Lehrberuf*. Bern, Stuttgart und Wien: Haupt.

Leschinsky, A. (1987). Warnung vor neuen Enttäuschungen. Strukturelle Hindernisse für eine Schule der Gerechten Gemeinschaft. *Die Deutsche Schule*, 79, S. 28–43.

Lind, G. (1993). *Moral und Bildung. Zur Kritik von Kohlbergs Theorie der moralisch-kognitiven Entwicklung*. Heidelberg: Asanger.

Luhmann, L. (1986). Grundwerte als Zivilreligion. Zur wissenschaftlichen Karriere eines Themas. In: H. Kleger &. A. Müller (Hrsg.), *Religion des Bürgers. Zivilreligion in Amerika und Europa*, S. 175–194. München: Kaiser.

Mortimore P. (1997). *New Developments and Findings in School Effectiveness and School Improvement research from an international perspective*. Paper presented at a school Effectiveness Special Interest Group Meeting at the 1997 AERA Annual Conference, Chicago.

Mosher, R. (1979). A democratic High School: Damn it, your feet are always in the water. In: ders. (Hrsg.), *Adolescents' Development and Education: A Janus Knot*. Berkeley: McCutchan, S.497–516.

Mosher, R. (1990). *Democracy: If you can keep it*. Beitrag zum Jahreskongreß der Association for Moral Education (AME) in South Bend, IN.

Oser, F. (1995). Selbstwirksamkeit und Bildungsinstitution. In: W. Edelstein (Hrsg.), *Entwicklungskrisen kompetent meistern*. Heidelberg: Asanger, 1995, S. 63–73.

Oser, F. (1995). Wann lernen Lehrer ihr Berufsethos? In: A. Leschinsky (Hrsg.), *Die Institutionalisierung von Lehren und Lernen. Beiträge zu einer Theorie der Schule. Festgabe für Peter Martin Roeder*. Weinheim & Basel: Beltz, 1995, S. 235–243, 1995.

Oser, F. & Althof, W. (1992). *Moralische Selbstbestimmung. Modelle der Entwicklung und Erziehung im Wertebereich. Ein Lehrbuch.* Stuttgart: Klett.

Power, C., Higgins, A. & Kohlberg, L. (1989) *Lawrence Kohlberg's Approach to Moral Education.* New York: Columbia University Press.

Rusch, G. (1986). Verstehen verstehen. Ein Versuch aus konstruktionistischer Sicht. In: N. Luhman & K. E. Schorn (Hrsg.), *Zwischen Intransparenz und Verstehen. Fragen an die Pädagogik.* Frankfurt/M.: Suhrkamp, S. 40–71.

Schellhas, B. (1994). *Die Entwicklung der Ängstlichkeit in Kindheit und Jugend. Befunde und Längsschnittstudie über die Bedeutung der Ängstlichkeit für die Entwicklung der Kognition und des Schulerfolgs.* Berlin: Max-Planck-Institut für Bildungsforschung, Studien und Berichte 55.

Schreiner, G. (1987). Schule als "Moral Democracy". Zu neueren amerikanischen Versuchen, in Schulen Gerechte Gemeinschaften einzurichten. *Die Deutsche Schule, 79,* 13–27.

Selman, R. L. (1984). *Die Entwicklung des sozialen Verstehens. Entwicklungspsychologische und klinische Untersuchungen.* Frankfurt/M.: Suhrkamp.

Solomon, D., Watson, M., Schaps, E., Battistich, V., & Solomon, J. (1989). Cooperative Learning as Part of a Comprehensive Classroom Program Designed to Promote Prosocial Development. In: S. Sharan (Ed.), *Current Research on Cooperative Learning.* New York: Praeger.

Strittmatter, A. (1986). Berufsbelastung des Lehrers: Zahlen, Fakten, Auswege. Sachverhalte und Überlegungen zur Berufssituation des Lehrers, Belastungen und Möglichkeiten, sie zu ertragen. *Schweizerische Lehrer-Zeitung, 8,* 7–14.

Wassermann, E. (1980). An alternative High School based on Kohlberg's just community approach to education. In: R. L. Mosher (Ed.), *Moral Education. A First Generation of Research and Development.* New York: Praeger. pp. 259–278.

# 33

# Control at Work:
# Issues of Specificity, Generality, and Legitimacy

Norbert K. Semmer

## INTRODUCTION

All over in psychological writing, there seems to be much agreement that people profit from the conviction that they are able to influence their own affairs (e.g. Frese, 1989, Seligman, 1975, Flammer, 1990; Rotter, 1966). Its positive effect have, for instance, been shown for dealing with stress (Jerusalem & Schwarzer, 1992), enhancing learning and performance, and well-being in general (Bandura, 1992).

It comes to no surprise that this topic plays an important role in the psychology of work as well. In numerous writings, representing quite diverse approaches, control has been regarded as beneficial. Although different writers use different labels, such as autonomy, decision latitude, control, degrees of freedom, the decisive element is basically the same: the possibility of making decisions about one's own activities and the conditions under which they are to be performed (Frese, 1987, 1989).

## CONTROL AS AN INDIVIDUAL DIFFERENCE VARIABLE

Note, however, that with regard to much of the research in the area of work, the emphasis is somewhat different. Basically, there are two different foci in this type of research. One is concerned with individual differences, that is, people's tendencies to hold rather general beliefs about the possibility to exert control (Rotter, 1966) or specific expectations about their personal capacities to deal effectively with a given problem (Bandura, 1992). The other is concerned with the possibilities for control that are offered by specific work environments, and, thus, with environmental contingencies.[1] This latter perspective is dominant in work psychology.

---

[1]Of course, Rotter's concept of internal vs. external control is also concerned with environmental contingencies. It reflects, however, individual tendencies to perceive such contingencies (generalized beliefs). In contrast, measures of work

555

This is not to say that research on individual differences in generalized control beliefs does not exist in the area of work (cf. Ganster & Fusilier, 1989). There even exists a work locus of control scale (Spector, 1988. Nevertheless, the majority of studies assesses locus of control as a general construct. This research indicates, for instance, that internals tend to have higher job aspirations and are more likely to end up in jobs they like. Also, there are more internals among workers in supervisory positions and among women who chose a career rather than homemaking (cf. Furnham, 1992; Hurrell & Murphy, 1991). Furthermore, the general picture from research on locus of control which implies more ill-health among externals, is rather consistently found in the occupational area as well (Hurrell & Murphy, 1991). With regard to a buffering role of locus of control, that is its capacity to attenuate the impact (or the perception) of stressors, there is not very much work related research, and what there is has produced mixed evidence. There are some studies, however, which indicate that the relationship between stressful circumstances and stress reaction may be stronger for externals than for internals. Internals, however, seem to respond more strongly to attempts to restrict their freedom of action (Hurrel & Murphy, 1991).

In a similar vein, there is research in the domain of work that deals with constructs which are related to locus of control, such as sense of coherence (Antonovsky, 1991), self-esteem (Brockner, 1988), and, especially, hardiness (Kobasa, 1988; Orr & Westman, 1990). In general, this research yields a similar picture: Positive effects in general, yet many conflicting results, and less than clear conclusions about the nature of the effects, especially with regard to effects on appraisal of stressors, occurrence of stressors, coping efforts, and affective and physical reactions (see Semmer, 1996).

## CONTROL AS A CONCEPT IN JOB DESIGN AND STRESS AT WORK

The thrust of control-related research in the area of work is concerned with the control options that specific working conditions are offering. This issue has a long tradition in work psychology. This tradition stresses the negative impact of a Tayloristic work design with its emphasis on breaking down tasks into as small pieces as possible, prescribing exactly what to do when and how they are to be performed, thus reducing skill, planning and thinking, and control over one's activities as much as possible (Taylor, 1911).

Such anti-tayloristic concepts and the activities associated with them were stimulated especially by the socio-technical approach to job design (cf. Herbst, 1974Richter, Jordan, & Pohlandt, 1994; Trist & Bamforth, 1951) and related developments in Europe and the United States (e.g. Davis, 1972; Davis &

autonomy aim at assessing the different nature of such contingencies as they exist (or are perceived to exist) in different work environments.

Cherns, 1975; Emery & Thorsrud, 1969; Ulich, 1994; Warr, 1976). Their emphasis on autonomy on the group level is shared by concepts on the individual level (Hacker, 1986; Hackman and Oldham, 1980; Turner & Lawrence, 1965; see also Oldham, 1996).

These concepts have stimulated quite a bit of activity in terms of change projects as well as research, and autonomy has become a major issue of research related to job design. Autonomy often has been shown to be related to performance. Thus, in Spector's (1986) analysis, adjusted r is .26. However, there is evidence pointing to an interaction between autonomy and other characteristics, notably feedback: Autonomy seems to be related to performance only when feedback is provided (Ganster & Fusilier, 1989; Dodd & Ganster, 1996). In change projects which typically involve group work, autonomy has often shown to improve not only job satisfaction, but also productivity (cf. Beekun, 1989; Goodman, Devadas, & Hughson, 1988; Guzzo, Jette, & Katzell, 1985). These effects are, however, not uniformly achieved and by no means automatic. Many conditions have to be met if positive results are to be obtained. The change process has to be carefully planned and executed, management support is indispensable, as are careful considerations of training needs, pay regulations, or availability of resources that are needed to successfully deal with the increased responsibility. Factors like these often result in "autonomous" work groups where the autonomy desired is not really achieved, or not maintained. Where it is achieved, other changes such as increased work load and time pressure sometimes counter the positive effects of increased autonomy (cf. Antoni, 1996; Buchanan, 1989; Seppälä, 1989; Ulich, 1994). Also, some of the effects are indirect and will only show when appropriate measures are taken, as in the study by Wall, Kemp, Jackson, & Clegg (1986) which did not show direct effects on productivity; however, the same work output was maintained without the necessity of a supervisor. Furthermore, there is evidence that these effects occur mainly in complex work environments ("high-variance systems," Wall, Corbett, Martin, Clegg, & Jackson, 1990; cf. Wall & Jackson, 1995). Nevertheless, and despite all ambiguities and inconsistencies which inevitably characterize such research, it can be concluded that increased autonomy does offer great potential for increasing productivity (Antoni, 1996; Ulich, 1994; Wall & Jackson, 1995).

While much of the theoretical underpinnings of research on autonomy in job design has been based on motivational considerations (Emery, 1972; Hackman & Oldham, 1980), cognitive effects have long been proposed and investigated, especially by the "action regulation" tradition in German work psychology (e.g. Hacker, 1985; see Frese & Zapf, 1994; Wall & Jackson, 1995). These mechanisms most notably involve anticipating problems and dealing with early signs of system failures so that their actual occurrence is prevented (Wall, Jackson, & Davids, 1992).

Affective reactions continue to be of major interest, however. And so it is not surprising that the issue of control occupies quite a central role in research on stress at work (Frese & Semmer, 1991; Kahn & Byosiere, 1992; Murphy, Hurrell, & Quick, 1992; Richter & Hacker, 1997; Warr, 1987; 1996), and quite a few chapters and books on stress at work deal specifically with control issues (e.g. Ganster & Fusilier, 1989; Jones & Fletcher, 1996; Sauter, Hurrell, & Cooper, 1989; Steptoe & Appels, 1989; Sutton & Kahn, 1987).

In recent years, a model proposed by Karasek (1979; see Karasek & Theorell, 1990; Theorell & Karasek, 1996) has attracted special interest. It assumes a combination of high demand and low decision latitude ("high strain jobs") to be especially detrimental to health. Research tends to support the detrimental role of high demands as well as the positive effects of control. However, research for their interaction is rather weak. In addition, the "decision latitude" scale typically used in this research combines aspects of control with those of complexity and thus goes beyond the measurement of control. Furthermore, many analyses have been conducted on the level of occupations rather than individuals (see Ganster & Fusilier, 1989; Jones & Fletcher, 1996 Kasl, 1996). Despite such ambiguities, altogether quite impressive support for the importance of control at work for well-being and health, especially coronary heart disease, has been accumulating from research based on this model (cf. Haynes, 1991; Theorell & Karasek, 1996).

This conclusion is also supported by studies that use more narrow measures, such as the "autonomy" measure of Hackman & Oldham (1980) or measures similar to it (Semmer, 1982; 1984). Thus, a meta-analysis by Spector (1986) showed adjusted $r$s of .37 with general job satisfaction, -.33 with physical symptoms and -.37 with emotional distress. In addition, performance effects of stress often are found to be moderated by control (Bowers, Weaver, & Morgan, 1996).

Despite the basic convergence with regard to the general trend, there is, of course, quite some controversy as to the exact nature of the effect. Frese (1989) distinguishes between various mechanisms: (a) stressor reduction (control over stressors), (b) fitting the stressor to the person (confronting the stressor at a time when one is best suited to do so), (c) the "Minimax-hypothesis" by Miller, (1979); (being able to determine the maximum amount one is willing to take), (d) Persistence in (problem-oriented) coping, and (e) control satisfying a basic "need for control." Methodologically, there is much controversy about issues like linear vs. nonlinear effects, main vs. interactive effects, objective vs. perceived autonomy, etc. And, as one would expect in this type of research, there is much conflicting evidence concerning all these issues. Nevertheless, the general conclusion does seem justified that, in general, control at work has positive influences on satisfaction, well-being, and productivity (see Jones & Fletcher, 1996; Karasek & Theorell, 1990, or, more cautiously, Ganster & Fusilier, 1989).

## SPECIFICITY, GENERALITY, AND LEVELS: THE ROLE OF CONTEXT IN JUDGING POSITIVE AND NEGATIVE EFFECTS OF CONTROL

My conclusion that, "in general," positive effects of control are found, is not meant to deny the many inconsistencies by which this research is plagued. It is mainly meant to emphasize that these inconsistencies should not blind us with regard to the general picture that is emerging. Nevertheless, it is the inconsistencies and the controversies that drive both research and theory. One of the issues that has been subject of considerable debate as well as the focus of refined measurement attempts, concerns the question of specificity vs. generality.

It has already been mentioned that Karasek's (Karasek & Theorell, 1990) measure of job decision latitude is often criticized for being too broad, encompassing aspects of skill as well as of control (cf. Kasl, 1996). However, many even regard the very concept of autonomy as too global. Thus, Breaugh (1985) suggests to break it down into "method autonomy" (e.g., "I am allowed to decide how to go about getting my job done"), "work scheduling autonomy" (e.g., "My job is such that I can decide when to do particular work activities"), and "work criteria autonomy" (e.g., "I have some control over what I am supposed to accomplish"). While the third of these sub-dimensions may be relevant only to people in higher echelons, it is especially the first two that have been taken up in other research (timing control and method control in work by Jackson, Wall, Martin, & Davids, 1993; Wall, Jackson, & Mullarkey, 1995).

It makes sense that such a finer distinction could grasp relationships which otherwise may go unnoticed because the effects are very specific. Thus, Wall et al. (1995) confirm the Karasek model in finding an interaction of control and demands in predicting anxiety, but only for the method control subscale, not for its combination with time control into a more general measure of control. Furthermore, they report an interaction between the two subscales in predicting anxiety, such that the combination of both low timing control and low method control is especially detrimental.

Such distinctions could also help in unraveling relationships between specific types of stressors specific types of control, and/or specific outcomes. For instance, if one has to work in an environment which is noisy at certain times (e.g., traffic peaks), it should be time control that is especially helpful, as it enables one to carry out more complex tasks at quiet times (see Averill's (1973) concept of "control of confrontation").

Thus, breaking down the concept of control into more specific components certainly does seem a fruitful way. As an aside, it is interesting to note that a similar discussion is taking place with regard to social support, where the specific matching of type of support and type of stressful situation is an issue (cf. Cohen & Wills, 198).

At the same time, however, it also seems promising to go the opposite way and to ask if control over the situation at large, rather than over the stressful situation at hand, may be an important aspect that sets the agenda for the impact of a specific stressful situation (see also Jones & Fletcher, 1996).

Why should the greater context have such an impact? If we distinguish between the immediate situation and the broader context, we may find that we are able to cope with any single stressor but at the same time are unable to prevent stress situations from reoccurring.

Thus, I may be able to cope with a high workload by increasing effort. If, however, this leads my supervisor into believing that I can cope with this workload on a permanent basis, he or she might give me a new work assignment as soon the current one is finished. In this way, I have control over the immediate assignment but not over the overall context.

As long as a stressful experience is not traumatic in itself but rather of the type of minor stressors that we typically encounter in daily working life, the evidence suggests that the negative impact on health does not stem from *single* stressful experiences. On the contrary, stressful events that one successfully copes with can become a source of increased self-esteem and self-efficacy (Schaefer & Moos, 1992; Thoits, 1994). Only if the stress experience becomes chronic, negative effects are to be expected (Kasl, 1992). Being chronic implies lack of control, but not necessarily with regard to the single stressor but rather with regard to the continuous reappearance of stressors.

The main question then becomes if one is in control with regard to the situation as a whole, at least enough to maintain an acceptable balance between aversive and beneficial aspects.

This shift of focus may be important because it suggest a much greater substitutability of control efforts at various levels. Furthermore, it directs attention to the costs that are associated with control efforts and thus highlights potentially negative aspects of control, an aspect that deserves much more attention. Finally, taking the question of substitutability even further, one may ask if not only control at various levels may act as substitutes for one another but also if other resources may act as substitutes for control.

## Substitutability of Control Efforts

If faced with a stressor such as overload, one may be able to control the immediate stressor, for instance, by declining to take over an additional responsibility as long as he or she is overburdened with the current one. One may, however, be unable to decline this new assignment because one's supervisor insists, yet gain strength from the conviction that, if things become unbearable, one can leave the situation as a whole—for instance, because one estimates rather high the chances to find an alternative job. (This, of course, is at the heart of Miller's (1979) Minimax-idea: I can control the maximum amount of stress that I am willing to accept). If, on the other hand, one feels trapped in the situation, the very same stressor may lead to much greater stress at any level of its individual controllability.

A finding by Gardner (1978) nicely illustrates this point. He quite successfully replicated results by Glass & Singer (1972) regarding performance decrements after a period of uncontrollable noise. However, during his series of experiments, a statement of informed consent became mandatory which included the right to withdraw from the experiment at any time without penalty. Subjects that received uncontrollable noise under this condition did not show performance decrements after uncontrollable noise whereas those without the statement of agreement did.

Thus, it may be that the important aspect is not necessarily having control at a given level but rather having control at any one level. And it may well be that control at higher levels is even more important in the long run, simply because its range is greater.

## Costs of Control

Restricting the focus on the immediate stress situation is also likely to lose sight of another phenomenon which becomes apparent only in the larger context: the issue of the costs of control (Semmer, 1990; Thompson et al., 1988.

Schönpflug (e.g. Schönpflug & Battmann, 1988) has emphasized that any coping effort should be analyzed with regard to its costs. So far, however, the discussion about negative effects of coping have concentrated on coping efforts that do not tackle the problem itself, such as avoidance coping. Avoidance coping may be effective in the short run but carry great risks in a longer perspective (Suls & Fletcher, 1985). However, problem-oriented coping, even if it is effective, also carries its risks.

Three aspects come to mind with regard to these costs. They are (a) negative side effects of control efforts, (b) control as a limited resource, and (c) the mental burden implied by the act of exercising control.

1. *Negative side effects of control efforts.* Often, one may be successful in exercising control over the situation at hand but, by doing so, create problems in other areas (see Schönpflug & Battmann, 1988, for a discussion of this).

   Thus, one may cope successfully with being overburdened by working extra hours. This, however, may lead to one's spouse complaining about a partner who is seldom at home and does not share household and family responsibility in an acceptable way. Or it may lead to coworkers becoming suspicious, accusing their colleague of trying to impress the boss in order to be promoted. Or it may simply lead to exhaustion which, in turn, impedes the ability to effectively deal with difficulties.

2. *Control as a limited resource.* Furthermore, not only may efforts to control the situation have side effects or long term costs. In many cases, control is a resource that diminishes when used, and thus must be allocated with care.

   For instance, one may, indeed, be able to decline a new assignment. Doing so, however, reduces the possibility to do this again, since one may appear unmotivated or incapable if the argument of being overburdened is used too often. Similarly, filing a complaint may be an effective way of controlling interpersonal stressors such as unfair treatment. Doing so repeatedly may, however, create an image of being quarrelsome. And quit-

ting one's job may, indeed, be a successful way of exercising control, but
if one keeps changing jobs, prospective employers may become suspicious about one's commitment.

Thus, using resources may undermine these very resources, and to see
one's resources diminishing may in itself become stressful (Hobfoll,
1989).

3. *The burden of exercising control.* Unless one can use routine programs
that go without effort, exercising control is in itself an activity that demands cognitive capacity: One needs to decide about which ways of exercising control are most feasible, what their potential side effects are, if it
is wise to use this resource now or if it should be kept for later use, etc.

Battmann (1984; for a short description in English see Schönpflug (1986)
describes an instructive example. His experiment simulated the task of
supervising a number of department stores. Explicit instruction to plan
one's daily activities paid off, but only for subjects high in intelligence.
For those low in intelligence, however, planning involved an additional
demand on their more limited resources.

Apart from the drain on cognitive resources implied by the very act of control, the emotional implications may also be costly. Control typically is not an
all-or none phenomenon but rather a matter of degree (Frese, 1989; Thompson et
al., 1988). Therefore, the possibility exists that one's control efforts will not be
effective, leaving the person with even less resources in a still unchanged situation. Anticipating this, and dealing with the uncertainty involved in taking an
appropriate decision, may in itself become a source of stress (Schönpflug, 1986;
Schönpflug & Battmann, 1988; Thompson et al., 1988). The same applies to the
calculation of potential side or long term effects discussed in the previous section. As a result, the person may really have to deal with two problems - the
stressful situation at hand, and the calculation of the costs and benefits of exercising control under conditions of uncertainty.

In a situation where the person is stressed already and his or her momentary
resources are already weakened, calculating the efficiency of control options may
become a seriously stressful task in itself. Again, this speaks against regarding
control as something that is important only for the stressor one is encountering
but rather for an explicit consideration of context.

## Losing Options by Exercising Options

Oesterreich (1982) has developed a concept which he calls "efficiency-
divergency." Based on a general concept of control, he postulates that people tend
to chose courses of action that are most promising in terms of achieving goals
(efficiency) but at the same time keep open as many options as possible (divergency). This concept implies that people prefer to keep open their options, to be
able to take many decisions as late as possible, which also means that they do

not like to unduly constrain themselves. Empirical research confirms many features of the model (Oesterreich, Resch & Weyerich, 1988; Resch & Oesterreich, 1987).

Now, it may be possible to keep at least some options open when taking a decision. This usually is not possible to a great extent. On the contrary, many decisions restrict further possibilities for deciding anew (Baltes, 1997).

Thus, calling a certain person for help may increase my dependence on this person and possibly restrict my possibilities of asking somebody else for help (e.g. because this person uses certain methods which then excludes people who are not experts on this methods from helping, or because other people may resent that they have not been asked in the first place). Improving my skills in a certain area restricts my possibilities of becoming an expert in another area. Gaining the privilege of receiving mostly task assignments that match my special skills will further increase my skills in this area but restrict my possibilities of developing skills in other areas.

This anticipation of control restrictions by exercising control may be stressful in itself. Furthermore, calculating these risks may add additional cognitive and emotional burdens, as argued above.

Again, in order to decide on this, one has to take account of the context at large, and it would not be wise to concentrate only on the stressful tasks at hand.

A special case of this is the issue of decisions that one is free to take, but only on an all-or-nothing basis. Once the decision is taken, however, it carries with it many restrictions that now one has to put up with. Thus, being promoted into a management position will imply that one's day may be dictated by external demands to a greater degree than before (see Yukl, 1994). In a similar vein, taking up the responsibility for a new project may well imply that the necessities of this project will dictate much of one's time and activities as long as the project is running. So, there are likely to be times when one feels quite out of control; nevertheless, the fact than one has taken the basic decision to enter this situation by him- or herself is likely to alter the perception and evaluation of this lack of control. This certainly deserves more attention in research.

## Substitutability of Resources

The possibility to control things probably is one of most important resources one can possess. It is, however, certainly not the only one. Social support is another resource the importance of which is well established, even though there are still arguments about the exact mechanisms (e.g. Cohen & Wills, 1985; Quick, Nelson, Matuszek, Whittington, & Quick, 1996; Sarason, Pierce, & Sarason, 1994; Schwarzer & Leppin, 1991; Winnubst, Buunk & Marcelissen, 1988). A wide array of personal resources can be added, such as self-esteem (e.g. Brockner, 1988), self-efficacy (Bandura, 1992), sense of coherence (Antonovsky, 1991), optimism (Scheier & Carver, 1992), hardiness (Kobasa, 1988), explanatory style (Peterson & Seligman, 1984), or locus of control (Rotter, 1966). Of course, it can be argued that many of these contain at least element of control. However, this is only part of the picture. Aspects thus as hope (Quick et al., 1996), optimism (Scheier & Carver, 1992) imply a belief that things will develop well even in the absence of one's own possibilities to exercise control. And there is one category that keeps coming up in many of these concepts an in practically all discussions of this area, and that is "meaning." Semmer (1996), summarizing the characteristics of "resilient people," included as one of the protective elements the ability to interpret single events as parts of a broader, and meaningful, pattern (besides the tendency to expect the environment to be basically benign and the tendency to expect things to be controllable and to perceive oneself as capable of influencing them).

What is important here is the idea that it is not any specific resource that may count but rather the total amount of resources in general (see Hobfoll, 1989). This is exemplified by Holahan & Moos (1990). They used a "resource composite" consisting of personal (self-confidence and easygoingness) and social (family support) resource measures and showed that this predicted psychological functioning either directly (for people with few stressful events) or indirectly (via approach coping, for people with many stressful events). A similar argument has been made for coping, where in many cases it is possible to successfully use a variety of strategies (McCrae, 1992).

Note that this argument does not necessarily contradict the idea that resources should match situational demands. Rather, it is important to distinguish between any single situation on the one hand, and long-term circumstances on the other. It may well be that any given situation requires rather specific resources, although this may well imply a range of resources rather than any single one. Unless we are dealing with situations that keep reoccurring in very similar ways, however, in the long run it may be more important to have a broad repertoire of resources, because that way we are better equipped to deal with a variety of different circumstances.

## Balance of Aversive and Rewarding Aspects of the Work Situation

To expect any job situation (or, for that matter, any life situation) to be without stressful experiences would be quite naive, and it is wise to prepare for negative experiences to occur (see the concept of a "realistic job preview" which avoids disappointment by new employees through emphasizing not only the positive side of a job offer but also its drawbacks (Wanous, 1992). And it seems that stressful experiences can be accepted even if they cannot be controlled as long as the overall situation offers enough positive aspects to make the balance look right. By this mechanisms, the importance of a single stressful situation may be reduced.

This may well be behind the finding by Scheier, Weintraub, & Carver (1986) that optimists are better able to accept an uncontrollable situation. Since they are optimistic in general, the overall balance of the situation is maintained, as they still are expecting many positive things to occur.

At the same time, however, a stressor may become "unduly" devastating if it is experienced as offsetting this balance. Thus, one may accept all kinds of difficult and straining situations quite calmly because by accepting them one expects to positively influence future events, such as being promoted. As long as this expectation exists, this person may accept not being in control without undue suffering.[2] If the expected reward does not occur, however, it is not only the single event that it important. Rather, it becomes so extremely stressful because it conveys the information that all the stresses one has endured are not, and perhaps, never will be, offset by corresponding rewards (Siegrist, 1996).

Again, this argument shifts the focus from the single experience to the broader context. This may be a longer time interval (as in the promotion example) or a balance across domains, as when non-control over some domains is accepted in exchange for valued resources in other domains.

## LEGITIMACY AS THE OVERARCHING CONCERN

The last paragraph has already led to a perspective of social exchange: It is the overall balance that counts more than the specific stressful experience, and in a resourceful context even rather severe life events are not necessarily devastating but may, indeed, be a source of strength (Schaefer & Moos, 1992). In stress research, this issue of balance has been forcefully argued by Hobfoll (e.g., 1989) as well as by Schönpflug (e.g., Schönpflug & Battmann, 1988).

Since most of the daily stressors we encounter do not involve threats to our physical integrity but rather to our psychological integrity, the question of balance inevitable leads to the issue of reciprocity. This is at the heart of a model developed by Siegrist (e.g., Siegrist, 1996, Siegrist & Matschinger, 1989). He is concerned with an imbalance between effort and rewards. High effort may be induced by "extrinsic" demands (e.g., job duties) or by "intrinsic" demands which stem from a trait he calls "immersion," characterized by a high need for approval, competitiveness and hostility, impatience and irritability, and inability to withdraw from obligation. Rewards are conceived in terms of money, esteem, and status control. The latter refers to a secure occupational status, whereas in low status control this status is threatened, for instance by forced downward mobility, by status inconsistency, that is, a position that does not correspond to one's educational background, or by (actual or possible) redundancy.

---

[2]There is a German proverb stating that "learning years are not master years," implying that the relatively powerless position of an apprentice is (a) justified and (b) transitory, thus suggesting that this situation of reduced control be accepted by the apprentice.

In an impressive series of studies, Siegrist has shown that an imbalance of effort and rewards is predictive both of cardiovascular risk factors and of cardiovascular disease (see Siegrist, 1996, for a summary of this work).

The question of reciprocity is, of course, intimately related to the issue of fairness and justice. If organizations are perceived as being unfair, as violating the obligations ascribed to them in what is called the "psychological contract," typical stress emotions, such as anger, are likely to occur (cf. James, 1993; Morrison & Robinson, 1997; Rutte & Messick, 1995).

The same event can elicit very different reactions depending on the perceived fairness of management actions in terms of procedural and interactional justice (Greenberg, 1993; Konovksy & Brockner 1993). And, much in line with the concept of (im)balance between effort and rewards, perceived unfairness seems to have stronger implications when prior commitment was particularly high (Brockner, Tyler, & Cooper-Schneider, 1992).

Fairness, in turn, depends on the perception of which actions are legitimate in a given context of social exchange.

In interviewing people about work stressors, we have repeatedly been surprised by the low significance many people attached to stressors that many out siders would consider quite aversive, such as cleaning incontinent people in a geriatric hospital. The nurses' typical comments to this emphasized that this was "part of the job." And it turned out that a slight change in context, from a legitimate part of one's role to an illegitimate demand, would drastically alter the appraisal of an otherwise unchanged action. Thus, having to open and close the window for a patient who cannot move would be considered acceptable - unless the nurses perceived that patients might be able to do this at their own least some of the time. Then the comments changed to something like "we are not a hotel crew here", and the very same act was considered quite stressful.

Based on these informal observations, we are investigating this issue in a more systematic way in ongoing research. The first step was to devise a questionnaire which contained vignettes that describe the same act but different degrees of legitimacy. An example from a questionnaire for hospital staff would be: "You have to search for archived X-rays for hours". Legitimacy would be varied by continuing that the X-rays are needed (a) for better serving a patient who was seriously ill vs. (b) for a research paper of one of the doctors. Throughout the questionnaire, the illegitimate version was considered to be significantly more stressful than the legitimate one (Berchtold & Woodtli Andrini, 1998) and similar results were obtained in an industrial production setting (Gutknecht & LaFaso, 1997).

These considerations, and the first results obtained, fit very well with findings reported by Peeters, Schaufeli & Buunk (1995) about research with secretaries and policemen. They write: "Both studies showed that stressors that are *typical* for a profession—such as overload for the secretaries and dealing with victims of accidents for policemen—are appraised as least "significant." For COs, problems with prisoners are very typical stressors and it is probably because of this reason that this type of stressful event is perceived to be least "significant." Apparently, employees *expect* that some stressors are indissolubly connected with their profession, and as a result of this they do not perceive them to be very significant." (p. 471).

Another for this phenomenon comes from Gundykunst & Ting-Toomey (1988). Using data from Babad & Wallbott (1986) and Wallbott & Scherer (1986), they investigate the relationship between culture and reactions to injustice. With regard to Hofstede's (1991) dimension of "power distance," they report that anger as a reaction to injustice is less common in cultures where power distance is high. In other words, where arbitrary and inconsistent behavior of superiors is taken for granted, the unfair treatment experienced, and the reduced control associated with it, is less stressful than where a smaller power distance implies a demand for more consistency and reciprocity on the part of the supervisor.

It has long been recognized that people do not aspire control in situations where it would be more legitimate for somebody else to exercise control, because this person possesses more of the necessary skills (Thompson et al., 1988). Thus, passengers of an air plain will usually be quite willing to leave control over the airplane to the pilots. What should be added to this is that this legitimacy may not only stem from the specific skills somebody possesses but also from more normative considerations about legitimacy: Non-control may well be acceptable if it is either legitimate in itself (as with a supervisor in cultures of high power distance), or part of an overall situation which is considered legitimate in terms of a fair balance between aversive aspects, such as lack of control, and desired rewards in one's working situation.

Note, however, that this issue concerns situations where control will not be claimed (or even rejected). This is not to be confused with control-rejection as a personality trait (Frese, 1992). The general tendency to reject control resembles more the protective style of people with low self-regard (Tice, 1993), and the aim seems rather to avoid the risk of failure and blame (a motivation often found behind rejection of control - Thompson et al., 1988). Not surprisingly, then, Frese (1992) reports that being high in control rejection does not protect against the negative influence of stressful situations, and Frese et al. (1994) find direct association of control rejection with indicators of poor well-being.

While such a "defensive" lowering of control aspirations does not seem a promising strategy (cf. Semmer, 1996), there is evidence that, on the other hand, the inability to yield control may also be damaging. This seems to be typical of the famous Type A Behavior pattern. Type A's show a tendency to maintain control under all conditions (even conditions where control cannot be attained), and they react strongly—both behaviorally and in terms of cardiovascular reactivity—to threats to control (Contrada & Krantz, 1988; Edwards, 1991; Glass, 1977). Siegrist and associates (Siegrist, 1996) have shown that such a high need for control was associated with an elevated risk for cardiovascular disease over a period of 6 years, independent of other influencing factors. And there is evidence that this is associated with the tendency to set goals that are too high and therefore carry a great risk of failure (Ward & Eisler, 1987).

Thus, it seems that it is neither wise to claim nor to reject control under all circumstances. Rather, a balance between the two seems to be optimal. To judge whether or not such a balance is achieved, it is important to carefully look at the amount of various types of control offered in the work situation. At the same time, however, control at various levels of generality, the costs of exercising this control, the balance of non control with rewards, and the legitimacy of this whole constellation should be taken into account much more than has been done so far.

## REFERENCES

Antoni, C. H. (1996). *Teilautonome Arbeitsgruppen*. Weinheim: Psychologie Verlags Union.

Antonovsky, A. (1991). The structural sources of salutogenic strengths. In C.L. Cooper & R. Payne, (Eds.), *Personality and stress: Individual differences in the stress process* (pp. 67–104). Chichester: Wiley.

Averill, J. R. (1973). Personal control over aversive stimuli and its relationship to stress. *Psychological Bulletin, 80,* 286–303.

Babad, E. Y. & Wallbott, H. G. (1986). The effects of social factors on emotional reactions. In K. S. Scherer, H.G. Wallbott, & A.B. Summerfield (Eds.), *Experiencing emotion: A cross-cultural study* (pp. 154–172). Cambridge, UK: Cambridge University Press.

Baltes, P. B. (1997). On the incomplete architecture of human ontogeny: Selection, optimization, and compensation as foundations of developmental theory. *American Psychologist, 52,* 366–380.

Bandura, A. (1986). *Social foundations of thought and action: A social cognitive theory*. Englewood Cliffs, NJ: Prentice-Hall.

Bandura, A. (1992). Exercise of personal agency through the self-efficacy mechanism. In R. Schwarzer (Ed.), *Self-efficacy: Thought control of action* (pp. 3–38). Washington, DC: Hemisphere.

Battmann, W. (1984). Regulation und Fehlregulation im Verhalten. IX. Entlastung und Belastung durch Planung (straining and relieving effects of planning). *Psychologische Beiträge, 26,* 672–692.

Beekun, R. A. (1989). Assessing the effectiveness of sociotechnical interventions: Antidote or fad? *Human Relations, 42,* 877–897.

Berchtold, I. & Woodtli Andrini, T. (1998). *Stress und Zumutbarkeit von Arbeitsaufgaben im Spital.* (Stress and legitimacy of tasks in a hospital). Unpublished bachelor's thesis, University of Bern, Department of Psychology.

Bowers, C. A., Weaver, J. L, & Morgan, B. B. (1996). Moderating the performance effects of stressors. In J. E. Driskell & E. Salas (Ed.), *Stress and human performance* (pp. 163-192). Mahwah, NJ: Lawrence Erlbaum Associates.

Breaugh, J. A. (1985). The measurement of work autonomy. *Human Relations, 38,* 551–570.

Brockner, J. (1988). *Self-esteem at work*. Lexington MA: Lexington Books.

Brockner, J., Tyler, T. R., & Cooper-Schneider, R. (1992). The influence of prior commitment to an institution on reactions to perceived unfairness: The higher they are, the harder they fall. *Administrative Science Quarterly, 37,* 241–261.

Buchanan, D. A. (1989). High performance: New boundaries of acceptability in worker control. In S. Sauter & J. J. Hurrell, & C. L. Cooper (Eds.), *Job control and worker health* (pp. 255–273). Chichester: Wiley.

Cohen, S. & Wills, T. A. (1985). Stress, social support, and the buffering hypothesis. *Psychological Bulletin, 98*, 310–357.

Contrada, R. J. & Krantz, D. S. (1988). Stress, reactivity, and type A behavior: Current status and future directions. *Annals of Behavioral Medicine, 10*, 64–70.

Davis, L. E. (1972). The design of jobs. In L. E. Davis & J. C. Taylor (Eds.), *Design of jobs* (pp. 299–327). London: Penguin (originally published in 1966).

Davis, L. E. & Cherns, A. B. (1975). *The quality of working life* (2 vols.). New York: Free Press.

Dodd, N. G. & D. C. Ganster (1996). The interactive effects of variety, autonomy, and feedback on attitudes and performance. *Journal of Organizational Behavior, 17*, 329–347.

Edwards, J. E. (1991). The measurement of Type A Behavior Pattern: An assessment of criterion-oriented validity, content validity, and construct validity. In C. L. Cooper & R. Payne, (Eds.), *Personality and stress: Individual differences in the stress process* (pp. 151–180). Chichester: Wiley.

Emery, F. E. (1972). Characteristics of socio-technical systems. In L. E. Davis & J. C. Taylor (Eds.), *Design of jobs* (pp. 177–198). London: Penguin (originally published in 1959).

Emery, F. E. & Thorsrud, E. (1969). *Form and content in industrial democracy.* London: Tavistock.

Flammer, A. (1990). *Die Erfahrung der eigenen Wirksamkeit. Einführung in die Psychologie der Kontrollmeinung.* Bern: Huber.

Frese, M. (1987). A theory of control and complexity: Implications for software design and integration of computer systems into the work place. In Frese, M., Ulich, E. & Dzida, W. (Eds.) *Psychological issues of human-computer interaction in the work place .* Amsterdam: North-Holland.

Frese, M. (1989). Theoretical models of control and health. In S. Sauter & J. J. Hurrell, & C. L. Cooper (Eds.), *Job control and worker health* (pp. 107–128). Chichester: Wiley.

Frese, M. (1992). A plea for realistic pessimism: On objective reality, coping with stress, and psychological dysfunction. In L. Montada, S.-H. Filipp, & M. J. Lerner (Eds.), *Life crises and experiences of loss in adulthood* (pp. 81–94). Hillsdale, NJ: Lawrence Erlbaum Associates.

Frese, M., Erbe-Heinbokel, M., Grefe, J., Rybowiak, V., & Weike, A. (1994). "Mir ist es lieber, wenn ich genau gesagt bekomme, was ich tun muß": Probleme der Akzeptanz von Verantwortung und Handlungsspielraum in Ost und West ("I prefer to be told exactly what to do": Problems with accepting responsibility and control in East and West). Zeitschrift für Arbeits- und Organisationspsychologie, 38, 22–33.

Frese, M. & Semmer, N. (1991). Streßfolgen in Abhängigkeit von Moderatorvariablen: Der Einfluß von Kontrolle und sozialer Unterstützung. In S. Greif, E. Bamberg & N. Semmer (Hrsg.), *Psychischer Streß am Arbeitsplatz* (S. 135–153). Göttingen: Hogrefe.

Frese, M. & Zapf, D. (1994). Action as the core of work psychology: A German approach. In H. C. Triandis, M. D. Dunnette & L. M. Hough (Eds.), *Handbook of industrial and organizational psychology, Vol. 4* (pp.271–340). Palo Alto, CA: Consulting Psychologists Press.

Furnham, A. (1992). *Personality at work. The role of individual differences in the workplace.* London: Routledge.

Ganster, D. C. & Fusilier, M. R. (1989). Control in the workplace. In D. L. Cooper & I. T. Robertson (Eds.), *International Review of Industrial and Organizational Psychology 1989* (pp. 235–280). Chichester: Wiley.

Gardner, G. T. (1978). Effects of federal human subjects regulations on data obtained in environmental stressor research. *Journal of Personality and Social Psychology, 36,* 628–634.

Glass, D. C. (1977). *Behavior patterns, stress, and coronary disease.* Hillsdale, NJ: Lawrence Erlbaum Associates.

Glass, D. C. & Singer, J. E. (1972). *Urban stress: Experiments on noise and social stressors.* New York: Academic Press.

Goodman, P. S., Devadas, R., & Hughson, T. L. G. (1988). Groups and productivity: analyzing the effectiveness of self-managing teams. In J. P. Campbell, R. J. Campbell, and Associates (Eds.), *Productivity in organizations* (pp. 295–327). San Francisco: Jossey-Bass.

Greenberg, J. (1993). The social side of fairness: Interpersonal and informational classes of organizational justice. In R. Cropanzano (Ed.), *Justice in the workplace. Approaching fairness in human resource management* (pp. 79–103). Hillsdale NJ: Lawrence Erlbaum Associates.

Gutknecht, S. & La Faso, L. (1997). *Stress und Zumutbarkeit von Arbeitsaufgaben in der Produktion.* (Stress and legitimacy of tasks in industrial production). Unpublished bachelor's thesis, University of Bern, Department of Psychology.

Gundykunst, W. B., & Ting-Toomey, S. (1988). Culture and affective communication. *American Behavioral Scientist, 31,* 384–400.

Guzzo, R. A., Jette, R. D. & Katzell, R.A. (1985). The effects of psychologically based intervention programs on worker productivity: A meta-analysis. *Personnel Psychology, 38,* 275–291.

Hacker, W. (1985). Activity: A fruitful concept in industrial psychology. In M. Frese & J. Sabini (Eds.), *Goal directed behavior: The concept of action in psychology* (pp. 262–284). Hillsdale, NJ: Lawrence Erlbaum Associates.

Hacker, W. (1986). Complete vs. Incomplete working tasks—a Concept and its Verification. In G. Debus, & H.W. Schroiff (Hrsg.), *The Psychology of Work and Organization.* (S. 23–36). Amsterdam: Elsevier.

Hackman, J. R. & Oldham, G. R. (1980). *Work redesign.* Reading, MA: Addison Wesley.

Haynes, S. G. (1991). The effect of job demands, job control, and new technologies on the health of employed women: A review. In M. Frankenhaeuser, U. Lundberg, & M. Chesney (Eds.), *Women, work, and health: Stress and opportunities* (pp. 157–169). New York: Plenum.

Herbst, P. G. (1974). *Socio-technical design: Strategies in multidisciplinary research.* London: Tavistock.

Hobfoll, S. E. (1989). Conservation of resources: A new attempt at conceptualizing stress. *American Psychologist, 44,* 513–524.

Hofstede, G. (1991). *Cultures and organizations: Software of the mind.* New York: McGraw-Hill.

Holahan, C. J. & Moos, R. H. (1990). Life stressors, resistance factors, and improved psychological functioning: An extension of the stress resistance paradigm. *Journal of Personality and Social Psychology, 58,* 909–917.

Hurrell, J. J. & Murphy, L. R. (1991). Locus of control, job demands, and health. In C.L. Cooper & R. Payne (Eds.), *Personality and stress: Individual differences in the stress process* (pp. 133–149). Chichester: Wiley.

Jackson, P. R., Wall, T. D., Martin, R., & Davids, K. (1993). New measures of job control, cognitive demand, and production responsibility. *Journal of Applied Psychology, 78,* 753–762.

James, K. (1993). The social context of organizational justice: Cultural, intergroup, and structural effects on justice behaviors and perceptions. In R. Cropanzano

(Ed.), *Justice in the workplace. Approaching fairness in human resource management* (pp. 21–50). Hillsdale NJ: Lawrence Erlbaum Associates.

Jerusalem, M. & Schwarzer, R. (1992). Self-efficacy as a resource factor in stress appraisal processes. In R. Schwarzer (Ed.), *Self-efficacy: Thought control of action* (pp. 195–213). Washington DC: Hemisphere.

Jones, F. & Fletcher, B. C. (1996). Job control and health. In M. J. Schabracq, J. A. Winnubst, & C. L. Cooper (Eds.), *Handbook of work and health psychology* (pp. 33–50) Chichester: Wiley.

Kahn, R. L. & Byosiere, P. (1992). Stress in organizations. In M. D. Dunnette & L. M. Hough (Eds.), *Handbook of industrial and organizational psychology, vol. 3* (pp. 571–650). Palo Alto CA: Consulting Psychologists Press.

Karasek, R. A. (1979). Job demands, job decision latitude, and mental strain: Implications for job redesign. *Administrative Science Quarterly, 24*, 285–308.

Karasek, R. A. & Theorell, T. (1990). *Healthy work: Stress, productivity and the reconstruction of working life.* New York: Basic Books.

Kasl, S. V. (1992). Surveillance of psychological disorders in the workplace. In: G. P. Keita & S. L. Sauter (Eds.), *Work and well-being* (pp. 73–95). Washington, D. C.: APA.

Kasl, S. V. (1996). The influence of the work environment on cardiovascular health: A historical, conceptual, and methodological perspective. *Journal of Occupational Health Psychology, 1*, 42–56.

Kobasa, S. C. Q. (1988). Conceptualization and measurement of personality in job stress research. In J. J. Hurrell, Jr., Lawrence R. Murphy, S. L. Sauter, & C. L. Cooper (Eds.), *Occupational Stress: Issues and developments in research* (pp 100–109). New York: Taylor & Francis.

Konovksy, M. A. & Brockner, J. (1993). Managing victim and survivor layoff reactions: A procedural justice perspective. In R. Cropanzano (Ed.), *Justice in the workplace: Approaching fairness in human resource management* (pp. 133–153). Hillsdale, NJ: Lawrence Erlbaum Associates.

McCrae, R. R. (1992). Situational determinants of coping. In B. N. Carpenter (Ed.), *Personal coping: Theory, research, and application* (pp. 65–76). Westport, CT: Praeger.

Miller, S. (1979). Controllability and human stress: method, evidence, and theory. *Behavior Research & Therapy, 17*, 287–304.

Morrison, E. W. & Robinson, S. L. (1997). When employees feel betrayed: A model of how psychological contract violation develops. *Academy of Management Review, 22*, 226–256.

Murphy, L. R., Hurrell, J. J., & Quick, J. C. (1992). Work and well-being: Where do we go from here? In . In J. C. Quick, L. R. Murphy, & J. J. Hurrell (Eds.), *Stress and well-being at work: Assessments and interventions for occupational mental health* (pp. 331–347). Washington, DC: American Psychological Association.

Oesterreich, R. (1982). The term "efficiency-divergency" as a theoretical approach to problems of action-planning and motivation. In W. Hacker, W. Volpert, & M. v. Cranach (Eds.), *Cognitive and motivational aspects of action* (pp. 99–110). Berlin: Deutscher Verlag der Wissenschaften.

Oesterreich, R., Resch, M. G., & Weyerich, A. (1988). Bevorzugung und inhaltliche Bewertung von Handlungsfeldern unterschiedlicher Natur. *Sprache & Kognition, 7*, 144–161.

Oldham, G. R. (1996). Job Design. In C. L. Cooper & I. T. Robertson (Eds.), *International Review of Industrial and Organizational Psychology, Vol. 11* (pp 33–60).

Orr, E. & Westman, M. (1990). Does hardiness moderate stress, and how?: A review. In M. Rosenbaum (Ed.), *Learned resourcefulness: On coping skills, self-control, and adaptive behavior* (pp. 64–94). New York: Springer.

Peeters, M. C. W., Schaufeli, W. B., & Buunk, B. P. (1995). The role of attributions in the cognitive appraisal of work-related stressful events: an event-recording approach. *Work and Stress, 9*, 463–474.

Peterson, C., & Seligman, M. E. P. (1984). Causal explanations as a risk for depression: Theory and evidence. *Psychological Review, 91*, 347–374.

Quick, J. D., Nelson, D. L., Matuszek, P. A. C., Whittington, J. L., & Quick, J. C. (1996). Social support, secure attachments, and health. In C. L. Cooper (Ed.), *Handbook of stress, medicine, and health* (pp. 269–287). Boca Raton, FL: CRC Press.

Resch, M. G. & Oesterreich, R. (1987). Bildung von Zwischenzielen in Entscheidungsnetzen. *Zeitschrift für experimentelle und angewandte Psychologie, 34*, 301–317.

Richter, P., Jordan, P., & Pohlandt, A. (1994). Bewertung und Gestaltung vollständiger Tätigkeiten im Rahmen eines sozio-technischen Ansatzes. In B. Bergmann & P. Richter (Hrsg.), *Die Handlungsregulationstheorie. Von der Praxis einer Theorie* (S. 253–268). Göttingen: Hogrefe.

Richter, P. & Hacker, W. (1997). *Belastung und Beanspruchung*. Heidelberg: Asanger.

Rotter, J. B. (1966). Generalized expectancies for internal versus external control of reinforcement. *Psychological Monographs, 80*, 1–28.

Rutte, C. G. & Messick, D. M. (1995). An integrated model of perceived unfairness in organizations. *Social Justice Research*, 1995, 8, 239–261.

Sarason, I. G., Pierce, G. R., & Sarason, B.R. (1 994). General and specific perceptions of social support. In W R- Avison & I.H. Gotlib (Eds.), *Stress and mental health* (pp. 151–177). New York: Plenum.

Sauter, S. L., J. J. Hurrell, & C. L. Cooper (Eds.); (1989). *Job control and worker health*. Chichester: Wiley.

Schaefer, J. A. & Moos, R .H. (1992). Life crises and personal growth. In B. N. Carpenter (Ed.), *Personal coping: Theory, research, and application* (pp. 149–170). Westport, CT: Praeger.

Scheier, M. F., Weintraub, J. K., & Carver, C. S. (1986). Coping with stress: divergent strategies of optimists and pessimists. *Journal of Personality and Social Psychology, 51*, 1257–1264.

Scheier, M. E. & Carver, C. S. (1992). Effects of optimism on psychological and physical well-being: theoretical overview and empirical update. *Cognitive Therapy and Research, 16*, 201–228

Schönpflug, W. (1986). Behavior economics as an approach to stress theory. In M.H. Appley & R. Trumbull (Eds.), *Dynamics of stress* (pp. 81–98). New York: Plenum.

Schönpflug, W. & Battmann, W. (1988). The costs and benefits of coping. In S. Fisher & J. Reason (Eds.), *Handbook of life stress, cognition and health* (p. 699–713). Chichester: Wiley.

Schwarzer, R. & Leppin, A. (1991). Social support and health: A theoretical and empirical overview. *Journal of Social and Personal Relationships, 8*, 99–127.

Seligman, Martin E. P. (1975). *Helplessness. On depression, develoment, and death*. San Francisco: W. H. Freeman.

Semmer, N. (1982). Stress at work, stress in private life, and psychological well-being. In W. Bachmann & I. Udris (Eds.), *Mental load and stress in activity. European approaches* (pp. 42–52). Amsterdam: North Holland.

Semmer, N. (1984). Streßbezogene Tätigkeitsanalyse. *(Stress-related job analysis)*. Weinheim: Beltz.

Semmer, N. (1990). Streß und Kontrollverlust (stress and the loss of control). In F. Frei & I. Udris (Eds.), *Das Bild der Arbeit* (pp. 190–207). Bern: Huber

Semmer, N. (1996). Individual differences, work stress and health. In M. J. Schabracq, J. A. Winnubst, & C. L. Cooper (Eds.), *Handbook of work and health psychology* (pp. 51–86) Chichester: Wiley.

Seppälä, P. (1989). Semi-autonomous work groups and worker control In S. Sauter & J. J. Hurrell, & C. L. Cooper (Eds.), *Job control and worker health* (pp. 291–306). Chichester: Wiley.

Siegrist, J. & Matschinger, H. (1989). Restricted status control and cardiovascular risk. In A. Steptoe & A. Appels (Eds.), *Stress, personal control and health* (pp. 65–82). Chichester: Wiley.

Siegrist, J. (1996). Stressful work, self-experience, and cardiovascular diesease prevention. In: K. Orth-Gomer & N. Schneiderman (Hrsg.), *Behavioral medicine approaches to cardiovascular disease prevention* (pp. 87–102). Mahwah, NJ: Lawrence Erlbaum Associates.

Spector, P. E. (1986). Perceived control by employees: A meta-analysis of studies concerning autonomy and participation at work. *Human Relations, 39,* 1005–1016.

Spector, P. E. (1988). Development of the work locus of control scale. *Journal of Occupational Psychology, 61,* 335–340.

Steptoe, A. & Appels, A. (Eds.); (1989). *Stress, personal control and health.* Chichester: Wiley

Suls, J. & Fletcher, B. (1985). The relative efficacy of avoidant and non-avoidant coping strategies: A meta-analysis. *Health Psychology, 4,* 247–288.

Sutton, R. I. & Kahn, R. L. (1987). Prediction, understanding, and control as antidotes to organizational stress. In J.W. Lorsch (Ed.), *Handbook of organizational behavior* (pp. 272–285). Englewood Cliffs, NJ: Prentice-Hall.

Taylor, F. W. (1911). *The principles of scientific management.* New York: Harper & Row.

Theorell, T. & Karasek, R. A. (1996). Current issues relating to psychosocial job strain and cardiovascular disease research. *Journal of Occupational Health Psychology, 1,* 9-26.

Thoits, P. A. (1994). Stressors and problem-solving: The individual as psychological activist. *Journal of Health and Social Behavior, 35,* 143–159.

Thompson, S. C., Cheek, P. R., & Graham, M. A. (1988). The other side of perceived control: Disadvantages and negative effects. In S. Spacapan & S. Oskamp (Eds.), The social psychology of health (pp. 69–93). London: Sage.

Tice, D. M. (1993). The social motivations of people with low self-esteem. In R. F. Baumeister (Ed.), Self-esteem: The puzzle of low self-regard (pp. 37–53). New York: Plenum.

Trist, E. L. & Bamforth, K. W. (1951). Some social and psychological consequences of the longwall method of coal-getting. *Human Relations, 4,* 3–38

Turner, A. N. & Lawrence, P. R. (1965). *Industrial jobs and the worker.* Boston: Harvard University.

Ulich, E. (1994). *Arbeitspsychologie* (3rd ed.). Zurich: Verlag der Fachvereine & Stuttgart: Poeschel.

Wall, T. D., Corbett, J. M., Martin, R., Clegg, C. S., & Jackson, P. R. (1990). Advanced manufacturing technology, work, design and performance: A change study. *Journal of Applied Psychology, 75,* 691–697.

Wall, T. D. & Jackson, P. R. (1995). New manufacturing initiatives and shopfloor job design. In A. Howard (Ed.), *The changing nature of work* (pp. 139–174). San Francisco: Jossey-Bass.

Wall, T. D., Jackson, P. R., & Davids, K. (1992). Operator work design and robotics system performance: A serendipitous field study. *Journal of Applied Psychology, 77,* 353–362.

Wall, T. D., Jackson, P. R., & Mullarkey, S. (1995). Further evidence on some new measures of job control, cognitive demand and production responsibility. *Journal of Organizational Behavior, 16,* 431–455

Wall, T. D., Kemp, N. J., Jackson , P.R., & Clegg, C. W. (1986). Outcomes of autonomous work groups: A long-term field experiment. *Academy of Management Journal, 29,* 280–304.

Wallbott, H. G. & Scherer, K. R. (1986). The antecedents of emotional experiences. In K. S. Scherer, H. G. Wallbott, & A. B. Summerfield (Eds.), *Experiencing emotion: A cross-cultural study* (pp. 69–83). Cambridge, UK: Cambridge University Press.

Wanous, J. P. (1992). *Organizational entry* (2nd ed.). Reading, MA: Addison-Wesley (p. 209).

Ward, C. H. & Eisler, R. M. (1987). Type A behavior, achievement striving, and a dysfunctional self-evaluation system. *Journal of Personality and Social Psychology, 53,* 318–326.

Warr, P. (Ed.); (1976). *Personal goals and work design.* Chichester: Wiley.

Warr, P. (1987). *Work, unemployment, and mental health.* Oxford: Oxford University Press.

Warr, P. (1996). Employee well-being. In P. Warr (Ed.), *Psychology at work* (pp. 224–253). London: Penguin.

Winnubst, J. A. M., Buunk, B. P. & Marcelissen, F. H. G. (1988). Social support and stress: Perspectives and processes. In S. Fisher & J. Reason (Eds.), *Handbook of life stress, cognition and health* (p. 511–528). Chichester: Wiley.

Yukl, G. (1994). *Leadership in organizations* (3rd ed.). Englewood Cliffs, NJ: Prentice Hall.

# Author Index

# Subject Index